The Dynamics of Defeat

To My Parents

Contents

List of Illustrations   xi

Introduction   1

A Note on Primary Sources   7

1   The Challenge of Insurgency: South Vietnam,
    1954–1965   11

    The Diem Regime, 11
    Americans and Diem, 23
    Strategic Hamlets, 33
    Chaos After Diem, 38

2   The Front Victorious: Hau Nghia Province
    Through 1965   45

    The Creation of a Province, 45
    The Party, the Front, and Revolutionary Struggle, 54
    Futile Efforts to Stem the Revolutionary Tide, 68

3   Prospects for War: On the Eve of American
    Intervention   85

    The U.S. Army Confronts a Dilemma, 85
    Revolutionary Military Forces, 93
    South Vietnamese Assets, 102
    The American Strategic Debate, 105

4   Search and Destroy: The Big-Unit War, 1966–1967   117

    War Begins for the 25th Division, 117
    The Military Environment, 127

5   Sword and Shield: Pacification Efforts, 1966–1967   141

"Revolutionary" Development, 141
The U.S. Army and the Village War, 147
Continued American Frustrations, 155
A Violent Struggle, 167

6   Battle: The Tet Offensive, 1968   193

The Origins of the Tet Offensive, 193
The Tet Offensive in the Saigon Area, 199
The Tet Offensive in Hau Nghia Province, 205
The Results of the Tet Offensive, 215

7   The Accelerated Pacification Campaign   223

A Change in Allied Strategy, 223
Attitudes Toward Friend and Foe, 226
The Political Status of the GVN, 234

8   Battle: The Tet Offensive, 1969   241

The One-War Concept, 241
A New Offensive, 242
The Front Wounded in Hau Nghia, 247

9   The Pacification of Hau Nghia Province, 1969   255

The Phoenix Program, 255
Strengthening Regional and Popular Forces, 262
Village Development, 268
Allied Discord, 272

10   High Tide for the Allies: 1970   283

An Early-Year Lull, 283
The Cambodian Invasion, 286
The Departure of the 25th Division, 289
Rural Security, 293
GVN Land Reform, 298
The Front Reacts, 300

11   Last Battles: 1971–1973   309

A Year of Preparation, 309
The 1972 Offensive, 315
The Last Act, 319

12   Reflections on the War   323

Notes   337
Glossary of Terms, Abbreviations, and Acronyms   357
Selected Bibliography   361
About the Book and Author   365
Index   367

Illustrations

Maps

South Vietnam   xiv

Provinces in Saigon Area: III Corps Tactical Zone (III CTZ)   xiv

Hau Nghia Province: Districts, Capitals, Villages   xv

Hau Nghia Province: Terrain and Lines of Communication   xvi

Photos

An American jet bombs suspected enemy positions on the outskirts of a hamlet in Cu Chi district during the 1968 Tet Offensive   181

Ground fighting spills over into the hamlet itself during Tet 1968   182

Relatives mourn a child killed in the 1968 Tet Offensive fighting   182

American advisors inspect a South Vietnamese militia outpost near Bao Trai in late 1966   183

Front forces destroyed a militia outpost between Bao Trai and Hiep Hoa in 1966—a frequent occurrence during this period of the war   183

Revolutionary Development Cadres assemble in Bao Trai in 1967   183

An armored personnel carrier (APC or "track") is damaged by a mine near Hoc Mon Bridge on the Hau Nghia/Gia Dinh border   184

A dead comrade is evacuated by infantrymen of the 25th
Division during the Tet Offensive   184

A soldier of the 25th Division lies wounded by a U.S. claymore
mine that was captured and detonated by the enemy   185

The men of a Joint Vietnamese-U.S. Combined Reconnaissance
and Intelligence Platoon (CRIP) were a tough bunch   185

A patrol boat with American infantrymen aboard cruises the
Vam Co Dong River   186

U.S. infantrymen fly out on helicopters for a search and destroy
mission in 1967   186

This South Vietnamese militia outpost was established in 1969
in Due Hue district   187

This militia outpost, seen from the ground, was located in
territory long controlled by the Front   187

A B-52 strike on the Ho Bo Woods in 1967 is observed from
the outskirts of the Cu Chi base camp   187

The 25th Division base camp at Cu Chi in 1968 brings a bit
of stateside army life to Vietnam   188

An enemy rocket scored a hit in the Cu Chi base camp during
the 1968 Tet Offensive   188

This one-room schoolhouse was damaged by Front mortar in
1969   189

The Hiep Hoa sugar mill, once one of South Vietnam's major
industrial facilities, was heavily damaged and home to enemy
snipers by 1969   189

Combat infantrymen of the U.S. 25th Division search an
unidentified hamlet in Cu Chi district in 1968—an anxious
and fearful experience for Vietnamese villagers   190

Villagers eagerly participate in a 25th Division Medical Civic
Action Program (MEDCAP) in 1968   191

Members of the 25th Division band, wearing helmets and flak
jackets, entertain the people of Cu Chi   192

An American Psychological Operations unit distributes leaflets
in 1967 to the accompaniment of a blaring loudspeaker   192

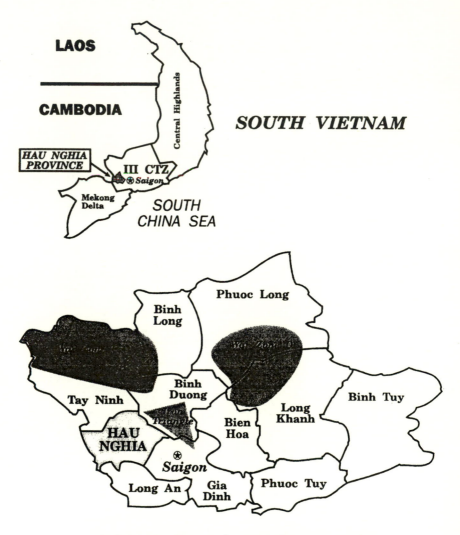

PROVINCES IN SAIGON AREA
III Corps Tactical Zone (III CTZ)

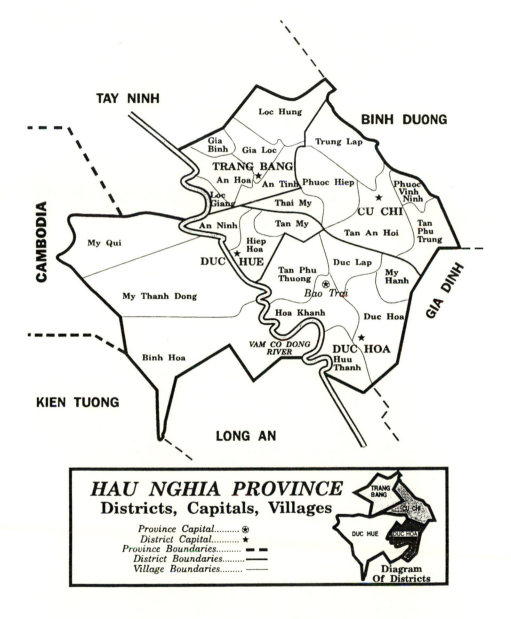

TAY NINH

BINH DUONG

CAMBODIA

GIA DINH

Loc Hung

Gia Binh
Gia Loc
TRANG BANG
An Hoa
An Tinh
Phuoc Hiep
Loc Giang
Trung Lap

Phuoc Vinh Ninh

CU CHI

Thai My

Tan My

An Ninh

Tan An Hoi

Tan Phu Trung

My Qui

Hiep Hoa

DUC HUE

Tan Phu Thuong

Duc Lap

My Hanh

My Thanh Dong

Bao Trai

Hoa Khanh

Duc Hoa

VAM CO DONG RIVER

Binh Hoa

DUC HOA

Huu Thanh

KIEN TUONG

LONG AN

HAU NGHIA PROVINCE
Districts, Capitals, Villages

Province Capital.......... ⊛
District Capital.......... ★
Province Boundaries.......... ▄ ▄
District Boundaries......... ▬▬▬
Village Boundaries......... ▬▬▬

TRANG BANG

CU CHI

DUC HUE

DUC HOA

Diagram Of Districts

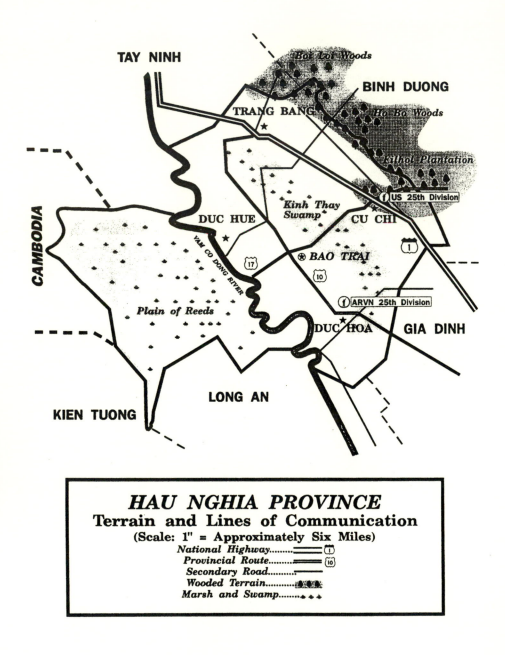

HAU NGHIA PROVINCE
Terrain and Lines of Communication
(Scale: 1" = Approximately Six Miles)

National Highway.........

Provincial Route..........

Secondary Road...........

Wooded Terrain.............

Marsh and Swamp.........

Introduction

This book is a history of the war in Hau Nghia province, Republic of Vietnam, during the period of 1963–1973. Hau Nghia, formed in October 1963, was a small entity even in Vietnamese terms. Furthermore, because it was a South Vietnamese administrative unit only and not recognized by the National Liberation Front (NLF), Hau Nghia no longer exists. Therefore, on the face of things, it might appear that a lengthy study concerning the course of war in Hau Nghia makes little sense. However, an examination of the conflict in this small province is valuable on two levels for students of the Vietnam War.

First, the province was the key administrative unit in rural South Vietnam. The provincial administrations had far more authority over the local population than did lower political entities, such as the district or village. Individual province chiefs, usually field-grade army officers, wielded the power of a satrap. Anything done in Saigon that touched the lives of rural citizens went through the province capital for direct implementation or delegation below. Hence, economic planning, public works, primary education, and health care were administered on the province level. More importantly, during the period in question, most political initiatives and many of the military efforts aimed at destroying the Communist-led insurgency in South Vietnam were either planned or controlled at the province level. American combat divisions normally established their tactical areas of responsibility, and thus the course of their operations, on the basis of provincial boundaries. American Province Senior Advisors (PSA) were among the most important individuals in the massive advisory effort. Therefore, a province study has great value. Although the major decisions of the war were made in Saigon or Washington, an examination of a microcosm of the struggle at the province level makes possible a clear and basic understanding of the military and political dynamics, the nuts and bolts of revolutionary warfare, that characterized this unique and crucial struggle.

Secondly, Hau Nghia is an excellent province to examine. Situated between Saigon and Communist bases along the Cambodian border, Hau Nghia intrinsically had great strategic importance. Furthermore, unlike many provinces in the Central Highlands, Hau Nghia was almost entirely populated by ethnic Vietnamese, so it is not necessary to consider the special circumstances caused by the presence of non-Vietnamese hill tribes. Unlike the cities and some coastal areas, Hau Nghia was inhabited mostly by peasants who represented the largest and politically most important segment of South Vietnam's population. In addition, though it was usually present and always important, the "big-unit war," so prominent just south of the Demilitarized Zone (DMZ), did not totally engulf Hau Nghia and make the local insurgency unrecognizable due to the constant infusion of outside forces. Conversely, in contrast to some provinces in the Mekong Delta where American units never operated and the war remained at a much lower level, in Hau Nghia province, Americans played a large and critical role. Most importantly, Hau Nghia was in the heartland of the insurgency. For political and strategic reasons, it was typical of the type of area in which Saigon had to prevail if it had any hope of long-term survival. Therefore, both sides made a great and sustained effort to triumph there. From beginning to end, the battle was fierce and closely reflected both the ebb and flow of the general struggle and the structural strengths and weaknesses of the contending forces.

This project has a somewhat curious genesis. A year before the fall of Saigon, which surprised me along with everyone else, I was stimulated to think deeply about the war through my acquaintance with several American officers and civilians who had been a part of the large advisory effort in rural Vietnam. These men were disappointed and bitter because of their experience. As I later found out, they and many other veterans of the pacification campaign believed that the mode of operations developed by the U.S. military command in Vietnam was inappropriate to the political struggle in the rural areas because it relied far too heavily on the application of conventional military power.

In the view of these officers, dependence on military measures had two very serious defects. First, an overemphasis on the military sphere caused a poor allocation of human and financial resources. The army's fixation on wasteful big-unit "search and destroy" operations led to the neglect of less costly and more sophisticated measures that could have brought security and well-being to rural Vietnam. Changing the political orientation of the peasantry from hostility or apathy toward Saigon to genuine support should have been the object of U.S. efforts, and Americans should have pursued the destruction of the enemy's military units only when it suited this larger political aim. Military operations should never have been allowed to become an end unto themselves. Second, these officers maintained that the violence coming from U.S. and South Vietnamese military operations was both counterproductive and morally reprehensible. The "big-unit" war brought grief, suffering, and material destruction to the Vietnamese countryside. Innocent victims of the violence were driven to either hatred of the government or numb war weariness. In either case, the enemy benefited. Small pockets of goodwill developed by various aid projects were often destroyed in an instant by something as catastrophic as a needless air strike or as minor as a thoughtless American soldier shooting a water buffalo. My friends also were saddened deeply by the harm done to the U.S. Army. Although not defeated militarily, its effectiveness was impaired and its reputation damaged by this degrading, fruitless conflict.

At the time, I was very impressed by these arguments because they were intellectually cogent and showed a high degree of ethical sensitivity. The collapse of South Vietnam proved beyond all doubt that something had gone very wrong, and it added greatly to my desire to make some contribution toward understanding the debacle. Therefore, upon receiving funds from the Center for Military History in Washington, D.C., I decided to write a history of the war in Hau Nghia province that would illustrate how an inappropriate use of force shackled the American war effort and contributed to defeat. Implicit in this argument was the belief that a more rational effort made toward "nation building" in rural South Vietnam might well have led to a favorable outcome of the war. Such a point, I believe, would have been worth making.

But during the past few years of research and composition, I have changed my views almost entirely. Although I still believe that a study of the war in Hau Nghia province is of great interest, I now do so because, in my opinion, it shows that the problems facing the Americans in Vietnam were insurmountable once President Lyndon Johnson decided to intervene. I now believe that, because of unalterable structural characteristics of both the South Vietnamese government and the U.S. Armed Forces, the number of actual options available to Americans in Vietnam was very low. Rather, I am impressed with the enormous difficulties that stood in the way of pursuing any greatly different policy, military or political, that could have spared us defeat in Vietnam. Indeed, four points drawn from a study of Hau Nghia province, briefly stated below, illustrate why, in my opinion, the difficulties we faced were virtually beyond solution, given the political and military realities that existed in Vietnam, the United States, and the world arena.

First, as shown distinctly in Hau Nghia province, the Government of Vietnam (GVN) lacked legitimacy with the rural peasantry, the largest segment of its population. Throughout its sad history, except in a very few areas, the best the GVN was able to gain was the acquiescence of the rural population; deep and genuine support was rare. There were good reasons for this. The peasantry perceived the GVN to be aloof, corrupt, and inefficient. Many, probably most, Americans with any experience in rural Vietnam shared this perception. The GVN lacked legitimacy because, in most important respects, it represented a continuation of the political and social structure established over the years by the French colonial administration. South Vietnam's urban elite possessed the outward manifestations of a foreign culture and often professed an alien faith. More importantly, this small group held most of the wealth and power in a poor nation, and the attitude of the ruling elite toward the rural population was, at best, paternalistic and, at worst, predatory. Nor did the ruling elites, understandably, ever show any desire to take measures that would endanger their position.

Faced with these realities, American efforts to change the political attitude of the rural population toward the GVN from acquiescence to genuine support failed again and again. Furthermore, every American political or economic effort in the countryside was aimed at reform or raising the material standard of living. With the partial exception of Nguyen Van Thieu's tardy and limited land reform program, neither the GVN nor the Americans ever proposed a fundamental change in the social or economic makeup of South Vietnam. This is not to argue that the Government of Vietnam was a particularly bad one when judged by the standards of other postcolonial regimes. Rather, history and geography condemned the GVN to face a unique and brutal challenge coming from North Vietnam and its instrument, the National Liberation Front. The problem facing the GVN was not to regain legitimacy lost but, rather, to establish legitimacy in the first place. Therefore, not only did Saigon have to crush the Front, it had to establish a political base at the same time. And this daunting task had to be accomplished before fatigue neutralized the indispensable American support required to counter a threat from the North that might exist for an indefinite time. The cumulative weight of these tasks was too great for the GVN to bear.

The second factor that ultimately frustrated allied efforts, illustrated so well in Hau Nghia province, was the great strength of the Communist-led National Liberation Front in the rural areas. The Front was the direct descendant of the Viet Minh and thus antedated the GVN. It offered a forceful and convincing vision of an alternate future. The Front was also the agent of the Democratic Republic of Vietnam (DRV), which was both powerful and completely dedicated to extending its sovereignty over the entire country. At the time of American intervention on the ground in 1965, the Front occupied and administered almost all of Hau Nghia province, along with large portions of South Vietnam as a whole. Although it had few qualms about employing ruthless tactics, such as the everpresent assassination campaign, the Front nevertheless enjoyed widespread support among the peasantry. In sharp contrast to GVN officials, Front cadres were perceived by most peasants as honest, efficient, and, coming as they did from the ranks of the peasantry, more responsive to the rural population. Among the peasantry, the Front was often supported, usually respected, and always feared. Furthermore, despite the great risks involved, the Front was usually more appealing than the GVN to the bravest, most intelligent, and most politically aware of the rural youth. To young men and women from the countryside, the Front offered the idealistic vision of a unified socialist Vietnam. It also recruited and promoted on the basis of merit and offered to the ambitious an opportunity to help govern the new Vietnam. The alternative offered to young peasants by the GVN—conscription into the armed forces—was much safer but involved almost no chance of upward social or economic mobility. For this reason, Front leaders, in general, greatly surpassed their GVN counterparts in terms of commitment, determination, and morale. Consequently, the Front was able to establish an extremely formidable political apparatus in the countryside, protected by a large and highly motivated light infantry army. Unfortunately for the allies, the great strength of the Front meant that efforts to crush the NLF would require much time and a lavish use of force.

The third important consideration emerging from a study of Hau Nghia province is the fact that the Americans in Vietnam, despite many claims to the contrary, showed a keen appreciation, in theory and in practice, of the importance of the political struggle in the countryside. From the beginning of American involvement in Vietnam, there was an endless succession of political, military, and economic initiatives aimed at changing the political allegiance of the rural population. Most of these initiatives were inspired, planned, and partially implemented by American personnel. Indeed, U.S. military units, often criticized for wasting their efforts in fruitless search and destroy missions, spent a substantial amount of time during every phase of the war attempting to improve the position of the GVN in the countryside. Unfortunately for the allies, every effort to change the basic political relationships in rural Vietnam foundered because of the structural weakness of the GVN and the grim tenacity of the Front. Almost all "progress" from the allied point of view was coercive and entailed an essentially negative process: The Front could be weakened, principally through military attrition, but the GVN could not be strengthened.

Lastly, an examination of the war in Hau Nghia province strongly suggests that military force, much of it American, was the only method through which the allies could effectively combat the Front. Enemy military forces by 1965 were very formidable and represented a genuine threat. Until organized Front military units were defeated, forced to flee, or weakened through attrition, "nation building" was impossible. No amount of political sophistication or cultural sensitivity could alter the fact that a fierce and lengthy military campaign was essential. Furthermore, despite the maxim that the bayonet was the best weapon for counterinsurgency and an air strike the worst, it was impossible for the U.S. Army to fight the necessary military campaign without causing great destruction and much loss of innocent life. Under the best of circumstances, it was difficult to distinguish between friend and foe in Vietnam. And an inherently difficult situation was made worse when the Front frequently and intentionally provoked American fire into populated areas. Ideally, our soldiers should have been more discriminating in their use of violence, but it should come as no surprise that, under fire, they acted like the tired and scared men that they were. Violence in war is a historical given, not a variable. Moreover, the counterproductive aspects of the violence campaign must be weighed against the grim but undeniable fact that the huge number of Front followers killed, wounded, captured, or driven to surrender shook the Front very badly. Unfortunately for the United States, the long war of attrition required to weaken the NLF was simultaneously a crushing burden on the U.S. Army and led inevitably to a steady decline in public support for the war effort. Unfortunately for Saigon, the war of attrition ultimately fragmented the Republic of Vietnam and left it defenseless.

A note on terminology will be helpful. Inescapably, I have used many of the multitude of acronyms created during the Vietnam War. I have listed the original term for each acronym when first used, and a list of military terms and acronyms is included. In general, I used the terms most widely employed in the documents to describe the respective sides. Consequently, the Republic of Vietnam is referred to as the "GVN," "Saigon," or simply the "government." The National Liberation Front is referred to as the "Front" or the "NLF." The People's Revolutionary Party, which was a branch of the Vietnamese Workers Party (the Communist Party of North Vietnam), I have referred to as the "Party." Except when they appear in quotes, I have avoided the derogatory terms used by the opposing sides to refer to each other, such as "Viet Cong" or the "Saigon puppet regime."

This research would have been impossible without the aid of the Center of Military History (CMH) in Washington, D.C. The fine staff of CMH, currently producing a multivolume history of the Vietnam War for the Department of the Army, rendered every possible form of aid. Despite the large number of classified documents I was required to use, the U.S. Army never hindered my research in any way; rather, army officers and employees were invariably helpful and generous with their time. As I understand it, the army has taken the very sensible attitude that honest research on this painful topic can only serve to gain a fuller picture of the truth, and, even if critical of army policy, this will be an improvement over the extreme vilification that characterized many works done during the war itself.

I have also received valuable assistance from Douglas Pike and Steve Denny at the Indochina Archives, a branch of the Institute of East Asian Studies at the University of California. I have used many of the Archives's collection of interviews and interrogations that the Rand Corporation and others conducted during the war with defectors and prisoners of war. The Indochina Archives also supplied me with a translation of a remarkable document, *Vietnam: History of the Bulwark B2 Theatre* by General Tran Van Tra, commander of the Front's ground forces. Using these resources, I have tried to incorporate the other side's perspective of the struggle.

Lastly, I am grateful to the many American veterans of the war in Hau Nghia province who helped me. Several advisors have provided me with a retrospective view of the American war effort in the countryside, and dozens of former soldiers of the 25th Infantry Division have contributed taped interviews, letters, and other documents. Their help has given me invaluable insight into the alien, intense, and dangerous world of the combat infantryman in Vietnam. A complete list of all of the people interviewed can be found in the Note on Primary Sources.

I also would like to note that, although I believe the entire war was a miserable chapter in our history, this project is analytical and very impersonal in tone. Any researcher working on the Vietnam War is confronted by bewildering and complex ethical and moral questions. For the purposes of this work, however, I have accepted the moral validity of warfare in general and of the Vietnam War in particular. Doing otherwise would have jeopardized my purpose of explaining the structure and tempo of the war. I hope that an understanding of the deadly coherence that governed the struggle will help the reader to comprehend the strange, chaotic, and sinister atmosphere that surrounded this dreadful conflict.

A Note on Primary Sources

This project is based almost entirely on primary sources. All records of the Hau Nghia advisory team and all CORDS documents employed can be found at the Current History Branch, U.S. Army Center of Military History (CMH), Washington, D.C. When suitable, I have listed the appropriate file. The records of the 25th Infantry Division and II Field Force are available at the Washington National Records Center, Suitland, Maryland. In addition, I have copies of all military records employed and most CORDS documents. The interviews of Front defectors recorded during the war by Rand Corporation and others can be found at the Indochina Archive, Institute for Southeast Asian Studies, University of California, Berkeley. Oliver Davidson, a young CORDS field-worker during the war with long experience in Hau Nghia province, was kind enough to allow me to copy a large number of his reports and notes from this period; these are referred to in the notes as "Davidson Papers."

I have given the complete title of any record employed when used for the first time in the notes and used a shortened title or abbreviation for further citations. However, to aid the reader, the following is a list of the most frequently used records, along with the abbreviations employed in the notes.

Headquarters, Advisory Team 43, *Hau Nghia Province Report* (hereafter cited as Hau Nghia PR, followed by appropriate date).

Headquarters, 25th Infantry Division, *Operational Report—Lessons Learned* (hereafter cited as 25th ORLL, followed by appropriate date).

Headquarters, II Field Force Vietnam, *Operational Report—Lessons Learned* (hereafter cited as II Field Force ORLL, followed by appropriate date).

Headquarters, MACCORDS III Corps Tactical Zone, *III Corps Tactical Zone Overview* (hereafter cited as III CTZ Overview, followed by the appropriate date).

Chester L. Cooper et al., *The American Experience with Pacification in Vietnam: An Overview,* (Contract Study, Institute for Defense Analysis, Arlington, Va., 1972), Vol. 3 (hereafter cited as Cooper, *American Experience with Pacification*).

I have also used a large number of interviews, mostly taped, and letters to the author. Unless noted otherwise, the interviews were conducted in the summer or fall of 1989. Interested parties may review any of this material. If the information derived from the interviews or letters pertains to matters of policy, I have cited it. However, to avoid unnecessary footnotes, I have not cited material dealing with impressions, anecdotes, or descriptions of the environment. Below is a list of the people who shared their thoughts and memories.

25th Infantry Division

Henry P. Bergson
Phil Boardman
C. W. Bowman
Charles Boyd
Daniel Breeding
Michael Call
Dale Canter
Robert Conner
Samuel L. Crouch
Todd Dexter
Col. Thomas Ferguson (Ret.)
Thomas Giltner
Kenneth Gosline
Dennis E. Hackin
Jerry Headley
Robert Julian
William Kestell
Robert Knoll
Gerald Kolb

Jay Lazarin
Jeri Liucci
Roger McGill
Maj. Gen. Thomas Mellen (Ret.)
Tim Menglekoch
Jim Murphy
Hector Nadal
Alan Neil
Del Plonka
Gregory Pybon
Lt. Col. Carl Quickmire (Ret.)
John A. Riggs
Tim Ross
Larry Rutt
Morgan J. Sincock
Sidney Stone
Dan Vandenberg
Maj. Gen. Ellis W. Williamson (Ret.)
Michael Willis

Advisory Team 43: Hau Nghia Province

Lt. Gen. Gerald Bartlett (Ret.)
Col. Carl Bernard (Ret.)
Col. James Bremer (Ret.)
Lt. Col. Frank Chance (Ret.)
Lt. Col. David B. Harrington (Ret.)
Brig. Gen. Stuart A. Herrington

Richard O'Hare
John Pancrazio
Lt. Col. Donald Pearce (Ret.)
Col. Andrew Rutherford (Ret.)
Col. Jack K. Weissinger (Ret.)
Lt. Col. Elliott R. Worthington (Ret.)

Others

Phillip Davidson
Bert Freleigh, AID

Colonel Donald Marshall (Ret.), CORDS
Hugh Stovall, 196th Light Infantry Brigade

I have used no anonymous material. I have omitted or changed the names of Vietnamese defectors or prisoners to eliminate the slight possibility that some individual might come to harm, but the original material can be consulted. I have also left out the names of a few American soldiers to spare them or others personal embarrassment.

1

The Challenge of Insurgency: South Vietnam, 1954–1965

The Diem Regime

By the fall of 1963, the Republic of Vietnam, headed by President Ngo Dinh Diem, was losing its war against the Communist-led National Liberation Front. As frequently happens in war, difficulties on the battlefield brought about administrative changes. Because the situation in the area northwest of Saigon was particularly grave, Diem decided to detach four contiguous districts from three provinces and form a new province between the Saigon suburb of Gia Dinh and the Cambodian border. This reorganization was accomplished by presidential decree on October 15, 1963. The new province was named Hau Nghia and was comprised of Duc Hoa and Duc Hue districts (formerly of Long An province), Trang Bang district of Tay Ninh province, and Cu Chi district of Binh Duong province. Saigon hoped that the change of boundaries would lead to a concentration of action in a strategically important area and thus aid the overall war effort. Whatever the merits of Diem's decision, it was purely administrative and in no way indicated a change of strategy. Consequently, the establishment of Hau Nghia was not a major event within Vietnam and went unnoticed outside the country. A month later, Diem was deposed and murdered.

It is grim coincidence that the murder of Diem and the creation of Hau Nghia occurred so closely together. Yet, for our purposes, the coincidence is helpful. While Diem was in power, the conduct of the war was in the hands of Saigon. Although U.S. aid was, from the first, essential and American officials frequently troublesome, Diem was very capable of maintaining an independent, although unsuccessful, policy against his enemies inside and outside the NLF.

After the deaths of Diem and his brother Ngo Dinh Nhu, the overall situation in South Vietnam changed fundamentally. From that point onward, the direction of the South Vietnamese war effort, to the extent that it had direction, was increasingly influenced or controlled by Americans. Although successive regimes in Saigon jealously guarded the political and economic position of the South Vietnamese ruling elites, they permitted the United

States to play the dominant role in formulating the war effort. Virtually every new policy attempted from 1964 until at least 1970 was American in origin, and whatever impetus existed for these policies came from American funds and often from American personnel. Hence, to a large degree, the war in Hau Nghia province was an American war from the beginning.

Yet, it would scarcely be possible to understand the course of events in Hau Nghia after 1963 without a general look backward at the years following the Geneva Conference of 1954.[1] In this period, the NLF gained both the political initiative over the Diem government and an increasingly favorable balance of political and military forces. Also during this period, Saigon attempted to combat the growing threat to its existence with methods that clearly foreshadowed later American efforts.

When the Geneva Conference adjourned in July of 1954, South Vietnam was in a state of near chaos. Economic uncertainty, the inherent difficulties of establishing a new government apparatus, streams of refugees, the bizarre activities of the religious sects and bandit groups, and malicious intrigues between French and American agents made impossible an orderly transition from colonial domination to independence. Even worse was the provisional nature of the Geneva Accords. The Final Declaration of the conference, calling for national elections in two years, was crippled from the start because it was left unsigned, only accepted orally, denounced by Saigon, and accepted only with reservations by the United States. Clearly, war or rebellion might return in the near future. Therefore, it is not correct to view the Vietnam conflict during the 1955–1959 period as a steady erosion of the Saigon government's power at the hands of Communist-led insurgents. Rather, a power vacuum existed throughout South Vietnam, which Diem rushed to fill.

Initially, Diem had several advantages. First, there was an undeniable war weariness and desire for some sort of stability on the part of the vast majority of the population, both rural and urban. Second, despite plots by the departing French, Diem had managed to secure the support of the United States. Backed by U.S. aid, which continued unabated after the Geneva Accords, Diem's promises of reform and prosperity were plausible. Diem had been anti-French, in contrast to top South Vietnamese military leaders and the completely discredited Emperor Bao Dai. Therefore, many non-Communist elements within the Viet Minh could be expected if not to support the new government, then at least to await developments and see if Diem could establish a genuine government. Most important, although perhaps not fully appreciated by Diem, was the attitude of the Communist leadership, both north and south.

Apparently, there were few illusions within the higher echelons of the Party concerning the likelihood of the nationwide elections and reunification talks agreed to at Geneva. Nevertheless, the Party had claimed that Geneva was a great victory; immediate action against Diem would contradict this line. It also dismissed the possibility of a truly popular Saigon government being established in the rural areas because of class conflict and structural contradictions. Furthermore, establishing a strong socialist government in Hanoi and rebuilding war-ravaged areas throughout the North was the top priority of the Party. Therefore, Party leadership adopted a two-pronged strategy: regroupment of essential cadres to North Vietnam and reorganization of a secret Party apparatus in the South. An underground cadre from Cholon later described the situation:

> The main guideline for the people who were to stay was there was to be no public violation of the Agreement. We were supposed to maintain our legal identities as ordinary citizens. Organizations were to be maintained at the most minimal levels; no written communications or papers were to be utilized in any way. The object was complete, total secrecy. . . . We were told that Diem might honor the Agreement or he might not. But in either case we had to continue the movement, keep people warmed up and keep the organizations going. If there really were elections, then we would be able to capitalize on the situation more quickly if the networks were in place. And if there weren't, we would be better prepared to resume the struggle. In any event, the Party could never sleep on its victories.[2]

Consistent with this strategy, most of the trained military cadres along with any technical specialists, moved north. Because the Geneva Accords theoretically offered protection to former resistance fighters, a sizable number of Party members in the rural areas registered with Saigon authorities and began a legal existence. However, the most dedicated Party members, who had managed to maintain a secret existence during hostilities, remained underground and totally reorganized the Party on the basis of a secret cell system. The main task of the illegal segment of the Party was to prepare political action in case of elections or to lay the groundwork for future political resistance if, as was believed likely, no elections were held. With memories still fresh of the 1945 Hanoi general uprising, which led to the establishment of the Democratic Republic of Vietnam under Ho Chi Minh, the Party directed much effort toward strengthening its position in Saigon. According to the Geneva Accords, no Communist military units were to be left in the South, but the new Party apparatus carefully established the nucleus for a new military strike force. Old weapons were taken to the North, and new ones were hidden. In areas where terrain allowed secret activity, small main force units remained in existence. Nevertheless, the primary attention of the Party was centered on the North, and the Party in the South was relatively disarmed.

With his most dangerous enemy occupied elsewhere and for the moment honoring the Geneva Accords, Diem amazed his many American detractors by moving quickly and skillfully to establish some sort of government in the South. First, in April 1955, he succeeded in crushing the Binh Xuyen, a well-entrenched criminal organization centered in Saigon. More bloodshed followed when the Cao Dai and Hoa Hao, two religious sects with private armies and originally allied with the Binh Xuyen, were also dispersed or forced to submit to Diem's authority. Strengthened by this show of force,

Diem next conducted a referendum that ended the Vietnamese monarchy and proclaimed himself president of a new Republic of Vietnam. All the while, Nhu, Diem's eccentric but powerful brother, developed the Can Lao political party and propagated a strange proto-Fascist "personalist" ideology.

Diem and Nhu knew perfectly well that the remnants of the Viet Minh would ultimately be their principal enemy. Indeed, Party-inspired mass demonstrations extolling the "victory at Geneva" were commonplace events. Therefore, while preparing action against the Binh Xuyen, Diem and Nhu initiated the Anti-Communist Denunciation Campaign, which rapidly developed into a manhunt directed against the Party. The hunt increased in scope and energy with each Diem victory. Predictably, the Cong An, Diem's police, were hardly discriminating. It proved easy to accuse any potential enemy of having Communist affiliations. Jails filled, and an uncommonly large number of prisoners were shot while attempting escape. According to a later study prepared for the U.S. Defense Department, "There can be no doubt, on the basis of reports of the few impartial observers, that innumerable crimes and absolutely senseless acts of suppression against both real and suspected Communists and sympathizing villagers were committed. Efficiency took the form of brutality and a total disregard for the difference between determined foes and potential friends."[3]

It may be that Diem created as many enemies as he neutralized with his indiscriminate approach. Nevertheless, his campaign left the Party reeling. In fact, the Party was quite unprepared for what had transpired. Although a strong clandestine tradition existed, the Party had organized quite openly in the rural areas while fighting the French; much of rural Vietnam had been, after all, totally under Party control. Furthermore, many underground Viet Minh followers had surfaced, and others had moved north. As previously mentioned, Party leaders had discounted the possibility of creating a strong central government. On the contrary, they were confident that chaos would continue and had hopes of a coup or general uprising in the near future. Diem's campaign, therefore, had the advantage of surprise. Party leaders were rounded up in the cities and, where possible, in the rural villages. Every time a cell, the Party's basic three-person organizational building block, was compromised, it had to be rebuilt. Often, a cell had to be reorganized many times over.[4]

With the situation in the South deteriorating and the Geneva Accords appearing more and more a dead letter, bitter debate began within the Party leadership on how best to proceed. Le Duan and others proposed a rapid switch to armed struggle. Truong Chinh, Gen. Nguyen Vo Giap, and other "northerners" urged patience. In December 1956, a compromise was agreed to at the Central Committee's Eleventh Plenum, calling for both continuing political agitation in the near term and long-range preparations for armed struggle. Southern cadres were not fully privy to these deliberations. Furthermore, they had to face the Cong An on a daily basis and were both fearful and impatient. Morale within the Party dropped, and many apparently felt betrayed by Ho Chi Minh and the Soviet Union. Because the Party had claimed publicly that the Accords would be carried out while actually expecting a quick end to the Diem regime, confidence in the judgment of the leadership fell and defections rose.[5] Diem had seized the initiative, and prospects for the Party seemed bleak. However, Diem could not yet claim victory. Saigon's authority had not yet been extended to cover the countryside, where some 80 percent of the population lived. By 1956, attempts by the Saigon government to achieve this control were under way.

Diem's efforts were both administrative and military. He began by abolishing the elective village councils that Bao Dai had established. In June 1956, Diem decreed, without benefit of statute as legally required, that, henceforth, elective councils would be replaced by three- to five-man committees appointed by the province chief.[6] Furthermore, four months later, Saigon proclaimed that the province chiefs would be appointed directly by the president and would be responsible for all administration within the province. In early 1957, the power of the province chief was further enhanced by making him commander of all military forces controlled by the province. From this time on, most province chiefs were ARVN (Army of the Republic of Vietnam) field-grade officers. These measures were all intended to centralize power within South Vietnam. However, because loyalty to Diem was obviously the first requisite for appointment, all too often the new province chiefs and lesser officials proved to be corrupt cronies of Nhu or one of his allies.

While Diem was centralizing administrative power in his own hands, the South Vietnamese army was kept busy with sweeps through rural areas. After a village or hamlet was apparently cleared of enemy forces, a six-man Civic Action cadre team moved in, when available. The cadre teams, a personal creation of Diem and Nhu, were a transparent copy of the Viet Minh cadres who had played the central role in the struggle against France. They were necessary for Diem because he had virtually no political constituency in rural Vietnam outside Catholic areas. (Diem, the quintessential Vietnamese urban aristocrat, knew almost nothing about agrarian life. His few journeys to the countryside while president were carefully stage-managed affairs.) Team leaders reported directly to a presidential office and, in theory, operated independently of village and province officials. A primary role for a cadre, on paper, was to serve as a sort of people's ombudsman, capable of passing complaints against bad officials directly to Saigon. The cadre teams were to gain the confidence of the villagers by living with them and by establishing self-help projects, made possible with U.S. aid. Once the proper rapport had been established, the cadres were to propagandize against the Communists and praise Diem and the Can Lao Party. Villagers, no doubt wisely, would go through the motions in more or less good humor. Gerald Hickey, the prominent American anthropologist, witnessed some propaganda meetings:

> Every Saturday evening there is a hamlet Communist denunciation meeting, and the hamlet chief and five-family leaders are responsible for seeing that all male residents over 18 years are in attendance. On the fifteenth day of

> each lunar month there is a general Communist denunciation meeting held at the dinh [communal temple]. . . . Villagers dutifully assist at these meetings, but most do not appear particularly attentive. Some squat outside the dinh chatting in low tones while a few read newspapers. After one denunciation meeting, a young farmer regaled his friends in one of the nearby shops by imitating the speaker of the evening.[7]

According to the recollections of a cadre leader of this period, many villagers simply disbelieved the message: "We were supposed to explain why the communists were bad and why the people must follow the government. But during the Resistance the communists had been the only ones in the village to fight against the French, so when we tried to explain that the communists were evil people, the villagers just didn't listen to us."[8]

The Civic Action cadre teams were a parody of political development. Aid programs, when properly and honestly administered, were welcomed by the peasants. Corruption, however, was the rule. Team members were well paid; consequently, like the military and civilian administrators, they were usually appointed because of political or family ties rather than merit. Invariably, they came from outside the area and rarely were from rural backgrounds. Diem's cadres differed from the Party's in yet another respect: Regardless of their independence, the Civic Action cadres were yet another projection of state power coming from the outside. There was no internal recruitment or organic link with the community, two fundamental characteristics of the Viet Minh and, later, the Front cadres. The Civic Action cadres were *in* rural Vietnam, not of it. Furthermore, beyond some strange and foreign ideology and a few material trinkets, they had nothing to offer. Their task was futile, and their role was minor. They are worth mentioning only because they foreshadow the large and theoretically crucial Revolutionary Development Cadre program launched by Americans ten years later.[9]

As Saigon attempted to extend its control throughout the countryside, it was forced to face the explosive issue of landownership. In the years before World War II, landholding patterns in Cochin (which is what the French called the southern third of Vietnam) had degenerated, in the words of an American economist, into a static "mechanism for widespread economic exploitation and social abuse."[10] Large French and Vietnamese absentee landholders dominated the Mekong Delta especially. The upper 2.5 percent of landowners held approximately 45 percent of the land. With the population expanding and new land progressively more expensive to develop, the result was a steady increase in rent demanded of tenants, until it reached 40 to 60 percent of the annual rice harvest. At the same time, caloric consumption declined after 1930. Many of the landless lived on the edge of survival. Naturally, the Viet Minh were quick to capitalize on this situation. When war against France began, French-held land and large Vietnamese-owned estates were confiscated, and remaining large landowners were driven into the cities. This land, in turn, was distributed to the landless. Small landowners were left in peace, reflecting the Viet Minh's united-front strategy. Where land was still rented, limits were placed on rents and tenants assured of long-term rentals. As might be imagined, this policy was extremely popular and earned for the Viet Minh the loyalty and gratitude of hundreds of thousands of poor peasants.[11]

The Geneva Accords in 1954 brought an uncertain situation concerning landholding. As the landowners constituted an important bloc supporting Diem and the Saigon government, Diem did not have the option of accepting the land redistribution that had taken place during the fighting as permanent. Rather, as Saigon extended its forces into the countryside, the landlords and their agents also returned. To prevent the worst type of exploitation seen during French rule, Diem, under American pressure, issued a series of regulations limiting rents to between 15 and 25 percent of the annual harvest, providing secure tenure rights, and limiting individuals to 100 hectares of cropland. Land over this limit was to be purchased by the government and resold to the peasants.

However, such measures, which would have been progressive thirty years earlier, had little appeal to peasants who had received land expropriated by the Viet Minh. Furthermore, in execution, Diem's program was a dreadful failure. To begin with, regulations concerning rents were frequently ignored. A 1967 U.S. study showed that rents in government-controlled areas were in the 25 to 40 percent range. Naturally, landlords held on to the best land if they were actually forced to sell a portion of their holdings. The decree did not cover land devoted to cash crops, and implementation of the program was laborious and required a great amount of paperwork. Loopholes existed in all phases of the program and were often exploited by the landowners to slow or stop implementation. Another counterproductive aspect of the program was the 100-hectare limit. Because only a few very rich landowners had title to more than 100 hectares, middle-level landowners were not touched at all. Worse yet, influential politicians and members of Diem's families used the program to gain ownership of much of the land expropriated by the government. Indeed, the GVN itself became the largest landlord in the country by far. Rents on government land went into the provincial coffers and were a prime source of graft. Frequently, local officials doubled as land agents for private owners or for government holdings. Lastly, Diem's measures did not truly come to grips with the problem of the landless peasant. In the Mekong Delta, where most of the peasants lived, figures from 1960–1961 show that 62 percent of all land was rented and only 22 percent of the peasantry owned all of the land they farmed.[12] Locally, distribution might be even worse. In Long An province (part of which was soon to be transferred to Hau Nghia), for example, only 10 percent of the 75,000 hectares of rented rice land was subject to expropriation. Due to delays and corruption, only some 3 percent of the estimated 35,000 families renting land in Long An ever gained title under the program.[13]

Diem's land policy soon proved a bonus for the Party. Not only was redistribution largely illusory but the peasants were also forced to sign contracts with the landowners, reaffirming the latter's rights of title. Naturally, the Party propagandized against Diem's program. The effect of the Party's efforts is well illustrated by the following account, given by a former Front military officer who was a landless peasant in Long An at the time of his recruitment:

> I was poor. I had lost my land. I didn't have enough money to take care of my children. In 1961 propaganda cadres of the Front contacted me. . . . They came to all the poor farmers and made an analysis of the poor and rich classes. They said that the rich people had always served the French and had used the authority of the French to oppress the poor. . . . Without any other means to live, the poor had become slaves of the landlords. The cadres told us that if the poor people don't stand up to the rich people, we would be dominated by them forever. The only way to ensure freedom and a sufficient life was to overthrow them. . . .
>
> When I heard the cadres, I thought that what they said was correct. In my village there were about forty-three hundred people. Of these, maybe ten were landlords. The richest owned five hundred hectares [1,236 acres], and the other had at least twenty hectares [49 acres] apiece. The rest of the people were tenants or honest poor farmers. I knew that the rich oppressed the poor. . . . So I joined the Liberation Front. I followed the VC [Viet Cong] to fight for freedom and prosperity for the country. I felt this was right.[14]

The land issue was only one among many that the Party exploited. Other economic ills, such as inflation, were attacked, along with the ubiquitous corruption of GVN officials. Diem's connections with the United States were condemned, as was his abrogation of the Geneva Accords. The charismatic Ho Chi Minh was contrasted in personal terms with Diem and Nhu. Therefore, the period 1957–1959 was a time of general recovery for the Party. Many of the most vulnerable cadres already had been imprisoned or killed in 1956; survivors were in safe areas or in deep cover. As the situation stabilized, much effort was concentrated on forming worker-peasant alliances and on proselytizing the peasant conscripts of Diem's armed forces. However, Party members were ready to concede that Diem's policies, particularly the land issue that so antagonized the peasantry, were more important than the Party's political work in aiding the recovery.[15]

Throughout 1957–1959 the Party adhered to the policy of political rather than violent resistance. However, because its apparatus had proven too vulnerable to the Cong An, Diem's secret police, the Party decided to answer in kind. Although the small main force armed units that survived Diem's 1956 offensive sought to avoid contact with government forces, another type of armed activity was initiated. Called tru gian by the Party ("extermination of traitors"), this revived policy, which had been employed heavily against the French, called for the assassination of government officials and agents considered dangerous to the Party.

The "extermination" policy was conducted in absolute secrecy. The Party denied responsibility for acts of terror and attempted to blame Saigon. The "traitors" picked for death fell into several categories. First and foremost were Cong An agents and other government officials who proved successful in tracking down members of the secret Party apparatus. Other victims included locally influential anti-Communist teachers, Civic Action Cadres who took their task too seriously, and local government officials. In the latter category, the Party was careful to target officials who proved honest and effective; the corrupt and inefficient were left in peace. Although some of the executions might have been the result of local vendettas, tru gian was unquestionably a premeditated policy with a long pedigree in the Party's history. (During and after World War II, the Party waged a ruthless campaign of assassination and intimidation against anti-Communist nationalist groups competing for leadership of the anti-French crusade.) It was a dangerous tactic. Just as many Vietnamese followed the Party because of their hatred for the GVN security services, relatives and friends of tru gian victims might well become enemies of the revolution out of hatred. Indeed, many of the most dedicated and skilled of the Party's opponents were driven by a desire for personal revenge. Nevertheless, the Party persevered in their role in the cycle of terror in Vietnam and, as shall be seen, later increased it greatly. There were very good reasons to do so. The "extermination" campaign protected Party cadres, sowed fear among GVN officials, and encouraged corruption and inefficiency on the part of government officials. In the words of a former Party leader in Dinh Tuong province, "In principle, the Party tried to kill any (government) official who enjoyed the people's sympathy and left the bad officials unharmed in order to wage propaganda and sow hatred against the government."[16]

It should be stressed, however, that, until 1960, even the extermination program was a small-scale and secret effort. The Party did not consider it as a move toward the armed struggle phase, during which the GVN would be challenged openly and assaulted with all possible vigor. The Party also kept secret its major role in sporadic fighting between GVN forces and remnants of the religious sects.[17] In general, despite pleas for armed resistance coming from many southern cadres, the Party leadership in Hanoi continued its political—as opposed to armed—strategy.

In Saigon, Diem appeared to be riding high. Government armed forces were lightly opposed and, thanks to U.S. aid, growing in size. Administration was expanded and tightened down to the village level. The government was increasingly able to collect taxes. A village militia (Dan Ve) and a Civil Guard (Bao An) were organized to protect village and district officials and installations, respectively. Cong An agents were active everywhere, identifying potential enemies of the regime. Diem convinced the Americans in Saigon (and he may have believed this himself) that continued insurgent activity was, in fact, a futile "last gasp" of a movement that had been defeated politically. In 1959, Diem launched his most intensive campaign against the Party. Military and Cong An operations increased steadily, and, in May, Diem promulgated Law 10/59, which provided for harsh punishment for virtually any antigovernment activity.[18]

In addition to the stepped-up offense against the Party, Diem and Nhu initiated an aggressive resettlement program. In February 1959, the government initiated the Agglomeration Centers plan, designed to resettle families suspected of sympathizing with the enemy with families considered loyal. The latter group would presumably keep the former in line. Understandably, potential "watchdog" families found this scheme most unappealing.[19]

In any case, it was upstaged in July by a population resettlement plan called the Agroville Program. This plan called for the construction of 80 large Agrovilles and 400 Agrohamlets by 1963. Agrovilles were to be constructed in areas where, for political or geographical reasons, government control was considered potentially vulnerable. Each Agroville was to be fortified and protected by militia and regular troops, and it was to offer advanced economic and educational aid to the villagers. Whatever advantages the Agrovilles theoretically possessed, the peasantry rejected them totally. The Agrovilles that actually were begun were constructed with forced labor that Diem considered national service. Although on paper the program was voluntary, in practice it entailed forced relocation; some peasants had to abandon lands cultivated for generations. Forced to leave family graveyards, many people were outraged. And corruption characterized the program every step of the way. In general, the Agroville Program justified the Party's conviction that Diem's policies would alienate the rural masses. Faced with resistance from the peasantry, the program was one of the first casualties when the Party decided to begin armed struggle. It folded in early 1961, barely 25 percent complete.[20]

Yet, in 1959, this defeat for Diem still lay in the future. His forces were pressing the Party harder than at any time in the past. In the words of a Communist defector, "If you did not have a gun you could not keep your head on your shoulders."[21] This impression is confirmed by a document captured in 1959 that was prepared by the Nam Bo Regional Committee (the highest Party organ in the South), entitled "Situation and Missions for 1959." Although concluding that the overall political situation was actually improving, the document clearly reflected the grave situation faced by Party members:

> Thus in the recent period, generally speaking, the enemy has created greater losses for the Party and for the popular movement than in previous years, and has been able to carry out a relatively greater number of plots, particularly those of an oppressive and a thieving nature, although the people's struggle movement against the enemy has also progressed, compared to previous years. . . . Basically, the movement is in a defensive position in the face of the daily increasing strength of the enemy's attacks.[22]

Perhaps the Party waited too long before striking back. Events, however, vindicated the leadership. Though doctrinal disputes in the politburo and pressure to adhere to Moscow's peaceful coexistence policy of the late 1950s played a role in the decision to delay armed struggle, much more important was the Party's view of the essential nature of Diem's regime. The Saigon government was considered by its very nature to be corrupt, repressive, and inefficient. The urban, and often Catholic, moneyed elite that supported Diem was viewed by the Party as predatory in relation to the rural masses.

Although the Party no doubt underestimated Diem in the short run, strategists in Hanoi believed that his military and administrative advances ultimately would count for nothing and actually would aid the Party. The leadership expected that Saigon's performance would prove to the peasants the truth of the Party's propaganda line. The Party was certain that, as Diem's administrative control of the rural areas extended, it would bring with it corruption, hated landlords, an unpopular draft and militia requirements, travel restrictions, bad administration, and an American presence that the masses would find humiliating. Thus, any apparent success for Saigon would be superficial and temporary. As Diem's regime revealed its true face to the masses, the Party was confident that an ever more favorable political situation would evolve. When the time was ripe, the Party would begin armed struggle, and the entire Diem apparatus, however imposing on paper, would collapse in short order. Events would show that the Party was entirely correct in its assessment. However difficult the local situation might become, the Party was determined to be patient and to allow Diem's oppression to create the political preconditions for armed struggle. The following quote from a high-level defector outlines Party policy at this time:

> The general situation, as I know from my own area, and as cadres from other areas told me, was that the cadres and the people were terribly anxious to cross to the armed phase, but that the Central Committee sought every means to prolong the political phase according to its concept of the "ripe situation." What is a "ripe situation"? It is one in which the masses have been brought to a point where, if not a majority, then at least a certain number must follow the path laid out by the Party: They must see no other escape from their predicament. How does one create a "ripe situation"? That is the purpose of political struggle. During that period Diem's terrorist policy was becoming more blatant day by day, and the alienation of the people from the government was becoming greater and greater. Thus the Party pushed the struggle movement, which increased the terrorism. But the more the people were terrorized, the more they reacted in opposition, yet the more they reacted, the more violently they were terrorized. Continue this until the situation is truly ripe, and it will explode, according to a saying of Mao Tse-tung: "A firefly can set a whole field ablaze." Yet for a firefly to set a whole field ablaze the field must be extremely dry. "To make the field dry" in this situation meant that we had to make the people suffer until they could no longer endure it. Only then would they carry out the Party's armed policy. That is why the Party waited until it did.[23]

In any event, the Party's patience provided ample rewards. In May 1959 (the exact date is uncertain), the Party Central Committee in Hanoi decided to begin armed struggle in closest coordination with continuing political struggle. This change in direction, eagerly sought by the southern cadres, quickly brought about a dramatic change in the overall balance of forces between Diem and his opponents. Throughout Vietnam, main force provincial battalions were reformed, and traditional base areas were rebuilt. Everywhere, preparations were under way to engage Diem's forces in selective combat.[24]

The switch to armed struggle was best evidenced by a sharp increase in terrorism. The "extermination of traitors" campaign was quickened in the last half of 1959. In early 1960, the Party launched a ferocious assault on Diem's rural political apparatus, highlighted by coordinated assassinations during the 1960 Tet celebrations of January 18–25. South Vietnamese figures supplied to the U.S. Embassy listed 233 assassinations in 1959, 143 of them taking place in the last two quarters. In the first five months of 1960, this figure surged to 780.

It is difficult to overrate the importance of the terror campaign. Previously, Saigon officials had virtual freedom of movement in the countryside. Many appointed officials lived in the villages to which they were assigned. But Party members had to move in extreme secrecy and were in continual peril. The great upswing in the "extermination of traitors" campaign changed the situation virtually overnight. Local officials were forced back into fortified compounds located in district or province capitals. Movement became hazardous. More hazardous still, on the part of an official, was a display of competence or genuine anti-Communist zeal. Most important, by forcing the government of officials back into the towns, the Party was able to reestablish its political presence in the countryside. Political agitation, political and military recruitment, administrative reorganization, and taxation could be undertaken with a degree of safety unknown to the Party for years, particularly at night.[25]

Ultimately, the Party's success in isolating the Saigon government from the rural population in most of South Vietnam would prove fatal to Diem. However, in terms of immediate impact in 1959, both domestically and internationally, the initiation of main force combat was nearly as important, and it more clearly represented the mortal threat coming from the Party toward the Diem regime. From the beginning, the Party's military efforts were characterized by careful planning, which, when combined with strict secrecy, ensured that insurgent forces would attack with local superiority. Regular combat began on 26 September 1959 when 2d Liberation Battalion ambushed two companies of the ARVN 23d Division, inflicted 26 casualties, and captured most of their weapons. A more spectacular assault occurred on 25 January 1960 when the same insurgent battalion, reinforced with local guerrillas, penetrated the compound of the 32d Regiment, 21st ARVN Division at Tay Ninh. The insurgents succeeded in killing 23 government soldiers and capturing a large number of arms. This assault was a very grim portent. According to Lt. Gen. Samuel Williams, head of the U.S. military advisory group, the defeat at Tay Ninh was a "severe blow to the prestige of the Vietnamese Army and an indication of the VC ability to stage large-size well-planned attacks."[26]

Taken individually, small military actions reduced Diem's power not a bit. Party-led forces were still far too small to threaten ARVN with defeat in the field. However, victories over Diem's army were excellent propaganda and served to raise the morale of those attempting to destroy the government. Developments were truly ominous from Diem's point of view. Not only were the insurgents quickly succeeding in destroying Saigon's control over the countryside and replacing it with a functioning administration, they were also establishing a military apparatus that could protect the insurgency and allow it to expand. In retrospect, it is clear that the Party seized the initiative from Saigon in late 1959–1960. It was not to be relinquished until well after American intervention. The speed of the collapse of Diem's rural political apparatus in many parts of South Vietnam is the best testimony concerning the Saigon government's lack of legitimacy in the countryside.

Americans and Diem

Although not aware of the true dimensions of the problem, U.S. intelligence analysts in the 1954–1960 period were well aware that Diem's support in the countryside was unstable.[27] Americans in Vietnam expressed, time and again, the need for reform and for honest administration. As we have seen, such prospects did not overly concern the Party leaders. They believed that Diem's government was corrupt and exploitative by nature and completely incapable of structural change. This estimation proved entirely correct. But Americans proved incapable of facing this fact.

Although it was no doubt true that the South Vietnamese government was in need of reform, those Americans arguing for policy changes were missing the central point. What Diem desperately needed was not simply a reform package; rather, he needed the cadres to carry out any change of policy. Faced with internal opposition, the Saigon government required a large number of young men from rural areas willing to risk their lives to defend the state. In this regard, Diem failed utterly. It was not enough to gain the acquiescence of the rural population. Many peasants, very likely most, cared little about affairs outside their village or hamlet and wished most strongly to be left alone in peace. And a majority of rural youth probably feared the rigors and dangers of joining the insurgency and therefore resigned themselves to conscription sullenly. But Saigon needed to recruit "the best and brightest" of the rural youth to lead the military forces and to man the rural administration. Unfortunately for Diem, it was precisely this group that entered the ranks of his enemies. As Jeffrey Race has shown so well, the incentives offered by the Party were much more compelling to brave and intelligent Vietnamese rural youth than those offered by Saigon. To the idealistic, the insurgents offered the vision of a remade and unified socialist Vietnam that would have a place of honor among nations of the world struggling against the vestiges of colonialism. The revolution also offered an avenue of social advancement more exciting than anything the government could propose: The insurgents would, after all, become the leaders of the new Vietnam. The Party offered young men and women a powerful vision of the future. In return, it asked absolute political dedication, obedience, and a willingness to face the very real prospect of death.

In the absence of genuine support in the countryside, Diem had little choice but to rely on force to confront the insurgents. Unfortunately for

Saigon, the government's military forces were crude instruments indeed, considering the political situation. Almost to a man, the leaders of ARVN had served the French. By 1953, the majority of the war effort against the Viet Minh in Cochin (the area that constituted most of South Vietnam after Geneva) was carried on by Vietnamese forces loyal to the French Union. Naturally, this did little to make the army popular. And ARVN could trace its history back only to 1955. As Bernard Fall pointed out, ARVN (unlike, for instance, the Indian army) was not able to base a tradition on military exploits under colonial rule.[28] In contrast, insurgent military forces traced their immediate heritage back to the early 1940s and were able to lay claim to Dien Bien Phu and other great victories against the French. Furthermore, the insurgents, with their pure nationalist credentials, could identify their work with the great military efforts in the distant Vietnamese past.

ARVN's development was shaped by the U.S. Army. Originally, American officers intended to create a small, relatively mobile force prepared to deal with insurgency. In 1955, Lt. Gen. John O'Daniel, commander of MAAG (Military Assistance Advisory Group), declared that "the Army will be above all, according to American ideas on the subject, a police force capable of spotting communist guerrillas and communist efforts at infiltration."[29] This goal, however, was quickly abandoned. Under Lt. Gen. Samuel Williams, commander of MAAG from late 1955 until 1960, American advisors supervised the creation of a conventional, Western-style land army—organized into divisions and corps, heavily mechanized (relative to other Asian armies), and road-bound. Influenced by the Korean War, MAAG planners wished above all to develop a force strong enough to defend against a massive invasion from the North long enough to allow reinforcement by American forces. Diem supported this development with enthusiasm for he hoped to build up a powerful army led by officers loyal to his regime. As the United States was allocating roughly 80 percent of its aid to the military sector, any financial considerations that might have inhibited ARVN's growth could be safely ignored by Diem.[30]

Since 1960, MAAG and the Pentagon have been sharply criticized for their policy and their failure to organize a land army more appropriate for guerrilla warfare.[31] In the words of Bernard Fall, the severest critic, "This 'Korean trauma' of American military planning in Viet Nam was utterly disastrous, for it created a road-bound, over-motorized, hard-to-supply battle force totally incapable of besting the real enemy (i.e., the elusive guerrilla and not the Viet-Minh division regular) on his own ground."[32] Such criticism is misguided. In the first place, Diem believed he could organize ARVN along American lines because the Cong An and local forces were sufficient and appropriate for dealing with his opponents. As we have seen, Diem was correct, in the narrow sense. Until the Party decided to begin armed conflict in 1959, the struggle in Vietnam, from Saigon's point of view, was a police action. During this decisive period, ARVN's presence would have been meaningless; it may well have been a liability. To fight the enemy "on his own ground," as Fall suggests, would have required ARVN to disperse throughout the heavily populated rural areas in South Vietnam. Such a deployment would have greatly increased daily contact between ARVN personnel and the agrarian population. In fact, a more difficult situation might have arisen because, unfortunately for Saigon, ARVN was one of the most thoroughly disliked institutions in rural South Vietnam. The authors of the *Pentagon Papers* noted that foreign observers in the late 1950s believed that "far from giving security, there is every reason to suppose that the army, buttressed by the Civil Guard . . . is regarded by the Southern peasant as a symbol of insecurity and repression."[33] The Party was waiting for the Diem government to show its repressive face before beginning armed struggle. The increased presence of ARVN could well have quickened the process, rather than retard it.

Furthermore, Bernard Fall and others have made a false distinction between the military means required to fight an insurgency and those required to wage a conventional war. Obviously, operations at the strategic level in the two types of war are fundamentally different. In a conflict such as World War II, one side can force its opponent to fight by threatening occupation of strategic objectives, ultimately the enemy's homeland. If enemy defensive forces are defeated, the enemy will make peace or friendly forces will occupy his homeland and physically disarm him. In such a conflict, efforts to occupy or defend strategic objectives will force both defender and attacker to form lines. Concentration of force at the appropriate point is requisite; forces are concentrated densely on the line, with the rear relatively unmanned. Therefore, the amount of territory actually occupied by forces will be very small relative to the total area of almost any country. Fronts may be very long, but they will also be very thin.

In an insurgency, however, two sides dispute the control of the same homeland. In theory, the entire country is a strategic objective for both sides will share a common source of supply and recruitment. Therefore, it is impossible to concentrate forces to make a line, and deployment tends to be dispersed. In conventional war, the attacker realizes the necessity for concentration if victory is desired. In an insurgency, the attacker (i.e., the insurgents), by dispersing forces, compels the defender (i.e., the government) to either do likewise or forfeit a military presence over most of the countryside. It was precisely this dilemma that faced Diem at the defeat of his rural apparatus in 1960.

Critics of MAAG claim that U.S. doctrine prevented ARVN from filling this gap. However, this claim is confused. Although the nature of an insurgency differs from that of conventional war, many of the military factors at the tactical level are alike. In both types of war, small-unit tactics are similar, revolving around the machine gun, the mortar, and the rifle. Therefore, any military unit, regardless of size, receives training in basic light infantry tactics. Nor is an American-style division a ponderous mastodon. In reality, it is quite flexible and can be broken down quickly, a proposition later confirmed again and again by American experience in Vietnam. In fact, a division-based army can be broken down more quickly than a battalion-based force can be concentrated, if necessary. It is equally confused to equate a road-bound, mechanized force with a slow force. The opposite is the case. Trucks are much faster than men, and mechanization, if at all properly maintained, brings mobility. Strategically, Saigon's forces were far more mobile than enemy forces until at least 1973. That the enemy was to compensate for this lack of mobility by stealth is a credit to the Party's military leadership. The fact that such stealth could not have been fully employed without the support or acquiescence of the rural population is yet another indicator of Saigon's political weakness in the countryside.

The problem for Saigon was again a lack of ideologues. ARVN was an ineffective instrument because many of its officers were poor and many of the soldiers sullen. Organizational change would not have altered this basic situation at all. If a "heavy" ARVN failed against the insurgents because of a lack of will to fight, it is reasonable to conclude that a "light" ARVN would have failed for exactly the same reason.

A similar situation existed regarding Diem's militia forces. One reason that MAAG argued in favor of a "heavy" ARVN was the belief that, potentially, the provincial militia (Civil Guard or Bao An) and the village militia (People's Self Defense Forces or Dan Ve) would be sufficient in combination with the police to provide local security. Consequently, MAAG argued that the militia should be lightly armed and as mobile as possible in its role as the primary antiguerrilla force. Diem, however, wanted the Civil Guard to be more heavily armed and capable of cooperating with ARVN. Americans believed Diem's position reflected his desire to use the Civil Guard, commanded by loyal officers, as a potential anticoup force. As usual, Diem had his way. In 1960, the Civil Guard was moved from the Department of the Interior to the Department of Defense. A later Defense Department study concluded that this move was "disastrous" for it removed any sort of rural defense force.[34] In this case, American observers were putting too much emphasis on organizational change. It is even difficult to understand why this particular organizational change was an error. In 1958, approximately one-third of the province chiefs were field-grade officers. By 1960, this percentage increased to roughly two-thirds, and by 1962, seven-eighths of South Vietnam's provinces were headed by military men. Because the province chief was also commander of the provincial militia, it is difficult to see why the transfer of the militia to Defense was anything more than a reflection of the actual state of affairs. Furthermore, although the militia was moved administratively to a different department, it still remained in the province. If well-led and supported by intelligence from the rural population, the Civil Guard would have been a difficult opponent for the poorly armed insurgents of 1960. As it was, the unmotivated Civil Guard avoided contact with the enemy and proved an ineffective reaction force. Its main task proved to be the protection of the provincial administration. In short, the Civil Guard was the type of institution to be expected in a country ruled by a fearful dictator who wanted, above all, to centralize power and who lacked a firm base of support in the countryside.

If the Civil Guard were bad, the village-based Dan Ve was worse. Civil Guard soldiers at least had six months of training and were equipped with basic infantry weapons. Soldiers of the People's Self Defense Forces, in theory, were volunteers protecting their own homes. In practice, peasants were forced to join, were given only the most rudimentary training, and were paid miserably and irregularly. Frequently, members either sympathized with the revolution or were outright infiltrators. Rather than carrying the war to the local enemy, Dan Ve forces were normally tied down protecting installations in pitiful fortifications. As the Civil Guard proved unable to react quickly, Dan Ve posts proved easy and tempting targets for the insurgents.[35] The Dan Ve was armed with a motley collection of old French and American carbines, and the insurgents often had better weapons than the Dan Ve by the early 1960s. Indeed, raids on Dan Ve posts were an important supply source of weaponry for the enemy.

Although the basic weakness of Saigon's military forces was quickly shown after 1960, the Party, as always, was careful to match political and military efforts. The decision to begin armed struggle necessitated the formation of a popular front directed against Diem. The Party always took pains to prevent the insurgency from being identified solely with Vietnamese communism. With the military struggle under way, Party leaders realized that it was neither possible nor desirable to deny the Party's role in the violence. Consequently, they established the National Liberation Front in December 1960. The NLF had representatives from several factions opposing Diem, in addition to the Party. The non-Communist opposition had a degree of autonomy, but the primary position of the Party, although not emphasized, was never concealed. Likewise, Party members held all of the key positions in the People's Liberation Army (PLA), established in February 1961, as the military wing of the NLF. As Diem and the United States were, by this time, attempting to convince world opinion that the insurgency was a tool of Hanoi, Peking, and Moscow, the Party also established a nominally independent southern Communist movement within the NLF. Founded in January 1962, the People's Revolutionary Party (PRP) proved useful in the propaganda battle. The peasantry took little notice of the formation of the PRP, realizing sensibly that it was new in name only. The new stress on the southern origins of the insurgency, however, was very effective in the world arena in countering the U.S. and GVN claims of foreign aggression against a sovereign South Vietnam.[36]

While the Party worked hard to create the political foundations for protracted struggle, insurgent forces stepped up their assault on Diem's administrative apparatus and military forces. According to U.S. figures, the People's Liberation Army had grown, by November 1961, to 25,000 men, organized into increasingly larger groups. Americans also estimated that the "terrorist-guerrilla organization," presumably referring to local force guerrilla units, had grown to 17,000. U.S. figures also estimated that insurgent forces had killed 500 GVN local officials and civilians, had kidnapped 1,000 more, and had inflicted 1,500 battle deaths on ARVN.[37] Bernard Fall maintained that, by the end of 1961, the NLF had completed an "arc of insurgency" around Saigon. The authors of the *Pentagon Papers* in retrospect reflected on the bleak nature of the situation:

> By late 1961, if not earlier, it had become clear in both Saigon and Washington that the yellow star of the Viet Cong [VC] was in the ascendancy. . . . The VC continued to hold the initiative in the countryside, controlling major portions of the populace and drawing an increasingly tight cinch around Saigon. The operative question was not whether the Diem government as it was then moving could defeat the insurgents, but whether it could save itself.[38]

The deteriorating situation in Vietnam was watched very carefully by the new Kennedy administration. For the first time, the problem of Vietnam was a top priority to an American president. This increased interest in Vietnam reflected not only the worsening situation but also John Kennedy's personal interest in the techniques of counterinsurgency. Indeed, Vietnam quickly developed into a laboratory for the creation of a whole new concept in foreign relations with developing nations. "Counterinsurgency," as envisioned by Kennedy, was a complex combination of guided liberal economic development and discriminating coercive techniques appropriate for a struggle that was simultaneously political and military.[39] Although this is not the place for an examination of the development of the Kennedy policy toward Vietnam, two related themes appear in this period that require some attention for they were to recur time and again during American involvement in Vietnam's village war. The first theme was the tendency of many American planners to view the difficulties faced by both Washington and Saigon in terms of defective organization. The second was the problem of to what degree, if any, Washington should exercise sovereignty over the internal affairs of South Vietnam.

Soon after his inauguration, Kennedy came to believe American efforts in Vietnam were being hampered by a lack of focus. As early as April 1961, he asked Deputy Secretary of Defense Roswell Gilpatric to develop a plan to help South Vietnam. Although Gilpatric's program was a modest effort in terms of funds and manpower requirements projected, it was noteworthy because it argued that American efforts would be significantly improved if a single coordinator was put in charge in Washington. On April 12, Walter Rostow delivered a memorandum to Kennedy recommending the "appointment of a full time first-rate back-stop man in Washington."[40] Apparently, both Gilpatric and Rostow had in mind Gen. Edward Lansdale, a past friend and advisor of Diem. But Lansdale had powerful enemies at both the Pentagon and State Department, and he was never employed as "the first-rate back-stop man." However, the search was on, and, at one time or another, several American officials served as top program coordinator. Ultimately, the organizational charts reached their most organized stage with the creation of Civil Operations and Revolutionary Development Support (CORDS) under former White House aide Robert Komer in 1967.

While American planners searched for the correct mode of organizing and coordinating Washington's efforts, they also attempted to identify the organizational weaknesses within Diem's government. As we have seen, the Party believed his government was doomed because of basic structural weaknesses that were beyond remedy. Americans realized well enough that Diem's regime was far from a model government, but all believed, to one extent or another, that the problems facing Diem could be alleviated or solved. In this regard, organizational change received a great deal of attention. In particular, American officials were disturbed by the lack of an overall plan on the part of Diem's government to direct efforts against the NLF. While in Saigon in October 1961, Gen. Maxwell Taylor, President Kennedy's military advisor, had an interview with ARVN Chief of Staff Duong Van Minh. Minh expressed fears that ARVN was losing the support of the people—a startling admission considering the source. Nevertheless, MAAG Chief General Lionel McGarr and newly appointed Ambassador Frederick Nolting, when reporting on the conversation to Washington, stressed the administrative problems brought up by Minh. As Nolting reported, "When analyzed, most of Minh's comments in military field are occasioned by lack of overall coordination and cooperation. This re-emphasizes absolute necessity for overall plan which would clearly delineate responsibility and create a team effort."[41]

A short while later, Nolting reported favorably on a plan put forth by Diem, at the urging of American officials, that established a National Executive Council patterned after the American National Security Council (NSC). Presumably, Nolting saw the proposed council as the appropriate vehicle for coordinating the war effort. In any case, he did not emphasize that Diem's brother Nhu was to head the council, although American officials in Vietnam had long argued that he was ruining Diem's government and that his removal was a prerequisite for the continued survival of Diem's regime.[42]

U.S. military advisors were particularly concerned with the establishment of an effective chain of command for ARVN and the militia. They were perplexed by Diem's policy of preventing close coordination between ARVN and the province chiefs. This policy, in American eyes, was attributable to Diem's desire to counterbalance ARVN with provincial forces and thus make a coup more difficult. ARVN itself did receive a unitary chain of command in this period, yet (if General Minh is to be believed) coordination between ARVN and the provincial administrations continued to be very poor.[43] Nor was any relief in sight. At no time was Diem willing or able to integrate his military and political apparatus. It is arguable that such integration never occurred in the entire sad history of the South Vietnamese government. The authors of the *Pentagon Papers* accurately summarized the results of such faulty integration:

> For President Diem's purpose this bilineal organization offered an opportunity to counterbalance the power (and coup potential) of the generals by the power of the province chiefs. It was a device for survival. But the natural byproduct

of this duality, in terms of the effectiveness of actions against the VC, was poor coordination and imperfect cooperation in intelligence collection and production, in planning, and in operational execution in the countryside, where the battles were fought—both the "battle for men's minds" and the more easily understood battles for control of the hamlets, villages, districts, and provinces.[44]

While much effort was expended in the attempt to clean up the organizational charts in Washington and Saigon, American officials were forced to face a much more complicated issue: What role should the United States play in shaping Saigon's domestic policies? As long as Diem was at least outwardly successful in protecting his regime, this problem did not often come up; Diem set policy, and the United States supported him. But when Diem's position weakened after 1960, Washington was forced to admit that the GVN had serious flaws. Although no consensus was ever reached in Washington concerning the exact nature of Saigon's weakness, at one time or another American officials advocated: the reestablishment of elective village councils, the removal of particularly corrupt officials (especially Diem's brother Nhu), the ending of blatant nepotism within Diem's regime, a decrease in pro-Catholic favoritism, an end to the repression and harassment of Diem's non-Communist opposition, and the granting of at least some real power to the national assembly. Interestingly enough, land reform was rarely mentioned in this period. Although Diem supported his brother to the end, he was clever enough to agree that U.S. reform proposals had great merit. However, he normally argued that reform could only come when stability in the rural areas could be achieved.

In general, the Pentagon agreed with Diem. Military advisors argued that he was unlikely to accept persuasion, considering his determination to appear independent of American control. Hence, the only leverage Washington had was the threat to curtail or lessen aid. But such a policy on Washington's part, it was feared, could only weaken Saigon's war effort. The result would be a coup, which would strengthen the insurgency, or an outright victory for the NLF. Therefore, the Defense Department took the position that it would be best to increase military aid and get on with the war.[45]

More determined reformers could be found in the State Department. One early proponent of the use of leverage on Diem was Ambassador Eldridge Durbrow, who, in December 1960, suggested that if Diem were incapable of building greater public support, the United States "may well be forced, in the not too distant future, to undertake the difficult task of identifying and supporting alternate leadership."[46] At this time, however, Durbrow's position was extreme in American circles. Indeed, events in late 1960 pushed the State Department in the opposite direction, away from putting pressure on Diem. In November 1960, a few ARVN officers attempted a coup. Although events are not at all clear, American agents apparently tried to manipulate the occasion by convincing the rebellious officers to bargain with Diem toward a solution that would allow him to remain in government with diminished power. While negotiations took place, Diem exploited this delay by summoning loyal troops to Saigon and crushing the coup. Whatever the actual American role in this incident, there was much concern in Washington that Diem had lost his trust in the United States and that actions must be taken to restore the American position. Much hope was placed on newly appointed Ambassador Nolting's ability to work well with Diem.[47]

Nolting indeed attempted to gain Diem's friendship and trust. However, as events turned against Diem, high circles in Washington were frequently faced with the problem of linking U.S. aid, or at least an increase in U.S. aid, with reforms in Saigon. Influenced by the Taylor-Rostow and McNamara-Rusk reports of November 1961, Kennedy authorized a cable to Nolting on November 14 that promised increased economic and military aid for Saigon. Nolting was instructed, however, to make clear that the aid program was conditional upon improvement of the South Vietnamese war effort:

> It is most important that Diem come forth with changes which will be recognized as having real substance and meaning. Rightly or wrongly, his regime is widely criticized abroad and in the U.S., and if we are to give our substantial support we must be able to point to real administrative, political and social reforms and a real effort to widen its base that will give maximum confidence to the American people, as well as to world opinion that our efforts are not directed towards the support of an unpopular or ineffective regime, but rather towards supporting the combined efforts of all of the non-Communist people of the GVN against a Communist takeover. You should make this quite clear, and indicate that the U.S. contribution to the proposed joint effort depends heavily upon his response to this point. You should inform Diem that, in our minds, the concept of the joint undertaking envisages a much closer relationship than the present one of acting in an advisory capacity only. We would expect to share in the decision-making process in the political, economic and military fields as they affect the security situation.[48]

Some interesting points appear in this cable. First of all, Nolting was told to phrase U.S. demands for reform in terms of their necessity for American and world public opinion rather than their necessity for a successful war effort per se. This thrust, however, may have been diplomatic in nature, designed to spare Nolting the unpleasant task of telling Diem that Washington believed his government was a failure as presently constituted. The remainder of the cable, however, is unambiguous in its call for a direct role for Americans in the determination of South Vietnamese domestic policy. Unfortunately, it was not made clear exactly how Washington wished to divide sovereignty over South Vietnam with Saigon. Nolting, or Diem for that matter, might well have asked the decisionmakers in Washington whether the concept of sovereignty allows for division between two nations.

In any case, Diem was not pleased by Kennedy's proposals, believing that they offered little and required much. An anti-American media campaign was launched in the government press. But Washington was not yet prepared to abandon Saigon or overthrow Diem, so there was little choice other than to back down. In December, the language of the original cable was "clarified" to express Washington's desire that the "partnership" between the United

States and South Vietnam be so close that any major actions should be subject to prior consultation.[49]

This exchange between Saigon and Washington was not the first nor the last time that the United States unsuccessfully attempted to force reforms on the South Vietnamese. Yet, it is possible to discern by this date the evolution of two schools of thought on dealing with Saigon. The first, most clearly expressed by Nolting and Lansdale, argued that the war, by definition, had to be fought and won by the South Vietnamese. They urged Washington to channel all its effort toward supporting the constituted government in Saigon. It should be made clear to the world, these men contended, that the United States was aiding a fully sovereign South Vietnam. Americans should restrict their efforts aimed at changing Saigon's domestic policy to persuasion and to setting a good example. Often implicit in this argument was the belief that Saigon's fundamental difficulties were due to the actions of a perfidious enemy, rather than to structural problems within South Vietnamese society. Always implicit in this argument was the conviction that the United States was not prepared to administer South Vietnam. Overt American control over events in South Vietnam, even if operationally possible, would be counterproductive in the Vietnamese countryside for it would confirm the Party's claim that South Vietnam was an American puppet; it would also be a global public relations disaster. They also believed that stressing Saigon's independence would mute the racial overtones of the situation that were never far below the surface.

A second school of thought argued for direct American intervention in South Vietnamese affairs if required for the war effort. Before Diem's murder, advocates of this school, which eventually included most of the State Department and the CIA, as well as many cabinet members involved with Vietnam, concentrated on a change of government in Saigon. When the ARVN generals who toppled Diem proved even more incapable of countering the NLF, many Americans, particularly those on the spot, began seeking ways of carrying out policy independent of GVN channels. From very early on, CIA and Army Special Forces were operating with nominal supervision from Saigon (or often from Washington, for that matter). In particular, Special Forces personnel working with the Montagnard hill tribes often shared the tribesmen's view that Saigon was just as much the enemy as the Party. Special Forces contempt for the Saigon government, according to later CIA chief William Colby, encouraged revolts against GVN during 1964 that were aimed at achieving Montagnard autonomy. Sadly, the hill tribes expected American support. But such support was obviously impossible, and the revolts were suppressed.[50]

The Montagnard affair was an extreme example of Saigon's powerful ally working in a direction that was not at all desired by the established government. Yet, it exemplified a tendency on the part of American personnel working in the countryside to seek methods of countering the insurgency that would be free of control from Saigon. Mundane matters such as how much, if any, money could be controlled directly by province advisors or

Agency for International Development (AID) workers reflected, to a large degree, the basic mistrust or even contempt of many Americans on the spot (and more than one South Vietnamese local official) for Saigon's ability to deal with events. As shall be seen, the tendency to seek means of fighting the war free from Saigon's control increased as direct American involvement grew. Soon, among Americans who knew Vietnam best, there was talk of "harnessing the revolution." Regardless of official U.S. policy, which remained until the end that Saigon was in charge of the "village war," many Americans came to agree with the NLF that the Saigon regime was structurally unsound. Unfortunately for all concerned, such pessimism rarely led to the conclusion that the game was already lost. Rather, it led those Americans discouraged with Saigon's war effort to seek ways of energizing and remaking South Vietnamese society from the ground up.

Strategic Hamlets

Sorely pressed by the Party, aware of growing unrest within his own armed forces, and increasingly apprehensive about American intervention in South Vietnamese internal affairs, Diem, in late 1961, started what would be his last effort to turn events against the Front and save his regime. His chosen vehicle soon became known as the Strategic Hamlet Program. As previously mentioned, Americans had long been urging Diem to devise a comprehensive plan of action for use against the insurgency. In September 1961, MAAG developed an elaborate Geographically Phased National Level Operation Plan for Counterinsurgency and urged its adoption by Saigon. At the same time, at Diem's request, R.G.K. Thompson, the principal architect of Britain's successful counterinsurgency effort in Malaya, was also at work developing a blueprint for a long-term campaign in rural South Vietnam.

Both plans called for a phased approach, beginning with clearing operations on the part of ARVN and followed by the construction of fortified hamlets, defended by a revitalized militia in conjunction with aggressive police operations against the Party's local apparatus. Both plans called for political reforms and economic measures, to be enacted as soon as possible, that would lead to a more prosperous life and thus secure the loyalty of the rural peasantry.

Naturally, there were differences in approach that led to some acrimonious and undignified bureaucratic infighting. MAAG, fearing the steadily growing main force insurgent units, wished to keep ARVN's role in rural pacification to the absolute minimum. Thompson wanted ARVN to operate for longer periods in areas undergoing pacification, to protect government cadres responsible for carrying out both economic reforms and the attack on the Party's rural apparatus. MAAG wanted to begin with operations in War Zone D, northwest of Saigon, and then to concentrate efforts on the provinces around Saigon. Thompson urged Diem to begin in the lower Mekong Delta where the insurgency was still relatively weak. In general, he urged a slower pace of operations than did MAAG.[51]

As Diem's execution of the Strategic Hamlet Program came to bear little resemblance to either plan, there is no point in trying to judge the merits of the respective approaches. However, the arguments presented in favor of each are early examples of a fundamental disagreement over the use of armed force during an insurgency, a disagreement that reappeared several times during the period of American involvement.

In the view of MAAG, the very existence of enemy main force units was a challenge that the government could not ignore. No matter what the future course of events, ARVN and revolutionary armed forces would ultimately have a showdown. To be successful, American officers believed that ARVN would have to develop military competency and an aggressive spirit. In MAAG's view, nothing could be more injurious to ARVN's development than having it tied permanently to a static defensive role. Furthermore, if its role were to protect the pacification effort, ARVN would either be forced to spread itself far too thin or concentrate in relatively restricted geographic areas, thus leaving much of the country in enemy hands and allowing the insurgents even more time to train and expand their heavy forces.

In the long run, MAAG feared, the insurgents would be strong enough to undertake larger and larger operations, which, if successful, would make a shambles of any political progress made by the pacification program. Therefore, MAAG wanted ARVN, as soon as possible, to initiate offensive operations against enemy main force units wherever they could be located. Even if large-scale operations failed to destroy large enemy units, it was reasoned, ARVN would maintain the initiative and lessen the danger of enemy offensives by neutralizing supply bases and assembly areas. Thus, even if operations were conducted in remote areas not vital in the political struggle because of low population density—areas that, in any case, were better suited for the use of massive firepower—ARVN would still be playing a vital role in wearing down enemy manpower and keeping heavy forces away from the populated areas. In a nutshell, this argument served to justify later U.S. search and destroy missions.

Proponents of the Thompson approach stood MAAG's arguments on end. Rather than seeing the advantages of keeping enemy forces away from the heavily populated rural areas, they stressed the importance of protecting counterinsurgency programs in exactly these areas over long periods of time. If enemy main force units choose to inhabit remote safe zones, they argued, ARVN would do well to leave them in peace for the immediate future. Instead, ARVN operations should be directed against the local guerrilla forces that might otherwise hinder GVN police activities and rural development programs. Furthermore, Thompson and his allies stressed that security must be long-term; only when the GVN had reestablished lasting control of an area should ARVN move on. Thus shielded, government cadres would have an opportunity to win the true allegiance of the population. As support for the government grew and as the enemy rural apparatus was weakened, the insurgency would find it ever more difficult to obtain resources and recruits for the main force units. Furthermore, if villagers could be convinced that it was safe to cooperate with the government, insurgent military forces would lose their near-monopoly on immediate local intelligence.

Thompson envisioned that the area under government control would continue to expand like a spreading "oil spot." As the insurgency was slowly deprived of its ability to recruit and gather local supplies and intelligence, the balance of forces would shift toward the government. The insurgency would lose the initiative, and uncommitted segments of the population would willingly align themselves with the government. Main force insurgent units would be forced either to engage the much more heavily armed ARVN or retreat ever further from populated areas. Lacking military protection and losing local support, the insurgent political apparatus could be slowly ground down. Ultimately, the entire insurgency would collapse.

There was nothing new in the Thompson approach. The theoretical foundations of the "oil spot" strategy had been well developed by the French during the nineteenth century. In practice, similar strategies have been employed as long as there have been empires and rebellions. Nevertheless, the "area security" approach, which became the American name for the "oil spot" strategy, came to be viewed as an alternative to the search and destroy policy of attrition. As shall be seen, in practical terms, the line dividing the two approaches was not at all clear. Furthermore, to the extent that the two approaches did require a different mode of operation, both evidenced fatal flaws in the Vietnamese environment.

In any event, the Strategic Hamlet Program as carried out by Diem and Nhu proved to be a catastrophic failure. The program's leadership ensured an erratic course. Nhu himself, a proto-Fascist and mentally unstable drug addict, exercised overall control. Col. Albert Pham Ngoc Thao, head of the National Police and Nhu's deputy in charge of the program, was a Party member and longtime Front agent. (Thao also played a major role in the Diem coup.)[52] As urged by both MAAG and Thompson, Diem chose to begin efforts in a single province. However, Binh Duong, the province chosen, was not a relatively secure province as Thompson would have preferred. Rather, it was in the center of the "arc of insurgency" around Saigon. Apparently, Binh Duong was chosen because of its undeniable strategic importance, situated as it was between War Zone C and War Zone D northwest of Saigon. In addition, some pacification activity had already begun in Cu Chi district (later part of Hau Nghia). Code-named Operation SUNRISE, the construction of strategic hamlets was begun on 22 March 1962 at Ben Tuong hamlet in Ben Cat district. Trouble began at once. Most peasant families refused relocation and had to be forced to new homes. Journalists noticed that very few young men were among those relocated. Yet, the presence of GVN forces prevented armed interference by insurgents. Relocation and the construction of fortifications and facilities proceeded more or less on schedule. Although somewhat skeptical, Americans in Saigon were encouraged by the energy displayed by the government and even more so by the growth of what appeared to be a coherent national campaign.

Soon, the local experiment at Ben Tuong was expanded nationwide. Under the direction of Nhu, all government efforts in the countryside were subordinated to the new program. The year 1962 was proclaimed the "Year of Strategic Hamlets."[53]

The immediate goals of the Strategic Hamlet Program were ambitious, and the pace was rapid. Nhu planned the construction of 12,000 hamlets by the end of 1963, enough to have housed virtually the entire rural population of South Vietnam. By April 1963, Saigon reported that nearly 6,000 hamlets, housing over eight million peasants, had been completed. Although later assessments of the program showed these numbers to have been inflated, there can be no doubt that, bankrolled by the United States, Nhu's program succeeded in affecting the lives of a great number of villagers. Other numerical indicators were favorable to Saigon, as well. The number of insurgent defectors rose. Taxes collected in rural areas stabilized after two years of steady decline. Insurgent incidents declined. Yet, none of Diem's efforts were accompanied by any of the political reforms considered necessary by Washington. Indeed, official relations between Saigon and Washington grew cooler and more distant. This state of affairs could only have pleased Diem. As long as the Strategic Hamlet Program appeared to be succeeding, it served as the perfect solution for his problems. Washington would continue to aid Saigon as long as there was apparent success in the countryside. Diem and Nhu, however, had complete control over the Strategic Hamlet Program and need not have feared American infringements on Vietnamese sovereignty.[54]

American reaction to the Strategic Hamlet Program was curious. Washington was well aware that Diem and Nhu were not implementing reforms that Americans believed necessary for a successful war effort. However, reports of military progress were accepted as truth with little critical evaluation. At the Honolulu Conference in July 1962, Secretary of Defense Robert McNamara was told by Gen. Paul Harkins, first head of the newly organized Military Assistance Command, Vietnam (MACV), that military progress had been substantial and would continue. McNamara recognized the "tremendous progress" made in the prior six months and concluded that in all probability the insurgency would be well under control by late 1965. Plans were authorized to prepare a phased American withdrawal as soon as South Vietnamese military personnel could be trained to take over essential tasks from U.S. support groups and advisors.[55]

As late as October 1963, with Diem's government on the verge of collapse, McNamara and Maxwell Taylor, head of the Joint Chiefs of Staff (JCS), would report to Kennedy and the National Security Council that the military phase of the conflict was going well, that South Vietnamese strategy was sound, and that U.S. military withdrawals could actually begin in the near future.[56] Gen. Bruce Palmer, later Gen. William Westmoreland's top deputy, described the McNamara-Taylor report as "so unrealistic as to be almost ludicrous."[57] There were a number of more pessimistic and realistic voices trying to be heard. Col. John Paul Vann had already made a name for himself in the army's highest echelons with his criticism of ARVN, the GVN, and General Harkins. Vann was scheduled to brief the JCS in June 1963, but this meeting was canceled at the direction of Maxwell Taylor. Vann's beliefs were widely held by American advisors. Even at MACV, then Brig. Gen. Richard Stillwell, Harkins' chief of operations, was candid within the army concerning ARVN's weakness.[58] It is difficult to ascertain whether mistaken assumptions were due to poor in-country reporting or to faulty interpretation in Washington. Perhaps, as suggested by General Palmer, wishful thinking in Washington was motivated by the upcoming presidential election. In any case, the fact remains that at no period during the entire U.S. involvement in Vietnam, with the possible exception of 1975, were American impressions of the overall situation at more variance with the actual state of affairs than during the Strategic Hamlet Program.

In reality, the entire program was an irrelevant response to the insurgency and consequently doomed from the outset. From the Party's point of view, the program no doubt caused some problems. Large-scale population relocation, by definition, required reorganization of the local Party apparatus. In some instances, the fortified hamlets posed problems of entry. Overall, however, the insurgency reaped political dividends from the program.[59]

In the first place, all of the problems besetting the Agroville Program were amplified. Peasants bitterly resented relocation. Often, the new hamlets made no sense economically. The supposed benefits of the program, such as improved sewage or more school rooms, were in no way commensurate with the sacrifices imposed on the peasantry. Normally, these benefits did not appear anyway, and forced labor was employed to build fortifications. Because of Nhu's personal supervision and his stress on an ever-quickening pace of operations, execution of the program took on a frantic quality, and local officials routinely reported half-completed projects as finished. In the second place, the entire program was coercive and did nothing to answer any of the problems fueling the insurgency. The administration remained aloof and was often corrupt. Officers remained arrogant and inefficient. In short, every unscrupulous and inefficient characteristic of the Diem regime was emphasized and amplified by the Strategic Hamlet Program. The aggressive policy intended to save Diem was, in reality, hastening his end.[60]

Furthermore, the entire program was founded on erroneous military assumptions. The fortifications employed were designed to prevent small groups of guerrillas from entering the hamlets. If the insurgents assaulted a fortified hamlet in strength, heavy government militia forces or ARVN units were supposed to serve as reaction forces. However, because the hamlets were sprouting throughout the countryside, real protection was impossible. This made little difference when the fortifications were real only on paper: In such instances, the insurgents continued to operate normally. When, however, a fortified hamlet threatened to have the impact desired by Saigon, i.e., the denial of access to the peasantry, insurgent main force units were capable of striking heavy blows. This state of affairs was best illustrated in Ben Cat district itself, the site of initial efforts. Despite the priority status of Ben Cat, Front units, in broad daylight on 16 June 1962, ambushed an eleven-vehicle ARVN convoy, killing over thirty ARVN soldiers and two American officers serving as advisors. Civilian sabotage of the road prevented early relief. Such a large ambush would have been difficult or impossible for the insurgents without the support or at least acquiescence of the local population. By April 1963, most of the statistical indicators still bringing much satisfaction to Washington began a downward trend. Shortly thereafter, the precarious state of the Strategic Hamlet Program was dramatically illustrated when, on 20 August 1963, insurgent forces overran Ben Tuong hamlet, the site of the original pilot project.[61]

While Diem was engaged in a life and death struggle with the Party, he also chose to openly confront the Buddhist leadership of South Vietnam. Few periods during the Vietnam War are as poorly documented or understood as the Buddhist crisis. What role the Party may have played is particularly obscure. Diem was already losing the rural struggle, and chaos in the cities strained his regime to the breaking point. Increasingly isolated, he steadily lost any ability to control events. On 1 November 1963, Diem and Nhu were murdered during a coup led by the army and at least tacitly approved by the United States.

A coup was a fitting end for the Diem regime. Outside the Catholic community, Diem and his brother were unmourned, and, for a short time, officers who had participated in the coup were popular heroes. The regime had completely failed to create a stable and broad base of support in the society. Whether another individual possessing judgment superior to Diem's could have accomplished his goals is impossible to guess. Certainly, the obstacles facing any independent, non-Socialist South Vietnamese government would have been imposing; the margin of error for anyone heading a Saigon government was, at best, very small. Nevertheless, the fact remains that Diem's efforts were inadequate, and his regime was a disaster for the United States. Bui Diem, Saigon's ambassador to the United States during Thieu's regime, later lamented the Diems' mark on Vietnamese history:

> For the newly created country of South Vietnam, it was a national tragedy, another opportunity squandered by the failure of leadership. Just as Bao Dai's human weakness had aborted the possibility of successful nationalist effort against the French, so the character flaws of Ngo Dinh Diem and Ngo Dinh Nhu thwarted the chance to build a democratic nationalism that could have counterbalanced Vietnamese communism. The consequence was that South Vietnam created a tradition of authoritarian rule that had only the negative virtue of anticommunism to recommend it. And the two-decade-long history of the country was to demonstrate that, as a principle of social cohesion, anticommunism by itself was dismally inadequate.[62]

Chaos After Diem

The Strategic Hamlet Program died with Diem and Nhu. The new Duong Van Minh government was quick to abandon it. With Diem's security apparatus in disarray, it soon became clear that much of the "progress" that had so pleased MACV had been fictitious. Peasants who wished to leave the hamlets did so. Many local government officials viewed the collapse of the program as a "blessing in disguise."[63]

If the fall of Diem and the end of the Strategic Hamlet Program were "blessings" for the rural population of Vietnam, they soon proved something less from the American viewpoint. Whatever hopes Americans held concerning ARVN's ability to serve as a foundation for a stable government, strong enough to battle the insurgency on its own, were quickly shattered. Between January 1964 and June 1965, there were six major changes of government and two more unsuccessful coups. Instability in Saigon was reflected in the rural areas by a massive turnover of administrative personnel. Naturally, NLF activity increased, and the insurgency gained control of more and more of the countryside. Revolutionary forces were particularly successful in expanding and consolidating their control of the area around Saigon. Nor were any of the successive governments in Saigon able to control or mobilize the urban population. Buddhist groups were unappeased. Students rioted frequently. Every account of this period stresses the existence of an atmosphere of suspicion, confusion, and chaos in Saigon itself.[64]

In fact, the United States was faced with a calamity in South Vietnam. The failure of the Diem regime to build a legitimate government created a power vacuum fully as serious as that existing after Dien Bien Phu. Yet, there existed no new Diem capable of even an attempt to fashion any sort of national political apparatus. The Party had done its work very well. In the rural areas under its direct control, the Party had created a complete administration able to tax the population, to propagandize and educate, and to support a growing military establishment. In areas not under direct Party control, its cadres had infiltrated everywhere. The policy of terror was undeniably successful in exerting a presence for the insurgency throughout the country: Not only was anti-Communist zeal made very dangerous but the tendency toward neutrality among peasants with doubts on the aims or methods of the Party was greatly increased. In short, the Party had seized for itself much of the rural population for a power base, and most areas not under direct control were neutralized. The only exceptions in rural Vietnam were areas populated by Catholics and adherents of the two major religious sects, the Cao Dai and Hoa Hao. Unfortunately for Saigon, the religious minorities did not cooperate. In any case, it was, by definition, impossible to base a national government primarily on the support of religious minorities. Nor was the situation much better in the urban areas. The small middle class and intelligentsia lacked any sort of unity or political vision. They might fear the Party and support the army, but the support was frequently halfhearted and conditional. Some political groups in the towns and cities espoused neutralism and hence were unacceptable to Washington. To be sure, those manning the government apparatus, where it still existed, could be counted on to oppose the Party; they would, after all, have the most to lose if the revolution were to succeed. However, under

Diem, the civil service and police had proven to be inefficient and corrupt. There was no reason to expect any fundamental improvement.

Only the army remained to serve as a base for an anti-Communist regime in South Vietnam. Because the army lacked internal institutional unity and was principally occupied in making coups, no meaningful initiatives against the Party, coming from the South Vietnamese themselves, were possible in this period of chaos. Although not well recognized at the time, an entirely new period in the struggle for South Vietnam was beginning. Whatever the faults of Diem, he had proved successful in keeping the management of the war effort firmly in his hands, despite his near absolute dependence on U.S. aid. The police action against the Party during the 1950s, the Agroville plan, and the Strategic Hamlet Program were all initiatives planned and carried out by Saigon. Considering the level of aid coming from Washington, Americans had had a remarkably small role in the actual determination of policy. After Diem's murder, the situation was altered drastically. Virtually every major policy in Saigon's war effort against the insurgency was American in inspiration. This state of affairs was to exist until the withdrawal of U.S. forces.

This is not to say that the United States took over the war after the Diem coup. Although it is true that anything substantial that was tried was American in inspiration, the South Vietnamese remained very sensitive about outward displays of sovereignty. In addition, the South Vietnamese retained veto power over U.S. actions. Occasionally, as when they refused suggestions concerning a combined command under American leadership, this veto power was overt. Normally, however, if some American inspiration was of little interest to the Vietnamese, they would render it harmless by inaction.

This new state of affairs was quite apparent during 1964. As the Front was making gains everywhere, Washington was desperately trying to promote a more stable and effective regime in Saigon. In particular, Saigon was pressed to mobilize all sectors of society behind the war effort. Gen. Nguyen Khanh, the new strongman, readily agreed and announced imminent mobilization in March. However, specifics were slow in coming. As various decrees started filtering from Saigon, it soon became clear that mobilization would be something less than total. In fact, the strength of South Vietnamese armed forces grew less in 1964 than it had in 1963. Talk of nonmilitary mobilization came to nothing. In another instance, General Khanh a U.S. suggestion that an American "brain trust" advise the Vietnamese cabinet, but there is no sign that anything at all was done by the new advisors. Similarly, when Khanh was pressed for the removal of particularly corrupt officers and officials, he would agree, then delay removal, and finally transfer or even promote those in question.[65] These are just a few examples of Saigon's willingness to issue decrees, agree to new policies, and participate in joint studies without anything of substance taking place.

The best example of a key American initiative frustrated by Vietnamese indifference was the Hop Tac Program, the only major attempt at pacification to take place during 1964–1965. Hop Tac, the Vietnamese term for "cooperation," was originally proposed by Ambassador Henry Cabot Lodge in June 1964 and supervised by General Westmoreland, newly installed at MACV, and his staff. The new program was intended to be an intensive pacification effort for the area surrounding Saigon. It supposedly would include a closely coordinated effort to integrate all pacification plans for the provinces surrounding the capital, which included Hau Nghia, Binh Duong, Long An, Bien Hoa, Phuoc Tuy, Phuoc Thanh, and the capital district of Gia Dinh. The plan envisioned the creation of successively pacified concentric rings spreading outward from Saigon. In a phrase that became a joke in the U.S. mission, MACV briefed officials on the creation of "rings of steel" that would spread from Saigon, eventually securing the entire area from the Cambodian border to the South China Sea. When successfully completed, Hop Tac would be duplicated in other vital areas of the country until the insurgency was eventually destroyed.

Despite talk of "rings of steel," Hop Tac was actually the latest version of the spreading oil spot. Operations were to begin with clearing sweeps by ARVN. In the second phase, ARVN would protect police and Civic Action cadres who would be working on improving the people's welfare and rooting out the insurgents' apparatus. With the government firmly in control and the people grateful for their improved circumstances, a revitalized militia would take over security duties, and ARVN would move on to repeat the process.

Although Hop Tac was not the catastrophe that the Strategic Hamlet Program became, it, too, illustrated the weakness of the Saigon regime. The operation began on 12 September 1964 with an ARVN sweep through some enemy-held pineapple groves west of Saigon. The area to be entered had not been occupied by government forces since 1960. The ARVN unit soon ran into a minefield and took numerous casualties, and the action was immediately broken off. The next day, the ARVN unit was back in Saigon participating in a new coup.[66] Eventually, the operation was begun and was able to register statistical gains that pleased MACV. However, wishful thinking on the part of Americans concerning Hop Tac was not widespread. Although the official line remained that Hop Tac was a partial success and was preventing a "siege" of Saigon, it was common knowledge that the program was another failure. A special study made by the embassy in October 1964 concluded, "Generally speaking, Hop Tac, as a program, does not appear to exist as a unified and meaningful operation."[67] In September 1965, when beginning his second tour, Lodge requested another assessment of the program from the embassy. The conclusions could not have pleased the ambassador: "Hop Tac did not achieve its original goals primarily because they were completely unrealistic and did not take into account the difficulty of the task. These goals were set quite arbitrarily and with no regard for the available resources and strength of the enemy."[68] In February 1966, Lodge received another briefing, where it was acknowledged that Hop Tac had failed to register any real progress in the preceding year. Rather, it was reported, security had actually declined in Hau Nghia and Gia Dinh. By the time the Hop Tac Program was quietly buried in July 1966, insurgent forces around Saigon had increased considerably. The security situation was so bad that MACV was compelled to deploy three U.S. battalions in the inner ring around Saigon, which was to have been the first "ring of steel" in the original Hop Tac plan.[69]

In retrospect, Hop Tac can be seen as essentially a paper exercise. Despite all of Westmoreland's efforts to portray it as a Vietnamese operation, it was American from top to bottom.[70] The planning was done by the MACV staff and translated into Vietnamese. The Vietnamese were cynical about the entire program and felt it was something that had to be done to keep the Americans happy. Furthermore, the program was one of the first to be publicly identified as American, and it suffered in consequence. To the extent that Hop Tac was identified with a Vietnamese leader, that leader was General Khanh. And with the fall of Khanh, the new leadership gave it even less attention.[71]

No doubt, Vietnamese indifference toward Hop Tac was an obstacle to any sort of genuine progress. Yet, there is little reason to believe that a genuinely enthusiastic effort on the part of Saigon would have made much difference. The major problem afflicting Hop Tac was the same problem afflicting the whole of Saigon's war effort: governmental instability. As we have seen, chaos in Saigon had long been predicted by the Party and was seen as a natural reflection of the Saigon regime's fundamental lack of legitimacy. And, as the Party also predicted, when government forces weakened, revolutionary forces grew ever stronger. This is precisely what happened during the Hop Tac period.

The balance of forces, which had tipped against the government in 1960, was growing even more unfavorable to Saigon. On 20 July 1964, about the same time that Lodge was pressing for a mobilization of South Vietnam, the Party called for a "general mobilization" in the South, requiring every male from eighteen to thirty to serve in revolutionary forces. Approximately one-third of those eligible refused service and fled, but another third accepted combat duties. The remainder agreed to transport duties and the like. As a consequence of mobilization, main force units grew in size and strength. Through the latter part of 1964 and all of 1965, PLA forces grew increasingly bold in challenging the more heavily armed ARVN units in the field, and insurgent forces scored victories almost everywhere. In May and June of 1965, despite the start of air attacks on North Vietnam and initial deployments of the marines near Danang, ARVN suffered a series of catastrophic defeats. Losses on both sides soared: ARVN lost 1,672 men during a single week in June. By the beginning of July, MACV rated five ARVN regiments and nine separate battalions as ineffective. Eleven of ARVN's fifteen training battalions had to be disassembled to provide immediate replacements for combat units. To make matters worse, most ARVN units suffered defeat because of military incompetence and cowardice, rather than any inferiority in numbers or firepower. In short, by the summer of 1965, ARVN was well on the way toward complete collapse.[72]

American response to the steady deterioration in South Vietnam after mid–1964 was, of course, the bombing of the North and the deployment soon thereafter of U.S. ground forces. The latter decision, in particular, was to completely change the nature of the war in South Vietnam. Heretofore, the conflict had been harsh and difficult for those concerned. Yet, if one wished, it was often possible to sit on the fence and await the eventual outcome. In many rural areas, the pace of life was not profoundly altered. All of this changed with the arrival of U.S. troops. However difficult the war had been for the people of South Vietnam, the level of violence increased to a remarkable degree after American intervention. Virtually overnight, an already bitter revolutionary conflict was transformed into another of the violent and vicious wars that sadly have marked this century.

2

The Front Victorious:
Hau Nghia Province Through 1965

The Creation of a Province

Over twenty years after his tour of service, a combat veteran of the U.S. 25th Infantry Division recalled that Hau Nghia province was "green and fertile. I loved to watch the wind move through the rice paddies like waves. It was beautiful, like Iowa is beautiful." Many other Americans echoed this man's words, describing Hau Nghia's natural setting as "verdant," "lush," like a "semitropical paradise." But though many found the panorama pleasing, few admired the works of man in this part of Vietnam. The inhabitants had enough to eat, but they lived in bleak surroundings: "miserable," "run down," and "impoverished" were typical adjectives used to describe hamlets in Hau Nghia. Americans unfamiliar with the developing world were not the only people to hold such impressions. Anthropologist Gerald Hickey, one of America's most prominent authorities on rural Vietnam, described the area as "poor" even in Vietnamese terms and noted that a typical peasant in Hau Nghia "tends to live on a very narrow subsistence margin." Rural poverty in South Vietnam normally fed a strong revolutionary current, and this was certainly true in Hau Nghia. Indeed, it was part of the revolutionary heartland. Consequently, descriptions of Hau Nghia always include reference to the scars of war. Soldiers remember the odd smell of napalm and the eerie appearance of defoliated woodland. In the words of one officer, "Flying over the province by helicopter, one could see that Hau Nghia had been very heavily fought over. In some areas the ground resembled lunar landscape for miles on end, so close together were the shell holes."[1]

Hau Nghia was located northwest of Saigon. To the east, it shared a border with Gia Dinh province, which surrounds Saigon, and with Cambodia to the west. Its other neighbors were Binh Duong province to the northeast, Tay Ninh province to the northwest, Kien Tuong province to the southwest, and Long An province to the southeast. Geographically, Hau Nghia was a small province in Vietnamese terms. Roughly pentagonal in shape, it measured approximately 43 (north-south) by 50 (east-west) kilometers. Duc Hue and Duc Hoa districts, originally parts of the major Mekong Delta province of

Long An, were utterly flat and low-lying, with intermittent swamps and marshlands. Vietnam's huge and inhospitable swamp, the Plain of Reeds, extended well into the southwest portion of Duc Hue. The smaller Kinh Thay Swamp, a 5-mile-wide strip, ran diagonally from southeast to northwest, roughly parallel to the border between Duc Hue-Duc Hoa and Trang Bang-Cu Chi. North of the Kinh Thay, the terrain begins the almost imperceptible transition leading from the Mekong Delta (to the south) toward the Central Highlands (to the north). This transitional zone, beginning in Cu Chi and Trang Bang and extending north into Binh Duong and Tay Ninh provinces, is called the Mekong Terrace or the Piedmont. Though still flat, the elevation is slightly higher there, the land somewhat dryer and interspersed with woodland instead of swamp. Men and vehicles can easily traverse this area at any time of the year, a very rare circumstance in Vietnam. For this reason, the French constructed Highway 1, an all-weather road, going from Saigon through Cu Chi, Trang Bang, and Tay Ninh and on to Phnom Penh. A few smaller roads, only some 200 kilometers in all, connected the district capitals and larger hamlets. Two wooded areas, called Boi Loi Woods and Ho Bo Woods by the Americans, straddled the border between Hau Nghia and Tay Ninh-Binh Duong. Small patches of woods and shade trees were found throughout the province.

The eastern branch of the large Vam Co Dong River (sometimes called the Oriental by Americans) flowed across the province from northwest to southeast. A large segment of Duc Hue district, comprising 30 percent of the province, lay to the west of the river. Several small streams feeding either the Vam Co or the Saigon River to the northeast ran through Hau Nghia. These, in turn, were linked by canals in some spots.

The climate in Hau Nghia was typical of the area. The summer monsoon or rainy season was very wet and lasted from May through October. The winter monsoon, relatively dry and somewhat cooler, ran from November through February. From February through April, Hau Nghia was hot and dry. The average rainfall was 75 inches annually.

Although small in area, Hau Nghia was densely populated, as is the rule in and near the Mekong Delta. No precise census could ever be conducted, but the province had between 240,000 to 260,000 inhabitants at the time of American intervention. Over the following years, the population declined, perhaps to under 200,000. In 1965, the province ranked fortieth out of forty-three in terms of area but twentieth in terms of population. Ethnically, the population was almost entirely Vietnamese, with only a scattering of Chinese, Montagnards, and Khmers. Although a precise breakdown in terms of religion is not possible, it is clear that a majority of the population followed both Buddhist practice and Ong Ba, the peasant religion of Vietnam. The Cao Dai sect was strong in Hau Nghia, attracting about 10 percent of the inhabitants. In addition, approximately 15 percent of the population were Catholic, many having resettled along Route 1 from the North after the Geneva Convention.

The civilian economy was almost entirely agricultural. Some 47,000 hectares (one hectare = 2.5 acres) were under cultivation. As the population declined, so did the amount of land cultivated. The primary crop was rice. A major sugar refinery operating in the village of Hiep Hoa was the only industrial facility of any importance at the time of American intervention, but it did not continue to operate for long. The small nonagricultural portion of the work force was primarily employed in small, family-run businesses. Hau Nghia had no natural resources of any consequence.[2]

When the U.S. 25th Infantry Division arrived in January 1966 and established its base camp at Cu Chi, Hau Nghia was controlled almost entirely by the NLF and had been for some time. The inhabitants of Hau Nghia were not new to insurgency. Rural Vietnamese living northwest of Saigon saw French imperialism at its worst. Cash-crop agriculture, dependent on a large supply of cheap landless laborers, was a prominent feature of the area. A large French estate, the Filhol rubber plantation, played a dominant role in the economy of Cu Chi. Extensive sugarcane plantings, also owned by French interests, existed along the Vam Co River in Duc Hue. The cane was processed at the French-owned sugar mill at Hiep Hoa village. The mill, actually a complex of several buildings, was one of the largest industrial facilities in southern Vietnam. Other estates produced peanuts and pineapples. Consequently, after 1946, the area became a Viet Minh stronghold. Indeed, the French made little effort to exert a continuous control over the districts northwest of Saigon, concentrating instead on controlling the major towns and keeping the roads open during the day. Small forts and watchtowers sprouted throughout the countryside. Static defenses were no great danger to the insurgents. The frequent ground sweeps and air attacks, however, were another matter and things to be feared. To counter superior French technology, Viet Minh forces took advantage of the relatively dry and well-drained soil in the Cu Chi area and began construction of a sophisticated network of tunnels, some 50 kilometers worth by 1954. Frustrated in their pursuit of the elusive Viet Minh, French forces did succeed, however, in leaving behind bitter memories of murder, rape, looting, and violence.[3]

After Geneva, many Viet Minh families from the Hau Nghia area went north.[4] During this period, the Party by and large honored the Geneva Accords and dismantled the bulk of its military apparatus in South Vietnam. A core for a new revolutionary army was nevertheless maintained. Where the people were sympathetic and the terrain allowed deep cover, small military units settled in for a long wait. Two of these areas were the woodland in Cu Chi and the Plain of Reeds, which extended into Duc Hue. (Indeed, the Party's guerrilla fighters often called themselves the Bung, which simply means "swamp.") Unhealthy conditions and boredom were common enemies, according to a later Party history, as forces "became idle and during these inactive periods their main elements could not develop but deteriorated spiritually as well as organizationally."[5] Despite these difficulties, the effort was well worth it from the Party's point of view; when the decision was made to begin armed struggle, the military nucleus was ready. These deep-cover safe zones also allowed the top political leadership to operate in security very early in the conflict. Along the Vam Co River on the Tay Ninh-Cambodian border, for instance, the National Liberation Front was formed and its headquarters established. COSVN (Central Office in South Vietnam), the Party's headquarters and the real nerve center of the revolution, set up next door.[6]

It is difficult to trace events in the Hau Nghia area in the period between the Geneva Convention and the Party's decision to begin armed struggle in 1959. The new Diem government, according to interviews done in 1965 by an American military study group, was initially accepted. However, the villagers soon resented the loss of village autonomy and the appointment of unfamiliar officials. The activities of the Nhu family brought further discontent, particularly concerning the favoritism shown the Catholics and the great power wielded by the Can Lao Party. The population was further discontented by the "corruption and cruelty" of the local administration. Well before 1959, the Americans concluded, the Front was operating vigorously, especially in Cu Chi district.[7]

This account is confirmed by a district-level Party cadre from Cu Chi who later defected. This man, who became a moderately high-ranking Party member, came from a poor peasant family and received only one year of schooling. He described his childhood as "miserable because of working and war." He recalled that for many people, life in his village of Trung Lap was good in 1956–1957, with some villagers even owning motorbikes. Nevertheless, Party cadres were active from the beginning, portraying Diem as a cruel despot who did not even have a family. (This later point was a common one. Diem was contrasted with Ho Chi Minh, another bachelor. Ho was pictured as a man who had "married" the revolution and thus sacrificed his personal happiness for the people. Diem's lack of a wife and children, on the other hand, was considered "unnatural" by family-oriented rural Vietnamese and attributed to homosexuality.) According to the cadre, the people of Trung Lap were urged to overthrow Diem and bring peace to the country. The peasants were receptive to the Party's message because of "discrimination" by the government. Diem's manhunt against Viet Minh sympathizers further frightened many villagers, especially when his agents beheaded suspects in neighboring hamlets. In 1960, insurgent military forces began to pressure the hamlet and forced the government to abandon its fort. When the government lost its permanent presence, the Front was free to organize the hamlet for further revolutionary struggle.[8]

An assistant platoon leader in the Cu Chi local force battalion, who surrendered in October 1965, recalled that his village came under Front control in October 1960. His decision to join the Front was prompted by antagonism toward GVN militia forces and an insensitive village government. As happened in many other areas in Cu Chi, this man's hometown was made into a "combat village," complete with trenches and other fortifications. The village was organized politically. Every ten families formed a group and every three families formed a cell; chiefs of the family groups were individuals with family members fighting for the Front. When asked why other men in his battalion had joined the Front, the platoon leader replied, "Some joined the Front because their folks had joined the Resistance against the French. Since their folks went on fighting the GVN they chose to stand by their side. Some joined because they didn't like to be drafted in the ARVN; some were dissatisfied with the GVN. There were many causes, I can't name them all."[9]

The revolution was also strong in Trang Bang from an early date. A low-level Front military defector from Loc Giang village, one hamlet of which was the district capital of Trang Bang, recalled that the Viet Minh had been very strong in the village and had "produced many Communists" during the French war. Consequently, when the Party began its propaganda campaign in earnest, it concentrated on those families who had been supporters in the recent past: "They only put emphasis on the former Khang Chien (Resistance) families in order to motivate more hatred in them for the GVN. The hatred for the GVN spread from these families to others." One issue that particularly antagonized villagers, according to this man, was the practice of forced labor—district officials would require villagers to work in the construction of district facilities. In 1960, open revolt was in progress and the government presence reduced to the areas within gunshot of its military fortifications. The defector estimated that 90 percent of the population of Loc Giang cooperated with the Front, and about 50 to 60 percent followed willingly. At about the same time the Front was beginning a policy of instigating mass demonstrations against Diem throughout South Vietnam. One of the first large ones, drawing some 5,000 demonstrators according to Front sources, took place in Loc Giang on 21 January 1961. A similar sized demonstration took place the same week in Duc Hoa.[10]

In other parts of the province, progress for the Front was slower. In 1970, a middle-level defector from the Party recalled the collapse of governmental authority in a hamlet belonging to the large and important village of Hiep Hoa in Duc Hue district, site of the sugar mill. Originally a field hand for a rich landlord (and, as such, at the bottom of the Vietnamese social hierarchy, this man was recruited to serve as a village guerrilla in late 1962. At the time of his recruitment the insurgent apparatus in his hamlet consisted of four men. At that point, local insurgent forces were poorly armed and tried to avoid contact with the Hiep Hoa militia. Within a few months, this man was made hamlet finance and economy chief and was nominated to provisional membership in the Party. Front tax collection in the hamlet began in earnest in 1963, yet the villagers were not yet eager to pay. The defector estimated that only 5,000$ were collected that year. (South Vietnam's currency was the piaster. In 1965, the official exchange rate was 60$ = $1U.S. Thus, the amount collected was less than $80.00.) His own pay was 2$ per day and 20 liters of rice for the month. Yet, the Party was growing in strength, and, after the fall of Diem, its fortunes in Hiep Hoa improved dramatically. In 1964, the defector recalled, everyone in the hamlet paid their taxes to the Party, and revenues increased to nearly 20,000$.[11]

As mentioned in the previous chapter, when the Party decided to commence armed struggle in 1959, Diem's difficulties multiplied rapidly in much of rural Vietnam. In areas where the Front was active, GVN officials were forced to retreat behind barbed wire at local outposts every night. They stayed there for the remainder of the war. In August 1961, Diem and Nhu responded by authorizing the start of planning and personnel training for Operation SUNRISE, the pilot project for the Strategic Hamlet Program. Implementation began on 22 March 1962 in Binh Duong province. At first, the central government tried to conceal its role, but it was well known that Nhu was personally controlling the enterprise. By this time, the cult of counterinsurgency was well established in Washington, and great hopes were pinned on the Strategic Hamlet Program. Publicly, the initiative was both supported and heartily praised by American officialdom in both Saigon and Washington.

In theory, the Strategic Hamlet Program was a comprehensive combination of coercive, organizational, and assistance measures that would simultaneously drive the Front away, reestablish government control, and bring a better material life to the peasants. According to the plan, the entire hamlet was to be fortified, the militia strengthened, and a census conducted. In addition, "suspect" families relocated near a military post for easy surveillance, and each family would be assigned to a five-family cell, where it was to become part of a larger self-help and intelligence network. The hamlet administration would also be restructured, the people would be organized into various government groups, and public works programs were slated to begin. It was based on a set of assumptions all of which had to be correct for the program to succeed. Above all, Saigon assumed that the Front was a threat coming from outside the hamlets, i.e., a military threat. If so, then the stress on fortification and denial of access made sense. The GVN also assumed that the Front's appeal was based on malicious propaganda, which could be countered by GVN Civic Action cadres and government organizations. The peasantry, in Diem's view, was essentially content and would be happy again if administration improved and some physical improvements were made in the hamlets. In practice, all of these assumptions were dubious, and the program developed into a calamity.

The course of the disaster was charted by Dr. Gerald Hickey and John C. Donnel, two American researchers who knew Vietnam well and studied the program closely. One of the hamlets they examined was Xom Hue in Tan An Hoi, the largest village and capital of Cu Chi district. Xom Hue was one of the first hamlets to undergo the process and received the direct attention of Saigon officialdom. Difficulties in Xom Hue, therefore, could not be explained away as the result of a lack of attention by the authorities. The problems that arose, on the contrary, were structural and a perfect illustration of the weakness of the Diem regime.

Xom Hue was a very large hamlet with a population of some 1,700. The peasants were forced to build an extensive network of earthworks that surrounded the entire hamlet. This included a ditch five feet deep and ten feet wide with a rampart of similar size, both studded with bamboo spears. In front of the ditch, a fence of bamboo and barbed wire was constructed. The bamboo was requisitioned from the villagers without compensation, thus denying them their emergency "cushion crop," which was only sold in lean times and took three years to regrow. The time required for construction also prevented the peasants from planting tobacco, the major dry season cash crop in Xom Hue. When not digging, male villagers had to join in Republican Youth military and political training that consisted of "doing the manual of arms with a 5-foot bamboo staff, and reading slogans in unison."

To make matters worse, work parties of up to 150 persons were forced to work in hamlets as much as 100 kilometers distant. Contrary to government promises, villagers in these work parties were not paid and had to either buy their own lunches or, (as was frequently the case for poor peasants) go hungry. Villagers from neighboring Trung Lap, also unpaid, were forced to help their Xom Hue brethren construct facilities for Cu Chi district headquarters. Corvée labor, Hickey and Donnel pointed out, reminded peasants of the "hated French," and GVN rationalizations that similar measures were employed in North Vietnam had little impact in Xom Hue. Nor was there any way for the peasantry to express its discontent. Despite some administrative reorganization, any political activity critical of the government was strictly forbidden.

Few families in Xom Hue were relocated. The ten that were moved were supposed to receive 1,000$ (about $14) and help in reassembling their homes. Once again, the GVN's promise was broken. (Although Hickey and Donnel do not mention it, both undoubtedly knew that funds authorized for such projects were frequently siphoned by officials somewhere along the graft pipeline.)

The security component of the program offered little as a trade-off for the economic sacrifices and harsh labor extracted. Front military forces did not attack Xom Hue, although they were very active in Ben Cat and probably could have done so. Perhaps there was no reason to attack. The fortifications were designed to keep the Front out, but the Cu Chi district chief estimated that 60–70 percent of the hamlet residents had divided loyalties and would cooperate with the Front. The "enemy," therefore, was already inside Xom Hue. Perhaps Nhu realized this, despite public proclamations. As he told Hickey in August 1961:

> People say that our cadres should go out, work with the peasants and establish a relationship of affection and confidence with them to learn their needs. But if the cadres do this, they are overwhelmed by the people's claims and demands. The only thing for the government to do is issue orders and back them up with force.[12]

A highly publicized ceremony was held to commemorate the completion of the Xom Hue Strategic Hamlet in the summer of 1962. A large reviewing stand filled with Vietnamese and American officials was surrounded by hundreds of Vietnamese troops. Nhu himself presided. Hickey came to observe with Homer Biggart of the *New York Times* and the famous French journalist François Sully. With his "anger rising steadily," Hickey listened to officials describe the wonderful future in store for Xom Hue's peasants. It was a bizarre scene. Tanks had blocked off the roads, and no villagers were allowed to attend for "security" reasons. Hickey asked an American colonel whether it was not the point of the entire Strategic Hamlet Program to provide security. The answer was stony silence.[13]

Security was a pressing issue indeed for the GVN in Cu Chi district by 1962. This point was driven home to Hickey and Donnel when they visited a neighboring village while studying Xom Hue:

> John and I also went to Trung Lap, which was very scary and strange. A teacher we were talking to suddenly leaned forward and said that we should not be there. She said that a hamlet chief had been found dead in a well the night before. We were in a rented Citroen 15 (one of those marvelous get-away cars like Joan Crawford sped around the French countryside in during the wartime movies), and we had problems on a road with thick forest on either side. It had an eerie air about it, and the next day at that very spot an ARVN unit was mauled in a well-laid ambush by the Viet Cong (who had spent a week preparing for it.)[14]

Hickey and Donnel knew that unless the Strategic Hamlet Program was utterly reshaped it was going to fail. Despite sharp and acrimonious criticism from both American and South Vietnamese officials, they prepared a report and gave a series of high-level briefings that vividly showed the self-defeating nature of the centerpiece of Diem's war effort in rural Vietnam. When Diem was overthrown, the junta in Saigon ended the Strategic Hamlet Program immediately, citing as reasons many of the points raised by Hickey and Donnel.

In the meantime, however, the Strategic Hamlet Program was rushed forward in Cu Chi and Trang Bang, along Highway 1. Unlike the residents in Xom Hue, thousands of villagers here were forcibly relocated away from Front-controlled hamlets off the road. This was a very sensitive issue. Many peasants bitterly resented relocation for both religious and economic reasons. Ironically, many of the relocated people were, no doubt, potential supporters of the GVN; the revolutionary nature of the Front frightened many of the most traditional Vietnamese peasants. The Party could never completely hide its anticlericalism (one of the few good propaganda points for Saigon), and many of the most devout followers of Ong Ba, the indigenous peasant religion, looked at the Front with suspicion. Ong Ba, however, stresses ancestor worship and the veneration of gravesites, and removing the family from their ancestors was therefore a blasphemous act. The bulk of the peasantry was undoubtedly less religiously inclined, but, at the very least, relocation entailed a huge inconvenience for the peasants would have to walk a long distance to their new land. To do this with little or no compensation, as was normally the case, added serious insult to an already grievous injury. Had Saigon been stronger and able to support the Strategic Hamlet Program, the Front would have been threatened. As it was, Diem handed the Front another marvelous propaganda issue and further alienated thousands of villagers.[15] In the words of a Front indoctrination cadre, asked in his interrogation why people in the Hau Nghia area turned away from the government in this period:

> People don't like to be looked on and treated as VC. People don't like Strategic Hamlets and New Life Hamlets whenever they are compelled to resettle in an area far from their fields or working places. Villagers don't like to be drafted. They are dissatisfied with self-defenders and village officials who behaved badly with the village girls. The most important causes of dissatisfaction are indiscriminate attacks on villages and being considered and treated as VC.[16]

Despite the concentration of GVN forces in the area because of the Strategic Hamlet Program, Saigon's position continued to erode northwest of the capital. Some time in late 1962 (the precise date is unclear), the GVN established a special tactical zone along the Binh Duong-Tay Ninh and Long An border. The problem was that Front forces were active on both sides of the Kinh Thay Swamp. Because GVN provincial forces patrolled in their own territory and would rarely cross boundaries in pursuit, insurgents could simply slip into the opposite province in case of a contact.[17]

Administratively, the obvious next step was taken on 15 October 1963 when Diem proclaimed the existence of Hau Nghia province. Diem, who had literary interests, chose the name himself; it means "deepening righteousness." At the same time, he directed that a small hamlet in Duc Hoa district be renamed Khiem Cuong, meaning "modest but vigorous," and made it the province capital. In theory, Khiem Cuong would serve well because of its central location, roughly equidistant from the four district capitals. Military forces based at the province capital would be well located to serve as a reaction force. The choice also avoided any sign of favoritism (and opportunities for graft) for any particular group of district officials; Diem would begin the province with a clean slate. In reality, however, the new capital was a Front hamlet, dirt poor, terribly vulnerable, and thus miserably situated and poorly suited for its task. Nor were the local peasants impressed with the new state of affairs. They refused to adopt the new name of Khiem Cuong and continued to call their hamlet Bao Trai, or "round farm." (Everyone, Americans included, followed the peasants' lead on this matter, and I shall do likewise.) Because of the danger and poor living conditions, GVN officials considered Hau Nghia a hardship post from the beginning.

Diem's decision to create Hau Nghia province reflected the downward spiral of the South Vietnamese war effort. The growing debacle in the countryside exacerbated the Buddhist crisis in the cities. On 1 November 1963, ARVN launched a coup, murdered Diem and Nhu, and established a junta to run the country. South Vietnam was thrown into chaos.

The Party, the Front, and Revolutionary Struggle

Diem had been murdered by his generals, but he was destroyed by the Front. By late 1963, the Party had succeeded in fashioning a revolutionary movement that the GVN could not handle. Soon, American and North Vietnamese intervention would change the nature of the conflict in fundamental ways. Consequently, at this point, it is appropriate to analyze in greater detail how the Front operated in Hau Nghia province. By doing so, we can examine the indigenous "people's war" in South Vietnam at high tide, before the intervention of outside forces. Hopefully, it will also be possible to better appreciate the depth of the catastrophe that faced Americans in Vietnam when they stepped in after Diem's demise to prevent a Front victory.

Although other scholars have described the organizational structure of the Front and Party in great detail, a summary is required here.[18] Because the general direction of the insurgency was firmly in the hands of the Party, the highest organizational echelon was the Central Committee in Hanoi. No major policy was developed without its consent. Operationally, however, the second echelon—the Party's bureau of southern affairs, called COSVN by the Americans—was more important. In practice, the distinction between COSVN and the Central Committee was not rigid; some members of COSVN were also members of the Central Committee, thus allowing the bureau to set policy on all but the most vital matters. Although overall policy was determined at COSVN or the Central Committee, descending organizational echelons were responsible for implementing directives in a manner appropriate to local conditions. Directly beneath COSVN were several interprovince zones or regions, serving primarily as liaisons between province committees and higher authorities. Regions had limited policy functions and hence were subject to frequent changes in boundaries. All of Hau Nghia province was in the enemy's B2 Theater, a large area directly controlled by COSVN that included part of the GVN II CTZ (Corps Tactical Zone) and all of III CTZ and IV CTZ. Because COSVN gave so much attention to the area around Saigon, the districts in Hau Nghia were normally under the operational military control of a succession of special zones or military regions.[19] More extensive political duties were assigned to the various province committees. (As previously mentioned, Hau Nghia was a GVN administrative unit and was not recognized by the enemy. The opposing sides recognized differing provincial and district boundaries in other areas of the country, a situation that caused some confusion. On enemy maps, Cu Chi district included a portion of GVN Ben Cat district and was a part of Binh Duong province, Duc Hue and Duc Hoa were part of Long An province, and Trang Bang was recognized by the NLF as a district of Tay Ninh.) Provincial committees were charged with developing plans for the implementation of COSVN directives in a manner that took into account local conditions. The district committees had a supervisory and liaison role and functioned for the province committee in a manner similar to that of the regions vis-à-vis COSVN.[20]

Although the village committee was the lowest echelon on the organizational chart, it was considered by the Party to be the most important for the purpose of waging revolutionary war. The Party worked tirelessly at strengthening the village apparatus. The village chapter, made up of small cells of Party members, was directly responsible for the implementation of Party policy at the village and hamlet level. This included everything from propagandizing the masses to collecting taxes to finding recruits for the local military units. Everywhere, Front organizations, such as the Farmers' Liberation Association or the Women's Liberation Association, were organized to more fully mobilize the peasantry. The emphasis placed by the Party on the village yielded crucial dividends. Because the insurgents, whether Party members or not, were locally recruited, they were able to identify directly with the rural population and exploit bonds of family and friendship. The revolutionaries were personally intimate with the population and therefore could identify, pressure, intimidate, or, if necessary, eliminate individuals opposed to their movement. Unless someone was picked for promotion or assigned service in main force divisions, followers of the revolution rarely had to leave their home provinces and normally operated in or near their home hamlets. This situation not only was good for morale but also made possible the superb intelligence apparatus that was characteristic of the insurgency. The Party's village emphasis also facilitated timely and relentless propaganda. As Jeffrey Race has pointed out, the Party was careful to subordinate every political effort to the struggle with the GVN and to keep the village apparatus from developing into a mere administrative unit.[21]

In general, the Party and Front were skillfully organized, combining the ability to centralize policy formulation and implementation, on one hand, with the ability to react to local conditions and events, on the other. The Party leadership combined organizational brilliance with an uncanny ability to exploit genuine grievances, put their opponents in the worst possible light, mobilize political-military action, generate fear among their enemies, and, most importantly, convince supporters that victory was inevitable. Political, psychological, physical, and military factors continually interacted in the Party's calculation. The weave of revolutionary warfare was so complex that it is difficult to know where to begin to unravel it for the purposes of analysis. The land issue, however, is an obvious place to start.

In a traditional agrarian society, even one like Vietnam where much was changing quickly, the individual's relationship to the land is central to economic and social existence. Just as land was fundamental in determining wealth and status, it was fundamental in defining political position. Indeed, more than anything else, it was the land issue that ultimately brought Diem to ruin. As detailed in Chapter 1, Diem attempted to restore the position of Vietnamese landlords who had been dispossessed by the Viet Minh. Although he tried to placate the peasantry with a feeble and corrupt land reform plan, his land policy, as recounted by a founder of the NLF, was a disaster:

In the countryside he destroyed at a blow the dignity and livelihood of several hundred thousand peasants by canceling the land-redistribution arrangements instituted by the Viet Minh in the areas they had controlled prior to 1954. He might have attempted to use American aid to compensate owners and capitalize on peasant goodwill; instead he courted the large landholders. Farmers who had been working land they considered their own, often for years, now faced demands for back rent and exorbitant new rates. It was an economic disaster for them. . . . The result of all this was a frustrated and indignant peasantry, fertile ground for anti-Diem agitation.[22]

With the land issue, Diem provided the Party leaders with a perfect tool to begin the process of integrated political and military struggle that the Party called dau tranh. At any given phase of the war, debate took place within the Party over which strategy was appropriate to the balance of forces as they existed at the moment. Nevertheless, the leadership was always in agreement on one point: Political struggle and military struggle must be linked continually. The hammer and anvil was a common metaphor. Political struggle, naturally, had to dominate in the initial stage of a protracted conflict. Measures had to be calculated to simultaneously increase the power of the revolution and decrease the power of the "puppet" regime. Eventually, persuasive and coercive measures were directed toward every sector of Vietnamese society and all organs of the GVN's political-military apparatus. First of all, however, the Party had to nurture its revolutionary core, the foundation upon which the entire effort was based. In Hau Nghia, as in much of rural Vietnam, this core was the landless peasantry.

Hau Nghia province was not destitute, but it was poor. Land in Hau Nghia, unlike that in the Mekong Delta proper to the south, did not allow double rice harvests. The population density, however, was high. Consequently, many peasant families lived an existence that was uncomfortably close to dire need. Although precise figures from Hau Nghia are not available, the number of landless peasants must have been very high. As previously mentioned, large plantations were a prominent fixture during the French period. According to GVN figures from 1964, in the southern region of South Vietnam, which included Hau Nghia, 44.4 percent of the peasants were landless in 1961. Another 28.5 percent rented some land, and only 22 percent of the peasants farmed their own land exclusively. In land area, this meant that 62.5 percent of land was rented and 35.2 percent privately owned. Large landowners, in Vietnamese terms, dominated. According to an exhaustive American study done in 1968, the upper 9.5 percent of landowners owned 54.7 percent of the land in the same southern region in 1966. On the other end of the scale, the bottom 26.6 percent of the landowners owned less than one hectare and accounted for only 2.5 percent of the land owned.[23] In neighboring Long An province, the percentages were even more unbalanced: In 1968, 79 percent of the peasantry were landless.[24]

Students of the Vietnam War have long realized the critical nature of the land issue for the Party. Douglas Pike wrote:

"He should own the land who rubs it between his hands each season," runs an ancient Vietnamese proverb, expressing the great hunger that only the landless who work the land can ever fully understand. In a primarily agrarian society such as Vietnam, concern for land and land tenure problems is second only to concern for weather, and the NLF in those areas where land was a major issue, the Mekong Delta and the coastal lowlands, made full use of it. . . . Cadres were instructed to turn every issue into land terms.[25]

Gabriel Kolko maintains that the struggle for land was "the single most important issue not only of the war in the south after 1960 but in the entire history of the Revolution."[26]

Despite the importance of the issue, it is a very tricky one to analyze because of its multiple manifestations. Obviously, it touched on material conditions. Landless peasants, for instance, had to do stoop labor. Unless a landless peasant had the good fortune of having sustained access to fertile land, housing would be of the crudest variety and diet monotonous, even if adequate. A poor landless peasant would probably own almost no consumer goods. Psychological stress stemming from uncertainty over the future added a bleakness to life. Land, along with the family, was security. Bad weather, political disturbance, or blight could turn a marginal existence into a nightmare very quickly. Likewise, social status was largely determined by landholding. Village affairs were traditionally dominated, although not exclusively so, by landowners. Weddings, funerals, and Tet celebrations, so important in village life, were usually very meager affairs for a poor peasant. Even gravesites, so central to Ong Ba, were far more humble for the landless. Having only labor to sell, few landless peasants could afford to properly educate their children.[27] Obviously, these inequities provided boundless opportunities for Front cadres with an equalitarian message preaching class conflict.

There was considerable debate within the Party over what constituted a "class enemy" and a "landlord." The requirements of revolutionary warfare posed a dilemma for the Party that had no obvious solution. On one hand, by their very nature, "Front tactics" required reaching out to a large part of the social spectrum. Indeed, it was central to dau tranh to have political struggle across the entire social spectrum at all times. On the other hand, the "base element" of the revolution, the poor peasantry and urban workers, had to be convinced that the social struggle was uniquely theirs. Only if this were done could the Party ask for the sacrifices inherent in the struggle. This presented no problem in the area of propaganda and indoctrination: As will be seen directly, the Party was skilled at developing propaganda themes to suit every group. However, in terms of social action in realms controlled by the Party, principally "liberated areas" and within the Front apparatus itself, the problem was direct and pressing. The debate was entirely tactical because, as shown in dramatic fashion by the bloody "land reform" carried out in North Vietnam during the late 1950s, collectivization was considered the ideal answer to the land question. This fact, of course, was not advertised to the peasants who had "reactionary" views on the matter.

In general, the Party accepted a rather lenient definition of "landowner," The Party line on the subject was described by a middle-ranking civilian cadre of the Central Nam Bo (an area including Hau Nghia) Propaganda Culture Indoctrination Section. The man was from Duc Hoa and was assigned to work in a liberated zone in Duc Hue district. Although he was considered to be from a "good element" of society because of his Front sympathies, he was not asked to join the Party because he was well educated and his father-in-law was a large landowner. As he later described it, his section was employed in "propaganda, mass culture, indoctrination and training work. The word 'mass' here refers only to workers and agricultural laborers. The Section is supposed to follow the thinking of the mass in order to put it right and to strengthen it." The man gave a succinct definition of "landowner":

> Those who live on their agricultural revenues and don't work at all with their hands. They hire laborers or collect land rent. The amount of their property differs according to the region. Landowners who have sold their land are still considered landowners and may be denounced as are others in their class.

The man also gave a more comprehensive description of the Party's view of the class structure in the countryside:

> The VC classified the country people as follows:
> A. Exploiter country people:
>   1. Entirely [hoan toan] exploiters and our enemies, that is the landowners.
>   2. Exploiters to a certain degree and our allies for the time being, that is the rich farmers who don't work much.
> B. Middle farmers classified as:
>   1. Middle farmers, near the rich farmers, somewhat exploiters.
>   2. Middle farmers.
>   3. Middle farmers, just up-graded from poor farmers. The middle farmers are further classified as old and new middle-farmers. The latter are those who have been up-graded since 1945 and are considered worthier than old middle farmers.
> C. Poor farmers who have only little and and whose work is the main source of revenue.
> D. Landless farmers.

It should be pointed out that the "poor" and "landless" farmers listed above would have constituted at least 70 percent of the population of Hau Nghia province.

Any researcher using the interrogation reports of Front and Party defectors must be struck by the extremely high proportion of poor peasants among them. A very typical example was given in 1966 by a former squad leader in a Front main force battalion operating in Hau Nghia province, who recalled his decision to join the Front:

> I became active in the Front in January 1964. I was working as a laborer in a ricefield about a kilometer from my village when a VC cadre came and

persuaded me to join the Front. . . . He said I would be working for the people and the nation, and thus for the liberation of the peasants from feudalism and landlordism and the nation from American domination. Besides I would be given 2 hectares of land which I would then be able to farm as my own. . . . The aim that appealed to me most was the overthrow of landlordism, as I believed land would be distributed to the peasants, particularly to those who worked for the Revolution. . . . I was dissatisfied with my life, because my family was very poor. I only thought of having land to help my parents lead a better life.[28]

In practice, the Front moved carefully in the matter of land redistribution. The details were left to the village cadres and, as might be imagined, had to be worked out with great care to minimize painful and divisive disputes among tenants. For the most part, they were careful not to antagonize middle-level peasants. Large holdings owned by absentee landlords or the GVN were confiscated and distributed to the tenants, with most peasants receiving between one-half and one hectare of land. Rents, where still paid, were frequently less than 10 percent—a much lower total than was the case in GVN areas. The Front also introduced a policy of progressive taxation that both lowered most peasants' tax bills considerably and discouraged the ownership of surplus land. Land was distributed conditionally. Peasants were expected to support the Front with taxes, with membership in mass organizations, or, if necessary, militarily. If a peasant refused to do so, his land could be lost. Obviously, all the advantages gained by Front reforms would be lost if the GVN prevailed. Thus, the land reform program was more than a strategy to gain popularity. Above all, it was aimed at gaining peasant commitment to the Front.[29]

As the Front began to prevail in Hau Nghia, the land distribution process was started. In Loc Giang village, for instance, the Front had controlled most of the hamlets since 1961. Land distribution, however, did not begin until at least one year later. A Front rallier from Loc Giang, quoted earlier, recalled that land was allocated on the basis of need and family size: A family of four might get half a hectare, a family of eight, an entire hectare. This man believed that yields increased only somewhat, if at all, but he did not see increased production as the major reward: "The only good thing in land distribution was that the poor didn't have to work as hired laborers any more, because they had their own land to work on."[30]

Difficulties were inevitable. Although the details are not clear, apparently the Front was initially too aggressive at redistribution in some locales and antagonized middle-level peasants. The education officer of Tay Ninh province (which included Trang Bang district until October 1963) had served first the Viet Minh and then the Front for over twenty years; he recalled that, in 1961, a furious debate took place over the pace of redistribution. In some areas, he recalled, land had been distributed to middle-level peasants. Later, the Party reversed course and wanted to "inflict punitive measures" against class enemies. This included redistributing the land given to some well-off peasants in favor of the very poor. Militants carried the day in Tay Ninh, but, as time went on, the Front increasingly sought "solidarity with middle farmers."[31]

The Party used the land issue to begin the momentum of revolutionary struggle. It touched many people, it was immediately understandable, and it led to direct commitment on the part of many toward the Front. If the Party's position on land struck a chord with the peasants, an issue that they knew intimately, then it was natural for them to believe the Party on issues that were more distant and unfamiliar. Yet, the struggle in rural Vietnam was far more complex and dynamic than a simple matter of grievance and response. In many respects, commitment was more important than any particular issue. Certainly, the method of transmitting the message was as important as the message itself.

Various Front mass political organizations had a crucial role in the indoctrination of the peasantry. The Farmers' Liberation Association was the largest and most important. Among others were the Women's Liberation Association and Youth Liberation Association. Within these, various cadres worked at "educating" and developing the "class consciousness" of the peasantry. Mass gatherings, study sessions, and Chinese-inspired self-criticism meetings were continual. In the words of one captured education cadre from Hau Nghia, the Front "assigned a great many people to the education mission in order to continuously develop the culture of the people." The rallier from Loc Giang recalled, "There were all kinds of cadres for all categories of the villagers. Young men had young man cadres, young women had young woman cadres, old men had old man cadres and old women had old woman cadre, etc."[32]

The theme stressed most often was class hatred. If the class enemy could be linked with foreign imperialism, all the better. The following propaganda motif came from Duc Hue:

This village-chief's family has its members educated in town. They are pilots and officers for the Americans and the puppet government. His sons and grandsons strafe and bomb our village and hamlets. By that you can see that landowners always go hand in hand with the imperialists to fight against us peasants and workers.[33]

The national appeal was also used with the peasantry to great effect but was secondary until American intervention. The following is a line developed for Front schools in the Hau Nghia area:

There is only one Vietnam Nation. There is only one Vietnamese People. North and South are under the same roof. Therefore when the Americans come to Vietnam, it is the duty of the Vietnamese people to throw them out of the country. They come here as aggressors. They come to invade Vietnam, therefore the Vietnamese people are determined to chase them out of the country, to liberate the South and to unify the nation.[34]

Naturally, the GVN was constantly mocked and criticized. Inflation, high prices, corruption by officials, and "decadent" Western culture were all recurring themes.

The Front also exploited resistance to conscription. Although many young men drafted by the GVN were able to serve near home, the Front offered the opportunity to avoid uniformed service altogether. Before American intervention, the Front usually refrained from forcing young men to join revolutionary military forces. Membership in one of the various organizations was sufficient commitment initially. Naturally, Front cadres hoped a young man would volunteer for more arduous and risky tasks as indoctrination and peer pressure did their work. As the military defector from Loc Giang remembered:

> Most of the fighters were draft dodgers. At first, the cadres said they could come to their area to dodge the GVN draft without having to work for the Front. The cadres let them go free for a few months before they started forming study sessions for these draft dodgers and sending female cadres to proselyte them.[35]

Even when a young man chose to "hold the Front's gun," service had its attractions. A hamlet guerrilla lived a largely civilian existence at home and played a military role only when necessary.

Convincing someone to join main force military units that required full-time service away from home was much harder. The indoctrination cadre asserted that even Party members were often reluctant to leave their home villages for risky service with main force units. He also recalled that young men were hiding from both the Front and the GVN outside many villages, being fed secretly by their families. Front cadres would do their best to convince these families to have their sons come home.[36] More testimony on the subject comes from the interrogation of current affairs chief of the Youth Group Committee from Trang Bang district. This man had fought the French, gone north in 1954, returned to Trang Bang in 1963, and surrendered in 1966. He claimed that most young men were war weary:

> I've dealt with youths of three areas—contested areas, weak areas and deep areas. Most of the youths in the deep areas have relatives working for the VC, so they support the revolution. Moreover, they are poor. They either join the Front troops or stay home to do farming, but they hide themselves when the GVN or Americans make operations to the area. The youths in contested areas are pacifistic, they avoid both sides. We call them uncommitted youths. They don't work for the GVN and don't work for the Front full-time, they only dig trenches, build combat fences, etc. These kinds of youths follow whichever side makes better propaganda. The youths in weak areas, like cities and strategic hamlets, don't approve of communism and VC, but they don't want to be drafted by the GVN because they think they will be killed by the VC in battles. Therefore, they try all means to avoid the draft. These kinds of youths have low morale in serving the revolution, so we select the good ones among them to educate and propagandize.[37]

As this quote illustrates, it was one thing to create a climate of sympathy for the aims of the Front but quite another to actually mobilize individuals to face the risks and harsh life required to carry the revolution to victory. Grievances alone, no matter how genuine, do not make revolutions. The direction, inspiration, and energy for struggle had to be supplied by the Front cadres.

It is impossible here to do justice to the role played by the cadres from top to bottom. The Party, of course, was an archetype Leninist organization. Consequently, the top cadres made policy and expected it to be implemented faithfully down each rung of the organizational ladder. Local initiative, however, was expected and encouraged. Local cadres also had the key role of reporting on the local situation, which was crucial for Party strategists in determining the balance of forces and creating appropriate policy.

Equally important, local cadres served as examples of revolutionary virtue. They were expected to be honest, sincere, and brave. After the war, COSVN commander Gen. Tran Van Tra defined revolutionary virtue and explained its importance:

> Virtue is manifested in behavior between people, between the general and the specific, in the family and in society. Everyone must love and respect each other, and be faithful, sincere and loyal. . . . It must be Vietnamese morality and communist morality, which combine to form the virtue of Ho Chi Minh. . . . If words are not accompanied by action they have no value, theory not demonstrated by reality is only empty theory. Every individual must be exemplary in study, work, combat, production, and one's way of life, and life in an exemplary, close-knit family and an orderly, harmonious society. If we are not exemplary no one will listen to us, and if families are not harmonious and exemplary there is no way to create an orderly, just society.[38]

General Tra was describing an ideal. It was an ideal, however, that Front and particularly Party cadres took very seriously. Compared to their GVN counterparts, Front cadres had many advantages. GVN officials were usually members of the urban elite. In contrast, because most Front cadres came from rural Vietnam and frequently were from the area in which they operated, they dressed like, lived like, and thought like the local peasantry. Whereas GVN officials, whether honest or corrupt, received status and material benefit from their position, Front cadres worked for a pittance. Standard pay was 3$ (about 3 cents) per day and 20 to 25 kilos of rice per month. The military rallier from Loc Giang, quoted earlier, described the propaganda advantages of this point:

> The cadres always cultivated hatred toward the GVN in the people during study sessions. Why could they do that? Because they said they didn't get paid to work as cadres for the Front; they worked because the Front has the just cause to work for.[39]

Mistreatment of villagers on the part of GVN officials or soldiers was a continual grievance. The Hiep Hoa finance cadre, also quoted earlier, recounted the Party's policy on personal behavior:

> I should point out that all VC cadres are subject to a very strict set of rules of behavior laid down by the Party. For example, a cadre may drink, but may not get drunk. Drunkenness is punishable by dismissal, although I have known of cases where individuals have been given several warnings for this offense. No cadre may steal anything, especially from the people. A stolen chicken from a farmer will result in dismissal from the Party.

The same man described the Party's policy toward the issue of civilian casualties, an area where the GVN was frequently indifferent:

> Mistreating the people is a very serious offense, although sometimes a regrettable incident occurs when innocent civilians are killed or wounded by one of our mines or booby-traps. In Hiep Hoa, whenever this happened, we would always attempt to visit the family to offer apologies, and explain that the incident was an accident of war. It was bad for our cause when this happened, and we always tried to smooth over the damage when possible.[40]

A different rejoinder might be used if the war damage was material only. A production cell leader in a tiny arms factory in Cu Chi described how the Front handled complaints from villagers concerning battle damage to their hamlet:

> Peasants would complain to neighbors that VC hiding in houses were to blame for damage (which was slight); VC would answer, "We would not complain if we lost our lives to defend the people, so why do the people complain loudly when they suffer a little damage to their property? You have no constructive spirit."[41]

The cell leader also described the deep impact made on villagers by the cadres' willingness to sacrifice:

> People knew life with ARVN was much easier: They got paid monthly and suffered no hardship. The VC life is very hard. The VC used the earth as their beds, and the open sky as their mosquito nets. This was what the people said, but in the meeting organized by the VC they said that their life was full of glory and their death full of greatness. They asked the people to join the Revolutionary movement. Besides, their attitude toward the people was very courteous; therefore, the people were very glad to join the VC.[42]

Finally, the same man recalled the excellent behavior of Front military forces when in the area, in sharp contrast to ARVN's reputation for haughty conduct:

Front soldiers came frequently to help build combat villages and fight ARVN. The population liked them very much because they were always ready to help them with their pit digging or their gardening. The people listened to them very eagerly whenever they told the stories of their lives. All the young men in my hamlet who were to be drafted by ARVN joined the Front.[43]

Front cadres tirelessly dispensed indoctrination and propaganda to villagers. The primary recipients of the Front's message, however, were the cadres themselves. Even the lowest-level cadre was required to attend training courses. The ideological component of these courses for village cadres did not contain elaborate Marxist analysis: their Leninism was decidedly secondhand. A longtime province-level education cadre noted that most village or hamlet cadres had only a vague idea about communism and, in the recent past, were "merely oppressed people" that had risen, thanks to the Front, to become "some sort of VIP in the village." They were content with their lot and followed the ideological lead of their superiors without question. Higher up the ladder, however, cadres received more and more extensive training in ideological matters. Whereas hamlet and village cadres followed the Front primarily because of rural issues, such as land, higher cadres tended to stress the international struggle against "American Imperialism."[44] Whatever the precise motives of the individuals involved, the Front was very successful in instilling in their political cadres a faith in their cause and a powerful faith in ultimate victory. As we shall see, enough of them kept this faith, despite extraordinary military pressure, to frustrate the American war effort in the Vietnamese countryside.

Regardless of a cadre's level, self-criticism sessions were frequent. These sessions were normally a type of group therapy with members of the group criticizing and praising themselves and others. Cadres were urged to always remember that they were there to serve the people and should never forget the lot of the poor peasant. Another aim of self-criticism was the prevention of complacency and self-delusion. The Cu Chi district youth secretary was asked during interrogation to explain the Party's reasons for self-criticism:

Because they want the people to tell the truth. Because they think that if we are doing wrong, the only way we can be corrected is to do it ourselves, not to wait until the other person does it. You don't have to wait until the other person corrects you. Do it yourself, purge yourself. Secondly, it's a method of self-help and we also need the help of the other people.[45]

If a cadre were suspected of losing this zeal or, worse, becoming corrupt, self-criticism was more akin to a trial than therapy. Under such circumstances, the individual was well advised to confess promptly if guilty. If he did not, and was later found to be culpable, punishment, in one cadre's words, could be "stiff, very stiff."

Various internal difficulties impeded Front efforts. After 1960, a large number of "regroupee" cadres came to the South after having lived and trained in the DRV since the Geneva Accords were signed in 1954. This was not a north/south problem per se because most of these individuals were southern born. Their experiences and perspectives were different, however. The regroupees were frequently given senior positions and expected the respect and deference they believed their due because of their long experience and sacrifice. Military regroupees had more experience in handling larger groups of men than did their younger counterparts. The more recent cadres believed that the regroupees frequently had lost touch with southern conditions. In the military area, younger fighters had experienced combat against modern weapons (such as helicopters and armored personnel carriers) employed by ARVN since 1962, which had not been used during the Viet Minh period. There was also the apparently well-founded suspicion that a few of the regroupees had grown weary of struggle and came to the South because of homesickness or hatred of life in the North.[46]

Illicit love affairs also were a frequent cause of morale problems. Sexual morality in rural Vietnam was traditionally quite conservative. The Front pointed to prostitution, drug use, and other forms of moral debauchery as manifestations of a malignant capitalist culture being imposed on Vietnam by the United States. In general, the Front tried to pose as the defender of traditional Vietnamese family values. On the other hand, the Front took a very progressive stance, in Vietnamese terms, on women's equality. Women were widely employed at all levels of the revolution, except main force combat. Consequently, a great many young men and women found themselves together outside traditional settings. As recalled by the finance cadre from Hiep Hoa, the Front tried to encourage a puritanical code of conduct:

> Second wives and mistresses are forbidden. If the woman is single, the punishment is dismissal. If she is married, the punishment may be confinement as well as dismissal. It does not matter if the woman is the wife of a fellow-VC cadre or of a GVN soldier or official. The first is frowned upon because it can only create dangerous dissension in the ranks. The latter is regarded as dangerous because of the security risk of consorting with the wife of an enemy.[47]

Nevertheless, pregnancy, jealousy, and other domestic strife was very common. One cadre recounted a most uncomfortable incident in Duc Hoa:

> I lived in a security cadre's house near the GVN post. One day a drunkard in the neighborhood shouted: "You false revolutionaries, you have availed yourself of the revolution to make a woman pregnant, then have abandoned her." I asked my host to go out and make him hold his tongue. He reluctantly went out but didn't succeed. Later I was told that he himself was the culprit. Such cases were very common in the country since young men and girls are working together.[48]

The youth secretary from Trung Lap showed resignation when commenting on a similar incident: "The whole country's in heat. Especially when the people are mixed up, all thrown in together there, it's bound to happen."[49]

The Front also had difficulty dealing with the sensitive issue of religion. Although the Front publicly supported freedom of individual worship, the Party's anticlericalism was well known. In earlier years, the French had gained the support of two native Vietnamese sects, the Cao Dai and Hoa Hao. Diem had later turned on both of these sects. The Catholics, of course, were a cornerstone of both the French and Diem regimes. In Hau Nghia province, there were substantial numbers of both Cao Dai and Catholics. (The Cao Dai "Vatican" was in neighboring Tay Ninh province.) The Front made extensive efforts to infiltrate the Cao Dai, apparently with some success. Having many members from the urban merchant class, the Cao Dai were never pro-Front, but Front appeals went a long way toward neutralizing them and keeping them from aligning strongly with the GVN. As shall be seen, Cao Dai areas in Hau Nghia were frequently neutral zones, which, from the Front's point of view, was good enough.[50] Catholics were a different matter altogether. The Front tried to win over Catholics and was successful with some individuals. For most Catholics, however, Catholic memories of conflict with the Party were too powerful to overcome. An important political and education cadre recalled that, even with the help of two priests the Party was thwarted in An Hoa, a large Catholic village in Trang Bang district:

> I would like to say that the Catholic clergymen were here prior to the arrival of the French Colonialists and they are still to some extent the last bastion to defend the western regime. Let's take this example, in An Hoa village where I sent many of my agents to carry out our civilian proselyting, we had the cooperation of two Fathers who had worked for the Front for many years, but we still could not defeat the efforts of the Catholic groups. The Catholic group in the An Hoa village could provide the National Government with more than 1,000 soldiers. Although the Fathers tried hard they could only present a very small body of soldiers to us.[51]

The Catholics in An Hoa had good reason to fear for the future of their faith. As recounted by a North Vietnamese officer who commanded the Cu Chi main force regiment, the Front's policy of religious toleration was only tactical:

> They feel that the socialist citizen will drop religion after awhile when they get to know the reasons, which will surface naturally later. . . . Had they bothered the churches and pagodas, they would have been subjected to much criticism. They will strive to destroy the religions slowly through education of the cadres and the people. The destruction will be slow and will follow that path.[52]

Despite all difficulties, Front cadres built on a foundation left by the Viet Minh and succeeded in creating a sympathetic political climate in Hau Nghia province. An American researcher studying Hau Nghia in 1968 was startled to find some families that had supported the Viet Minh-NLF for three generations. The researcher remarked on how deeply the Party's view of events had penetrated:

> The everyday speech patterns of the people of the district reflect the characteristic expressions of the Viet Cong. Peasants referred to the central government as "Diem-My" (Diem-American) usually followed in VC terminology by "clique" or "gang."[53]

In 1962, Gerald Hickey made a strikingly similar observation on the attitudes of the people of Cu Chi:

> The people here have learned from early childhood to view reality through the prism of Viet Cong ideas, beliefs and prejudices. Success in turning these people toward actual allegiance to a nationalist government would thus require extraordinary measures applied over a long period of time.[54]

Yet, the Front's success in rural areas like Hau Nghia was not entirely due to its great ability to exploit real or imagined grievances and present an alternate view of the future. The cynical manipulation of fear in all of its manifestations was a central component in the Party's theory and practice of struggle. Most notorious was the brutal use of terror against enemies of the revolution. The Party was careful to direct its violence at the very worst or very best of GVN officials. "Punishing" (the Party's euphemism for murder) a despicable official gained the Party popularity; killing good officials sowed fear. By making efficiency and anti-Communist zeal very dangerous, the Party encouraged bad and dishonest administration in GVN areas. This, in turn, reinforced negative feelings toward Saigon on the part of the villagers. A low-level civilian cadre later described this process in a hamlet in Cu Chi:

> People said that all the good officials were either killed or chased away by the VC and they were replaced by bad officials. The VC started in 1960, killing first the Village council member in charge of police and then the hamlet chiefs. . . . All the other government officials were afraid and resigned their positions under threats from the VC; the village chief, the finance members, the Secretary of the council, all resigned. The council member in charge of police was replaced by a Civil Guard from the outpost. He was very haughty and arrogant. The new village chief was a stranger in the village. He was disliked by the population because he often tried to squeeze money.[55]

Despite later Party efforts to pass off much of the terror campaign as the unauthorized work of "overzealous" cadres, there can be no doubt that virtually all assassinations were premeditated and came by order of high Party officials. The veteran political and education cadre quoted earlier discussed precisely this point during his interrogation:

> I can say that for every act of terrorism that happened in that province, then that is the work of the Party secretary, because he is the only one who is

responsible for this kind of action. He directs all security agents to commit such acts of terror. . . . As far as killing or slaughtering is concerned, I can say that sort of thing is done entirely by the decision of the higher authority. Of course in every country or in every region there are some bad guys who act upon their own will. In the Front such a person would be subjected to punitive measures.[56]

Probably more important than genuine acts of terror was the climate of fear and disorientation that such deeds created for those people who were undecided or indifferent toward the struggle. After all, if the GVN could not protect its own functionaries, what could a simple villager do? Questioning any Front policy would bring accusations of "reactionary thinking." A doubter would certainly be wise to watch his or her tongue, as a loose word might well be relayed to supporters of the revolution and become the topic in a self-criticism session. Furthermore, Front propaganda relentlessly propagated a stream of disinformation about the GVN and Americans. When the Front took over a hamlet, it was common to force the villagers to destroy their identity cards, thus putting them in danger of arrest if they ventured into GVN areas. Low level supporters of the Front were told that the GVN would torture them if they attempted to switch sides. U.S. aid projects were pictured as sinister tricks. The cumulative effect was to greatly encourage supporters of the revolution and intimidate both opponents and those sitting on the fence.

Futile Efforts to Stem the Revolutionary Tide

The Front's job in Hau Nghia was made much easier for a time thanks to the anti-Diem coup. Although many of Diem's policies had been very helpful to the Front and prospects for an eventual Front victory were extremely bright, Diem and Nhu had waged war with tenacity, if not wisdom. The new junta proved unable to assemble any sort of government and fell prey to a new strongman, Gen. Nguyen Khanh. The result was another calamity for Saigon. In the words of Bui Diem, a keen observer of the GVN:

> With this development the purposeless rule of the generals gave way to the buffoon antics of a man whose serious moments were rare. . . . In retrospect the regime of Nguyen Khanh put an end to the idea of bringing alive in South Vietnam a democracy vital enough to ward off the political and military challenges of the Vietnamese Communist Party.[57]

Despite the fact that there was no real hand on the tiller, orders continued to issue forth from Saigon. In early 1964, Saigon began the Hop Tac Program, intended to strengthen the regime's position around Saigon. Although the general outlines of the operation were established by American planners in Saigon, each province was ordered to submit pacification plans that would best suit its particular environment.[58]

As Hau Nghia had just been formed and was under serious pressure from the Front, it is difficult to imagine that any detailed planning took place. Nevertheless, the provincial leadership in Bao Trai was expected to follow a five-step guideline established in Saigon to impose some degree of uniformity on rural operations throughout the Republic of Vietnam. The first step was to be a military clearing action, during which insurgent main force units were to be defeated or chased from the area. Once an area was cleared, government forces were to proceed to the second step, which required the construction of New Rural Life hamlets. To be certified complete, a New Rural Life hamlet had to meet six criteria: (1) the completion of a census designed to facilitate the destruction of the insurgent "infrastructure," (2) the creation of an effective hamlet militia, (3) the construction of appropriate fortifications and military facilities, (4) the establishment of an adequate communication system with higher headquarters to aid the rapid dispatch of reserves in case of assault, (5) the organization of the hamlet population into age groups in order to begin unspecified "New Rural Life activities," and (6) the election or appointment of a hamlet administration committee. While the New Rural Life hamlets were being constructed, the third step, which involved the insertion of government Rural Development cadres, was to take place. Step four called for the creation of an integrated hamlet-village-district-province self-defense apparatus. Step five was the mobilization of the population into specialized groups, such as farmers' associations, youth groups, etc., which would somehow generate support for the government.[59]

As can be readily seen, the Hop Tac plan was vague, repetitious and more than a little muddled. It was also very ambitious. If all five steps, including the six criteria, could actually be carried out in any area of meaningful size and if this process could be progressively spread to neighboring areas, the insurgency would be completely destroyed. Conceptually, the five-step plan was as irrelevant as the Strategic Hamlet Program: If the government had been strong enough to carry it out, there would have been no insurgency in the first place.

In reality, despite the attention to the Saigon area due to Hop Tac, the GVN in Hau Nghia province was fighting for its life. Although the NLF rainy season campaign in 1964 was widespread throughout Vietnam, Hau Nghia was particularly hard hit. In June, Duc Hoa district town was assaulted by a strong enemy force and nearly overrun. In this action, easily heard from Saigon only twelve miles to the east, insurgent forces were repulsed only when two government artillery pieces were depressed to zero elevation and used for direct fire at point blank-range.[60] Soon thereafter, the Duc Hue district town was evacuated, leaving only one hamlet in all the district west of the Vam Co Dong River in government hands and ceding a third of the province to the Front. Hiep Hoa, a village on the east bank of the Vam Co Dong, was designated the new district capital of Duc Hue. Several hamlets in Duc Hoa were transferred to the administration of Duc Hue to give the truncated district a larger population. Next, communications between

Hiep Hoa and Bao Trai were severed with the fall of a government outpost at La Cau. Pressure on the province capital was stepped up from another direction when the major village of Hoa Khanh, roughly three miles southwest of Bao Trai, was abandoned, thus severing direct road communication with Duc Hoa district town. Further enemy gains were made north of Trang Bang district town and along Highway 1 near Cu Chi.[61] Many Vietnamese officials doubted that Hau Nghia would be able to survive and predicted that it would be broken up and the districts returned to the original provinces.[62]

As the situation rapidly deteriorated, the GVN, with American guidance and support at every step, increased its efforts to fight the insurgency by destroying its economic base and disrupting the social fabric of the areas where the Front was strongest. After the Diem coup, the GVN halted forced relocations in Hau Nghia province. Indeed, from this point onward, overt population relocation was very rare in the province. In its stead, however, a series of violent measures with the same intent and result were employed against many of the sparsely populated areas in Hau Nghia. These means included defoliation, air attack, and indiscriminate artillery bombardment of what later were to be called "free fire zones." All these controversial tactics resulted from the nature of revolutionary warfare. Following the classic Chinese revolutionary model and its experience in the war against France, the Front was eager to create "liberated zones" in areas under its control. It had a very expansive definition of "liberated" and frequently used the term to describe territory where its influence was strong and its presence uninterrupted. Under that definition, all of Hau Nghia province, apart from a few fortifications, was liberated. What Front leaders really desired, however, was to establish zones where their control was absolute and the population could be entirely mobilized for revolutionary struggle. These zones would be sources of both manpower and rice, and they would serve as areas for training and rest for military units. Obviously, nearby contested areas could be pressured or attacked much more easily. And above all, the zones would stand as models of the just and equitable new society the Front hoped to create. Naturally, the Front foresaw the continued expansion of liberated zones, a sort of spreading "oil spot" in reverse. From the GVN's point of view, some areas in Hau Nghia province had already become or were in danger of becoming genuine liberated zones; thus, they had to be attacked. These areas included anything west of the Vam Co River and a thin strip running along its eastern bank. Off-road areas along the Binh Duong-Tay Ninh border with Cu Chi-Trang Bang in or near the Ho Bo-Boi Loi Woods were totally Front-controlled. Smaller zones existed in the Bao Trai area and along the Kinh Thay Swamp.

Defoliation, begun in late 1962, was widely used along the Vam Co and the wooded areas in the northern portion of Hau Nghia. Later, it was liberally used in any local area considered a likely ambush site. Defoliation had two aims. Most of the effort was devoted to destroying vegetation that covered the movement of troops and cadres. In theory, aircrews sprayed only uninhabited tracts and avoided fruit trees and croplands. A much smaller, outright crop destruction effort was also undertaken, directed at areas entirely under insurgent control. Although not proclaimed loudly, the GVN and Americans both expected and hoped that defoliation would force villagers to leave Front areas and move to regions that had a GVN presence and were thus safe from spraying. To a certain extent, they were undoubtedly correct. A middle-level education cadre in Duc Hoa witnessed the defoliation of a large inhabited stretch of land on both sides of the Vam Co near Bao Trai. He estimated that two-thirds of the crop of the villages of Hoa Khanh and Binh Hoa was destroyed, with sugarcane and manioc particularly hard hit. In this instance, the government had warned the village in advance and had invited the inhabitants to move to GVN areas for assistance. According to the cadre, the rich and middle-level peasants, about 40 percent of the village, did move to the towns, leaving their sons behind in hiding and sending for them only when assured that ARVN would not draft them immediately. He further estimated that about 30 percent of the population moved westward into the Plain of Reeds or Cambodia. A further 30 percent stayed. Those who moved west or remained, the cadre contended, were poor or landless farmers, the "basic classes of the revolution." The cadre also revealed that the regional Party committee had originally seen defoliation as an "immense danger." Apparently, they initially overestimated both the extent to which the GVN and Americans would employ the tactic and the toxicity of the sprays. As it became obvious that most areas of the province would not be sprayed, Front cadres used the issue vigorously for propaganda, portraying it as an "inhuman, cruel and barbarous act."[63] This was not a difficult claim to make. Interviews on the subject conducted in Cu Chi by Americans indicated the peasantry's deep hatred of the policy. One farmer pointed out that during the French war it was possible to flee to uninhabited areas and survive, but that course of action was no longer possible. He also cautioned that destruction and fear, rather than political conviction or hatred of the Front, was the major reason for people moving to GVN areas.[64] It is impossible to estimate how many people were affected. Spraying was not done at all in most parts of the province, and, obviously, defoliation had to remain limited. A massive use of herbicides in every area with a Front presence would have meant the utter destruction of Hau Nghia province, a pointless act for the GVN. Nevertheless, many Americans who served in Hau Nghia after 1966 recalled the scores of small abandoned hamlets and widespread destruction of trees and vegetation in some areas.

Air and artillery attacks were similar in intent and result. Before American intervention in the ground war, effective close support of ground troops in battle by tactical air power or artillery was a rare commodity. Providing advice and training on these matters was very high on the list at MACV until 1965. Simple air or artillery bombardment of a Front-controlled zone was another matter, however, and well within the competence of the men involved. Informal "free fire" zones developed and were routinely shelled or bombed. In Hau Nghia, these zones usually were the same areas that were sprayed with herbicides: i.e., along and west of the Vam Co in the

Boi Loi-Ho Bo area. The cadre from Loc Giang recalled that, beginning in early 1965, his hamlet, which was off the road near a wooded area, became the target of intensive bombardment: "There is bombing almost every day, many times a day, and artillery shellings are countless." Despite Front pleading, over half of the population left for Trang Bang district town, leaving behind "cadres' and fighters' families." The man claimed that most villagers said they blamed the GVN for the air attacks but that some used the attacks as an excuse to flee from the Front. Another cadre serving in Duc Hue described conditions in a hamlet near the Vam Co:

> In the country it was absolutely impossible to hold meetings during the day. Moreover, after a bombing, people often left the country for GVN areas or didn't pay attention at the meeting. We tried to comfort them but they attended the meeting absentmindedly. Even the cadres' families settled in secure areas. Sometimes they left for Cambodia or GVN areas. Since the cadres weren't able to make their families confident, they didn't succeed any better in reassuring people. . . . The Front forbade people to sell their buffaloes and paddy, or dismantle their houses, but if the village or a nearby village had just been bombed, they secretly dismantled their houses, sold their buffaloes and paddy and let their families settle elsewhere. The men remained because they had no GVN papers and didn't like to risk the reputation of having followed the pirates (GVN and Americans). Young men usually remained because they were afraid of being drafted by the GVN. . . . If any young men were killed by air attacks or shellings, the VC said: "At home you also risk death, you had better go and fight."[65]

In February 1965, the U.S. Air Force began tactical operations in South Vietnam. Shortly thereafter, Arc Light B-52 raids began. Front zones in Hau Nghia were early and frequent targets of the B-52s. An assistant platoon commander of the Cu Chi local force battalion described one of these first attacks in the Ho Bo area:

> The area bombed was covered by rubber trees. All of the houses were outside of this area. We ran out after the first bombs exploded. I saw four planes with long wings. Gusts of wind reached me, as in a storm. Trees and men were shaken. The earth quaked. My ears were sore. . . . All the trees in the bombed area were uprooted or cut down. No one, no house was hit.[66]

By the time American troops arrived in Hau Nghia in January 1966, most free fire zones had become largely depopulated. Although U.S. air and ground forces pummeled Front base zones continually, most of the violence suffered later by civilians was triggered by combat, rather than indiscriminate area attack. It is difficult to assess the results of the GVN-American depopulation policy at this stage of the war. On one hand, most villagers continued to live in contested areas where the GVN presence was, at most, a daytime phenomenon. Taxation, proselyting, organizing, and recruiting never stopped in most areas in this phase of the war, and Front military forces used the remote areas in Hau Nghia during the entire conflict. In addition, there can be no doubt that many of the people driven to the towns or hamlets near the road were sympathetic to the GVN or at least hostile to the Front. The GVN, therefore, also forfeited a chance to create a base of support in many areas of the province, which might have developed if the tide of the war had changed. On the other hand, the defoliation and bombardment campaign did prevent the development of a progressively larger, fully functioning state-within-a-state just outside the capital. Also, fear of attack did shake the resolve of many who were otherwise sympathetic to the Front. Virtually all of the cadres quoted in this research defected because of exhaustion or fear of death. War weariness sapped the morale of Front supporters just as it did followers of the GVN. Lastly, it should be pointed out that the Front viewed the spraying-bombardment campaign as a genuine threat and went to great lengths to prevent peasants from leaving their native hamlets.

Nevertheless, the GVN could not fight the war entirely from the air. Therefore, General Westmoreland decided to move an ARVN division into Hau Nghia. The unit ultimately selected was the 25th Division stationed in Quang Ngai province, near the demilitarized zone. Unfortunately for the government cause in Hau Nghia, the ARVN 25th was known to be a particularly poor unit in a not very illustrious army. Gen. Cao Van Vien, later chief of the Joint General Staff in Saigon, reportedly rated the 25th as the worst division in any army in the world.[67] It is impossible to determine whether the unit deserved such a dismal rating—it surely would have had many competitors. In any case, the move to Hau Nghia crippled the division. As in most ARVN units, recruits were generally from provinces in or near to the area of operations. When the 25th was redeployed to Hau Nghia in April 1964 and its headquarters established at Duc Hoa district town, the desertion rate soared. In an attempt to alleviate this problem, some of the soldiers' families were moved in or near Hau Nghia, as well. But it quickly became apparent that neither the dislocated families nor their new neighbors were at all pleased with this policy. In his memoirs, Westmoreland admits that the redeployment of the 25th was a "mistake"—one of the few times the word appears in that document. It would have been more efficient, the general concludes, to have raised an entirely new division.[68]

It is possible to outline the effects of the ARVN 25th's deployment and overall government efforts in Hau Nghia in mid-1964 because a village study was commissioned by MACV. Hop Tac was a MACV program, and R. Michael Pearce, an American researcher from the Rand Corporation, was therefore asked to study the evolution of this village as "it passes from insurgent control through pacification to government control."[69] In the course of this assignment, Pearce spent two months of late summer and early fall 1964 in Duc Lap village, Hau Nghia province. Although the author of the study was very cautious in his assessments, the findings serve to illustrate the political disaster facing the government at this time in Hau Nghia.

Duc Lap, situated barely two miles from Bao Trai on a main provincial road to Cu Chi, was chosen for the study because it was considered one of the very few villages in Hau Nghia secure enough to be examined over any extended period. "Security," however, was a most relative term in Duc Lap. Although clearing operations around the village had begun in April, two of the six hamlets of Duc Lap were not considered safe enough to enter at all. A very large number of families inhabiting the remaining four hamlets had been forcibly relocated from areas off the road. Ap Chanh, the hamlet judged most secure, served as headquarters for an ARVN battalion and contained that unit's three mortars. The presence of a force as large as an ARVN battalion prevented outright assault on Duc Lap, but it failed to provide the sort of security required for a comprehensive pacification effort. Even in Ap Chanh, insurgents were able to enter in daylight and kidnap officials. All four government hamlets were continually harassed by mortar attack, sniping, and frequent mining of the roads. The two "insecure" hamlets, however, were relatively free from harassment because, according to the villagers, many families and relatives of the local guerrillas lived there.[70] Furthermore, whatever security the government troops gave the inhabitants in their direct proximity, ARVN mortars were "a thing to be feared" by the families living off the road. This fear was very well founded, as can be seen by an incident in November when the ARVN battalion commander and his American advisor were killed by friendly short mortar rounds, fired from the compound at Ap Chanh. To make matters worse, ARVN armored personnel carriers frequently damaged local crops.[71]

A very bad relationship existed between the inhabitants of Duc Lap and ARVN soldiers. The battalion commander apparently did much to prevent bad treatment of the villagers, once even apologizing to the village chief on behalf of an enlisted man who had punched the chief in the face. Yet, his efforts could not erase the distrust historically held by the rural Vietnamese toward their own soldiers. Villagers were particularly angered by the very poor road discipline showed by the ARVN truck and jeep drivers who regularly hurtled through hamlets at high speed, oblivious to the safety of those in the way. (This complaint was later to be leveled at the Americans, time and again.) Villagers also complained of an arrogant attitude on the part of soldiers' wives toward the permanent inhabitants. Apparently, something of a low point in civil-military relations was reached in Duc Lap when the alleged carelessness of one of the wives led to a major fire, destroying many homes. Although the government refused to compensate those who had lost their homes, many ARVN dependents were moved out of the immediate area.[72] None of these matters were petty because bad ARVN conduct toward villagers was a major propaganda theme employed by the Party.

Pearce also pinpointed a final and rather obvious difficulty concerning ARVN's presence: Because there were far more villages than battalions, government forces would eventually leave. He concluded, somewhat ruefully, that unless an effective militia was created before the departure of ARVN, insurgent main force units would return to Duc Lap within days or even hours. Unfortunately for the government cause, efforts to create such a militia floundered in Duc Lap.[73] After the Diem coup, the new government changed the name of the village-based People's Self Defense Force to the Popular Forces (PF); the province-based Civil Guard was renamed the Regional Forces (RF). The "backbone" of village defense was a 25-man Popular Forces platoon. The men of this platoon were members of the Hoa Hao sect and had been deployed in Duc Lap from their homes in An Giang province some time in 1961. A better illustration of the government's long-term weakness in Duc Lap could hardly be found: Not only was the government unable to raise a local militia in Duc Lap, it was forced to deploy one from a far-off delta province, consisting of adherents to a minority sect who would presumably be politically reliable. It is impossible to evaluate the actual performance of the Hoa Hao platoon—it is perhaps telling that, after three years of operations in an insurgent stronghold, only of its two men had been killed. At best, the platoon was able to provide some protection for the village administration chief and his relatives who, like GVN officials throughout rural Vietnam, were forced to retreat each night to the hamlet fort. This latter consideration can hardly be blamed on the Hoa Hao: In later years, elements of an American division, an ARVN division, and a greatly expanded militia likewise were unable to provide genuine security for the government administration anywhere in Hau Nghia at night.

In accordance with the Hau Nghia pacification plan, a major duty of the ARVN battalion was organizing and training the locally recruited Popular Forces. Although this effort had just begun at the time of the Rand study, the progress was not encouraging. Recruitment was a major difficulty. Although the Rand researcher did not consider the question of how many youths of Duc Lap village had entered or were entering the ranks of the NLF, there can be no doubt that the number was sizable. From the young men remaining and not conscripted by ARVN, GVN officials planned to raise a company of 74 men, who would be stationed in platoons in the four "secure" hamlets of Duc Lap.

Considering the enemy strength, it is not surprising that it was difficult to find volunteers. The village chief and the Hoa Hao platoon leader both claimed that the village finance officer threatened to confiscate ID cards from youths reluctant to volunteer. Because it was impossible to travel outside a hamlet without an ID card due for of being arrested as an insurgent or ARVN deserter, this was a most potent threat. The ranks gradually began to fill, although never to full strength. Typically, most progress was made in Ap Chanh. That hamlet's contingent was trained, began limited operations with the battalion, and even sprang a successful ambush on a group of local guerrillas. The platoons from the other hamlets, however, barely developed at all. One 20-man platoon had only 1 trained soldier. Another 26-man platoon had not been issued arms. Overall, there was a woeful lack of combat experience, although the company commander had seen service with ARVN and with French Union Forces fighting the Viet Minh.[74] Considering the crucial role assigned to the local militia—protecting the GVN pacification cadres and freeing ARVN to spread the "oil spot"—it is readily apparent that the entire pacification effort in Duc Lap was being built on an extremely weak foundation.

Despite all these difficulties, the various security efforts were the bright spot for the government in Duc Lap. In theory, attaining relative security was a means toward the end of improving the material condition of the population and creating freely given support for the Saigon government. However, each nonmilitary effort in the pacification of Duc Lap was an abject failure. Given the local sentiment, such an outcome was inevitable. In the estimate of the village chief, 70 percent of the population of Duc Lap was pro-NLF, 30 percent was neutral, and only 1 percent openly supported the government. He further observed that virtually every family in the village had someone actively working for the Front.[75] Under such conditions, decent administration, progovernment propaganda, and any programs leading toward economic betterment had to come from the outside. Unfortunately for Saigon, it was in these areas that the government was weakest.

Orderly administration of Duc Lap, even under the "improved" security conditions, was very difficult. Nominally, the village was a part of Duc Hoa district, and any dealings with the provincial administration at Bao Trai should have gone through Duc Hoa. In reality, however, Duc Hoa had little or no say in the affairs of Duc Lap. Although only 9 miles directly south of Duc Lap it was completely isolated from that village and from Bao Trai. To reach Duc Lap from the district town, one had to travel through Saigon, thence to Cu Chi, and on through Bao Trai—a trip of over 45 miles. Therefore, all matters requiring the attention of higher authorities went through province channels at Bao Trai. Village officials, however, were reluctant to deal with provincial officials who were much higher on the administration charts. When they did, results were often unhappy. Furthermore, the proximity to Bao Trai, as well as the importance given to operations in Duc Lap by province authorities, served to encourage provincial interference in small affairs. All of this fostered intrigue. The Rand researcher, with obvious dismay, detailed the maneuvers leading to the replacement of the apparently competent village chief.[76]

Government propaganda efforts failed utterly. Although facilities for circulating government information were built in four hamlets, they remained unmanned for lack of an experienced information officer. Officials distributed posters widely, but they quickly were ripped down from bulletin boards by children or used to plug holes in the walls of dwellings. Government newspapers were distributed but rarely read. Sometimes, ARVN psychological warfare officers read messages over loudspeakers attached to helicopters, but they were rarely heard because the helicopters had to maintain sufficient height to protect them from small arms fire.

The Rand researcher contrasted the dismal government effort with the technically crude but politically sophisticated propaganda effort run by the Party. Government corruption, alleged U.S. imperialism, and forced relocation were popular themes. Furthermore, Party propaganda could be very timely.

Pearce recounted that one afternoon a South Vietnamese jet accidentally dropped a bomb near a hamlet. Although no one was injured, the better part of one family's rice crop was destroyed. Soon thereafter, NLF pamphlets appeared reciting the incident, noting that the government refused to make compensation (which was true), and claiming that the act was deliberate and inspired by Americans, which, strictly speaking, it was not. Apparently, because only one bomb was dropped, the population accepted the government's claim that the incident was an accident. There were, however, requests that government aviators "tie" the bombs on the wings more tightly.[77]

Measures intended to raise living standards were paltry and haphazard. The government built two pigpens in Ap Chanh and distributed some fertilizer. There was talk of cheap loans for more pigs but no action. In reality, talk of economic betterment during this period made little sense. The villagers were poor to begin with, and, unfortunately for Saigon, economic conditions were actually worsening. Inflation was rising, credit was difficult to obtain, and military action frequently damaged crops.[78]

Pearce did, however, single out government efforts at raising education standards as the most successful in the pacification program. Although classrooms were overcrowded and were run on split shifts, attendance was very good. Yet, even this "bright spot" was very likely illusory. Teachers admitted that political subjects were entirely ignored in favor of straight academic subjects. This was done, they claimed, to give the children the best possible chance at passing the crucial fifth grade examination, which would determine if they had even a chance at a high school education. The only way for a Duc Lap child to obtain a secondary education was to both pass the exam and be lucky enough to receive a government scholarship to the high school in the district town. Pearce posed the question of whether the meager opportunities in the educational field might not aid insurgent recruitment; however, he did not reach any conclusion.[79] Such intellectual timidity was entirely unwarranted. As previously mentioned, the Party recruited and promoted on the basis of class origin and merit—exactly the opposite of the method used by the Saigon government, where positions of responsibility were almost entirely monopolized by the urban elites.[80] Nor should Pearce have been especially impressed by the fact that the insurgents allowed the schools to function peacefully for it was well known that the insurgents sent their own children to government elementary schools.[81]

A final comment on the Rand study is in order. Although the author catalogued one failure or setback after another, he did not come to the conclusion that all his evidence inescapably pointed to: that all the government efforts were failing and that if such trends continued Saigon was certain to lose the war in the very near future. Perhaps MACV did not want to hear such conclusions. Whether or not that was the case, Pearce actually blamed the villagers for Saigon's failures:

If pacification is to succeed in Duc Lap, it cannot be just a one-sided government handout program but must have the cooperation of the government and the people, both giving what is theirs to give. From the standpoint of the village population, their biggest contribution to pacification will be a change in attitude toward the government. They must show a willingness to help build an effective local government system and support and defend that system.[82]

This was an incredible conclusion. In 1964, there was not a single reason for the rural peasantry to change its attitude toward the government. The insurgency was obviously succeeding, and the government was totally unable to protect potential opponents of the Party. Furthermore, there were very few incentives to support the government in the first place. In harsh reality, activists in rural Vietnam willing "to help build an effective local government system and support and defend that system" were almost exclusively on the side of the Front.

Despite the deployment of the 25th ARVN and continuing Hop Tac activities, the government's position in Hau Nghia eroded still further during 1965. In April, someone inside betrayed an ARVN Ranger outpost near Bao Trai, and insurgents annihilated a company of men as they slept. A Popular Forces outpost at Ap So Do, astride the road connecting Bao Trai to Trang Bang and Hiep Hoa, was overrun in the late spring. At about the same time, guerrillas destroyed a similar outpost on the route from Bao Trai to Duc Hoa district town. In both cases, the province officials had to disband the PF units. A short time later, insurgent forces attacked and heavily harassed Duc Lap village, threatening to isolate Bao Trai totally.[83]

Until this time, very few Americans had witnessed events in Hau Nghia province. But, as the advisory effort increased, so did the number of Americans in the countryside. In March 1965, John Paul Vann was sent to Hau Nghia province to serve as AID advisor. Although not yet the public figure that he later became (particularly in recent times due to Neil Sheehan's major biography), Vann was already well known to both journalists and prominent American officials in Vietnam. He had long experience in Vietnam, first as an army officer and later as an employee of AID. According to Bruce Palmer, Westmoreland's chief of staff, Vann was a "legendary figure, admired and respected throughout Vietnam . . . and probably knew Vietnam better than any other American of his day."[84] Many Americans believed that Vann possessed a nearly unrivaled knowledge of the actual conditions in the Vietnamese countryside. He was also known for his outspokenness and refusal to accept unduly optimistic—or outright false— reports on pacification. Vann's ideas on how the United States should conduct the war will be examined in some detail later in this volume. For the present, it is sufficient to note that he had been appointed AID representative to Hau Nghia, according to Palmer, "because it was infested with Viet Cong, yet close enough so that the U.S. mission in Saigon could keep an eye on him."[85]

As things were going from bad to worse in Hau Nghia, Ambassador Lodge, recently reappointed to Saigon after Barry Goldwater's presidential campaign, gave General Lansdale the unenviable task of coordinating the civil activities under American control that were intended to foster political development and pacification. Daniel Ellsberg, newly arrived in Vietnam, was a member of the Lansdale team. One of his duties was to report on field trips he made to gather information that might be of value for American aid to pacification. In October 1965, Vann invited him to visit Hau Nghia. Ellsberg's report on his visit, written shortly thereafter, was widely circulated in Saigon and at the Pentagon.[86] At the time of his Hau Nghia report, Ellsberg was still in agreement with U.S. objectives in Vietnam, if not entirely so with the tactics employed. His report essentially relayed Vann's assessment of the situation in Hau Nghia, and it offers a vivid and unique picture of the catastrophe facing Saigon in 1965. Vann's views were no doubt better informed than those of the Rand researcher. They were also more pessimistic and certainly closer to the truth.

When Ellsberg arrived in Hau Nghia in mid-October 1965, road communications were in a shambles. Vann had graded each section of road in the province as "passable—not hazardous," as passable but "slightly," "moderately," "extremely hazardous," and as "impassable." He preferred driving his own Scout over these crude and rugged roads to traveling in convoy. On roads he considered "moderately hazardous," Vann drove briskly, about 80 to 90 kilometers per hour. On "extremely hazardous" roads, he would drive 90 to 110 kilometers, with his rifle pointed out the window and grenades ready. Although there was always the danger of sniping or outright ambush (Vann's assistant was ambushed in early 1966 and held prisoner for seven years), mines were the most common danger. These mines could be very elaborate and extremely powerful; an informant had once led Vann to a string of 20 105mm shells controlled by a single wire. On occasion, the enemy constructed mines using as much as 200 kilos of plastic explosive, although 15 to 20 kilos were more common. Clearing mines was a daily chore for Regional Forces and frequently led to casualties. Of course, civilians also were victims: On one especially dangerous 2-kilometer stretch of road, eighteen people were killed in a month.

Road conditions were indicative of the appalling state of security in Hau Nghia. Government forces responsible for security were failing miserably. One regiment of the ARVN 25th operating in Hau Nghia, Vann pointed out, failed to kill a single enemy during the entire month of August 1965, despite claims of having conducted 1,400 small-unit actions, over 600 of these at night. Vann concluded that these figures reflected fictitious patrols or actions so predictable that they were simple to evade. ARVN's dismal performance may have been due to military incompetence or to enemy penetration of regimental headquarters. But more sinister motives may have been at work. The ARVN regiment's U.S. advisor told Ellsberg,

"Nearly every regimental plan is changed in many ways by 25th Division headquarters, and virtually every change is such as to reduce the chance of contact or to allow the VC an avenue of escape: changing the axis of approach, removing the block force, leaving an open flank."

If the advisor's assessment was correct, it indicated the divisional leadership was either incredibly incompetent, cowardly, or, worse yet, treasonous. At this stage of the war, if Vann's analysis was accurate, failure to engage insurgent forces was not due to any great difficulty in finding them. Enemy patrols at night would verbally taunt Popular Forces outposts. Insurgents laid mines regularly, with the same spot often mined for days in a row. A platoon made up of enemy defectors had no trouble making contact and, despite being very poorly armed, killed several insurgents.

Popular Forces were, by and large, no more effective than ARVN at providing any semblance of security for the population. According to several advisory personnel, PF soldiers almost never ventured from their outposts at night. Furthermore, Vann claimed to have received intelligence that PF forces would make accommodations with the NLF, promising inactivity in exchange for a minimum of harassment. Asked if such accommodations were tacit, Vann replied:

> Hell no, it's not tacit. We get the information; while those VC workers are out there, tearing up the building and making a hell of a racket, they're yelling right into this post: "We're your brothers. Why are you working for the Americans and the traitors in Saigon?" And most of the time where these little deals are made, the PF leader or hamlet chief has talked face to face with the VC commissar.[87]

Penned up in their outposts, unwilling or unable to venture out at night, the Popular Forces were able to protect only themselves and those government officials who may have slept at the outposts. Any villagers who may have harbored genuine resentment toward the NLF were in no position to take action. Ellsberg's summary of the situation is apt:

> Most of the posts in Hau Nghia are along major routes, guarding roads rather than villages; even those associated with a village are at one end, on the outskirts. The "security" they provide the villagers at night is not even problematic. And the arrogance of the VC, tearing up roads, killing hamlet officials, and abducting messengers from buses virtually at the front gate of the outposts underlines the point.[88]

Accommodation was apparently not restricted to government military forces. Dong Hoa Bac, a small hamlet in Hiep Hoa village, was the only hamlet in Hau Nghia west of the Vam Co Dong River still nominally under government control. Vann believed that this, too, was fiction. In his opinion, the hamlet was run by the enemy and survived only by accommodation. Furthermore, Vann believed that the Hiep Hoa sugar mill itself, the largest commercial facility in Hau Nghia, continued to operate only through accommodation. Owned jointly by French interests and the GVN, the mill had not been attacked since its construction in 1923 and sported paned glass windows. Intelligence indicated that the mill's special status was due to a very sizable tribute paid each year to the NLF. Unknown to Vann at the time (although the truth hardly would have come as a surprise), Truong

Nhu Tang, then director of the government sugar monopoly, was secretly a founding member and top official in the Front.[89]

If Vann's opinions were at all accurate, government administration fully matched the government's military effort in terms of futility. Although he worked well enough with the province chief and did single out the Duc Hoa district chief for praise, he characterized the Duc Hue district chief as perhaps the most corrupt in Vietnam. That inefficiency and corruption were the rule rather than the exception is clearly indicated by Vann's description of many of the "self-help" projects that theoretically were important components of the pacification effort:

> The province chief calls them "help self." The theory is that they're what the people want, and they'll contribute the labor. The villagers ask for schools, clinics, soccer fields; but somehow the request comes up through the village and district chiefs, and the people usually turn out to want new hamlet offices. The people aren't interested in working on that, so we end up buying labor and using a contractor anyway.[90]

However, Vann's major criticism of government officials did not involve personalities or the touchy question of corruption. Rather, he believed, as did the Party leadership, that government personnel were incapable of representing the peasantry due to class differences. The major problem in the countryside, according to Vann, was that "the present leaders, bureaucrats, and province and district officials do not come from, think like, know much about, or respond to the wishes of the rural majority of the population."[91] No doubt, more than one government official privately agreed with Vann. In any case, the province chief perhaps best summed up the situation in Hau Nghia when he told Ellsberg, "There are two hundred and twenty thousand people in Hau Nghia, and two hundred thousand of them are ruled by the VC." He added. "I am not a province chief; I am a hamlet chief."[92]

At about the same time that Ellsberg arrived in Vietnam, Gen. Harold K. Johnson, then army chief of staff, had lunch with Bernard Fall, the famous historian and internationally recognized expert on Vietnam. In the course of their talk, Fall challenged some basic demographic facts on Vietnam supplied to Johnson by his staff. After later examining these discrepancies and learning that Fall was correct in each case, Johnson realized that many basic statistics and matters of factual detail concerning Vietnam were unknown to army personnel. More importantly, he concluded that the army had no coherent picture of the essential problems faced in Vietnam and consequently lacked a long-term program of action. To help remedy this situation, Johnson commissioned, in July 1965, a study charged with "developing new sources of action to be taken in South Vietnam by the United States and its allies, which will . . . lead in due time to successful accomplishment of U.S. aims and objectives."[93]

To carry out this study, a group of middle-range officers were chosen, possessing not only outstanding military records but also advanced academic degrees. For eight months, these officers studied the history of Vietnam, developed historical parallels with other nations, studied the organization of the U.S. agencies involved, interviewed returning officers, and made field trips to Vietnam, many to the countryside. Titled *The Program for the Pacification and Long-Term Development of South Vietnam* (PROVN), the study was submitted in March 1966.[94] Because PROVN is an important document, its findings will be examined in the next chapter in conjunction with an analysis of the "Vann thesis." At present, PROVN is of interest because the authors chose Hau Nghia province for detailed study; it illustrated well the problems facing the GVN in the countryside. PROVN's Hau Nghia study also presents the most complete picture of the situation in this province at the time of the arrival of the U.S. 25th Division and the beginning of the "American" war.

Although not stated in so many words, the PROVN findings lead inescapably to the conclusion that, by the end of 1965, the NLF had won the war in Hau Nghia province. PROVN estimated that the insurgents controlled 53 percent of the population and "influenced" 42 percent more. Government control was put at less than 5 percent. The authors further estimated that 4,291 insurgents were active in Hau Nghia, broken down into the following categories: a 60-man "provincial hard-core" company, 1,085 cadres, 987 irregular guerrillas, 979 secret self-defense corps, and 1,180 people's self-defense corps. Enemy forces were credited with the ability to disrupt the economy, control lines of communication, and recruit, tax, and "terrorize" the population. Enemy control, according to the American officers, was due to efforts to identify the insurgency with the problems of the villagers, the exploitation of kinship ties and the use of "a 'sweet' approach, supplemented by terroristic murders, kidnappings, and torture." Furthermore, the CIA representative in Hau Nghia concluded that 98 percent of the insurgents in the province were local and that they neither got nor needed substantial aid from Hanoi—in particular, they were capable of producing their own grenades and other weapons locally.[95]

In the face of enemy energy and strength, government forces, as described in PROVN, were capable of only feeble efforts. A MACV advisor to an ARVN unit operating in Hau Nghia believed ARVN's ineffectiveness was due to an overall lack of leadership, an unwillingness to delegate authority, and a lack of will to close with the enemy. He also believed troop strength to be too low. The advisor further noted that men in the Popular Forces were miserably poor and so badly paid that many of them had to desert to feed themselves. One of the officers assigned to PROVN who visited Hau Nghia commented that, despite years of advice from the U.S. Army, routine Vietnamese operations demonstrated a lack of understanding of the basic fundamentals of security and showed no attempt at troop discipline or population control. Snipers were countered by suppressive artillery fire rather than aggressive small-unit actions, even though this meant extensive damage and loss of life for local inhabitants. As an example of ARVN ineptness, the PROVN visitor cited an occasion when an entire ARVN battalion based in Cu Chi waited until midday to relieve an outpost only two kilometers down the road that had been attacked the night before. Relief consisted of collecting the wounded and dead.[96]

The PROVN study also noted the weakness of the government's nonmilitary efforts in Hau Nghia. The USOM (U.S. Operations Mission) (AID) advisor, presumably John Paul Vann, claimed that, even though some of the local officials were "totally corrupt," the worst corruption existed at the corps level. The positions of province and district chief were for sale at known prices. Beyond corruption, administration was very inefficient. Cu Chi district, for instance, had been designated a "pilot district" for the Hop Tac Program and therefore was to receive special allocations of funds and manpower to carry out pacification. Yet, the Cu Chi district chief complained that, even though hundreds of dollars worth of artillery ammunition was expended every day, the district was chronically short of manpower and received almost nothing in the way of medical supplies. The Cu Chi district advisor added that construction efforts, except for schools, were at a virtual standstill. Schools were constructed eagerly, the advisor believed, because the enemy sent their children there.

To the extent that the PROVN researchers were able to determine the sentiments of the population, government weakness was again revealed. A behavioral scientist, assigned to PROVN, interviewed villagers and concluded that the local inhabitants judged the GVN and the Front above all on their respective ability to provide security. Obviously, the government was considered the inferior of the two in this regard. Interviews also indicated that, where the government's presence was felt (which was only near the district towns and Bao Trai), the inhabitants did not believe that the government had any genuine interest in their welfare. Officials were aloof and shunned contact with individual villagers. In contrast, the PROVN researchers noted, the NLF made every effort to identify the movement with the problems of the villagers.[97]

The situation in Hau Nghia by the end of 1965 was perhaps not entirely typical of the country as a whole. Certainly, the insurgency was stronger there than in some provinces, but the situation was not at all unique. Several other provinces (some of which, like Long An or Binh Dinh, were larger and more important than Hau Nghia) had likewise fallen under the nearly complete control of the NLF. Unfortunately for Saigon, these provinces had important characteristics in common—they were ethnically Vietnamese, heavily populated, and agricultural. Given that a majority of South Vietnam's people were ethnically Vietnamese, non-Catholic, and rural, it is readily apparent that, by 1965, Saigon had lost the allegiance of the largest and most important segment of the population. Consequently, the government was in a very nearly hopeless position. Only the badly flawed ARVN stood in the way of victory for the NLF. And, during 1965, ARVN was being destroyed piecemeal. It is impossible to determine how much time may have passed before the Front would have forced a favorable political or military outcome to the war. It *is* possible, however, to conclude that only the introduction of American ground forces temporarily prevented the fall of the anti-Communist government in Saigon.

3

Prospects for War: On the Eve of American Intervention

The U.S. Army Confronts a Dilemma

Every aspect of the war in Hau Nghia province after 1965 revolved around the use of force on the part of the U.S. Army and Air Force. However, before considering the actual course of operations by U.S. armed forces and, in particular, their role in the political struggle for Hau Nghia province, it is necessary to examine some aspects of the earlier experience that both shaped and limited the mode of employment of the American military in South Vietnam.

Although there is a certain continuity in the American military tradition, principally passed on through the service academies, the modern U.S. Army was born on the battlefields of Europe in 1944. Regardless of any strategic errors the Allies may have committed, the tactical performance of American and British ground forces was very impressive. Though numerically superior, the force ratio facing the Western Allies (roughly 3:2) was nowhere near as favorable as that facing the Soviet Union (roughly 3:1 or even more). Yet, in ten months, the Western Allies routed an experienced foe and, while doing so, inflicted many more casualties than they themselves suffered. Considering the numbers involved and the magnitude of the victory, the cost in blood paid by British and American troops was very low. Leaving aside the British, the U.S. Army developed a mode of operations so effective that it has influenced American and Western military operations on land to the present day.

The superiority of the U.S. Army did not result from better officers, soldiers, or weapons. In many respects enemy forces were superior in each of these categories. The army was, however, totally superior in two critical areas—tactical air power and technical-support services. Tactical air power slowed enemy deployments and supply and often supplemented artillery for direct support. American superiority in technical and support services, though less obvious in effect, was just as important as mastery of the air. U.S. soldiers were well fed and benefited from the best medical support in the world. American divisions were lavishly supplied and, in contrast to enemy units, normally kept up to or close to authorized strength by an enormous "pipeline" of men and matériel. Drawing on the world's largest supply of technically proficient civilian manpower, the U.S. Army was totally mechanized, had enough engineers to allow it to function well in any terrain, and benefited from excellent battlefield communications.

Because of all of these factors, the makeup of American combat units grew more and more complex. The Combat Command system used for U.S. armored divisions, which utilized complete combined arms teams at the regimental level, was the most complicated combat organization in any army and was copied by the German Bundeswehr after the war. In general, American units of all types excelled at the use of combined arms. In particular, American artillery was faster to react on both offensive and defensive missions than that of any other army. This fact made American units very dangerous to attack and on numerous occasions (the Kaserine Pass and the Ardennes are good examples) saved U.S. forces from suffering the full consequences of poor deployment. It is noteworthy that, during the entire war, large American formations were forced to surrender only twice: 12,000 men at Bataan and 9,000 during the Battle of the Bulge. The British lost more than this combined total at both Singapore and Tobruk, and every other major army suffered massive defeats totally beyond the American experience.

The United States fought a rich man's war against Germany and Japan and would do so again in Vietnam. Whenever possible, money in the form of firepower was expended instead of blood. To do this, the U.S. Army created the largest "tail" (i.e., the highest percentage of support personnel relative to combat troops) of any army in the world. Just as it did later in Vietnam, the system had its critics. Perhaps the Americans, particularly officers, were overly concerned with creature comforts. Perhaps the system, because of its size, was often inefficient and marked by corruption. Perhaps the American system did a poor job of distributing the risks of combat: Those relatively few soldiers that did fight often had to fight too much. Yet, whatever the drawbacks, the lavish support given American divisions gave them firepower at least equal to that of any nation and staying power that was unmatched. Above all, the American system worked.

Nothing happened during the twenty years between the end of World War II and the beginning of full-scale war in Vietnam to cause the U.S. military to doubt the effectiveness of its mode of operations. In Korea, a small American contingent prevented the complete occupation of the country by North Korean forces. The ensuing counteroffensive succeeded in virtually destroying the North Korean Army. The greatest accomplishment, however, came in November 1950, when China intervened. American units were at the end of an overly extended supply line, incompetently deployed, and taken by surprise. Despite these disadvantages, every American division escaped entrapment and regrouped. U.S. infantry repeatedly defeated horrifying "human wave" ground attacks with superior firepower. Within months, a counteroffensive was under way that stabilized the situation and inflicted massive casualties on the Chinese. During the ensuing diplomatic stalemate, the Americans proved adept at substituting firepower for manpower and at keeping their own casualties at a relatively low level.

After Korea, the U.S. military concentrated both on defining the role for ground forces in the nuclear age and on increasing the mobility and firepower of its divisions still further. During the Kennedy administration, with both the White House and Congress showing great interest in conventional military capabilities, the army and Marine Corps were the beneficiaries of increased budgets. Troops were issued new rifles capable of automatic fire, and armored personnel carriers (APCs) came into general use. The extraordinary developments in the field of electronics transformed battlefield communications and intelligence gathering. The most innovative development was the introduction of the airmobile concept, with its reliance on a very large number of helicopters. It was a perfect example of the rich man's warfare. Airmobile units were very expensive, difficult to maintain, and required huge numbers of support personnel to keep them operational. Nevertheless, their introduction was probably the most significant tactical development in conventional land warfare since the development of the armored division in the late thirties. With the helicopter, American commanders were able to ponder the implications of operations more mobile and complex than any undertaken in the history of warfare.

The armed forces sent to Vietnam were by far the best ever sent to war by the United States. The developments outlined above gave American forces unprecedented mobility and firepower. Field-grade officers, with very few exceptions, possessed experience in either World War II or Korea or both. Discipline, always a problem for the U.S. Army, was good. Because the army had done a better job than most institutions in American society at opening doors for racial minorities after World War II, it possessed a fine cadre of NCOs and junior officers. Morale was excellent. In the words of one officer interviewed, "In 1965, the U.S. was fat and sassy. The army was too."

Although the army and Marine Corps were splendid military instruments, several factors that contributed importantly to their strength severely restricted the type of operations that could be conducted in Vietnam. In the first place, the U.S. military, with its excellent record of impressive achievement at little cost in American blood, was extremely casualty conscious. This reflected both American democracy and the essentially civilian character of American society. Conscription made this preference even more pronounced. Therefore, it was army doctrine to substitute firepower for manpower, "bullets for bodies," whenever possible. To generate the needed firepower, a very large logistical "tail" was essential. The elaborate and dramatically successful medical support system was also very manpower-intensive. For political reasons and to boost morale, the army believed it had to provide unprecedented creature comforts to its men, further contributing to the size of the support element. The combat contingent was even lower because of the frequent need to use combat troops directly or indirectly to guard the enormous air bases, logistical centers, and the divisional base camps.

The combat battalions supported by this massive structure were very flexible, exceptionally mobile, and extremely powerful. Despite six years of war and scores of major engagements, American ground forces did not lose a single battle in Vietnam. Yet, the factors that made American units so formidable in battle also dictated that they be relatively few in number. Consequently, U.S. commanders in Vietnam were reluctant to disperse what combat strength they did possess in an attempt to control the largest possible area with the fewest possible men. Rather, commanders sought important objectives, usually enemy main force units or safe zones, that would allow them to concentrate the forces available and use the maximum amount of firepower. This tendency was particularly marked before 1969, when the enemy was employing large main force units in almost every part of Vietnam. Within this context, the large-unit war conducted by the United States during the first three years possessed a compelling internal logic. The logic of the situation, however, thwarted the desires of many Americans concerned with the village war, who wanted to have U.S. forces widely dispersed and employed directly in support of the various pacification plans.

Second, if the "big tail, sharp teeth" structure of American ground forces limited the number of U.S. units available for the village war, it also made them very tricky instruments of policy when they were so employed. American firepower was always present, and units rarely operated beyond the range of artillery firebases. Weather permitting, tactical air support and helicopter gunships were quickly available. Therefore, if fired upon, U.S. units, regardless of size, struck back quickly and powerfully. To be sure, a set of rules of engagement (ROE) existed that defined the conditions under which artillery and air support could be used. In planning offensive operations, U.S. units had to receive permission from both American and Vietnamese higher echelons for the unrestricted use of firepower. In particular, the establishment of free fire zones required extensive clearance procedures. Additionally, in normal operations, air and artillery support was authorized only when organized resistance was encountered: Sniping was excluded from this category.[1] But it would be wrong to put too much stress on the importance of these regulations. In essence, they were commonsense procedures. The army command was quite aware that its forces possessed the firepower to cause wanton destruction. Officers were equally aware that unnecessary desolation on a grand scale would be counterproductive to the war effort, bad for discipline, and unacceptable to public opinion. As it was, vivid images of violence, relayed home by the ubiquitous press, eroded support for the war. Yet, even if rigidly adhered to, the regulations permitted the use of huge amounts of firepower. And, as events would show, the South Vietnamese rarely objected to the American commanders' choices of weaponry. This is hardly surprising for ARVN was, if anything, quicker to utilize whatever support available than were U.S. units. Furthermore, the ROE were not always understood properly by American officers; they were also frequently ignored. Lastly, the ROE were bitterly resented by many combat officers who sincerely believed that they increased American casualties.[2]

Understandably, the innate destructiveness of U.S. combat operations outraged sensitive people in America and abroad. It also to frustrated scores of American civilians and military personnel concerned with reorienting the political allegiance of the South Vietnamese population. Many were to condemn our operations as self-defeating, which, as shall be seen, was true in many respects. However, the destructiveness of U.S. operations did not result from a particular type of deployment or a doctrine that was easy to change. Rather, it resulted from the very structure of American ground forces. The first duty of any commander, whether he leads a squad or a division, is the protection of the men under his command. Sadly, in war, the best way to protect one's own soldiers is to kill the enemy or drive him away. In the U.S. Army, this meant the use of firepower, even if this entailed the risk or certainty of civilian deaths. It was this motivation, far more than the much-publicized drive to raise the "body count," that accounted for the vast majority of civilian casualties caused by American fire. One might wish that things had been otherwise, but it is ahistorical to be surprised that they were not.

Structural limitations on the use of U.S. military power were compounded at first by strategic muddle. Initially, American commanders lacked a conceptual framework for operations in Vietnam. In public, military leaders went to great lengths to show that the U.S. Army had experience conducting operations against guerrilla forces. They pointed to successes against the British, the Indians, and Filipino insurgents. Except in the most theoretical terms, however, such examples from the distant past were meaningless. In fact, American ground forces had never participated in a large modern counterinsurgency campaign. Nor were American officers quick to examine the fate of armies that had. Col. A. J. Bacevich, a keen student of the army during the fifties, has recently pointed out that the military paid scant attention to the French debacle in Indochina:

> The Army's perspicacity did not extend to a recognition of "revolutionary warfare" as a peculiar type that the Army would confront. American officers did not draw any profound conclusions about the war in Indochina. Little discussion of the French failure there appeared in American military journals. That which did appear was seldom helpful. Even Bernard B. Fall, an analyst of insight and experience, was telling American readers in late 1953 that the French experience could provide only "a few general lessons." Fall said that the Indochina war "cannot be considered a modern war since one of the opponents is entirely devoid of armor and air power."[3]

Although it is true that counterinsurgency training was in vogue during the Kennedy administration, especially at the Special Warfare School at Fort Bragg, this training was aimed at the creation of elite units, such as Special Forces, and at the development of a cadre of highly skilled advisors. The regular line officer concentrated on the traditional tasks of leading men in battle and the management of ever more complicated military operations. Therefore, officers leading units, when first deployed in Vietnam, were not sure what was expected of them. Gen. Lew Walt, commander of the marines sent to Vietnam in 1965, was later most candid in this regard: "Soon after I arrived in Vietnam it became obvious to me that I had neither a real understanding of the nature of the war nor any clear idea as to how to win it."[4]

It is not surprising that General Walt was confused. In mid-1965, his superiors had not yet determined either the size of the U.S. troop commitment or the proper method of employment. The Joint Chiefs of Staff and General Westmoreland, with the support of Walter Rostow and Dean Rusk in Washington, favored an American presence large enough to permit offensive operations against enemy main force units as soon as possible. Ambassador Maxwell Taylor and George Ball argued for sharply limited American force levels and the employment of U.S. troops in and around strategic "enclaves." While this argument was taking place, most interest in Washington was concentrated on observing the effects of the bombing offensive against the North.[5] Hanoi's refusal to negotiate combined with ARVN's catastrophic defeats in late spring-early summer, tipped the strategic argument in Westmoreland's favor. As the situation in Saigon, with the fall of the civilian Quat government, was nearing chaos, the Americans believed that they were facing a desperate situation. Consequently, the military operations authorized for the remainder of 1965 were hurried, makeshift affairs lacking a central direction other than preventing ARVN's immediate collapse. As Westmoreland later put it, "If President Johnson was determined to succeed in Vietnam, as General Johnson communicated to me, I saw no solution, while awaiting results from the bombing and expanded ARVN forces, other than to put our own finger in the dike."[6]

The intense and frantic campaign of the 173d Airborne Brigade was a good example of early U.S. military operations. The 173d was deployed to Bien Hoa in May 1965, where it provided base security while Washington debated the role of U.S. ground forces. In August, the brigade was redeployed to the distant Pleiku-Kontum area in the Central Highlands, where it began active combat operations. In September, the unit was redeployed to Binh Duong province near Saigon, where it operated north of Ben Cat district town. In October, the 173d made a sweep into the "Iron Triangle," an important enemy haven in Binh Duong. The brigade moved another hundred miles the following month to Binh Tuy province. Soon thereafter, it returned for a short rest in Bien Hoa, after fighting in five different provinces in as many months. On New Year's Day 1966, the 173d went into battle, launching the first major American operation in Hau Nghia province.

In the beginning of December, two Front main force battalions began assembling along the Vam Co River in preparation for Tet attacks in Duc Hue and Duc Hoa districts.[7] To protect Bao Trai, the 173d launched a "spoiling attack," Operation MARAUDER, which began on 1 January 1966. It entailed a three-battalion airmobile assault on both sides of the Vam Co just to the south of Bao Trai. The battalion operating west of the Vam Co and the adjacent battalion across the river failed to make contact, but the remaining battalion, also operating on the east bank, took heavy fire upon landing, and a firefight ensued. During the battle, the engaged American battalion sought in vain to locate the flanks of the enemy unit it faced. Confronted by sustained artillery fire and air strikes, the enemy withdrew and broke contact. Although the Americans did not realize it at the moment, the enemy retreat was a small-scale disaster for the Front. While policing the battlefield the next day, the Americans discovered 98 bodies killed by artillery fire.[8]

From the military point of view, MARAUDER is a good example of the flow of battle in Vietnam during this period of the war. Most of the 173d failed to make substantial contact at all, and fighting consisted of short, sharp exchanges. The battalion that did make contact failed to fix the enemy unit and was unable to prevent its withdrawal. The major American "success" for the day took place when an artillery barrage, targeted according to doctrine on likely retreat routes, decimated an enemy unit assembling for retreat. Because 98 of the 131 "confirmed" enemy killed in action during the entire operation died together in just a few moments, it is clear that random firepower, rather than the exertions of over 1,500 U.S. infantrymen, dealt the heaviest blow.[9]

From the American point of view, however, the outcome was the result not of luck but of the very nature of army operations. Though the vast majority of bombs and shells, to say nothing of small arms ammunition, landed harmlessly, the infinitesimal remainder was capable of inflicting fearsome losses on enemy forces, especially if they were caught in the open. Most operations, therefore, yielded little or nothing, and a small number resulted in short, violent flurries where both sides would take limited losses. A very few operations caused the rapid annihilation of an enemy unit. Unfortunately for the soldiers of the NLF, the Americans conducted a great many operations.

MARAUDER was the most violent battle since the formation of Hau Nghia. As shown previously, government units during this period were afraid of engaging the insurgents in battle, and when battle took place, it was at the Front's initiative. During MARAUDER, however, the pattern was reversed. It is impossible to determine whether the insurgents accepted battle willingly, but they were soundly beaten in either case. The amount of firepower brought to bear against the NLF units was completely without precedent in Hau Nghia. American artillery fired over 9,000 rounds—3,400 in support of the battalion that achieved contact. In addition, 127 tactical air sorties were flown in support of the 173d.[10] Although these figures were later surpassed many times, they represent the quantitative leap in violence that took place after American combat units entered the war.

MARAUDER also illustrates the almost complete lack of coordination in the early period of U.S. involvement between American military actions and any sort of activities aimed at strengthening the government's political position in the countryside or, perhaps more to the point, preventing its further erosion. In particular, the 173d was not fully prepared to deal with the refugees caused by its operations. Refugee policy, as acknowledged by the operation report, was "somewhat confused."[11] Originally, the Americans planned to evacuate all refugees "generated" west of the Vam Co River, an area that was entirely controlled by the Front, to the care of 25th ARVN and the Hau Nghia province administration. Quickly, however, it became clear that facilities and supplies were inadequate to deal with the numbers involved. Hence, government authorities instructed the 173d to evacuate only adult males. In addition to 43 prisoners and 61 enemy "suspects," 507 refugees were moved east of the Vam Co.[12] It is impossible to tell how many came willingly in opposition to the NLF or in fear of U.S. operations and how many were simply abducted by the Americans at the request of the GVN. It is perhaps significant that the Americans listed the refugees in the operation report as "enemy losses."

U.S. activities to gain the goodwill of the population were restricted to various good deeds under the general listing of civic action. Brigade doctors and dentists treated some 1,400 refugees and villagers. Brigade engineers landscaped the schoolyard in Bao Trai. Soldiers gave away food and candy to children. (In a later operation the 173d distributed T-shirts to children with the brigade emblem and the motto "173d Airborne All the Way.") Efforts to convince the villagers of the government's sincerity and the enemy's perfidy consisted of six airdrops of 295,000 leaflets.[13]

On 8 January 1966, the 173d departed Bao Trai for further operations in Binh Duong. It is impossible to assess the impact of MARAUDER. Perhaps an enemy attack was thwarted, and a good portion of an enemy battalion or its equivalent was mauled. On the other hand, over 500 people were driven from their homes. Most importantly, the brigade was there and gone within a week. With the departure of the 173d, the government was left with the same resources that had proved so inadequate in the past. In the operation report, it was claimed that "the Brigade's presence in Bao Trai improved the government's position and the image of U.S. and Allied Forces in Hau Nghia Province and VietNam."[14] It is not unreasonable to be quite skeptical of this assertion.

Although the 173d Airborne operated in Hau Nghia only for a short while, Westmoreland had already decided that the province was important enough to warrant a continuous U.S. military presence. In December 1965, planning groups from the U.S. 25th Infantry Division (not to be confused with the ARVN 25th Division that also served in Hau Nghia) began arriving in Hau Nghia to prepare for the division's deployment from Hawaii. The American war in Hau Nghia province began in earnest with the deployment of this division, and for over four years, the "Tropic Lightning" Division waged war in or near Hau Nghia. During this period, both the operations of the 25th and the political and military efforts of the Saigon government made possible by the American presence transformed the nature of the war in Hau Nghia in almost every respect. However, before beginning to chart the new course of war in Hau Nghia, it will be helpful to review the strategic significance of the province and to reconstruct as accurately as possible the balance of political and military forces at that time. Such a review will illustrate the magnitude of the problem facing American and South Vietnamese forces and also make intelligible the military and political operations subsequently undertaken by both sides.

Revolutionary Military Forces

Just as the Party waged revolutionary warfare as a synthesis of political and military dau tranh, its military forces were a synthesis of main force, local force, and guerrilla units operating on an interrelated battlefield consisting of agricultural lowlands, highlands, and cities. The intricate but robust military organization controlled by the Party ensured that the struggle for Hau Nghia province would be an extraordinarily difficult one for the Americans. And the geographical location of Hau Nghia, lying at the nexus of the three types of battlefield, ensured that it would be extremely important.

Because political and military operations were always integrated, the military structure used by the enemy was thoroughly wedded to the political apparatus. At the top of the military apparatus were the main force units. Although they were the fewest in number, the most powerful components of the enemy's military structure were the regular North Vietnamese divisions (People's Army of Vietnam or PAVN). Employed in the far north and in the Central Highlands at the time of American intervention, PAVN units were controlled either directly by Hanoi in one of the PAVN theaters or by COSVN. PAVN units did not appear in Hau Nghia until 1968, although they were in Tay Ninh much earlier. Less well trained and less heavily armed but nevertheless formidable (and nearly always superior in morale and skill to their ARVN counterparts) were the NLF main force units. Although such units normally operated on a battalion or regimental level, by 1966, two divisions, the 5th and 9th, had been formed and were operating under COSVN in B2 Theater in the provinces around Saigon. Main force independent regiments, controlled by COSVN or military region headquarters, were also active. Two of these regiments were operating in and around Hau Nghia in the spring of 1966.

Local force units, controlled by province headquarters if organized by battalion or by district headquarters if organized by company, had somewhat less training and fewer heavy weapons but were still capable of engaging ARVN and were more than a match for GVN militia units. Therefore, local force units were always a serious threat to pacification efforts of any sort. The three NLF provinces which contained the districts of Hau Nghia controlled four local force battalions: Long An had the 2d Independent and the 506th; Binh Duong had the Phu Loi, and Tay Ninh had the 320th. Each of these battalions at one time or another fought in Hau Nghia. In addition, each district in Hau Nghia was the home of a local force company. Both main force and local force units were very flexible and capable of breaking down into small units and operating as guerrillas if required.[15]

Just as the village was the heart of the insurgent's political apparatus, so, too, was it the ultimate base for the military effort. Every village controlled or contested by the NLF had a force of local guerrillas. Although poorly armed and not well trained in the finer points of the military craft, they were very important for several reasons. In the first place, the village was the initial training ground for soldiers later promoted to higher units because of valor and political awareness. Second, guerrillas had important military functions. They were primarily responsible for mining roads and laying booby traps and were capable of springing an ambush. As conditions demanded, they might serve as guides, porters, or extra combat muscle for local or main force units. They were also a vital part of the enemy's intelligence-gathering network. In addition, the guerrillas provided protection for both the local political cadres and for more important cadres passing through the area. The major role of the local guerrillas, however, was political. On the village and hamlet level, they provided a continuous armed presence that encouraged supporters of the revolution and intimidated opponents.

It is very difficult to give the number of local guerrillas with precision. Americans estimated in March 1966 that between 100,000 and 200,000 were operating nationwide. Figures for enemy combat units were undoubtedly more accurate. This same estimate put PAVN strength at 38,000 and NLF main and local force units at 63,000 and growing fast.[16] Whatever the exact figure, 25th Division intelligence, in early summer 1966, concluded that virtually every hamlet in Hau Nghia was able to raise a squad of guerrillas, every village one or two platoons. Overall, the 25th credited the enemy with having the equivalent of six battalions of guerrillas operating in Hau Nghia.[17] If one calculates 8 men to a squad, the total would be over 1,200. Clearly, enemy local forces greatly outnumbered the GVN militia in Hau Nghia, which, in theory at least, was supposed to deal with the local guerrillas.

In military matters, however, numbers rarely tell the entire story. In this respect, the Vietnam War was similar to most others. For instance, in the field of weaponry, it would appear that the Americans and South Vietnamese possessed an overwhelming advantage. Enemy forces, after all, entirely lacked air support, mechanized transport, and, for the most part, field artillery and armor. Revolutionary forces, nevertheless, possessed certain advantages that partially compensated for their relative disadvantage in firepower. Terrain in much of Vietnam, including Hau Nghia, facilitated secret movement. An astonishing array of ingenious fortifications, ranging from simple bunkers in hamlets to elaborate tunnel complexes in redoubts or "combat villages," helped conceal insurgent troops and protect them from air strikes and artillery. The intelligence network employed by the NLF was excellent in every respect, and what technical means the enemy possessed for intercepting allied radio communications were well used. The insurgency's strength in the countryside, although enabling revolutionary forces to move without being seen, made similar movement by Americans and South Vietnamese virtually impossible on the ground. Many Front agents joined the army of civilian workers employed at U.S. installations and provided useful intelligence for the revolution. More importantly, Party cadres and sympathizers had infiltrated the GVN at every level. Though it is impossible to document, it is wise to assume that every major offensive operation undertaken by ARVN and most of those undertaken by U.S. forces were compromised to some degree.

Revolutionary military forces could not match the heavy and sustained firepower brought to bear by American aircraft and artillery, but they did benefit from the many advances made in the field of small and medium infantry weapons during and since World War II. This was especially true for main force and local force units that were organized to engage American or ARVN units in pitched combat. Although the first enemy weapons captured were mostly obsolete rifles and carbines of many different types and nationalities, American and North Vietnamese intervention on the battlefield prompted the Soviet Union, China, and North Vietnam itself to send an increasingly large supply of moderately sophisticated and very effective infantry weapons for distribution to Front forces. Consequently, throughout 1966 and 1967, insurgent troops received better weapons in every category. The famous AK47 assault rifle and the K50M, a North Vietnamese version of the standard World War II Soviet submachine gun, were rugged and formidable automatic weapons. They were both widely used by Front fighters long before most ARVN soldiers received the comparable M16 rifle. Local force units also received different types of Soviet bloc machine guns, the heaviest of which were very useful against helicopters and posed a limited threat to aircraft. Though enemy units, other than the North Vietnamese Army (NVA), lacked artillery, they frequently used light, medium, and heavy mortars with deadly effect. Although (with rare exceptions on the part of the NVA) revolutionary forces lacked armored vehicles, allied tanks and the more widely used armored personnel carriers were regularly attacked with recoilless rifles, small antitank guns, mines, or the ubiquitous RPG (rocket propelled grenade) rocket launcher, an improved Soviet version of the German Panzerfaust. Various types of simple free-flight missile launchers, the largest with a range of about ten kilometers, were useful for long-range bombardment of towns or military base camps.

The local guerrillas, for the most part, lacked the more sophisticated weapons listed above, but they were still capable of fulfilling important military missions. Mines and booby traps, many locally produced, were the most lethal weapons they used. Although crude in design and often made of cardboard or wood, antipersonnel mines were a major nemesis for allied infantrymen, and larger mines were capable of seriously damaging armored vehicles. Furthermore, as main force and local force units were refitted, the best of the older weapons were handed down. Vietnam was a country awash with weapons, and a shortage of small arms never troubled any of the combatants. Hence, guerrillas were able to inflict a painful level of attrition on allied forces, even when main force units were in hiding, refitting, or in action elsewhere.

The mutually supporting structure of main force, local force, and guerrilla units permitted a wide range of operations and an astonishing economy of force. For instance, due to their political strength in the countryside, Front military forces were able to redefine the concept of mobility. They generally operated without benefit of motorized transport. Consequently, the Front's ability to pre-position food and supplies was critical. Front leaders called this technique "feathering the nest in advance." Whenever possible, supply was handled locally. Most taxes paid to the Front came in the form of rice, and bulk rice was stored in caches all over rural Vietnam. In addition, peasant supporters were required to keep a small reserve of rice on hand at all times, ready to be either dispensed to fighters on the move or sold for small amounts of cash. The advantages of this system were described by a cadre from Duc Hoa district:

> Cash taxes were forwarded to higher headquarters, but rice taxation was kept by the finance section of the village committee and stored in "safe" peoples' houses. When combat units passed through the village they simply requisitioned rice from the finance section. People were also expected to keep one jar of rice for the village guerrillas and one bushel of paddy in reserve to sell to mobile units when necessary. Thus our military units had many advantages: They didn't have to carry rice and could carry more ammo. They also didn't have to warn a village in advance of their arrival and thus safeguarded the security of operations.[18]

Village guerrillas or other villagers conscripted for the purpose aided in the transport of necessary military supplies. Of course, the nature of the terrain limited the size and number of units capable of secret movement, but the capability existed to some degree throughout Vietnam. Therefore, the Front was able to maximize one of the greatest inherent advantages held by insurgents in revolutionary warfare: Because they do not have to defend any precise geographic point and their opponents must defend many, insurgents always have targets of opportunity. When operations went smoothly, Front forces were able to prepare and train for a specific mission well in advance, prepare psychologically for the moment of violence, gain surprise, and achieve local superiority of force at the point of attack. Furthermore, the Front was frequently able to synchronize a series of surprise attacks, assaulting with what Front officers called "miraculous speed." Small groups of local guerrillas, commandos, or sappers might launch diversionary strikes in preparation for main force assault. As events were to show over and over, no part of Vietnam was totally immune from the threat of attack. Even if proper operations were not called for, military harassment in the form of ambushes, mortar attacks, sniping, and mines was an everyday reality in most of Vietnam.

The results of this state of affairs gave the Front two great advantages. In the first place, the strategic initiative was almost always with the Front. If it wanted battle, it could always have it. Conversely, if revolutionary forces wished to lower the level of violence for a time, that, too, was possible. The high level of integration of Front forces allowed one component to take up the slack from another if the situation demanded it. For instance, if combat losses in a main force unit were high, recruitment or conscription from village guerrilla units could be stepped up. If allied pressure in a certain area succeeded in weakening the village apparatus, main force units could be broken down and delegated to the villages. This was an important factor because North Vietnamese manpower, ultimately employed in the village war as well, was a nearly inexhaustible military resource. The Front's military apparatus was intricate but very sturdy. As long as the political will existed to carry the revolution forward, there was no obvious place or easy way to attack it.

The second advantage possessed by the Front lay in the intricate disposition of forces on both sides that resulted from this war without front lines. The manpower available to the GVN, though numerically high, was dispersed throughout the countryside, defensively or statically deployed. Maps of rural Vietnamese areas that were colored as GVN-controlled, Front-controlled, or contested resembled a pattern of "leopard spots"—an analogy used fondly and frequently by Front leaders. Therefore, it was extremely difficult to bring the GVN's numerical superiority to bear. The psychological dynamic was also important. Because even the most secure GVN-controlled areas were usually close to a contested or Front-controlled zone, a small Front attack— a "false alarm"—would precipitate defensive sweeps and other operations that would wear forces down. After the war, the American scholar Hung P. Nguyen identified the crippling effect this had on GVN forces:

> All in all, this strategic disposition and system of coordination was intended to create maximum uncertainty and insecurity and to tie down the bulk of government forces in territorial security missions, thus inducing all the elements of friction that eventually wear down a much larger military machine.[19]

More testimony on the subject comes from Gen. Tran Van Tra, then head of B2 Theater and commander of Front military forces. In his recent memoirs, General Tra describes the results of military dispositions on GVN leaders:

> They were very afraid of the interspersed, "leopard spot" configuration on the battlefield. Our forces were everywhere, even in their urban areas and in their capital. . . . Each party member and soldier, and each small unit, in turn, had a source of support in our larger units—platoons, companies, battalions, or larger units—scattered all over the various areas, in temporarily occupied areas, the contested areas, and the areas contiguous to our free areas. That was a system from which we could not lose a single link. It was an all-encompassing strategy of revolutionary war which caused the enemy troops to suffocate, to worry apprehensively day and night, and think that all places had to be defended and they could be safe only with large forces.[20]

Considering all factors, the enemy had a very good light infantry army. The "barefoot guerrilla" image, cultivated by the Front and accepted by many abroad, was a grotesque parody of reality. Nevertheless, Front forces had serious deficiencies that hurt them on the battlefield, particularly when on the offensive. The logistic system that gave them such a wide reach did have major weaknesses. The process of gathering supplies was not only time-consuming but also vulnerable to allied spoiling operations. Even when the collection of supplies went smoothly, the amount accumulated was never large by American standards. Therefore, enemy units were short on staying power and punch. Lacking air support and heavy artillery, it was very difficult for them to "soften up" an objective prior to assault. Consequently, the enemy was often forced to rely on frightfully dangerous infantry onslaughts that often failed with catastrophic results. In addition, it was very difficult for Front forces to develop momentum once an attack began. The shock effect coming from "miraculous speed" was substantial, but once the initial storm was spent, allied units had far greater staying power and strategic mobility. Battles initiated by Front forces, therefore, had to be sharp but short affairs. Extended fighting played directly into the strength of the GVN and the Americans. The Front was well aware of these problems and usually showed great caution before accepting a battle. Nevertheless, by 1966, revolutionary military units were in place and very capable of dealing heavy blows.

The most serious deficiency, however, was the sheer danger inherent in fighting opponents with much greater firepower. The major reason that U.S. forces relied so heavily on very expensive weapons systems was that American commanders realized that "fire kills." As noted earlier, these commanders were trained to substitute "bullets for bodies" whenever they could. To the extent that it was possible, ARVN followed the American model. Front forces did not have this luxury, and they were potentially vulnerable to random attack at virtually any time. Front fighters often had to live in hideous tunnels for temporary protection. While there, they might meditate on the very real possibility of being buried alive or burned to death. Base areas, chosen because of their difficult terrain, were often inherently unhealthy places to live, and malaria was a perpetual problem. The Front did what it could to offer its followers medical assistance, but efforts were, by necessity, crude. Rapid medical evacuation from the battlefield, so critical for American morale, was utterly out of the question. For all these reasons, serving with the Front was physically arduous and an extremely dangerous enterprise. Whatever the precise casualty ratios, there can be no doubt that serving in a Front combat unit was a much riskier proposition than serving with ARVN, much less with the Americans.

The sheer danger of fighting Americans was made even more perilous, from the point of view of the Front, because U.S. intervention threatened to blunt one of the most powerful weapons available to the revolution: the aura of inevitable Front victory. The Front propaganda machine was put into high gear to steel the nerves of the fighting forces. Their task was particularly urgent because the Front had promised imminent victory at the beginning of 1965, only to have it snatched away by the arrival of American troops. Political cadres who served with every Front military unit and conducted continual indoctrination did what they could to convince the soldiers that American morale was low and that U.S. troops could not fight well on an unconventional battlefield without knowledge of the terrain and local conditions. They were also told that the U.S. Army was a "losing Army" that had only won World War II because of the A-bomb and had taken a beating in Korea. Grossly exaggerated stories of Front victories over Americans and tales of individual heroics on the part of Front soldiers were staples of "emulation" propaganda campaigns.[21] Cadres themselves were given a more sophisticated interpretation of events. A propaganda cadre from Duc Hue stated at his interrogation that, in late 1965, Front leadership issued revised instructions and guidance entitled "New Situation and New Duties," which was the basis a program aimed at raising fighting morale. The program was begun in Duc Hue district in December. Cadres were told to emphasize the political strengths of the revolution and to be confident of victory. Although marred by some military bravado, the analysis of the situation given by the Party to the cadres proved in some aspects to be remarkably accurate:

> Abroad we have the unanimous support of many countries, including many capitalist ones. The movement against the war in Vietnam and American imperialism is spreading even in the U.S. The USSR continues to increase its aid to Vietnam. . . . The enemy has only some technical advantages. . . . They're at a loss to choose among three paths: to withdraw from Vietnam, to go on, or to extend the war to the North. They don't agree with each other. Their soldiers' morale is low. The Americans can't bear such losses in money and men for long. . . . The fact that the Americans are making negotiation proposals demonstrates their weakness and their defeat.[22]

As events would show dramatically, the Front succeeded in assuring its most committed supporters. For most cadres, belief in the justice of the cause did not waver, nor, more importantly, did faith in ultimate victory. In a fundamental sense, American intervention, so disastrous for the Front in most areas, helped it in one way. Prior to the appearance of U.S. ground troops, the nationalist issue was an abstract one for many Vietnamese, unification of Vietnam was certainly not the primary issue in the countryside before 1965. Foreign intervention, however, made Front claims on the dangers facing the fatherland very compelling for many. Hatred of Americans was a powerful political and psychological weapon in the hands of the Front, and it used it well.

The Front needed every weapon at its disposal for the struggle in Hau Nghia province because certain geographic realities dictated that both sides would put forth the maximum effort. The Party always viewed the war in Vietnam as an integrated political-military struggle taking place on three battlefields: the cities, the agricultural lowlands and delta, and the jungles and mountains. It was not that one battlefield was more important than the others but that each had its specific place in the overall strategic picture. Efforts in the cities struck at the enemy's political base and hindered the GVN from accumulating a foundation of support. Urban organizing was also supposed to prepare for an ultimate "general uprising," which would paralyze the GVN's nerve center. The struggle in the agricultural lowlands, where the bulk of the people lived, was likewise crucial and was the principal locus for political dau tranh. The political momentum coming from mass support was indispensable. Taxes, rice, and manpower all came from the lowlands. The terrain, however, favored guerrilla war and not decisive battles. Consequently, Front military forces in the lowlands had the twin tasks of protecting the insurgency's political apparatus and of tying down as much of the GVN's manpower as possible to prevent it from being used in more important locations. Main force units, organized in divisions and possessing as much power as possible, were viewed by most Party leaders as the decisive weapon. Because the wooded terrain of the north and the Central Highlands allowed concentrations in the face of hostile air power and because the firmer soil allowed for mechanized transport, the highlands were the obvious place for main force divisions to operate. Ultimately, Party leaders believed, the final blow would come from this region. Until that time, the wooded areas and mountains were the battlefield of choice upon which to engage the powerful U.S. battalions; in the rugged terrain, American firepower would count for less. Tactical victories over U.S. units, which in fact never came, appeared to be very possible. If nothing else, the highlands were a good place to fight a campaign of attrition.

All three regions intersected in Hau Nghia province, and Saigon lay in close proximity. Gia Dinh province, a special administrative zone including Saigon, was Hau Nghia's eastern neighbor. The Saigon suburbs started with the village of Hoc Mon, a mile or so to the east of the Hau Nghia border. Roughly six miles east of Hoc Mon lay the great Tan Son Nhut Airbase, the location of the headquarters of both MACV and the Vietnamese Joint General Staff. To the east of Tan Son Nhut was the capital itself. As Saigon was easily the most important strategic prize in the country, the GVN naturally deployed a large number of forces in direct proximity. Highway 1 through Hau Nghia constituted a likely avenue of approach for any attack on Saigon coming from Tay Ninh or Cambodia.

For its part, the Front spared no effort to construct heavily fortified base areas in the provinces around the capital. Northwest of Saigon, these base zones all featured wooded terrain and firm ground. Closest to Saigon was the Iron Triangle in Binh Duong province. (One point of the "triangle" was the village of Ben Sec, made famous by journalist Jonathan Schell. Ben Sec was just across the Saigon River from Trang Bang district.) Directly south of the Iron Triangle were three smaller zones that were very nearly contiguous: the Boi Loi Woods, the Ho Bo Woods, and the Filhol Plantation. The Boi Loi was mostly in Tay Ninh and the Ho Bo in Binh Duong, but both intruded into Hau Nghia. The Filhol was just to the north of Cu Chi district town. The Front used these areas for staging, supplying, and, when possible, training its main and local force units. Although the inhabitants of a few scattered and tiny hamlets continued to live and farm in these areas, they were sparsely populated by 1966. Ideally, the Front would have liked to create true "liberated" zones complete with a large civilian population in place, directly supporting the military effort. But, as shown in Chapter 2, GVN and American bombardment and chemical attack prevented this, and most civilians moved to safer areas near the major roads. Because of the continuous threat of attack, the Front built elaborate tunnel complexes, including hospitals, small arms factories, and headquarters. These tunnels linked many contested hamlets with the base zones, and smaller tunnel complexes existed throughout the area. Mai Chi Tho, Saigon Party chief during the war and brother of North Vietnamese Foreign Minister Le Duc Tho, later described these zones close to the capital: "Cu Chi was a springboard for attacking Saigon, the enemy brain center. It was like a thorn stabbing in the eye."[23]

If the safe zones around Cu Chi were like a thorn in the eye, then War Zone C, which included most of the northern half of Tay Ninh province, was like a club aimed at the skull. War Zone C was the headquarters for both the Front and COSVN. A large area, dominated by a strangely isolated mountain named Nui Ba Den, it was the terminus for a major branch of the Ho Chi Minh Trail. On the Cambodian side of the border, a large military complex critical for the Front war effort was developed. Front main force and PAVN units were always in War Zone C in considerable strength. Indeed, throughout the war, Saigon feared that the Front would try to seize Tay Ninh City and establish its capital there. Although this never transpired, War Zone C became one of the most fiercely contested areas in Vietnam and the location of some of the bloodiest battles in the war. It was also uncomfortably close to Hau Nghia province.

Hau Nghia province also shared a border with Cambodia. Along its border with Duc Hue district, a portion of Cambodia called the "Parrot's Beak" by the Americans juts well to the east and at one point is only some thirty miles from Saigon. To make matters worse for the GVN, the area in Duc Hue that lay between Cambodia and the Vam Co River (except for a solitary Special Forces camp) was a portion of the Plain of Reeds, a famous Front base area that extended well into the Mekong Delta. The importance of Cambodia for the Front war effort can hardly be overstated. The famous Ho Chi Minh Trail served as a military lifeline to North Vietnam. More important logistically was the supply route reaching to the Cambodian port of Sihanoukville. But Cambodia was more than a supply pipeline. It was the site of training and rest areas for combat units, and the entire border region served as a backdoor through which Front fighters or cadres could flee if pursued, making them very hard to trap. More critically, Cambodia served as a true "liberated zone." Thousands of Vietnamese peasants had settled along the Cambodian border over the years, and they were joined in the early sixties by thousands more, fleeing combat and air attack. These border areas could be mobilized fully for revolutionary war, a point made by a high Front cadre who rallied in Trang Bang:

> I would like to point out that we over here, in GVN-controlled areas, we are mistaken when we say that the Cambodian border is merely a supply route to use in lieu of the Ho Chi Minh Trail. It is not so. Cambodia is now a real

source of manpower and supplies for the VC. It was not merely a supply route but an actual storage area. . . . As you already know, in Cambodia we have lots of Vietnamese communities. The young men of those communities mostly join the Front and return to this country to serve the Front.[24]

Just to the south of Hau Nghia lay the Mekong Delta, the heartland of rural Vietnam. Although not sharing all the characteristics of the riverine terrain of the Mekong provinces, Duc Hue and Duc Hoa districts were part of the upper delta. Directly south lay Kien Tuong and Long An provinces and the Mekong Delta proper. Fierce political struggle, so prominent in the delta battlefield, was a daily fact of life to the people of Hau Nghia.

Naturally, Hau Nghia province also possessed intrinsic importance to both the GVN and the Front. The military manpower and production coming from the province's 240,000 people was a strategic prize worth winning. However, it was the geographical factors outlined above that led both sides to commit significant resources to the struggle in Hau Nghia. It was a strategic highway of great importance, and lines of supply and communication running either way between the delta and Front military zones passed through Hau Nghia province. Likewise, infiltration, illicit commerce, and communication of all sorts between Saigon, the bases, and Cambodia went through the province. Lastly, military blows directed at Saigon itself might be based in or pass through Hau Nghia. Obviously, the Front appreciated all of this. It had already expended great resources in the area by 1966 and had nearly succeeded in ejecting the GVN from the province.

South Vietnamese Assets

Compared with the strong and dynamic political-military apparatus created by the insurgents, the resources available to the South Vietnamese government in Hau Nghia were paltry. Only Bao Trai, the district capitals, and a few other hamlets were even contested by Saigon, and the GVN political apparatus indigenous to Hau Nghia was in shreds. Although no total of the number of GVN militia forces in Hau Nghia exists for early 1966, force levels must have been very low, considering the situation in the countryside. A sizable number of National Police (NP) were assigned there (over 700 by December), but they were without value outside the towns. Many were perpetually "on leave" in Saigon. Although some of the most skilled and dedicated anti-Communists worked for the NP, most Americans had contempt for the organization because of its notorious corruption and incompetence. This lowly opinion was shared by the Vietnamese people; both they and the Americans referred to uniformed members of the NP as the "white mice," in reference to their white helmets. In any case, because road movement was so difficult and most of the province was controlled by the enemy, a sizable majority of the NP sat behind the barbed wire performing administrative tasks in Bao Trai and doing nothing to project a GVN presence on the countryside.[25]

Nor was the 25th ARVN Division, elements of which operated in Hau Nghia, much of an asset. As noted in Chapter 2, ARVN units in this province had crippling problems. Although possessing enough heavy weaponry to stay in the field, ARVN was continually plagued by poor training and miserable leadership. Some of this was the work of the Front for the Party went to great lengths to weaken ARVN internally in every possible way. Indeed, "action among the military" was an integral part of dau tranh. Front agents had penetrated the ARVN at every level, and American officers were convinced that every large ARVN operation was compromised. Interrogation of Front prisoners of war showed, over and over, that Front military units frequently had several days notice of large ARVN operations. Common soldiers were accused of being "puppets" in the hands of American imperialists and were the targets of specially designed propaganda campaigns stressing the class differences between officers and men. The draft was likened to corvée labor or slavery. Consequently, desertion rates in ARVN divisions were painfully high, often reaching 10 percent per month, and sustained combat would send these rates higher yet. When this total is added to often serious combat losses, it is easy to understand why ARVN units had to be retrained again and again. In addition, although ARVN was manned by peasant and urban conscripts, a majority of field-grade officers were from the urban elite, and many were Catholic. Therefore, prospects for promotion, especially if a soldier had a rural background, were dismal. Pay was likewise miserable, a particularly serious problem if the soldier had a family.[26]

Like every division in ARVN, the 25th was crippled by the political intrigues of the high command. Operations of this division were so pathetic that the intelligence advisor working for John Vann in Hau Nghia was convinced that Col. Phan Truong Chinh, division commander, was a Front agent.[27] The real debilitating factor, however, was junta politics. Colonel Chinh was a friend of Premier Nguyen Cao Ky. The ARVN 5th Division, stationed immediately to the south of the 25th, was commanded by an ally of Ky's rival, Gen. Nguyen Van Thieu. Ky, therefore, had ordered Chinh to orient the bulk of the 25th southward to serve as an anticoup force. He also ordered Chinh never to commit more than one battalion of each regiment to combat at any one time. Consequently, Chinh had his hands full guarding installations and opening the main roads periodically so that produce could go into Saigon and supplies could reach towns under GVN control. Seeking battle with Front forces was not on the itinerary.[28]

ARVN was far from useless, however. Much of the criticism directed toward it during the war by U.S. military personnel resulted from an unfortunate but understandable lack of empathy for the different reality facing South Vietnamese soldiers. As risky as combat was for American servicemen, they had set tours of duty and were sent home upon completion. But ARVN conscripts were in the war, in one way or another, for the duration. In addition, no ARVN unit could count on the supporting fire or medical evacuation assistance that was routine in the U.S. Army. Caution in battle, therefore, was natural. Indeed, although mediocrity was the norm, ARVN possessed numerous skilled and courageous officers and men. Many NCOs had seen long service and understood the tactics of the enemy. Many junior officers were genuine anti-Communists and eager to wage war more vigorously. And several French- or American-trained field-grade officers were fine tacticians. Therefore, if the correct combination of good leadership and adequate support existed for a particular unit, it might be capable of distinguished service, especially if attacked. However, as the turnover in the officer corps was heavy, a good unit might deteriorate very quickly. Conversely, however, a bad unit could not be quickly transformed into a good one. Unfortunately for Saigon's efforts in Hau Nghia, the ARVN 25th, as previously noted, was a very poor division. Nevertheless, no matter how bad it was, without its presence the GVN would have been driven out of the province completely.

Although GVN resources in Hau Nghia were meager at the beginning of 1966, no South Vietnamese reinforcement was possible at the time because of continued governmental instability in Saigon. Between March and May, the ruling military council headed by Ky and Thieu faced a series of crises with the Montagnards and the Buddhists. Some Americans feared civil war and the disintegration of ARVN. After some tense moments, including the real possibility of fighting between the U.S. Marines and ARVN, Ky and Thieu prevailed.[29] As usual, when Saigon was in turmoil, government efforts in the countryside ground to a standstill. Although the crises at Hue and Danang proved to be the last of a progression that had begun with Diem's murder, no one knew this at the time, and the GVN's position eroded even further.

Saigon's prospects in Hau Nghia in early 1966 were utterly dismal. Without outside aid, the government soon would have been completely ejected from the province. As conditions in Long An and Binh Duong were every bit as critical, Saigon was faced with near collapse in the crucial area west of the capital. The GVN desperately needed an infusion of military muscle to avoid imminent catastrophe. This infusion, of course, was provided by the U.S. Army.

Just as American intervention had rescued the GVN in the country as a whole, the arrival of the U.S. 25th Division reopened the struggle for Hau Nghia province. Ultimately, the task assigned to American ground forces proved overly ambitious and poorly thought out, but the presence of a U.S. division was a great asset. The 25th, in particular, was one of the best divisions in the U.S. Army. With its permanent home in Hawaii, the 25th is known as the "Tropic Lightning Division." It had distinguished itself during World War II, first at Guadalcanal and later at Okinawa. During the Korean War, it played an important role in the perilous Yalu campaign. Because the 25th was intended for operations in the Pacific, much thought had been given through the years to the problems of conducting operations in tropical areas. In preparation for deployment to Vietnam, the division constructed a dozen replicas of Vietnamese hamlets in Hawaii to aid in realistic training. Maj. Gen. Frederick C. Weyand, the 25th's first commander in Vietnam, was an innovative officer and proved to be, as shown later by his much deserved promotion to army chief of staff, one of the finest American generals to serve in Southeast Asia. Organized into three brigades of roughly equal strength, the 16,000 men of the 25th fully possessed the great firepower, rapid mobility, and lavish support typical of all U.S. divisions.

Although the 25th had responsibilities outside Hau Nghia and was heavily engaged in Tay Ninh province, at least one full brigade normally operated out of its base camp at Cu Chi. Therefore, virtually overnight, the numerical military balance in Hau Nghia shifted in favor of Saigon. This military side of the balance of forces was not as important (at least in eyes of the Party) as the political side, but it was important nevertheless. And though the goal of comprehensive security for the population of Hau Nghia continually eluded allied forces, American ground troops were indispensable. They were used to guard installations, open roads, make difficult or impossible enemy main force operations, impede insurgent political activities during daylight, and occupy hamlets controlled by the NLF for years. Most importantly, the presence of the 25th promised a breathing space for Saigon during which it would have the opportunity to create forces appropriate to a renewal of the political struggle for Hau Nghia.

The American Strategic Debate

Although American ground and air forces constituted the major U.S. contribution toward the military struggle, American advisors, mostly military men, contributed what they could to the political struggle. They had been active since the formation of ARVN in 1954. In the early years of the Diem regime, American civilians, working either for the U.S. government or for one or another of the volunteer agencies active in Vietnam, were busy dispensing advice on agriculture, economic development, and other such activities aimed at "nation building." As long as Diem appeared successful at governing the country, little thought was given in Washington to the role of the advisory program. When Diem began to falter, however, Vietnam quickly became the major laboratory for developing a coherent response to the dreaded Communist strategy of "wars of national liberation."

In the Kennedy years, American theories concerning counterinsurgency assigned the advisors a critical role. As best enunciated by General Lansdale, America's near legendary Clausewitz of counterinsurgency, the U.S. advisor was to be the principal catalyst for the development of a Vietnamese government both just and strong enough to defeat the insurgency. He wanted the advisory effort manned by a small elite of civilian and military cadres, possessing a genuine understanding of and affection for Vietnam and its people. Advisors were to get out into the countryside, where Lansdale believed the real struggle was taking place, and there develop an honest rapport and friendship with their Vietnamese "counterparts." As "rapport" (a ubiquitous buzzword in the advisory effort) developed, U.S. advisors would "energize" (an equally ubiquitous buzzword) the South Vietnamese war effort not so much by offering advice as by serving as role models for Vietnamese officials. Advisors would also act as competent and honest conduits for U.S. technical and financial aid. Lansdale did not want American advisors to actually run rural Vietnam on their own authority; indeed, the principal goal was the development of an honest and responsive Vietnamese rural administration. According to this theory, the power of American example would lead Vietnamese local officials to increasingly take the initiative toward building a just and prosperous society. Lansdale also argued that the advisory effort should be autonomous and sheltered from bureaucratic interference from either Saigon or Washington. He also wanted advisors to have an indefinite tour of duty.[30]

On the last two points, Lansdale did not get his way. Advisors remained firmly within the established military and civilian channels, with a one-year tour of duty. Nevertheless the vague but ambitious role assigned them was accepted by Kennedy, and the effort quickly grew larger than envisioned by Lansdale. Throughout the early sixties, more and more provinces were assigned American advisors, and ARVN divisions all had advisory groups. In 1964, military advisors were assigned to ARVN battalions and to most districts in Vietnam.[31]

Despite the increasing size of the advisory effort, these were years of frustration. ARVN's military performance showed little or no improvement despite years of effort on the part of the Americans in charge of training and the development of combat doctrine. On the political front, events proved equally disappointing. In spite of the efforts made at developing rapport at the local level, hopes that an American presence in the Vietnamese countryside would lead to reform from the bottom up proved totally unfounded. Consequently, advisors grew frustrated and soon began a futile search for some type of direct leverage that they could use to force the Vietnamese government to take actions on the local level that were desired by the advisors. This search met with failure repeatedly. In reality, the U.S. advisors, if anything, lost whatever meager authority they possessed in the early sixties. The American province advisor was initially required to approve provincial plans before AID funds were issued in support of pacification projects. In December 1964, USOM scrapped the joint sign-off system and allowed Vietnamese province chiefs to requisition AID commodities on their own authority. Despite objections from the field and some second thoughts on the part of USOM, the State Department succeeded in preventing the return of the sign-off system on the grounds that it would stifle initiative within the GVN.[32] Simultaneously, U.S. advisors were dealt another setback. MACV, under pressure from the province advisors, instituted a four-month trial program that gave district advisors direct control over the disbursement of a small amount of U.S. funds. The trial program was judged successful, and MACV proposed making it permanent throughout the country. However, Saigon protested loudly that this plan was an attempt by the United States to undermine the GVN's sovereignty. The plan was abandoned soon thereafter.[33] A similar example of Saigon's stubborn defense of its administrative authority took place in the summer 1965. At a time when the GVN was in mortal peril, USOM accused the province chief of Binh Tuy of misusing $250,000 of AID funds. When the GVN refused to do anything, USOM took the unprecedented step of halting all assistance to Binh Tuy and withdrawing its personnel. Saigon capitulated on the issue and removed the province chief. But this small victory was a Pyrrhic one for the issue had received press coverage and the GVN had lost face. Ambassador Lodge, consequently, made it clear to USOM that he did not want to see a repeat performance.[34] He got his wish.

By 1966, frustrated American field-workers had found an articulate spokesman in John Paul Vann. As noted in Chapter 2, Vann had been the AID advisor in Hau Nghia at the beginning of his steady rise to the top of the U.S. establishment in Vietnam. His thoughts on the war are of interest because they represented the beliefs of many of the Americans serving in the countryside, in closest contact with the village war. They are also of interest because, taken together, the various components of the "Vann thesis" offered a very different analysis of the problems facing the Americans in Vietnam than was current in Washington or Saigon. In addition, because Vann had an alternative diagnosis of the problem, he also suggested an alternative prescription for treatment. In fact, had he and his supporters won the day, the American conduct of war in Vietnam would have been very different. Several participants in the war effort and some scholars, including William Colby, Robert Komer, Andrew Krepinevich, and Guenter Lewy, have argued after the fact that had the United States fought the "village war" advocated by Vann instead of the "big-unit war" conducted by Westmoreland it might well have achieved its basic goal of maintaining an independent, non-Communist South Vietnam and thus have avoided a humiliating defeat.

The official explanation of U.S. policy in Vietnam presented from Washington and the U.S. Embassy in Saigon served as the point of departure for the Vann thesis. According to the official version of events, American bombing of the North and intervention in the ground war were justifiable responses to direct North Vietnamese aggression against a sovereign state. The insurgency was portrayed as a creature of the North. The deployment of PAVN forces south of the DMZ was widely used to justify the American ground presence. And the success of the insurgency was explained as the result of cynical manipulation of an unsophisticated population by Communist cadres, direct aid from the North, and, most importantly, the ruthless use of terrorism. Although no one argued that the GVN was a model government, the problems facing Saigon were portrayed as stemming directly from the insurgency itself; once freed from the outside threat, the GVN would and could improve. The government in Saigon, whatever its imperfections, was always defended as being greatly preferable to the harsh Communist regime in the North.

Though Vann, a staunch anti-Communist, certainly agreed with the last point, he and his supporters viewed the entire insurgency as a symptom of the crisis facing Saigon rather than its cause. In a widely circulated paper prepared by Vann and some disciples in September 1965, entitled "Harnessing the Revolution in South Vietnam," he argued that the major problem facing the GVN was its structural inability to adapt to a genuine social revolution that had been under way in Vietnam for decades. As Vann argued:

> The existing government is oriented toward the exploitation of the rural and lower-class urban population. It is, in fact, a continuation of the French colonial system of government with upper-class Vietnamese replacing the French. Although the wealth of the country lies in its agricultural production, it is the agrarian population which is realizing the least out of either the technological advancements of the twentieth century or the massive assistance provided by the U.S. The dissatisfaction of the agrarian population was manifested against the French, held in check during the early years of Diem, and has become increasingly evidenced each year since the late fifties. It has obviously been fanned by communism; today it is largely expressed through alliance with the NLF. The understandable concern of the U.S. with the communist involvement in the revolution has obscured the fact that most of the objectives of the revolution are identical to those for which Americans have long fought and died.[35]

Although somewhat vague concerning the aims of the "social revolution," Vann believed nothing could be achieved unless Vietnam established a government run by "leaders who come from, think like, and are responsive to the majority." Communism was not, however, seen as the answer. The Vietnamese peasantry, Vann believed, wanted nothing of collectivized agriculture, regimentation, or state-encouraged atheism. Vann maintained that the NLF was strong not because of the inherent appeal of Marxist socialism but because the GVN had forced virtually all non-Communist progressive elements into an alliance with the Party. The NLF was an unstable coalition of necessity, Vann argued, not an unshakable alliance. Because solid support for either the Party or the GVN was, in reality, very thin, the possibility still existed, he believed, to isolate the Party if the GVN were reshaped and made attractive to non-Communist elements within the NLF. If the GVN were transformed from a reactionary to a revolutionary government, then not only would the Party lose much of its direct support but also the government could begin to mobilize the large portion of the rural population that was, in fact, neutral.

None of these ideas were new in American circles. Lansdale had said much the same thing years before. What made Vann and his supporters stand out was their contention that the GVN was incapable of reforming itself. Although he recognized that many honest GVN officials wanted a better life for the people, Vann contended that even well-meaning officials had proved that "they are incapable of surmounting a system of which they are both a product and a participant and have a vested interest in perpetuating." Under such conditions, he argued, the United States must force the GVN to change and save itself. To accomplish this, Vann believed,

Americans had to become directly involved with the internal affairs of Vietnam at every level.

Vann was very vague on what particular actions should be taken. Perhaps he was being cautious. He continually prodded the American establishment in Vietnam, but always as an insider. He realized the dangers of being too specific on sensitive matters. Nothing, for instance, was said about land reform, a purge of particularly corrupt officials, or a fundamental redistribution of wealth and power. However, he did propose that the Vietnamese province chiefs be given much more power at the expense of the central government to prevent the corrupt, ponderous, and inefficient administration at the ministerial level from stifling any initiative in the countryside. American province advisors, Vann contended, should be given enough real power to ensure that the newly strengthened provincial administrations would fight the village war vigorously and effectively. He also proposed an extensive program of political indoctrination aimed initially at provincial officials, then slowly spreading throughout the administration, the military and eventually the population at large. Lastly, Vann suggested that the soundness of his proposals be tested in three designated provinces.[36]

Because he believed that the major problems facing the GVN were its own policies and weakness, rather than enemy strength, Vann was highly critical of the U.S. military policy that he saw develop. The countryside, rather than the enemy safe zones, was the major theater of operations for Vann, and he was appalled by the profligate use of American firepower. He ridiculed the standard defense of free fire zones that argued that any peasant who chose to stay in one of these zones after warning was given was a Communist supporter and therefore responsible for his or her own safety. Vann believed that this policy, regardless of questionable ethics, was counterproductive to the point of stupidity. Civilian casualties would ultimately harm the GVN, as embittered relatives turned to the NLF. Furthermore, he argued, depopulating areas also drove off the neutral or potentially pro-GVN segment of the population, thus yielding even more territory to insurgent control and enabling the Party to concentrate its efforts in contested areas. In general, he feared that an emphasis on firepower, air strikes, and electronic gadgets threatened to obscure the vital importance of the political struggle in the villages and hamlets. Therefore, he wanted to keep the U.S. military presence as limited as possible. The number of American units that were required, Vann argued, should be deployed in heavily populated rural areas where they could help in the village war. Moreover, American troops should use massive firepower only for defense against overt attack. At all other times they should rely on discriminating small-unit tactics. If U.S. forces discovered enemy soldiers entrenched in a village and could not dislodge them without undue risk, it was preferable, according to Vann, to ignore or blockade them rather than call in mortars, tanks, artillery, or aircraft. As the war progressed, when Vann was asked (as he often was) what immediate action the United States could take to strengthen the war effort, his stock answer was "remove an American division."

Although he wished to see the U.S. military involvement kept as limited as possible, Vann realized it was necessary to some degree to prevent the outright collapse of South Vietnam. He also had no doubts about the necessity of a U.S. presence in its totality; only Americans could force the GVN to do what was required. Furthermore, because Americans must take the lead in reshaping an entire society, their presence would have to be of very long duration. Nor did he question the basic wisdom of U.S. involvement. Indeed, Vann and his supporters believed that the struggle in Vietnam was part of a larger epic that was critical for the entire free world:

> Vietnam occupies the center of a work stage in a drama potentially affecting the destiny of all mankind. It is the scene of a civil war, the target of external aggression, the forum for an East-West confrontation, and the testing ground for all forms of economic, psychological and military warfare. Most baffling of all, Vietnam has thus far been its own worst enemy.[37]

Vann was not alone in calling for a more thoughtful conduct of the war than was possible during the frantic 1965 ground campaign. The high-level officers who produced the PROVN study mentioned in the preceding chapter argued, as had Vann, that the problems facing the GVN were due more to deeply rooted social and political difficulties than to Communist subversion or North Vietnamese aggression. The military elites running South Vietnam, argued PROVN, disdained the rural population, believing themselves to be the masters rather than the servants of the people. A large number of GVN officials and officers, according to PROVN, were driven by sordid personal motives and viewed government service solely as an avenue for financial gain through corruption. Members of the small but prosperous urban middle class were likewise disdainful of the rural masses. However, the middle class also had contempt for the GVN, was suspicious of the crude and uncivilized Americans, and frequently regarded the NLF with respect or even admiration. Therefore, many urbanites, PROVN maintained, viewed the war as a struggle between the military and the insurgents and therefore sought detachment. The peasantry itself, according to PROVN, was fatalistic, war weary, and suspicious of a government so prone to breaking its word. The PROVN authors believed the peasants could be won over, but only if change and its benefits were thrust upon them from the outside and not the reverse. The Vietnamese people, in general, were portrayed in PROVN as difficult to motivate and reluctant to sacrifice for abstract ideals. This last point, however, was believed to be potentially beneficial for the U.S. effort: "Because of a reluctance to stand on principles, the Vietnamese are quite vulnerable to manipulation within the framework of an appropriate social reward and punishment system." Obviously, the Party viewed this last point differently.

The PROVN study argued forcefully for a powerful American presence in Vietnam for an indefinite period. Although the authors echoed West-moreland in stressing the great importance of defeating the enemy main force units and preventing the insurgency from gaining outside support, they emphasized that the "object beyond the war" was the construction of a society that would be politically and economically strong enough to stand on its own:

> People are the decisive elements of that "object which lies beyond" this war. The GVN, with U.S. support, must orient on this point of decision. This fact, too often mouthed without real understanding in the now trite phrase "winning the hearts and minds of the people," must guide all of our future actions. This significant point is stressed: The current battle for the villagers of South Vietnam may well be one of the most important and decisive conflicts in world history. PROVN focuses on this central battle; all other military aspects of the war are secondary.[38]

Because of the high stakes in the village war, the PROVN study warned against any tendency to allow military operations to obscure the fact that rural construction or pacification efforts would ultimately decide the outcome of the struggle. Although pressure should be kept on the main force units, U.S. ground forces, PROVN recommended, should be assigned whenever available to pacification duties under the control of the U.S. province advisor. As the GVN was so feeble and the war so important, PROVN was blunt in advising that Americans cease worrying about South Vietnamese and world opinion on the issue of Vietnamese sovereignty. Rather, PROVN argued, only direct American control of many facets of the "nation building process" offered the possibility of success. Like John Vann, the PROVN authors wanted to see far more authority given to the province chief. They further recommended that American advisors receive real power through the control of resources and that their opinions be taken into account on matters pertaining to the removal of corrupt officials and the promotion of promising young Vietnamese officers and administrators. In addition, PROVN called for the immediate appointment of a single manager for the U.S. pacification effort to end interdepartmental rivalry and confusion. Scores of further recommendations were made, some major, others somewhat trivial. Yet, throughout the study, there was a continued emphasis on the importance of the village war and the necessity for Americans to play a direct role in it.[39]

In May 1966, the PROVN study was forwarded to MACV. At the request of the JCS, Westmoreland and his staff studied PROVN and promptly relayed a cable to the Pentagon containing MACV's appreciation of the document. According to MACV's interpretation, PROVN called for two major initiatives: the creation of a single organization charged with coordinating all U.S. military and political efforts and a greatly expanded American intervention in South Vietnamese internal affairs. MACV claimed to be in agreement with the first initiative and briefly recapitulated efforts already made in that direction. Westmoreland's staff also reminded the JCS that a comprehensive reorganization of the military and civilian pacification programs had to be authorized in Washington, not in Saigon. On the second initiative, however, Westmoreland voiced serious doubts. Though agreeing that the United States should seek to affect Vietnamese policy through "constructive influence and manipulation," MACV stressed the dangers inherent in direct American management of the war effort:

> MACV considers that there is a great danger that the extent of the involvement envisioned could become too great. A government sensitive to its image as champion of national sovereignty profoundly affected by the pressure of militant minorities, and unsure of its tenure and legitimacy will resent too great involvement by U.S. Excessive U.S. involvement may defeat objectives of U.S. policy: development of free, independent non-communist nation. PROVN properly recognizes that success can only be attained through support of Vietnamese people, with support coming from the grass roots up. Insensitive U.S. actions can easily defeat efforts to accomplish this. U.S. manipulation could easily become an American takeover justified by U.S. compulsion to "get the job done." Such tendencies must be resisted. It must be realized that there are substantial difficulties and dangers inherent in implementing this or any similar program. . . . Our goals cannot be achieved by Vietnamese leaders who are identified as U.S. puppets. The U.S. will must be asserted, but we cannot afford to overwhelm the structure we are attempting to develop.[40]

Westmoreland further observed that any reorganization of the present American apparatus would be more effective if it were phased and gradual, to prevent the hampering of existing programs. He also cautioned that any plans to greatly expand the U.S. role in "revolutionary development" on the province and district levels must take into account the great shortage of properly trained American civilian and military personnel who understood the subtleties of rural Vietnam well enough to do more good than harm. Due to these objections, Westmoreland recommended that PROVN be reduced from a "blueprint for action" to a "conceptual document" that might aid the NSC in developing further American efforts in Vietnam.[41] As usual, Westmoreland prevailed, and PROVN was condemned to virtual obscurity.

Professor Lewy, in particular, claims that Westmoreland's treatment of the PROVN study was one of several examples showing that MACV did not understand the political nature of the war. As we have seen, many Americans argued much the same thing at the time. Such criticism, however, does not consider the differing perspectives toward the war that reflected the different arenas of the participants.

From Washington, far from the frustrations of the village struggle, the war was viewed within the context of overall U.S. foreign and domestic policy. President Johnson and his closest associates were convinced that the greatest threat to South Vietnam came from the North. They were also sensitive to the constraints on U.S. policy stemming from both domestic and world public opinion. They believed it was essential to portray the war as an example of naked enemy aggression that had to be countered. The "Munich" precedent was recalled sincerely in Washington, but it was also necessary to justify the war itself: A policy based openly on the assumption that the GVN was corrupt, rotten, and basically responsible for the conditions that led to the insurgency would have been extremely difficult to defend.

There was little doubt in the minds of Johnson, Rostow, and others that the United States could bring a better life to the South Vietnamese (and, hence, win them over to the GVN) if the Americans could both neutralize North Vietnamese efforts and properly organize U.S. involvement in the countryside. Therefore, Washington concentrated on the bombing campaign and on various efforts to streamline and reorganize the pacification campaign. Leverage was continually discussed, but little was done in the face of objections from the GVN, the U.S. Embassy, and MACV. On the issue of direct American participation in South Vietnamese internal matters, considered secondary in any case, Washington continually yielded to the embassy and MACV, the two institutions, it was reasoned, that should know best.

For field-workers like John Vann, the most important political arena was the South Vietnamese countryside. Day in and day out, they faced the corruption and inefficiency that characterized the GVN. Frustration was the rule as Vietnamese officials proved unwilling or unable to address problems which the Americans considered critical for the transformation of rural South Vietnam. Delays, mismanagement, or outright corruption in Saigon discouraged not only Americans but many conscientious South Vietnamese officials, as well. Several of the latter actually encouraged Vann and other Americans to develop lines of authority independent of Saigon. It must be emphasized that Vann and his supporters believed that the insurgency was the natural consequence of the misguided policies of a corrupt and archaic regime. Therefore, they were quite willing to risk the consequences, both in Vietnam and abroad, of having the Americans labeled "imperialists" and the GVN marked as a U.S. "puppet," especially because foreign and domestic opponents of U.S. policy already were describing the situation in exactly those terms. The alternative, Vann believed, would be either outright defeat or a longer and more violent war.

The perspective from MACV and the U.S. Embassy was very different. Although they were well aware that serious problems existed in the countryside, high-ranking American officials in Saigon were continually forced to deal with the problems resulting from GVN instability. Both Westmoreland and Lodge had been in Vietnam long enough to have witnessed the floundering of one initiative after another, as coups or domestic unrest brought the governmental apparatus to a standstill. If John Vann was unconcerned about the GVN's image as a sovereign and independent government, Westmoreland and Lodge both realized that the GVN was already suffering serious difficulties on precisely that topic. "American imperialism," for instance, was a major issue during the Buddhist struggle movement that culminated in near anarchy in Danang and Hue in early 1966. Both the embassy and MACV held the well-founded fear that U.S. ultimatums to the GVN might have devastating immediate effects, even if the policies proposed would be ultimately beneficial. Furthermore, Americans in Saigon were more aware than anyone else of the immense problems caused for everyone by the rapid buildup of U.S. military forces: Overloading the GVN with radical reforms might well have caused complete paralysis.

Nor was it ever U.S. policy to redistribute wealth and power in South Vietnam. The few groups there that actively opposed the insurgency (the ARVN officer corps in particular) could hardly be expected to continue to resist the NLF if the Americans sought to deprive them of their wealth and status in return for U.S. support. Therefore, the embassy generally favored the line of least resistance concerning relations with the GVN. Lodge spared no effort to persuade Vietnamese and American officials of the crucial importance of the pacification effort, but he also argued that ultimately this was a South Vietnamese responsibility.

In the military sphere, Westmoreland sought to relieve, as quickly as possible, most ARVN units with U.S. divisions in the fight against the NVA and other main force units. He gave several reasons for this approach, and the village war figured prominently in many of them. First of all, Westmoreland realized that ARVN had taken a fearful beating and badly needed time to regroup. Pacification and security duties were, however, still feasible for weakened South Vietnamese units. Furthermore, he argued that Vietnamese forces were far more able to deal with the rural population than were U.S. units made up of soldiers ignorant of the language and culture. Although he never said as much, Westmoreland undoubtedly knew that relations between American combat infantrymen and Vietnamese villagers would frequently be marked by mutual hatred and loathing. In essence, he called for a division of labor between U.S. and South Vietnamese forces. American units, whenever possible would seek out enemy main force units and provide a "shield," behind which the South Vietnamese could regroup and turn their efforts toward the countryside.[42] Westmoreland put it best himself in a vivid if somewhat strange manner:

> In an effort to explain this kind of warfare in simplest terms, I occasionally likened the political subversives and guerrillas to termites persistently eating away at the structural members of a building, analogously, the structure of the South Vietnamese government. Some distance away hid the main forces, or big units, which—mixing my metaphor—I called "bully boys," armed with crowbars and waiting for the propitious moment to move in and destroy the weakened building. Only by eliminating the bully boys—or, at least, so harrying them as to keep them away from the building—was there a possibility of eliminating the termites or enticing them to work for our side, an essential though systematic and tedious process.[43]

Westmoreland had other concerns, as well. Despite the air campaign, the DRV was both willing and able to accelerate infiltration of troops and supplies. Military formations of the NLF were likewise expanding. As Westmoreland had fewer than 200,000 U.S. troops at his disposal at the beginning of 1966, he was very mindful of the catastrophic effects that would result from a single American defeat in battle. Though there was little possibility of a debacle on the scale of Dien Bien Phu, a smaller defeat, similar to the destruction of the French Groupement Mobile 100, was a genuine possibility. The French, after all, had lost scores of small and medium-sized engagements. As we shall see in the next chapter, an entire company of the Tropic Lightning Division was very nearly annihilated soon after its initial deployment to Hau Nghia. Several similarly perilous engagements took place in 1966 throughout Vietnam. Consequently, Westmoreland, for good reason, was very reluctant to disperse his forces and instead sought battlefields where U.S. units could operate in mass. He also was eager to employ American troops in areas where they could use their artillery and air power with as few restrictions as possible. Both of these considerations reinforced Westmoreland's conviction that U.S. ground forces should concentrate on defeating main force units and that the pacification campaign should be left primarily to the South Vietnamese, with American military participation on an ad hoc basis.[44]

Westmoreland's strategy has been labeled "search and destroy," "war of attrition," or "the big-unit war." None of these labels is totally satisfactory for each implies a never-ending series of multidivisional operations, such as CEDAR FALLS. In fact, most U.S. units conducted at least a portion of their operations in heavily populated areas, with the aim of crushing local guerrilla formations and reestablishing at least the outward manifestations of GVN control. A better description for MACV's mode of operations would be "the parallel wars concept." Although U.S. units emphasized operations against individual main force formations or enemy safe zones and South Vietnamese units emphasized pacification operations, the division of labor was never rigid. Westmoreland and MACV were, however, quite consistent in insisting that the chain of command within U.S. and South Vietnamese forces be kept separate. Therefore, Westmoreland, with the support of the embassy and the South Vietnamese government, resisted any idea of a joint command like that employed in Korea or the large-scale encadrement of U.S. and South Vietnamese units. American and Vietnamese forces would coordinate their various operations, but each would be responsible for successful implementation of plans within their respective spheres. Both partners would, in essence, fight parallel wars. This state of affairs was well suited to Westmoreland's desire to engage main force units whenever possible. It was also well suited to the desire of the embassy and the South Vietnamese to have the GVN appear sovereign in its own house.

Implicit in this arrangement was MACV's reluctance to station American troops more or less permanently to a specific, heavily populated district or province on pacification duties for this would ultimately involve U.S. officers and advisors in day-to-day administration. Far better, from the point of view of both MACV and the embassy, were vigorous offensive operations intended to gain time for the establishment of a stable GVN that, whatever its faults, would then have the opportunity to better its position in the countryside. As shall be seen, Westmoreland's strategy came unraveled not because the goal of destroying main force units was not worth attaining but rather because it proved impossible to accomplish within an appropriate amount of time and with acceptable losses. As shall also be seen, the American experience in Hau Nghia province fosters doubts concerning the wisdom or applicability of the alternative strategy endorsed by Vann, the PROVN authors, and, later, many others.

In general, the balance of forces existing in Hau Nghia at the beginning of 1966 heavily favored the revolutionary troops. The Front, led by the Party, had succeeded in establishing a sophisticated political apparatus with broad-based support. Enemies of the revolution were driven to the remaining government outposts, killed, or silenced through intimidation. Neutral elements of the population were no threat to the revolution as long as the government was kept on the defensive. Revolutionary military forces were both numerically and qualitatively superior to those available to the GVN alone in Hau Nghia. Furthermore, military units of the NLF were increasing in size and receiving more effective weaponry. On the other hand, the government political apparatus had been nearly crushed in Hau Nghia. The GVN's presence extended only to a few important villages located on major roads and protected by fortifications and government troops. Life was hazardous for government officials even in the most "secure" areas, especially at night. Both ARVN and the government militia proved incapable of thwarting the extension of NLF control in Hau Nghia. American advisors, in theory so important for the war effort, had little authority or influence, and U.S. political and economic programs intended to bring a better life to the people were confused and uncoordinated. Only American military intervention offered hope for the future, but it was hampered by confusion and deep differences concerning how best to proceed.

4

Search and Destroy:
The Big-Unit War, 1966–1967

War Begins for the 25th Division

Although the GVN's position in Hau Nghia was extremely precarious in January 1966, the arrival of the U.S. 25th Division gave the American–South Vietnamese allies an always qualitative and sometimes quantitative superiority on the battlefield. This was apparent to all concerned, and American commanders were eager to press forward without delay with military operations. As we shall see in the next chapter, 25th Division command was very aware of the importance of the political struggle in Hau Nghia and allocated considerable resources in that direction. Nevertheless, most operations had the clear but elusive goal of destroying Front military units. Although it will require backtracking in the narrative, U.S. operations aimed at the destruction of revolutionary military units for the years 1966–1967 should be examined as a whole. Scores of major operations and thousands of minor ones undertaken by the Tropic Lightning Division during this period all had the same objectives: preempting attacks by revolutionary forces; destroying enemy supply depots and fortifications; and, most importantly, killing the Front's soldiers. U.S. operations in this period were also quite similar in size and tempo. Furthermore, search and destroy missions were only indirectly connected to other initiatives in the countryside. After considering the U.S. military campaign, it will be possible to analyze the American and South Vietnamese political effort during this same period, an effort that also utilized force as its major component.

In January 1966, the 25th Infantry Division, like the other army and Marine Corps divisions, was a well-designed and very powerful instrument of military force. Army planners in the preceding decade, reacting to the perceived requirements of the nuclear battlefield and, later, to Kennedy's "flexible response" doctrine, stressed adaptability of organization and the ability of divisional units to operate independently. The simple but rigid "triangular" division based upon regiments was replaced by a more specialized and fluid organization based upon three brigades. Normally, the division's combat assets were divided more or less equally among the brigades, but, if the situation demanded it, commanders would not hesitate to load up one at the expense of another. The 25th Division's nine infantry battalions constituted the heart of its fighting strength. Made up of four line infantry companies, a support company, and headquarters (HQ), a full-strength infantry battalion in Vietnam had a paper strength of 920 men. Two of these battalions were mechanized and included large numbers of armored personnel carriers, which served both a transport and a shock role. Infantrymen of the Tropic Lightning Division had fearsome punch behind them. Four artillery battalions were available, each consisting of four batteries with six 105mm howitzers apiece. A fifth artillery battalion possessed heavier 155mm and 8-inch howitzers. The 25th Division also had tanks serving with an attached armored battalion and a reconnaissance squadron of armored cavalry. An integral aviation battalion gave the division a limited airmobile capability. (The bulk of helicopter and other aviation assets were controlled by higher headquarters in Vietnam. Competition for these assets was fierce among the divisions, but the 25th could normally count on substantial capabilities.) Many support units sustained the combat elements.

Beginning in 1952, the JCS had developed a series of contingency plans for intervention in Vietnam. Because the 25th Division was based in Hawaii and intended for employment in the Pacific, it figured prominently in all of them. Obviously, officers of the 25th watched developments in Vietnam with intense interest in the early sixties, and many division personnel served in Vietnam as advisors, support troops, and door gunners before full-scale intervention. Officers stressed small-unit tactics and counterinsurgency techniques in training, and mock Vietnamese hamlets were constructed in Hawaii to lend realism to the training. Nevertheless, despite long preparation, the actual demands of wartime deployment created totally unexpected dilemmas and something resembling chaos. Westmoreland decided in mid-1965 that the 25th would join a powerful force he was creating in the Saigon area. However, when the situation in the central highlands started to disintegrate, MACV decided to send the first component of the 25th deployed to Vietnam, the 3d Brigade, to Pleiku. Key personnel and supplies were stripped from other units to bring 3d Brigade up to strength. Remaining combat elements were allocated to 2d Brigade, which began heading to Cu Chi in January 1966. The haphazard deployments had left 1st Brigade an organizational shambles, and two battalions were therefore brought in from Alaska to reconstitute it. Consequently, for the first few months of service in Vietnam, the 25th Division at Cu Chi was, in essence, a one-brigade division. The 1st Brigade deployed in late spring. Later in the year, the 3d Brigade of the 4th Division was put under 25th operational control, initiating a trade for the 25th's original 3d Brigade that was sent to Pleiku. This transfer was completed in August 1967.[1]

Unlike their later comrades, the first contingents of soldiers from the Tropic Lightning Division were deployed by sea to Vietnam. They were jammed into a hot ship in tropical waters, a physically unpleasant experience. It did, however, allow the men to get their emotional bearings and contemplate what lay ahead. Robert Conner, whose departure had been delayed for several weeks while he awaited his requisite eighteenth birthday, later recalled this experience:

> It was a miserable couple of weeks. We did our push-ups early in the morning to avoid burning our hands on the deck. The rest of the day we tried to stay on the shady side of the ship, avoided spitting windward, and read dirty books. . . . The bunks were about 18 inches apart and the isles about the same distance wide. There were big arguments, and we started to get on each others' nerves. But in the back of your mind, you knew the guy you were arguing with was your buddy and you would have to fight beside him.

According to Conner, spirits were high and the men very well trained. However, in a deeper sense, like so many of their predecessors in U.S. military history, the men of the 25th were unprepared for a foreign war:

> We thought we were tough and streetwise, but we were really ignorant. Most of us didn't really know where Vietnam was. If we were going to the Far East, why did we keep sailing west? . . . In the distance, land was breaking. As we looked, we wondered why we were coming to a country like this. We sat in the harbor for two days. Back in training, they had told us the VC wore black pajamas. There were sampans all around the ship, and everyone wore black pajamas. Were they all the enemy?

Before anything else could be done, the 25th Division had to establish a base of operations within Vietnam. Advance parties had chosen an abandoned peanut field just north of Cu Chi district town and directly south of the Filhol Plantation. The site was picked because it was just off Highway 1, the ground was suitable for heavy vehicles, and the land was uncultivated. Highway 1, at this time, was vulnerable to interdiction along its entire length. In addition, Vietnamese officials and U.S. advisors in Hau Nghia had warned the 25th that the already famous "Tunnels of Cu Chi" extended into the area, but their counsel was unheeded. Consequently, constructing the base camp necessitated a low-level but frustrating military campaign. The first troop convoys were large and heavily escorted. Ambushes, however, were still frequent. Transport personnel began modifying their vehicles, welding steel plating onto the trucks and installing sandbags and machine guns on top. Driving much faster than safety dictated, the trucks and other vehicles kicked up clouds of the reddish dust that covered this part of Vietnam. Upon arrival, the first troops busied themselves constructing a bleak collection of tents, foxholes, and crude field fortifications, as well as a tiny airstrip. Men put their cots on the ground (or mud, depending on the weather). Water was trucked in and used sparingly. Sniping from outside and also apparently from inside the perimeter was continual. Soldiers discovered a few tunnels that were preserved for training purposes. During the day, U.S. patrols swept through many of the numerous hamlets in the vicinity of the base camp and succeeded in capturing some hidden rice and a few weapons. Sharp but short exchanges of fire with local guerrillas were common, resulting in small numbers of killed and wounded on both sides. On most nights, small enemy units probed the heavily guarded perimeter and frequently launched mortar attacks. They were answered by cautious and tentative night patrols and a large amount of preplanned artillery fire targeted at points where division intelligence guessed the attacks might originate from. Soon, soldiers learned to sleep through outgoing artillery fire but to wake up immediately and run for bunkers at the sound of "incoming."

Within months, the base camp at Cu Chi had grown much larger and more elaborate. Engineers constructed a large airstrip and a small hospital. Cabin-like tent kits, with wooden floors and superior circulation, replaced the general-purpose tents. Wells were dug and showers constructed. Modern plumbing was never a fixture, however, and burning feces gave the camp a wretched odor that every veteran of the 25th recalls. Over time, each battalion set up its own little home inside the larger perimeter where men, when not on perimeter duty, could rest and recuperate in relative safety for brief periods between field operations. Much of the drudgery of camp life, so hated by past generations of American soldiers, was performed by a small army of local Vietnamese who were eager to make money doing everything from filling sandbags to washing laundry. (Naturally, as everyone knew, many employees were Front agents.) Elaborate mess facilities were constructed, complete with ice machine and ice-cream maker. The men showed great ingenuity in the venerable art of scrounging for creature comforts: Indeed, Cu Chi became the source of all sorts of luxuries for field units and advisory teams. Engineers built outdoor movie theaters and athletic facilities, and, because Cu Chi was close to Saigon, various USO (United Service Organization) groups often stopped by and entertained. Danny Kaye gave a show that some "lifers" swore was identical to the one he gave in World War II. Actress Ann-Margret was an early visitor, and the men named a large outpost on the northeast perimeter, a site of frequent attack, in her honor. Brothels in Cu Chi district town, needless to say, did a very good business. By the end of 1966, the Cu Chi base camp was a small city.

The camp was undoubtedly a necessity. It served many of the functions fulfilled by "the rear" in every modern war. Front forces and PAVN used their base zones and Cambodia in a similar manner. The big difference, of course, was that the Front political apparatus in the hamlets allowed a portion of their military effort to be self-supporting; manpower and food for the Front came from the hamlets themselves. In contrast, the 25th Division had to import everything. The dependence on the Cu Chi base camp and the smaller versions constructed later had serious implications for the U.S. war effort. The safety and comfort available at Cu Chi acted as a magnet for every soldier eager to get out of the field, and a bureaucratic momentum developed, leading to a proliferation of camp jobs. This momentum was strengthened by the army's understandable policy of transferring combat soldiers to Cu Chi when they were "short," i.e., when they had a month or less left in their one-year tours.

More to the point, however, Cu Chi and its supply lifeline on Highway 1 were obvious targets of attack and needed to be defended constantly. Throughout the war, a very high percentage of operations conducted by the 25th Division were designed to prevent mortar attack and ground harassment on the base camp and to keep roads open. Road security operations had secondary advantages in that they aided the local economy by quickening commerce. But sweeps around the camp, which rarely resulted in contact, offered no such benefits. Instead, they were dangerous affairs for Front guerrillas laid a multitude of mines and booby traps in areas likely to be swept. Force expended to defend the base camp was force that could not be projected for larger strategic or tactical purpose. Yet, the dilemma persisted: The extensive measures undertaken to defend the camp could not provide total security (and Cu Chi was regularly harassed and periodically attacked throughout the war) but, had nothing been done to protect the camp, Front forces no doubt would have been glad to attack it far more frequently and violently.

Fortunately for both the men of the Tropic Lightning Division and the population of Hau Nghia, the Front did little to hinder the 25th's deployment. The relative quiet in Hau Nghia reflected decisions made elsewhere by Front and DRV military leadership. U.S. ground intervention precipitated a fierce strategic debate in Hanoi on how best to confront the new military situation. On one side was General Giap, who argued that American firepower was too great to be faced in large battles. Furthermore, Giap contended, PAVN must be held in reserve in case the United States invaded the DRV itself. The Front, he proposed, should concentrate on protracted guerrilla war, wear down American forces and keep the main force units in reserve. Gen. Nguyen Chi Thanh, commander of COSVN, and Le Duan argued that Front forces could fight the Americans if the terrain and conditions were favorable and thus should selectively accept combat if the Americans pressured the base zones. Part of Thanh's calculation may have been the desire to draw U.S. troops away from the populated areas and into the Vietnamese hinterlands, thereby giving the Front's political apparatus the opportunity to strengthen itself further so it could better support the expansion of main force units. In any case, the latter group prevailed, and Giap was ordered to increase infiltration from the North and begin a new theater of operations south of the DMZ. The hamlets would be quiet, but the jungles very bloody.[2]

Although establishing the base camp necessarily dominated their earliest efforts and Division Headquarters were not activated until 26 March, General Weyand and his staff were already looking ahead. Upon deployment to Hau Nghia, the 25th Division was ordered to accomplish a number of missions. First on the list and first in importance was the order to conduct search and destroy missions within the division's tactical area of responsibility (TAOR), which included all of Hau Nghia, most of Tay Ninh, and part of Binh Duong. Second, the 25th was instructed to be prepared to participate in search and destroy missions outside the TAOR when called upon by II Field Force Vietnam, the U.S. headquarters for all units operating in III

CTZ. The third mission was to aid the GVN with its revolutionary development campaign in the national priority area of Hau Nghia. The remaining missions were essentially commonsense ones, such as securing the Cu Chi base camp or being prepared to aid beleaguered friendly units.[3]

Like other U.S. commanders, the officers of the 25th had no intention of fighting an indefinite campaign of low-level attrition (although this was exactly what ultimately resulted). Rather, they intended to annihilate the revolutionary main force units within the divisional TAOR through a series of major operations. Battalion commanders of the 25th were advised that "a battalion must begin an operation with the idea in mind that the VC must be methodically dug out and ground to dust."[4] In pursuit of this objective, the division planned six major operations (a "major operation" involved a battalion or more; a "minor operation" could be conducted by any unit from a squad up to a battalion) for April 1966. Five of these were search and destroy missions. The sixth was a pacification operation that shall be investigated in Chapter 5.

Operation CIRCLE PINES, the first search and destroy mission undertaken by the 25th Division, is worth a brief examination because it exemplifies the flow of battle in Vietnam at those rare but violent times when U.S. and enemy main force units actually collided. The objective of CIRCLE PINES was the destruction of enemy redoubts in and around the Ho Bo Woods in Binh Duong and Hau Nghia provinces and the annihilation of two battalions of the 165A main force regiment, reported to be operating in the area. The job was given to the 2d Brigade of the 25th Division, a task force made up of three battalions including armor, mechanized infantry, and foot soldiers. It was the first operation in Vietnam in which an American armored battalion was employed.[5] On paper, it was to be a classic "hammer and anvil" maneuver. The armor and mechanized infantry battalions were instructed to seek engagement near a rubber plantation north of the Ho Bo Woods, destroy fortifications, and then turn south, where the infantry battalion would be stationed as a blocking force, ready to intercept enemy troops that presumably would be fleeing U.S. tanks and APCs.

CIRCLE PINES got under way very smoothly on 29 March. However, enemy troops proved adept at utilizing the heavy cover and their own extensive fortifications to avoid pitched battle. For six days, the men of 2d Brigade destroyed fortifications and searched for hidden rice and ammunition caches with only fair results. The desired battle did not materialize, although there were sharp, sporadic contacts. On 4 April, the mechanized and armored battalions wheeled southwest with the intention of passing through the blocking forces and assembling at the village of Trung Lap, just inside Hau Nghia, to bring CIRCLE PINES to a close. In late afternoon, the armored battalion arrived in Trung Lap. The mechanized infantry battalion, however, discovered a very large rice cache and therefore was late getting under way. Soon thereafter, the mechanized forces ran into an estimated company of enemy infantry. Two APCs were knocked out, leading the U.S. commander to call in artillery and deploy for battle. But on this occasion, the enemy again successfully withdrew. Nevertheless, this skirmish had important consequences. The infantry blocking force had been preparing to join the rest of the brigade in Trung Lap. Late in the afternoon, however, two companies, situated about two miles apart, were ordered to deploy defensively for the night and await the arrival of the delayed mechanized battalion the next day. These two companies, at approximately 120 men each, were potent forces but were too separated to effectively support each other. The armored battalion had completed assembly at Trung Lap, and both companies were, in effect, isolated. Similar tactical situations would occur thousands of times during the coming years in Vietnam without incident. But on this occasion, the 25th Division came perilously close to suffering a humiliating defeat in the first pitched encounter with large, main force Front units.

The threatened unit was Company A, 2d Battalion, 27th Infantry Regiment (*Wolfhounds*), which was serving as the eastern blocking force. American officers reconstructed events immediately afterward and concluded that PLA forces had quickly recognized the vulnerability of Company A and had succeeded in rapidly concentrating an entire battalion of the elusive 165A Regiment, reinforced with local guerrillas (making a force of at least 400 men), for a massed attack on the company perimeter from every direction. The objective, the Americans believed, was the total annihilation of Company A. On this occasion, however, the fortunes of war favored the Americans. Wisely, the battalion commander deployed two squads outside the company perimeter to establish ambushes. One of these squads sighted three Vietnamese and opened fire without result. With the original ambush compromised, the squad leader moved and set up a new position. At 0410 hours, over 100 enemy soldiers stumbled into the newly laid ambush and, simultaneously, the company perimeter was assaulted from every direction. Luckily for the Americans, their ambushing squad dislocated an important portion of the assault at the most critical moment. The battle lasted for an hour. Front fighters penetrated the company perimeter at many points, and hand-to-hand combat, one of the rarest events in modern war, took place. Company communications broke down, and the three platoons fought, in essence, separate engagements. Toward the end of the battle, U.S. artillery began to appear. Nevertheless, all three platoons were in desperate shape and low on ammunition: One platoon had distributed the last of its small arms ammunition. However, the Front battalion, no doubt fearing increasing U.S. artillery fire, as well as the coming of dawn, broke off the battle at 0530. After the battle, American officers concluded that a final enemy assault would have destroyed Company A.

In just over an hour, Company A suffered 12 men killed and 42 wounded, a devastating total for a short engagement. The 25th Division's intelligence could only estimate enemy losses. Thirty bodies were found, but American officers believed that far more dead and wounded had been evacuated. One of the Vietnamese found dead on the barbed wire had been employed by the 25th as an interpreter for their civilian employees at base camp. Whatever the relative totals, the engagement had been a "near run thing," and U.S.

commanders, though proud of the tenacity of their own men, were impressed by the professionalism shown by the PLA. The division prepared a special report detailing the engagement, which was widely circulated among other American units.[6]

In its entirety, Operation CIRCLE PINES highlighted the advantages and disadvantages of the opposing forces. The 2d Brigade claimed to have killed 157 enemy soldiers, with another 300 possibly dead. Tons of supplies and ordnance, but only 52 weapons, were captured. Hundreds of small fortifications were destroyed. In return, the brigade lost 30 men killed and another 195 wounded.[7] During the operation, American units were able to move about at will, and, due to superior firepower, the attrition rate probably favored the Americans in large- and small-scale encounters. When pressed, American soldiers fought hard, although it took timely artillery and more than a little bit of luck to spare the division a major defeat. Front main force units proved themselves capable of avoiding contact with superior U.S. forces, reacting quickly to timely intelligence, concentrating a large force at a vulnerable point, and launching a major assault.

It is important to emphasize that the single major engagement during CIRCLE PINES took place at the Front's initiative. Only in the critical areas of firepower and staying power did the Front units prove deficient. Yet, American commanders were impressed by their enemy's performance, and in the special report prepared after the assault on Company A, they recommended that, in the future, battalions, rather than companies, should be used to establish independent perimeters in areas where the enemy was active. No doubt the experiences of 2d Brigade—and especially that of Company A—served to reinforce the already strong tendency of American officers toward operations in mass, supported with a heavy reserve of firepower and conducted in a very prudent manner.

In many respects, CIRCLE PINES was not a typical search and destroy mission. It proved to be the most violent encounter for either side until the massive multidivisional Operation CEDAR FALLS nearly a year later. The near destruction of Company A was the most perilous moment for the 25th Division until the Tet Offensive in 1968.

Of course, this was not apparent at the time. Neither the failure of 2d Brigade to bring the enemy to battle on American terms nor the assault on Company A deterred General Weyand from authorizing a great number of search and destroy missions. Four more took place in April.[8] In the quarterly period of May to July 1966, there were seventeen more.[9] The August to October quarter, during which the division was allocating more time to area control pacification operations, was a period of relatively low main force activity. Nevertheless, five large search and destroy operations took place then.[10] Although divisional records for the November to January period are unfortunately not available, neither Hau Nghia province reports nor the II Field Force records for this period indicate that any activity of notable scale took place, other than preparations for CEDAR FALLS.

There is no reason to investigate any of these operations in detail. They were approximately equally divided between battalion- and brigade-level operations and lasted from between a couple of days to two or three weeks. Almost all were either in Hau Nghia or on the Hau Nghia-Binh Duong border, although two were in Tay Ninh and one in Long An. Virtually every part of Hau Nghia received attention at one time or another, but the Ho Bo-Boi Loi woods area was the main theater of operations. At no time did the Tropic Lightning Division succeed in bringing a large enemy main force unit to battle, regardless of the size or duration of the individual operation. Naturally, this meant fewer casualties for both sides. Rarely did the Americans claim to have killed over 75 of the enemy, although "possible" enemy casualties were often listed as much higher. American battle deaths did not often exceed fifteen.

There were, of course, some bright spots from the American point of view. During the large search and destroy operation of 16–27 May 1966 (code-named WAHIAWA), U.S. troops captured an uncommonly large amount of supplies and claimed to have killed 144 enemy troops in the Ho Bo and Boi Loi woods. The division was pleased with WAHIAWA, and confidently claiming that the manpower and material losses suffered by the enemy had reduced the combat effectiveness of nearby main force units considerably and predicting that enemy operations planned for the near future had been disrupted. Although this latter assertion may well have been correct, enemy main force units were reported to be returning to the Boi Loi Woods in June. On another occasion, U.S. troops trapped an entire enemy platoon, killed 11 men, and captured the remaining 19. Soon thereafter, a cache of 107 weapons was discovered, one of the largest captured in Vietnam. A few days later, on 7 June, a battalion on a search and destroy mission discovered a grenade factory capable of producing 400 to 500 grenades a week.[11]

However, in many respects, the forces of the NLF were doing very well. Most importantly, PLA units, although often under heavy pressure, continually demonstrated their ability to avoid pitched battle. The ingenuity and bravery of the "hard-core" revolutionary soldier was frequently acknowledged by American officers. Revolutionary soldiers also worked hard at refining tactics to somehow compensate for U.S. firepower. For instance, on occasion, enemy units would "hug" an American unit, making it impossible to use artillery. The Americans countered this technique by having helicopter gunships fire at enemy positions from a distance of 40–50 meters, a dangerous tactic for the valuable gunships.[12] In addition, NLF units were rapidly being upgunned, and more and more captured weapons were from the Communist countries. In June 1966, enemy troops began using the RPG-2 rocket launcher, thus making the battlefield much more dangerous for American APCs and the previously invulnerable tanks.[13] Lastly, NLF units continued to show an impressive ability to move at night. No matter how hard U.S. soldiers would work at clearing an important area, such as the Ho Bo Woods, NLF units were able to reinfiltrate and force the Americans to repeat an operation again and again.

With the exception of the Tet Offensive, the big-unit war for the 25th Division peaked in intensity during the first five months of 1967. Search and destroy missions tended to increase in size and duration. Most of the fighting, however, took place outside Hau Nghia province. Elements of the 25th participated in Operation ATTLEBORO in late November 1966 in Tay Ninh, which was the largest operation of the entire war to that point. The hard fighting in this operation, as well as that that took place in earlier efforts in the Ho Bo-Boi Loi area, helped convince Westmoreland that the Front would fight for its base zones. In the following months, he tested this thesis on a very large scale.[14]

In January 1967, 2d Brigade, along with attached forces, served as the blocking force for Operation CEDAR FALLS, a multidivisional campaign aimed at destroying enemy forces and installations in the Iron Triangle. On the first day of CEDAR FALLS, elements of 2d Brigade collided with the battalion headquarters and attached company of the 165A Regiment. After a sharp engagement, during which, according to some prisoners, 50 enemy soldiers had been killed, the enemy successfully withdrew. For the duration of this massive operation, 2d Brigade scoured the Hau Nghia-Binh Duong border, destroying fortifications and seizing supplies. Nevertheless, when the "hammer" supplied by 1st Division and others finally struck the "anvil" supplied by 2d Brigade, few enemy troops were caught in between. Lt. Gen. Jonathan Seaman, commander of II Field Force, however, claimed a great victory: "A major portion of the enemy's base and control center for operation against the Capital Military District has been destroyed. This represents the loss of an investment of twenty years." Whatever the merits of General Seaman's claim, enemy forces returned to the Iron Triangle within weeks of the termination of CEDAR FALLS.

Shortly thereafter, elements of the 25th Division took part in Operation JUNCTION CITY, one of the largest and most violent of Westmoreland's multidivisional search and destroy operations. It lasted from 22 February to 14 May 1967 and was aimed at the destruction of the 9th NLF Division in Tay Ninh's War Zone C. This task was very nearly accomplished, although not in the manner envisioned. JUNCTION CITY, in fact, developed into a massive CIRCLE PINES. Despite the efforts of thousands of U.S. troops, as well as a smaller number of ARVN soldiers, large-scale battle took place only when the NLF division took the initiative in the form of assaults on smaller American units. All these assaults failed. One of them—on Firebase Gold at Suoi Tre, guarded by two companies of the 25th Division's 3d Brigade—was one of the bloodiest battles of the war. Despite the presence of U.S. air and artillery, an entire regiment of the 9th Division assaulted the firebase at dawn. U.S. artillery was forced to fire at point-blank range. After four hours, the attack was broken off. Thirty Americans were dead, with another 109 wounded, and over 600 enemy dead were collected around the perimeter.[15]

JUNCTION CITY was the last large multidivisional search and destroy operation undertaken by the Tropic Lightning Division. Thereafter, with the advent of the summer monsoon in May, the size of such missions again decreased, although the tempo did not. Operations resembled those of the same period in 1966. Although the 3d Brigade, 4th Division, finally transferred to the 25th on 1 August and operated in Tay Ninh, the remainder of the division concentrated in Hau Nghia. Again, the Ho Bo-Boi Loi woods area received most of the attention.[16] And again, enemy units, particularly when aided by monsoon weather, proved able to avoid battle. As in 1966, the division devoted most of its efforts during the wet summer monsoon to pacification operations.[17]

With the beginning of the relatively dry winter monsoon in November, division intelligence noted an increase in enemy main force activity. Consequently, the Tropic Lightning Division prepared for a new round of search and destroy operations on what had become very familiar ground. In November, for the first time, a North Vietnamese Army regiment, the 101st that was attached to the 9th NLF Division, was identified in Hau Nghia in the Ho Bo-Boi Loi woods area. The sighting came as a surprise and was explained as an attempt by the North Vietnamese to secure a large portion of the rice harvest for shipment north.[18] Considering the events of early 1968, this interpretation may well have been in error. In any case, 2d and 3d Brigades set out in vain pursuit. Soon thereafter, 2d Brigade was sent into the Iron Triangle, while 1st and 3d Brigades began another assault on War Zone C. Once again, the now-familiar pattern was repeated as U.S. units failed to fix enemy units, and combat took place when the enemy attempted to overrun an isolated unit. A particularly grim example of this occurred on 1 January 1968 when two regiments of the NLF 9th Division assaulted a 3d Brigade firebase in War Zone C. When finally forced to retreat, the enemy left behind 355 dead.[19] American losses were 21 killed and 149 wounded.

Further search and destroy operations nearly ceased after 10 January when General Weyand, at this time commanding II Field Force (all U.S. units in the provinces around Saigon), became convinced that an enemy attack was coming. With perhaps the finest American display of generalship in the entire war, Weyand convinced Westmoreland to allow him to begin redeploying U.S. and ARVN units closer to Saigon in response to signs of an impending NLF offensive during Tet 1968.[20] As we shall see, Weyand's move had major consequences for the war, both in Vietnam in general and in Hau Nghia in particular.

The Military Environment

The above account of operations by the 25th Division gives events a coherence that would have been utterly invisible at the time to most of the fighting men involved. To a certain extent, combat soldiers in all wars are hard put to grasp the connection between their efforts and a larger military purpose. One of the primary reasons that the U.S. government has subsidized the writing of very detailed operational histories of recent wars is the belief that it owes it to veterans to illustrate how the contributions of their small units fit into the "big picture." However, the war in Vietnam posed some unique challenges to U.S. soldiers that are an intrinsic part of this story and that also led to certain policy implications. It is therefore worthwhile to analyze the military environment confronting the men of the 25th Division in Hau Nghia province.

One of the great strengths of the Tropic Lightning Division in the first two years or so of war was a generally high level of morale, stemming from an intense group cohesion. This was especially true for the initial contingent of men who had trained together for extended periods in Hawaii and arrived with their units intact. Thomas Ferguson, a lieutenant colonel and division signal officer at the time of deployment, later recalled the "oneness" felt by the men:

> There was a total willingness on everyone's part to sacrifice for the common purpose. We all knew each other and treated each other like equals. We were able to throw individual mission statements out the window and subordinate our individual interests to the common good. General Weyand had a strong positive attitude and helped us face every problem. In Hawaii, we had developed realistic operational procedures that lessened the need for detailed orders. We all had a great latitude for action. Our officers and NCOs were outstanding. A trust existed among us that is hard to put into words today.

An enlisted man in the division's armored cavalry squadron added that he not only knew everyone in his unit but most of their families, as well. A captain in the same unit, who had served with it for over two years in Hawaii, claimed that he knew every one of his 190 or so men by their first names. Later officers, following MACV's disastrous policy of a six-month officer rotation (derisively called "ticket punching" by enlisted men), could rarely make a similar claim.

As the months progressed, casualties accumulated, and the initial one-year tours began to come to an end. The cohesion of the 25th as a division began to suffer as replacements arrived piecemeal. Gerald Kolb, an enlisted man who arrived in the summer of 1967, described the disorientation of a typical arrival in Vietnam by air from the United States:

> A hush came over the cabin of the plane. All of the joking, singing, and cajoling stopped. You could have heard a pin drop. The stewardess was crying, and some of the men were, too. When the door of the plane opened, we were hit with a musty, rank, urine-like odor. It was very hot. We passed a bunch of guys whooping and hollering: They were going home. My God, what a low, low feeling.

Men entering the combat zone in this manner had to undergo the difficult process of fitting into a unit already in place. They were aided by a special one-week combat training course at Cu Chi, called "charm school" by some men, that every replacement had to go through. In addition, the 25th Division command, realizing how crucial it was for morale, made sure that the men received mail every day, even when in the field. Yet, none of this could substitute for shared experience, which came quickly for most soldiers.

Indeed, within the combat units, the fighting spirit remained very high. Michael Willis, an infantryman who arrived in August 1967, described the process:

> When I arrived at the *Golden Dragons* [2d Battalion, 14th Infantry Regiment], morale was high. In pitched battles we gained experience surviving. The guys got much closer and would sort of hook together. We would try to watch over and protect some of the weaker guys. We developed an arrogance: We weren't going to die, the enemy was.

It should be pointed out that the men of the 25th Infantry Division received virtually no political guidance. In contrast, Front and NVA soldiers received continuous, systematic, and very effective indoctrination from the political cadres who accompanied every unit. American soldiers naturally thought about the purpose of their presence in Vietnam, but most explained it in either personal or very vague, general terms. Doing one's duty, seeing war, serving the country, or stopping communism were all common reasons for service. But fierce ideological commitment to a political purpose was extremely rare. On any given day, this state of affairs probably did not matter. The men's commitment to each other—and to self-preservation—was sufficient to make most units in the 25th Division generally fearsome in battle. A massed attack on an element of the Tropic Lightning Division, with its skill and firepower, was a virtual death sentence for any opponent. Nevertheless, few men of the 25th were disappointed if a contact were not made, an ambush not sprung, a battle not fought. If soldiers thought an officer was overly aggressive, incompetent, or willing to needlessly risk lives for career promotion, unit morale would plummet. For most men, the main goal was to serve honorably, look out for one's friends, and go home. In the words of one combat veteran who came over with the initial contingent, "Morale was high and most people believed they were doing the right thing. But soon, everyone was counting the days. The subtle objective was to go home."

Such sentiments were most understandable. For fighting men, Hau Nghia province was a miserable and dreadfully dangerous place to serve, and for most Americans, the climate and the land itself were enemies. C. W. Bowman, a combat infantryman serving with the 25th Division during 1967, described Hau Nghia province:

> During the dry season, the temperatures frequently reached 110 degrees or more during the day. You can only imagine how the heat intensified the odors of garbage, compost, and manure. The ground would get so dry that the dirt would turn to dust. When the trucks and other vehicles would drive down the roads, there would be great clouds of fine red dust and you'd just be coated with it. You were already soaking wet from sweating, so the dust would just soak into your clothes and your skin. After a time, it would even get into the pores of your skin. So if you'd take a bath, you'd still be dingy grey or red, depending on the area you were in. It would actually stain your body.

The dust accumulated in such quantity, another soldier recalled, that at the very start of the rainy season, before it turned to mud, large clouds of dust pummeled people in the middle of a downpour. It was the heat, however, that punished the men in the field. C. W. Bowman remembered the effects:

> We would hump through the boonies with anything from 80 to 100 pounds of gear on us. I saw people suddenly pass out, just have all of their energy drain out of them from the heat. We'd be so tired that when we stopped along the trail somewhere, just to take a five-minute break, two or three guys would just fall asleep or pass out, it was hard to tell which. We would sweat so hard our shirts would get crusted from the salt leached from our bodies. It just got to the point that when you did move through the jungle it was one foot in front of the other. It was all you could do just to keep going. If you did come into contact, you'd forget about all of the humping and strain and stress: A couple quarts of adrenalin pumping through your heart gives you the strength to do what you need to do.

The rainy season began in late spring. Tropical thunderstorms of frightening intensity transformed the terrain almost overnight. Lightning killed two men and injured fifteen more in late April 1966. On other occasions, lightning detonated claymore mines, scaring one soldier "absolutely, totally, utterly witless." Mosquitoes, other insects, and snakes thrived. Above all, the rain, even as it filled the rice paddies and brought sustenance to the population, meant mud and rot. Once again, Bowman offered vivid testimony:

> When the monsoon started, that's when it really got tough. . . . Sometimes it rained for two or three days straight, sometimes it rained for a week straight. That was the time everything started to rot and mildew. Things just disintegrated from constant moisture. That's when everyone started getting ringworms. Guys would have chunks of hair fall out of their heads from ringworms; one time I counted over 100 ringworms on myself. You couldn't be out in the paddies more than three or four days before your feet would start rotting. There was trench foot, and guys couldn't walk because of the plantar warts on their feet. Some guys got malaria.

The fatigue and disorientation, bad enough during the dry season, were even worse during the rains. Bowman continued:

> We did a mission near Trang Bang in the middle of the night. It was raining so hard that you had to grab the web gear of the guy in front of you so you didn't lose contact. Anyway, it was raining so hard we were up to our knees in water. All of a sudden, I heard a terrific splash, I turn around and my friend Mike was down on the ground rolling around. I thought he had stepped on a punji stake. He was cussing and mumbling. I said, "What happened Mike?", and he told me he had fallen asleep. That gives you an idea how tired we were sometimes.

The physical wear and tear on the men was dreadful. Combat veterans of other wars could sympathize with the plight of Bowman and his comrades:

You averaged three or, if you were lucky, four hours of sleep a night. I've got photos of all of my friends and you can see, especially in the black and white photos, our eyes are sunk back in our heads; we have dark circles around our eyes, like somebody punched us in the eye. All of us were skin and bones. It was a joke among all of us that if we wanted a strong guy to carry the machine gun what we needed to do was crawl back to base camp and get one of the clerks because every time we went there we saw guys from muscle city trying to punch keys on the typewriters. Out in the field, we looked like a bunch of drowned rats. . . . It's amazing how fear can keep you awake all night and keep you going the next day, but it reaches a point where you have to try to get your buddy to stay awake for you because you're saying, "I have to sleep. I don't care if they come up and slit my throat or shoot me in the head, I just can't take it any more."

No one in the 25th Division was absolutely safe or, for that matter, truly comfortable at any time. Men were often killed or wounded at the Cu Chi base camp during mortar attacks or probes. Smaller base camps established by brigades or temporary firebases constructed by artillery battalions were even more vulnerable. However, most fighting and dying was done in the field. Field operations, usually battalion- or company-sized, might last from two weeks to two months. Although helicopters, armored personnel carriers (called "tracks" by the men), and trucks were typically used at some stage, leg infantrymen spent most of their time on foot. All combat units in the field were seriously under strength at virtually all times. The casualties were so frequent, illness so pervasive, and what one man called the "call of the rear" so strong that an element of the 25th Division at 70 percent of paper strength was in very good shape. Periodically, field strength was far lower. Veterans recalled 60-man companies (164 men paper strength) and 13-man platoons (42 men paper strength). One result of this was that infantrymen carried as much ammunition as they could, far more than standard load. An infantryman in Vietnam lugged an extraordinary array of lethal equipment: twenty or more loaded magazines for his rifle, extra rounds for the squad's M-60 machine gun, CS or smoke grenades, hand grenades, claymore mines, and sometimes plastic explosives for destroying bunkers and tunnels. Toting all this weaponry added greatly to fatigue. Another result of low field strength was that ground units were even more dependent upon artillery, helicopter gunship, and air support for their survival. Without supporting fire, infantry units would have faced possible annihilation each day in the field. Every man in the bush knew this, and units became psychologically dependent upon outside support. As shall be seen, this situation caused serious dilemmas for the pacification program.

Tactical intelligence was quickly out of date and frequently unreliable. By the time radio intercepts, prisoner interrogations, or captured documents were analyzed, the moment for action had usually passed. The alternative to acting on specific intelligence was "beating the bush," i.e., putting infantry units in harm's way, waiting for an attack, and calling in fire support. Carl Quickmire, a troop commander in the 25th Division's armored cavalry in 1966, later described the tempo of operations in Hau Nghia province:

It essentially amounted to going out and beating the jungle every day and every night looking for the enemy. There were all kinds of fancy names given to the "tactics": search and destroy, cordon and search, sweep and search, anvil and hammer, etc. and etc. But it all amounted at the tactical-unit level to going out, looking for the enemy and trying to kill him. Despite all of the highfalutin gadgets, intelligence, for the most part, was extremely poor. We did not know who we were looking for or where to look, in most cases. We frequently were ambushed, sometimes due to our own stupidity, for taking the same route or setting a daily schedule or setting a certain established routine.

The sheer frustration of these operations, of "going around in circles," as one former soldier put it, produced immense mental strain. There were too many miles, too many dangers, and too few American fighting men in the field to establish a permanent presence throughout Hau Nghia or much of rural Vietnam. Attrition, in theory, was a means toward the end of eroding the enemy's will. But to the men on the spot, killing appeared to be the end in itself. Because destroying units (rarely accomplished) and killing the enemy (frequently done) were the objectives, rather than seizing and holding territory, American units visited the same places over and over. With no end in time or place in sight, self-protection was at the top of every small unit's list of priorities. Firepower was substituted for aggressive small-unit tactics. Many American fighting men during the war and after criticized the passivity of allowing air and artillery to be the principal tools of destruction. Undoubtedly, there were times when skillful ground assault would have saved American lives and waiting for support was exactly the wrong thing to do. Nevertheless, infantry assaults are dreadfully dangerous. They require excellent training, superior élan, and good luck. A bad officer, confused men, or an unfortunate break can turn a ground attack into a bloodbath in an instant. Many Front units were well trained and had great spirit. Yet, their attacks on U.S. forces failed repeatedly. Relying on fire support may not have been the best way to win the war, but it probably was the best way to stay alive. There was great heroism, but it frequently worked against short-term tactical objectives. Wounded men became the center of countless small engagements. "Uncommon valor" was indeed a common occurrence if it involved saving a comrade's life or moving forward to help a trapped American unit. It was much less common if it were in pursuit of a higher body count. Jay Lazarin, who served with the *Wolfhounds*, one the army's best infantry units, later reflected on these matters:

> Over my one-year tour, my unit went to those two areas [along the Vam Co in Duc Hue district] numerous times, made serious contact with the VC, and sustained many casualties from both firefights and booby traps, yet we never stayed put there long enough to keep the area clear of the "the enemy" or to block his travel routes. So, as the year wore on, each time we knew we were going back to these places, we (the experienced ones) mumbled out loud about going back for the express purpose of trying to see who could kill more of the other. . . . We were certainly not ashamed of what we were doing and

went about all our operations trying to do our best. Yet, the most troubling aspect was always the knowledge that as soon as we left, they would be back, and, most likely, so would we. . . . Each time we took casualties, they became our priorities, and medevac missions took first place in most thinking on the scene. I am not saying that this was bad; from a grunt's point of view, that's how we stayed alive or survived injuries. It just didn't seem aggressive enough then or certainly now. I'm not now sorry for it; this kind of tactic probably kept most of us alive.

Fear of mines and booby traps added another ingredient to a dismal psychological brew. Michael Call, another 25th Division combat veteran, reconstructed a mental dialogue that thousands of his fellow soldiers undoubtedly had:

We begin to walk with our eyes fixed on the ground, looking for some telltale sign we should avoid. I ask myself, "Is that little thing ahead the three prongs of a Bouncing Betty (a mine that springs up to about waist high before going off) or just three blades of grass?" As my right foot moves in front of my left foot, I carry on a debate within my mind on whether I should place it down on *that* rock just ahead or behind it. Or in front of it. Or to the side of it. But now I face another dilemma. If I choose to step to the side of the rock, which side do I choose? These gooks are very clever. They must figure that I will want to place my foot on hard ground. So, maybe they put the mine under the rock. Maybe I shouldn't place my right foot anywhere near that rock. Maybe I should move over to the left a little or to the right. Then again, why not place my foot in the step of the guy ahead of me? But he is already too far ahead. And if you walk too close to him, he will get pissed off because if I trip a mine he'll get blown away too. What to do with my right foot? I say, "I can't stand on my left foot forever." I finally put my right foot down and nothing happens. My next decision is what to do with my left foot, which, in the act of walking, comes up when the right foot goes down.

There was very good reason to fear mines. Del Plonka, a platoon leader in the 25th Division's *Golden Dragons* battalion, recalled the fate of a comrade just outside of Cu Chi:

There were these things called stick mines. It's nothing more than taking a dead piece of wood attached to a mine with a trigger device—you knock the stick over and it goes. Usually, they used land mines, and land mines are designed to blow up tanks. Needless to say, when this young man tripped this stick mine and it went off, he lost both legs immediately. He was more or less split open from the groin area up to his neck. The best I could do was put him in a poncho. It was a very sickening sight, seeing all that blood and seeing that poor young man with that face just looking at you with those bewildered eyes, and, well, it stays in your mind.

Although trapping and annihilating Front units proved easier to do on the map than in the field, there were areas in or very near Hau Nghia province where some sort of contact with the enemy was easy enough to find. Most of the abandoned Filhol rubber plantation was situated just to the north of the Cu Chi base camp across the Binh Duong border, but smaller portions of it lay directly adjacent to the base camp to the north, east and west. To the men, it offered a "serene but very eerie vista." Hundreds of huge rubber trees, planted decades previously, stood in perfect rows, their tidiness upset by the scrub that had grown up between them. It was heavily mined and booby-trapped and served as cover for passing Front units or infiltrators attempting to harass Cu Chi.

Much worse were the Ho Bo and Boi Loi woods, a large wooded area touching Binh Duong, Tay Ninh, and northern Hau Nghia; troops frequently lumped them together simply as "the Ho Bo." Ho Bo was a Front base zone of long standing. Consequently, B-52 and fighter bomber attacks were frequent. The area had been sprayed with chemicals many times without really clearing the canopy. Needless to say, Ho Bo, a free fire zone, was constantly shelled. Yet, the Front was well dug in and defended the area tenaciously. For this reason, troops from the Tropic Lightning Division visited the Ho Bo over and over. The men hated it. For one thing, as vividly described by Michael Willis, the Ho Bo had some of the worst terrain in Hau Nghia:

> It was the thickest terrain I ever saw. Think of a rose bush in the United States. Now imagine one as round and thick as a bus, with spikes that look like French bayonets. Don't forget the leeches that walk along the ground and the half-inch- to inch-long black ants waiting for those leeches to snatch them. Everything was eating everybody.

The terrain was even more daunting because clearing it with a machete brought the risk of setting off a booby trap. Small cuts from the thorns and sharp leaves easily infected and scarred the men. An ambush or firefight was always a possibility. Jerry Liuci, who joined the 25th's famous 2d/27th Battalion (*Wolfhounds*) in late 1967 shared his unpleasant memories of the Ho Bo:

> We took an Eagle Flight [helicopter assault] to an area that will always have a certain amount of fear for me, a place called the Ho Bo Woods. It was filled with thick brush and trees. There were small trails going to who knows where. . . . This area was definitely Charlie's stronghold. We found tunnels, caches of weapons, underground hospitals, spider holes, booby traps, you name it. It definitely gave you that eerie feeling every time you went there because the VC that you fought in the Ho Bo Woods were hard-core, fight-to-the death kind of characters. It gave you a lot of respect for these guys: They were definitely hard and seasoned.

Another area visited frequently by elements of the 25th lay along the Vam Co River. In this expanse, the Front had constructed dozens of well-hidden bunkers to shelter the units continually in transit to and from Cambodia. As was normally the case in Hau Nghia before the Tet Offensive, typical engagements along the Vam Co were short, chaotic affairs. In the summer of 1967, however, a Front main force unit near the village of An Ninh in Duc Hue district, dug in along a horseshoe bend in the riverbank, accepted battle. After a fierce air and artillery bombardment, the *Manchu* battalion made a mass helicopter assault. C. W. Bowman was a participant and gaves a graphic picture of a large engagement in Hau Nghia from the American side of the battlefield:

> As we were coming in, I could see and hear the rounds hitting the chopper; they were tearing holes inside the door. The guy alongside of me got shot in the neck on the way in. Just prior to when we came in, they had fired six thousand rounds of artillery and bombed it all morning. But you could see two choppers burning on the ground anyway. They dropped us off in the middle of the horseshoe, and when we jumped out we immediately sank up to our hips in the mud of the rice paddies. . . . After the chopper took off, Charlie was still shooting at us, and we had to crawl through the mud until we got behind a dike. We were pinned down there all that day. They called in air strikes all around us. They called in artillery. We assaulted the wood line three times, and we got run out three times. One time we assaulted, our own gunships opened up on us and killed and wounded a bunch of guys. We laid there all night in the mud and water. We couldn't get any of the wounded out that day or night: You could hear them moaning back in the rear area. Charlie was probing the perimeter all night. The next day, most of us were soaking wet and wrinkled and covered with leeches from lying in the water all night. The battlefield was covered in smoke, like a fog. The next day, our officers said they were going to walk artillery in front of us as we assaulted the wood line. When we were assaulting it, I watched the artillery throw mud and trees up in the air, and the only thing I could think of was "damn, this is just like the movies." It was like I stepped out of my body and walked around myself and then stepped back in myself and continued the assault. We fought for the rest of the day and swept the horseshoe. We blew up the trenches and the bunkers and did a body count. Everyone wanted a body count.

The great firepower available to U.S. units had its military drawbacks. Because there were few logistical or financial restraints on its use, artillery was used for every conceivable purpose. The most common fire mission was "H&I" (harassment and interdiction), blind firing at Front base zones or likely lines of communication. This was a controversial tactic for many combat officers believed that H&I caused only a handful of casualties in return for the effort and money spent. Samuel Crouch, who served with the 25th's 155mm battalion that fired the division's heaviest artillery, recalls that, sometime in mid-1967, his battery alone fired 200,000 shells in less than a year's service. The men estimated that this worked out to $34 million worth of ordnance, most of it for "H&I." Furthermore, about 1 percent of the rounds that were fired did not explode on impact because of faulty fuses. Thus, as critical officers pointed out, Front areas were littered with tons of usable explosives. Naturally, these "dud" rounds were converted into powerful mines and booby traps used to kill American soldiers. In addition, landing zones for helicopter assaults were lavishly "prepped" by air and artillery bombardment. Many officers were convinced that this tactic ruined surprise and allowed the enemy to avoid battle (which was no doubt viewed as a blessing by many of the men).

Above all, fire support is one of the most complex of military missions, and mistakes do take place. When something went wrong, American soldiers were threatened with disaster from their own side. In the fall of 1966, Bob Conner's company, on a joint operation with ARVN near the Vam Co in Duc Hue district became involved in a large firefight. South Vietnamese Skyraiders were called in, and in the moments that followed, Conner and his comrades were subjected to a napalm attack, a common enough experience for their Front opponents:

> We saw the plane and heard the bombs falling to earth. Fortunately, the napalm hit right between our platoon and the one next to us. For a split second, it took the oxygen out of the air. That smell of burning soap or whatever it is, gasoline, kerosene, the fumes, and everything were all up your nose, and your eyes were running. And just for a few moments, you're gasping for breath, and you're hollering and screaming. . . . The whole battle took less than thirty minutes. It felt like eternity. It's like you miss part of your life.

Night operations were a common experience for everyone involved with the struggle for Hau Nghia. In most parts of the province, like so many areas in Vietnam, "Charlie ruled the night." American officers, long critical of South Vietnamese timidity after dark, were determined to contest this. Beginning immediately after the 25th arrived in Vietnam, commanders of the Tropic Lightning Division sent their men out on hundreds of night ambushes, and more ambitious tactics were sometimes tried. In the fall of 1967, the 3d/4th Armored Cavalry squadron began night sweeps down Highway 1 between Cu Chi and Trang Bang. The M-48 tanks, with their 1,000,000-candlepower xenon searchlights blazing from the turrets, led APCs down the road as infantrymen walked on either side. Obviously, such a force could not surprise anyone. Rather, the Americans were offering "bait." hoping for an ambush and a chance to use their fearful power. One night, as recalled by Gerald Kolb who was just in from the United States, the Front obliged. Kolb's account affords a glimpse at the chaos inherent in night fighting. Also, like Bob Conner's memory of his brush with cremation from napalm, it provides some idea of what it must have been like for the Front soldiers doing battle with the Americans:

> One particular night, they ambushed us pretty good from one side of the road. They told us later it was about 30 VC, but, of course, we didn't know that because it was about midnight when it happened. They opened up with machine guns, rocket launchers, RPGs, whatever. Our tanks and tracks kept going a little bit and stopped to return fire immediately. One of the tanks was firing beehive rounds point-blank. That tank caught on fire, but the guys kept on pumping out the M-60 and the 90mm: Finally, the stuff got so hot and was popping so much they had to jump out. I got into this ditch I was walking next to with two other green guys. We covered our heads and our butts pretty

good, and we started to return fire at the tree line about a quarter of a mile away. I dropped my M16 into the mud and was out of action for a few minutes. About this time, the column started to withdraw. We didn't dare get up because their side was firing, our side was firing, and tracers were going about three or four feet over our heads. We were just scared shitless. They withdrew. We were left behind, three green guys who had been there about a week or ten days.

About five to eight minutes later miniguns came in on Hueys. The bull moose was on the loose. What I mean by that is that the minigun was firing away up in the sky: There was this real low roar, right over us. We didn't dare get up because, at that distance, they would think we were gooks. So we stayed there and waited for the bullets to rip through our backs. That was done in about ten minutes. Then we heard some artillery come up and some 90mm tank guns fire. There were explosions all around us. That went on five or ten minutes. From our own guys; they thought we were dead, they told us later. About half an hour later, the tracks and tanks returned. We were waving our arms and yelling. You never saw anybody jump up on an APC so fast in your life, that's about six feet off the ground. We found out later that they just about shot us thinking we were VC. What happened was that no one had been killed or hurt except for one guy who cut his hand opening an ammo can. The VC took it pretty bad.

It is extremely difficult to assess the outcome of the 1966–1967 campaign waged by the 25th Division against the main and local forces of the NLF in and around Hau Nghia. In the strategic realm, U.S. forces failed to either annihilate enemy units in big battles or to permanently clear major NLF redoubts. Furthermore revolutionary forces continually evidenced a high degree of technical skill at maneuver, and incredible bravery, if questionable judgment, during their always vain assaults on American units. Lt. Gen. Bernard Rogers, who helped plan CEDAR FALLS-JUNCTION CITY, gave a typical U.S. assessment of his opponent's methods of war in a report written after the operations:

With respect to the enemy contacted during the two operations, we found most of them dedicated, well-disciplined, persistent, tenacious, and courageous, often displaying more "guts" than sense. It was a sheer physical impossibility to keep him from slipping away whenever he wished if he were in terrain with which he was familiar—generally the case. The jungle is usually just too thick and too widespread to hope ever to keep him from getting away; thus the option to fight was usually his.[21]

However, there can be little doubt that the numerous search and destroy missions prevented enemy main force units from operating as they wished. It is obviously impossible to guess what revolutionary forces would have done had the Americans elected not to assault the safe zones. In this regard, it should be remembered that, from the safe zones in the Ho Bo-Boi Loi woods area, Front units were within easy striking range of Cu Chi and Trang Bang. Likewise, the safe zones along the Vam Co River threatened Bao Trai and Duc Hoa. Yet, even in this case, the picture remains murky.

Despite the thousands of fortifications destroyed and weapons captured and the tons of other supplies taken, revolutionary forces, in many ways, were stronger at the end of 1967 than they were in January 1966. Certainly, their weaponry steadily improved, and main force units increased in size. The Front's political apparatus was able to maintain a supply of manpower, and North Vietnam's involvement in the war steadily increased, raising the levels of both men and supplies. All of this was made abundantly clear during Tet 1968.

In the final analysis, the war fought by the 25th Division, typical of the entire U.S. military effort in this period, developed into a war of attrition despite American intentions to the contrary. It should be emphasized that the large search and destroy missions were only a part of this war of attrition. Overall, most of the violence took place during the never-ending series of small-unit actions. Whether an American unit was on a search and destroy mission, a pacification operation, static security, or at rest, small-unit ambushes, sweeps, and patrols continually took place. For instance, during the August to October 1966 quarterly period, the 25th Division undertook ten major operations and 1,211 minor ones. Contact with the enemy occurred during every major operation and in 113 of the minor actions. All these totals are typical. So, too, are the staggering figures of ordnance expended by the 25th Division during this same quarter: U.S. artillery fired 160,000 rounds of ammunition, killing at least 100 people; nearly 3,000 tactical air sorties were flown in support of the 25th and were credited with killing another 41; and 9,000 helicopter gunship missions were flown, adding another 35 to the total dead. Land operations during this quarter, according to U.S. figures, resulted in 313 confirmed enemy killed and several times that number probably killed.[22] Overall, figures for 1966–1967 are much higher. For the months March through October 1966, the division claimed 1,225 enemy confirmed killed and several times that figure estimated dead. Thereafter, the figures increased. For the February to April 1967 quarterly period, due to heavy fighting during the dry season, the division claimed 1,588 confirmed enemy killed. After this quarter, divisional records ceased making estimates of overall enemy killed, although they continued to list enemy losses in individual operations. Although these figures were estimates, almost certainly too high, and undoubtedly included a large number of innocent civilians, they are indicative of the high price paid by revolutionary forces to wage war against an American division.

Nevertheless, it was likewise very dangerous to serve in the U.S. Army. Whatever the actual losses inflicted on revolutionary forces, the 25th Division, like every American unit, kept careful and totally accurate figures concerning their own losses. For the period of 1 January 1966 to 1 August 1967, the divisional strength averaged about 12,000; it rose to about 17,000 after the inclusion of 3d Brigade. During this nineteen-month period, excluding the November 1966 to January 1967 quarter for which figures are unavailable, the 25th Division had 592 men killed in battle, 42 men killed from nonbattle injuries, and 5,568 men wounded. If the missing quarter were added in, the figures would, of course, be higher yet. Consequently, a soldier beginning his one-year tour with the 25th had a better than 33 percent chance of being killed or wounded; in line units, this percentage was naturally much higher. Although most Americans sent to Vietnam were relatively safe, the men who were in harm's way fought one of the bloodiest wars in American history.

In retrospect, it is clear that the Americans were losing the war of attrition. With sickening regularity, the weekly U.S. casualty reports were relayed to the public over network news, with a predictably adverse effect on support for the war. The only way such losses could be justified was if the pain endured contributed toward the "object beyond the war," i.e., the revival of the South Vietnamese government. To ascertain whether such a revival was taking place, it is necessary to return and examine the political-military struggle waged over Hau Nghia province during the two years before the Tet Offensive.

5

Sword and Shield:
Pacification Efforts, 1966–1967

"Revolutionary" Development

During late 1965 and early 1966, just as the 25th Division was being deployed to Cu Chi, there was a marked increase of interest shown by U.S. policymakers in the struggle for the allegiance of the South Vietnamese rural population. This struggle was sometimes called "the other war," "the battle for hearts and minds," "the village war," or, most commonly, "the pacification campaign." The emphasis on pacification was due primarily to three factors. First, most Americans dealing with Vietnam believed correctly that U.S. intervention in the ground war had saved South Vietnam from collapse and therefore that certain military and political assets could safely be allocated to a renewal of the struggle in the countryside. Second, most U.S. policymakers believed, mistakenly, that the ground war was going so well that there would soon be an improvement in rural security—the prime requisite for a successful pacification effort—due to the anticipated absence of enemy main force units. Third, Lyndon Johnson, faced with an open-ended war, wanted desperately to convince American and world opinion that the United States was succeeding not only in defeating enemy military forces but in building a stronger and more just society in the South, as well.[1]

The increasing concern for pacification was best exemplified by the various pronouncements coming out of the three conferences attended by Johnson and the GVN leadership—Honolulu in February 1966, Manila in October 1966, and Guam in March 1967. In each, there was a great deal of shallow chatter concerning the "social revolution" that was to be brought to the Vietnamese people by the GVN and the United States. Likewise, at each meeting, South Vietnamese officials praised their own efforts aimed at bringing a better life to the rural population and promised even more enthusiastic efforts in the future. No doubt, much of the verbiage was for the benefit of the press.

Yet, the proceedings of the conferences, as well as other documents concerning the "other war," lead to the conclusion that President Johnson and some of his closest advisors had only the vaguest conception of how to proceed in countering the revolution that was already under way in Vietnam. Johnson, in particular, seemed to believe that pacification entailed essentially an increase in public works and preparations for elections.[2] Ambassador Lodge, the quintessential "other warrior," favored the creation "on the precinct level or equivalent thereof" of a civilian "counter-terrorist organization." This organization, in Lodge's view, would conduct a census, issue identification cards, monitor the movement of people and goods, organize local defense, and "go through each hamlet with a fine-tooth comb to apprehend the terrorists."[3] In other words, Lodge endorsed methods almost identical to those already attempted by Diem, Khanh and Ky. Furthermore, Lodge advised Johnson that it was vital to "saturate the minds of the people with some socially conscious and attractive ideology, which is susceptible of being carried out."[4] What this "attractive ideology" should look like and where it might come from were questions left entirely unanswered.

Robert Komer, appointed by Johnson after the Honolulu Conference to coordinate U.S. pacification efforts from the White House and soon to be in charge of the pacification program, was not concerned with seeking any conceptual breakthrough for American efforts other than the Revolutionary Development Cadre, which shall be discussed presently. Rather, Komer believed that the GVN as it was then constituted, aided by a more organized American effort, would succeed in destroying the insurgency: "Wastefully, expensively, but nonetheless indisputably, we are winning the war in the South. Few of our programs—civil or military—are very efficient, but we are grinding the enemy down by sheer weight and mass."[5]

Despite the fact that U.S. intentions concerning the war in the countryside continued to be somewhat ill defined, the White House did decide that American efforts should be better organized. Consequently, after each of the three conferences, the organizational charts were streamlined. After Honolulu, Deputy Ambassador William Porter was put in charge of coordinating various civilian efforts without, however, having his new authority institutionalized. After Manila, the various components of the United States Information Agency (USIA), the Central Intelligence Agency (CIA), and AID were combined and designated the Office of Civil Operations (OCO) under Porter's leadership. After Guam, the process was completed when OCO was redesigned as CORDS and transferred to MACV under the direct leadership of Robert Komer. (This entire process was characterized by some very undignified bureaucratic infighting between MACV, the embassy, CIA, and the other agencies.) Consensus was also reached that an ever greater percentage of ARVN's strength should be allocated directly to pacification duties, without, however, any change in the chain of command in favor of more direct control over troops on a sustained basis by the province chief. Hence, despite some protests on the part of the ARVN high command, 50 percent of ARVN was assigned to pacification duties for the 1967 Combined Campaign Plan, with more slated to participate when not involved in tactical offensives.

Regardless of some grumbling on the part of a few ARVN generals concerning the undignified nature of pacification duties, the Americans made a concentrated effort to show the world that the GVN fully supported the new reemphasis on the pacification campaign. At each of the high-level conferences, Ky, Thieu, and others made glowing pronouncements about GVN intentions to bring a new and better life to the rural population. Furthermore, Americans were very pleased with the appointment of Maj. Gen. Nguyen Duc Thang to head the GVN pacification campaign. Americans considered Thang a good soldier and a dynamic administrator with a genuine concern for the rural population. Robert Shaplen, the widely read correspondent for the *New Yorker*, also believed that these very qualities led Ky and Thieu to distrust Thang.[6]

However, regardless of Thang's personal qualities or the actual extent of his power, the GVN quietly indicated that its view of what actually constituted social revolution or a new life for the people was not the same as that held by any American seriously expecting fundamental change. This divergence of views was clearly evidenced by two questions of terminology. Lodge disliked the term "pacification" because it evoked memories of the French during the First Indochina War. Nor was he pleased with the phrase "rural construction," which was the literal translation of the Vietnamese Xay Dung Nong Thon and served as formal designation for General Thang's ministry. Because Lodge believed "rural construction" suggested public works rather than "revolutionary uplift" (which he advocated), the ambassador asked each member of the Mission Council to create a new and more appropriate translation after the conference. Westmoreland, perhaps showing his chilly response to the whole effort, recommended that the literal translation be kept and no more thought given to the matter. Lodge, however, was not put off and chose the new term "revolutionary development" to characterize the entire effort in the countryside. With Ky's agreement, he decreed that the GVN Ministry of Rural Construction be officially translated as the Ministry of Revolutionary Development (MORD). Nevertheless, the Vietnamese used the new term only when discussing something in English with a U.S. official. In fact, they soon even dropped the word "rural," which left simply the Ministry of Construction or Bo Xay Dung. Nor did Lodge's semantic acrobatics impress many Americans, as the term "pacification" continued to be used almost exclusively in conversation.[7]

Another matter involving both terminology and policy highlighted the differing attitudes held by the Americans and South Vietnamese regarding the pacification campaign. For some time, many Americans in Vietnam, John Paul Vann among them, had been urging that the GVN undertake policies designed to split off non-Communist elements of the NLF from their associations with the Party. One method urged was a more comprehensive amnesty plan. For many years, the GVN had operated the Chieu Hoi ("Open Arms") Program, which promised amnesty to anyone voluntarily defecting from the NLF. Rarely were any of these "ralliers," the term applied to those surrendering, in high-level positions within the NLF. But the

Americans wished to entice influential revolutionaries, presumed to be discontented with the methods of the Party, into active support of the GVN. It was hoped this could be achieved through a program of "national reconciliation," which promised not only amnesty but also a position of suitable responsibility within the GVN or ARVN to those high-level ralliers believed to be genuinely converted. Consequently, due to American urging, the communiqué from the Manila Conference of October 1966 declared the existence of a new "national reconciliation" campaign. Because the GVN was cool toward the whole idea, the communiqué was vague concerning any actual differences between the new program and the already established Chieu Hoi effort. But the GVN actually had no intention of instituting any program resembling that desired by the Americans and was quite content to maintain the long-standing policy of granting amnesty after surrender. Nor was there any intention of employing large numbers of important ralliers within the government apparatus. Therefore, the GVN delayed for three months after promising the Americans that an announcement of the new program would be made internally. When the pronouncement finally came, the new campaign was translated as "national solidarity" rather than "national reconciliation" and signified no change whatsoever in the status quo.[8]

Both these matters concerned much more than semantics. Not every faction in the U.S. hierarchy advocated social revolution; MACV, for instance, was always distant on the matter. However, those that did (if "revolution" was defined in terms of major reform rather than a substantial redistribution of wealth and power) were faced with determined opposition from the GVN. The aim of the Saigon government remained exactly what it had been under Diem: crush the revolution without altering the social and political structure of South Vietnam.

Regardless of the differences between Washington and the GVN, the actual pacification plan drawn up for 1966 was, in most respects, similar to those of preceding years. As usual since Diem's murder, the United States took the lead in planning, and planners once again employed the familiar oil spot concept. Though work was to be continued in hamlets and towns where programs were already under way, the planners decided that over 900 new hamlets were to be pacified and another 1,000 cleared of enemy troops. They renamed the military clearing phase the "peace restoration phase"; after clearing, a hamlet would move to the "new life development phase." During this latter period, GVN personnel would conduct a census, install some sort of government apparatus, spread progovernment propaganda, organize a militia, construct fortifications, and move against the Front political apparatus. Finally, the government would institute various economic programs that would presumably lead to a rise in the standard of living. Hamlets that underwent this process were to be designated New Life hamlets. Once they were completed, government forces would move on and duplicate the process in an ever-widening area.[9] Priority areas continued to be the provinces in Hop Tac, including Hau Nghia, as well as the coastal areas of Binh Dinh and Quang Nam provinces.[10]

The 1966 plan, however, did boast of a new and theoretically vital component—the Revolutionary Development Cadre (RDC). Although cadre teams had been employed during and since the Diem period, their function was paramilitary and administrative, and, in general, their role was very minor. However, in 1965, a locally organized South Vietnamese cadre team of some fifty men came to the attention of the CIA because of its apparent success protecting the government's position in a village of heavily contested Binh Dinh province. The team's organizer and leader, Maj. Nguyen Be, was a former Viet Minh officer, a rare individual in ARVN. He impressed the Americans with his zeal, competence, and honesty. Major Be argued that the GVN must employ the same methods used by the Party to be successful in the countryside, and his cadre team, therefore, had a political emphasis. The members were locally recruited, ideologically anti-Communist, and strictly disciplined. They did their best, although poorly armed, to keep enemy local guerrillas from entering the hamlets in which the team was operating. Team members also assisted the villagers in constructing a fish refrigeration plant. Although propagandizing for the GVN, team members also attempted to side with villagers when confronted with corrupt officials, and their personal behavior and honesty were reported to be exemplary. Above all, the cadre team was to serve, according to Be, as the essential conduit between the government and the people of the countryside. The team would bring the government's message to the people and, in return, present the just grievances of the population to the government. The entire cadre team concept, as Be acknowledged, was patterned after the political cadres system employed so successfully by the party.[11]

Whatever the actual performance of Major Be's little team in Binh Dinh, William Colby and others were enthusiastic and brought the concept to Lodge, who, as might be expected, was equally impressed. Here, after all, were his "precinct workers," presumably capable of dispensing "some socially conscious and attractive ideology, which is susceptible of being carried out." Americans quickly decided to extend Be's cadre team concepts nationwide. They established a training center for Revolutionary Development Cadre teams (RD Cadre) at the seaside resort town of Vung Tau, just outside of Saigon. After the first director of training proved corrupt, Major Be was put in direct charge of the training center, and the overall program was the responsibility of General Thang and MORD. General Thang planned to train 5,500 men in each fifteen-week course, with the aim of having 19,000 cadre members in the field by the end of the year.[12]

For a while, U.S. officialdom warmly embraced the RD Cadre team concept. The program was a primary topic of conversation at Honolulu. In April 1966, after his first trip to Vietnam, Komer reported to Johnson that the cadre program, although it had problems, was "the most promising approach yet developed." Komer was so enthusiastic that he wished to build an additional large training center that would double the number of men trained. This plan, however, did not prove feasible and was dropped. A report prepared for Ambassador Porter in April 1966, which was quite gloomy in most respects, spoke optimistically of the RD Cadre and described the team concept as "the basis of the present pacification program."[13]

In theory, the RD Cadre Program was unique because it promised to address the most serious problem faced by the GVN: lack of support in the countryside. Every other component of the pacification program was aimed either at direct repression of revolutionary forces or at raising the material standard of living without changing the political status quo. The RD Cadre Program, however, might become a vehicle for grassroots political reform and a catalyst for genuine political commitment on the part of the rural population. To be sure, the cadres had a military and intelligence function. Organized into teams of 59 men, 41 of the members had the task of providing hamlet security and eliminating the Party's political apparatus. Two men were to specialize in military intelligence and psychological warfare. The remainder of the team was supposed to assist villagers in the organization of local government, dispense agricultural information, and promote public health. Team members were instructed to wear peasant clothes and to live and eat with the villagers.[14] Four principles were to guide team members:

1. The cadre were to be the link between the people and the government of Vietnam.
2. The people were the main force, and the cadre were to be their guides.
3. The old life was to be destroyed, and, in its place, a new life was to be created. The result of the creation of a new life would be the New Life Hamlet.
4. The cadre were guided by the Ministry of Revolutionary Development's policy and doctrine and by the people's will.[15]

In addition to these principles, the RD Cadre teams were to act in accordance with 11 criteria, consisting of 98 works. The 11 criteria were listed in order of priority. The first priority, understandably, was the "Annihilation of the Communist Underground Cadres." The second criteria, however, had an aim unique in the pacification program. Entitled "Annihilation of the Wicked Village Dignitaries," this criteria instructed team members to investigate corrupt officials and forward their information to Saigon, where action against dishonest functionaries would presumably be taken.[16] It is easy to understand why many Americans were enthusiastic about the RD Cadre Program. On paper, it looked like what many of them had long been seeking—a program manned by Vietnamese themselves that promised to pressure the enemy political apparatus, provide additional security, and, just as important, bind the people and government together through an honest and responsive local administration.

There were other reasons for high hopes in U.S. circles. The newly promoted Colonel Be at Vung Tau was an honest and thoughtful figure. Many Americans were openly or secretly fascinated by the techniques employed by the Party, and Colonel Be was impressive because of his understanding of the enemy's strategy and his attempts to emulate it. Hence,

Colonel Be became a "VIP" and received many important American visitors at Vung Tau, where they would witness inspiring ceremonies. On one notable occasion, Colonel Be gave Vice President Hubert Humphrey a pointed lecture on corruption in the GVN, which was at variance with the "party line" coming from MACV and the embassy.[17]

Yet, there were problems from the outset. Because the program was so quickly expanded, training periods lasted only ten weeks. Although Be wished to recruit team members locally, this proved impossible; consequently, most of the cadres were from urban areas. Because the cadres received a draft exemption, many volunteered for less than patriotic motives. More importantly, as Be himself stressed, the RD Cadre Program could not fulfill its ambitious aims unless real power was actually delegated to the villages and hamlets that the teams were supposed to transform. Considering the makeup of the GVN, this delegation of power was unlikely from the outset and, in fact, never took place.

The U.S. Army and the Village War

As everyone recognized, however, neither the RD Cadre Program nor any other component of the pacification campaign could begin to function until enemy troops were cleared out of targeted villages and some sort of basic security was established during the daylight. As already shown, this was an especially acute and difficult problem in Hau Nghia province. According to 25th Division records, GVN control of the province "extended only to the maximum range of supporting weapons located in the Vietnamese military installations immediately surrounding the four district capitals and the province capital."[18]

Yet, this "control" was conceded by American officers to be tenuous even in daylight. Enemy forces were capable of harassing any location in the province and frequently did so. The ARVN 25th Division headquarters at Duc Hoa received particular attention from enemy snipers. Two militia outposts in Cu Chi district were described as "little more than prisons in basically VC controlled hamlets."[19] Road mining and ambushes of both military and civilian traffic were common.

Ollie Davidson, a young civilian assigned to the Hau Nghia advisory team to work in Trang Bang district, arrived in Hau Nghia in late May 1966. As he later recalled, the enemy held all of the off-road hamlets in the province. Travel was possible only in small convoys and only before 4:00 P.M., and the road between Cu Chi and Bao Trai was particularly dangerous. According to Davidson, everyone—military and civilian alike—went armed.[20] The dismal situation in Hau Nghia was well known in higher circles. Lodge considered Hau Nghia to be the worst province in Vietnam from the point of view of the government.

With GVN forces so hard pressed, the U.S. 25th Division was the major asset available to the allies at this stage of the war for a resumption of the battle for the control of Hau Nghia, just as it was the major asset employed in the campaign against organized revolutionary military units. Although every U.S. division was concerned with the pacification campaign to one degree or another, the officers of the 25th were concerned with the problems involved to a degree unequaled in the army. There were several reasons for the high degree of pacification activity on the part of the Tropic Lightning Division. In the first place, compared to units fighting in the Central Highlands or near the DMZ, the 25th was not faced, in the early stages of the war, with quite the same degree of threat from enemy main force battalions, although, as recounted in Chapter 4, the division attempted engagement at every opportunity. Second, population density in Hau Nghia was quite high. Basic military matters, such as securing the base camp and main lines of communication, made participation in the village war unavoidable.

In addition, General Weyand believed that the pacification campaign would ultimately be crucial in determining the outcome or at least duration of the conflict. He had prepared the 25th in Hawaii for "area security" counterinsurgency tactics, and it is unlikely that any army units were as well prepared for service in Vietnam. After the war, Gen. Bruce Palmer contrasted Weyand, an advocate of area security, with William DePuy, commander of the 1st Division and Westmoreland's former deputy, who was an advocate of the big-unit war. The 1st and 25th Divisions were neighbors in Vietnam, and differences in approach, combined with a competition for resources, led to some bitter disputes between officers of these famous units. Many 25th Division officers, for instance, were convinced that DePuy had Westmoreland's ear and used it to gain military assets and publicity.[21] Whatever the merit of these convictions, Americans working with the pacification program found Weyand very cooperative.[22]

Furthermore, General Westmoreland had his eye on Hau Nghia. In April 1966, he commissioned a MACV staff study to make recommendations on U.S. policy toward ARVN units that were found to be particularly ineffective. The study concentrated on the ARVN 5th and 25th Divisions and recommended several strong actions, including breaking up the defective units. This was too much for Westmoreland, but he did authorize greater association between the Tropic Lightning Division and the ARVN 25th and agree to consider a greater role for U.S. troops in pacification duties in Hau Nghia.[23] Lastly, the summer monsoon comes to the upper Mekong Delta approximately between May and October. During this period of heavy rainfall, much of the terrain is submerged. Therefore, large-scale, sustained operations for either side were extremely difficult at this time of year. Pacification operations, however, being localized and smaller in scale than most search and destroy missions, were still feasible and were an attractive alternative to inactivity.

As soon as the 25th Division had established its base camp at Cu Chi, Weyand began preparations for the village war. Informally, he instructed the 1st/5th Mechanized Battalion to do what was possible to develop hamlet security in Cu Chi and Trang Bang districts. One battalion of the *Wolfhounds* (1st/27th) was assigned similar duties in Duc Hoa, the other (2d/27th) in Duc Hue. The first major attempt to expand the area under some sort of government control in Hau Nghia province began in late April 1966. Code-named Operation MAILI, the 1st Battalion, 27th Infantry (*Wolfhounds*) was ordered to secure the hamlets in and around Duc Lap village (the same area, coincidentally, examined in Chapter 2 because of a 1964 Rand Corporation study). A later analysis of 25th Division duties in Hau Nghia gave a good summary of the situation prior to MAILI and of the intentions of the operation:

> Provincial Route 8 is the only usable road leading into the province capital from Saigon via Route 1 through Cu Chi. It was essential that the hamlets along this road be secured in order to insure the maintenance and security of this key route. Route 8 also cuts across a major Viet Cong supply and communication corridor leading from Long An province to VC base areas in Tay Ninh and Binh Duong provinces. Since October 1965, ARVN forces had been repeatedly attacked and driven away from their positions along the route by the Viet Cong. The result had been that the previously thriving hamlets had been almost completely evacuated by the residents. The road had been mined or interdicted with roadblocks almost daily during the seven months prior to MAILI, making travel difficult and hazardous. The hamlets in the area up to 6 kilometers to the northwest and southeast of the road had been unmolested sanctuaries for Viet Cong local guerrillas for months. Except during an occasional ineffective sweep by ARVN forces stationed at Bao Trai, the people of these hamlets had experienced no contact with the GVN. Although not considered to be active Viet Cong sympathizers, they nevertheless had been forced to make accommodations with the VC in order to survive.[24]

MAILI got under way on 27 April. On each day for the next two weeks, American troops cleared part or all of a hamlet in the operational area. Once these were "secure," GVN officials inserted a Vietnamese "Go Team," consisting of National Police, psychological warfare troops, intelligence troops, and medical personnel. Police searched each dwelling, checked credentials, and dispensed propaganda. The American Duc Hoa district advisor accompanied the "Go Team" to provide liaison with 25th Division forces. Vietnamese "Counter Terror" troops, later renamed the Provincial Reconnaissance Units (PRU), helped U.S. troops establish ambushes. On five occasions, battalions of the ARVN 25th joined in operations. Security was sufficient to allow the construction of a new militia outpost at Duc Hanh B, a hamlet directly astride Route 8. American and South Vietnamese personnel conducted several hundred MEDCAPs (Medical Civic Action Programs). In addition, U.S. troops distributed "Helping Hands" kits, containing clothing, soap, candy, and other small items, to hundreds of villagers. This latter program was unique to the 25th and was funded by the State of Hawaii.[25]

Throughout MAILI, American soldiers were on the alert for combat. U.S. intelligence believed that every hamlet in Duc Lap had some local guerrillas. Additionally, it was known that three Front main and local force battalions had been operating nearby during April. In one sweep, American soldiers stumbled into a hastily abandoned enemy field kitchen, estimated to have been serving breakfast to approximately 100 men. Every day and night,

American troops conducted sweeps, patrols, and ambushes. Normally there was no contact whatsoever, although the men found and destroyed over 200 bunkers, many of them very elaborate. Occasionally, American forces suffered mortar attacks or sniping, and soldiers discovered and disarmed scores of crude but effective mines and booby traps, some very powerful. Some of the mines, however, did their gruesome job, accounting for the majority of the 22 men wounded during MAILI.

Yet, even during relatively quiet operations such as MAILI, anxious moments arose. Just after midnight on 5 May, elements of an American company established an ambush. Front forces, consisting of two main force and one local force platoon (approximately 50–75 men), according to later estimates, located the American position. A brief exchange began but quickly ended when the Americans detonated deadly claymore mines. An hour later, however, the Front units assaulted the American ambush from the northeast, southwest, and southeast. A vicious firefight ensued and lasted for an hour. American troops brought in artillery, and reinforcements hurried to the scene. By the time the enemy had withdrawn, 5 American soldiers had been killed and 5 people were wounded, one of whom was a Vietnamese guide. Americans claimed to have killed 31 enemy soldiers.[26] The 5 dead were the only Americans killed during MAILI.

After two weeks, MAILI was concluded and the *Wolfhounds* returned to Cu Chi. It is of some interest to take a brief look at what the Americans thought had been accomplished by this operation. Interestingly, the division did not emphasize the 47 enemy claimed to have been killed and the 21 "Viet Cong suspects" captured, even though those were very respectable totals for a battalion-level operation of any type. Rather, U.S. officers believed that the most significant result was that the Front had been denied at least the outward vestiges of control over an important area for a limited time. They claimed that MAILI had discredited the revolution in the eyes of the villagers and that the operation had proved that American soldiers "contrary to Viet Cong propaganda, are not unfeeling, blood-thirsty brutes." In addition, officers were impressed by the fact that one of the hamlets, Duc Hanh B, had tripled in population during the operation and that commerce had quickened. Furthermore, the Americans claimed that the GVN had extended its influence into each of the hamlets in the operational area, pointedly remarking that many of these hamlets had not been ventured into by government officials for years. They were also impressed by the "Go Team" and with the general level of effectiveness of joint American-Vietnamese operations. Lastly, they were pleased with the level of coordination between division forces and the district advisory team.[27]

It is difficult to assess the validity of any of these claims. Certainly the *Wolfhounds* had a very difficult assignment. Most of Duc Lap had been under revolutionary control for many years, and the Party constantly stressed the "hate Americans" theme. It should also be recalled that, in 1964, the village chief told Michael Pearce, the Rand researcher, that 70 percent of the villagers of Duc Lap supported the Front, 30 percent were neutral, and only 1 percent sided openly with the government. Considering the course of events in Hau Nghia in the two years since the Rand study, there is no reason to assume that popular attitudes had changed in favor of the government during that period—the reverse is much more likely. The 25th Division pacification report said nothing about this, although the after action report on MAILI recorded that at least one American ambush had been compromised by the villagers. The report also detailed the total failure of American ambushes to surprise the enemy, despite the fact that sizable enemy units were operating in the direct vicinity. The tactical victory, if losing 5 men should be considered a victory, happened during a firefight started by the Front.

The perceived improvement at Duc Hanh B may well have been an illusion or at least partially so. Although province reports do verify that a considerable increase of population did, indeed, take place, it did not necessarily follow, as claimed by the 25th Division, that this indicated a desire to live under the GVN. It was certainly possible that many of people who returned to Duc Hanh B had grown disillusioned with the Party and genuinely wished to live under the GVN, but it is also reasonable to assume that many villagers believed that Duc Hanh B would be one of the few places in the operational area relatively safe from potentially violent U.S. military operations. There is another reason to doubt that the population shift in Duc Lap had much to do with any great swell of sympathy toward the GVN: The Americans made absolutely no claim that they had harmed the Party apparatus in Duc Hanh B or any other hamlet in the least. In addition, the local enemy military units were still completely intact. Consequently, anyone fleeing to Duc Hanh B for political reasons would be little safer there from possible retaliation than in any other hamlet of Duc Lap. On the other hand, the new militia post was garrisoned, and military traffic during daylight between Bao Trai, less than two miles from Duc Lap, and Cu Chi greatly increased throughout 1966, indicating that the GVN had established some outward manifestation of a presence. Considering the fact that the GVN had been completely expelled from Duc Lap, it is understandable that the situation after MAILI was considered "progress" by the Americans.

Whatever the actual impact of MAILI, Front forces wasted no time making an impressive show of force. As previously noted, by the time of U.S. intervention in Hau Nghia, NLF forces had succeeded in virtually isolating Bao Trai and its garrison that was principally made up of the 49th ARVN Regiment. Supply to the surviving GVN outposts in the immediate area was possible only through the use of heavily escorted truck convoys, which were continually harassed and ambushed. Communications between Bao Trai and Hiep Hoa, the new capital of Duc Hue district (the original capital west of the Vam Co River had been abandoned the previous year) were particularly bad. Goaded by the Americans, the 49th ARVN made several attempts during May to reestablish communications between the two towns and to clear the east bank of the Vam Co in the Hiep Hoa area. In response to these ARVN thrusts, Front units of undetermined size stormed Hiep Hoa on the night of 26 May. Holding the town for hours, the Front captured many weapons, shattered the local militia, and destroyed a small GVN naval unit on the river. The Hiep Hoa sugar mill, the only real industrial facility in the province, was occupied. More ominously, scores of government officials or sympathizers were kidnapped or killed outright. According to U.S. officers, "by storming the district capital and site of Hau Nghia's only significant industry the VC were able to effectively demonstrate their mastery over Hau Nghia's political and economic life."[28]

Faced with a situation that was still deteriorating, as the assault on Hiep Hoa graphically illustrated, the 25th Division quickened the pace of pacification operations. One battalion spent the month of June operating near Trang Bang district town. Another was sent to the area between Duc Hoa district town and Bao Trai. Yet a third operated between Bao Trai and Hiep Hoa. All of these operations resembled MAILI. American soldiers destroyed bunkers, sprang an occasional ambush, captured rice and weapons, carried out psychological warfare, and did good deeds in the villages. American units cooperated with ARVN and GVN "Go Teams." Officers involved claimed that, because of these operations, U.S. troops became increasingly adept at utilizing timely intelligence as they grew more familiar with the area and improved liaison with GVN forces. No doubt, there was some validity to this claim for the number of enemy prisoners of war and suspects captured was far higher than the number claimed to have been killed. These operations were widely publicized, and one received a visit by General Thieu and General Weyand; Thieu was made an "honorary *Wolfhound.*"[29]

All these operations highlighted a strange new U.S. tactic, called the "County Fair." These exercises were all nearly identical. American and Vietnamese units would surround a targeted hamlet as secretly as possible during the early morning. At first light, soldiers would sweep through the hamlet, search "hooches," check identification cards, and cart off any draft-age males or other suspicious figures. Until this point, a "County Fair" was indistinguishable from a normal hamlet sweep. These, however, included efforts to charm the villagers. After the hamlet was searched, the 25th Division band would give a concert, on one occasion at the unlikely hour of 7:30 A.M. The province chief or some other high official would give a speech, and medical personnel would then conduct MEDCAPs and dispense "Helping Hand" packages. Finally, cooks from the 25th Division would make lunch for the entire hamlet.

Again, it is difficult to judge the effectiveness of the coercive aspect of this tactic. U.S. officers claimed that timely intelligence was gathered, although the number of suspects apprehended was never large. Americans furthermore claimed that the various festivities improved relations between U.S. soldiers and the local population, though one observer noted that the villagers seemed somewhat bewildered by the affair.[30] A differing view was given by two American relief workers who termed the concept a "ludicrous example of insensitivity" toward Vietnamese culture. They also repeated the opinion of one villager present during a "County Fair" in another province of Vietnam: "How would you feel," one said, "if a bunch of burly foreigners invaded your hamlet, took away your men, and played weird foreign music to 'entertain you'?"[31] Lt. Col. Andrew Rutherford, the American province senior advisor in Hau Nghia from June 1966 through April 1967, witnessed a few of these affairs and later described them as "ham-handed and clumsy attempts to win over the people." Apparently, 25th Division officers concurred with Rutherford's estimate. The sweeps continued throughout the war, but after late 1966, the band and cooks stayed home.

From the U.S. point of view, violence was low-level. As usual, mines were the major nemesis of the infantrymen and accounted for most of the wounded. On the night of 28 June, however, the 25th Division experienced one of its harshest moments of the entire war. As was done every night, several ambushes were set by U.S. patrols. One 12-man patrol near the Vam Co River was assaulted in the morning by a mixed formation of local guerrillas and local force soldiers. Although firing could be easily heard at the battalion command post, radio communications were severed immediately, thus preventing accurate artillery fire and ground reinforcement. The patrol was annihilated.[32]

Overall, both the leading officers of the 25th Division and the U.S. advisory team in Hau Nghia claimed to have been pleased with the results of the division's pacification effort. In reference to MAILI-type operations, the division reported:

Although the operations are not spectacular by the standard of VC body count, this combined effort is highly successful. In one such operation, a hamlet of ten families became one of thirty families. Such action as this disrupts and eventually destroys the VC infrastructure, while at the same time it adds to the prestige and respect of all participants.[33]

A later assessment, in reference to all four pacification operations in Hau Nghia, was even more optimistic:

Through pacification efforts such as those discussed above lies perhaps the most logical approach to the MACV "Hearts and Minds Program." Although results are never dramatic and occasional reversals are to be expected, these operations are critical to ultimate victory of ARVN and FWMAF (Free World Military Armed Forces) in South Vietnam. VC main forces and their base areas must obviously be constantly sought and destroyed concurrent with these pacification efforts in order to prevent these forces from exerting their influence in the pacified area. With proper distribution of military forces and assets, pacification and search and destroy operations can be undertaken simultaneously to win the war on both fronts.[34]

Lieutenant Colonel Rutherford, the PSA, agreed with these assessments, noting that ARVN's performance had increasingly shown "flexibility and aggressiveness." He further claimed that "the close and continuous contact between the US and ARVN forces through daily staff and commanders' meetings has infused new confidence in the Vietnamese, enhanced mutual confidence and facilitated a rapid exchange of information."[35]

During the summer and fall of 1966, the 25th Division continued to operate heavily in Hau Nghia. All of the operations were labeled "search and destroy," but many closely resembled the four pacification efforts just described. Although the Ho Bo and Boi Loi Woods were the main theaters, nearly every area of the province was visited at least once by American combat troops. In addition to the many search and destroy-pacification operations, the division employed other tactics. One widely used technique was called "Roadrunner." The object of this type of exercise was to demonstrate the ability of U.S. units to go where they wished by sending heavily armed task forces over major and secondary roads, regardless of mines and obstacles. Officers hoped Roadrunners would have a psychological effect on friends and enemies alike as a demonstration of American resolve and military power.[36]

Another technique employed, called "Checkmate," was designed to deny the use of provincial roads to the enemy by establishing random checkpoints manned by American and Vietnamese personnel. Frequently used, Checkmates rarely succeeded, although ARVN deserters were often apprehended. For instance, during the August to October quarter, soldiers conducted 26 Checkmates, searching of over 2,800 vehicles and over 28,000 people. They claimed to have captured 1 enemy, along with 21 "suspects."[37]

Road clearance, however, was, in theory, a job for ARVN and the GVN militia. It was a tedious, frustrating, and frequently dangerous mission. John Pancrazio, a member of the 4-man Cu Chi district advisory team in 1966, later recalled the cycle he witnessed while working with the militia:

> Road clearance was almost a game. The VC would block the roads and booby-trap the roadblocks, and we would go out at daylight and blow up the booby-traps and clear the road and repeat these actions time after time. Once in a while, the VC would spring an ambush just to keep it interesting, and we would try to figure out where they were going to establish their next roadblock and set up an ambush at night to try and foil it. On those occasions when they attacked our compound, we would head for the bunkers. . . . weather the attack, beat it back, stay on alert for the rest of the night, and start the entire cycle of road clearance again at dawn. On many occasions, I had conversations with villagers during the daylight hours and found them dead in the wires following an attack that night.

U.S. participation in psychological warfare for the provinces near Saigon was handled by specialists at II Field Force. The 25th Division also had a small "psywar" team. The major effort was a lavish program of leaflet drops. During the same August to October quarter, II Field Force dropped or otherwise distributed 160 million leaflets in the provinces around Saigon. The major theme stressed in these leaflets was "surrender or die." They also used the "sweet approach," emphasizing the good qualities of the GVN along with appeals to the homesick. A leaflet pertaining directly to 25th

Division activities is a good example of the latter appeal, although the threatening undertones should be noticed:

[English Translation: Side 1] The U.S. soldiers of the 25th Infantry Division have been in your area making it safe by clearing the area of the VC. You have only seen a small part of our massive strength. This mighty force, known the world over, stands ready to make your life safe. [Side 2] Your friends, the U.S. soldiers of the 25th Infantry Division, are here to help you. We will give you medical assistance when you need it. We can build schools, bridges, and roads to make life easier for you. Help us together to defeat the VC forever.[38]

The 25th Division also attempted to capitalize on recent events for propaganda purposes. A military victory or, better yet, a Front atrocity was a good subject for propaganda leaflets and posters. On one occasion in 1967, a civilian bus on the way to Saigon hit a mine near Trang Bang, killing some thirty people, and doctors at the 25th Division hospital treated the survivors. Division psychological warfare officers put together a propaganda campaign stressing Front cruelty and American humanitarianism. Perhaps as a result, mine incidents along that stretch of road declined greatly for several months.

Continued American Frustrations

Although the power of the 25th Division was sufficient to prevent the destruction of the GVN's position in Hau Nghia province, the overall U.S. effort was seriously hampered by a number of factors. In the first place, the American pacification effort in Hau Nghia was very poorly organized at this stage of the war. Davidson later recalled that, when he arrived in Hau Nghia in mid-1966, there was no definition of "pacification," nor any centralization of effort. The various representatives of MACV, AID, the Office of Civil Operations, and CIA were constantly involved with personal and interagency battles, and each attempted to establish a personal relationship with the Hau Nghia province chief. Furthermore, Davidson recalled,

Allocation of resources was always poor and badly utilized. AID resources (for Hau Nghia) were stolen, disappeared, never arrived, and then misused when we received them. Since resources were only allotted for certain things, we traded one commodity for something we could not afford to buy but vitally needed for some project.[39]

On his own initiative, Davidson established a warehouse system for commodities he was responsible for, to protect them from the Vietnamese and other U.S. agencies.[40] There is no reason to doubt any of this testimony for the confusion in the pacification effort was well known in both Saigon and Washington and led to the various reorganizational schemes mentioned earlier in this chapter.

Secondly, relations between the U.S. advisors and the Vietnamese authorities were often very difficult. Cultural differences naturally caused problems, and language difficulties were particularly vexing. (Although Vietnamese has a Roman alphabet, it is extremely difficult to learn.) Davidson recalled that only one member of the Hau Nghia advisory team that he was acquainted with spoke Vietnamese.[41] As time went on, more and more Americans received language training. One officer who went through such training admitted that, though capable of basic communication, he was unable to understand the idiom used by the peasants. He also added that other Americans were in awe of his apparent ability and considered him fluent, and he maintained that only a handful of Americans in all of Vietnam were truly fluent in Vietnamese. This testimony has the ring of truth. Therefore, communication was almost always conducted through Vietnamese interpreters who, especially at the lower levels, were frequently incompetent. When the message was clear, interpreters also frequently changed the content of communications to keep those involved happy and to prevent anyone from "losing face."

More basic to the problem of difficult relations between American and Vietnamese personnel, however, was the ambiguous position of the U.S. advisor. As mentioned earlier, these advisors were urged to develop "rapport" with their "counterparts." In theory, close personal relationships would develop, leading to the creation of a bicultural brotherhood of warriors dedicated to a common cause. Each side would learn to appreciate the unique strengths and capabilities of the other, and both would profit. Most of this was rubbish, of course. Many advisors genuinely admired Vietnamese culture, and some formed personal relationships of great depth and enduring value. Most were certainly far more sensitive to the fearful plight of the civilian population than were American soldiers. Nevertheless, many advisors grew contemptuous of the corruption and inefficiency of GVN officials. In their turn, the urban Vietnamese elite, the group from which most officers and officials came, considered Americans to be uncultured boors who had to be tolerated but were best kept at a distance. Socially, the two groups, by and large, kept apart, despite the fact that the advisory compounds at province or district were usually very close to the respective GVN headquarters. Exceptions abounded, but the fusion of skills and emotions generally remained a chimera.

Corruption and inefficiency, always linked, caused more problems than anything else. In training, advisors were cautioned that actions taken by local officials, which might seem incomprehensible, were often only the "Vietnamese way." On the other hand, it was part of the advisor's duty to help rationalize and energize the Vietnamese war effort. Consequently, they were instructed to identify individual officials who, for one reason or another, were hampering progress. The monthly Hau Nghia province reports and OCO/CORDS documents were filled with examples of U.S. advisors trying to remove various Vietnamese officials. For instance, Lieutenant Colonel Rutherford had a long running feud in 1966 with the Vietnamese official in charge of public works and vigorously sought his removal. Finally, in November, the offending official was apparently removed. The PSA reported, "His loss will be the province's gain."[42] The next month, however, this official was back at work, and Rutherford was again forced to plead to the province chief that Saigon consider action. There is no way to ascertain whether the PSA was correct in his assessment. Often, complaints against officials concerning incompetence or corruption were based on rumor, and, on many occasions, an individual Vietnamese might be vilified by one American advisor and praised by another. Therefore, no attempt will be made here to detail these various conflicts or determine the validity of U.S. complaints. It is sufficient to note that hardly a month went by in Hau Nghia, throughout the war, without a member of the advisory team attempting to initiate some type of action against one or more Vietnamese officials. Sometimes they succeeded, although usually they did not. The job of advisor was a frustrating one, especially so because advisors were vulnerable to manipulation in Vietnamese personal rivalries.

The military advisor was in an equally sensitive position. In many respects, it was a more difficult position for the actual responsibility for command in the field was, on occasion, unclear. A very good example of the problems facing the military advisors was the "Chinh-Hunnicutt affair." As noted in Chapter 3, Gen. Phan Troung Chinh, commander of the ARVN 25th Division that was headquartered at Duc Hoa district town, was a controversial officer. Known for his intelligence and skill as a poet, Chinh had important friends higher up the chain of command. MACV, however, considered Chinh a weak and hesitant combat commander. Some Americans thought he was so bad that he must have been an agent for the Front. Colonel Hunnicutt, the senior advisor for the ARVN 25th, was described in the *Pentagon Papers* as "a dynamic, competent officer assigned to improve effectiveness." Relations between the two men were evidently not good. Finally, Chinh, in an order of the day, accused Hunnicutt of seeking his removal and that of other Vietnamese officers, of bypassing the chain of command, and of destroying the "spirit of cooperation between Americans and Vietnamese." The press got wind of the story, and articles were written arguing that this feud challenged the entire position of the U.S. advisory effort. Westmoreland quickly moved to conciliate the Vietnamese. Chinh apologized for the order of the day and published a memorandum stating that no attempt had been made to disparage the advisory effort and that all was forgiven. Hunnicutt rotated home, and the dispute was over. Shortly thereafter, MACV distributed a new pamphlet for advisors, urging them to understand Vietnamese ethnocentrism and to deal with Vietnamese culture on its own terms.[43] None of this would have amused the American soldiers who were fighting along the Vam Co Dong because, the soldiers believed, the ARVN 25th was unable to fulfill its mission.

Nor did the American advisors always see eye to eye with the command of the Tropic Lightning Division. Because of the manpower and resources available to the 25th, the division had a great deal of "clout" in the affairs of Hau Nghia. Ollie Davidson remarked that "division was King—when they said jump, you jump."[44] The advisors did not always jump quickly enough. Although the Hau Nghia advisory team was quick to praise the 25th Division, problems did come up. Lieutenant Colonel Rutherford's tour ended early because of disputes with the 25th over support for the pacification program. As shall be seen, two other PSAs suffered the same fate later in the war.[45]

Despite these problems, the situation in Hau Nghia at the end of 1966, in American eyes, appeared to have improved in some respects. The number of ralliers under the Chieu Hoi Program climbed steadily throughout the year. By year's end, 529 Hoi Chanh (the name given individual ralliers) had surrendered in Hau Nghia. This was a large number and pleased the advisors because it was more than double the number they had expected for the year.[46] However, they recognized that this number was less significant than it might have appeared. In the first place, only a handful of the Hoi Chanh were Party members, and none of these held positions of authority. Despite bounties offered for weapons, only a handful were recovered. The overwhelming majority of the Hoi Chanh were people conscripted into service by the Front for the least important tasks, such as porters. Many were nothing more than members of one Front organization or another. In short, the program had almost no appeal to the dedicated political cadres or armed guerrillas important to the revolution. Second, interrogations revealed that neither allied propaganda nor any latent desire to live under the GVN were determining factors in the choice to rally. Rather, the most vital reasons, in order of importance, were (1) constant hardship and too much time spent in holes, (2) fear of death, (3) hard work for little or no pay, (4) homesickness, (5) lack of food and (6) false promises by Party cadres concerning future compensation. Interrogations further revealed the millions of leaflets distributed had little impact because many ralliers were semi- or totally illiterate. Intelligence officers also learned that, on occasion, Front troops carried Chieu Hoi leaflets with them so they could, if necessary, pretend to rally rather than be captured and imprisoned. Some officers referred to the program as "VC R&R" (rest and recreation).[47] Third, the number of ralliers was sustained only during periods of heavy fighting on the part of American or ARVN troops; a direct connection, in the opinion of U.S. advisors, existed between intensive American operations and the number of ralliers. For instance, the largest number of ralliers surrendered during August, a month of furious activity within Hau Nghia by the 25th Division. Of the 91 Hoi Chanh in August, 23 were women and children very likely seeking the relative safety of GVN territory, who no doubt represented an insignificant loss from the point of view of the Party.[48] The number of ralliers in November dropped to 23 as the 25th Division prepared for the coming big-unit operations. The PSA also believed this drop was due to better command control by the enemy and to the fact that the less committed had already rallied.[49]

Although the Chieu Hoi Program provided a simple means to implant clandestine agents in GVN territory, the Front was a mass organization and viewed the program as a serious threat. Cadres continually propagandized against it and spread rumors that Hoi Chanh would be tortured and imprisoned. If that failed, the Front treated most ralliers as prodigals and attempted to win them back. If necessary, ralliers were simply conscripted again and watched more closely. An indoctrination cadre serving in Duc Hue described the process:

> The hardest cases were the soldiers who gave up their weapons and defected, usually during a move. They went back to their villages and told everyone why they had deserted. They made people lose their faith in the Front. We didn't bother them for a time, then we sent them to a reeducation session. Depending on the results of reeducation, they would be assigned to the main force, the guerrilla force, or the laborers' organization. These laborers were assigned to work in fighting areas and each working period lasted for three to six months. Moreover, they were not fed by the Front and had to carry their food with them.[50]

This leniency reflected the difference between the Vietnamese and American attitudes toward treason or betrayal. The struggle was long and tiring. Most families, in addition, had members on both sides of the conflict, adding a strange and complex personal chemistry to the war that continually bewildered Americans. The NLF naturally welcomed GVN defectors and spent much effort proselytizing government forces. By the same token, just as the Front was careful with ralliers, the GVN treated ARVN deserters very mildly. However, behavior acceptable for the masses was strictly forbidden for cadres, and any cadre who defected was a prime candidate for assassination. In extreme cases, "revolutionary justice" included killing the offender's family, as well.

American advisors were also pleased by another development. As mentioned earlier, the GVN militia in Hau Nghia was in a decrepit state until the deployment of the Tropic Lightning Division. By mid-1966, however, recruitment for the Regional and Popular Forces (RF/PF) was once again under way. In July, 32 soldiers were recruited for the militia, and, by December, the number was up to 360. Overall, during the July to December 1966 period, the Hau Nghia advisory team claimed that 1,114 men had been recruited for the RF/PF.[51] In the context of 1966, little was expected and little was achieved in operational terms by the militia. Nevertheless, the militia expansion program would ultimately cause serious problems for the Front.

Although the GVN was making some progress in increasing numerical strength, the much-vaunted RD Cadre Program foundered in Hau Nghia during 1966. By midyear, there were three 59-man teams working in various hamlets. The number rose to five in October.[52] Despite the fact that the RD Cadre Program was run by the Americans (first by the CIA and later by CORDS), the advisory team in Hau Nghia never had any reason to highly value efforts on the part of the cadre teams. Davidson recalled that the cadres came from areas outside the province and that many Americans considered them little better than draft dodgers.[53] Furthermore, because the RD Cadre Program was identified with the Americans, Vietnamese officials gave it little or no support. On some occasions, personal rivalries sprang up between the team leaders and the district chiefs.[54] American advisors believed that the cadre teams were failing to accomplish any of their important objectives, except for census-taking. In September, the PSA complained: "The RD Cadre are still not accomplishing their intended mission, particularly in the destruction of the Communist infrastructure. This is the primary reason for the lack of achievement in hamlet pacification."[55] In fairness to the RD Cadre, it should be pointed out that "neutralizing" the local political apparatus of the NLF was nearly an impossible task in 1966. Some enemy cadres were in "deep cover" and therefore extremely difficult to identify. Those revolutionary cadres who functioned openly simply left their hamlets at the approach of allied force and retreated to hamlets controlled by the Front (a category that still included a majority of the hamlets off the roads) or went into hiding, guarded by local guerrillas. They returned when they wished at night or even during daylight. In spite of American urging, the cadre teams rarely spent the night in their hamlets, contending that the security situation made this impossible. One group, according to the advisors, did not spend a single night in their assigned hamlet during the four months of their activity. The Americans claimed, in addition, that "VC harassment has been from negligible to non-existent."[56] This last claim was something of an exaggeration for two attacks on team members caused the death of two cadres in August and three in September. However, the American advisors attributed the success of the September attack to a failure by the cadre team to construct their assigned local defenses.[57] Hence, if U.S. reports are at all accurate, the cadre teams were doing little to attack the enemy political apparatus or improve local security. Nor were there any indications that the RD Cadre Program was doing anything to bring the population and the government closer together. The opposite may have been the case, as the following account indicates:

> During weekly visits to the new cadre groups, there was never a time that a total of 59 cadres could be accounted for. . . . Cadres have come up with a "novel idea." In order to maintain sufficient manpower, a group went to a neighboring village, collected all available young men, and set them to work in the target hamlet. There must have been some form of coercion used for, late in the afternoon, several of the laborers bolted and, although fired upon by the RD Cadres, managed to escape. Since the next planned location of the RDC group is the hamlet from which the young men were impressed by the cadres for labor, it is somewhat doubtful that the spirit of camaraderie and mutual understanding, so greatly desired by the ministry, will have much opportunity to flourish.[58]

An earlier report indicated the disappointment on the part of the advisory team concerning the whole RD Cadre Program:

Although group leaders report that 75 percent of the six-point criteria has been met in their hamlets, there is little to indicate that this is true. Until constant, conscientious, and detailed inspection by Vietnamese officials is forthcoming, it is doubtful that there will be much improvement in future reporting periods. . . . If the program was completely under Vietnamese control, GVN officials might be more energetic in improving cadres.[59]

After the war, Lieutenant Colonel Rutherford was even more critical of the RD Cadre Program. He believed that the lack of local recruitment was the most critical failing. Although some of the team leaders were "sincere, real go-getters," most members hated rural life and looked down on villagers. The numerous disputes that arose with the locals and the practice of forcing villagers to work on various projects did more damage than the various bright spots in the effort did good. In a word, Rutherford concluded, the RD Cadre Program was "worthless."[60]

Overall, it can be seen that the pacification campaign waged by the GVN and the U.S. Army in Hau Nghia during 1966 met with decidedly mixed results, especially when considering the very high price paid in terms of blood and treasure. On one hand, the GVN was no longer in danger of being swept from the province altogether. The government was able to exert some sort of presence in areas that it had not dared enter in many years. Heavy military activity on the part of the 25th Division inflicted serious losses on the enemy and, no doubt, made it more difficult for the Front to operate than had been the case a year earlier. In the few areas where a strong government presence was continuous, commerce was beginning to revive as compared to the economic paralysis existing at the beginning of the year (although the effects of this were at least partially offset by a 50 percent inflation rate caused by U.S. intervention and damage done by military operations).[61] Lastly, militia recruitment was again under way.

On the other hand, the Front remained in control of most of the province at night and much of it during daylight. The Party's political apparatus had not been touched. As shown vividly by the occupation of Hiep Hoa in May, Front military units were completely intact and capable of dealing heavy blows, despite the proximity of U.S. troops. This point was made again later in the year. Although they avoided contact during the 25th Division's spring and summer effort in Hau Nghia, Front forces resumed large-scale activity in the winter as U.S. units prepared for their huge dry season search and destroy missions. In November, Front forces overran and destroyed two militia watchtowers.[62] In December, the enemy launched two separate company-sized attacks on Bao Trai that, according to advisors, led the population of the capital to wonder aloud whether ARVN would ever be able to protect them.[63] Ominously, despite heavy losses, the Front was able to keep its forces up to strength through local recruitment. The advisory team reported in December that, in spite of the increase in large-scale enemy activity, there was no evidence "to indicate the presence of nonorganic VC forces operating in Hau Nghia."[64] Nor was the security situation much improved. In October, the advisory team observed that "most of the roads and the areas along them now belong to the government during *daylight hours* (emphasis added). Most of the hamlets away from the road, despite continuing military operations, are contested or belong to the Viet Cong."[65] Lastly, it should be observed that any progress on the government side came not from new ideas or greater energy but rather from the application of military force, mostly American, and other coercive measures. The RD Cadre Program, the only initiative aimed at improving the relations between the rural population and the GVN, foundered badly. None of this augured well for any future revival of the GVN that Americans believed crucial for a successful outcome to the war itself.

Interestingly enough, Ambassador Lodge viewed the situation in Hau Nghia quite differently. In August 1966, he sent a long cable to President Johnson and Secretary Rusk, outlining his assessment of U.S. efforts in Hau Nghia. In this cable, Lodge extolled the efforts of the 25th Division and informed Washington that "it is good to report that many of the things which we used to hope for—and dream about—are taking place. . . . In Hau Nghia today we are winning; they are losing. Our side is clearly coasting along as the Americans say." Although he did admit problem areas, Lodge claimed that 53 percent of the province was under GVN control and that the enemy's share had fallen to 32 percent, a figure that, he added, was still above the national average.[66] In fairness to Lodge, it must be pointed out that he had seen the collapse of the GVN in and around Hau Nghia during earlier years, and anything favorable no doubt looked like great progress. Yet, to validate the figures given—and thus the original assumption that "we are winning"—Lodge would have had to equate any government presence with control. As has been seen, the U.S. advisory team did not make such an assumption.

It is impossible to determine whether the cheerful views of Ambassador Lodge made any impression on President Johnson or other war leaders. Another report, derived partially from Hau Nghia province, may have had influence. In October of 1966, Secretary of Defense Robert McNamara made one of his whirlwind tours to Vietnam. After visiting Saigon and 1st Division Headquarters, he came to Cu Chi. General Weyand and his staff briefed the secretary on the 25th Division's area security operations. Although McNamara noted with displeasure the fact that the 25th had recorded a lower "body count" than had the 1st Division, he claimed to be impressed with Weyand's stress on pacification.[67]

We know now that McNamara's will was steadily beginning to crack. He had already learned to distrust the Pentagon's assessments of both the bombing campaign against North Vietnam and the ground war in the South and was leaning instead on the much more pessimistic analysis coming from the CIA. Nothing he saw in Saigon or Cu Chi could have improved his morale. Immediately upon returning, he prepared a long and important report for President Johnson, concluding that "I see no reasonable way to bring the war to an end soon." The big-unit victories and high body count were the only bright spots, according to McNamara, and they were not enough. His description of the pacification program was very pessimistic; it could just as well have been a description of Hau Nghia province:

Pacification is a bad disappointment. . . . Pacification has, if anything, gone backward. As compared with two, or four, years ago, enemy full-time regional forces and part-time guerrilla forces are larger; attacks, terrorism, and sabotage have increased in scope and intensity . . . we control little, if any, more of the population; the VC political infrastructure thrives in most of the country, continuing to give the enemy his enormous intelligence advantage; full security exists nowhere (not even behind the U.S. Marines' lines and in Saigon); in the countryside, the enemy almost completely controls the night.[68]

McNamara's central recommendation was that U.S. force levels be stabilized, negotiations begun, and all efforts made to prepare the American people for a war of indefinite duration. The political catastrophe in Washington was already beginning to unfold.

As previously indicated, the entire pacification effort received ever-growing attention through 1966 and early 1967. Concern for the "other war" increased even more when the Joint Chiefs of Staff requested troop increases that would have raised force levels to 670,000 U.S. personnel in Vietnam and that would have required the mobilization of reserves. This request was opposed by virtually every group outside the military, primarily on the grounds of domestic politics. Indeed, during this period, there was a growing fear throughout the administration that public approval of the war was waning and that steps would have to be taken to keep the blood tax and financial costs as low as possible as the only way to convince Hanoi that the United States was determined to persevere. Within this political context, it grew fashionable to argue that the resources already allotted were adequate if the pacification campaign could be made to succeed. The stakes involved with the pacification campaign were probably best put by Alain Enthoven, assistant secretary of defense and head of systems analysis, in a memo to McNamara dated 1 May 1967:

As MACV himself said before the Congress, the enemy "believes our Achilles' heel is our resolve." They believe that public opinion in the United States will eventually force our retirement. And they could be right. As for our own goals, I see only one way of establishing stability in Vietnam. We must match the nationalism we see in the North with an equally strong and patient one in the South. No matter what military success we may achieve, if we leave before that is done, there can be no stability, and we will have lost everything we have invested in South Vietnam. Indeed we will jeopardize much of the general stability in the world which we bought at the price of the Korean War. Therefore, I see this war as a race between, on the one hand, the development of a viable South Vietnam and, on the other, a gradual loss of public support, or even tolerance, for the war. Hanoi is betting that we'll lose public support in the United States before we can build a nation in South Vietnam. We must do what we can to make sure that doesn't happen. We must work on both problems together: slow the loss in public support; and speed the development of South Vietnam. Our horse must finish first.[69]

Despite the fact that the pacification campaign was increasingly viewed as absolutely critical for success, the 1967 effort differed only slightly from that of 1966. Principally, there was less emphasis on the RD Cadres (although they remained theoretically preeminent) and somewhat more on the attack against the political apparatus of the Party and NLF. In short, the 1967 effort was more of the same but with greater intensity.[70]

As in 1966, the war in Hau Nghia during 1967 revolved around the activities of the 25th Infantry Division. Most of the division spent the dry season campaigning in the Iron Triangle and, later, in War Zone C. Nevertheless, troops were made available for pacification-search and destroy operations in Hau Nghia. From 1 December 1966 through 14 May 1967, the 25th ran Operation ALA MOANA along Highway 1, east of Cu Chi and in the area north and northeast of the base camp. For this type of operation, ALA MOANA was particularly violent and, from the American point of view, quite successful. Highlighted by a vain enemy assault on an isolated company that cost assaulting forces over 100 dead, 25th Division claimed to have killed 381 enemy, detained an additional 650, and captured 120 tons of rice. Portions of 2d Brigade spent the month of March sweeping the banks of the Vam Co River, claiming another 67 enemy dead. Other battalions, on an on-and-off basis, were assigned to clearing operations between Cu Chi and Trang Bang district town with little contact.[71]

With the approach of the summer monsoon rains, 1st and 2d Brigades returned from the "big-unit war" and prepared for an all-out pacification offensive in Hau Nghia province. From 13 May to 7 December, 2d Brigade conducted Operation KOLEKOLE. Until the beginning of October, KOLEKOLE took place in Duc Hue and Duc Hoa districts, particularly in the vicinity of Bao Trai and the district capitals and along the Oriental River. After early October, the center of activity shifted to areas north of Highway 1, including a district of Binh Duong province. From 18 May to 7 December, 1st Brigade conducted Operation BARKING SANDS in Cu Chi and Trang Bang district concentrating on Route 1 and the district capitals. Both of these lengthy operations were similar in scope, objectives, and results. In reality, they were both a series of numerous small operations that resembled the 1966 pacification effort of the 25th. Men ran sweeps, patrols, and ambushes throughout the province. "Roadrunners" were run and "Checkmates" established. The 25th Division command ordered numerous combined operations with the militia. Dozens of hamlets were the targets of "Cordon and Search" operations, which resembled the "County Fair" without the band concert. Following Westmoreland's earlier call to "make them part of our victories," 2d Brigade worked closely with ARVN. The 1st Brigade was less active in this regard for most ARVN activity took place in Duc Hue and Duc Hoa. U.S. troops captured a staggering amount of ordnance. During KOLEKOLE, 284 weapons were captured; during BARKING SANDS, another 240. Interestingly, both of these figures are considerably higher than normal relative to the body count claimed and perhaps indicate very serious enemy losses. In addition, during KOLEKOLE, over 40,000 small arms rounds and 27.5 tons of rice were seized; BARKING SANDS figures were 102,000 rounds and 133 tons of rice. For the two operations, it was claimed that over 10,000 bunkers and 1,200 more elaborate fortifications were destroyed.[72]

Just as in 1966, heavy activity on the part of the 25th Division caused a large increase in the number of ralliers: In the May to July quarter, when the division was most active, 556 Hoi Chanh surrendered in Hau Nghia.[73] Province records, however, made no mention of any important enemy ralliers. Ollie Davidson recalled that the Chieu Hoi Program was plagued by a lack of support on the part of the Vietnamese because it was an American initiative. He further observed that the program was a method for "recycling VC."[74] Nor was life very pleasant for those choosing to rally: an American advisor described the Hau Nghia Chieu Hoi Center as "deplorable."[75]

During all of the operations of the 25th, particular attention was given to improving the principal lines of communications in Hau Nghia. Slowly, all of the major provincial roads were improved to allow all-weather travel. As U.S. military activity was keeping insurgent operations to a minimum, it grew ever easier to travel throughout the province. For the first time since the creation of Hau Nghia, each of the district capitals had relatively secure daytime communication with Bao Trai.[76] American advisors were particularly pleased during July, at a time when enemy activity was described as being at "an all-time low," because the PSA was able to convince General Chinh of the ARVN 25th (whose helicopter was grounded in Bao Trai) to return to Duc Hoa by road, an act that "would have been unheard of anytime in the past three years even if the road was trafficable."[77]

As the 25th Division concentrated so heavily on the roadways, most of the Civic Action (CA) projects run by division were allocated to those hamlets astride the major roads, especially Highway 1. Thousands of MEDCAPs were performed. The "Helping Hand" program was terminated in October after the distribution of 250,000 parcels. Typically, the division congratulated itself for such gestures. Concerning "Helping Hand," which, at best, had little significance, the division reported, "The entire 'Helping Hand' concept was extremely worthwhile and has gone a long way toward winning the 'other war' in Vietnam."[78] Tropic Lightning Division personnel also were frequently assigned to various self-help projects, such as well-digging, constructing sanitation facilities, and dispensing raw materials for village programs. It is difficult to ascertain how such activities were received by the population, although it was reported that "in many cases, VN people show little interest or desire to better themselves and perform physical labor only when they receive supplies, material, and equipment from U.S. Forces. Some have the attitude that the U.S. forces should not only supply them, but also do the physical labor to complete the project."[79]

Yet, despite any improvements in commerce due to safer travel during the day and despite the numerous good deeds performed, 25th Division activities along the roads had counterproductive aspects. For instance, during

"Cordon and Search" operations, it was routine to detain anyone found suspicious for any reason; during BARKING SANDS, division records state that 35,000 individuals were detained.[80] A large majority of these people were questioned at roadblocks and never apprehended, and most of those arrested were released after interrogation by GVN personnel. Nevertheless, the experience could hardly have been pleasant. A POW (prisoner of war) captured in Cu Chi told division intelligence that, although U.S. operations were making it more difficult to recruit in his district, former detainees were easily persuaded to join the Front.[81] In addition there were nearly daily incidents concerning bad road discipline on the part of American vehicles, resulting in injuries and damaged crops.[82] The population was so angry over such incidents that the Hau Nghia province chief and General Chinh persuaded the 25th Division to halt night "Roadrunners" along Highway 1 between Cu Chi and Trang Bang.[83]

During the year, the 25th Division spent much effort to improve the performance of the militia. In this period, there was a great deal of talk about instituting some sort of combined command arrangement, such as that employed extensively by the French. John Paul Vann was a particular advocate, believing that ARVN was a failure and that only a direct injection of U.S. troops and commanders would improve the situation.[84] Westmoreland, on the other hand, believed that Operation FAIRFAX, a large combined operation in Gia Dinh, had proved that, unless they operated independently, Vietnamese forces would leave everything to the Americans.[85] Although large-scale encadrement projects were never used extensively, the 25th Division experimented with what was called the Combined Lightning Initial Project (CLIP). CLIP envisioned the combination of one American squad, one ARVN squad, and one militia squad to operate out of an outpost. The experiment began in May, but, despite favorable comments in the records, it was terminated in October.[86] In its place, the division established the first of many Mobile Advisory Teams (MATs). Made up of one American officer and a few enlisted men assigned on a temporary basis to militia units, MAT teams became the focus of the U.S. effort to enhance militia training. In addition, at the urging of the Hau Nghia advisory team, the 25th created an experimental Combined Reconnaissance and Intelligence Platoon (CRIP), which brought together American and militia personnel in a joint reconnaissance unit. The new unit was successful, and Westmoreland became interested. Other divisions established CRIP platoons, and the 25th continued to use them throughout the war.[87]

Whatever the success of these various experiments, the militia and ARVN had trouble coping with an upswing in enemy activity late in the year when most American units moved out of Hau Nghia. On 16 October, Bao Trai and Duc Hoa received simultaneous mortar attacks, causing many casualties. In September, a militia reaction force was ambushed; the 20 casualties included the Trang Bang district chief.[88] In November, 2 cadre teams were attacked in broad daylight, killing 4 members and wounding another 12, and there were reports that enemy units had reequipped and recovered in morale since the American summer monsoon offensive in Hau Nghia.[89] For the time being, Vietnamese forces were able to secure most of the province in the absence of U.S. forces, but that situation, as the Tet Offensive would make evident, was actually the choice of the enemy. Overall, work with Vietnamese militia forces led to some unhappy conclusions on the part of the 25th officers:

> In recent advisor/training missions with RF/PF forces, D Troop Aero Rifles have found that RF/PF shortcomings are attributable more to lack of RF/PF command and leadership than lack of training. They appeared reluctant to disrupt the local balance of power and have explicitly voiced fear of retribution if VC are aggressively pursued. This is partially understandable in view of their lack of appropriate weapons and low ammunition supply. Their only indirect fire support comes from 60mm mortars for which they have but a few rounds per weapon. However, they are capable of sound tactical maneuvers at squad, platoon, and company level. *They lack only the will to kill VC.* (emphasis added).[90]

Violence was low-level but steady, as the figures indicate. During KOLEKOLE, 2d Brigade claimed 797 enemy killed; lst Brigade claimed 320 enemy dead, with another 760 possible. The killing was two-sided: 2d Brigade lost 148 killed and 876 wounded during KOLEKOLE; lst Brigade did not list its losses for BARKING SANDS but did remark that the "kill ratio" for the operation was 1:2.77 in favor of U.S. forces. Overall, for the two quarters lasting from 1 May to 31 October 1967, the 25th Division lost 264 men killed in action, 2,570 wounded, and another 16 men killed in accidents.[91]

A Violent Struggle

It is appropriate at this point to take a closer look at the validity and the actual significance of the "body count" figures used by the Americans to measure the level of violence or, in military parlance, the "attrition ratio" that existed during the Vietnam War. In the study of any war, figures concerning casualties or force levels should be very suspect. In such recent conflicts as World War I and World War II, estimates of the total number killed or wounded vary considerably. Estimates of civilian casualties are even less clear. This is all quite understandable, especially considering the fact that accurate accounting techniques are of very recent origin and flawed under the best of circumstances. Other factors complicate things. In the first case, armies are notoriously prone to overestimating their opponents' losses for the simple reason that it makes them look good. Secondly, governments frequently have a vested interest in showing the world and their own people how much their nation has suffered due to the perfidy of an enemy. This is particularly true if peacetime difficulties are being blamed on wartime damage and suffering. Nor do historians have an interest in making the war they are studying less destructive or less dramatic than is commonly thought. All of these factors will drive up estimates of casualties. In most cases, from the historian's point of view, the unfortunate fact is that no one ever did know and no one ever will know the precise level of violence that occurred during a given conflict.

A similar uncertainty exists regarding the Vietnam War. American units kept exact records concerning the numbers of their own soldiers killed and wounded, so at least one part of the picture is clear. Any doubts on this subject, expressed by some cynical opponents of the war, have been put to rest dramatically with the construction of the Vietnam War Memorial in Washington. And, due to the deep U.S. participation in every level of the GVN war effort, it is likely that the usual estimate of 224,000 South Vietnamese military personnel killed in action is very accurate.

Actual enemy losses and civilian casualties, however, are another matter. On one hand, the body count procedure was, on paper at least, quite elaborate. Nevertheless, it was well known that command pressure in many instances tended to inflate these figures, especially if it appeared that enemy casualties were, in truth, fewer than American in a given engagement. Duplication of count was also frequent. Every veteran assisting in this research thought that the body count was very inaccurate. In the words of one, "If you see two arms, two legs, and one head laying on the ground, you've got five bodies. No! Make it ten. Blood trails, don't you know. By the time a report gets typed and sent to Saigon, they've chalked up at least ten more dead VC. It was ridiculous." Furthermore, it was normal to classify all of the dead in an engagement as enemy. Ollie Davidson recalled that every body was automatically classified as "VC."[92] The imperfections of the body count procedures were well known at MACV and in Washington and were the subject of often furious debate between the military and civilian analysts at the Defense Department.

Interestingly enough, enemy units also had a body count procedure. As revealed after the Tet Offensive by the captured commander of the main force regiment that included the Cu Chi battalion, Front units received "rating points" for the number of allied troops that were estimated killed in action. Furthermore, these estimates had to be forwarded to higher command levels even if direct superiors believed them to be bogus. In addition, an individual main force soldier who killed five Americans or the individual guerrilla who killed three was awarded the prestigious title of "Heroic American Killer." The temptation to make false claims of Americans killed can be imagined. By and large, the prisoner stated, body count claims sent to COSVN and Hanoi were seriously exaggerated.[93]

Honest research, however, must treat very carefully the arguments over actual enemy losses and actual enemy force levels for these disputes were not, in fact, over statistics but rather over the proper way for the United States to conduct the war. MACV contended that, even if its body count figures were inflated in the field, the number of enemy losses not accounted for due to the retrieval of the dead, wounded, and weapons on the battlefield, as well as those enemy killed due to long-range air and artillery bombardment, more than compensated for inflated figures. These arguments validated Westmoreland's attrition strategy and were used to support requests for more divisions. The civilians in the Defense Department, however, often with CIA support, used captured enemy documents to argue that enemy losses were considerably less (from 30 percent to 50 percent lower) than claimed by MACV and that both the NLF and the NVA were having no trouble filling or increasing the number of units.[94] Furthermore, the civilians argued that, because the enemy usually had the initiative on the battlefield, enemy forces could decrease their own losses by refusing battle, regardless of U.S. force levels. These conclusions were used to oppose requests for more troops and to suggest a curtailment of multidivisional operations. There were problems, however, with the civilian figures, as well. Enemy documents had to be assumed to be both legitimate and accurate, assumptions that the military doubted for it was well known that the enemy grossly over-estimated U.S. losses. Nor could it be assumed that the enemy even knew their actual losses, especially concerning hamlet guerrillas and auxiliaries.

Similar confusion existed over the number of civilian casualties. The only hard numbers on this subject were derived from hospital statistics, but these were of little help in estimating the number of people killed in Front areas. Nor was it at all easy to determine, in many cases, the definition of "civilian." On the hamlet level, the NLF regularly employed conscripts, often over military age, to serve as porters and to help evacuate dead, wounded, weapons, and other supplies from the battlefield. Furthermore, enemy forces would evacuate weapons from the battlefield whenever possible, even if they were not able to reclaim dead comrades. Both of these facts were used by the military to justify a liberal definition of "combatant" as opposed to "civilian" and to explain the low ratio (25 to 33 percent) of weapons captured to dead claimed. As opposition to the war grew, however, and various congressional committees investigated civilian casualties, it was normal for the "doves" to seek the highest possible estimates of civilian casualties. From many circles, the charge of "genocide" was leveled at the United States. Here again, figures were being used for political purposes, in this case to end the war entirely. Since the war, similarly high estimates have been used to portray the U.S. war effort as uniquely barbaric. Rarely have people really wanted or tried to find the most accurate estimate possible.[95]

Professor Guenter Lewy has taken a long and sensible look at the various statistical arguments. He has concluded that civilian deaths for the entire war (1965–1974) in both North and South Vietnam were 587,000 or 45 percent of a total of 1,313,000 people killed by and on both sides. Lewy has also concluded, almost certainly correctly, that Vietnam was not an unusually cruel war in this unusually cruel century.[96] Therefore, the figures presented in this research are not meant to be taken as exact; they are only meant to serve as an imprecise indicator of the relative level of violence. There can be no doubt, whatever the real figures were, that a very large number of people were killed in Hau Nghia and that many of them were noncombatants.

The whole question of civilian casualties in Hau Nghia province is intimately related to both the attitudes held by American combat soldiers toward Vietnamese villagers and the nature of military violence in the war itself. These matters are difficult to analyze for they deal with complex questions of ethics, political morality, and the honor of the American armed forces. Furthermore, the evidence is complicated to handle. Anecdotal accounts can be used to support almost any claim, if one chooses to do so. During the war and since, many writers have used first-person narratives to create a picture of a confused and disoriented U.S. Army gone berserk, of soldiers routinely committing criminal and atrocious deeds for no purpose. Popular fiction and several motion pictures have spread this image further. Consequently, great care and sensitivity must be shown when trying to create an accurate depiction of what was typical behavior by American soldiers. Neither whitewash nor false condemnation serve any historical purpose. Unfortunately, no evidence exists that will lead to precise results. The following account is based upon certain indirect evidence, the records of the 25th Division and the Hau Nghia advisory team, and the personal accounts of fifty-four individuals, most either 25th Division combat veterans or American advisors. The conclusions drawn may be imperfect. However, the issues involved are too important to avoid.

There were very few areas in Vietnam where American soldiers had closer and more sustained contact with rural Vietnamese than in Hau Nghia province. For reasons not at all apparent in retrospect, the army did almost nothing to prepare soldiers for the "culture shock" (and the term is a good one) that all of them encountered when coming to Vietnam. Almost all of the veterans—most just out of high school and not "senator's sons," as one put it—stressed how totally ignorant they were about the Vietnamese and their culture. They were also unprepared for the poverty of Vietnam. Initial reactions were usually a mixture of curiosity and disgust. Bob Conner, a 25th Division rifleman, had a typical reaction upon arrival in 1966:

> The country was amazing. I looked around, and I said, "My God: I have never in my life seen anything like this." I would never dream in a million years that they still used ox carts; and these things they call water buffalo, big great-looking animals with rings in their noses and a funny way of looking at you. . . . The country was stinking and poor; it was from another era.

During the short in-country training course provided by the 25th Division at Cu Chi, soldiers were told about the battle for freedom and the importance of protecting the local population from the enemy. At the same time, veterans would informally be telling newcomers not to trust any Vietnamese at any time. Vietnam veterans invariably stress that one of the most frustrating and vivid impressions of the war was that it was impossible to tell the difference between friend and foe. Thomas A. Giltner, a platoon leader in the *Wolfhounds* in late 1966, put it well:

It was the hallmark of the war: You could never tell who was the enemy and who was not. Therefore, you treated everybody with suspicion and distrust. The enemy was everywhere and everybody at all times, and we were the foreigners in their country.

Obviously, this was a particularly difficult situation in Front strongholds like Hau Nghia province. Many veterans commented that the villages in the 25th's area of responsibility were full of "VC sympathizers." One man who was with one of the first units deployed to Hau Nghia said of the inhabitants of Cu Chi village, "You could readily see the hate in the eyes of the people there." Many men were sympathetic, in their own way, to the plight of the villagers. Rural Vietnamese were frequently described as equivalent to "pawns" or as being "between a rock and a hard place." Several 25th veterans would have echoed Thomas Giltner's sentiments about the civilians: "They were pathetic farmers caught in the middle of a tragic conflict that they did not understand and who really wanted to be left alone to follow their ancestral ways."

The rumor mill worked overtime in Vietnam. Extreme and bizarre cases of violence (which, if they happened at all, were extremely rare) became grossly exaggerated. There were stories of civilians putting battery acid in Cokes that they sold or putting ground glass in ice shavings. All sorts of grizzly tales concerning prostitutes and unwary patrons also made the rounds. In addition, villagers were credited with knowing more than they probably did. American soldiers were bitter about a lack of intelligence from the village, without realizing that many military activities on the part of the Front were, in fact, highly secret and known only to the cadres. Front main force units routinely slipped by American ambush patrols during night movements when every prudent villager was indoors. Furthermore, mines and booby traps, which caused so much anger in American soldiers, also took a dreadful toll on Vietnamese civilians.

Nevertheless, the American soldiers' distrust toward Vietnamese villagers was, above all, founded on dreadful reality. Regardless of what U.S. pacification pundits in Washington or Saigon were saying about separating the guerrillas from the civilians, the combat soldiers knew very well that the Front fighters who were inflicting so much pain on them were in and from the hamlets. The dreaded mines, for instance, often were laid by villagers as they watched U.S. troops approach from a distance and guessed the likely line of approach. The soldiers knew such things, but they could rarely find the individual perpetrators. Instead, they blamed the village. It was an ugly chemistry. Jay Lazarin described the situation:

The "friendly" civilians were seen as no such thing. To us, there were no friendly civilians, only ones who posed no immediate threat. But because they were perceived as (at best) harmless for the moment, they were treated with relative ambivalence. We let our guard down with them a bit more, as we sat around their villages during area sweeps. The friendly villages around Duc Hoa were always a pleasure to sweep because we knew it was an easy operation with very low risk. . . . But even these friendly villagers slept in their underground bunkers when we were around, and, as darkness came, our attitude toward them changed. We felt that they knew where the VC were, and they would never warn us if an attack of some sort was coming. So, in the morning, after even an uneventful night, the villagers were always looked at in a different way, one that reinforced our mistrust of anything non-American and, in retrospect, one that reinforced our ignorance of their dilemma.

C. W. Bowman expressed similar sentiments but stressed the ambivalence and confusion of 25th Division combat soldiers:

Our guys were mostly teenagers and thought most about whores. A lot of us didn't try to understand the people or make friends: Everybody was a zip, gook, or animal. New guys would give candy to kids: Vets would throw it at them and try to hit them. Some of the guys hated them. . . . A lot of us wanted to be friends with civilians, but we knew you couldn't trust them. There were a lot of VC sympathizers. . . . You'd like to get to know them, but you couldn't. Often, command-detonated mines were blown off before we'd enter a village. We'd sweep it and find only mama-san. We'd go into a hooch and find fifty pair of chopsticks and other small things. You knew the village had VC. . . . The children were great, and very smart. We felt sorry for their poverty, living in their straw hooches and dirt floors. But they always smiled, and we taught them to swear. But when friends started to die from booby traps and you don't see the enemy, men became embittered and grew hard-hearted. You had to be to survive.

The struggle in Hau Nghia was extremely harsh. Acts of cruelty on the part of American soldiers toward civilians were common enough. On the roads, Americans driving trucks or armored vehicles often ran civilian traffic into a ditch on purpose, sometimes causing injury or even death. On at least one occasion during a search and destroy operation, two civilians, after being ordered by Vietnamese interpreters not to move, were shot as they attempted to flee. Animals were shot for no reason. Soldiers were cautioned against killing water buffalo, but some could not resist the temptation, probably not realizing that the material damage done was far worse than "torching a hooch." Throwing rocks or shooting slingshots at civilians was considered sport by some. Many soldiers pushed around the slight Vietnamese, and some administered beatings. U.S. interrogators working through their Vietnamese interpreters often employed physical intimidation and the threat of worse when questioning someone suspected of knowing where the elusive enemy had just fled. Racial obscenities and insults were routine. Dead soldiers were mutilated by both sides.

However, there is no evidence whatsoever of willful murder. It is very possible, even likely, that murders took place. Yet, they were almost certainly extremely rare. Many veterans are outraged by the image that still exists in some quarters today of the American soldier as indiscriminate killer. Several of the men responding to this research eagerly confronted the issue and vehemently denied that any such thing took place in their units. They insist that most American combat soldiers fought a very hard war honorably. The evidence encountered for this research strongly supports this claim.

The best evidence that indiscriminate violence was very much the exception can be seen in the actions of some of the Vietnamese civilians themselves. American units in the field drew large numbers of small entrepreneurs wherever they went. The hawkers and prostitutes, regardless of what they thought of American combat troops, obviously felt safe enough to be around them on a daily basis. Dan Vandenberg, a 25th Division rifleman, described a typical road-clearing sweep outside Trang Bang district town:

> It was like a circus. Walking with us were girls and kids selling soda, beer, cigarettes, lighters, jackets, etc. You name it, they had it. If they didn't have it, and you asked for it, they'd have it the next day. Naturally, there was a "fun girls" contingent. It looked like a parade. As soon as they wouldn't go any further, we got uneasy real fast, I'll tell you. If we wanted to know what we were going to do the next day, we'd ask the civilians. They'd know before our commander knew.

On a larger scale, hamlets near U.S. bases invariably grew greatly in size due to commerce. This represented more than a desire to live in a safer area: Any GVN-controlled village or district town would do as well for that. Rather, it was due to a desire to make money off the U.S. Army. Economically and socially, this may have been a bad thing, but it was certainly not the action of a population terrified of wanton brutality on the part of American soldiers.

Even under these extremely difficult conditions, there were acts of kindness and compassion between American combat soldiers and the villagers. By and large, soldiers liked the crowds of children that invariably gathered around them during nonhostile missions. Units sometimes "adopted" children with birth defects or war wounds, gathering money and seeing that they received medical treatment. Efforts like "Helping Hand" probably had little importance in the larger scheme of things, but soldiers derived satisfaction from dispensing the little gifts. Accompanying one of the frequent MEDCAP missions was extremely popular duty for soldiers. It was relatively safe, but many fighting men appreciated its affirmative qualities. MEDCAPs were even more popular with the villagers and invariably attracted big crowds. One medical technician commented that "on a MEDCAP you could alleviate more suffering in a day than you could in an American hospital in a month." No doubt, in a larger sense, the medical effort was self-serving, but the men conducting it genuinely believed they were helping people in need.

Nihilistic mayhem was not the cause of death and destruction in Hau Nghia province. Combat operations, however, frequently were. As examined previously, U.S. units relied heavily on firepower both to accomplish their mission and to save the lives of American troops. In the "boonies," the equation was a simple one for the mission was simply "kill VC." Consequently, in places like the Ho Bo, firepower could be employed pretty much at will. When operating in populated areas, however, a contradiction appeared. In theory, American troops on pacification duty were there to protect the villagers and support the GVN's efforts to create political support, on one hand, and "kill VC" with the least possible cost in American lives, on the other. U.S. combat methods were well enough suited for the second half of this mission, but they were very bad for the first.

The officers of the 25th Division were well aware of this dilemma but could find no good solution for it. It is difficult to generalize about the use of firepower by the 25th because so much was up to the officer on the spot. Thomas Giltner, a platoon leader in late 1966, gave a good description of the situation:

> Our battalion decided that if we were approaching a hamlet, we presumed it was hostile. Unless we observed something, no fire was used. We certainly did not use reconnaissance by fire. We were very careful inside these villages, but that was all. If fired upon, you tried to estimate how big the enemy unit was. But you never really knew unless you were very close. You could usually tell if it was a very small or overwhelmingly large force. But you can't see the enemy. It is an "on the spot" judgment. At that time, we would use all force necessary within reason. Most engagements were short: The enemy would hit us and run. Sometimes, we had tactical air, but that was usually only with a battalion-sized force. Sometimes, gunships were right with us overhead or standing by or waiting on-call at the airfield. We had indirect fire: Both artillery and mortar forward observers were with us, so we could dial up anyone we needed. You had to know exactly where you were on the map: That was crucial for survival. So the firepower level differed. Sometimes, there was too much, but we always assumed the worst. We had no desire to harm villagers, even if they were VC sympathizers.

Giltner also expressed the common impression that Front guerrillas would exploit a reluctance to fire:

> If and when the VC perceived our reluctance to fire on a certain area, they would exploit it to the hilt. They would hit us from a village or hamlet they thought we were reluctant to fire upon. Or else they would fire outside a village and retreat into a hamlet thinking we wouldn't fire back: But on those occasions, they were badly mistaken. We would protect the people if we could, but we were certain to protect our people and our mission.

It is crucial to appreciate one aspect of this horrid dilemma. American soldiers were not willing to do anything to jeopardize their lives just to lessen the danger to noncombatants. The desire to keep U.S. casualties low was a far more powerful part of the dynamic leading to civilian casualties than was any desire on the part of the men to gain a good "body count." Officers knew that, though a high body count looked good on their records, a high number of "US KIA" (killed in action) looked a lot worse. Consequently, when restrictions on the use of firepower were placed on "secure" hamlets, they were bitterly resented and frequently ignored, and officers who believed that tactical finesse could replace firepower were unpopular. Bob Conner expressed the view of many fellow infantrymen on this subject:

> I remember one time we had a colonel who said he did not believe in using soldiers where he could use artillery or air strikes: Hey, I like that. And we had the artillery and tanks and air strikes all the time. But somehow or another, he got promoted or moved, and we got another colonel in there who was just the opposite: He did not believe in artillery and air strikes when he could use manpower. How stupid.

The men paid a psychological price. Almost every combat infantryman was a witness to utterly horrific sights and incidents. This was not the intention of U.S. operations, but it frequently was the result. Heartbreaking images of crushed, burned, and mutilated old people, women, and children have been and continue to be a loathsome burden for combat veterans. Nevertheless, Jay Lazarin expressed the conviction of almost every infantryman in Vietnam:

> When you are trying to survive, there is no such thing as too much firepower. We were not military tacticians or logistics people; we were infantrymen trying to kill them before they killed us.

There were three types of tactical situations that involved fighting in villages. The first, very common in 1966 and 1967, was, in essence, the occupation of Front villages or hamlets. As examined in Chapter 2, Front-liberated zones had long been subject to heavy air and artillery attack, and many villagers fled to areas closer to the major roads where GVN attacks were less fierce. Throughout the 1966–1967 period, this steady change in population distribution continued in Hau Nghia as people were relocated to or fled to hamlets along the roads, and several small hamlets off the roads were bulldozed or destroyed by fighting.[97] The remaining major villages, long under Front control, presented particularly difficult problems. Their size and relative proximity to GVN-controlled towns had offered protection in earlier times. Naturally, such hamlets were primary objectives for the 25th Division and ARVN pacification efforts. But many of these were "combat hamlets," honeycombed with tunnels and spider-holes and thus prepared for defense. Areas like these had to be swept over and over again, and firefights and destruction were regular occurrences. In early 1967, Davidson visited the large village of Loc Giang, astride the Vam Co River in Trang Bang district, shortly after it was reoccupied by U.S. and GVN forces during KOLEKOLE and BARKING SANDS (after having been controlled by the NLF for four years). He reported that the population had decreased from 7,000 to 3,000 since 1963. Only a one-kilometer circle in the center of the village had been spared air strikes and H&I fire from allied forces, and many people had fled to Trang Bang. Although some continued to work their land, Davidson estimated that over half of the rice fields and most of the sugarcane fields had been abandoned for fear of retaliation by either side. Similar circumstances existed throughout the province.[98]

The situation for the refugees was very harsh for few were considered eligible for government assistance. Because Hau Nghia was so close to Saigon, most long-term refugees fled to the capital to find shelter in the shantytowns or large refugee camps. But the few centers established for refugees in Hau Nghia were miserable affairs. The III CTZ refugee advisor told the Hau Nghia PSA that every effort would be made to remove the refugees from one settlement in Duc Hoa to an area "where they can live like human beings."[99]

A second tactical situation was far more common and confronted the 25th Division throughout the war. Villages that already were considered relatively friendly or had been recently occupied through division or ARVN operations had some sort of GVN presence during the daylight; many had forts and militia contingents. Whether considered secured or contested, however, no hamlet in Hau Nghia was genuinely safe from the American point of view. Consequently, a sorry situation developed there during the summer monsoon, as insurgent troops began to infiltrate hamlets along the roads at night (an easy task because the militia and ARVN rarely patrolled after sundown) in order to fire on American military vehicles the next day. Hamlets involved in 25th Division Civic Action programs were often singled out. Frequently, the U.S. response was to return the fire with automatic weapons and tank cannon, causing predictable damage—just as the enemy hoped. These short engagements did not lead to the total destruction of hamlets, but they were very ugly and very frequent. The attitude of the American soldiers on the spot was that if the villagers did not warn them of enemy infiltration, the villagers were responsible for their own safety. Faced with this danger, a nightly civilian exodus took place to the district towns, and those people staying in the hamlets constructed small bunkers in their dwellings. Despite protests on the part of U.S. advisory personnel, no one had a good answer for what one officer described as the "too-little too-much violence dilemma."[100] The Hau Nghia PSA observed that greater American activity had led to an increase in enemy terrorism. He further concluded that "the civilians are often caught in the middle; therefore, their security has been reduced. It is believed that this present situation is unavoidable if the GVN and allied forces are to defeat the VC in Hau Nghia."[101]

A third tactical situation arose when Front or NVA main force units occupied a hamlet or, worse yet, assaulted a town. At the very least, this meant serious destruction. If the enemy wanted to have a major battle, villages could be destroyed. These tragedies were common during the large offensives of 1968 and 1972. A smaller example took place in October 1967 at Loc Giang. After the village was cleared by U.S. troops during the summer, an ARVN Ranger unit was assigned there for protection. On the night of 29 October, enemy forces attacked the ARVN compound and penetrated the village—an assault that was costly for the enemy and ARVN alike.

More to the point, the Front executed a number of civilians thought to have been cooperating with the GVN. When Ollie Davidson returned to Loc Giang after the attack, he found even more damage and a very frightened population.[102]

In theory, the major rationalization for U.S. combat operations was to allow the GVN to regroup and expand its authority behind the American shield. But during 1967, U.S. and GVN efforts in this direction foundered despite the very close proximity of the shield. Successfully holding elections was the GVN's major accomplishment, particularly important because President Johnson was deeply concerned to show the world that the United States was protecting a functioning democracy. In Hau Nghia, province officials, the cadre teams, and the advisory group worked hard to ensure that elections would take place in every hamlet that was even moderately secure, and U.S. field-workers watched the electoral process very closely. As was typical throughout Vietnam, party affiliation followed religious divisions, rather than easily identifiable ideological positions; the NLF, of course, was excluded from elections entirely.[103]

Field-workers did not report cases of outright fraud, although it was believed that local officials in Hau Nghia, as elsewhere, were instructed to promote the Thieu-Ky ticket. For instance, during public meetings, which were not well attended, officials would schedule Thieu supporters to speak first, an important advantage in a field of seven candidates.[104] The Thieu ticket, because of Catholic support and official pressure, was widely expected to win a plurality in Hau Nghia. However, despite proclamations from Washington, field-workers were not able to detect much enthusiasm for the elections.[105] According to the Hau Nghia PSA, "General attitude appears to be that the Thieu-Ky ticket will win, that the election will not reflect the true views of the majority, and that the results will have little or no effect on the current prevailing conditions in the country."[106]

On election day, 3 September 1967, the cadre teams, the National Police, the militia, and U.S. troops did their best to guard polling areas. For reasons of their own, Front forces did nothing to disrupt the polling. Despite predictions to the contrary, Truong Dinh Dzu, a political unknown who made his mark by calling for talks with the NLF, won a plurality in Hau Nghia, Binh Duong, and Tay Ninh. He lost in Long An narrowly and finished second to Thieu in the country as a whole. He was jailed by Thieu shortly thereafter, but there was much speculation about Dzu's success and what role, if any, was played by the Front.[107] Whatever the actual case, CORDS personnel were very cautious in their assessment of the election:

The year of 1967 had a principal objective that influenced all pacification programs—the transition from a government by decree to that of a fledgling democracy. Success depended on two critical factors: (a) preparation of the public to accept individual responsibility and to participate in the formation activities, and (b) building confidence in the minds of people in officials whom they have chosen as their leaders. The success of the first precept was self-evident in view of the high percentage of the populace participating in the elections. The success of the second has yet to be demonstrated.[108]

Elections were the bright spot. If the opinion of the advisory team is at all accurate, the RD Cadre Program did no better in 1967 than in the previous year. In April, the PSA claimed that the creation of the required number of Real New Life hamlets (Ap Doi Mois) was stalled because of weak cadre leadership. The population of Duc Hanh B, a hamlet that received a great deal of attention in the pacification program, even appealed to have their team removed.[109] Although the three teams operating in Duc Hoa district were staying at their hamlets overnight, the three teams in Cu Chi refused to do so, citing a lack of security even though there had been no recent attacks by the enemy.[110] One team in Cu Chi was singled out for what passed as praise in Hau Nghia:

> The Tan Bac hamlet RDC (Revolutionary Development Cadre) team, Cu Chi District, is rated as the number two team in the province. It continues to excel in leadership, team attendance, high morale, and understanding of the program. Although the team appears busy and capable, no significant accomplishments were produced outside of assisting with the hamlet election.[111]

Later in the year, however, the other two teams in Cu Chi were reported to have "failed miserably." These two teams were moved the next month for the people wanted them out.[112] Concerning the RD Cadre Program, what is missing in the U.S. records is what is important. For the entire year of 1967, not a single RD team was credited with aiding security, harming the Party apparatus, or doing anything to improve the position of the government in the rural areas. The entire RD Cadre Program, along with the Ap Doi Mois, had turned into a paper exercise with little real importance.

Although the GVN cadres failed in attacking the revolutionary political apparatus, so had everyone else. Not a single important figure was reported to have rallied. The Special Branch of the National Police did have a small network of informants, but it was reported that the population found them "repugnant" and refused to cooperate.[113] Later in the year, the Hau Nghia advisory team stated,

> Intelligence activities by the National Police have not been very successful. They are not directing their primary interest toward gathering information on the VC infrastructure, which should be their main responsibility. This is especially true in areas undergoing pacification.[114]

It should be pointed out that Col. Nguyen Ngoc Loan's National Police concentrated their activities in the cities with considerable success. It should also be pointed out that, in heavily contested rural areas, any policeman showing efficiency and zeal was in dreadful danger of assassination by the Front. In the latter part of the year, CORDS and the CIA began instituting provincial and district intelligence centers to correlate intelligence data on the Front's apparatus, but for this period, all that was accomplished was the identification of a large number of suspects. Apprehensions were almost nil.

The militia and ARVN forces did not prove particularly successful at providing the local security as they were assigned to do. When U.S. units were in the vicinity, enemy forces would disperse and security would improve. Yet, it was noted that neither ARVN nor the militia were active at night, thus enabling infiltrators to enter hamlets undergoing heavy pacification activities.[115] The example of the aforementioned Loc Giang village was not unique.

It is not at all simple to assess the outcome of the allied effort in Hau Nghia during 1967. As in the previous year, much depended on what aspect of the situation was being compared to the earlier situation. Davidson observed that, to those who had seen Hau Nghia in early 1966, the situation at the end of 1967 appeared tremendously improved. The government was functioning to one degree or another in some areas where it had previously been ejected, and road communication and commerce improved greatly in 1967. Yet, the cost had been high to both the population of Hau Nghia and allied soldiers. Despite the large number of revolutionary soldiers killed, the main force units and, to a lesser extent, the local guerrillas showed themselves capable of rebuilding. Security, though outwardly improved, was still haphazard, and the insurgent political apparatus had not been seriously hurt. There were also few signs that the government had improved its political position in the countryside. The Revolutionary Development team at the 25th Division knew this very well. They had prepared a color-coded chart showing the security status of each hamlet in their area of operations. Another chart had a graphic representation of how the "area security" concept was supposedly working and how 25th Division efforts fit into the overall American-GVN pacification effort. The charts were used for briefings that 25th officers called the "horse and pony show." In the words of one officer involved in these briefings, everyone at division knew that the charts "had no counterpart in reality whatsoever." Other U.S. statistical indicators, which were later viewed as markedly overoptimistic, showed that the GVN's position was still precarious. The Hamlet Evaluation System (HES), begun in early 1967, rated hamlets on a letter scale, (A, B, C, D, E, VC—"B" was considered an acceptable rating; "VC" is obvious); during September, HES listed no hamlets as "A," 17 as "B," 37 as "C" (contested), 24 as "D," 7 as "E," and 67 as "VC."[116]

After two years of war involving U.S. troops, the Front still held the political initiative in Hau Nghia. Unfortunately for the GVN, this situation existed in many parts of Vietnam. According to a CORDS report:

> The hardest idea to sell in most parts of III CTZ [the provinces around Saigon] is that the GVN is truly interested in the welfare of its citizens and will protect them against exploitation by either the VC or corrupt officials. There are few concrete evidences to support this theme and quite a few rather obvious examples to refute it.[117]

It must be emphasized again that anything of importance that was accomplished in Hau Nghia during 1966–1967 was due to coercion and violence, most of it supplied by U.S. forces. The "carrot" was minute compared to the "stick." Although Americans in the field wished to see the population slowly begin to rally behind the GVN, the rural population at best (from the American point of view) remained caught between two powerful forces. This was to remain true for the next two years as the fury of the Tet Offensive ebbed and was followed by the strongest allied effort of the entire war.

An American jet bombs suspected enemy positions on the outskirts of a hamlet in Cu Chi district during the 1968 Tet Offensive. (Photo by Hector Nadal, a 25th Division combat photographer)

Ground fighting spills over into the hamlet itself during Tet 1968. (Photo by Hector Nadal)

Relatives mourn a child killed in the 1968 Tet Offensive fighting. (Photo by Hector Nadal)

American advisors inspect a South Vietnamese militia outpost near Bao Trai in late 1966. In this stage of the war, most militia units stayed in their outposts after dark. Consequently, the Front controlled Hau Nghia province at night. (Three photos on this page by Andrew Rutherford)

Front forces destroyed a militia outpost between Bao Trai and Hiep Hoa in 1966—a frequent occurrence during this period of the war.

Revolutionary Development Cadres assemble in Bao Trai in 1967. In theory a crucial component of the pacification campaign, the South Vietnamese RD Cadre Program was, in reality, a failure.

An armored personnel carrier (APC or "track") is damaged by a mine near the Hoc Mon Bridge on the Hau Nghia/Gia Dinh border. Mines were a continual plague for the 25th Division. (Photo by Hector Nadal)

A dead comrade is evacuated by infantrymen of the 25th Division during the Tet Offensive. (Photo by Hector Nadal)

A soldier of the 25th Division lies wounded by a U.S. claymore mine that was captured and detonated by the enemy. The location is uncertain, but the wooded terrain is typical of the Ho Bo-Boi Loi Woods. (Photo by Todd Dexter)

The men of a Joint Vietnamese-U.S. Combined Reconnaissance and Intelligence Platoon (CRIP) were a tough bunch. Lightly armed but mobile, CRIPs were a rare success in the field of combined operations. (Photo by Hector Nadal)

A patrol boat with American infantrymen aboard cruises the Vam Co Dong River. Ambushes by both sides marked the river war. (Photo by Hector Nadal)

U.S. infantrymen fly out on helicopters for a search and destroy mission in 1967. They are over Trang Bang district on an "EAGLE FLIGHT" operation. (Photo by C. W. Bowman)

This South Vietnamese militia outpost was established in 1969 in Due Hue district. Increasing militia strength was a prime component of the pacification campaign. (Photo by Richard O'Hare)

This militia outpost, seen from the ground, was located in territory long controlled by the Front. It was mortared and harassed constantly throughout 1969. (Photo by Richard O'Hare)

A B-52 strike on the Ho Bo Woods in 1967 is observed from the outskirts of the Cu Chi base camp. (Photo by C. W. Bowman)

The 25th Division base camp at Cu Chi in 1968 brings a bit of stateside army life to Vietnam. (Photo by Sidney Stone)

An enemy rocket scored a hit in the Cu Chi base camp during the 1968 Tet Offensive. Even the relative comfort of the camp was precarious. (Photo by Sidney Stone)

This one-room schoolhouse was damaged by Front mortar in 1969. Americans built these little schools by the dozens. They were frequently attacked by the Front, usually when vacant. (Photo by Richard O'Hare)

The Hiep Hoa sugar mill, once one of South Vietnam's major industrial facilities, was heavily damaged and home to enemy snipers by 1969. Americans avoided its interior. (Photo by Richard O'Hare)

Combat infantrymen of the U.S. 25th Division search an unidentified hamlet in Cu Chi district in 1968—an anxious and fearful experience for Vietnamese villagers. (Photo by Hector Nadal)

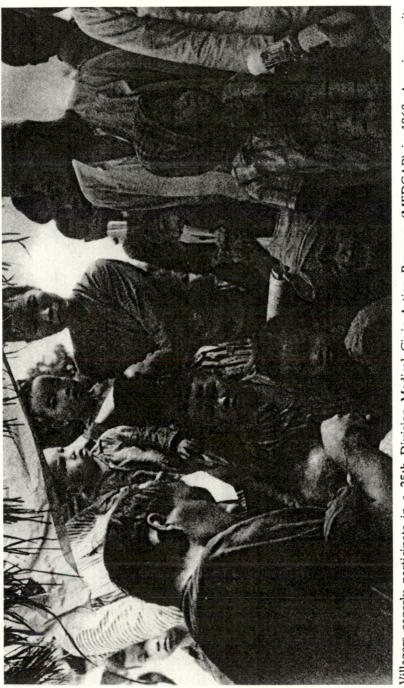

Villagers eagerly participate in a 25th Division Medical Civic Action Program (MEDCAP) in 1968. American units performed thousands of MEDCAPs, a genuinely affirmative program. (Photo by Hector Nadal)

Members of the 25th Division band, wearing helmets and flak jackets, entertain the people of Cu Chi. (Photo by Hector Nadal)

An American Psychological Operations unit distributes leaflets in 1967 to the accompaniment of a blaring loudspeaker. American units frequently attracted a crowd. (Photo by Thomas Giltner)

6

Battle: The Tet Offensive, 1968

The Origins of the Tet Offensive

Although they recognized that the position of the GVN in Hau Nghia and some other "hard-core" provinces, such as Binh Dinh and Long An, was still precarious at the beginning of 1968, American political and military leaders generally were pleased with the apparent course of the war. They believed that U.S. military pressure was slowly forcing enemy main force units away from the populated areas. Americans anticipated that ARVN and territorial forces increasingly would be able to defend the cities, "secure" rural areas, and extend government control farther and farther into Front territory. On the military side, the views that Army Chief of Staff Harold Johnson expressed to a journalist were representative:

If you exclude the two northernmost provinces of South Vietnam, just south of the Demilitarized Zone, you find that the major forces of the enemy have already been largely broken up. They will have an occasional ability to mount an attack in a force of up to 2,500 in poorly coordinated attacks. But this will be periodic and somewhat spasmodic, because I do not believe that they any longer have the capability of regular, planned reinforcement.[1]

Other officials in Washington, trying to build support for the war effort, gave similar, if more general, descriptions of the situation. President Johnson, in a news conference on 17 November 1967, declared that "the fact that the population under free control has constantly risen . . . is a very encouraging sign . . . overall we are making progress."[2] A few days later, Ambassador Ellsworth Bunker claimed the GVN had increased its control from 55 percent of the population to 67 percent.[3] The next week, Vice President Humphrey told "Meet the Press" that the allies held both the political and military initiative.[4] The most highly publicized expression of optimism came from General Westmoreland, who had gone to Washington to deliver a "progress report." On 21 November, he told the National Press Club that "I am absolutely certain that, whereas in 1965 the enemy was winning, today he is certainly losing." Although the general cautioned against any expectation of a clear-cut military victory, he pointed out that it had taken until mid-

1967 to prepare the logistical base for sustained operations and that presently the enemy faced the full force of U.S. arms. He further predicted that, "in two years or less," American forces would be able to begin to shift the combat burden to ARVN and disengage.[5] Robert Komer evidenced even greater optimism in a cable sent to Lieutenant General Khang, commander of III CTZ, on 1 January 1968: "I do believe that with all RVNAF [Republic of Vietnam Armed Forces] and Free World Forces taking the offensive in 1968, together with greatly stepped-up operations against the VC infrastructure, victory will come within our grasp."[6]

To be sure, there were a number of "in-house dissenters." As previously indicated, Secretary McNamara was increasingly plagued with serious doubts. Gen. Earle Wheeler, chairman of the JCS, claimed steady progress but credited the enemy with considerable military strength and cautioned "that there may be a communist thrust similar to the desperate effort of the Germans in the Battle of the Bulge in World War II."[7] The II Field Force intelligence, predicting a major enemy effort, estimated that the enemy was capable of making multibattalion attacks anywhere in III CTZ.[8] John Paul Vann was among the least optimistic of officials. In November, he circulated a paper highly critical of ARVN and the militia, and he was known to be skeptical of HES figures, the computerized data used to chart the pacification campaign.[9] A typical story about Vann circulated around Saigon in early 1968:

> John Vann followed the Big Three (Westmoreland, Komer, Bunker) into Washington in December. As usual, his line was considerably less optimistic. But he said nobody in Washington wanted to hear it; after all, they had just had the word from the horse's mouth. Anyway, Vann, after much standing around in corridors, was finally given an audience with Walt Rostow. Rostow listened somewhat impatiently for awhile and then told Vann something like this: "Vann, I know your pitch; I read all the reports, but don't you agree that the war will be over by July?" Vann shot back: "Oh, hell, no, Mr. Rostow; I'm a born optimist—I think we can hold out longer than that."[10]

Whatever the views of Vann and a few others, most U.S. officials believed that Allied efforts were succeeding to one degree or another on virtually all fronts. Consequently, there seemed to be no reason for a major change in direction in the American conduct of the war. As devised by CORDS, the 1968 pacification program was to have been a continuation of the 1967 effort, with a greater emphasis on identifying and eliminating Front cadres under the new Phoenix program.[11] Westmoreland and MACV planned to concentrate the U.S. military campaign once again on the border areas, most notably south of the Demilitarized Zone. The II Field Force intelligence believed, by November 1967, that enemy main force units were massing in the northwest area of III CTZ on both sides of the Cambodian border. Therefore, MACV decided to launch a series of large offensive operations near the Cambodian border to seal off the area and keep enemy forces from intruding deeply into the CTZ. Direct responsibility for the defense of Saigon and the Capital Military District was shifted to ARVN.

Within a circle with a radius of roughly 50 kilometers from Saigon were situated the four U.S. divisional base camps of II FFV (Field Force, Vietnam), as well as the Long Binh-Bien Hoa complex. As originally planned, only 14 of the 53 available American combat battalions would have been inside the base area circle at the time of Tet. Some would have been up to 150 kilometers away, and all would have been dependent upon air transport and, more to the point, functioning airfields for quick redeployment.[12] As part of the projected 1968 dry season campaign, the 25th Division was ordered in December to deploy the 1st and 3d Brigades in northern Tay Ninh province for Operation YELLOWSTONE in War Zone C. The 2d Brigade was widely dispersed on pacification operations in Hau Nghia and parts of Binh Duong and Long An. For two weeks in December, elements of 2d and 3d Brigades were detailed to an ad hoc operation aimed at the destroying an NVA regiment unexpectedly sighted in the Ho Bo and Boi Loi woods. During all these efforts, familiar patterns soon were reestablished. The NVA regiment eluded U.S. forces, and violence during the pacification operations was steady but low-level. Contacts in War Zone C were sporadic except on 1 January, when an NVA regiment launched a grim assault on a 3d Brigade firebase. Although American units suffered the painful loss of 29 killed and 159 wounded, the attackers were seriously mauled, leaving behind 355 men killed.[13]

It may have appeared that the 1968 campaign was going to be a virtual repeat of 1967, but disturbing indications of a major change in enemy strategy began appearing in late December and early January. American intelligence received persistent reports that Front cadres were justifying an extremely heavy tax levy on the grounds that a decisive offensive was imminent. Enemy main force units in northwestern III CTZ either disappeared from the allied order of battle or were detected moving closer to the base area circle. Front local force units were receiving both NVA replacements, which had rarely happened before, and heavier weapons. The area around Saigon, previously designated Military Region 4 by COSVN, was reorganized into four subregions, a move clearly indicating the possibility of fighting near the capital.[14] According to the new COSVN organization, Cu Chi and Trang Bang districts were included in Subregion I (SRI); Duc Hue and Duc Hoa were included in Subregion II (SRII). Lastly, there was a marked increase in enemy military activity throughout Vietnam during the first week of January: The allies claimed that enemy losses during that week were the highest of the entire war. In III CTZ, the most important action took place on 8 January when a large enemy force, estimated by the South Vietnamese at 700 men, attacked Bao Trai. Because the Hau Nghia advisory team had more pressing tasks during the first week in February than writing the January report, details are somewhat sketchy. However, as reported in the *New York Times*, Front forces killed 27 South Vietnamese soldiers and policemen, raised their banners in the marketplace, and held most of the town for three hours before withdrawing.[15] This attack, so close to Saigon, was yet another indication to II Field Force intelligence that the enemy intended to carry the war into the heart of III CTZ, particularly when captured documents revealed preparations for a series of attacks on provincial towns, including Cu Chi.[16]

For all of these reasons, Lieutenant General Weyand, commander of U.S. forces in the provinces around Saigon and a former intelligence officer himself, sought a major alteration in American deployments for the area under his command. On 10 January, he met with Westmoreland and requested a delay for several large U.S. operations. Westmoreland was well aware of menacing enemy movements throughout the country, especially in the North, and he granted Weyand's request.[17] Consequently, Weyand ordered a steady redeployment of American battalions throughout III CTZ. In line with this movement of forces, 3d Brigade moved away from War Zone C to southern Tay Ninh. Elements of 2d Brigade reinforced the Hau Nghia-Binh Duong border. Overall, by the end of January, 27 American battalions were inside the base area circle, 22 outside, and 4 deployed near Khe Sanh—a virtual reversal of the original plan.[18] As January progressed, there was no reason to regret any of these moves for it was becoming even more clear that the Front was planning a major effort. The scope and intensity of this effort, however, was not properly appreciated, as often happens in the murky field of military intelligence.[19]

One might well sympathize with U.S. intelligence analysts in 1967–1968. Even with two decades of hindsight available, much of the history of Tet is still unclear today. Apparently, the chain of decisions leading to the Tet Offensive began in Hanoi in early 1967. As recounted earlier, a basic split existed in Hanoi between COSVN and Le Duan, on one hand, and Truong Chinh and General Giap on the other. COSVN was eager to escalate the struggle, even if this required fighting pitched battles with the Americans. General Giap and his allies advocated "protracted war," with its emphasis on political struggle: The decisive blow would be delivered after an exhausted United States had been forced to leave the field of battle. In early 1967, COSVN argued that a decisive offensive was possible the following year. We do not know the exact course of the debate, but COSVN apparently argued that many aspects of the situation were favorable. Despite U.S. exertions, the Front's main force strength was growing, their units were being supplied with more powerful weapons, and the military resources of the DRV were increasing greatly. The political situation, they seemed to believe, was likewise favorable. Fundamentally, the Front's position in the countryside was still extremely strong. Despite many paper victories on the part of the allies, Front cadres dominated or contested virtually all of rural Vietnam. Because of the fighting and economic dislocation (both resulting from American intervention), South Vietnamese cities were filling at breakneck speed. Signs of hatred toward the United States and contempt for the GVN were easy enough to find in the growing urban slums of Saigon or other cities, and the U.S. political position, both domestically and internationally, was declining quickly. Whatever the precise argument, the time was ripe, COSVN argued, for a decisive blow. Despite pleas for caution from Giap and others, Le Duan and the advocates from COSVN defeated their opposition and secured the support of the politburo for a supreme war-winning effort the following dry season.[20]

After the Tet Offensive disintegrated into the military debacle it proved to be for the Front, U.S. commentators and analysts developed two explanations of Hanoi's intentions, with very little evidence for either. In the first scenario, the politburo never expected a decisive victory in Vietnam; the real target of the Tet Offensive was the American public. Perhaps Hanoi lost more men than it wished, this argument goes, but the psychological defeat dealt to the United States was more than worth the blood expended. Indeed, the Tet Offensive is seen here as the turning point of the war, leading to the destruction of President Johnson and, ultimately, to U.S. withdrawal. The validity of this analysis is widely accepted but not self-evident: American resolve was plummeting before Tet, and it is difficult to see why it was to Hanoi's advantage to force out a war leader as miserable as Lyndon Johnson. But even if the "military defeat, psychological victory" interpretation for Tet is correct, there is no evidence at all that American will was Hanoi's primary target. No doubt, public opinion in the United States was a factor in the decision, as it was in everything done by the Party. Attacking the enemy's will, after all, was an integral part of dau tranh. It was no coincidence that, in late 1967, the DRV made signs that it would consider diplomatic negotiations without preconditions. Nevertheless, if the Tet Offensive was some sort of titanic gambit, with the sacrifice of Front manpower planned at the outset for political advantage, Hanoi has never made this claim. Indeed, during and since the war, the Party has been surprisingly mute on the entire subject of Tet, in stark contrast to the stream of accounts concerning other episodes of the war.

There is even less reason to think that the North Vietnamese politburo compelled the southern-based NLF to undertake a suicidal offensive, leading to the destruction of any independent impulses within the Front. Increasing northern domination of the Front may have been the result of the Tet Offensive, but it certainly was not the intent. COSVN was actually dominated by southerners, and it had been instrumental in Tet's inception. Military operations south of Hue (that is, in B2 Theater) were planned by General Thanh and, after his death in July 1967, by General Tra at COSVN, who also commanded assaults by Front units. Giap and PAVN controlled the northern battles. PAVN lost heavily during Tet in the areas where it could realistically fight. Front forces had to take the initiative in the Saigon area and the Mekong Delta; there was no military alternative. Infiltrating large numbers of North Vietnamese regular regiments deep into the South Vietnamese heartland without detection would have been impossible. Thus, if there was going to be a surprise assault throughout South Vietnam, the Front would have to commit its armed strength to the maximum. Certainly, the Front's officers and men did not fight as though they thought they were going to lose.

Instead, there is every reason to believe that the Front leadership thought it had a realistic chance to win the war in very short order. Although the Tet Offensive failed in most political and all military categories in Vietnam, if not in the United States, the original plan of operation, as events of 1975 indicate, was plausible. It failed because the Party overestimated its own strength and underestimated its opponents. History is filled with similar folly.

The offensive was predicated on three assumptions. First, the Hanoi planners believed that a very high level of strategic surprise could be achieved. Second, the Party assumed that ARVN units would melt away or even change sides if a devastating blow could be delivered against the ARVN command and GVN political structure. Third, Front planners believed that the urban population would aid Front forces and precipitate the fall of the government as ARVN and the National Police were collapsing. This would be the semimystical "general uprising," the mass expression of revolutionary will that would leave the enemy prostrate. Once formed, a new government would agree to a cease-fire and expel the Americans. The Party did not plan to defeat the bulk of U.S. forces in the field, although an assault on Khe Sanh might have taken place if events elsewhere were favorable.

To achieve victory, the Party planned a three-stage offensive lasting throughout the dry season. In Phase I (September 1967 to early January 1968), PAVN attacks would draw U.S. units toward the hinterlands. As we have seen, the 25th Division had some fierce battles in this period and originally was preparing for a dry season campaign in War Zone C. Weyand's redeployment was a dreadful blow to COSVN. Phase II, beginning during the Tet holiday, would entail a massive nationwide attack on the cities, towns, and allied communication centers. The timing of the Phase III final blow would be based upon the outcome of Phase II. During this climactic stage, all reserves would be committed, and victory would be assured.

Had the first two assumptions proven valid, the entire effort might have turned out differently. To cause an ARVN collapse, the Front planned a lightning blow against major ARVN headquarters and military installations throughout the country. In Saigon, this meant a coordinated assault by the six local force battalions, permanently operating in the Capital Military District, against the great U.S. bases at Long Binh and Tan Son Nhut. Elements of the 5th NLF Division were to hit the Bien Hoa complex simultaneously. The Front hoped to seize or neutralize these critical objectives to make any major American reinforcement difficult or impossible or, at least, to tie down U.S. forces in a fight for their bases, keeping them away from Saigon proper. COSVN planners also ordered sapper units to simultaneously assault the presidential palace, National Police headquarters, ARVN command installations, and the U.S. Embassy; as much of Saigon as possible was to be seized. All these objectives were to have been accomplished within the first twenty-four hours.

Concurrently, attacks on provincial and district capitals throughout the country would serve to prevent or slow allied reinforcement of Saigon and other major cities. In addition, some Front units were assigned the task of interdicting critical roadways. Everywhere, political cadres were to propagandize, thus increasing the psychological pressure on the GVN. The Front planned to multiply and exploit the initial shock by greatly reinforcing the local force units in Saigon with more heavily armed main force and divisional units; this reinforcement was promised within two to five days. By this point, Front planners expected confusion and psychological paralysis to be nearly total as ARVN units began to fall apart. In the resulting chaos, Front cadres within Saigon would instigate strikes, riots, and violence against the GVN and Americans in the city. A second wave of assaults was planned for the middle of February to finally shatter the GVN.[21]

However, as events would show, all the Party's basic assumptions behind the Tet Offensive were in error. The Party's military commands made a serious tactical blunder by commencing their offensive in the north a full twenty-four hours before attacks began throughout the rest of the country. Because of this inexplicable error, Thieu canceled the cease-fire and put ARVN units, still weakened by ill-considered furloughs, on a heightened state of readiness. American garrisons at the critical enemy objectives of Bien Hoa, Long Binh, and Tan Son Nhut were placed on red alert just hours before the assault. The military phase of the Tet Offensive in and around Saigon was virtually doomed before it began.

The Tet Offensive in the Saigon Area

Before examining the Tet Offensive in Hau Nghia province, an overview of the fighting around Saigon is in order. Indeed, the battles in Hau Nghia were an adjunct to the greater struggle for the capital. The attack began in the early hours of 31 January 1968. Although units guarding installations in Saigon were on alert, the 25th Division was caught by surprise. Sidney Stone, who, at the time, was the division historian and worked closely with 25th Division intelligence personnel, recalled the chaos that ensued:

> I shared a Quonset hut with Division Intelligence, and no one around me knew anything. There was just speculation all the time about when we were going to get mortared again. . . . We knew there was an NVA regiment around Dau Tieng, but nobody had an inkling about attacks in our direct area. . . . I was awakened about 3:00 A.M. by a real large boom. It was the first time that we had those large rockets coming in. . . . We were surrounded by the better part of a main force regiment. We were cut off from Saigon by another regiment. I am sure there was at least one regiment attacking Tan Son Nhut. We didn't have any artillery because it was forward for the dry season operation north in Dau Tieng. We just didn't know.

Front main force attacks on Long Binh and Bien Hoa failed badly after fierce fighting. The sapper assaults, despite anxious moments at the U.S. Embassy and elsewhere, failed to paralyze command control. Although slow to react, ARVN units stood their ground and nowhere collapsed. There was a crisis, however, at the huge Tan Son Nhut air base. Located on the northwest fringe of Saigon, Tan Son Nhut was the site of MACV and ARVN headquarters and probably the single most important objective attacked by the Front during Tet. A Front regiment attacked and breached the base perimeter in the first hours of the offensive, fighting off an ARVN counterattack. Fortunately for the allies, the 3d/4th Cavalry Squadron (the 25th Division's armored reconnaissance unit) was strung out along Highway 1 between Trang Bang and the Hoc Mon Bridge directly astride the Hau Nghia-Gia Dinh border. One of the battalion's missions was to aid Tan Son Nhut. As Sidney Stone remembered, "They have a saying in armor: 'regas, bypass, haul-ass,' and that's what the 3/4 did. They took off like a bat out of hell for Tan Son Nhut." The troop stationed at the Hoc Mon Bridge, a small force of about half a dozen armored personnel carriers and a single tank, managed to push directly through and attack Front infantry in the flank at the decisive moment. In its turn, the U.S. unit was also overrun. The attack on Tan Son Nhut was stalled, however, and, by early morning, the remainder of the 3d/4th and elements of the *Wolfhounds* had arrived. Fighting was hard, but the critical moment had passed.

By 3 February, NLF units were on the defensive within Saigon and Cholon. Promised reinforcements were committed late or piecemeal—or did not arrive at all. By 5 February, ARVN was given the exclusive responsibility for clearing Saigon-Cholon, and U.S. units, which by this time were streaming toward the capital, were given the task of clearing the areas surrounding the city and, as American commanders desperately hoped, of preventing enemy withdrawal. During the first two weeks of February, U.S. units engaged in heavy fighting along Highway 1, particularly near the village of Hoc Mon in Gia Dinh province directly across the Hau Nghia border, as Front units first attempted to reinforce the battle for Saigon and later attempted to protect the withdrawal of defeated battalions. Deadly, company-sized engagements, previously rare events, took place every day. Dennis Hackin, a crewman on a "track" during Tet, recalled the Hoc Mon landscape: "For the first time Vietnam really looked like the documentary war footage I grew up watching on television. Up a road on both sides was a burned-out village. Tanks, tracks, trucks, jeeps were burned and destroyed." Larger set-piece battles were likewise frequent. Jeri Liuci, an infantryman with the *Wolfhounds*, later described a night assault on his company's perimeter near the Hoc Mon Bridge:

There were a lot of VC in the area. One night we could smell a lot of pot through the woods, probably some of it was our own. We heard a lot of noise, yelling and screaming, we even heard *Take Five* by Dave Brubeck as dusk was coming on. We just had this gut feeling it was going to be heavy. We dug in a lot better than usual. We had triple concertina wire set up, claymores, trip wires, and we even cut some fields of fire. . . . Our platoon went out on night ambush. About 0200 we heard lots of fire from the perimeter. There was squawking on the radio between our companies. There was penetration on the bunker line, and the enemy was repulsed. It got really heavy: We could see tracers and explosions. "Puff the Magic Dragon" was called in. This antique plane just lumbered around, but when he opened up with those gattling guns, it was quite impressive. The noise and the sound were unbelievable. . . . We humped in just before dawn, and fighting was still going on. There were over a hundred bodies. Later that day, we found more surface graves. . . . To give you an idea of how steadfast the people we were fighting were, I found a dead VC medic who had tied himself to a bamboo clump, with a morphine syringe stuck in his arm, as he was bleeding to death. He had an RPG at the ready with the safety off. Another guy was clutching one of our claymores: He was going to try to command-detonate himself on our perimeter. Amazing.

By 19 February, the first phase of the Tet Offensive had been defeated in Saigon. However, bitter fighting continued on and off around the capital in the weeks that followed. Casualties in the 25th Division grew steadily. On March 2, the division suffered one of its worst defeats of the war. Company C of the 4th/9th (*Manchus*) battalion was ambushed and annihilated outside Saigon. Forty-eight men were killed and 29 wounded in less than half an hour. That engagement, however, was a grim aberration in a string of allied military victories. On 5 May, the Front attempted another attack on Saigon with even larger forces than the first, without, however, attempting to carry out attacks in other parts of Vietnam. In a period of a few days, the Front suffered a terrible defeat for most units failed to penetrate the U.S. screen around Saigon that had been established after the original attack.[22]

The Tet Offensive displayed glaring deficiencies within the Front's military apparatus. However clever Front forces had been in confusing allied intelligence, the actual fighting showed they had neither the command control to wage a multidivisional battle nor the staying power required to prevail in sustained combat.

Interesting testimony concerning Front failures during Tet comes from a speech given during May 1968 by a high-ranking prisoner of war, captured in October 1967. At the time of capture, the prisoner was the direct assistant to the chief of indoctrination division, COSVN. At one time, he had been a corps commander and held a rank equivalent to general: As such, he was one of the highest-ranking prisoners taken throughout the war. There was little reason to doubt the man's testimony; he was a prisoner, not a defector, and he predicted and desired a Front victory. It is therefore unlikely that he believed his remarks would be self-serving. The translator of his remarks noted that, whenever he referred to U.S. forces, he used an old idiomatic term that is used when an elder speaks to children. In his speech, the prisoner gave a classic example of the Party's view of dau tranh, or integrated political-military struggle. He claimed that, during Tet, the Front was attempting a revolution by combining a general offensive with a popular uprising. The way in which the Party would achieve its revolution was by utilizing the concept of "Three Merging Points for One Goal." The first of the three "merging points" was the "military mission," that is, efforts toward increasing strength on the battlefield. The second mission was political, aimed at building Front support and exploiting contradictions within Vietnamese society. The third mission was military indoctrination, which aimed at weakening the fabric of ARVN through propaganda, family appeals, and exploitation of the class differences between officers and enlisted men. In this context, he claimed that: the Tet Offensive was not a "normal military operation;" rather, "it is a way of applying the three merging points for one goal at the highest level in order to attain a decisive victory, that is, to destroy the South Vietnam government. In that case, we would have a final victory." The prisoner went on to outline the calculations that led to the offensive:

> We dared to begin the offensive because the strategic opportunity was there. What is that strategic opportunity? We realized that, after the dry season of 1967–1968, the U.S. forces had made every effort to attack us. But they didn't achieve the purpose that they expected. The reason I'm not talking about the RVNAF here is that the main force that truly wants to defeat us is the U.S. force, not the RVNAF. What is more, there is the problem of the elections in the States. The Doves try to put pressure on the Hawks, the ones who are responsible for the war in Vietnam, by agitating the antiwar movement in the United States. In that condition, we thought: If we attack the cities and can overthrow the South Vietnam government and remain in those cities, the Americans cannot muster sufficient reaction to overcome that situation; if we cannot get a victory in this Tet Offensive, we can at least make an echo in international opinions—especially in American public opinions. In this case, we participate directly in the antiwar movement in the United States and help the Doves win in the election, bringing the advantage to us. Thirdly, we had the tactical opportunity. We knew that, before Tet, General Westmoreland himself had announced that the VC would start a big fight for the sake of politics. And your intelligence agencies with the information of our situation surely knew that we were going to attack. . . . Big fighting, but how big? How will they employ their forces? What is the concept of the fighting? . . . So, even at the most vigilant places, there were only about 50 percent of the forces on defense. But there were also places with only 5 percent on the defense! That is why, though we were not strong in military forces, we still hoped that we could enter the cities and take them over.

The prisoner also gave an interesting analysis of the conditions that led to failure in the Tet Offensive. First of all, he admitted that the Party had seriously underestimated the esprit de corps of the ARVN officers. Second, he maintained that the Party leaders had badly misread the conditions in the urban areas. They had assumed that the masses were eager for revolution. They found out, however, that the relative prosperity within the cities (a prosperity that the prisoner considered false, coming as it did from the American presence) had seriously dampened revolutionary potential. The prisoner recalled that the 1945 General Uprising, centered in Hanoi, succeeded because the people were near starvation. He claimed, moreover, that U.S. intervention had harmed the Front both directly, by disrupting the expansion of the political cadres, and indirectly, by fostering a psychological militarization of the struggle. Both factors disturbed the equilibrium between the "three merging points":

Our direction is toward a general offensive, a revolution with the main objective being the RVNAF. Now, the main objective is also the U.S. forces. Is that concept, that slogan still right? Our higher ranks didn't answer that question! . . . But, in fact, we had to face a new situation developing for us. The lower ranks pay no attention to the political movement and to the military indoctrination mission. So, from the years of 1965–1966 until now, the political struggle movement has been in serious decline. At the same time, in the battlefields and in the military aspect, we were forced to put all our effort to developing our forces to deal with the new situation. Because of that, the relationships among the three points were more disproportionate, and the military faction could take advantage of the opportunity to burst into the cities, although the movement of the people in cities and the military indoctrination mission couldn't work together. . . .

The war is really furious at this time. When the Americans entered the war, the quantity of bombs and ammunition was twice as much as in World War II and three times more than in the Korean War. So, our bases in the jungles, our liberated villages, none of those places were quite safe for us. Some of our country bases can be considered as being swept completely. Our strategy is based on the people. Our basic means is the people. But if the people all went to the safe areas, we lost that basic means—especially the means for conducting the military indoctrination mission and for the political struggle. . . . We did not have safe conditions, and, consequently, we could not form cadres—political and military indoctrination forces—to catch up with the military forces. . . .

In this kind of war, the war between two forces, the longer it lasts, the more experiences we have. If we only use military strength to fight one another, we cannot know who will be defeated. If our side is armed with the AK47, your side also has the AR15. Modern type meets modern type, strength meets strength, and we will fight all the time, none will be defeated. Consequently, the political mission becomes important. But the average leader, when he gets modern weapons and the organizations are all set up, becomes proud and despises politics, the military indoctrination! It sounds strange here, doesn't it? But that is the fact. Because it is easy to envision military action, but it is hard with the political ones! For example, with any kind of weapon—it doesn't matter—you kill three enemy, capture three guns, everyone sees that. But the political activities—the politics also have battlefields, the battlefield of our thought and the enemy's thought—bring about the conditions leading to the victory of the military forces. But that modern weapon with a limitless effect is not recognized by anybody! . . . You already know that, in any war, the military group is always superior, the ones who handle military forces. A good leader is the one who concentrates the most troops. People have more affection for the military man, the one who, in their minds, sacrifices more. The one who has the weapon in his hand has the most prestige. So, any policy supported by the military forces will develop and progress vigorously—no one can stop it. And if it is in opposition with any policy, then only God can save that policy! The pride in our military system usually leads to mistakes in policy, bringing harm to the political and military indoctrination aspects.

The prisoner freely admitted that the failure of Tet would be a serious setback for the Front. He further predicted (correctly, as events were to show) that peace talks would entail more fierce fighting. He believed, however, that the superior organization and political sophistication of the Party, coupled with the continuing contradictions within Vietnamese society, would pave the way for ultimate victory by the NLF.[23]

As might be expected, the American view of the Tet Offensive was rather different. Above all, U.S. military intelligence was convinced that the enemy had suffered losses of unprecedented size. The fighting in the provinces around Saigon alone for the period 31 January to 19 February, according to U.S. estimates, cost the Front 12,614 men killed, 864 men captured, and 3,089 weapons lost. American losses were put at 453 killed and 3,625 wounded; ARVN suffered 471 killed and 1,290 wounded. The second wave in May was almost as violent and constituted an even greater military defeat for the Front for no psychological blows, such as the fall of Hue in February, were delivered to compensate for the losses.[24] In both phases of Tet, Front forces lost an unusually large number of crew-served weapons, a clear indication of heavy losses and tactical blunders. There were other reasons for the U.S. military to believe that the outcome of Tet had been favorable:

> The VC/NVA Tet offensive aimed at no less an objective than winning the war with one stroke aimed at the heart of political and administrative power in South Vietnam-Saigon. Militarily it was a complete failure for the VC. Its political impact is both harder to judge and beyond the scope of this report. But it must be concluded that whatever political gains were made were bought at an enormous cost to both VC and NVA in terms of trained men and organized units. It was a price which neither North Vietnam nor the NLFA (National Liberation Front Army) can afford for long. The amount of damage done to US and ARVN forces was slight by comparison, and out of the battle ARVN emerged with an unprecedented rise in self-confidence. The civil cost was considerable, but not catastrophic, nor permanent. NLF claims to represent the people were shown to be patently false as the popular uprising—a central assumption in NVA planning—failed to materialize in spite of the sudden display of NVA/VC strength throughout III CTZ. The continued weakening of "war of liberation" techniques has been shown as North Vietnam increasingly has had to replace VC losses by outside infiltrators and not by NLFA recruitment. This in turn has been reflected in the lesser guerrilla skills of NVA units when operating near populated areas, making their detection and defeat easier, and forcing them to rely more on outside support and better weapons to survive and operate. The impact of the Tet offensive on the course of the war has yet to be determined, but it is clear that it has brought the war closer to resolution either by military or political action.[25]

Yet, despite these favorable (from the allied point of view) factors, the U.S. military was obviously shaken by the size and intensity of the Tet Offensive. They were disappointed that the civil population had not provided warning and were well aware of the psychological damage done to the American war effort:

The enemy moved sizable groups of personnel and significant material support into Saigon and other critical areas before the offensive began. Friendly forces were not warned of these actions by the local population which was either indifferent to, passive, or was afraid of enemy reprisal in the event his presence was disclosed. Allied forces had no information base in the local population.
. . .

The VC and NVA are capable of infiltrating all the supplies they require to sustain their operations. Surveillance, control, and interdiction of waterways in III CTZ are inadequate to stop this flow. . . .

The enemy turned a decisive military defeat into a psychological gain. Despite heavy losses, he mounted an offensive of sizable proportions and demonstrated his capability to conduct coordinated attacks by fire and maneuver over widely dispersed locations. Politically he gained worldwide attention and may have enhanced his position at the current peace negotiations.[26]

The Tet Offensive in Hau Nghia Province

In most areas of Vietnam, the Tet Offensive, however violent at its peak, lasted for a relatively short period; most of the heavy fighting was over by March. The second phase in May was essentially confined to the area around Saigon. By summer, the GVN had begun a very rapid recovery, and in many areas the situation had returned to "normal." Unfortunately for the people of Hau Nghia, events in their province took a very different course. There, the Tet Offensive initiated a period of intense fighting and fearful destruction that lasted a year and a half. When lulls occurred, they were measured in weeks, rather than months.

There were three principal reasons for the increase in violence. In the first place, Hau Nghia was a transit point for Front and NVA main force units. Men and supplies going to and from Saigon passed through Hau Nghia in very large numbers. Resident local force and guerrilla units were always active. Consequently, the pressure on Hau Nghia was almost unrelieved. And resident forces were in action in all phases of the Tet Offensive. Retreating main force units brought U.S. forces with them in hot pursuit. In short, when the pressure was off Saigon, it usually shifted to Hau Nghia. Second, because the allies did not wish to see a repeat of Tet (although a smaller one took place in 1969), Hau Nghia became the target of a furious pacification campaign that was much more intense than that of either 1966 or 1967. Third, when peace talks began in May 1968, both sides, anticipating the possibility of a cease-fire, pushed hard to achieve political and military success. Therefore, Front forces sometimes stood and fought in situations where they would have previously evaded battle.

By October 1969, the Front had lost the military component of this stage of the war in Hau Nghia province. This defeat allowed the GVN to extend control over the province to an unprecedented, although not complete, level. Unfortunately for the allies, the flood tide for the GVN in Hau Nghia corresponded to the period of American withdrawal. By 1971, the Front began a slow but incomplete recovery. By 1972, the province was once again violently contested.

The Tet Offensive began in Hau Nghia province on 31 January with an attack on Duc Hoa town, home of the ARVN 25th Division's headquarters, by elements of a local force battalion. The assault began at dawn, and Front forces quickly occupied the marketplace and raised their banners. Within three hours, two resident ARVN battalions reoccupied the town. Because the Front unit retreated quickly and fighting was light, it is likely that this initial attack was intended to divert the attention of the local ARVN forces from the crucial early battles around Saigon.[27]

Early the next morning, a far more violent attack took place on the Cu Chi district headquarters. Front forces occupied much of the town and penetrated the advisory compound. (Ironically, but perhaps not coincidentally, the Cu Chi district advisor had been killed in an ambush two days before Tet.) Front infiltrators in the militia opened the jail, and, while the attack was in progress, Front mortar teams launched a fierce bombardment at the 25th Division base camp, inflicting many casualties. The mortar bombardment continued after sunrise, a previously unheard of event. After nine hours of fighting, ARVN, the Hau Nghia militia, and U.S. units dislodged the attackers. Cu Chi town lay in ruins.[28]

Major Donald Pearce was rushed to Bao Trai to take over the Cu Chi position left vacant by the previous advisor's death in action. To enter Cu Chi, he accompanied a two-company sweep, led by the province chief. He later described the situation in Cu Chi:

> We entered Cu Chi in the morning. . . . To enter the district compound, we had to step over the bodies of two dead VC. After we stepped over their corpses, the district chief greeted us. John Paul Vann arrived by helicopter and asked if I was ready for the job. "Yes, sir" I replied. (What else do you say?) Actually, I had hoped for an overlap period with the acting district advisor, but he was a civilian and had taken off when the fighting started. The only thing standing in the district compound was the AID trailer, and it was full of holes. The advisory compound was burned to the ground, and all of the records destroyed. . . . The town was a smoking ruin. It was damaged very badly and ceased being a viable economic center for at least six months. Recovery did not really begin until July.

Simultaneously, elements of a main force regiment occupied the large village of Tan Phu Trung astride Highway 1, on the Hau Nghia side of the border with Gia Dinh. Like the attack on Cu Chi, the occupation of Tan Phu Trung was intended to interdict Highway 1 and thus prevent American reinforcement of the battles around Saigon, particularly in the Hoc Mon area that was just a few kilometers to the east on Highway 1. This objective was only partially accomplished for 25th Division units succeeded in pushing through. Nevertheless, by 2 February, Highway 1 was intermittently closed. Unlike the smaller units that assaulted Duc Hoa and Cu Chi, the Front forces in Tan Phu Trung fought in place for thirteen days until they were finally dislodged by two battalions of the 25th Division on 15 February. Front infantry dug in deeply and used the local fortifications that had been constructed over several years for their own benefit. U.S. commanders used everything at their disposal, including air attacks and direct fire by 8" howitzers to destroy Front positions. The village was virtually destroyed.[29] Major Pearce witnessed the fighting and the aftermath:

> In the end, Tan Phu Trung was totally destroyed. There wasn't anything over two feet tall still standing. There were bomb craters everywhere and bloated bodies of the enemy in green uniforms all over. The bodies were bulldozed into bomb craters and covered. The whole area was leveled and then smoothed over with road graders.

While large-scale fighting occupied the attention of allied units, Front local forces and guerrilla units overran seven militia outposts during February. American intelligence believed that, in at least four of these cases, defeat was the result of treachery. Major Pearce saw the results of one of these betrayals at an outpost in Cu Chi:

> This outpost was built from American ammunition boxes filled with dirt and covered over—a pretty substantial little outpost. Every man in that outpost was killed, and a great many of them were still lying in their hammocks in their little fighting positions they had built in the outpost. The lieutenant in charge was lying there very quietly and peacefully; he had been shot in the back of the head. None of the bodies were hanging out of the hammocks. It had to be a coordinated thing, like "on the count of three, pull your trigger." The gate and the wire were open. It was very obvious this place had been taken from the inside.

The most violent incident of this type occurred at the La Cau outpost in Duc Hue district on 6 February. Before the attack, Front agents serving in the militia opened the gate and deactivated the defensive claymore mines. Thirty-seven PF troopers and two MAT advisors were killed in their bunkers. Fifteen additional soldiers deserted with their weapons.[30] La Cau was the first outpost to be overrun in Hau Nghia since June 1967; another PF platoon, manning an outpost within sight of the Cu Chi base camp, deserted to a man and was not heard from again.

Heavy ground attacks began again on 18 February when local force units attacked the Duc Hue district headquarters in Hiep Hoa. During the fighting, the town was heavily damaged and the sugar mill virtually destroyed. The following day, the village of Tan Hoa, just south of Hiep Hoa, was occupied by Front local force units. As at Tan Phu Trung, the occupiers of Tan Hoa stood and fought for four days until finally forced out by ARVN.[31]

Although there were short lulls, fierce fighting continued during March and April as large units from both sides traveled through and operated in Hau Nghia. Many of the Front units mauled in the Saigon area retreated to Hau Nghia. In March, elements of eight enemy battalions were within the province, as opposed to four during February. In addition, American intelligence estimated that the Front had roughly 850 local village guerrillas in action. In response to enemy movements around Saigon, General Weyand at II Field Force once again redeployed his units. He temporarily relieved the 25th Division of responsibility for portions of Tay Ninh province and shifted most of its units into Hau Nghia, Binh Duong, and the Capital Military District. Several U.S. battalions were active along Highway 1 and other lines of communication in Hau Nghia, attempting to clear roads and prevent Front resupply for another attack on Saigon.

Throughout this period, local guerrillas did their best to slow American and ARVN units on the roads. The road connecting Bao Trai and Duc Hoa, for instance, was effectively closed.[32] Bill Kestell, a crewman in a 25th Division APC, described the impact of this type of harassment:

> Round a bend—there's a barricade—flankers out—herringbone formation—clear the road for the engineers to get by to check for mines and booby traps. Then either blow them or push them out of the way with the articulated scraper. Then pull in your flankers—mount up and take the point to the next barricade. Sometimes, you could see two or three beyond the one you were working on. And always the questions—how many eyes are watching you? Be careful not to get careless or let your guard down just because nothing has happened yet—or yesterday—or last week. To cover twenty miles or less might take the better part of a day!

Small-unit actions were sharp and steady, and bigger battles were also common. On four occasions in March and once in April, U.S. and ARVN units succeeded in engaging enemy battalions. Americans claimed to have killed well over 100 men in each engagement, while sustaining minimal casualties themselves.[33] Although Front forces spent most of this period refitting for the second phase of Tet, they, too, launched sporadic attacks. In March, three more outposts were overrun, and another was taken in April.

Although there was a lull in the fighting elsewhere in late March, North Vietnamese regulars entered the war in Hau Nghia province in a dramatic way. On 25 March, three PAVN battalions assaulted Trang Bang district town, beginning one of the largest battles to take place in Hau Nghia province during the entire war. Although the precise PAVN objective cannot be ascertained, the size and ferocity of the assault indicates that the attackers wanted to seize and hold the town.[34] Major Frank Chance, the Trang Bang senior advisor, described events:

> The attack began early in the morning, about 0400 with mortar and small arms fire directed at the district headquarters. The fighting moved into the marketplace and escalated with machine guns and rockets. Our RF/PF (the militia) resisted fiercely. The province chief brought up a force from Bao Trai. The 25th Division intervened with all of the firepower it could muster. There was fighting in the streets and on the rooftops. When it was over the next morning, I personally counted over 300 dead NVA. We brought in bulldozers to bury the dead. We had to wear our gas masks to quell the odor of death. It was a complete defeat for the enemy.

The battle, however, continued. Remnants of the Front regiment fleeing Trang Bang stumbled upon elements of a U.S. mechanized infantry company and overran it. Bill Kestell, who miraculously survived the encounter, remembered seeing a "sea of NVA" before his "track" was blown up. The pursuit and sporadic fighting continued for two more days before what was left of the PAVN force retreated into Cambodia.

In May, action around Saigon again reached a feverish pitch. The 9th NLF Division, which had not been fully committed in earlier fighting, used Hau Nghia province as the staging area for a renewed assault on the capital. Altogether, sixteen main and local force Front battalions were identified in the province throughout the month. As previously recounted, the second phase of Tet ended in quick defeat for the Front. But in Hau Nghia, because of the rapid movement of forces from both sides, combat raged virtually every day. Cu Chi was again vainly assaulted by the Front and heavily damaged.[35] Three 25th Division battalions with ARVN support succeeded in nearly surrounding a main force regiment astride the Vam Co Dong. In a three-day battle, the enemy unit was nearly destroyed: As such, this action constituted one of the very few "textbook" tactical operations conducted by the division throughout the war.[36]

Although the assault on Saigon was turned away by the middle of the month, a battle on 27 May probably best exemplifies the military futility of Front efforts during the second phase of Tet. During this encounter, elements of the Front 273d Regiment assaulted a full battalion of the 25th Division (4/23d Mechanized Infantry), deployed in a night defensive position in a pineapple grove in the southeastern corner of Duc Hoa district. The U.S. unit was on full alert. The Front soldiers employed human-wave tactics to attack an American position garrisoned by nearly as many men as the attackers and possessing far greater firepower. The results were predictable: The Americans claimed 243 enemy killed, compared to a loss of 6 men dead. U.S. soldiers also captured 33 crew-served weapons, a sure indication that they had smashed their enemy.[37]

During June, NLF main and local forces began to retreat from the provinces around Saigon, and fighting fell off markedly. Nevertheless, 25th Division units stayed close to the Saigon area. As usual, when enemy units moved through Hau Nghia on their way to Cambodia and War Zone C, small-unit actions were numerous. However, a short lull began as the Front retreated and allied forces both contemplated the full meaning of the Tet Offensive and pondered future action. At this point, it is possible to take a closer look at the impact of Tet on the overall situation in Hau Nghia province.

The Tet Offensive very nearly destroyed the pacification program in Hau Nghia and made a complete mockery of GVN claims that it was able to protect the rural population. Of course, this was the predictable result of the failure of the allied "shield" to protect the populated areas from incursion by NLF main force units. Neither the Regional nor Popular Forces, much less the RD Cadres, were intended to stand their ground against the better-trained, more highly motivated, and more heavily armed main and local force Front units. This was particularly true by the beginning of Tet for the local force units were significantly upgunned with the general issue of the AK47 assault rifle. In this category, even ARVN was at a disadvantage because old American carbines were still general issue. However, ARVN was more than able to compensate for this weakness through artillery and air support. The territorial forces, at this stage of the war, were rarely afforded such luxury unless operating with an ARVN or U.S. unit. Thus, as these units were pulled back to protect Saigon, clear Highway 1, and guard the major towns, the soldiers of the RF/PF, huddled in their often meager outposts, were in a very difficult situation. No doubt, this state of affairs had been anticipated by the Front: A plea to the soldiers of both ARVN and the RF/PF to desert and aid the revolution was the primary propaganda theme used early in the offensive.[38] Although this plea had little effect on ARVN, it had some success with the territorial forces. Altogether, 12 of Hau Nghia's 66 outposts fell during the first 6 months of 1968. American intelligence was convinced that, in several cases, the fallen outposts had been betrayed by members of the garrison secretly working for the Front. For the period of 1 January to 1 July 1968, the Regional Forces lost 134 men killed in action, against 246 deserters; Popular Forces lost 68 men in battle, as opposed to 432 deserters. Though most of the RF troopers eventually returned to duty, only 5 PF soldiers went back. A large portion of the Hau Nghia Popular Forces, therefore, had been working for the Front all along.[39]

The failure of the militia, however understandable, led to a nearly total collapse of security in the rural areas of Hau Nghia. According to one American observer in the province:

Neutralization, not the destruction of outposts, seems to be the VC aim. Every time Charlie goes by a post, he takes a slap at it. This keeps the RF/PF inside, out of contact with the villagers. . . . Villagers interviewed say that they worry only about living from day to day, moving back and forth to escape the fighting. Few now attempt to rebuild destroyed or damaged houses, or, it seems, to try to plant a crop for the coming year. . . . The villages are, at least for the present, enemy controlled, and the best efforts of forces within the province seem hardly to hinder enemy movement toward the capital.[40]

Although to one degree or another this bleak situation held true for the entire province, Duc Hue district was in particularly bad straits. According to a Rural Technical Team survey conducted in May, the government's position in Duc Hue during February "hung by a thread. During this period the VC unquestionably controlled the GVN population of the district." The team further reported that one-third of the district's Popular Forces had deserted and that many had gone over to the Front.[41]

As might be expected, the collapse of security in Hau Nghia brought an end to the pacification program; during this period, according to the PSA, the "pacification program ground to a halt." In particular, he claimed that "during February, the RD effort in Hau Nghia province was nearly shattered by the VC Tet Offensive."[42] Although the Front made no particular effort to target the RD Cadre teams, and few members were killed or wounded throughout the offensive, the fighting forced the teams back into the government-controlled towns. All the efforts of the cadre teams during the preceding year and a half had no effect on the Front's ability to penetrate hamlets. The deputy province chief, in charge of security, estimated that the Front could penetrate any hamlet in Hau Nghia, including the 1967 New Life hamlets. Although the RD Cadres made some effort to resume activities during the short lull of April, the May attacks stopped them again.[43] These factors led to an expression of disgust by a member of the Hau Nghia advisory team:

> The GVN is for the most part ineffective in previously pacified areas. Upon the departure of the RD Cadre teams, the RD hamlets are abandoned and any programs that may have been started by the cadre collapse in short order. There does not appear to be anything of a lasting nature built in the RD hamlets and especially disappointing is the fact that this includes any kind of a popular base for the central government. . . . Confidence in the ability of the GVN to furnish security must be given to the people of this province before any significant progress in pacification can be made. This confidence will be established when security becomes in fact real.[44]

Other facets of the pacification program also stumbled. Advisors castigated the Vietnamese Information Service (VIS) because of its uselessness in the face of the great upsurge in Front propaganda. Efforts to identify and attack the NLF political apparatus made no headway whatsoever for the RD Cadres and the National Police were busy protecting themselves. The Cu Chi district Phoenix headquarters was abandoned in February, and the American advisor for the Hau Nghia Phoenix Program was killed in April.[45] Naturally, nothing could be done against the Front apparatus in the many areas of Hau Nghia that the GVN temporarily abandoned.

CORDS also had picked a bad time to begin organizing the People's Self Defense Force (PSDF). The idea of this program, close to the hearts of both Colby and Komer, was to arm and organize the broad masses of the rural population and thus somehow involve them directly in the struggle against the Front. Later, this program developed into something of a farce in Hau Nghia. In any case, as reported by Ollie Davidson at the time, Trang Bang district officials distributed a paltry number of weapons. One of the officials underscored the absurdity of the situation when he commented sardonically, "If the soldiers returned to their outpost every night, then it would be the people who were the main fighting unit and the soldiers in reserve. This was not how, he said, it was designed to be."[46]

Because the fighting during the Tet Offensive centered upon the cities and towns, many areas in rural Vietnam escaped the violence. In Hau Nghia, however, destruction was very widespread, especially to hamlets astride Highway 1 in Cu Chi and Trang Bang districts. As previously examined, the large village of Tan Phu Trung, the scene of a two-week battle, was devastated. The GVN claimed that 1,039 families there had been left homeless during the fighting—11 villagers killed and 21 wounded.[47] The 25th Division reports gave the even higher estimate that 80 percent of the village had been destroyed.[48]

Major Pearce recalled the efforts made to reconstruct the village:

> Members of village staff and our people laid out a completely new village. For tactical purposes, everything was laid out at 90° angles, with a well in the middle of town. Every villager was allowed to come back, but some were unhappy because they wanted to rebuild on the exact same spot as before for religious reasons. We wouldn't let them. We designed a prefab house package with a cement floor and tin roof and made of wood. Before assembly, these houses were banded with metal and stockpiled. We had a big ceremony. We were trying to win hearts and minds after we had, during the course of battle, destroyed their entire village. The village chief had his plan, and before I left the village had been completely rebuilt. It was one of largest civic action programs we were able to pull off.

Although Tan Phu Trung was the hardest hit, other villages, including Tan An Hoi and Phuoc Hiep in Cu Chi along Highway 1, Trang Bang district town, Hiep Hoa, and Bao Trai all suffered serious damage. In April, prior to the heavy fighting of May, the GVN estimated that 3,095 families in Hau Nghia were homeless.[49] The PSA estimated that 30 percent of the population of Hau Nghia had left the province during February.[50] The situation in May was described by Lt. Col. Carl Bernard, the new PSA, in a message to John Paul Vann:

> The pacification effort in Hau Nghia has been submerged by the flood of main force battalions moving to and from Saigon area and the U.S.-ARVN efforts to destroy them. The concern of the Vietnamese, official and nonofficial, has turned to security and no time or effort is being spent on any other subject. Six heavy contacts, all within earshot of heavily populated areas, have taken place since 1 May. There have been 52 attacks on outposts since 1 May resulting in total of 253 ARVN and RF/PF casualties. The psychological impact of these incidents has been incalculably bad. I have valid reports of civilians from outlying hamlets in Trang Bang who had formerly spent the night in the district capital. They now go further into VC-controlled territory for security. They avoid GVN-controlled areas because they consider them all targets for imminent attack and subsequent rescue by U.S. and ARVN forces. In Cu Chi alone, there were 452 houses destroyed. From Tet on, 70 percent of Cu Chi's commercial and light industry has been destroyed and no efforts made to rebuild. The big marketplace in Cu Chi town has been forbidden the people by the VC, and they are deathly afraid to violate this order.[51]

The situation in Hau Nghia was made even worse because the areas that suffered the most had been scenes of the most intensive pacification activities in preceding years. The various civic action programs performed by the 25th Division had centered on the villages along Highway 1. Tan Phu

Trung, in particular, had been the recipient of much effort. (Richard Nixon had visited there when he was vice president.) A goodly portion of its population had come from the North after 1954 and had later been supplemented by villagers relocated from destroyed hamlets off the road.[52] No doubt, a good deal of political capital was used up by the allies in these areas due to their obvious inability to protect the population. In addition, members of the advisory teams noticed a change in the migration of population. Previously, when fighting had centered around hamlets off the road, villagers had moved to government-controlled areas. During Tet, however, with the fighting taking place in the areas where the government was strongest, many villagers fled to hamlets controlled by the Front.[53] Certainly, this was a reasonable response on the part of the villagers, and the Front propagandized heavily in this direction. Nevertheless, this movement of villagers sheds doubt on earlier American claims that those civilians moving into government areas were essentially "voting with their feet" in favor of the GVN.

The sheer violence of the Tet Offensive created a dangerous and very ugly chemistry between U.S. soldiers and the local inhabitants. It must be stressed that only the major engagements have been outlined in this account. During the first six months of 1968, the numerous battles were continually punctuated with smaller clashes. American soldiers were fearful, enraged, and extremely quick to retaliate against the smallest enemy action; many held personal grudges against individual hamlets. This sorry situation, so difficult to control, drew an angry response in July from Major Pearce:

> The past month has seen several incidents in which very few VC and very few shots fired in anger triggered U.S. troop reaction which resulted in rather extensive destruction of property and the death of 13 civilians and the wounding of 8 more. In the cold light of post-facto investigation, it would seem that the retaliatory measures taken by the U.S. troops in an attempt to defend themselves were vastly out of proportion to the threat that existed. To return a few AK47 rounds with the main gun on an M48 tank and thus destroy homes and kill sleeping civilians is wrong and is a problem, with many pros and cons involved. The people openly question this tactic.[54]

After the war, Pearce recalled that road incidents, sometimes purposeful, led to the death or injury of many civilians during this period. There were almost daily episodes of needless property destruction and other acts of cruelty by American soldiers. The worst situations, however, developed when Front harassment provoked U.S. fire. Pearce recalled:

> For the first six months of 1968, soldiers of the 25th Division were absolutely paranoid about ambush. One round over an American head would bring forth a huge response. Any Vietnamese were assumed to be VC and treated as such. [The American soldiers] would fire blindly at the first tree line. I have seen hamlets destroyed by helicopters after taking small arms fire. Troops would always report that they found enemy bunkers, even though we kept

telling them that every house had a bunker for protection from our fire.
. . .

Once I sifted through remains of some houses destroyed in a village on
Highway 1 toward Trang Bang. I found a grandmother and four children
suffocated from flames. They were unmarked. Things like this were not unusual
and used to break my heart. . . .

They used to destroy in a few minutes time all that I could possibly conjure
up with all the civic action programs and begging and pleading and whatever
else you could think of. They could counteract what I could do in a month
in three or four minutes.

It was cruelly paradoxical that these tragic encounters took place as the
25th Division was attempting to tighten its rules of engagement concerning
artillery. Inhabited areas were put off-limits to artillery fire unless the military
situation clearly required it. Major Pearce had great difficulty in getting
artillery support for the Cu Chi district militia outposts because many of
them were in abandoned hamlets. The maps, however, were not updated
and showed inhabited areas. The ironic result, as described by Pearce, was
that the Front was able to manipulate American restraint, just as in other
instances it would manipulate American quickness to use firepower:

The VC were very smart. They moved in and around inhabited areas as shown
on the map and used them as staging areas because they knew that U.S.
artillery would not fire on them. I let more VC go free and observed them
moving across country than I ever killed with artillery fire.

The security vacuum created by the withdrawal of allied units from much
of Hau Nghia allowed NLF cadres to tax on an unprecedented scale.
Interesting testimony concerning this phase of the Front's activity comes
from a middle-level defector interrogated in 1971. This man had joined the
Party in 1963 but was expelled the next year for taking a second wife.
Because he no longer had protection from the Party, he fled to Cambodia
in 1965 and settled in the Front sanctuary of Ba Thu. By 1965, Ba Thu
was already a major rear area for the NLF, providing a secure place for
training, supply, and rest. In late 1967, as the Front prepared for its supreme
effort, the defector was offered the position of deputy village finance and
economy chief for the rural hamlets of Hiep Hoa village. Because the man's
second wife had married someone else, he yielded to pressure and returned
to Hiep Hoa in January 1968:

I accepted the offer, and, in January 1968, I returned to Hiep Hoa. At this
time, I believed that the impending General Offensive would succeed, and the
war would end soon after. . . .

My first job after returning to Hiep Hoa was to conduct a massive taxation
campaign. To do this, we had the support of an unprecedented number of
troops. Under normal conditions, the village guerrillas were responsible for
the security of finance and economy cadre during taxation. In early 1968,
however, there were several main and local force units in the area. While

large-scale attacks were being made on GVN-controlled areas and bases, we had conducted a widespread taxation campaign, supported by our village guerrillas and some elements of the external forces. Everyone in Hiep Hoa was asked to give one-third of the value of his crops and animals. The people were told that this was the money needed to finance the final drive to expel the Americans and bring down the puppet government. As a result, we were able to collect over 1,700,000$ during 1968 in Hiep Hoa.[55]

The Results of the Tet Offensive

A survey of the situation in Hau Nghia province at the end of June 1968 illustrates the numerous setbacks suffered by the government. Although Bao Trai was attacked twice, fighting finally began to slow as main force units withdrew from the province. Security, however, remained very bad at night because RF/PF units would retreat to their outposts, fearing they were outgunned by Front forces. By the end of the month, the RF/PF was seriously understrength. According to the province report, "travel on all roads in Hau Nghia is a perilous proposition."[56] Forty-nine people lost their lives due to mines on the roads during the month. RD teams returned to their hamlets but only during the daylight. Because so many had fled to Saigon, the National Police were numerically understrength and essentially confined to static defense. Consequently, little was done to target and attack the estimated 1,100 members of the Front apparatus that U.S. intelligence estimated to be active in Hau Nghia. The Chieu Hoi Program showed disappointing results, and, due to the fighting, schools had been closed, thus preventing the completion of the schoolyear. The fighting had also crippled commerce and destroyed the sugar industry.[57]

Nevertheless, despite all calamities, it would be a mistake to overestimate the extent of GVN-American setbacks suffered due to the Tet Offensive in Hau Nghia province. If the allied political and military efforts in the previous two years had been genuinely successful at shaking the Front and altering the political allegiance of the population, then Tet would have been a total disaster for the GVN. However, such success had not taken place. Any "progress" achieved by the allies had been coercive in nature and measured in terms of villages occupied and administered in daylight, outposts manned, roads controlled, territorial soldiers recruited, Hoi Chanh collected, and, above all, number of enemy killed.

There is no credible evidence that the population of Hau Nghia believed that either the GVN or the Americans could bring genuine security, much less honest and effective administration. This was quite understandable, considering the fact that virtually every hamlet in Hau Nghia, regardless of the degree of GVN presence, had a resident Front apparatus of one size or another, backed up by some sort of military force in direct proximity. None of the social or political conditions that had led so many peasants in Hau Nghia to follow the Front in the first place had changed. Thus, no GVN-inspired "social revolution" had been short-circuited by Tet. The Front continued to recruit, although with more difficulty due to the vast allied military presence. Before Tet, the Front was always able to get its message across, and, however stunning Tet appeared to be to the Johnson administration, the American news media, and even the urban population of South Vietnam, the people of Hau Nghia could have held few illusions concerning the great strength of the Front. The GVN lost little that was fundamental in Hau Nghia because they had gained nothing fundamental before Tet. Therefore, most of the setbacks were temporary, and, once the military situation permitted, the allies proved quite capable of restoring and even improving the position of the GVN in Hau Nghia province.

The situation of the Party and the Front after Tet, however, was quite different. Their losses, both material and psychological, were real and proved long-lasting in Hau Nghia. Obviously, the Tet Offensive yielded great political dividends abroad, as anticipated by the Front: Very possibly, these dividends were even more substantial than hoped for. The crazy-brave sapper assault on the U.S. Embassy must be considered one of the most successful small-unit actions in the history of modern warfare.

Nevertheless, it would take time before the political advantages gained abroad would be felt in Vietnam. The setbacks suffered by the Front, however, were felt immediately. In the first place, it had failed to deliver on its promise to end the war rapidly. It must be pointed out that, though the NLF had always predicted success and would continue to do so, Front cadres had told the masses, just before Tet, that victory was imminent. They had intended to inspire their supporters to make the maximum effort. Yet, the great endeavor had ended in failure. Second, the "military indoctrination" mission had not succeeded for the most part, even in Front strongholds like Hau Nghia. Although many Hau Nghia militiamen went over to the Front or fled the fighting and others remained immobile in their forts, some units fought stubbornly. More importantly, ARVN units in the province, if the opinion of the advisory team was valid, put up a good fight after the initial shock was over.[58]

The best example of skilled and intrepid defense by GVN forces took place when two Front battalions attacked Bao Trai on 6 May. The apparent objective was the Hau Nghia province headquarters, although it is not clear whether the Front wished to occupy the town. Front sappers penetrated to the center of Bao Trai but were killed while placing their charges. Led by Col. Ma Sanh Nhon, the Hau Nghia province chief, the militia stood firm during the attack. The next day, helped by villagers who pointed out concealed Front positions, the militia ejected the remnant of the attacking force. American advisors were extremely pleased with events. The Front was defeated in a psychologically important place and suffered heavy losses. Because local forces handled the situation without U.S. aid, Bao Trai suffered little damage, and few defenders or civilians became casualties. It was a "low-tech," low-cost victory by the Vietnamese themselves, just the sort of thing that John Vann and his supporters hoped to see. The question raised by the battle at Bao Trai, from the American point of view, concerned what could be done to foster a more general distribution of the conditions that had made the victory possible: good leadership, good soldiering, and popular support. As we shall see, much of the next four years was spent trying to find the answer.[59]

Lastly, Front forces in Hau Nghia suffered unprecedented losses, although it is impossible to determine their extent. In particular, the local force units were heavily engaged throughout Tet and certainly suffered grievously. Interesting evidence concerning the Tet Offensive in Hau Nghia from the point of view of Front forces is contained in a very large document captured in October 1968. The document, prepared for COSVN Subregion 1 Headquarters and dated 30 June 1968, is an official report on the operations of the Cu Chi District local force units, covering the first six months of 1968. Like an operational report from an American division, most of the report is concerned with establishing an enemy order of battle, guessing enemy capabilities and intentions, and quantifying anything that could be quantified. Yet, some portions are revealing. Perhaps reflecting the view of the captured Front general quoted earlier, who stated that "the main force which truly wants to defeat us is the U.S. force, not the RVNAF," American forces are referred to as "the enemy," "U.S. forces," or the "Americans" in this document. South Vietnamese units of any type, when referred to specifically, were invariably called "puppet" forces or troops. Another interesting characteristic of the report is the preposterous number of victories claimed. If this report were taken seriously, COSVN would have believed that the local forces operating in Cu Chi district did not suffer a single defeat and inflicted murderous losses on the U.S. 25th Division. The Cu Chi local forces, which included one battalion, five companies, and several smaller units, claimed to have killed nearly 6,000 U.S. troops, primarily during fighting against the Tropic Lightning Division. The actual casualties suffered by the 25th between 1 February and 1 June 1968 were 883 killed and 3,679 wounded in fighting against main force, local force, and guerrilla units in five different provinces. The following strange account of a mutiny by 25th Division soldiers, which may or may not have actually occurred—and certainly not as described, indicates that Front leaders, like their American counterparts, found it difficult to "know the enemy":

In the battle fought at Trang Bang, Go Dau, elements of the 2d Brigade, 25th U.S. Infantry Division, were ordered to go to the aid of a U.S. unit there. They ran away to hide themselves, refusing to get aboard the planes. Their commanders pursued and caught them, beat them mercilessly, and shaved their heads. A number of others struggled against the order, cried, and fasted.[60]

Yet, despite fanciful claims of unending victories, more sober testimony is contained in the Cu Chi report. As the following quote indicates, the Cu Chi local force leaders were willing to acknowledge the difficulties caused by allied firepower, although they were surprised that it would be used on hamlets long built-up and pacified:

The enemy activities have created a number of difficulties for us in the fields of attack preparation, transportation, and movement over open terrain and caused human and material losses to us. . . .

In summary, the enemy tactics consisted primarily of using armored vehicles, helicopter gunships and war planes to destroy the battle area even in strategic hamlets.[61]

The report also illustrates the grievous losses suffered by Front units that saw heavy fighting during Tet. At full strength, the 7th Local Force Battalion, the major unit of Cu Chi forces, had 320 men. By the end of Tet, it had lost 122 killed and 116 wounded—a 74 percent casualty rate that, in military terms, is considered ruinous.[62] Other units under control of Cu Chi District suffered 231 killed and 187 wounded out of an undetermined number of effectives, although it was mentioned that one company that had 60 men at full strength was down to 15; another 26 men were captured, and 20 more deserted.[63] Because any headquarters must have a more or less accurate estimate of its own forces, these figures are probably accurate: It is unlikely that a unit would overestimate its own losses. Therefore, the Cu Chi report validated allied claims that Front forces suffered unprecedented losses during the Tet Offensive.

There is other evidence that the offensive caused a serious setback to the NLF in Hau Nghia. The Hiep Hoa deputy finance chief quoted earlier recalled that he was "extremely discouraged" and "frightened by the losses which we had taken." His further remarks illustrate very well the problem caused by the Front's military debacle:

We had lost many cadre during the 1968 offensive and its aftermath. The result was that many cadre were making it to the top who in former times would have never been considered. . . . My own operations were becoming more and more difficult and dangerous. The taxation situation had deteriorated tremendously, because the people were disenchanted with us. We had promised to topple the puppet government with the General Offensive and had collected extremely heavy taxes on the basis of this pledge. In 1969, when I attempted to tax again, the people were angry about this. This attitude, combined with the decimation of our cadre and the enemy build-up, resulted in a great drop in taxes collected. From January to October 1969, we were only able to collect 300,000$ in all of Hiep Hoa as compared to 1,700,000$ in 1968.[64]

The American officer who interrogated the defector from Hiep Hoa later recalled that the experiences of this man were far from unique—many defectors considered the Tet Offensive a disaster. Brig. Gen. Stuart Herrington, the interrogator and at the time (1971–1972) a captain in the U.S. Army attached to the Hau Nghia advisory team, contended after the war that Tet resulted in "the near death of the Southern Communist movement—insofar as native *Southern* cadres are concerned."[65] After being captured during the summer, the acting commander of a Front regiment, which included a Cu Chi main force battalion, revealed that, whereas at the beginning of Tet his regiment was at full strength and manned by 95 percent native southerners, by the beginning of the second phase of Saigon attacks in May, half his men were replacements from PAVN.[66] Also, Jeffrey Race found that the material, human, and psychological losses suffered by the Front during Tet were an important factor in its serious decline in Long An province after 1968.[67]

The most definitive commentary on the Tet Offensive comes from General Tra. After June 1967, he commanded COSVN's military forces and thus had a leading role in both planning and controlling the offensive. Considering Tra's position, it would have been difficult for him to completely condemn the effort. In his memoirs, he claimed that Tet was a "strategic blow" to the United States. Nevertheless, as the following quote indicates, Tra clearly believed that the Tet Offensive as actually carried out was a mistake and that a different road could and should have been followed. The Party erred, according to Tra, in allowing emotional factors to cloud its determination of the balance of forces, a serious blunder in Marxist terms:

> However, during Tet of 1968 we did not correctly evaluate the specific balance of forces between ourselves and the enemy, did not fully realize that the enemy still had considerable capabilities and that our capabilities were limited, and set requirements that were beyond our actual strength. In other words we did not base ourselves on scientific calculation or a careful weighing of all factors, but in part on an illusion based on our subjective desires.

The results of allowing hope to cloud analysis were catastrophic losses and a severe blow to the revolution:

> For that reason, although that decision was wise, . . . we suffered large sacrifices and losses with regard to manpower and material, especially cadres at the various echelons, which clearly weakened us. Afterwards, we were not only unable to retain the gains we had made but had to overcome a myriad of difficulties in 1969 and 1970 so that the revolution could stand firm in the storm. Although it is true that the revolutionary path is never a primrose path that always goes upward, and there can never be a victory without sacrifice, in the case of 1968, if we had weighed and considered things meticulously, taken into consideration the balance of forces of the two sides, and set forth correct requirements, our victory would have been even greater, less blood would have been spilled by the cadres, enlisted men, and people, and *the future development of the revolution would certainly have been far different* (emphasis added).

In most heavily populated areas of Vietnam, the summer of 1968 was a welcome respite from the violence of the preceding months. NLF main force units withdrew to their sanctuaries, and local force and guerrilla units attempted to avoid fighting while desperately trying to replenish their ranks. The GVN and CORDS concentrated their efforts on Operation RECOVERY, an intensive effort aimed at resettling refugees and repairing the widespread physical destruction. Even the people of Hau Nghia experienced a short lull in the violence during July, as the 9th Front Division retreated to War

Zone C and other units avoided contact; there was not a single enemy-initiated action during the entire month. As the enemy withdrew from Hau Nghia, more 25th Division units, principally elements of 2d and 3d Brigades, poured into the province. The American military position in Hau Nghia was strengthened even further in June when two powerful battalions of the 10lst Airborne Division, recently redeployed from the north after the relief of Khe Sanh, were put under the operational control of the 25th Division. One of the new battalions participated in the last major battle of the Tet Offensive in Hau Nghia, routing a main force battalion along the Vam Co River on 27 June.[68]

With any threat from main force units temporarily lifted, the 25th Division began an ambitious pilot project in Duc Hue district. A frequent criticism of army pacification techniques was that their duration was too short: Whatever benefits were gained during operations were quickly lost when U.S. units pulled out. Consequently, the 25th decided to deploy a full battalion in Duc Hue district and leave it there for an extended period. American officers hoped that this method of deployment would benefit long-term security, increase operational capabilities as American personnel grew intimate with the details of the terrain, and aid in the collection of local intelligence as villagers learned to trust the soldiers. More importantly, officers hoped that villagers either hostile to the Front or neutral in the struggle would be persuaded that the GVN, with U.S. aid, could protect them on a sustained basis. Operational priorities were somewhat different than they had been on previous pacification missions. Rather than seeking out Front combat units, the battalion officers were instructed to target enemy support elements, guides, porters, supply assistance troops, guerrillas, and, above all, members of the Front political apparatus.[69] Furthermore, a concentrated effort was made to cooperate with territorial units, although a Vietnamese request that U.S. squads be placed in outposts was rejected. Both the division and the advisory team were pleased with the project, particularly when one raid resulted in the capture of seventeen Front cadres, a very good day's work in Hau Nghia.[70] Soon thereafter, the 25th Division greatly expanded this project.

The Hau Nghia administration and the U.S. advisory team utilized the lull, caused by enemy withdrawal and the overall lessening of enemy activities due to the rainy season, to reestablish the outward manifestations of the pacification program. The RD Cadre teams were once again out in the hamlets, despite reports that some were alienating villagers through improper conduct. In addition, the advisors doubted that anything would be accomplished even after completion of the requisite number of tasks and steps; the province report ruefully noted that most of the "outer-belt" hamlets being pacified (that is, those hamlets constituting the spreading "oil spot") had been pacified before. The territorial forces were slowly rebuilt, although it was noted that they still failed to project local security due to a lack of offensive operations.[71]

The "miracle rice" pilot project, one of the very few economic programs that had the potential to make a major improvement in the rural population's standard of living, also foundered in Hau Nghia. Promising yields several times greater than normal, U.S. agricultural advisors pushed this program heavily, and over 200 farmers in Hau Nghia agreed to accept the new seed. However, the seed arrived late, the Vietnamese agricultural service chief got drafted (thus crippling the educational program), and many farmers grew wary of the added investment in fertilizer and insecticides that was required. In the end, only sixty farmers accepted the seed. As might be expected, 1968 was a very inauspicious year to begin agricultural experimentation. Some demonstration plots were destroyed by tracked vehicles. Travel to and from markets remained a very hazardous proposition. And, to add insult to injury, there was a local drought. The Hau Nghia agricultural advisor noted sadly in October that local farmers were demoralized by the six months of virtually nonstop fighting they had endured and, because of their despair, were allowing much good land to lie fallow.[72]

During the summer of 1968, the advisory team began pressing for improvements in local administration. Because Hau Nghia was poor, backward, and very dangerous, Vietnamese officials had long considered it a hardship post. This situation grew worse after Tet due to the general mobilization decreed by Thieu, leading to increased draft calls. As previously mentioned, American advisors at every level in Hau Nghia struggled perpetually, but vainly, against perceived corruption and incompetence. In this period, however, the advisory team grew ever more vocal concerning corrupt and shoddy administration, particularly when not a few officials took unauthorized, extended leaves to escape the Tet Offensive. A typical exasperated complaint came from the PSA in October:

One of Hau Nghia's enduring problems has been the repeated assignment of dishonest, ineffective and cowardly officials to this province when they fail to measure up elsewhere. Some examples: The former deputy for administration arrived in July after having exhausted all possible sources of appeal to avoid this assignment. He was timid and refused to leave the towns unless absolutely necessary. He submitted his resignation in October and vanished before the request was acted on. The former Chieu Hoi chief will be court-martialed for selling Hoi Chanh status to three Vietnamese of Chinese extraction from Cholon. His predecessor also was jailed for corruption. The III CTZ police chief told provincial police chiefs that those refusing to behave would be transferred to outlying provinces. That assignment in Hau Nghia is in fact used as punishment for policemen is shown by two assignments which recently came to light, one an alcoholic and the other a suspected VC.[73]

For whatever reasons, these complaints received a hearing in Saigon as John Vann, Robert Komer, and William Colby all pressed Vietnamese officials to do something. During April 1969, Thieu visited Hau Nghia and personally promised efforts toward improving administration. Whether anything was actually done concerning this matter must remain an unanswered question, although praise for Vietnamese administration in Hau Nghia continued to be rare indeed.[74]

The comparative lull in violence ended in Hau Nghia during August. Early in the month, main force units attacked the base camp of the 49th ARVN Regiment at Duc Hoa, causing heavy casualties. Two weeks later, a Regional Forces outpost in Trang Bang was attacked. Although the defenders beat back the assault, the outpost was destroyed and had to be abandoned, causing an exodus of civilians to Trang Bang district town. On 28 August, the two battalions of the 101st Airborne intercepted a battalion of the 101st NVA regiment and destroyed it in northern Trang Bang district. This was undoubtedly most fortunate for the allies because the next day a large Front force attacked Trang Bang district town. In this instance, the garrison was alerted and put up stout resistance. An ARVN Ranger battalion, led personally by the Hau Nghia province chief, reacted quickly and put the enemy to flight. Although the number of enemy claimed killed was not large (31), territorial and ARVN losses were slight. The American advisory team, unaccustomed to witnessing a well-conducted battle on the part of the territorials, was extremely pleased, particularly because Vietnamese social welfare officials were on the scene that very day dispensing compensation. The commander of the Tropic Lightning Division also arrived promptly and personally decorated some territorial soldiers. The Trang Bang advisor believed that the battle was significant because the population witnessed a "clear Vietnamese victory in a fight for a very important objective."[75]

Due to a continued heavy American presence, Front units avoided contact throughout most of September, although low-level violence, as always, was kept up and a major battle took place. Because U.S. battalions took much of the pressure off territorial units, expansion of the RF/PF forces occurred. Recent territorial successes led the PSA to submit what for Hau Nghia was an optimistic report:

> The fear of imminent catastrophe that had demoralized most of the outposts and many of the district towns during the summer has been, in the main, dissipated. The widespread war weariness that is the product of so much tension appears to have rebounded in favor of the GVN. From all indication the people of the province would probably still settle for peace at any price, but GVN authorities have no intention of settling for less than complete control. The VC for the moment are able to influence only the more remote areas of the province during the daytime. Some of the determination of the top provincial authorities seems to be seeping down to the lower echelons and is becoming visible enough to be remarked upon. In sum, if hope is rising, and I believe that it is, it is nourished by war weariness, and the realization of the authorities that they cannot survive unless they establish control of the countryside, and the VC disappointment accompanying their failures. What happens in Hau Nghia is no longer determined exclusively by the VC. The GVN, aided by the American presence, has a firmer grip on the future.[76]

7

The Accelerated
Pacification Campaign

A Change in Allied Strategy

As the shock of the Tet Offensive dissipated, Americans at CORDS and MACV, surprisingly insulated from domestic events in the United States, grew more optimistic regarding the overall situation in South Vietnam. The jolt of Tet, on one hand, combined with ARVN's good showing, on the other, appeared to jar the Thieu regime out of a lethargic stupor. Thieu's general mobilization, which Americans had long called for, was greeted with great enthusiasm at the embassy. In addition, the Front atrocities at Hue and elsewhere, widely publicized in Vietnam if not in the United States, had both scared and angered a large number of urban "fence sitters," to the benefit of the GVN. More importantly, GVN setbacks in the rural areas proved to be considerably less harmful than originally feared: In this regard, it should be remembered that very few provinces experienced violence as intense or long-lasting as that in Hau Nghia. Furthermore, even skeptical Americans in Saigon grew convinced that the Front's psychological and material losses had been very great indeed. Lastly, there was the possibility, however remote, that the diplomats in Paris might quickly agree to an in-place cease-fire. Therefore, at the urging of Komer, Colby, and Gen. Creighton Abrams, the new head of MACV, Thieu launched the Accelerated Pacification Campaign (soon dubbed the "APC"), the first edition of which began on 1 November 1968 and lasted for three months.[1]

There was little that was conceptually new with the Accelerated Pacification Campaign. What separated it from previous efforts was the amount of resources committed, particularly the number of U.S. troops. GVN forces were ordered to quickly reoccupy any villages or hamlets lost to the Front during Tet. In addition, allied planners targeted for pacification over 1,000 hamlets throughout the country that were considered contested or Front-controlled. The major innovation of the APC was the demotion of the RD Cadre teams. The security mission heretofore assigned to the RD teams was assigned to the militia units that GVN officials were ordered to install permanently as soon as a hamlet was cleared. If militia units could not be recruited locally, they would be brought in from neighboring areas. Planners split the RD Cadre teams in half, assigned them to "secure" hamlets, and ordered them to concentrate on gathering intelligence, conducting local elections, and aiding economic development.[2] No longer the theoretical spearhead of "revolutionary development," a naive goal at best, the RD Cadre teams became merely another component of the overall pacification program and not a very important one at that.

In the military sphere, the change in operations was more pronounced. Previously, during late fall and early winter, American units were engaged in or preparing large operations aimed at enemy main force units in the hinterlands. In late 1968, however, Abrams ordered many American units to join ARVN in support of the APC. Main force units were to be attacked if in direct proximity; if not, they were to be ignored for the time being. U.S. forces were authorized to attack local Front base areas, such as the Ho Bo Woods, but were to stand on the defensive near large enemy redoubts, such as War Zone C, attacking them only indirectly with artillery and air power. Mammoth search and destroy missions like CEDAR FALLS became a thing of the past. A more defensive alignment was developed: Another Tet-style attack on the cities was to be avoided at all cost. Nevertheless, if PAVN wanted to have a battle, it knew where to find one. Indeed, the 25th Division fought fierce battles in Tay Ninh province in late 1968 and throughout 1969. MACV ordered American commanders at all levels to stress joint U.S.-Vietnamese military operations. In short, the mode of operations already employed by most American units during the rainy season was to be extended into the winter, with even more forces used.

As has been seen, pacification activities in Hau Nghia were basically coercive in nature from the very beginning, despite "revolutionary" programs or rhetoric coming from CORDS or the GVN. Force, much of it coming from the U.S. Army, was always the key component. The central position of force and coercion for the political struggle in Hau Nghia was rarely, if ever, more clear than during the Accelerated Pacification Campaign. The aim of the APC in Hau Nghia was quite simply to extend allied military control over as great an area of the province as possible. In contrast to earlier pacification initiatives, the APC involved virtually no talk about "revolutionary development" or any sort of social transformation. Rather, the goal was very simply to establish an armed GVN presence in contested or Front-controlled hamlets. Despite the formidable forces allocated, it was not an easy assignment. According to CORDS figures, which were often criticized as being overly optimistic, the Front's position in Hau Nghia as of 1 November 1968 was very strong. CORDS estimated that 57,600 people lived in "secure" areas, 71,200 lived in "contested" areas, and a further 53,700 lived in "VC" areas. Regarding numbers of hamlets, the figures were 38 "secure," 44 "contested," and 50 "VC."[3]

Maj. Gen. Ellis Williamson, 25th Division commander since August 1968 and previously commander of the 173rd Airborne during Operation MA-RAUDER in January 1966, was an enthusiastic supporter of the Accelerated

Pacification Campaign. To aid the APC, he began Operation COLORS UP, with the goal of bringing every hamlet within the Tropic Lightning Division's area of operation under some degree of GVN control by the end of January. Although the 25th Division continued to be active in neighboring provinces, Hau Nghia received the most attention, with all of 2d Brigade and part of 3d Brigade assigned there. Expanding the experimental program under way in Duc Hue district since July, one battalion from 2d Brigade was allocated to each of the three remaining districts for extended operations, and assets from 3d Brigade were employed where needed. In addition, an American platoon was assigned to each district in Hau Nghia to serve as the nucleus for a joint U.S.-territorial Combined Reconnaissance and Intelligence Platoon or "CRIP," a program that had been used on a smaller scale since 1967. Major General Williamson told his battalion commanders in no uncertain terms that he would not tolerate any "red hamlets," i.e., hamlets controlled by the Front, in Hau Nghia by the end of the APC.[4]

In addition to U.S. forces, many of ARVN's units were also allocated to Accelerated Pacification. For a time, two battalions of the ARVN 25th Division were put under the direct command of the province chief. This was a very unusual step, although American pacification proponents had long advocated giving the province chiefs more direct military authority. ARVN units had recently been strengthened by the allocation of M16 rifles, and to support the APC, the Americans also began supplying M16s to militia units. Hau Nghia Regional Forces began receiving theirs in November.[5]

The APC began on 1 November 1968 and was very well timed for operations in Hau Nghia. Front main force units, by and large, avoided contact when possible and prepared for a new round of heavy fighting during late winter and spring. Therefore, believing themselves safer than before from main force attack, American units employed company-, platoon-, and even squad-level operations to an unprecedented degree. As was usual for pacification activities, joint military operations were frequently used, and violence was low-level but unrelenting, with guerrilla units absorbing most of the pressure.

Numerical indicators, from the allied point of view, were very encouraging. Due to intensive Front propaganda and very tight command control, the number of ralliers under the Chieu Hoi program had slowed to a trickle throughout 1968 in Hau Nghia. In November, these numbers began to rise again: 40 Hoi Chanh rallied in November, 34 in December, and another 45 in January. At the end of December, CORDS estimated that 91,200 people now lived in "secure" areas, 61,600 lived in "contested" areas, and only 27,700 lived in "VC" areas.[6] The PSA reported at the end of January that the result of the APC "has been to reestablish a degree of GVN control over this province that has been unknown in the past."[7] Similar opinions were expressed at CORDS concerning all of III CTZ: "The Accelerated Pacification Campaign has been, thus far, the most successful GVN program attempted in this CTZ in the last three years. . . . This campaign has been the most successful on record with U.S. Forces providing superb support."[8]

Although the allies were successfully extending their physical control over large portions of Hau Nghia, serious difficulties concerning execution of the Accelerated Pacification Program soon arose. Coming in the confused aftermath of the Tet Offensive, the APC lacked elaborate preparation. GVN resources in Hau Nghia during this period were still very modest and were naturally stretched to the limit by this ambitious offensive. Some CORDS personnel who remembered the Strategic Hamlet Program under Diem were openly critical of the rapid pace, which was particularly worrisome in areas like Hau Nghia where local political resources were so paltry.

Attitudes Toward Friend and Foe

In addition, U.S. officers and men came into closer contact with Vietnamese military personnel, officials, and civilians than ever before. The result was a serious strain on Vietnamese-American relations in virtually every category. Indeed, a paradox central to the whole American effort in the "village war" was made very apparent. For the pacification program to succeed, a U.S. military presence in civilian areas was required. But, as previously related, this was always difficult and frequently dangerous for everyone concerned because of the unsatisfactory relationships that usually existed between villagers and American soldiers.

In the same vein, for GVN military forces to improve, most proponents of the "other war" advocated frequent and close collaboration between American soldiers and their South Vietnamese allies at the operational level. Joint operations were nothing new, of course; the 25th Division had employed them from the very beginning. Starting with the APC, however, and extending until American withdrawal, joint operations with ARVN and the militia in well-populated areas became routine. As shown countless times in World War II, relations between even close allies can be very difficult. Unfortunately for all concerned, military collaboration in Vietnam was made much more burdensome by an understandable but regrettable set of attitudes held by American combat soldiers toward both friend and foe.

Although such opinions were a matter of degree and there were exceptions, an overwhelming majority of American fighting men were contemptuous of their Vietnamese "comrades in arms." This was true throughout the U.S. involvement in ground combat. The reasons given by veterans for this animosity were remarkably similar: American soldiers believed that the South Vietnamese were unreliable and refused to do their share of the fighting. John Pancrazio, an advisor in Cu Chi, described a small operation with an ARVN unit in 1966:

> The majority of the armed forces could have more easily been termed armed farces! They were very poor fighters, with the exception of the Rangers, and were much more eager to avoid combat than to engage in it. When going on extended operations, they would carry live chickens to ensure they would have fresh meat, and they had absolutely no discipline, so the enemy could avoid them. On one particular occasion, I was forced to pull my weapon on an RVN

lieutenant in order to force him to proceed to a night ambush. His reason for not wanting to go to the planned site was "Boo Coo V.C. there. My Dai Vi [captain] will kill me if I go down there." My response was that he could die for sure right now or take his chances with his captain later. Needless to say, we proceeded to the ambush site where ARVN "noise discipline" ensured there would be no enemy contact that night.

Botching a mission intentionally was one thing: American units were known to do such things on occasion. However, when ARVN timidity endangered American lives, 25th Division soldiers were enraged. As related by Thomas Giltner, who served in late 1966 as a platoon leader, U.S. soldiers quickly learned to distrust both the combat skills and the honesty of their allies:

> The reports of ARVN sweeping through an area and encountering no VC were extremely dangerous to rely on. We were encouraged to run operations with the local ARVN units. They would be assigned an area to sweep, say at 0600 hours; a couple of hours later, we would follow in behind them and sweep the same area as part of the joint operation. We'd go in and, as soon as we'd arrive in the landing zone, well, you know the rest of the story: Sometimes we would meet hostile resistance, sometimes no resistance at all. We soon learned that these ARVN sweeps either never occurred or they were "search and avoid" missions. They were telling us things we wanted to hear.

Michael Willis, who served two combat tours beginning in 1967, emphasized the distrust felt toward ARVN:

> They were losers. They didn't have any initiative whatsoever. I guess it would have been hard knowing you might shoot up your brother or uncle. The 25th ARVN morale was the lowest of the low: The whole division would run. Apparently, some the spirit of the U.S. 25th rubbed off on them: I read that the ARVN 25th fought to the end in 1975. When we swept villages, ARVN would grab anyone and stick them on trucks and off they'd go. Good work! They just drafted VC. Chieu Hoi could have been planned by Hanoi. Thousands of people surrendered and ended up in ARVN. Wouldn't that cause dissension? The corruption was incredible.

Phil Boardman, a 25th Division rifleman and "tunnel rat," expressed his and his comrades' disgust at the time of Tet:

> We had absolutely no respect for ARVN. They wouldn't do a thing when we were around. They gave us some Kit Carson Scouts—former VC who were supposed to act as guides for us. We never trusted them. Anyway you looked at it, they were traitors to somebody. Hell, if ARVN could have fought, we wouldn't have been there.

During the fierce fighting of 1969, infantryman Dan Vandenberg developed a loathing for ARVN:

They were a joke. I despised the whole lot of them. They were all cowards. In the morning, their uniforms were spotless and weapons clean. They'd look the same at the end of day. We did all their work. We looked like tramps. For us to get new gear would take an act of Congress; The South Vietnamese always seemed to have a lot. We would rather go it alone: At least you only had to fight one enemy.

Alan Neil, who was with the *Wolfhounds* in most of 1970 (a period when Vietnamization was in full swing), was a bit more charitable but not much:

ARVN did their thing, and we did ours. That was fine with us, because the ARVN 25th was lousy. The fact was that we did a lot more fighting than they did. I have read a lot of books about the war in the last few years, so I know that ARVN could fight really well. But I never saw that side of them, and I never knew anyone that did. I think that when we were around they'd let us fight the war. If we weren't around, they'd fight. We never really understood them.

No doubt some of the animosity felt by American fighting men reflected cultural bias and racial antipathy. Nevertheless, what was truly striking was the contrast between the general contempt held by Americans for South Vietnamese soldiers and the nearly universal respect they had for their enemy. Without exception, every veteran assisting in this research expressed admiration for the cunning and courage of "Charlie." This respect was something they learned on their own in the field. Indeed, many soldiers later complained about not being warned properly during training about the skill and resourcefulness of their battlefield opponents in Vietnam. As Michael Willis recalled,

We were told the VC were farmers by day and guerrillas by night. One day at the end of an eight-hour battle, I asked our lieutenant, "When do these farmers go home to milk the cows?" There was certainly no affection involved. As one man put it, "Your average VC was a tough little bastard, but no one was bothered by killing him."

Yet, in a curious way, American soldiers affirmed their own skill and courage by acknowledging similar traits in their enemy.

Some of the same men criticizing ARVN in the quotes above expressed very different views of their foes. A brief inspection of these views offers a splendid illustration of the asymmetrical nature of the attitudes held by most American fighting men toward their allies and adversaries. Concerning the opponents he faced in Cu Chi district in 1965–1966, John Pancrazio wrote, "The majority of the enemy were dedicated fighting men and women. They truly believed in their cause and many of them, especially the NVA, were good and fierce fighters." Dan Vandenberg, who learned to detest ARVN while slogging through Trang Bang district in 1969, later said of the other side, "Charlie was really good. Everyone at least respected his abilities. The NVA were damned good, and they wouldn't chicken out. They had to take more than we did. We didn't have to go through bombing and artillery. What they took was incredible."

Thomas Giltner, who had discovered that intelligence supplied by ARVN could endanger his own men, had studied Asian warfare at Fort Bragg before coming to Vietnam. His opinions of the Front guerrillas he encountered in Hau Nghia were more informed than the average, but they undoubtedly echoed those of his *Wolfhounds*:

> We faced mostly local VC, peasants armed with World War II rifles and no heavy weapons. They were taking on the best army in the world. They received their training from the local cadres. We respected them from day one. . . . Following Sun Tsu's teachings, they always hit us where we were the weakest. They always decided when, where, and how to fight us; on what terrain and under what conditions; and when to break away and melt into the local populace or go back down into their tunnels. They decided when to conduct ambushes or raids, plant booby traps, employ snipers, infiltrate U.S. areas, or gather intelligence. They did an awful lot with an awful little. . . .
>
> They were tremendously inventive. We used to capture homemade rifles created out of metal pipes and bits of fence post. We never put out antipersonnel mines: We knew they would be dug up and used against us. Claymores were strictly accounted for, but they still were stolen. We always worried about Charlie getting sophisticated weapons. Once our whole battalion was roused out at night and sent looking for a starlight scope which was lost. We found it. We really worried about him getting a field piece. . . . The Vietnamese were just so ingenious. We all knew they were poor, not stupid.

American officers knew that their men respected the people they were fighting. Some of them worried about the effect this had on morale and attempted to discourage what one soldier called "Charlie worship." Lt. Jerry Headley, a platoon leader in 1969 with the 25th Division's 3/4th Armored Cavalry Squadron, recalled that such efforts were futile:

> A lot of people talked about how good the enemy was. Some men called him Sir Charles or similar things. He was a very good fighter and very disciplined. He had been fighting, and his uncles and his fathers had been fighting, for years. Some officers didn't like us to honor the enemy, but we did anyway.

Many men of the Tropic Lightning Division singled out PAVN for particular praise. They understood the conventional tactics that PAVN normally employed and greatly admired the courage required for the mass infantry assaults that were the hallmark of the big battles in Tay Ninh. They rarely distinguished between PAVN and the elite main force Front units that fought in a similar manner. The men had somewhat different views of the Front guerrillas; the intense frustration caused by coping with guerrilla tactics was frequently translated into hatred. Nevertheless, the resourcefulness and courage of village guerrillas was acknowledged. Indeed, stories of Front cleverness and tenacity have become a staple among American combat veterans. During the Tet Offensive near Trang Bang, Bill Kestell witnessed a good example:

> We had parked *The Ugly American* [Kestell's "track"] along the wall. It was just past sundown. I was in the hatch, and Larry was also up top. We were just talking when a sniper in a tree across the road took a shot at us. I can still see the muzzle flash. I think I loosed a short burst with the .50 (the .50-caliber machine gun, the track's main armament) at the flash. I caught hell from the lieutenant for giving away our position! Really. . . .
> That night we were mortared. Big deal—gooks dropped every single round short. Boy, these guys are really lousy shots. FNG (Fucking New Guy). . . .
> When we got south of Trang Bang Bridge these same lousy shots took out EVERY IMPORTANT TARGET IN THE COMPOUND—RIGHT FROM ROUND 1. When you have a fixed target that's known, you plan your lines of fire, check this with short rounds, and, when you're ready, add 200–300 yards and fire for effect. They took out TOC—COMMO—COUNTER BATTERY—THE WHOLE THING!

Naturally, American soldiers tried to explain to themselves why their Vietnamese enemies on the battlefield routinely showed courage and tenacity and their Vietnamese allies frequently did not. The U.S. Army, as always was the case concerning larger issues of the war, was utterly mute on the subject. Racial or cultural explanations were worthless because there were Vietnamese on both sides. Consequently, American fighting men correctly interpreted the situation in political terms. They recognized that Front followers were fighting for a "cause." (Most soldiers, however, did not really know what the "cause" was, although many recognized that hatred of the United States had much to do with it.) American soldiers usually explained South Vietnamese military shortcomings in terms of bad leadership and corruption on the part of GVN officials and ARVN officers. They could also see the class differences between ARVN's officers and men. Richard O'Hare, a member of the Duc Hue advisory team, commented on the later point:

> Concerning South Vietnamese leadership, there was a real difference between officers and men. The officers were urban, spoke French, and were often Catholic. The soldiers were rural Buddhists. The officers were always immaculately dressed and never helped with manual labor. There was a real feeling of aristocracy. The officers treated their troops and NCOs like dirt. We believed that some of the officers were VC, VC sympathizers, or fence sitters.

The asymmetrical views held by U.S. soldiers toward friend and foe did not help morale. Although Front propaganda directed at Americans was crude and had virtually no effect, some soldiers talked about being on the "wrong side." Others compared their role to that of the British Redcoats during the American Revolution. Mostly, the political confusion increased the tendency on the part of U.S. soldiers to shut out such concerns from their minds altogether and to fight the war for themselves and their immediate comrades. Lieutenant Headley recalled that even his politically unsophisticated troopers in the armored cavalry were troubled about these matters:

> If there was a national strategy, it never filtered down to the regular soldier. Everyone knew that the South Vietnamese governments, no matter who they had in there, were all corrupt. We all wondered: Why do we want those guys in there? Are they any better than the guys we are fighting? There just seemed to be no goal. This was very distressing. I was surprised how much even the young soldiers were aware of this.

On an official level, these negative attitudes often manifested themselves and lessened the effectiveness of joint efforts. Personnel of the Tropic Lightning Division were particularly incensed by what they believed to be insufficient support by ARVN and the GVN for their pacification effort. This problem drew the following remarks from the Duc Hoa senior advisor in January 1969:

> In anticipation of the acceptance of the 1969 Pacification Plan, U.S. forces operating within Duc Hoa were positioned to support the program by occupying company-sized operational bases within or near key hamlets. It was understood (or misunderstood) by the U.S. commander that the Vietnamese would simultaneously insert ARVN forces and government officials to provide the GVN influence necessary to pacification. This has not occurred and the efforts to date by the U.S. units without this assistance appear, in part, to have been futile.[9]

A special report prepared by 2d Brigade on its support for the APC during December reveals similar frustrations on the part of American officers:

> Their feeling is that they have taken many risks to adjust their disposition of forces to back up the APC and that the GVN has not fulfilled its duties by taking advantage of the voids opened in the VC-controlled areas in order to establish government control. . . . It is almost inevitable, given the unwieldiness of the GVN bureaucracy, that the APC will not transpire so efficiently as expected. It is also not probable that any U.S. units will long tolerate the frustration that this unwieldiness causes, inasmuch as they are used to action being taken when necessary.[10]

An incident reflecting the often difficult relations between American and Vietnamese units in the field was later recounted by Captain David Harrington, an officer attached to the Hau Nghia advisory team. Sometime during the period in question (the exact date is uncertain), an ARVN battalion supported by Regional Forces, both under the command of Lieutenant Colonel Nhon, the Hau Nghia province chief, was operating just north of Highway 1 near the Cu Chi base camp. No contact took place during the morning. At 1400 hours, everyone present could hear the beginning of an engagement between an undetermined enemy force and elements of an American battalion, roughly a kilometer or two to the north but outside the assigned area of operation for the Vietnamese units. Soon, the American battalion commander radioed the Vietnamese and requested that they move quickly to seal off the area of contact, a distance of about three to five kilometers. As shall be seen, Lieutenant Colonel Nhon was a very controversial figure in American circles. However, even many of his severest critics—and they were severe indeed—admitted that he was one of the best and bravest combat officers in ARVN. Nevertheless, no doubt realizing as well as anyone that a three-kilometer march in Hau Nghia could be a very dangerous proposition, Nhon demanded helicopters before he would release some of his troops. The American commander again urgently requested assistance but was turned down unless helicopters could be obtained. Two hours later, a message came through that helicopters would be available by 1630. Lieutenant Colonel Nhon replied that it was too late and that his operation was terminated. The Vietnamese returned to base with the 25th Division battalion still engaged.

There is no way nor any reason to make judgments on such incidents. The advisor involved recalled that the American commander was still enraged later. Nevertheless, the Vietnamese went away believing they had been expected to do the dirty work on the ground, knowing full well that U.S. units employed air assets whenever possible. The Americans, whether fully justified or not, believed they had been let down by their ally. Such incidents were not everyday occurrences, but they happened often enough to cause lasting bitterness.[11]

As previously mentioned, the allocation of sizable U.S. forces to pacification duties had long been advocated by many American field-workers. The assignment of long-term operations to American battalions in specific districts was considered a particularly wise move. Yet, here, too, problems were encountered. It was reported in January 1969 that the commander of the ARVN 25th Division was opposed to granting U.S. battalions long-term areas of operations within Hau Nghia because it was harmful to the government's image and compromised its sovereignty. The province chief had similar opinions. Captain Harrington, a member of the advisory team at Bao Trai, later described the uneasy pattern of relationships that existed in late 1968 between many of the advisors and Vietnamese officials:

Frankly, I think that the quality of the Vietnamese personnel in Hau Nghia was pretty low. The people who grew up in Hau Nghia didn't want anything to do with the Government of Vietnam. So all of the officials and the RD Cadres were from the outside. Nobody in their right mind wanted anything to do with Hau Nghia. ·Officials were sent there as punishment. . . .

The counterpart relationship was difficult. A lot of it was a matter of personalities. The cultural differences were great, of course. But Nhon, the province chief, wanted his people to remain distant from us. So I was never close to my counterpart. Nobody had close relationships with their counterparts that I could see. This was at the directive of the province chief. I heard it was better in the district headquarters.

According to Captain Harrington, the quality of American personnel assigned to work closely with the Vietnamese was not always high either:

> When I was there they were starting the Mobile Advisory Teams. The idea was a good one in theory. Four U.S. personnel would live with a PF platoon in their compound. At first, the Americans were regular combat personnel. You had better believe that no line officer was going to send his best people to MAT team duty. They always came in bunches of about a dozen, with no transport, radio, or anything. They had no special training and knew nothing of the language. It took them half of their eight-week tour to get settled in. These PF forts could be nasty little places. Our guys were kind of stranded. The execution of the program left much to be desired. It improved later when they set up special MAT team training.

Furthermore, because U.S. force levels during the Accelerated Pacification Campaign in Hau Nghia were higher than those of ARVN and the GVN apparatus and militia were stretched to the limit, American troops often operated in populated areas with little or no support from the Vietnamese. When this happened, explosive situations could arise.

As recorded at the time by Ollie Davidson, such an ugly situation developed in Hau Nghia during December 1968. The area in question was An Tinh village, composed of six hamlets just south and southeast of Trang Bang district town. Three of the hamlets were astride Highway 1 and therefore received a great deal of American attention. The 25th Division infantrymen called two of the hamlets "Dodge City East" and "Dodge City West" because "there was always a shoot-out when we came to town." American units began intense operations in An Tinh in early December, initially only during daylight. According to Davidson, An Tinh was dominated, if not controlled, by the Front. As a result, the hamlets were defended by small units, and, over the years, the Americans periodically took casualties. Enemy forces took advantage of well-constructed and cleverly hidden defensive positions that made it very difficult for American troops to operate. Although this was not the war at its most violent, it was war at its most frustrating, and American troops soon held a grudge against An Tinh. Some of the population was relocated, much of it fled to Trang Bang, and portions of the village were heavily damaged. Unfortunately for the Americans, local Vietnamese forces were already allocated elsewhere. To facilitate secret entrance and exit to the hamlets of An Tinh, Front cadres had forbidden the villagers to cut heavy concentrations of bamboo and undergrowth. Consequently, the Americans brought in their "Rome Plow" bulldozers to clear obstructions. Despite the efforts of some officers and advisory personnel, the bulldozers cleared virtually everything, including many valuable fruit trees. In addition, Americans would search houses, and if they contained what the soldiers believed to be combat installations, they, too, were destroyed.

This sad situation defied solution. American soldiers "in the grass" could hardly be expected to care about fruit trees if they provided cover for enemy troops. Nor can there be any doubt that many of the "bunkers" found were indeed fortifications and therefore justifiably destroyed. On the other hand, fruit trees were an important part of the livelihood of a poor population, and the destruction of them could hardly improve attitudes toward the GVN or American soldiers. Also, as noted above, it was common practice for villagers to build bunkers for their own protection from artillery or mortar attacks and firefights. Davidson believed that many of the homes destroyed were in this category and not used by the Front. Whatever the case, Americans began camping in the hamlets overnight, and operations in the area were extended for over two months, as advocates for a greater role for U.S. troops had long urged. As Davidson put it, "Slowly the hamlets were eaten away by small VC initiated incidents and massive U.S. retaliation." At least 200 homes were totally destroyed, and 3,000 refugees fled to Trang Bang. In February, U.S. forces withdrew for a time in reaction to the new round of heavy combat during Tet.[12]

How often such sad situations arose in Hau Nghia is impossible to determine precisely. However, according to province reports for the period of 13 September to 30 January 1969—a time of intensive operations but few large battles—583 families in Hau Nghia received compensation for war injuries and damage.[13] (It was not clear whether compensation came from the GVN or the United States. The United States paid compensation to Vietnamese villagers if American units were involved, regardless of which side was directly responsible for death, injury, or property damage.)[14] Whatever the negative impact of such operations on the Front, Davidson was bitter:

> The abandonment of the village [An Tinh] on February 8 is viewed as good and bad by the people. It is good if the U.S. leaves the area and peace can return even under the VC's control. It is bad because now the total area is cleared for artillery and rounds fall there day and night. There is no security in An Tinh, for the people or the U.S. troops. The day after moving out, the U.S. convoy was ambushed on the main road at 4:15 in the afternoon. Security, where???[15]

The Political Status of the GVN

The first stage of the Accelerated Pacification Campaign had an even more serious problem. Although the APC brought the GVN an unprecedented level of daylight control in Hau Nghia—certainly greater than before the Tet Offensive—there was no reason to believe that its poor political relationship with the population had changed in the least. The GVN was not stronger; the Front was weaker. Above all, the GVN was stretched very thin in Hau Nghia, and its position could again be contested in a dramatic manner, as soon happened. This was recognized at the time. At the end of December, Davidson wrote,

> The APC program is going pretty well, because military operations have kept the VC from doing too much in this soft spot. The plan goes forward, but it is only occupation, not pacification.[16]

Captain Harrington later commented on the pacification effort of this period:

> Overall, I think the pacification program in Hau Nghia showed some positive results in terms of influence of the GVN over the territory, but the hard facts were that the GVN was an interloper in most of the places there.[17]

The situation was best described by Lieutenant Colonel Bernard, the PSA, in the December 1968 report:

> These operations, however, have not greatly influenced our uncommitted population to change from their status of *attentiste*. The ability of the local VC to use terror and intimidation to discourage cooperation with GVN is partially impaired but much of the province's uncommitted population is not yet aware of this, and it is not likely to become persuaded of it soon. In short, the province's most commendable actions, bolstered by the extraordinary efforts of the 25th U.S. Infantry Division, amount to an occupation of what had been VC-dominated territory. It is not yet pacification. The essential first, occupation and the provision of security, is well under way. The frequent mortarings, occasional assassinations and infrequent minings initiated by the VC serve to shake the people's confidence in GVN presence as much as our military successes build it up. Despite this, we appear to be moving slowly towards the consolidation of governmental authority, the real goal of this province's programs.[18]

Just when the first phase of the Accelerated Pacification Program came to an end on 31 January 1969, the Nixon administration, openly committed to ending U.S. participation in the war, took office. The massive intervention of American ground troops had transformed the war in Vietnam in almost every category; the withdrawal of those same troops would have a similar impact. Therefore, this is a good point to review the balance of forces existing in Hau Nghia province at the beginning of 1969 in comparison with the balance existing in early 1966. It is a difficult comparison to make for the relative position of the two sides differed depending upon the level of analysis.

Had someone familiar with Hau Nghia in early 1966 visited the province three years later, the person's reaction would certainly have been that the allies had made great progress. In 1966, the GVN lacked any meaningful presence outside military base camps, district towns, a few Catholic hamlets, and the province capital. Bao Trai was under siege. The GVN political apparatus had been nearly destroyed, and the Front openly controlled most of Hau Nghia. Even the few GVN strongholds hosted a powerful Front presence. No place in the province was safe from attack by main force units operating from strongly held base areas. And no government official was safe from Front retribution. The Front had the strong support of a large, although undetermined, percentage of the rural population and through fear ensured the neutrality of most of the rest. Travel during daylight was possible only with a military convoy, and many stretches of road were impassable even then. At night, every government official, along with the entire militia (pitiful as it was), was forced to seek safety behind fortifications, thus completely yielding the province to the Front after dark.

On the other hand, in many respects the situation had nearly reversed by the beginning of 1969. The large number of American troops gave the allies great combat power. ARVN had increased in numbers, improved its armaments, and, though it was far from an ideal fighting force, its achievements during and after Tet had proven that it was capable of good service. In particular, the ARVN 25th Division could no longer be described as the "worst division in any army of the world" for its performance during 1968 had been adequate. The Regional and Popular Forces were much larger, possessed modern weaponry, and, by sheer mass if not any great skill in fighting, were beginning to make their presence felt, as shown by the fighting in Bao Trai in May and Trang Bang district town in March and August 1968. The massive armed presence of the allies enabled the GVN to extend its physical presence into hamlets totally given up three years earlier. Front base areas, constantly swept and harassed, were no longer safe havens but rather very risky areas from which to operate. The allied armed presence also allowed relatively safe travel during daylight on the major roads, and commerce had greatly improved. Although much of the population and most officials still had to retreat behind barbed wire and sandbags after sunset, extensive American night operations made the dark dangerous for Front cadres. In short, according to outward manifestations of control, the GVN had improved its position greatly. In this regard, it should be pointed out that the Front was stronger in Hau Nghia than in most provinces and that the relative increase of control by the GVN was in many places even greater.

Despite all of these factors, no one in American circles was predicting quick victory in Hau Nghia. Even CORDS statistical indicators conceded that nearly half of the population of Hau Nghia lived in "contested" or "VC" territory, despite three years of bloody operations by a splendid fighting division, the U.S. 25th Infantry. However much these operations harmed the Front, they made a shambles of much of the province, and Hau Nghia apparently lost a large number of its people. In January 1969, CORDS estimated that 180,500 people lived in Hau Nghia. Though no totally reliable census was ever taken, Americans had estimated in early 1966 that at least 200,000 lived in the province, and estimates from early 1965 had run up to 240,000 people. The exodus is hardly surprising considering the many hamlets relocated or damaged, in addition to the lure of quick American money to be found in the large cities.

Furthermore, there was a population shift within Hau Nghia. Except during Tet, most of the fighting took place in areas where the Front had once been strongest; therefore, many people either moved or were relocated to hamlets at least outwardly controlled by the GVN. Both population shifts surely hurt the Front, making it much more difficult to gather food or recruit. During 1966, the Front was expanding in Hau Nghia and was largely self-sustaining, very likely sending out much more in terms of taxes, food, and recruits than it was receiving in the way of weapons; by 1969, however, the Front in Hau Nghia was growing dependent on all types of aid from the North.

Nevertheless, the GVN was never able to convert Front weakness into government strength. As before, the GVN in Hau Nghia was totally dependent upon forces from the outside—and not just from U.S. troops and ARVN conscripts. As always, GVN officials were from areas beyond the province to a startling degree. So, too, were the RD Cadres, and even reinforcements for the RF/PF often had to come from other provinces. Government ideologues, those individuals willing to face death and subordinate everything for the war effort, came from the urban elites and religious minorities or they hated the Front because of personal vendetta. The rural population, which made up most of Hau Nghia, remained, at best (from the point of view of the GVN), apathetic and very war-weary. None of this augured well for the social or political rejuvenation required for the GVN to ensure its survival in the face of pressure from its ruthless but committed enemy to the north, regardless of the outcome of the struggle against the Front.

Therefore, in many respects, the Front had done very well during the three years beginning with 1966, in both Hau Nghia and all of Vietnam. Although its their position had weakened materially, what the Front yielded was given up only after intense struggle, and Front military forces shouldered most of the burden against the Americans, particularly in the provinces around Saigon. Meanwhile, the blood spilled by the men of the 25th Division, multiplied many times over by other U.S. units throughout Vietnam, had a devastating effect on public support for the war in the United States. The continuing presence of the Front in so many areas of Vietnam, a fact obvious to journalists, made hollow any official U.S. claims of progress, even when they were warranted. Painful losses, lack of identifiable progress, and distrust toward American leadership led to a mood of frustration and cynicism, not only in large and important segments of the American public but within the military, as well. Problems of morale and discipline, which grew slowly after 1966, assumed menacing proportions during 1969 and grew steadily worse as U.S. withdrawal proceeded—no one wanted to be the last to die in Vietnam.

Yet, not all of this was obvious to either side at the beginning of 1969. Though it was very clear to all concerned that the war effort was increasingly in trouble in the United States and that the new administration would likely be reluctant to increase the level of American ground forces, there was no sign that the United States would capitulate—the only outcome acceptable to the Front or to the North at the time. Everyone was aware of the possibility of American troop withdrawals, but no one, including President Nixon, knew precisely the pace at which they would take place. Despite the fact that the squabble over table shape had ended in Paris and negotiations were under way, the only aspect of the situation that was certain was that the war would continue. In this situation, the Party had reason for optimism. It still completely controlled some portions of Vietnam and contested a much larger area. The Front political apparatus existed to some extent even in rural areas claimed to be secure by the GVN. Its propaganda machine was still in very good working order and capable of projecting the Front's message in Vietnam and abroad. And even in areas where the Front was weak, small forces could terrorize the population through mortar attacks or, more frequently, through the "extermination of traitors" campaign.

Nevertheless, there were problems of great magnitude to be faced by the Front. In the summer of 1968, General Abrams redeployed three powerful units—the 1st Cavalry Division, the 101st Airborne Division, and the 3d Brigade of the 82d Airborne Division—from the northern provinces to the Saigon area. This was a clear sign that multidivisional operations in the remotest areas of the country would be less frequent and that heavy American pressure against the heartland of the Front was to be expected. Both ARVN and the militia were being increased in size and receiving more powerful armaments. Above all, the Front had to face the consequences of unfavorable military attrition rates. According to figures carefully assembled by the civilians of Systems Analysis at the Pentagon, a group that MACV believed constantly too pessimistic in reading figures, Front combat strength peaked August 1967, with 63,500 men under arms. By June 1968, this figure had dropped to 50,700. Far greater losses were suffered by guerrilla forces which peaked in January 1967 at 126,100; by June 1968, this figure had fallen to 51,200. Therefore, despite recruitment, Front force levels had fallen dramatically.[19]

Few, if any, aspects of the conduct of the war by the Americans have received more criticism than an alleged fixation on military attrition, as measured by the body count. It is certainly true that killing followers of the Front or forcing their capitulation did nothing to strengthen the allegiance of the population toward the government. Indeed, many of the methods required for the violence were counterproductive politically. Nevertheless, is impossible not to recognize the serious nature of the problem facing Front leadership due to crippling battlefield losses. Countless historical precedents illustrate the unpredictable chemistry at work within a military unit, whether a squad or an army. Losses cause fear, and battles cause physical exhaustion. The greatest test of military leadership is ascertaining what can be asked from the troops. Invariably, fighting takes a heavy toll on the bravest and most highly motivated men, and a drop in quality, even if not in quantity, frequently accompanies battle deaths. Operations become tentative on some occasions, with troops reluctant to close. On other occasions, disaster can strike due to strained communications or incompetent leadership. Everywhere, the margin for error narrows. Eventually, an entire army can crack, as happened to the Army of Northern Virginia in early 1865 and to the Germans in the fall of 1918 and again in the winter of 1945, despite the fact that simple manpower totals indicated that continued resistance was possible. Of course, this is precisely what happened to ARVN in 1975. And the Front was facing exactly this process at the beginning of 1969. Losses had been heavy for years and terrible during 1968. Despite effective propaganda, recruitment was more difficult because of the expansion of GVN control—and, no doubt, because it became increasingly clear that to follow the Front very likely meant death.

The Front had been shaken in 1968 and badly required a respite to prevent a downward spiral. The greatest danger to the Front, even greater than U.S. and GVN exertions, was that the leaders of COSVN and the politburo in Hanoi would ask too much. This is precisely what happened during 1969, and it brought the Front close to destruction in much of South Vietnam, including Hau Nghia province.

8

Battle: The Tet Offensive, 1969

The One-War Concept

The change in emphasis away from big battles in favor of pacification, begun during the Accelerated Pacification Campaign as an ad hoc response to the battlefield situation, became enshrined as official policy in early 1969. There were several reasons for this turn of events. First of all, there was a new administration in Washington. Nixon had not yet enunciated the Vietnamization strategy, but it was no secret that both he and Kissinger were displeased with Westmoreland's conduct of operations. In January, a Kissinger article appeared in *Foreign Affairs* in which he called for a new strategy in Vietnam, geared toward reducing American casualties, protecting the South Vietnamese population, strengthening South Vietnamese armed forces, and broadening the base of the GVN. This was a good description of the "one-war concept" a popular buzzword in late 1968 for pacification. It was also a reasonably good description of the Accelerated Pacification Campaign. Undoubtedly, MACV planners were well aware of this and eager to please their new boss.

But General Abrams and his planners were not just trying to gain favor in Washington. Abrams himself had long shown a greater interest in the village war than had his predecessor, William Westmoreland. In 1966, Abrams had received the PROVN study, examined in Chapter 3, and was impressed with its stress on the importance of comprehensive security in rural Vietnam. In the summer of 1968, he formed a small team of relatively junior officers, some of whom had worked on PROVN, and charged them with developing a plan of action based upon the concepts in that program. It is unclear whether Abrams was privately critical of Westmoreland's mode of operations or whether he believed that conditions had changed, that the big battles and the Tet Offensive had created the correct environment for "one war." In either case, Abrams personally supported the findings of the new task force, which were dubbed "son of PROVN," against spirited objections on the part of some of his subordinate commanders. The objective of the 1969 Combined Campaign Plan was officially "protection of the people," rather than destruction of the enemy.[1]

Abrams's shift in emphasis reflected a powerful momentum that had developed from the Accelerated Pacification Campaign. Indeed, at the beginning of 1969, Vietnamese officials in Saigon and the Americans at CORDS unanimously believed that the Accelerated Pacification Campaign had been a success and, hence, should be continued. Ambassador Bunker, who had coined the term "one war," was particularly enthusiastic. Thus, the White House, MACV, the GVN, and U.S. officials in Saigon were all in basic accord that the village war should have the highest priority.

There were no fundamental changes planned for the overall pacification program. The primary objective was the further expansion of GVN physical control in rural Vietnam. To support this effort, planners authorized a major expansion of Regional and Popular Forces and the new Civilian Self Defense Force. The Americans also wished to revitalize the Phoenix Program, a theoretically vital campaign directed against the Front's political apparatus that had been largely submerged by the Tet Offensive. Planners at CORDS set numerical goals for the number of hamlets they expected to see upgraded on the HES charts, the number of Hoi Chanh that should surrender, and the number of hamlets elections they wanted held.

As always, there were some minor innovations inspired by CORDS. It was commonly believed in U.S. circles that a major problem facing the GVN in the rural areas was the inability of the peasantry to somehow participate in local government. Therefore, the Americans pressed for hamlet elections whenever possible and wished to restore to the village some of its old importance in the administrative echelon. In addition, most Americans working with various "self-help" projects believed that the effectiveness of these programs was hamstrung by a lack of local participation. Consequently, there was much talk of monitoring and responding to the "true aspirations" of the people, rather than imposing programs from the top.

The GVN officials were perfectly willing to second such sentiments, as long as no one actually believed there would be any fundamental devolution of power from Saigon and as long as there was no danger to the continuing plunder of self-help programs. As always, whatever young idealistic Vietnamese or American officials might believe, the aim of the GVN was to crush the Front without fundamentally changing the power relationships existing in South Vietnamese society.[2]

A New Offensive

Nor had the North Vietnamese politburo and COSVN changed their goal. They still sought to expel the Americans, destroy the GVN, and seize power. The course of debate and deliberation inside the Party leadership during this period is particularly obscure. Apparently, there was a heated dispute over whether the 1968 Tet Offensive had been the correct strategy. Whatever the details, the Party never again made predictions of quick victory. In September 1968, a COSVN resolution called for "protracted war with transitional phases." In practice, the "transitional phase" decided on for the 1969 dry season campaign included another major military offensive.

Although the effort in 1969 did not reach the proportions of the Tet Offensive, it was, nevertheless, very sizable. The Party did not promise imminent victory, as it had with Tet. Nor did the 1969 offensive have ambitious territorial objectives. Rather, Party military leaders planned widespread attacks by fire, ambushes, and localized assaults. The generals in Hanoi and at COSVN did not intend to commit as many men as they had during the previous year, but they decided to employ elite sapper units and heavy weapons (principally mortars and rockets) more frequently. Also in contrast to 1968, American units and bases, which had been avoided where possible during the Tet Offensive, became prime targets. Negotiations were under way in Paris, and "talk-talk, fight-fight" was a venerable technique of revolutionary warfare that had proven its value in 1954. Certainly, the Party realized that, with the United States in domestic turmoil, increasing American casualties (particularly if accompanied by some local military victories) would have obvious political benefits.

In one important respect, however, the 1969 offensive was entirely different from the effort a year earlier: There was no possibility of surprise. Allied units of every type were on alert for a new round of heavy fighting, and U.S. intelligence carefully tracked the movements of enemy divisions. Throughout February, although contacts were few, allied units conducted spoiling operations in likely areas of approach and seized large amounts of supplies. Air attacks, including B-52 Arc Light sorties, were directed at safe zones. MACV made no secret of the fact that they expected heavy fighting. Nor, for that matter, did Front and North Vietnamese propaganda try to conceal the offensive. Captain Harrington recalled that, around Bao Trai before Tet 1969, men of the advisory team regularly saw lights moving in the distance and other signs of unusually heavy activity. As he put it, "Everybody knew something was up, but nobody knew exactly what."

The Party's 1969 dry season offensive highlighted the use of elite sappers. Under ideal circumstances, sapper units were made up of volunteers who received special training in infiltration techniques, explosives, and small-unit tactics. In theory, sappers would be able to overcome superior U.S. firepower with commitment, stealth, and combat skill. But in practice, these units frequently were filled up with conscripts and were even used as punishment duty. Nevertheless, splendid infantrymen were at the core of the sapper units. Like members of elite units in all armies, ideal sappers were arrogant, individualistic, and a little crazy. In the words of a PAVN sapper captured in Cu Chi in 1970:

> In the North, we received privileged treatment because we were known as a "suicide unit." We were dedicated to fighting. The morale factor is of utmost importance in the sapper service. Tactics and techniques come after. . . . In South Vietnam, the men lacked everything but were still very hedonistic. Unfortunately, conditions did not allow pleasure.[3]

In July 1969, the 25th Division captured the deputy commander of a Front sapper regiment during fighting in Cu Chi. Although he had joined the Viet Minh in 1949, the man was disgruntled with the Party and became a willing Hoi Chanh and stayed with the 25th for several months, helping American officers counter sapper tactics. According to his testimony, the heavy Front attacks in Tay Ninh during the summer of 1968 were intended to draw U.S. units away from Saigon so the capital could be struck once again during the coming dry season. This may explain the fierce fighting experienced by the 25th Division in August. Interestingly, he claimed that the aim of the 1969 offensive was not to seize Saigon but rather to reestablish the Front's position in the area immediately surrounding the city, where its forces had been decimated during Tet 1968. Through these attacks, the defector maintained, the Front would reoccupy "pivot points" with its main force units. When American and ARVN units moved against the "pivot points," Front local force and guerrilla units, reinforced with men from the DRV, would act against the GVN pacification program. He also supplied the principles of sapper warfare:

> Tactically, sapper action is not a set-piece fighting and therefore has a special nature. Its characteristic lies in patient endurance and hardship. To fight with sapper tactics it is necessary to detect every inadvertence in his defense—in the physical obstacles as well as in the psychology of the sentries. The sappers should find out enemy deficiencies in the location of sentries and obstacles, at the places the enemy considers as safe and sure. Exploiting the findings, the sapper then makes a penetration.[4]

The enemy winter-spring offensive began on 22 February 1969. American defenders easily disposed of sapper attacks and perimeter assaults against Bien Hoa and Long Binh. Four days later, however, enemy forces scored probably their biggest victory of the offensive when a PAVN sapper unit attacked the Cu Chi base camp. By 1969, the Cu Chi camp had grown into a bloated, sprawling complex that was a perfect target for a sapper attack. Various nondivisional rear service units had moved in with the 25th Division, expanding the perimeter. Large and valuable medium-lift helicopters, against protests from the division, were placed near the outer perimeter and were defended by one of these rear service units. Despite the fact that a major enemy offensive was already in progress, some of the men on the perimeter were complacent. Jim Murphy, a member of the 25th Division signal battalion, described the result:

> Cu Chi was a pretty quiet place until February 1969 when our little friends decided to pay us a visit. I remember that night because I was on guard, and I thought it was a piece of cake because I didn't have to go out on the perimeter. I got to guard the motor pool for a few hours. But at 4:00 A.M. we were rudely awakened by the sound of incoming rounds. I took a look out at our sector of the perimeter, and it was lit up like a Christmas tree. Sirens went off, and we were told to pile into the trucks. On the way out there, we ran right into an ambush, and the only way I could describe it was like being at a fireworks display and being about ten feet from all of those fireworks

going off. There was that rotten-egg smell of cordite. Needless to say, I was scared shitless.

The sappers killed 13 men and wounded another 26 and destroyed 9 helicopters. The attackers suffered only modest losses.

This attack was a sad and embarrassing moment for the 25th Division, but it soon proved to be the exception as American military superiority was quickly demonstrated throughout the Saigon area, the center of the enemy assault. Fighting remained furious until July, with several major battles every month near the capital. The heaviest fighting took place in Tay Ninh and the northern portions of Hau Nghia province. A Front attempt to seize Tay Ninh city caused particularly bloody battles for the 25th Division in June, and low-level but steady fighting took place in many areas.

There is no reason to chart the battles in detail. Most of the heavy fighting occurred when enemy units either assaulted isolated American or ARVN units and firebases or attempted to ambush supply convoys. For the first time in the war, the 25th Division did most of its fighting against PAVN, principally the 1st PAVN Division and the 101st Regiment. There were also clashes with the Front's 9th Division, the only large Front unit not principally manned by PAVN personnel. Several local force units were also encountered. Every large engagement was an American victory. So confident were U.S. commanders in their firepower that, on several occasions, they intentionally isolated their own units to provoke an attack. Often the ruse was successful and resulted in a lopsided victory. In fact, during the larger engagements, enemy units often evidenced a qualitative decline relative to earlier encounters, showing an inability to coordinate multiunit assaults.[5] The "tethered goat" tactic was risky, however, and not at all popular with combat infantrymen. Dan Vandenberg later described one of these bloody affairs outside Trang Bang during the 1969 offensive:

A company-sized ambush was a joke: Who are you going to ambush with sixty guys running around? We'd set up during the broad daylight in the middle of a rice paddy so Charlie would know exactly where we were. The brass hoped Charlie would hit us: Then they could call in jets and artillery. We would have been perfectly happy if nobody ever took a shot at us. Sure enough, one night Charlie hit us with everything he had. There were small arms, machine guns, mortar fire: The buttons on my shirt were too thick, I wanted to get closer to the ground. I was down to my last magazine, and everyone else was too. The resupply chopper arrived just in time; it was heaven sent. Jets came about the same time, and I'll give the pilots credit, they were good. They dropped napalm within fifty yards of our position. That shut up Charles for the rest of evening: We didn't hear a peep out of him. The next day, we went out but couldn't find a damn thing. You'd think even if we were the worst shots in the world, we'd hit something by accident. But we couldn't find a body. Our sister company found twelve to fifteen dead that had been hauled away, which was a lot. Charlie made a big deal about moving his dead, and he was smart. It was demoralizing because you'd rarely actually see any results. You began to doubt if you could shoot straight.

The violence slowed markedly in July as the main force units withdrew to War Zone C and Cambodia. Allied forces in the Saigon area claimed to have killed nearly 30,000 enemy in the period of 1 February to 31 July 1969. Whatever the figures actually were, they must have been extremely high as indicated by the capture of 2,700 prisoners, 11,296 small arms, and 2,200 crew-served weapons.[6] Such exorbitant losses of weapons and prisoners were a sure sign that enemy combat units were declining in quality.

American intelligence, after analyzing captured documents and prisoner interrogations, was convinced that Front forces and PAVN had taken a fearful pounding. There were many reports of a sharp drop in enemy morale, and enemy commanders made frequent appeals for more intensive political indoctrination to steady the troops. For the first time, enemy documents ceased to promise a military victory, calling instead for an indirect victory through political pressure. An officer of a local force battalion operating in Cu Chi district was captured after having served the Front since 1949; although remaining convinced of ultimate political victory, he admitted that his unit and others had been ordered to return to "Phase I" guerrilla activity for the first time since 1967. COSVN documents from Hau Nghia stated that operations in Cu Chi district were becoming very difficult and that the situation in Trang Bang was even worse, with the population growing afraid to cooperate with Front units.[7]

Because there were no dramatic battles (such as Khe Sanh or Hue during 1968) or spectacular media events (such as the sapper attack on the U.S. Embassy), the PAVN-Front offensive during 1969 received only a small portion of the press coverage in the United States that had been allocated to the great Tet Offensive. Yet, to the men of the 25th Infantry Division, it was every bit as violent as Tet 1968. Division intelligence estimated that greater casualties had been inflicted on the enemy than during the same period of 1968. American losses were very painful and nearly as great as the previous year. In the first three weeks of the offensive, 1,140 U.S. servicemen were killed, and the 25th Division was hurt badly. Between 1 February and 31 July 1969, it lost 509 men killed and many times that wounded.[8]

Multiplied throughout Vietnam by serious losses suffered by other American units, the attrition rate, even though much more favorable to the allies than during earlier years, fueled the antiwar movement and caused dissension and confusion within the new administration. As Kissinger related in his memoirs, the war threatened the ability of the new administration to govern:

Whatever our original war aims, by 1969 our credibility abroad, the reliability of our commitments, and our domestic cohesion were alike jeopardized by a struggle in a country as far away from the North American continent as our globe permits. . . . The comity by which a democratic society must live had broken down. No government can function without a minimum of trust. This was being dissipated under the harshness of our alternatives and the increasing rage of our domestic controversy.[9]

As described by Kissinger, the 1969 dry season offensive caused frustration within the administration because the rage directed toward the North was accompanied by a realization that little could be done about it. After fierce argument over the advisability of retaliation, Nixon decided on an air attack against a Cambodian sanctuary. Kissinger went on:

> These deliberations are instructive: A month of an unprovoked North Vietnamese offensive, over a thousand American dead, elicited after weeks of anguished discussion exactly one American retaliatory raid within three miles of the Cambodian border in an area occupied by the North Vietnamese for over four years. And this would enter the folklore as example of wanton "illegality."[10]

This raid soon developed into the famous "secret" bombing of the sanctuaries. More importantly, realizing that the American ground war must soon be terminated, Nixon announced the first installment of troop withdrawals in June. In addition, influenced by heavy U.S. casualties in general and the domestic furor over the battle at "Hamburger Hill" in particular, Nixon personally emphasized to General Abrams that American losses must be kept at a minimum and issued new orders to the effect that the primary U.S. mission was to enable Vietnamese forces to defend the country in the near future.[11] Thus, Front military exertions had paved the way for ultimate victory, however little Front forces were to participate in the final battle. Before savoring victory, however, the Front was forced to pay a very dear price.

The Front Wounded in Hau Nghia

The 1969 offensive in Hau Nghia began just after the original attacks on Saigon on 22 February. Fortunately for the population, Front and PAVN forces did not make major assaults on the towns. Nor did they attempt to occupy villages as they had during Tet. Furthermore, most of the large engagements of the next five months took place north of Highway 1 in relatively sparsely populated areas. Nevertheless, there were scores of mortar attacks, sometimes accompanied by sapper attacks and perimeter probes. For the most part, military and administrative targets received the enemy's attention.

As might be expected, the offensive put a quick, although temporary, end to the "progress" achieved during the Accelerated Pacification Campaign. The situation was made more difficult when several U.S. units were redeployed to Tay Ninh, where they remained until May. With the pacification effort once again submerged by big-unit warfare, the PSA, in late February, reported on the military and political quandary faced by the allies in Hau Nghia:

> Although we expected the attacks by fire after 22 February, they served to confirm that the VC could return in force. As a direct consequence of these attacks, our credibility as defenders of the population is seriously threatened.

. . . The major problem in this province is that it has too many VC. The ability of the VC to move supplies and men from their sanctuaries in Cambodia has been greatly impeded by a variety of means. It has not been diminished to the point where anything like security for the province population is possible. . . . In short, the variables in the Hau Nghia Pacification Program are the VC and the U.S. battalions. We were a great success during the APC when VC forces were withdrawn and we had a full U.S. brigade supporting our efforts. The VC have returned, and half of our brigade has departed. The current HES report reflects a downward trend with 43 hamlets dropping in security. Nine of these changes, affecting 13,000 people, were severe enough to cause a category change. This trend is likely to continue and, if unchecked, will cause a dramatic and very visible downgrading of security.[12]

As the fighting continued, allied forces scored one military success after another. Even territorial units put up stiff resistance on several occasions. Nevertheless, much of the pacification program remained stalled. As reported by the assistant senior advisor, the big battalions were still shaping the struggle in Hau Nghia at the end of April:

As long as the enemy is allowed to continue to use his sanctuaries in Cambodia, he will retain the capability of reinforcing his effort in Hau Nghia. If he is willing to pay the price, he can, at any time, bring the pacification effort in Hau Nghia to its knees. As long as a brigade of U.S. forces is present, the enemy must reckon with an exorbitant price. But should the U.S. brigade be withdrawn, he could count on a good return on his investment.[13]

The situation settled somewhat during May as U.S. units returned from Tay Ninh. In addition, seven new provincial force companies were deployed to Hau Nghia from neighboring provinces.[14] In June, the major elements of most of the enemy main force units withdrew, and local force units broke down and went into hiding. U.S. units quickly moved to fill the void left by the retreating Front and PAVN forces. To a greater extent than ever before, Hau Nghia province became the center of 25th Division activity. The 2d Brigade was deployed into Trang Bang and Cu Chi districts. At the end of June, 3d Brigade moved its headquarters to Bao Trai to take over responsibility for Duc Hue and Duc Hoa. At the end of July, the 3d Brigade of the 9th U.S. Infantry Division, operating in Long An province, was put under operational control of the 25th when its parent unit left for the United States.[15] At the beginning of summer, the Tropic Lightning Division was prepared for the most furious pacification offensive undertaken by U.S. forces in Hau Nghia. It was also to be the last.

The 1969 allied pacification offensive in Hau Nghia province began in July and lasted approximately nine months. Never had the allies concentrated so much manpower in Hau Nghia. The two U.S. brigades were supplemented by an ARVN regiment, 3,500 men in territorial units, 631 men employed in the RD Cadre teams, and another 500 members of the National Police. Against this powerful force, the enemy possessed the understrength elements of seven main force battalions and two regiments. On paper, these were formidable forces, but, in reality, only portions of most of these units were in Hau Nghia, the bulk of the manpower having shifted to Cambodia. All of the main force units were seriously understrength. So, too, were the dozen or so local force companies operating. In addition, American intelligence estimated that 1,100 political and administrative cadres were active in Hau Nghia, supported by approximately 700 guerrillas.[16]

The techniques employed by U.S. and South Vietnamese units were quite similar to those used during the Accelerated Pacification Campaign of late 1968. As enemy forces had uniformly dispersed and attempted to avoid contact, American units, too, broke down into smaller components. Platoon-level operations were common, and even squad-level operations were employed. The dispersion of U.S. forces, made possible by the absence of large enemy units, allowed the Americans to cover a much larger portion of the province than heretofore possible. In addition, although still eager to engage main force and local force units whenever possible, U.S. commanders made a dedicated effort to upgrade ARVN and the territorials. Joint operations were used more than ever before, with the territorial forces receiving special attention. The aim of the multitude of small joint operations, in addition to raising the proficiency of South Vietnamese units, was to provide day and night security for areas undergoing pacification.[17]

Militarily, the allied effort was a great success. The 25th Division alone claimed to have killed nearly 5,000 enemy during the period of 1 August 1969 to 31 January 1970. The true number must have been substantial because nearly 2,000 small arms, 150 crew-served weapons, and 500 prisoners were captured. U.S. losses dropped considerably from earlier periods and totaled 156 killed for the same six months.[18] Although there were few large encounters, medium- and low-level violence was constant. Two good numerical indicators of violence were the numbers of Chieu Hoi ralliers and refugees "generated." In the past, intense pacification operations, taking place so often in densely populated areas, always yielded many ralliers and refugees, but during the summer of 1969, these numbers soared. Whereas 86 Hoi Chanh surrendered in June, 258 capitulated in July. The numbers of Hoi Chanh remained high until November, with 234 in August, 330 in September, 384 in October, and 112 in November. Thereafter, the numbers declined again but never to the low levels of 1968. In June, the Americans estimated there were 4,663 refugees in Hau Nghia, in July, this number went up to 12,164 and peaked during September at 22,305. Most of the refugees were temporary and returned home quickly. Permanent refugees from Hau Nghia tended to gravitate toward the huge camps near Saigon or the capital's shantytowns. However, it is interesting to note that, in virtually every month, the numbers of refugees and ralliers either rose or fell together.[19]

Both 25th Division intelligence and the Hau Nghia advisory team gathered evidence that the Front was being pressed harder than ever before. Previously, virtually all of the ralliers had been low-level Front supporters. This category continued to be the largest, but, for the first time, important military and political cadres capitulated in significant numbers, a possible sign that the quality of the cadres had declined. During October, the Hoi Chanh included two company commanders, six platoon and six squad leaders, two deputy village chiefs, and a hamlet chief. In December, another company commander and twelve squad leaders capitulated.[20] Military attrition also took its toll on leading cadres as the commanders of Subregion 1 (the Front area including Cu Chi) and Subregion 3 (Long An) were killed in action.[21]

A primary goal of the pacification offensive was the separation of Front military units from the populated areas where they could receive support. Apparently, success in this regard was often achieved. As reported by 25th Division intelligence:

> More documentation was compiled on the deterioration of Subregion 1 as an effective political and military entity. The testimony of documents ralliers and prisoners contributed to the growing body of evidence which pointed to low morale, shortages of food and material, losses of large numbers of personnel and attempts to restructure the remnants of Subregion 1 forces. . . . Sources indicated that Subregion 1 units were still plagued with shortages of supplies and replacements, with no relief to be expected in the near future. Having lost the ability to launch full-scale military operations, Subregion 1 was now confronted with the rapid advances being made in the area of pacification and struggled to recoup its deteriorated influence in such traditional Viet Cong strongholds as Cu Chi District. Subregion 1 directives tended to reflect this reorientation, stressing security, propagandizing the people against the GVN, reorganization of components, and the elimination and screening of GVN sympathizers and personnel.[22]

The 25th Division also began a concentrated attack on the local Front guide network that was so critical for moving main force units through a given area. Careful and quiet intelligence work was required, but the results, according to General Williamson, commander of the 25th, were well worth it:

> As these guides were identified, we would swoop down in EAGLE FLIGHTS (small unit helicopter raids) and pick up members of the guide system. We almost never fired a shot on these raids. Little by little, we chipped away at his ability to move large units to battle. Our greatest damage was done to his units, however, as we destroyed their ability to use close-by "hide positions" after a battle. Most of their battles were short-raid type operations. They had to finish their operations and have their force hidden before daylight. Their escape from battle was nothing short of a frantic panic-filled flight. We were often able to find the choke points along their routes of flight, and when we could time our firepower with their passage we could tear units up so badly that many could not be committed again for months. I think the record will show that we were so successful in this type of operation that the undetected movement of large units deep inside South Vietnam was almost terminated by mid-1969.[23]

Furthermore, the division was pleased by the results obtained from the multitude of small-unit "area security" operations, as indicated by an evaluation made in January 1970:

> The effect of these small-unit reconnaissance operations has been to preempt the massing of enemy forces, destroy those forces which are contacted, and force the enemy into his Cambodian sanctuaries or deep jungles away from the major population centers in III Corps Tactical Zone. The results of these operations have been to inflict serious personnel losses on the enemy and to disrupt his supply activities. They have disorganized the enemy's usually scrupulous attack planning, imposed heavy personnel losses on the enemy while reducing friendly casualties, and deprived the enemy of the arms and supplies needed to sustain his attacks. The enemy units are not only being cut down in size but are losing their experienced leaders.[24]

In July 1969, Captain Henry Bergson took command of a company of the *Wolfhounds* operating along the Vam Co Dong River near Bao Trai. In previous years, this area would have been extremely dangerous because of its proximity to Cambodia. Throughout the summer and fall, Captain Bergson's company worked with ARVN, the Hau Nghia militia, and Cambodian mercenaries in the employ of American Special Forces and on converted World War II landing craft operated by the Vietnamese navy up and down the river. The battlefield environment grew so favorable that dispersed operations became the norm, allowing the *Wolfhounds* to saturate a much larger area than ever before. Later, Captain Bergson described his company's extremely successful campaign:

> At the beginning, we almost always operated in battalion- and company-sized operations. By the end, we were spread out in squad-sized ambush positions all over the map. We operated all along the east side of the river and went over to the west side on occasion. Booby traps caused most of the casualties, especially around Bao Trai. You name it—mines, command-detonated mines, punji stakes—we saw it. We didn't lose a single man killed when I was there due to direct fire. Only one was killed by a mine. We went up and down the river with the Vietnamese navy looking for trouble. We had a great Kit Carson scout. The closer to the river we operated, the more enemy caches we found. We were in and out of combat at a regular clip. In August and September, we sprang several good ambushes with real body count. It was an excellent company. . . . The VC were leaving the villagers alone and some of them were very friendly. The closer we got to the river, the farmers would come in right behind us and start reclaiming areas for rice cultivation. We could all see the progress, that the enemy was being pushed back.

Division intelligence at the time gathered substantial material that corroborated the accounts of General Williamson and Captain Bergson. For instance, one young officer who was captured revealed in interrogation that American small-unit operations had shut off most supply channels and that those units not in populated areas were barely eating enough to survive.[25] The II FFV intelligence received reports of Front soldiers stealing livestock, an almost unheard of event.[26] A document captured in October disclosed that desertion had become a very serious problem for the 268th Regiment, a usually solid Front main force unit, and that morale was dropping because of the problem.[27] Another document captured in October, a letter between two rear service cadres, read in part, "the situation in this area is extremely tense, since practically every unit down here has been stricken by hunger. Clinging to the Ben Chua area to purchase rice is a matter of life or death for all units."[28]

Front recruitment was also growing much more difficult. In August, some Hoi Chanh told the Hau Nghia advisory team that, contrary to normal practice, North Vietnamese troops were now serving in local force units. These reports were confirmed in November when a local force company commander revealed to 25th Division intelligence that most of his men were from the North.[29] A document captured in late November, classified "absolute secret," revealed that units subordinate to Subregion 1 had been unable to accomplish most of their objectives due to poor leadership. It also disclosed that all major efforts directed against the pacification program had failed because units were preoccupied with food procurement, a problem made more difficult because the population was moving toward GVN-controlled areas.[30] In late 1969, a PAVN lieutenant surrendered in Cu Chi to the 25th Division. In interrogation, he was asked whether he believed that the Front could launch another offensive in Cu Chi the coming year. His answer revealed the desperate military situation facing the Front:

Natural terrain features are mostly removed, and about 90 percent of the population is concentrated in strategic hamlets. Underground cadres have rallied to the Nationalist government, and only a few of them remain. If the VC send their troops to the area, they cannot avoid bloodshed. In addition, they will encounter the shortage of food supplies. It is very difficult for the Viet Cong to mount an offensive due to the demoralization of their troops and lack of support of the people. If the Viet Cong rashly mount an offensive, they will certainly sustain heavy casualties for nothing. They fear lack of food because that means more trips for rice, which are very dangerous.[31]

Although most of the evidence cited above dealt with the situation facing Front military units, there can be no doubt, as indicated by the soaring Chieu Hoi totals, that political cadres and support elements were in equally dire straits. Excellent testimony on the problems faced by the political cadres was given by the Hiep Hoa cadre already quoted in Chapter 6. This man had been promoted to Hiep Hoa finance and economy chief upon the murder of his predecessor by a drunken cadre who was trying to embezzle village funds. The names cited have been changed from the original document, and the term "OB" refers to a territorial fort. As described by this defector, the Front was battered by the 1969 allied campaign:

The military situation by the summer of 1969 was very bad. On 10 June, the Rung Tre OB was set up, and on 1 October, the An Thuan II OB was built.

These steps made it increasingly difficult for us to operate. We had to concentrate more and more of our activities in the Dong Hoa and Bao Trai areas, moving constantly from place to place. Control and discipline were difficult to maintain. . . . By October 1969, I had contracted malaria, and the military pressure was becoming unbearable. I requested permission from Chinh to go to Ba Thu (Cambodia) to recuperate. The permission was granted, and on 21 October 1969, I went again to Ba Thu. To the best of my knowledge, I was the only one who requested permission to leave Hiep Hoa, although many of us went to Ba Thu. Most of the others simply abandoned their posts and hurried to Ba Thu. Although it is true that no cadre is supposed to leave his village without permission, the situation at this time did not permit the usual procedures to be followed. For example, during the summer of 1969, Chinh was called to Cambodia for a four-week training course but was not able to return to Hiep Hoa for ten or twelve weeks because of the military situation. In any event, making contact at that time was difficult, and everyone had to fend for himself.

The former cadre also described conditions in Cambodia:

I spent the first month in a VC hospital in Ba Thu. After that, I lived with Nhuyen Van Trao. Trao was the assistant secretary, rear area. . . . Trao had been a guerrilla in Hiep Hoa. Like so many others, he had fled to Ba Thu to escape the military pressure of the front area. By this time, the Hiep Hoa "village-in-exile" had grown considerably. Trao's job was to keep track of the many Hiep Hoa natives who arrived in the area and attempt to keep them together. Most of us lived in the Dia Bai area. Trao was also responsible for keeping the rear area in touch with the front area. The flow of information here was mostly one way. That is, the people in the rear area were not very interested in keeping in touch with the front area. Most of us were in Ba Thu to escape the front. However, the cadre in the front area were constantly sending back messages of victories and the improving situation, in an effort to raise our morale and perhaps entice some of us to return. Trao had the task of disseminating this news. In addition, if a comrade in the front area was wounded, he would be brought to the border by the front area people. Trao would get a team together and pick up the wounded comrade at the border and take him to a hospital. Trao also performed this same function with supplies, which he and a team of volunteers would take to the border and turn over to a group from the front area. To the best of my knowledge, during this period, the people of the rear area always stopped at the border when carrying supplies or picking up wounded. One more job of Trao's was the welcoming of new arrivals from Hiep Hoa. He would get a group of volunteers together and build a house for the new arrivals. I think this was done more out of a desire to keep us all together than out of generosity or community spirit.[32]

The defector also revealed that the existence of the Hiep Hoa "village-in-exile" in Cambodia was not an exception but rather the rule. Exile village committees existed near Ba Thu for every major village in both Duc Hue and Duc Hoa districts. In addition, there were exile district committees from both Duc Hue and Duc Hoa.[33]

Because all signs indicated that the Front was weaker at the end of 1969 than at any previous time since American intervention in Hau Nghia and neighboring provinces, the officers of the 25th Division believed, with some reason, that their summer-fall offensive had been a great success. Divisional reports were more optimistic than at any time before. For instance, commenting on the period of July to October, the divisional report claimed a major victory:

> Prisoner-of-war interrogation and the large number of Hoi Chanh since mid-August clearly indicated the low morale of the enemy. This was due primarily to the relentless pursuit and destruction of enemy units and enemy inability to resupply his units or to evacuate wounded due to denial operations and population and resource control measures. The enemy had continued to sustain heavy casualties, was driven from many of his "secure" areas, and was critically short of food and supplies. Preemption through saturation surveillance, reconnaissance, and immediate reaction of massed fires had dealt the Communist insurgency in Tay Ninh, Hau Nghia, and Long An provinces another one-sided defeat.[34]

The situation appeared even brighter in Saigon. The Front was being pressed hard throughout the III CTZ, and the GVN presence had been extended everywhere. Although admitting some minor difficulties, CORDS officials were more than satisfied with allied efforts throughout 1969, as shown in the December report:

> Notwithstanding the foregoing, the progress made in pacification in the III Corps area during 1969 has been remarkable. If one recalls the situation a year ago, one cannot help but be impressed with the changes wrought. Only a minuscule percentage of the population remains "under VC control." Roads which were either closed or extremely dangerous are now teeming with civilian traffic. Curfew hours have been eased. Areas which lay fallow are back under cultivation. The harvest has been bountiful. The performance of territorial forces and their confidence in themselves has risen. Leadership continues to be spotty, but many units are experienced and combat-ready.[35]

Without doubt, 1969 was the best year for the allies both in Vietnam overall and in Hau Nghia province. Perhaps it would be more accurate to describe 1969 as the worst year for the Front because, regardless of the outward manifestations of progress, the GVN again failed to win the freely given support of the rural population in Hau Nghia province. As always, the "progress" resulted from the employment of force. But, as shall be seen directly, even the coercive components of the pacification program fell far short of decisive success. Efforts intended to win the support, rather than the grudging acquiescence, of the rural population continued to have little meaning, especially when measured against the constant violence inherent in the mode of operations used by both sides.

9

The Pacification of
Hau Nghia Province, 1969

The Phoenix Program

Although American and South Vietnamese efforts harmed the Front in 1969, most of the damage was due to military attrition and the number of defections caused by military pressure. The allies again failed miserably to attack the Front's political apparatus in an organized manner. This was a great disappointment for CORDS because 1969 was the first year during which the attack on the enemy apparatus was given top priority in practice as well as in word. To be sure, the critically important role played by Front cadres, especially those belonging to the Party, had long been recognized, and the destruction of the Front's political apparatus always was theoretically important in the various pacification campaigns. Yet, until 1969, both the efforts actually made in the field and the results obtained were quite minimal.

Despite the beliefs of many ignorant Americans to the contrary, the GVN was well aware of the importance of the Front's apparatus. Indeed, the shadowy and frequently violent war between the agents of the government and the insurgency had begun decades before with the French *Sûreté*, on one side, and various Vietnamese nationalist groups on the other. Diem incorporated the techniques, the files, and some of the Vietnamese personnel working with the *Sûreté* into the Special Branch of his National Police. Special Branch always considered the Party the most dangerous of Diem's many enemies and devoted great resources to the struggle against it. As recounted in Chapter 1, the National Police had great success until the Party began armed struggle and drove the GVN from most of the countryside. Obviously, from that point on, it was of no value whatsoever in rural areas until some sort of GVN presence was reestablished after U.S. intervention. The NP did, however, continued to campaign in the cities, with some success.

As might be expected, the earliest American campaign against the Party was run by the CIA. In the early 1960s, CIA agents began collecting information on the Front's political apparatus and opened an interrogation center in Saigon. For some murky reason, no terms then in use in the

English language were considered adequate to describe the structure they wished to destroy; hence, someone coined the term "infrastructure" to describe the Front's complex political apparatus. Naturally, the new word was grafted to the ubiquitous term "Viet Cong" and abbreviated to "VCI" (Viet Cong infrastructure).[1] Through 1968, the VCI were to be "eliminated"; thereafter, "neutralized" became the favored term. With the National Police crippled in the countryside, the CIA began organizing provincial "Counter-Terror Teams" in 1962, aimed at attacking the Front's cadres, especially those operating the "extermination of traitors" campaign. Soon thereafter, due to unfavorable press coverage, the name was changed to Provincial Reconnaissance Units, or PRUs.[2] Although the PRUs were controlled by the province chiefs in theory, the CIA ran the PRUs virtually as an independent arm of the agency after Diem's death, with only nominal direction or oversight from the GVN. The CIA sought this independence because the Front agents who had infiltrated every level of the GVN in this period of the war had been successful in totally sabotaging the clandestine effort against the Party. Although much general information concerning the PRUs was made public during various congressional hearings, the CIA has always guarded the details very closely. It is likely that much was never recorded on paper, especially early in the war when freewheeling CIA operatives were waging what almost amounted to a private war.

There were at least two CIA permanent representatives in Hau Nghia province at any given time. The advisors assisting in this research all admitted that they never really knew what the CIA representatives were up to. Although CORDS, in theory, was supposed to integrate the American pacification effort at every level, CIA activities were largely exempt. Presumably, coordination, such as it was, was handled at the very top. William Colby, made head of CORDS in November 1968, was a high CIA official and former station chief in Saigon. The CIA agents at Bao Trai ran the Hau Nghia PRU and the RD Cadre Program, which by its very nature was closely monitored and largely maintained by the GVN provincial officials and the U.S. advisory team. The PRU was another matter altogether, and advisors rarely knew anything about its activities.

Descriptions of the PRU personnel vary greatly. They were often characterized as fanatical anti-Communists, often bearing a strong personal vendetta against the Party and its followers. Sometimes, they are described as violent criminals and mercenaries. Many rumors of PRU operations circulated. One district advisor claimed that the Hau Nghia PRUs made raids into Cambodia and destroyed Front villages there. Another advisor recalled that the PRUs were very good at guerrilla tactics and frequently made contacts during their night patrols. And yet another advisor believed that they maintained their secrecy because they really were not doing very much. Whatever the truth (and this research has little to add to the matter), the PRUs were considered, proportionately, the most effective organization in the fight against the Front's apparatus.[3] Nevertheless, the PRUs were never strong numerically, numbering only about 4,000 nationwide in 1970, and their overall impact was necessarily very limited. As usual, the GVN was short on ideologues.

Other organizations were also supposed to struggle against the Front's apparatus. The National Police, which was gradually reinstalled in towns and large villages, was naturally charged with gathering intelligence, and ARVN and the militia had special intelligence platoons. In 1967, as previously mentioned, the 25th Division created a combined American-Vietnamese reconnaissance and intelligence platoon. In 1966 and 1967, the RD Cadre teams were, in theory, to lead the fight against the Front in the hamlets. But, as we have seen, they totally failed in this mission.

The formation of CORDS led to an initial attempt to centralize all the various efforts directed against the VCI. In mid-1967, Komer established a joint CORDS-CIA program, called Intelligence Coordination and Exploitation (ICEX), to bring some order out of the chaos of this important effort. Late in the same year, Thieu enlisted Vietnamese agencies in support of ICEX, and the program was renamed Phoenix or Phung Hoang in Vietnamese. In succeeding years, the Americans progressively pinned more and more hopes on the success of Phoenix. Nevertheless, it developed into one of the most important, if not most conspicuous, failures of the entire American war effort.

Before charting the frustrating history of the Phoenix Program in Hau Nghia province and elsewhere, it is appropriate to examine those characteristics of the Party's organization that made any organized assault upon it in the rural areas an extraordinarily difficult proposition. Although the Party had been able to operate quite openly in many parts of the country during the war with France, a clandestine tradition existed from the beginning. The Party was, after all, Leninist in origin. Nevertheless, severe weaknesses in security and organization led to harsh losses for the Party between 1954–1959. Through necessity, the underground cadres that survived the Diem years learned much about the fine art of clandestine operation. By the time of American intervention, Party and Front cadres had become quite expert at operating in a hostile environment.

This is not to say that the identity of every cadre was secret. In "liberated" or "contested" areas, important village-level cadres were well known to the population. These were the men and women that collected taxes, propagandized, or headed one of the various Front organizations. Villagers, of course, were warned never to cooperate with GVN agents, but competent investigators could frequently learn the identities of cadres operating in the open. Important cadres normally used a series of aliases that complicated things greatly. As a group, these village cadres, regardless of importance, were termed "illegal" for they operated more or less openly in violation, to say the least, of South Vietnamese law.

On the village level, "illegal" cadres were more likely than not Party members only if they held very important positions: About 25 percent of the cadres belonged to the Party, although some 75 percent of the village secretaries were members. Party membership was much more common at district level. At province level and above, any important cadre not belonging to the Party was a token figure, serving propaganda purposes. Naturally, Party members were the people that the Americans and South Vietnamese were most interested in apprehending.

Yet, even if identified, "illegal" cadres were very difficult to catch. Every villager was expected to give warning of approaching allied forces. This task was far easier if an allied operation had been compromised in advance. Important cadres would almost always sleep in the hamlets where the Front was strongest. Nearby, there would be a complex of tunnels and cleverly disguised bunkers where cadres could hide. If, despite precautions, the allies achieved surprise, every cadre had a bunker in the house where he was residing that gave him a very good chance of avoiding capture. District-level cadres of significant rank would normally reside in the strongest "liberated" village in their district and often had a squad or platoon of local guerrillas to provide security. A common tactic, if a raid were in progress, was for the guerrillas to initiate a firefight and lead pursuing soldiers away from fleeing cadres. Hiding places were even more elaborate at district level and normally protected by mines and booby traps. Cadres at the province level and above normally lived in the safest area of their province and rarely left it. If a province-level cadre did pay a visit to a district, local cadres made careful preparations and delegated the services of a local or main force unit for protection. Consequently, cadres at the province level and above were virtually untouchable and could only be hit indirectly through air attack or large military sweeps.

If apprehending "illegal" cadres was difficult, attacking the "legal" cadres was even more so. "Legal" cadres were so named because they operated behind the cover of a legal existence in contested or GVN-controlled villages, carefully concealing their affiliation with the Front. Every village in Hau Nghia had resident "legal" cadres. For self-protection, they employed a cell system, with each cell usually made up of three members. If one member was captured or rallied, the other two would flee for a time; the remaining cells would still be operating. This was possible for the identity of the legal cadres was known only to the village secretary. They acted as the eyes and ears of the revolution in GVN territory, and their presence, if not their identity, was known by every villager, making cooperation with the GVN very risky.

The whole situation was made even more difficult by the activities of the Security Affairs Section, the "Cheka" of the revolution. Security Affairs developed a system of informants that, to one degree or another, was independent of even the village secretary or his counterpart up the orga-nizational charts. These informants, unknown to other cadres (whether Party members or not), kept watch on important GVN figures and, of course, the activities of the other Party cadres. Presumably, Security Affairs even possessed agents at COSVN, and it was the Security Affairs section that often handled the "extermination of traitors" campaign. They were also the most difficult to identify and apprehend of all Party cadres. This was most unfortunate, from the point of view of the allies, because it made it almost impossible to end the terror campaign that was so crucial to the revolution. As long as Security Affairs could operate, it would remain dreadfully dangerous for any GVN official to show competence and zeal and even more dangerous for an important cadre to switch sides. The watchful eyes of Security Affairs also enabled Party leaders to maintain very tight discipline on important political and military cadres.[4]

Consequently, the Americans and Vietnamese seeking the destruction of the Front's political apparatus were faced with staggering difficulties. Nevertheless, CORDS recognized the critical importance of this apparatus and was determined to make the attempt. Above all, CORDS wanted to attack the VCI in an organized, discriminating manner, with heavy reliance on police action. To organize this approach, every province established a Province Intelligence and Operation Coordinating Center (PIOCC), and similar centers were established on the district level (DIOCC) as quickly as possible. The latter were considered more important operationally. All of these centers had American advisors.

The purpose of the DIOCC was to coordinate investigations concerning the identity and place of residence of local cadres. In theory, a suspect, once identified and investigated, was to be individually targeted and apprehended through arrest, if possible, or raid. The DIOCCs were also to serve as nerve points for intelligence gathering. In principle, they would allow quick reaction to fresh intelligence concerning the presence of an important cadre nearby or the meeting of a Front organization. Reaction forces, in such instances, would be whatever was available to the district chief at the moment, usually territorials. Units of the 25th Division were eager for such missions, although the call rarely came. On the province level, the PRUs might be employed. In theory, the National Police forces were to run these centers (without which the Phoenix Program had no meaning whatsoever), but, in practice, this task was usually left to the American advisor.[5]

On paper, Phoenix was a serious threat to the Front. Zealous, competent, and relentless police investigators, supported by quick reaction forces, would have been a mortal threat to Front cadres, legal or illegal. In reality, though, it proved a great failure and nowhere more so than in Hau Nghia province. This is not to say that the Front apparatus was not hurt badly during 1969. The Front was, of course, in serious difficulty by the end of the year at all levels. But, unfortunately for the allies, Phoenix had little to do with it. The numbers of cadres "neutralized" were much higher than at any previous time. In April 1969, CORDS estimated that there were 1,000 Front cadres operating in Hau Nghia, supported by somewhat over 3,000 service personnel. This latter category included porters or villagers willing to help construct fortifications.[6] Consequently, the Americans considered the service personnel to be of little importance and did not include them in the ranks of the VCI.

As was typical in Hau Nghia, the number of cadres killed, rallied, or captured went up or down depending upon the pace of U.S. military operations. In January, for instance, 9 cadres were accounted for, but the numbers soared during the summer and fall, with October being the most productive month when 63 "VCI neutralized" were reported. Altogether, the advisory team stated that 315 Front cadres had been eliminated in 1969, well over the quota assigned by CORDS at the beginning of the year.[7]

If true and even if most of the cadres were low-level, this would have constituted a serious blow to the Front. One officer later described the Vietnamese conflict as "the war of slippery figures." This was a particularly good description concerning figures emanating from the Phoenix Program. In the first place, it was very difficult to define what was meant by "VCI," the GVN included military cadres, but the Americans did not. Nor was it easy to determine at what level on the organization chart a cadre had to be placed to be considered a member of the VCI. In general, the Americans pressed for a more narrow definition of VCI than did the GVN. It was also extremely difficult to identify important cadres killed in action for the dossiers kept at the Hau Nghia DIOCCs were always described as miserable. Lastly, a large number of these figures were very likely fraudulent. District chiefs were given quotas of VCI to be neutralized. Such quotas tended to be viewed as report cards, and the temptation always existed to seriously distort or simply falsify the figures. John Paul Vann believed that a large number of cadres that were claimed to have been killed in action were, in fact, not cadres at all; many were not even followers of the Front.

Yet, even if the figures from Hau Nghia were accurate, the Phoenix Program failed badly in 1969. The most serious weakness, as revealed in several province reports, was that only a handful of the cadres killed or captured came from Phoenix activities. Almost all of the cadres that were reported to have been eliminated were actually killed in normal military operations or capitulated to the Chieu Hoi program. For instance, during September, there were 35 VCI neutralized. Of this total, 19 were Hoi Chanh, 13 were killed in regular combat operations by ARVN or the 25th Division, and only 3 were captured; only 1 of the captured was apprehended by Phoenix agents. At the end of the year, the advisory team reported that the Hau Nghia PIOCC had failed to target a single individual and was doing nothing with the information assembled.[8]

As so often happened when the Vietnamese showed little enthusiasm for an American initiative, the advisory team turned to the 25th Division. In December, a joint Phoenix–25th Division Military Intelligence center was established. American Phoenix advisors, with the aid of 25th Division Intelligence and with little Vietnamese help, developed dossiers and a "VCI mugbook" for important cadres they had identified.[9] Meanwhile, they faced another serious problem—the continued reluctance of important Front and Party cadres to rally. Throughout 1969, the Hau Nghia reports do not mention the capitulation of a single important cadre due to Phoenix. This was particularly serious because so few cadres were captured. Although the death of a cadre might impair Front activities for a time, it did no good at all for the Phoenix Program. Only through interrogation could dossiers be developed, and only through information held by important cadres could a concentrated assault on the "legal" apparatus be launched. Unfortunately for the GVN, important cadres rarely rallied and apprehension rarely took place, thus crippling the entire Phoenix effort.

Several factors account for the failure of the Phoenix Program in Hau Nghia during 1969. In the first place, as suggested earlier, the effort would have been difficult even in the best of circumstances. As it was, with the National Police not well thought of by the rural population and the people fearful of cooperating in any case, hard intelligence was very difficult to come by. Here again, the structural weakness of the GVN in the countryside seriously hampered the war effort. Second, many Americans working with Phoenix believed that GVN officials were apathetic because the program was so closely identified with the Americans. During May, this attitude was expressed by a CORDS official in Saigon:

> Many neutralizations are by chance, and few are the result of specific targeting. Command interest expressed at Saigon and Corps in Phung Hoang has not resulted in improved operations at province and district. Phung Hoang is still an American-inspired, American-style program that is accepted without enthusiasm by the Vietnamese. Phung Hoang has little momentum and, if left to the Vietnamese, would soon grind to a halt.[10]

This opinion was similar to hundreds expressed concerning any American-inspired plan. Unfortunately for the war effort, this included almost the entire pacification program. And, no doubt, there was some truth to such opinions. Vietnamese officials were sensitive to any charge that they functioned as U.S. "puppets," and, even under far better conditions, alliances have difficulties over problems of national pride. ARVN officers, in particular, were well known to consider any pacification duty to be undignified. Yet, this sort of analysis leaves much to be desired. The Phoenix Program—or something like it—was obviously a necessity if the GVN were to prevail in the long run, and Diem's police had certainly shown great zeal in attacking the Party apparatus before being evicted from most of the countryside. It is much more likely that fear of Front retribution played the most important role in the Phoenix failure. Penetration of the National Police by Front agents and the overall corruption of the GVN no doubt aggravated the situation.

This fear, of course, worked on GVN officials and potential ralliers alike. Although the Party showed little concern over many components of the pacification program (village elections, for instance, were not often interfered with), Phoenix was a serious threat, and the assassination squads of Security Affairs were quick to react. Whenever assassination figures were broken down in the province reports coming from Hau Nghia, many—very often most—of the victims were officials working with Phoenix or Hoi Chanh who were of some importance. For example, during June in Cu Chi district, 9 assassinations took place; 6 victims were connected with Phoenix.[11] Throughout 1969, 264 people were assassinated by the Front in Hau Nghia.[12]

Front leadership was well aware of the fact that some individuals would risk their own lives, but would not endanger loved ones. Consequently, many victims were relatives of officials or ralliers. This ruthless policy was sometimes counterproductive because many of the most efficient and zealous anti-Communists working for the GVN were driven by a thirst for revenge.

Of course, not all those killed by the Front were connected with Phoenix. An official or RD Cadre member considered honest, effective, and admired by the people was in dreadful danger. So, too, was an official who had earned the particular hatred of the local population through cruelty or especially blatant corruption.[13] Altogether, the "extermination of traitors" campaign was a crushing burden on the GVN, particularly concerning the Phoenix Program. It served as a powerful incentive for GVN officials to be both inefficient and corrupt. One form of corruption was particularly welcome by the Party: Americans received many reports of important Front cadres who, after arrest, were released due to well-placed bribes.[14]

Therefore, the Phoenix Program in Hau Nghia during 1969 was another paper exercise with little real value. In January 1970, CORDS estimated that 980 Front cadres were still operating in Hau Nghia. Earlier in the year, the PSA made a widely circulated quip that "more VCI are killed by Honda accidents, than by the Phoenix Program." The continued strength of the Front's political apparatus was recognized by American advisors and, in December, drew the following comment from the PSA:

> We believe that the first weeks of the enemy's winter campaign have revealed that the VC retain a viable political apparatus (although quite weak in some villages), but that this apparatus has been stripped of most of its guerrilla and local force protection. NVA and main force units operating at platoon and squad levels have taken over the job of the local forces of protecting tax collectors and proselytizing. . . . Local party infrastructures appear to be policing their ranks and learning how to survive in the pacification environment. There is at least a skeleton infrastructure in every village. . . . Rice taxation is often taking place during daylight.[15]

Strengthening Regional and Popular Forces

Although the energy put into the Phoenix Program was largely ill spent, some headway was made by the allies in another key component of the coercive side of their strategy: upgrading the Regional and Popular Forces. Although the role of the RF/PF in the Vietnam War received virtually no attention in the United States, by 1969, Americans on the spot all agreed that improving them was critical for a successful war effort. This was particularly true when U.S. troop withdrawals began. Recognizing that American ground forces were a dwindling asset, Thieu, with U.S. support, began a self-sufficiency program early in the year. As it expanded and received better arms, ARVN was to leave pacification duties and redeploy toward the border areas to assume the duties of U.S. combat units. The Regional Forces, operating either as companies or as combat groups resembling battalions, were to take over from ARVN, particularly in the war against local force units. The Popular Forces, normally operating as platoons, were to take over the duties of the Regional Forces and provide some sort of district security. The newly organized People's Self Defense Force and the RD Cadres were to be responsible for providing security in GVN-controlled villages. Thieu's plan was coherent but very ambitious. A failure at any level would imperil the entire effort.[16]

The effectiveness of the RF/PF was and is a very controversial subject in U.S. military and advisory circles. Many American officers and not a few advisors had utter contempt for the RF/PF, particularly the Popular Forces; very often these same people held negative views of the GVN and its forces in general. On the other extreme, some Americans who worked very closely with the RF/PF, often possessing some knowledge of the Vietnamese language and culture, were quick to sing the praises of the hard-pressed militia troops, frequently claiming they preferred to conduct operations with territorial units over either ARVN or U.S. units.[17] Several reasons existed for the great range of opinion concerning the territorials. Units of the RF/PF tended to operate more aggressively when under some sort of American supervision or when on joint operations with a U.S. unit because there was more confidence in combat and medical support and because of their fear of losing face in American eyes. Hence, many advisors saw the territorials working at better-than-average levels. Some advisors never served an infantry tour in Vietnam with U.S. forces and could not really make accurate comparisons. And, no doubt, some were trying to praise themselves when praising the units under their care. More fundamentally, however, territorial units varied tremendously in quality. Some, especially Regional Force companies, were well led and had some well-motivated soldiers. Such units, possessing excellent knowledge of the terrain, were capable of fine service. Had every territorial unit been the equal to the best in the various categories, the Front would have been smashed in short order. Sadly for the GVN, this was not the case at all. The majority of units performed quite poorly, and some, especially the PF platoons, were even worse than worthless for they were collaborating with the Front. It must be remembered, however, that the militia soldier, like his ARVN counterpart, was in the war more or less for the duration. Troopers were poorly paid and often poorly trained, particularly in the Popular Forces units. Again, competence and zeal were dangerous. Skill at engaging Front forces meant, in the long run, serious losses, with the best soldiers the most likely to be killed. To complicate matters, many militia soldiers had relatives or friends in the Front. In general, the RF/PF trooper, coming as he did from the rural masses, shared to a large degree the apathy and war-weariness afflicting the entire countryside.

With such considerations in mind, it must be concluded that, though some degree of progress was made in Hau Nghia concerning the RF/PF, it was more quantitative than qualitative. Numerically, there was a sizable increase. In April 1969, there were some 1,300 men serving in the Regional

Forces. Through recruitment and reinforcement from outside the province, this number climbed to 3,550 at the end of January 1970, organized into 31 companies and 5 combat groups. Although the number of men serving in the Popular Forces stayed about the same throughout the year at 1,800, the number of platoons was raised from 49 to 58.[18]

The number of contacts made by the Regional Forces was always much higher than those of the Popular Forces. Of course, contacts varied with the level of fighting initiated by the Front. In June, for instance, a time of considerable fighting, the RF made 100 contacts out of 1,101 operations; the PF had 86 contacts out of nearly 2,000 operations. In January 1970, with fighting at a low level, the RF averaged contacts on 1.7 percent of operations, and the PF on 0.8 percent. Though these totals were not impressive, the RF/PF, because of sheer mass, added appreciably to the attrition rate so harmful to the Front. Many of the cadres captured throughout the year were apprehended by the RF/PF, and, even when not successful, militia activities made it more difficult for the Front to operate for even more precautions had to be taken. This was not the case, of course, when accommodation had been reached with the local RF/PF unit.[19]

Sgt. Richard O'Hare, a member of the Duc Hue district advisory team, witnessed the slow and erratic spread of rural security in one part of Hau Nghia. Sergeant O'Hare's small team was based in a hamlet of Hiep Hoa village, the Duc Hue district capital, directly on the Vam Co Dong River. When he arrived in April 1969, the Front still controlled large portions of the district, and most of the population was "anti-American to say the least." The advisory team was housed in a French-built country villa that had belonged to Madame Nhu, the infamous "Dragon Lady" of the Diem era. At one time beautiful, the villa was run-down, pockmarked with bullet holes, and heavily fortified. In terms of the Vietnam War, however, it afforded opulent living. A short distance away was the sugar mill complex. Once one of the most important industrial facilities in South Vietnam, it had been occupied by PAVN during the 1968 Tet Offensive and ruined during the fighting. Although a few Vietnamese craftsmen operated some of the old French machine tools in one of the buildings, the rest of the complex was "rather spooky: There were large brick walls with no roof and wreckage lying all over the place." Despite the presence of a Regional Forces battalion in the hamlet, the advisors, fearing snipers and booby traps, rarely entered the complex.

The Vam Co Dong, nearly a half-mile across in places, dominated the strange tableau. With the exception of one small hamlet directly across the river from the sugar mill, the entire area west of the river was virtually uninhabited and hostile. A free fire zone for years, the low-lying marshy terrain west of the river was blanketed with bomb craters. The collection of craters continually grew, as Sergeant O'Hare found out on one of his first nights in Duc Hue when he was thrown out of his cot by the blast of a B-52 strike two miles to the west. O'Hare's team was about ten miles from the tip of the "Parrot's Beak" area of the Cambodian frontier and the major Front sanctuary of Ba Thu. Consequently, the area was a transit point for Front units of all sizes going to and from Cambodia. One of the primary jobs of the militia units stationed near the sugar mill was to interfere with this infiltration. Two advisors would accompany a militia operation, one walking at the front of a company and one at the rear. The American advisors all had advanced combat skills (O'Hare was a paratrooper), but their presence was desired by the Vietnamese not for the advice they could offer but because they had access to U.S. artillery, air, and Medevac support. ARVN had similar supporting units even closer, but the Vietnamese militia did not trust their countrymen's accuracy or timeliness and, therefore, came to rely heavily on American assistance. Because there were so few roads along the river, many operations were conducted with the aid of Vietnamese navy landing craft that ferried militia companies up- or downriver and carried them back. Militia units also conducted normal ground sweeps up the road toward Hiep Hoa village and occasionally tried a helicopter operation. According to O'Hare, these operations were characterized by lethargy and general ineffectiveness:

> We left at 9:00 A.M. and returned at 4:00. On most days, patrols were made: slow, gradual sweeps through the assigned area. We went slow so we wouldn't stumble on anyone. Occasionally, we came across something just as a blind hog would stumble on an acorn in the forest sometimes. It was not our intention to confront the enemy. . . . Every now and then, we would talk the Vietnamese into trying an ambush. Their way of doing this was to parade out while it was still light and come back about midnight. This was dangerous, and two of our patrols once ran into each other, and there were casualties.

Various small American units played a part. For several weeks, the 25th Division's elite Long Range Reconnaissance Platoon (LRRP) was based at the sugar mill for operations west of the river. This platoon, like all American units in this period of the war, was instructed to conduct joint operations with the Vietnamese. However, this rarely happened because the Americans feared, with good reason, that the Vietnamese would compromise one of their long-range missions into Front territory and bring about their annihilation. The result of this secrecy on one occasion was a near disaster when a U.S. forward air controller aircraft spotted the LRRPs west of the river and radioed the sugar mill, asking if the men under observation were friend or foe. The Americans at the sugar mill, not knowing where the LRRP was, signaled foe, and gunships moved to the attack, wounding several friendly troops.

The Duc Hue advisors also had frequent contact with riverine forces of the U.S. Navy. The navy operated patrol boats out of a small base downriver at Tra Cu in Duc Hoa district. The boats, mostly PBS MKIIs, were custom-designed, aluminum-hulled patrol craft, powered by pump jets giving them a one-foot draft. Although lightly armored and very vulnerable to attack, they were fast and powerfully armed with 30mm cannon and heavy machine guns. Patrol boats engaged in an often successful but dreadfully dangerous game of cat and mouse that the navy called "Eagle Float." At night, the boats would go upriver, cut their engines, and float downstream, watching their antipersonnel radar screens for anything that moved. Frequently, they intercepted Front infiltrators. On other occasions, they were victims of a Front ambush. One night, a boat was ambushed and sunk while rushing to the aid of the advisors at the sugar mill who were under ground attack. The attack was a feint, but the ambush on the river was real enough.

Americans also might be above the shoreline of the Vam Co Dong at night. In early 1969, the 25th Division aviation battalion developed a tactic widely copied by other units, called "Nighthawk." With this tactic, a helicopter was armed with a minigun, a 1,000,000-candlepower xenon searchlight from a tank, and a starlight night scope. The helicopter would fly along infiltration routes, as a crewman searched the ground with the starlight scope. If something was seen, the xenon went on and the minigun opened up. As might be expected from a tactic developed by the men on the spot with simple equipment that they knew would work, the technique was very successful.

When not busy on the Vam Co Dong, the advisors at the sugar mill had another mission in 1969 that was just as important: clear the road and establish a government presence in the area between Bao Trai and Trang Bang. When he arrived at Duc Hue in April, O'Hare was surprised to find major roads in Hau Nghia still impassable. Despite the presence of the U.S. 25th at Cu Chi, the ARVN 25th at Duc Hoa, and all of the other allied military forces in between, it was still extremely risky to travel the few miles between the two base camps. Direct ground communications existed between Bao Trai and Cu Chi but not between Trang Bang and Duc Hoa. The stretch of provincial Route 10 (called "number ten," after the Vietnamese slang for terrible) that passed through Duc Hue district between Bao Trai and Trang Bang was particularly bad. In early summer, one of the new militia companies brought in from another province was installed in a fort between the two towns. According to O'Hare, "We hit a nerve. We must have put the outpost right on a communication route. From the moment they arrived, our outpost was under mortar attack, machine gun fire, or rocket attack every night for weeks." Other militia units were formed and inserted in Duc Hue. Around the end of July, with the Front dry season offensive at an end, Duc Hue district started to grow quiet. By October, unescorted travel was possible on all major roads in Hau Nghia province.

On occasion, O'Hare dealt with members of the U.S. Army Special Forces, the famous "Green Berets." Over the years, Special Forces had constructed a series of camps and forts in remote areas all along the border manned by Cambodian mercenaries or indigenous hill peoples. Their role was to hinder infiltration and act as an early-warning picket line. Special Forces had built a camp near the sugar mill years before: When overrun in late 1963, it was the first compound lost in the war. In early 1966, the Green Berets established a new camp at the sugar mill. In January 1967, they set up another camp on the Vam Co Dong at Tra Cu, a site later shared with the navy. At the same time, the sugar mill camp was transferred several miles to the west, to the old Duc Hue district capital that had been abandoned years before.

The role of Special Forces in the war was controversial at the time and has been ever since. Many critics, Gen. Bruce Palmer for example, have argued that Special Forces were a drain on resources and a waste of skilled military manpower that was sorely needed by regular line units.[20] Others have argued that PAVN and Front forces had to devote considerable manpower to deal with the Special Forces camps. This research has nothing to add to this debate concerning Vietnam as a whole; the camps at Duc Hue and Tra Cu were almost never mentioned in province advisory reports and rarely figured in 25th Division documents. In late 1968, the 2d Brigade of the 25th used the Cambodian mercenaries from Duc Hue as a small part in a particularly successful employment of the "tethered goat" tactic of provoking enemy attack on a secretly reinforced firebase. The brigade commander later noted the Cambodians were bored, listless, and looked ready to desert. One advisor who visited the Duc Hue compound in early 1970 commented that the unit there had "the look of someone who was taking in their own laundry"—that is, they were so busy protecting themselves that they could not project power. That seems to have been a fair assessment of the role of Special Forces in the struggle for Hau Nghia province.

Despite the fact that some limited measure of success was achieved in upgrading the RF/PF, efforts to create a local self-defense force achieved very little. The People's Self Defense Force, normally referred to by its abbreviation PSDF, was originally formed in early 1968. Like the RD Cadre teams, the PSDF concept was pushed most heavily by CORDS chief William Colby. The PSDF, as envisioned by CORDS, was to become a mass organization with the mission of providing village- and hamlet-level security. Although the GVN planned to organize most villagers into support groups, those males in the 16–17- and 39–50-year-old age bracket would receive the old weapons discarded by the RF/PF, which received M16 rifles. In addition to providing security, the PSDF was seen by Colby as yet another vehicle to involve the rural masses in the struggle. For some reason, he believed that arming the population would show the confidence of the GVN in its own support in the rural areas, while proving at the same time that there was little danger in the approach because the Front already possessed superior weaponry.[21]

In any case, the PSDF, a minor effort during 1968, grew steadily throughout 1969. By the end of the year, Hau Nghia province officials organized 37,000 villagers into the PSDF and issued 4,700 arms.[22] Once again, if the substance of the program had matched the theory behind it, the Front would have been in mortal danger. If involvement with the GVN could be equated with commitment, then 4,700 armed villagers would have made recruitment, taxation and food procurement nearly impossible for the Front. In fact, the Front would have been defeated years earlier if the desire to support the GVN, which was necessary to make the PSDF effective, had existed.

As it was, the PSDF did almost nothing. On a few occasions, Front units attacked a PSDF group, very likely when it appeared that, due to local conditions and good leadership, a group did, indeed, serve as a threat. Invariably, when this happened, the Front scored a lopsided victory.[23] On other occasions, Front cadres entered a hamlet at night, disarmed the local PSDF, gave them a lecture, and left, sometimes taking new recruits with them.[24] Front losses due to PSDF activities numbered only a handful. This was a miserable performance, particularly given the fact that 4,700 armed members of the PSDF alone outnumbered all Front military units in Hau Nghia province. The poor showing by the PSDF could only have been explained if the Front had been ejected from the villages and hamlets of the province. But, of course, this was far from the case. Despite serious problems, the Front had a political apparatus in every village (although weak in some cases) and continued to tax, recruit, and propagandize, even if at a level lower than in previous years. Although CORDS officials would have undoubtedly been eager to cite any significant gains due to the PSDF, such claims were not forthcoming. The best that could be said came from a CORDS report in December: "The degree to which the PSDF will be useful in a security role, as well as acting as a political and social movement, remains to be seen."[25]

Village Development

As in every previous year, efforts to improve the conditions of life and change the political climate in the countryside from one of apathy or support for the Front to genuine support for the GVN failed badly. To be sure, province officials and U.S. advisors usually filled and often surpassed the various numerical quotas on development projects, village elections, and other such efforts.[26] Due to the successful military campaign, roads were once again open, and commerce improved. No doubt, some of the economic benefits from improved trade were offset by an inflation rate of 50 percent.[27]

Most of the economic benefits coming from the pacification campaign were quite insignificant. The miracle rice program of 1969 did little better than that of 1968. Although the spread of GVN control did allow a small increase in the amount of rice planted, farmers were reluctant to plant the new varieties because of past failures.[28] Altogether, peasants in Hau Nghia cultivated 40,000 hectares of rice during 1969, with the miracle varieties grown on only 374 hectares.[29] At American urging, the GVN made another attempt at some sort of land reform. For years, the GVN itself was the largest landlord in South Vietnam due to its holdings of expropriated French lands. In 1969, Hau Nghia officials made available 2,300 hectares of this expropriated land for distribution to those farmers already tilling it. To the 355 families who received title, the program was no doubt a blessing.[30] However, plans for more distribution were hindered because some 500 titles were in the names of farmers who could not be located due to the past fighting.[31] Furthermore, advisors estimated in August that of the 2,300 hectares of land left for distribution only 196 could be cultivated. The remainder was located in insecure areas west of the Oriental River.[32]

Nor was much substantive success achieved by efforts to revitalize local government on the village level. Such efforts, as usual, were American-inspired. Many CORDS officials believed that Diem had made a terrible error in 1956 when he abolished the elective village councils that had been established by Bao Dai. In their place, Diem installed appointed officials responsible to the province chief. In the same period, he increased the power of the province chief and appointed his allies to these very important positions.[33] Americans argued, quite logically, that this move had served to demote the village as an administrative unit. Appointed village officials might not even come from the village they were responsible for. And even if they were local inhabitants, it mattered little for the real power over local affairs rested with the province chief and, to a lesser extent, with the district chief. In these circumstances, the argument ran, villagers viewed the government as even more remote. Separated from the people, it grew difficult for officials in Saigon to learn of the "true aspirations" of the rural population. Because there was no accountability on the part of village or province officials to the people that they administered, corruption and arrogance became the norm. A vicious circle of corruption and alienation developed, Americans maintained, that created conditions favorable for the Party's cunning, although fundamentally dishonest, propaganda. The Party, of course, believed that this situation arose naturally from structural contradictions in Vietnamese society and had little to do with mistaken administrative policy.

CORDS was determined to restore a measure of self-government on the village level with the new Village Self Development Program. Whenever possible, village councils were to be elected, and these councils were, in theory, to be given some real power. The armed groups of the PSDF were under village control. So, too, in theory, was the local Popular Forces unit. In addition, village "checkbooks" were to be issued so that the council could plan and fund some of their own small-scale development projects.

Many Americans working with CORDS had high hopes for the new village program. On the most mundane level, they believed that locally initiated development projects would more accurately reflect the needs of the population. Too often in the past, development projects had included things like better offices for province officials. Additionally, CORDS hoped that elected officials, responsible to the people, would be far less prone to corruption. Some Americans also fervently hoped for more fundamental results. Although many, probably most, Americans at CORDS accepted the GVN's argument that Western-style democracy could not be created overnight during wartime, virtually all of them believed that genuine democracy was a highly desirable goal and, eventually, a realistic one. GVN officials did not openly challenge such thoughts, whether or not they actually believed them, and many young Vietnamese shared this vision for the future. But members of this latter group, very sadly, were in terrible physical danger of Front assassination if they attempted to turn words into deeds. In any case, Americans believed that the place to plant the seed of a genuine, socially responsive democracy was at the village level. The village council concept was, in many respects, the last U.S. attempt to "harness the revolution" and create a strong, pro-American society capable of weathering the storm that was certain to come.[34]

There were formidable obstacles facing the Village Development Program. The Vietnamese experience with elections in the past had not been a particularly happy one. Critics of the GVN outside of the Front routinely claimed that elections were rigged. The powerful Front propaganda machine dismissed the elections as a fraudulent effort done only to please the "puppet" government's American masters. As reported by Ollie Davidson, a not terribly funny joke circulated during early 1968 around Hau Nghia, indicating a measure of cynicism: "Question: If an election between Robert Kennedy and Lyndon Johnson for U.S. president were held in Hau Nghia, who would win? Answer: Johnson—but the election would be rigged."[35] More seriously, unless they were working secretly for the Front, most villagers, unsure about the outcome of the war, would be quite reluctant to serve in any GVN political organization. Therefore, as the situation developed, it proved difficult to find candidates. Just as importantly, the Village Development Program in no way meant a devolution of power from the province to the village level. The meager instruments of power given to the village councils were newly created, such as the PSDF, and the funds allocated were in addition to other development projects. Furthermore, it was very unlikely that any village official would dare stand up to a province chief in case of a dispute. In short, the power of the province chief and, by extension, the power of the centralized GVN was left completely intact.

The Village Development Program was not a complete break with the past. Elections had taken place in GVN hamlets and villages in previous years, although, if the Front were particularly strong, local governments were appointed. The village "checkbook" and the PSDF were the new elements, along with a greater degree of emphasis by CORDS on village development. Given the unpredictable pace of events in Hau Nghia province, the Village Development Program proceeded quite smoothly throughout the year. Problems did arise, of course. Although the Front did little to interfere with local elections, there was a lack of candidates in many villages. The village checkbooks were slowly issued, delays were caused because Hau Nghia officials doubted the competence of some of the members of the new village governments and insisted on checking their backgrounds. Additionally, as reported by the advisory team, province officials either did not understand the new "bottom to top" development concept or had little sympathy with the idea. During July, the first checkbooks were, at last, issued. By the end of October, all of Hau Nghia's 20 villages had elected governments with the checkbooks in hand. Additionally, 133 hamlets possessed elected governments, although, according to the new scheme of things, the village was the more important entity. Members of the advisory team professed to be pleased with the new development programs, claiming that village officials now had more prestige. Furthermore, CORDS estimated that 40 percent of the population had participated locally in the selection of development projects. These projects were small-scale affairs, such as livestock breeding facilities and fertilizer cooperatives.[36]

Despite elections and development projects, nothing fundamental had changed at the village level in the political or economic realm. Some evidence for this conclusion comes from the reports of specially trained teams of Vietnamese, working for CORDS, that were sent to the countryside to gain as objective a view as possible of local affairs. One such group reported from Hiep Hoa village during April that, of the thirteen candidates for village elections, seven were hamlet chiefs and the rest soldiers or government employees. They also reported that local inhabitants with popular prestige would not stand for election and that the people believed the results had been arranged in advance.[37] Another team reported from Hiep Hoa during July that the local population considered both village and hamlet officials to be inept and corrupt. Even elected officials required bribes for routine assistance on such matters as war damage compensation.[38] A larger survey of village committees in Hau Nghia province was submitted later in the year, it found that "in general . . . these committeemen have little work to do and sit at their desks in the village offices doing nothing or stay home. The Committeemen for Education and Culture and Agricultural Affairs have the most free time."[39]

Another large survey taken in July, aimed at determining the population's view of the concept of political opposition, revealed that the Hau Nghia peasantry believed that independent political activity was certain to get one in trouble with the GVN. The intelligentsia, though understanding the concept of opposition, viewed it principally as a means for an individual to gain personal power.[40] No doubt, such opinions reflected reality. In July, Charles Whitehouse, the III CTZ deputy for CORDS, received reports that the Hau Nghia province chief, a man often described in the province reports as overly preoccupied with domestic politics, was trying to prevent the creation of opposition political parties.[41] Whitehouse sent this report to Colby with the following comment:

> I suspect that this kind of thing is likely to occur in other provinces and it might be a good idea to have the GVN put out some kind of a circular enjoining the provincial authorities to comply with the letter and spirit of the new political parties statute. I am afraid they have a natural bent toward squashing any political activity which they don't initiate and must be made to feel that they are covered by Saigon if political ferment grows in their provinces.[42]

The lack of well-organized opposition parties was particularly disappointing because, in the opinion of CORDS III CTZ, Thieu's political allies had not organized on the province level and hence had "no base of popular support in III CTZ."[43]

The Front's reaction to the development side of the pacification program was interesting. Programs directed at improving material conditions did not seem to concern the Party. Several advisors noted that American agricultural advisors frequently went without harassment to areas in Hau Nghia that uniformed personnel were wise to avoid. Traveling unarmed and alone or in very small groups without escort, these individuals were dreadfully vulnerable to attack. Yet, they were largely unmolested. MEDCAPs given by the 25th Division were rarely harassed. Evidently, the Front leadership believed such efforts were harmless. Perhaps such gestures were appreciated by the peasants, and the Front did not wish to antagonize anyone over minor issues. As just mentioned, local elections and village council activities were likewise left in peace. No doubt, the Front realized that none of the reforms had substance. The same old rules imposed by the Front on local representatives of the GVN remained in force: Corruption and sloth were tolerated, but efficiency and zeal meant the risk of death.

Schools were treated very differently. Both the Americans and the GVN were very interested in expanding educational opportunities in rural Vietnam. Earlier in the war, the Front allowed GVN schools to function, as long as the teachers stuck to straight academic subjects. After the Americans intervened, they funded the construction of thousands of crude but functional schools in rural areas. U.S. military units, including the 25th Division, sometimes helped with construction. Obviously, at some point the Front began to view all of this as a threat. The school buildings, most of them one-room affairs, became prime targets of attack when unattended. One advisor witnessed a Front mortar attack, which he believed was intentional, at Bao Trai during a school recess, which killed and injured children. Richard O'Hare, a member of the Duc Hue advisory team, recalled the situation with bitterness:

> We were always building schools. They were simple cement block buildings with a tin roof. They had doors, but no windows or electricity. They were a big target and constantly attacked. The VC mortared them or blew them up at night. They must have thought that schools tied people to the government.

Major Pearce in Cu Chi recounted a similar situation and added that simple medical dispensaries were also subject to attack.

Allied Discord

Of course, what was really needed to make local political and economic development truly meaningful was peace. Unfortunately, that was one condition that could not be provided by the Americans or the GVN as long as the politburo in Hanoi and COSVN refused to capitulate. Measured against the physical destruction and psychological weariness caused by the war itself, any material or political benefits coming from the pacification programs were of little significance. Throughout 1969, as in previous years, the presence of large numbers of U.S. troops in close proximity to the population of Hau Nghia—absolutely required for the expansion of the government's physical presence and the weakening of the Front through attrition—was, by definition, accompanied by widespread destruction.

The violence was both intentional and unintentional. The Front continued its tactic of provoking U.S. retaliation against hamlets astride lines of communication. Like the "extermination of traitors" campaign, this tactic was ruthless but valuable from the point of view of the Front. It should be remembered that killing American soldiers was an essential part of the Front's strategy for its leadership was well aware of the corrosive effect casualties had on the U.S. war effort. Small-scale ambushes from cleverly concealed bunkers in or very near hamlets were an effective way of accomplishing this task at a relatively low cost. If such fighting led to hatred between American soldiers and the local population, all the better.

Mortar warfare caused particular problems. A continual duel took place between Front mortar teams and American infantry and counterbattery artillery. One particularly deadly mortar team regularly attacked Bao Trai with great accuracy. In early 1969, the team was captured. To the astonishment of all concerned, it was made up of women. Normally, Front mortar teams set up in the bush and attacked allied installations. Sometimes, however, they fired from positions in or near a hamlet when launching an attack by fire at an American or ARVN unit nearby.

An example of this tactic took place on 5 March 1969 in a hamlet of Duc Lap village. Duc Lap, quite close to Bao Trai, received very heavy allied pressure. Nevertheless, it was still a Front stronghold. This action occurred during the Front dry season offensive, which was characterized by the widespread use of mortar attack. About midnight, a U.S. artillery firebase some 200 meters away from Go Cao hamlet, located in a graveyard, received a mortar attack coming from a site in or near Go Cao. During the previous day, the American unit had received permission from the Vietnamese to establish countermortar grids near the hamlet. However, Vietnamese officials had refused permission to fire into the hamlet in case of attack. Despite this refusal, the Americans directed 81mm mortar fire toward the hamlet itself, killing one civilian and wounding ten others. Property and livestock were destroyed. Bao Trai was very nearby, and the province chief, Colonel Nhon, and the PSA, Lt. Col. Carl Bernard, arrived two hours later. Initial compensation was given on the spot. Despite this response, which for Hau Nghia was lightning-fast, Nhon and Bernard learned just after daybreak that the villagers were planning to march to the American firebase and stage a protest demonstration. Nhon immediately returned to Go Cao, accepted responsibility for the incident, and persuaded the villagers not to march. This incident provoked a furious protest from Nhon to the 25th Division.[44]

A counterpoint to this incident took place in August after both Bernard and Nhon had left Hau Nghia. Heavy restrictions were put on American firepower near Bao Trai because of the events in March. Front guerrillas and cadres quickly exploited this state of affairs and obtained a greater freedom of movement. Captain Bergson, commanding a company of the *Wolfhounds* near Bao Trai, described the outcome:

> Just as the sun set, right before dark, we could see the VC stream out of the hedgerows and go into the hamlets. All we could do was watch because we were close to Bao Trai and no fire was allowed. Our 81mm mortar team usually sat on its ass because it couldn't fire. On August 9, I decided to hit Charlie without clearance. That sunset, we opened up and hit them good. We killed thirteen men of the Duc Hoa local force company. I called in helicopters and got rid of the mortars.

A more violent incident took place in December, when a Front unit of undetermined size entered a hamlet in Trang Bang district, upon the withdrawal of an ARVN unit. American mechanized forces reacted, supported by aircraft. The hamlet was bombed and shelled, causing many casualties and the flight of 400 families. An RTT (Rural Technical Team) from CORDS reported shortly thereafter:

> Through the contact and intervention, the team found that most of the refugees have been effectively propagandized by the Communists so they show hatred toward the American troops because of the many casualties and damage they have caused. For instance, American tanks pushed down their houses, they often shot into their hamlets—people were killed and crops were damaged. They lived in anxiety night and day, they knew nothing of their future.[45]

Other, less dramatic incidents occurred with great frequency. Civilians were killed and injured in collisions with allied military vehicles. Two children were accidentally killed by U.S. troops in separate incidents. One high-ranking officer of the 25th Division, while flying in a helicopter, believed he spotted a Front banner in a village near the Cu Chi base camp; a reaction force sped to the scene, only to find that it was a Buddhist flag. There were frequent reports of mistreatment of villagers detained by American units, and Hoi Chanh sometimes received rough treatment from Americans. There were also reports of shots exchanged between American soldiers and RD Cadres.[46]

In this difficult atmosphere, something of a low point in American-South Vietnamese relations at the official level was reached in 1969. Many of the problems revolved around differing assessments in U.S. circles about the performance of Col. Ma Sanh Nhon. Nhon had always been controversial. Having spent four years in the United States, he spoke English fluently. He served as Chef de Cabinet for General Khanh and had been province chief in Hau Nghia since 1967. Although complaints or evaluations concerning one Hau Nghia official or another were a staple in reports from CORDS and the advisory team, no other official received even a fraction of the attention accorded Lieutenant Colonel Nhon. In addition, he was the closest thing to a national figure to serve in Hau Nghia. It is not at all the purpose here to make judgments concerning Nhon or his critics; such a task would hardly be possible. Nevertheless, a brief look at the "Nhon controversy" is of interest because it illustrated well some of the dilemmas of the joint American and GVN war effort.

On one point, most of Nhon's critics and defenders agreed: He was one of the best combat commanders in ARVN and often led his troops in person. For a time, he held the unusual dual position of Hau Nghia province chief and commander of the 49th ARVN Regiment. In April 1968, Nhon was relieved of his ARVN responsibility. Although, like virtually every important Vietnamese official in Hau Nghia, Nhon was accused by Americans of corruption, his administrative techniques caused most of the controversy.[47] Above all, several Americans denounced Nhon as dictatorial and overbearing toward his subordinates and reluctant to take U.S. advice. In a 1968 evaluation, a young American officer claimed that the bad personal relationship between Nhon and the Cu Chi district chief had led to paralysis in the development projects. Frustrated, the Cu Chi chief turned to the 25th Division for direct aid, an action that Nhon demanded to be stopped, claiming that American interference on the local level damaged the position of the GVN. All U.S. aid projects, Nhon stated, should be channeled through Bao Trai. The American evaluator recommended that Nhon be replaced.[48] Major Pearce later corroborated this report and added that, on more than one occasion, Nhon verbally humiliated the Cu Chi district chief in front of Americans. Pearce also recalled that Nhon and Major General Williamson, commander of the 25th Division, disliked each other intensely.

In August 1968, the assistant chief of staff for CORDS recommended that Nhon's insistence that all efforts be funneled through his office should be curbed through leverage or, if that failed, by Nhon's relief. Robert Komer, who received this recommendation, wished to encourage assertive behavior by Vietnamese officials and strongly disagreed with the report. Komer and Nhon were supported by Lieutenant Colonel Bernard, the PSA.[49] But despite Komer's initial disagreement, a recommendation from his office calling for Nhon's relief was issued in October.[50]

Nhon had his defenders in U.S. circles. He traveled widely throughout the province and was described as an eloquent speaker. He also defended the Vietnamese in disputes with the 25th Division. Some maintained that his dictatorial style was necessary due to the miserable administrators assigned to Hau Nghia. He was often described as being more "American-like" in demeanor than most Vietnamese and quite willing to make his positions known, regardless of matters of "face." Indeed, a common criticism was that, through his overbearing nature, Nhon tended to overwhelm U.S. advisors.[51] Regardless of American evaluations, Saigon deferred the matter, and Nhon continued to serve in Hau Nghia for a time.

In early 1969, Nhon, his subordinates, and some members of the Hau Nghia advisory team had a serious quarrel with some of the commanding officers of the 25th Division. It began in January when Nhon received reports that American interrogation teams were questioning prisoners without Vietnamese participation. He protested that this procedure was intended to deny Vietnamese intelligence and demanded that it be stopped. Because of this protest, the 25th Division issued a directive requiring joint interrogations. However, both Nhon and Bernard believed that joint interrogations were not always carried out.

Relations were strained further when the deputy commander of the 25th Division invited the Cu Chi and Trang Bang district chiefs to a Tet luncheon, scolded them for the presence of mines near an RF outpost in an American area of responsibility, and stated something to the effect that "U.S. soldiers were wondering just what kind of allies they had." The Cu Chi district chief replied that the outpost had been abandoned months before, which would have been evident if American soldiers had patrolled off the road. Because it is not Vietnamese custom to insult guests during a holiday luncheon, Nhon became very angry and refused from that point onward to enter the Cu Chi base camp and ordered his subordinates to do likewise. As later recounted by Major Pearce, another social event ended in a public relations disaster:

> I was at a party in Bao Trai where everyone was invited. Williamson arrived by helicopter, the pad was right outside. Nhon refused to go out and greet Williamson. Bernard pleaded with Nhon, but he sent a lieutenant anyway. Williamson was infuriated. The atmosphere was icy and sterile.

Relations were further strained shortly thereafter during the aftermath of the successful sapper assault on the Cu Chi base camp. Some officers of the 25th Division believed that lax vigilance on the part of Vietnamese forces had facilitated the attack. The Vietnamese charged, in return, that poor screening by the Americans of civilian Vietnamese employees at the base had compromised security. Somewhat later, the Trang Bang district chief claimed that he had been "ordered" to come to a meeting with 25th Division Intelligence. Nhon, always sensitive on such matters, repeated his ban on Vietnamese officials entering U.S. installations without his direct authorization. The cumulative results of such incidents led to seriously strained relations between the Hau Nghia administration and population, on one side, and the Americans, on the other. In March, Lieutenant Colonel Bernard wrote the following:

> There are many examples which show that both sides are competing to express distaste and disdain for one another. I suspect that this new surface irritation has a base in the 2 November speech of President Thieu which was received by the Vietnamese as a call to show their nationalistic spirit. . . . The inevitable incidents between Americans and Vietnamese are not glossed over or deliberately dampened by the commanders concerned as they once were. The only winners in these new antagonisms will be the Viet Cong.[52]

At the same time, relations between the advisory team and the 25th Division command also deteriorated. Adverse relationships between province advisors and American military commanders were common enough in

Vietnam. Frequent conflict reflected the contradiction inherent in the U.S. role in the village war. Advisors, if doing their jobs, wanted above all to guard the well-being of the province to which they were assigned. Only a few corrupt ones were content with falsifying reports and pretending that conditions were better than they actually were. Almost to a man, advisors believed that a more prosperous, secure, and coherent rural society was the aim of their efforts. For an advisor, a hamlet in smoking ruins was more than a tragedy; it was a defeat. Military commanders, however, saw their job differently. They were charged with hunting down the enemy and destroying him. Destruction was unfortunate, but it was viewed as an inevitable by-product of war. More to the point, as shown scores of times in Hau Nghia province alone, soldiers on the spot thought it was their highest duty to preserve their own men's lives, even if this meant civilian losses. Therefore, conflict between advisor and commander was very likely if both were doing their jobs as narrowly defined.

Frequently, this inherently tense situation reflected differences in background and training. In theory, province senior advisors were supposed to have a very broad outlook. It was their job to coordinate a myriad of activities, most of which were outside the normal military sphere. As in most armies, many American officers tended to see their role as above politics and cultivated a disdain for it. Advisors, however, were expected to operate in an intensely political atmosphere. The cultural sensitivity and knowledge needed for the development of "rapport" required intensive training, preferably in combination with a unique background. All too often, theory and practice failed to coincide, however, and many province senior advisors were ordinary officers given a training course and assigned to the field. Many of these men did a splendid job, and some did not. However, it is probably safe to assume that advisors coming "off the shelf" more closely reflected the attitudes of line commanders than did those men whose backgrounds provided unique qualifications for service in rural Vietnam.

Lt. Col. Carl Bernard, the Hau Nghia PSA during the period in question, possessed an ideal résumé for an advisor. As a young officer, he distinguished himself in combat as a member of Task Force Smith, the small ad hoc force sent to Korea in 1950 to blunt the initial North Korean invasion. In 1954, Bernard, one of the army's few truly fluent French-speaking officers, was assigned by Gen. Matthew Ridgway to examine the suitability of U.S. infantry for service in Indochina. The recommendations that Bernard collaborated on were strongly negative and reinforced Ridgway's determination to prevent American intervention in aid of France. Due to this experience, Bernard became closely acquainted with French writings on counterinsurgency. In the early sixties, he became one of the first instructors at the Special Warfare School at Fort Bragg. Along the way, he became friends with William Colby, Robert Komer, and John Vann and shared their belief in the primacy of the village war. In May 1968, Bernard was assigned to Hau Nghia as province senior advisor. He was popular with his subordinates and quickly earned their respect by insisting on absolute candor and honesty in their reporting to higher echelons.

If Bernard were an archetype advisor, Maj. Gen. Ellis Williamson of the 25th Division was an archetype combat commander in Vietnam. Wounded five times as a combat infantryman in World War II, Williamson prided himself on seeing war from the soldier's point of view. As an instructor of tactics at the army's Infantry School, he rewrote tactical manuals, stressing the importance of firepower. In line with most combat officers of his generation, his motto was: "We fight with bullets—not bodies." As he later put it, "I became thoroughly convinced that it was immoral for a commander to throw the bodies of his men at an enemy that was still firing weapons." He gained the reputation of being an excellent combat commander and, as recounted earlier, led the elite 173d Airborne Brigade in one of the first major American campaigns of the war.

The dispute between Bernard and the advisory team, on one hand, and Major General Williamson and the 25th command, on the other, followed several lines. In general, Bernard and several of his advisors were critical of what they believed was an overreliance on firepower during U.S. operations.[53] Major Pearce at Cu Chi, for instance, lodged numerous protests with the 25th Division concerning incidents of inappropriate conduct by U.S. soldiers. All the Americans at Bao Trai knew perfectly well that combat was unavoidable when enemy main force units wanted battle; as previously mentioned, such battles were all too common in this period. But aggressive use of American firepower, the advisors believed, should not be allowed to make a bad situation worse. Bernard was a great advocate of "aimed fire," discriminating small-unit tactics that emphasized rifles and grenades fired at identifiable targets, rather than heavy weapons and artillery directed at a general area. Since 1966, the 25th Division had steadily tightened its rules of engagement in inhabited areas. Nevertheless, the problem of Front-initiated incidents in the hamlets remained. Bernard argued that, unless there was a compelling reason to take action, the harassing enemy should be ignored or blockaded. One of the brigade commanders agreed with Bernard and tried to avoid firefights in hamlets, if at all possible. Most combat officers, however, reacted as they had been trained; responding fiercely and aggressively to enemy fire was the essence of the U.S. Army and not a reflection of any particular commander. In any case, the firepower issue was a continual irritant and created an ugly atmosphere of discord between the advisory team and the 25th Division, which made other disagreements even worse.

In addition, there was heated argument between members of the advisory team and the 25th Division over HES scores. General Williamson, as was well known at CORDS in Saigon, put heavy command pressure on his subordinates to raise HES scores throughout the division's area of operations. Lieutenant Colonel Bernard and some other advisors believed that this pressure could lead to incorrect scores and mislead higher echelons about the situation in Hau Nghia.[54] This was an extremely tricky issue. CORDS was very sensitive to the dangers inherent in incorrect reporting. With good reason, John Vann and many officials believed privately that incorrect reporting was one of the causes of American policy debacles in Vietnam in the early sixties. The Hamlet Evaluation Survey, frequently criticized in the press, was actually an attempt to develop some sort of objective criteria that could be used to measure the security status of individual hamlets and to avoid the foolish optimism of the past. Analysis of large numbers of HES figures over time could then be used to chart the relative course of the pacification campaign in any given area. The alternative to HES was a combination of body count and purely subjective appraisals by the advisors. But the danger of any reporting mechanism was that officials involved would treat it as a "report card" on themselves and thus put the best possible face on things. This was exactly what HES was designed to avoid.

Nevertheless, the reporting mechanism was always imperfect. At the field level in Hau Nghia, intentional deception was not the problem. All the advisors participating in this research believed their reports were honest, if not necessarily correct. Certainly, the HES scores coming from Hau Nghia province must have been sobering reading in Saigon: They were always among the lowest in the nation. Lieutenant Colonel Bernard made it very clear to all his subordinates that he expected absolute candor in reports. The practical difficulties, however, were substantial. The monthly HES scores were compiled by the small district teams; usually, one man was given the task. Richard O'Hare had the job in Duc Hue district and recalled:

> The reporting mechanism was something of a joke. I was supposed to visit every hamlet every month. I was also on operations with the RF/PF nearly every day. You couldn't do them both. So, sometimes I visited the hamlets, sometimes I didn't. Aside from that, it was bookkeeping, and nobody liked to do it.

The result of this state of affairs, ironically, was that Hau Nghia HES scores were lower than they should have been. Many small hamlets rated "VC" had actually been abandoned, but the district advisors sent in old reports anyway. Later in the year, this situation was rectified.

More to the point, evaluating the security status of a hamlet was largely a subjective task, regardless of how it was done. The lack of outward Front activity, for instance, might be a very good sign or a very bad one. From the point of view of Major General Williamson and the 25th Division, they had been ordered to support the pacification of Hau Nghia province and they were going to do it. At division headquarters, it might well have seemed that CORDS, which had long grumbled that the army had not paid enough attention to the village war, was now grumbling because it was paying too much. Williamson wanted to know exactly what was expected to raise HES scores, but the advisors refused to establish absolute guidelines. The result was further bad feeling.

A feud developed between Bernard and Williamson, which spilled over into Saigon. The situation was complicated by the fact that Bernard was one of Nhon's greatest supporters, and Williamson a strong critic. Such a disagreement was a major mismatch, with the advisor at the disadvantage.

It is not clear whether arguments with the 25th Division influenced the decision to transfer Nhon on 25 March. A few days later, CORDS transferred Lieutenant Colonel Bernard to another province.[55]

The problems for the Hau Nghia advisory team did not end with a change in personnel. Colonel Hanh, the new province chief, was a great disappointment to the Americans, although he came to Hau Nghia with a distinguished combat record. However, Saigon was very close, and, according to the advisors, Colonel Hanh's real interests were in political intrigue. Consequently, he was frequently out of the province and allowed administration to slide to levels even lower than before. Lt. Col. James Bremer, Bernard's replacement as PSA, dealt with Hanh exclusively through intermediaries, thus avoiding all matters of face. Their personal relations, rather than being based on rapport, were confined to a stultifying series of joint appearances at the many official ceremonies that characterized the job of province chief. Fortunately for the advisory team, Hanh's political fortunes turned sour quickly, and he was replaced in December. At the time of his departure, the advisory team reported, "The near total indifference and the harm he caused cannot be overestimated."[56]

Bad relations between the 25th Division and the advisory team continued. Lieutenant Colonel Bremer was fully briefed on the problems that had developed between Bernard and Williamson and was determined to get along with the division. The inherent tensions, however, were still very much in existence. Later, Bremer described the situation:

> We were interested in different things. Even though the formal mission of the division was to support pacification (in other words, me), they were interested in only one thing: body count. In their view, I and my team were there to charm the Vietnamese into providing local security for their base camps and firebases and to support their operations with intelligence information and with anything else they wanted. I was also supposed to secure the province chief's clearance within the minute at any time, day or night, for them to call in artillery fire onto any part of the province, populated or not, whenever they so desired. . . . Obviously, it couldn't work. It didn't help that the division commander was a major general and all the officers I had to deal with were brigadiers or full colonels while I, like Bernard, was a lieutenant colonel. And don't think they didn't take full advantage of it. . . . I remember one morning when John Paul Vann dropped in for a visit. He said to me, "I've heard some good things about you, mainly that you don't get along with the 25th Division. Any province senior advisor who gets along with that division isn't doing his job."

Like Bernard, Lieutenant Colonel Bremer could not sustain his position in the face of opposition from the 25th Division. He was transferred in August.

In September Major General Williamson rotated back to the United States, and, from that point on, relations between the advisory team and the division improved. Perhaps this was a matter of personalities. More likely, however, it was because, by September 1969, Hau Nghia province was a much safer place to be from the allied viewpoint. Roads that had never been traveled before were open, and fighting, which had caused most of the disputes between division and advisory team, was at an all-time low. The rights or wrongs of the disputes between the 25th Division and the advisors during Williamson's tour are not self-evident in retrospect. It was clear, however, that the 25th Division had delivered a fearful blow to the Front and had left it reeling.

10

High Tide for the Allies: 1970

An Early-Year Lull

Far from Hau Nghia province, the Nixon administration was faced with a quandary concerning Vietnam. All hopes for an early end to the war through negotiation had vanished. Internal opposition to the war effort was an increasingly serious problem and was beginning to poison the administration. On the other hand, the favorable trends evidenced in the fighting during 1969 indicated that Vietnamization might work after all. To help gain a frank and realistic assessment of the ground war, Kissinger dispatched his assistant, Alexander Haig, to Vietnam. Haig's findings were mixed. He concluded that the GVN had, indeed, expanded its control in the countryside to a considerable degree. He also noted, however, that Hanoi was showing no signs of capitulation and that Vietnamization had not yet been put to the test. British expert Sir Robert Thompson was more optimistic. He reported to Nixon that the GVN was in a winning position and would prevail against the Front within two years if American withdrawal were not rushed and aid continued to flow.[1]

Consequently, hoping to limit internal dissent and to give the GVN further opportunity to expand its control in the rural areas, the administration decided to continue the mode of operations used in 1969. U.S. forces would avoid costly and highly visible set-piece battles. Instead, while awaiting phased withdrawal, U.S. units would continue to upgrade GVN forces and help protect areas undergoing pacification. According to Nixon and Kissinger, the Cambodian operation was not foreseen at the beginning of the year.

In Hanoi, the future appeared most promising for the long term. Unlike many periods in the past, there was now unanimity over tactics. Giap (already planning the 1972 offensive), Truong Chinh, and other advocates of protracted war were ascendent. They were content to await American withdrawal and to target the political vulnerabilities of the U.S.-GVN coalition. Called dan va dam (talking and fighting), the object was to stimulate the "internal contradictions" of U.S. policy. Truong Nhu Tang, a high Front official, later described the technique:

There were, as all political cadre learned by heart, three currents of revolution in every people's war. The first two currents are the ever-growing international socialist camp and the armed liberation movement within the country in question. The third is the progressive movement within the colonial or neo-colonial power. Until the balance of military power decisively favored the revolution, it was this third current that had to draw the most energy. In this case it was American public opinion—the minds and hearts of the American people—that had to be motivated and exploited. Here were the internal contradictions that we sought to stimulate first of all, as we moved step by step toward our goal of isolating the Thieu government from its allies.[2]

Although they were masters at political psychology, international media theater, and disinformation, Hanoi's leaders knew that the single most valuable tool still in their hands to further weaken U.S. resolve was killing American soldiers. No great victories were required, nor was it necessary to keep the attrition level as high as it had been previously. It was enough to continue the sapper, mortar, and guerrilla war. Because of American deployments and disinclination to seek battles in the hinterlands, the Front would bear the brunt of the action once more. Hanoi no doubt worried about falling morale within the Front, but the cadres remained stolid, and PAVN could always supply replacements for Front units. No matter how grim things appeared to Front followers on the spot, some of their leaders could already see the outlines of the victory to come.[3]

The mission assigned the Tropic Lightning Division reflected the continuity in Nixon's Vietnam policy. The division's primary objective was to provide area security for villages and hamlets undergoing pacification. The 2d Brigade continued to operate mostly in Cu Chi and Trang Bang, the 3d Brigade operated principally in Duc Hue and Duc Hoa. The 3d Brigade of the 9th Division stayed under 25th control and remained in neighboring Long An province. Meanwhile, II FFV also ordered 2d Brigade to target remaining main and local force units, together with their vital support elements, in order to remove the critical military communications link between War Zone C and Saigon and thus lift any threat to the capital in the near future.[4]

The direction of the pacification program for 1970 was virtually unchanged, although increased numerical goals were set. The past weaknesses of the Phoenix Program persisted, despite an attempt to change the accounting procedures. CORDS personnel in Saigon decided that the figures of "VCI neutralized" were highly misleading. The arrest of a suspect was recorded as a "VCI eliminated" or a "VCI neutralized," but because the vast majority of suspects were released quickly, CORDS feared yet another program would fall victim to phony or padded figures. Therefore, it decreed that only suspects tried, convicted, and incarcerated could be counted as eliminations.[5] The Hau Nghia reports continued to list both the number of cadres eliminated and the number of cadres convicted; the former was always far greater than the latter.

The HES system also was altered, with greater emphasis put on security concerns as opposed to development projects. The more rigorous standards employed by the new HES/70 caused a downturn in the statistical war. (The decline was greater in Hau Nghia than in any other province in the country.) There is no way to ascertain whether HES/70 was any more accurate than the previous system. As previously noted, knowledgeable officials at CORDS only used the HES or HES/70 system to indicate broad trends, and they were more than aware of potential shortcomings. Nevertheless, the following comparison of HES/70 with the earlier HES figures for Hau Nghia is excellent evidence of the great difficulties continuing to face the allies in the province. According to CORD's analysis of Hau Nghia:

> Most of the HES-HES/70 disparity is traced solely to certain key security indicators; while the HES rates 98.3% of the population ABC in security, HES/70 similarly evaluates only 54.3%. Specifically the security areas of enemy military presence and activity are rated significantly lower in HES/70 than HES. For example, 78.6% of the Hau Nghia hamlet population resides in villages where at least a platoon-sized enemy local or main force unit is located nearby. The comparable HES indicator rates only 6.0% of the population in this same category. While the HES/70 reports that 43.9% of the province population lives in villages with a platoon of village guerrillas regularly present, the HES indicates only 10.0% similarly affected. According to HES/70, GVN hamlet chiefs are not present at night in hamlets containing 60.5% of the province population; the corresponding HES indicator is similarly rated for only 28.0% of the population.[6]

Thus, CORDS acknowledged that the Front still possessed a presence, varying in strength, in every area of the province. These figures, however, do not at all contradict the mound of evidence showing that the Front had been seriously weakened in the previous years. Clearly, the advisory team realized perfectly well that the Front was still very much in existence. Yet, a small number of cadres, supported by a remnant of guerrilla forces, was adequate to project a Front presence. Undoubtedly, overt Front control of hamlets in Hau Nghia had declined greatly. The one HES category that was totally accurate was "VC," and as noted earlier, this meant that the Front controlled the hamlet totally and that the GVN had no presence. In 1967, nearly half of the hamlets in Hau Nghia were in this category, by 1970, the GVN at least contested all of Hau Nghia's hamlets. Even the more pessimistic HES/70 figures claimed that there were no "VC" hamlets. To be sure, however, there were no "A" (pro-GVN) hamlets either.[7]

The pace of fighting in Hau Nghia during the winter and early spring of 1970 remained much as it had been since July 1969. Small unit and joint U.S.-South Vietnamese operations continued at a steady pace throughout the province. Although both the advisory team and 25th Division Intelligence predicted some upsurge in enemy activity, none took place for Front units continued to avoid contact.[8] The level of violence decreased somewhat from earlier months, but both South Vietnamese and U.S. forces claimed to have inflicted painful casualties on the enemy. Losses were serious enough that, in February, COSVN dispatched a PAVN battalion to Hau Nghia and broke it down into squads to reinforce local forces. The number of ralliers remained at a moderately high level, ranging between 78 and 95 per month. Tropic Lightning Division interrogations continued to indicate that morale was low in both NVA and Front units and that their operations were seriously hampered by disrupted supply services.[9]

In 1970, the American ground effort in the Saigon area began to wind down in earnest. The 1st Infantry Division, operating north of Saigon, was withdrawn early in the year. Consequently, the tactical area of responsibility for the 25th Division was greatly increased. In February, the 2d Brigade began to withdraw from Hau Nghia and was put under the operational control of II FFV in March.[10] To fill this void, the 49th ARVN Regiment took over the always difficult areas in northern Trang Bang and Cu Chi districts. This redeployment was considered the first major step toward Vietnamization in Hau Nghia. Battalions of 3d Brigade were instructed to support ARVN if necessary and to continue pacification operations throughout the rest of Hau Nghia.[11]

The Cambodian Invasion

Despite the phased withdrawal, the officers and men of the Tropic Lightning Division had one more act to play in the battle for Hau Nghia province. On 18 March 1970, Prince Norodom Sihanouk was deposed by Lon Nol. Cambodian forces, pitiful as they were, engaged NVA and Front units in the sanctuaries. The NVA reacted quickly and allocated many available units to an offensive against the new enemy. A large number of Vietnamese civilians, many having lived for generations along the ill-defined border with Cambodia, were massacred by Cambodian forces.

Seeing an opportunity to disrupt NVA activity with little risk, Thieu authorized a series of small raids across the border during April. In addition, he secured agreement for American support of a much larger operation. On 28 April, ARVN launched a large attack on the sanctuaries. On 1 May, U.S. units also crossed the border, including two battalions of 1st Brigade under the operational control of the 1st Air Cavalry Division. The rest of 1st Brigade entered Cambodia on 6 May. The next day, 2d Brigade was returned to the 25th Division, and it entered Cambodia on 9 May. On 7 May, elements of 3d Brigade, 9th Infantry, still under 25th Division control, passed through Duc Hue district and entered Cambodia in the Parrot's Beak region. Battalions of 3d Brigade continued their operations in Hau Nghia province and neighboring districts.[12]

A junior officer serving in a COSVN signal battalion, who was captured by the 25th Division, revealed that COSVN had been well aware that the attack was coming and had moved COSVN HQ and most of the NVA and Front main force units deeper into Cambodia. He also claimed that COSVN had twenty-four-hour warning of B-52 attacks in Cambodia.[13] Consequently, most of the opposition encountered by U.S. and ARVN units came from rearguard and service personnel. As it was, despite advance warning, American mechanized units moved quickly and very nearly captured the

Front's political leadership. Allied forces did smash the few main force units that were forced into battle. For American soldiers, the invasion was a steady series of small, fierce engagements as Front units fought to protect their retreating comrades. However, the major accomplishment was the capture of a staggering amount of food, arms, and military supplies. Quantities were so large that the allies had difficulties moving or destroying what they had captured.[14] By 30 June, all U.S. units were withdrawn, although ARVN continued its operations on and off for some time.

In retrospect, American participation in the Cambodian incursion, at least by ground units, can be seen as a monumental blunder. It is true that the turn of events in Cambodia gained time for Vietnamization and made it safer to quicken U.S. withdrawal. However, this significant benefit was gained by the Lon Nol coup itself, rather than the incursion. Far more important than the capture of supplies, which could have been accomplished by ARVN alone with U.S. air support, was the closure of the major supply line leading from the port of Sihanoukville to the sanctuaries. The enemy could have replaced the supplies in a few months, but the supply line was lost for the duration as Lon Nol's forces held the port until the bitter end. Although it is also true that American intelligence discovered after the incursion that it had disrupted some planned attacks, including one on Duc Hoa town, the scope of such attacks would have been, of necessity, quite limited because of the disrupted supply line and the allocation of PAVN forces to the battle against Lon Nol. Furthermore, any American soldiers spared in the attacks that were preempted must be balanced against the U.S. losses during the incursion, which were not high but were worse than in preceding months. Nor did the incursion help Lon Nol; if anything, the opposite occurred as U.S. and ARVN units pushed enemy units deeper into Cambodia. The real benefit to Lon Nol, if not the Cambodian people, was realized when the United States agreed to supply his forces. These supplies, however, did not arrive in large numbers until after American troops had withdrawn from Cambodia.

It is also probably true that ARVN gained in confidence due to the role it played. Yet, it is quite possible that ARVN would have gained even more self-respect had it fought alone, with only U.S. air and artillery support. Ironically, in contrast with the operation into Laos in 1971, an attack on the sanctuaries, even if on a smaller scale, was probably a task within ARVN's capabilities for it is doubtful that the enemy would have accepted a set-piece battle on the Cambodian frontier, within range of American artillery, with supply uncertain, and with fighting taking place to the rear. Above all, any military advantage gained by the Cambodian incursion must be set against the near madness that it spawned in the United States. Unwittingly, Nixon had seriously damaged prospects for the long-term aid to South Vietnam that he himself believed necessary to give Vietnamization a chance to succeed. Simultaneously, the Nixon administration began the long slide into the Watergate fiasco. Truong Nhu Tang, a high Front official, recalled that, once they had literally recaptured their breath, the leadership of the Front considered events in Cambodia to be a "resounding victory" because of the domestic debacle that ensued in the United States.[15]

Whatever the broader implications of the Cambodian incursion, it did serve to materially aid the GVN in the struggle for Hau Nghia. Although enemy combat units in the sanctuaries escaped, those operating in Hau Nghia had their supply lines cut and their rear service personnel roughly handled. U.S. battalions and RF/PF units continued operations in Hau Nghia during the entire incursion. The PSA reported, at the end of April, that enemy forces in Trang Bang and Cu Chi appeared to be "acting in a survival-related manner."[16] An assistant chief of staff to the main force Quyet Thang Regiment rallied in May and claimed that his battalions averaged only 60 men each and that morale was dropping.[17] Some days later, the deputy commander of Subregion 2 also rallied and testified that his men were suffering a crisis in morale and were near mutiny.[18] A rallier in Cu Chi revealed that his local force company was down to 5 men.[19] A medic from the DRV attached to a main force sapper unit in Cu Chi rallied in the summer. He testified that his unit had been separated from its headquarters in Cambodia, bringing hunger and disorientation. He also told American intelligence that many North Vietnamese soldiers had deserted in Cambodia and had joined the local population, fishing and farming. He also cautioned that the large number of ralliers was deceptive because some cadres were rallying to gain legal cover for continued revolutionary activity.[20]

The Hiep Hoa defector, quoted in earlier chapters, also gave interesting testimony concerning the chaos caused by the attack on the sanctuaries:

> In May 1970, we received warning that the ARVN was going to cross the border. . . . Many of us believed it and went to Van Bon, further west. However, some of our cadre did not believe the reports or waited too long to leave. These people, and almost all our supplies, were caught up in the invasion, which was a disaster for everyone. Afterwards, we had no food and had to begin to steal from the Cambodians just to survive. Chinh, of the Duc Hoa District Rear Area Committee, put out the word that everyone would have to be self-sufficient. Some cadre were even killed by the Cambodians when they were caught stealing food from them.
>
> It was at this time that I made the decision to return to Vietnam and rally. The situation seemed hopeless to me at the time, and although many of our cadre shared the same belief, no one dared talk about it. I know this because after I rallied, I met some of the cadre who were in Cambodia at that time. They told me that they, too, had decided to rally at this time.[21]

Although this man had to await his chance to rally, many in Hau Nghia province could do so immediately. During May 1970, 434 Hoi Chanh rallied, a greater number by far than either before or later. An additional 96 cadres were "neutralized," also a record number at the time. Understandably, the PSA reported in May that:

> The most significant event during this period and quite probably during the past several years was the total destruction of enemy base areas at Ba Thu

and Dia Gia (Cambodia). . . . It is certain that the effects will seriously hamper enemy operational capabilities for a long time to come.[22]

The Departure of the 25th Division

The withdrawal of American ground forces from Cambodia at the end of June signaled the beginning of a major redeployment in much of the Saigon area. The 1st Brigade of the 25th Division redeployed to northern Tay Ninh and northwest Binh Long provinces. Its previous area of operations in central Tay Ninh was given to the 25th ARVN Division. The 2d Brigade, previously operating in Hau Nghia, was redeployed near Xuan Loc in Long Khanh province. The 3d Brigade returned to more familiar ground and conducted pacification duties in Hau Nghia and Binh Duong during July. In August, however, 3d Brigade was instructed to cover the Saigon River corridor and, consequently, operated almost exclusively in Binh Duong and a portion of Tay Ninh provinces. Units attached to Divisional HQ at Cu Chi guarded the base camp. Although a few 3d Brigade operations spilled over into northern Hau Nghia, it was the 3d Brigade of the 9th Infantry Division that participated most significantly in the last few weeks of American ground combat in the province, operating principally along the Vam Co Dong River.[23] In August, ARVN and Hau Nghia Regional Forces companies were given the responsibility for securing most of Trang Bang and Cu Chi districts.[24]

The last phase of American ground activity reverted to the pattern established since the Accelerated Pacification Program began, with numerous small-unit and combined operations the norm. A particularly concentrated effort was directed at upgrading the RF/PF. In July, combat units attached to the 25th Division were instructed to detach one company for each district they operated in and assign it solely for work with Regional and Popular Forces. To a greater degree than before or after, enemy units avoided contact with U.S. forces. In the last quarterly period of operations in Vietnam, 39 men of the Tropic Lightning Division were killed and another 542 wounded. These totals were the lowest of the entire war but nevertheless showed that, with 600 casualties in ninety days, Vietnam remained, until the very end, a dreadfully dangerous place to be for American soldiers.[25]

As the summer wore on U.S. withdrawal proceeded rapidly. In early September, the 3d Brigade, 9th Infantry Division, began to stand down, a process that was completed by the end of the month. In November, 1st and 3d Brigades also returned to the United States. The 2d Brigade was once again put under the control of II FFV and operated near Bien Hoa until it, too, stood down in March 1971. On 15 December 1970, the Cu Chi base camp was officially handed over to the ARVN 25th Division. The ceremony was symbolic only because American combat units had actually left Hau Nghia province in September.[26] After nearly five years of unrelenting violence, the direct U.S. participation on the ground in the struggle for Hau Nghia province was over.

When the 25th Division left Vietnam, it was not the same organization that had arrived. As the war progressed, the U.S. Army was forced to operate under personnel policies set by the White House that were so inexcusably inequitable that they bordered on the criminal. Unquestionably, the quality of the personnel declined in some ways. In 1967, faced with growing manpower shortages, the army lowered intelligence requirements for its draftees, bringing in tens of thousands of recruits who, in better times, would never have worn a uniform. Michael Willis was nearing the end of the first of his two combat tours in the summer of 1968 when these new men began arriving in Vietnam:

> Some of the new guys were real dumb, I mean border-line retards. Out of ten, we would take nine and make them cooks. You sure didn't want people like that in the field. They wouldn't last, and they might get someone else killed, too. It was like we were trying to lose the war through mass extermination. To keep these people alive, you had to take even more responsibility.

Compounding this problem was a chronic shortage of veteran NCOs, so important to any army. By 1968, the army was training "shake and bake" NCOs straight out of boot camp. Virtually undistinguishable in age, background, and military experience from the other enlisted personnel, these men had difficulty exerting authority. Junior officers were increasingly drawn from Officer Candidate Schools as participation in ROTC plummeted. But even with accelerated training and lowered standards, the army was unable to make up the deficit of trained leaders. Thus, in the field, many squads were led by enlisted men instead of NCOs, platoons were led by NCOs instead of lieutenants, and so forth. In many cases, these men did a fine job; in other cases, their lack of experience hurt.

Outward standards of discipline certainly declined, as they always do in combat units: A rebuke concerning a minor infraction of rules would quickly be met with the rejoinder, "What are you going to do, send me to Vietnam?" The more serious and well-publicized problems of drugs and racial strife grew steadily at the Cu Chi base camp. There were rumors of "fragging," slang for attacks on officers by their men. In the base camps, all these problems could fester and feed off of each other, and the cumulative effects of these problems crippled the army for years after Vietnam.

Serious discipline problems were far less of a concern in the field. Combat soldiers knew they were safer without the men with serious psychological problems or drug addictions. Those with the lowest intelligence were also best left behind. This is one of the reasons that combat units in Vietnam were so seriously understrength. As one man put it, "Ten guys who cared for each other were a lot safer than twenty guys who didn't." No doubt, some units were better off than others. Yet, the evidence indicates that most combat units of the 25th Division retained a high degree of skill and cohesion until the end. Capt. Henry Bergson later gave his opinion of the company of the *Wolfhounds* he commanded in late 1969:

Morale was good. By the time we were out in field we were well rid of shirkers: We let them do what they wanted. It was the finest bunch of young Americans you could want. Most of the men were white, but race was never a question. There were some draftees and some college kids. We had some "instant NCOs," but they worked well, better than the lieutenants. We were pushing the enemy back, and we could see it. At the same time, no one volunteered to spend an extra day when the time came to go back to the world. . . . In December, I shifted to the Cu Chi base camp to finish my tour at battalion headquarters. There, you saw all of the problems that people read about: insubordination, drugs, black power. I was glad to get back to the States.

Alan Neil, a rifleman late in the war who served with the *Wolfhounds*, although not in Bergson's unit, had a similar recollection:

There wasn't a lot of cohesion in terms of larger units: the division or even battalion. I feel more of that now. The squads were close, however. There were problems back in camp, but we were almost never there. I know there were drugs and racial problems in Vietnam, but I didn't see them in the field. We had a job to do, and we looked out for each other. We were good infantry.

The biggest problem facing combat morale dealt not with pathologies but with politics. In-depth political discussion was rare in Vietnam, but every soldier there knew that Nixon was withdrawing the troops. Most American combat soldiers assumed that this meant that the United States was selling out South Vietnam. Before 1969, not many men could see a larger purpose in the war; after 1969, there were far fewer still. Nobody wanted to risk his life for a cause that he did not understand and that was probably lost anyway. Unquestionably, units grew very cautious. One infantryman estimated that his platoon "sandbagged" one-quarter of their night ambushes. Instead of proceeding to the ambush site, they would head to a local militia compound, bribe the Vietnamese with rations, and sleep. Other men called similar techniques "search and evade." The men would fight, but it was for themselves only. After the war, Dan Vandenberg described the feelings of his unit in late 1969:

Our morale was pretty good, but not even our John Waynes talked about winning. We could see that the war was going on just like before we got there and was going to continue after we left. We just wanted to do our time and get the hell out. We could care less about winning. Looking back now with hindsight, I guess we pretty much did the best job we could, considering that no one knew what they were doing or what they were trying to accomplish. If they did, they were keeping it a secret because they never told us.

The last account from the 25th Division comes from Jim Ross, who was with a mechanized battalion throughout 1970 and was one of the last American combat soldiers to serve in Hau Nghia province. His description of service in mid-1970 was strikingly like that made by men describing the war in 1966:

> Basically, our morale was pretty good. We were mostly from "Home Town America" and trying to do our duty. We were proud to be soldiers, but we couldn't really see the point of continuing the war with the outcome looking more and more bleak. We were in it together: When the shooting started, we did the job. There was more complaining about the elements than about the war. What would have been the point? We just tried to make the best of it and survive. . . . Most of our officers and men knew what they were doing. I never heard of renegade squads or anything like that. My Lai was bizarre, an unusual aberration. Things like it were strictly for the movies. The average soldier fought hard and well.

To the end, the 25th Division was a proud and skilled unit, but, according to Ross, the men knew better than anyone that their campaign in Vietnam had not gone well. Ross made this very clear in his description of his comrades' reactions to the news that they were leaving Vietnam:

> It was a relief for all of those going home; on the other hand, it was very distressing, very discouraging to think of turning over the entire area of operations of the 25th Infantry Division to the South Vietnamese army. We couldn't help but feel that it had all been for nothing. That nothing had been gained, that no forward progress had been made, and that things were basically about the way things were when we got there. The war was still going on, and the Americans were withdrawing. The reality of the combat situation within South Vietnam was worsening. All of the political talk, "peace with honor" and such things, had very little meaning in South Vietnam because everyone knew that, with each step we took to withdraw, the North Vietnamese and the VC were doubling their efforts to take over the country. We knew that when we left, the country would be overwhelmed by the VC and the North Vietnamese.

The 25th Infantry Division suffered 34,484 casualties in Vietnam, nearly 5,000 of them killed—more than any other division in the army. The Cu Chi base camp was handed over to ARVN without any ceremony. At the gate of the base camp, however, the GVN erected a large bronze statue of an American infantryman to commemorate the sacrifice of the Tropic Lightning Division. During the 1972 Easter Offensive, someone—it is unclear who—tore it down.

Members of the Hau Nghia advisory team, understandably, had mixed feelings concerning the withdrawal of U.S. combat battalions from the province. They had grown accustomed to the presence of the 25th Division. As the PSA remarked, "Looking to Cu Chi has become a way of life in Hau Nghia, even for Advisory Team 43."[27] As long as there were U.S. combat units in Hau Nghia, the war could not be lost outright. Their departure reminded every American remaining that the outcome of the war was, at best, still very much in doubt. Indeed, many of the advisors doubted that the GVN could survive in the long run. This made for an uneasy atmosphere. Advisors were professional soldiers, and it was very hard for them to face the prospect that all of their personal sacrifices and, more importantly, all of the sacrifices made by their beloved army might prove to be for nothing. Yet, there was also a certain satisfaction in knowing that the moment of truth had come. Prospects for the short term were good. The intense military pressure of the past three years had left the Front forces seriously weakened, and the enemy troops were avoiding contact at all costs. The advisors dared to hope that American withdrawal would promote greater self-sufficiency within the GVN and perhaps reveal strength and élan that had been missing in the past. Perhaps things might work out after all.[28]

Rural Security

While Front forces were trying desperately to regroup, the self-sufficiency program initiated by Thieu in 1969 reached fruition. By December 1970, ARVN was operating either in Cambodia or near the sparsely populated areas containing the remaining major sanctuaries. The Regional Forces were deployed in populated areas known to have a significant Front presence. The Popular Forces platoons, increased to 77 in number by the end of the year, were in both "contested" and "secure" hamlets. Regional Forces were significantly strengthened in December when Saigon established an independent RF artillery unit.[29] Armed members of the PSDF, over 6,000 strong by November, were given increased responsibility for village defense.[30] And with the Front on the defensive, the HES/70 scores steadily grew more favorable. In January, there were no hamlets listed in the "A" category, 27 in "B," 62 in "C," and 46 in "D." In October, there were 3 in "A," 88 in "B," 38 in "C," and 7 in "D," a clear reflection of the growth of outward GVN control throughout the province. Under such circumstances, the PSA saw some reason for hope, as he reported in December:

> On balance then, the GVN continues to be the winner. Greater resources are not well used, but progress is steady at all levels and attrition rate in combat favors GVN 2:1. An interesting year is before us, including presidential and lower-house elections. We will be especially interested in gauging both the will to win of GVN officials over the long haul and the GVN impact on a provincial populace which has an established tradition of sympathy for dissident political causes and resistance to central government control.[31]

By the end of 1970, the high tide of the pacification campaign in Hau Nghia province was reached. As always, most of the actual (as opposed to statistical) progress came from military pressure and attrition. Unfortunately for Saigon, the coercive elements of the war effort, despite the heavy losses inflicted on the Front, continued to show serious weaknesses. Fatally handicapped by the continuing fighting, even at a lower level, and the ruthless use of terrorism by Front cadres, attempts to create a political foundation for a strong state and efforts to raise the material standard of living made little, if any, headway.

As in 1969, the Phoenix Program remained a bitter disappointment in 1970. To be sure, the Americans believed there were some encouraging signs. Compared to earlier years, more information was coming out of the DIOCCs.[32] Above all, CORDS believed that the Front apparatus in Hau Nghia was continuing to decrease in numbers of cadres. In August, CORDS estimated that there were 493 Front cadres still operating in Hau Nghia, as opposed to just over 1,000 at the beginning of the year.[33] Although most of the cadres that were eliminated were low-level, the security affairs chief for Duc Lap village was captured in March on a Phoenix operation. Unfortunately for CORDS, the advisory team believed that almost everything of value coming from Phoenix was due to U.S. efforts. In addition, although the DIOCCs were identifying more cadres, virtually all of those that were "neutralized" came from combat, sweeps, and the Chieu Hoi program. For instance, of the 96 cadres accounted for in May (a record number at the time, due to the Cambodian invasion), none were apprehended by a Phoenix operation.[34] In addition, cadres apprehended, by whatever means, stood a very small chance of facing a lengthy incarceration. The maximum sentence for an "A"-category cadre, the most important, was two years, although this was sometimes extended. Only a handful of "A"-category cadres came from Hau Nghia. The more numerous "B"- and "C"-category cadres were rarely sentenced to more than one year of imprisonment. Normally, far more suspects were released than sentenced.[35] No doubt, the relative lenience of sentencing guidelines, which resulted in no small degree from a desire by CORDS to combat adverse publicity in the United States, prevented much injustice. Nevertheless, many Phoenix advisors were fearful that, due to corruption, investigative incompetence, or fear of the Front, a large number of important cadres were freed along with the innocent. The situation in Hau Nghia regarding Phoenix was repeated throughout South Vietnam.[36]

Although territorial forces continued to be a major factor in the war of attrition, a detailed study of their performance during 1970 revealed very serious defects. Col. Jack Weissinger, the Hau Nghia PSA from October 1969 until April 1971, was not pleased with the performance of either the Regional or Popular Forces. At the end of 1970, using district records, he compiled a statistical summary of the operations of each of Hau Nghia's 33 RF companies and 77 PF platoons. As of June 1970, the Regional Forces had approximately 3,500 soldiers, and the Popular Forces fielded another 500.[37] Throughout 1970, the Hau Nghia RF claimed to have killed 240 enemy and captured another 136. The PF figures were 69 and 45, respectively. Considering the force levels, these figures were not very high, but they did constitute a drain on the Front.

However, examination of individual units yielded very sobering findings concerning the Regional Forces. Throughout the province, a very small percentage of units accounted for a very large percentage of contacts made and casualties inflicted. Naturally, units willing to fight suffered higher casualties themselves. For instance, the most successful territorial unit in Hau Nghia was one of Cu Chi district's six RF companies. During 1970, this unit had 38 contacts, very few initiated by the enemy, and claimed to have killed 42 enemy and captured another 22. Had such a performance been the norm, the GVN would have crushed the Front in Hau Nghia very quickly. But, to Saigon's detriment, this unit was very much the exception. The remaining five companies in Cu Chi, totaled together, managed to kill only 18 enemy and capture 23. Again, these figures were for the entire year of 1970. Although the imbalance was not quite so great in the other districts, the trend was clear: A few RF companies did quite well, but most did very poorly.

This irregular performance was even more pronounced with the Popular Forces platoons that were assigned the critical task of village security. Overall, the PF claimed to have killed 69 enemy during 1970, with an additional 45 captured. The most successful PF unit was a platoon in Duc Hoa, which claimed to have killed 6 and captured 9 enemy throughout the year. The second most successful platoon came from Cu Chi and claimed to have killed 3 enemy and captured 5. Throughout the province, 43 platoons registered no enemy killed or captured; another 12 recorded 1 enemy killed or captured. The situation in Duc Hue district was so bad that Colonel Weissinger concluded that the district chief had given up the fight entirely. There, one platoon recorded 5 enemy killed and none captured during 1970. The 10 remaining platoons operating in Duc Hue killed a total of 1 enemy soldier—on an enemy-initiated contact at that—and captured none. All 17 RF casualties were suffered by the first unit. The remaining 10 platoons, which suffered no losses at all in a single year, were operating on a peacetime basis.[38] Many of them were operating near the Vam Co Dong, in the same region examined in the previous chapter. No doubt, some were the same units that Sergeant O'Hare made his leisurely daylight parades with. They were also operating in the same area where Captain Bergson's *Wolfhounds* were finding regular contacts. Some Americans defended the relaxed pace of RF/PF operations, pointing to the lack of residual violence and reminding impatient Americans that the South Vietnamese soldier was in the war for the duration and had to be cautious. Colonel Weissinger had little sympathy for such sentiments, commenting later that "the 3d Brigade of the 25th Division would suffer more casualties in Duc Hue in one day than all of the RF/PF did in one year. It was an insult."

There were serious implications to these findings. Colonel Weissinger, along with South Vietnamese intelligence, believed that the Front had infiltrated most units and had arranged an informal truce with many of them. He further noted that most units, particularly PF platoons, rarely received outside supervision on night operations. The supervision that was available was much more likely to come from U.S. MAT teams, rather than from South Vietnamese officials. MAT team supervision was problematical for the teams preferred billeting with the district advisors, instead of in the little militia forts. Colonel Weissinger further claimed that most of the night ambushes set by territorial units were compromised by either incompetence or predictable behavior. MAT teams struggled in vain to get militia units to vary their lines of march on the rare occasions that they went out at night. The result was "a charade with everybody playing a part." Due to this "charade," large areas of Hau Nghia province were never patrolled at night unless an American unit was nearby. Naturally, the Front knew exactly where these areas were. Lastly, Colonel Weissinger rejected the possibility that the worst units were failing to engage due to lack of opportunity, claiming instead that Front activity was spread throughout the province and that each unit could have made a contribution.[39]

Entire hamlets might reach accommodation with the Front. In Hau Nghia province, particularly in Trang Bang district, there were several hamlets that were predominantly Cao Dai or Catholic. The Cao Dai had difficult relations with the Front, and the Catholics were openly hostile. In other parts of the country, such areas might have been government strongholds. In Hau Nghia, however, an extreme anti-Front stance would have been suicidal, particularly in Trang Bang district so close to Cambodia and Front "liberated zones." Consequently, some of these hamlets apparently worked out a cease-fire. Captain Harrington remembered that, in late 1968, the Catholic hamlets clustered in An Hoa village, Trang Bang district, were more prosperous, quieter, and "less militarized" than the rest of the district. Colonel Weissinger once took Secretary of Defense Melvin Laird, another of the VIPs that made the short trip from Saigon to Hau Nghia, to the same area. He suspected that there was some sort of understanding between the Front and the Catholics. No doubt, the Front would have preferred support from these areas, but, if that were not possible, accommodation, generated by fear of the Front, was far preferable to active hostility.

The PSDF did almost nothing to fill the void in security. As in previous years, the number of enemy killed or captured by PSDF members was insignificant. Most weapons remained locked up in the village offices, and the small PSDF patrols were designed to protect officials, not the villages. Consequently, PSDF casualties were extremely low. As before, Front units would often penetrate a village, abduct and disarm PSDF members, give them a lecture, and let them go. An undetermined number of PSDF members defected to the Front, and, in most places in Hau Nghia province, the program was an utter waste of time and effort. After the war, Colonel Weissinger commented,

> The PSDF was a farce in Hau Nghia. We did an in-depth study of the PSDF, and it was one big lie. Some weapons were never issued out, and everyone who was supposed to be protected stayed inside the barbed wire. We had member after member of the PSDF open the gate so attackers could come in. It was just a miserable failure.

On those rare occasions when a PSDF unit threatened to seriously impede Front activities, reaction could be sharp. This was shown during June, when a unit was attacked by a local force company and lost 10 men killed, or by a more violent attack in January 1971, during which 20 PSDF were killed.[40] These were yet more examples of the dreadful dynamic of revolutionary warfare in Vietnam: Inactivity and incompetence were rewarded with safety, and military skill and anti-Communist enthusiasm brought the very real risk of death.

With the war still very much in progress, although at a lower level, and local security still highly problematic, most of the various programs designed to bring a better material life to the rural population and gain, in turn, their allegiance to the GVN remained irrelevant. To be sure, province officials filled or surpassed their quotas for projects authorized and completed. The rice harvest was somewhat better than during 1969, and the amount of land planted with miracle rice increased to 1,100 hectares, still a very small percentage of the total.[41] CORDS made another effort to reopen the Hiep Hoa sugar mill, the only manufacturing facility of any type in Hau Nghia, but continuing hostilities made the cultivation of sugarcane impossible. Even with subsidies, the project was not remotely profitable, and the effort was abandoned in November.[42] As usual, economic development in the midst of war proved next to impossible.

Many peasants in Hau Nghia continued to suffer dreadfully. Although the level of violence was less, a minimum of 7,000 refugees inhabited Hau Nghia throughout the year, and this number went up appreciably during the Cambodian incursion. In addition, the GVN continued, on occasion, to forcibly relocate peasant families to "secure" villages. Officials claimed, of course, that this was done to protect villagers from the fighting, which was true. However, the GVN also wanted to depopulate Front areas even further. This policy was typical of most counterinsurgency campaigns in history. It also was criticized bitterly by many Americans. Critics argued that relocation was unduly cruel, caused bitterness among its victims, and inevitably led to the importation of Front followers into GVN areas. The GVN and many other Americans defended the policy as a harsh but necessary means to deprive the Front of the human resources required for the insurgency. Regrettably, judging from the example of Hau Nghia province, the GVN was probably correct. Although all that critics of relocation said was true, the Front did everything possible to keep people in insurgent hamlets and to get relocated families to return.[43] In addition, relocation was not common, and most peasants fled on their own initiative. The withdrawal of U.S. combat units did not mean the end of the widespread use of artillery and airpower because ARVN units, in emulation of American operations, continued to use available assets in a lavish manner. For instance, during September, ARVN established a "no-civilian line" in northwestern Trang Bang district and authorized a liberal use of firepower in that area.[44] In total, Hau Nghia officials issued financial compensation to just over 4,000 war victims for deaths, injuries, and property damage throughout the year.[45]

GVN Land Reform

Under such circumstances, continuing efforts under the Village Self Development Program to revive the village as a meaningful political entity failed. Although many local projects were started, some of which were indeed voted on, the advisory team believed that most decisions concerning the nature of the projects were merely "rubber stamps" of the district chief's opinion. District advisors also reported that village chiefs only rarely exercised actual control of the PF platoons, as the district chiefs continued in reality to control these units. Despite high levels of participation, advisors believed that village elections continued to have little meaning. A report noted that, although participation in hamlet elections normally was about 90 percent, only 20 percent of those voting displayed any real interest in the outcome. Another report on elections in Trang Bang and Duc Hoa districts revealed that many candidates were poorly qualified and that many were soldiers only seeking a discharge. In addition, CORDS personnel in Hau Nghia concluded that most people voted out of fear of government reprisal; they also believed that the results were rigged.[46]

However, the one new GVN initiative had genuine impact. On 26 March 1970, despite fierce opposition, President Thieu pushed through a major land reform bill. Known as the Land-to-the-Tiller Law and abbreviated as LTT, this bill was the most ambitious effort on the part of the GVN to build support in the countryside during the entire war. To be sure, some sort of land reform program had existed since Diem, but earlier efforts lacked substance. In 1967, Thieu began issuing a series of decrees extending programs that were already established. Landlords were forbidden to evict tenants or collect past rents, and rents were frozen. No doubt even more wise was an order forbidding the army from reinstalling landlords in areas newly reoccupied. In addition, some government land was distributed to landless families. If any of these decrees improved the position of the GVN in Hau Nghia province, it was not noted by the advisory team. Agricultural improvements were largely submerged by the fighting, and many farms were abandoned. Also, these measures, though lessening the worst types of exploitation, were meager when measured against the Front's redistribution accomplished years earlier.[47]

American attitude toward land reform was inconsistent. It was always U.S. policy that some type of reform in the countryside should take place, but the precise nature of reform was never agreed upon. Many Americans advocated a radical program similar to the one already instituted by the Front. Others were more cautious, understandably fearing that a widely heralded redistribution of land might create severe administrative confusion if rushed and make the GVN appear to be breaking yet another promise. A few U.S. officials disagreed with land reform in principle, believing that private property rights were worthy of defense.[48]

Regardless of the attitudes of U.S. officials in Saigon, Thieu genuinely supported land reform efforts and went to great lengths to identify the new Land-to-the-Tiller Law with his personal leadership. His attitude was quite understandable for the LTT program went far beyond earlier reforms. Its principal feature was an immediate cessation of rents and the transfer of title to the persons actually farming the land. The old limit of 100 hectares of rice land permitted to one owner was reduced to 15, and landlords were promised compensation from the GVN. Although nothing ever went smoothly in Saigon, this program was not just another paper exercise. The percentage of tenant farmers (nearly 60 percent in 1970) fell to only 7 percent in 1973.[49]

As might be expected, many peasants in Hau Nghia were very interested in the LTT program, and, as reports in October 1970 noted, the program was "well understood." Thousands of applications for title were received by the village governments; some offices even ran out of forms.[50] Although cessation of rents took place immediately, the formal redistribution of land was necessarily time-consuming, and only a few hundred hectares legally changed hands in the first year. Of course, there was no way to construct a perfect formula for such a sweeping effort. ARVN soldiers, for example, might lose title to land they owned if relatives were farming it. Naturally, the Front propaganda machine picked up on this point and other inequities.[51]

It is not at all easy to determine the actual impact of the Land-to-the-Tiller Law in Hau Nghia. No doubt, it would have been revolutionary if passed in 1956. Nevertheless, it had one unavoidable flaw: It gave official approval to the land redistribution already undertaken by the Front. As Jeffrey Race has shown, this was a very controversial aspect of the law. Some GVN officials wanted the grant of title to go to those supporting the GVN, thus making the redistribution conditional on appropriate behavior. This, after all, was what the Front had done. Thieu rejected this, hoping instead to weaken or cut the link that tied many families to the Front. He was very likely correct in this policy for a conditional grant would have sharply increased tension in rural areas and could well have forced the "fence sitters" to make a commitment one way or the other, a risky proposition for the GVN in a province like Hau Nghia. Nevertheless, peasants who were unsure of the ultimate outcome of the war or who believed that the NLF would win continued to have a great incentive to cooperate with the Front.[52] On the other hand, the LTT was propagandized widely by the GVN, and it served to counter a basic Front argument that a GVN victory would mean the return of the landlords.

There was another problem with the LTT: It did very little to alter the basic power relationships that existed in Vietnam. Party cadres were quick to tell the peasantry that one should not feel grateful toward a thief who returns stolen property and to remind them that land reform from the GVN had only taken place because of Front policy. Furthermore, access to the power and wealth beyond the rural areas remained virtually closed to the peasantry for the South Vietnamese urban elites remained unchallenged.

Furthermore, it was very late in the day for politics in Vietnam. By 1970, the war had swept up everyone. The question was not so much who should win but rather who would win. Intrepid individuals, the ones who win or lose wars, had largely made their choices. Every family had relatives on one side or another or both, further influencing action. No doubt many people had forgotten why they were fighting. Political reforms, even a genuine one like the LTT, could only have an effect in the very long term. In the near term, the momentum of the struggle itself, which had built up over decades, would carry forward as before.

Therefore, it is likely that the Land-to-the-Tiller Law in a province like Hau Nghia, with its long history as a Front stronghold, would have increased any already existing tendencies of the population toward neutrality. Supporters of the Front gained nothing from it and would not change sides in any case. They, after all, desired revolution, not reform. So, though the LTT program could not hurt the GVN and probably helped it somewhat, most benefits of the program could only be realized if the bulk of the population believed that the GVN would win the war. But, as shall be shown directly, the opposite was the case.

The Front Reacts

Despite gains in the countryside, the Front's ability to alter strategy and change the mode and tempo of operations to meet changing circumstances continued to plague the allied war effort. COSVN did not necessarily react quickly because centralized decisionmaking at the top level could be a cumbersome process. Moreover, COSVN sometimes followed unsuccessful policies too long. For example, the Tet Offensives of both 1968 and 1969 continued far beyond the time of maximum impact, when measured against losses suffered. Nevertheless, when a policy proved unworkable, the Front could be quite flexible. For instance, when the U.S. Army and ARVN were decimating Front and NVA units in the first half of 1969, COSVN withdrew its main force units and issued a resolution sometime in June or July ordering a return to guerrilla activity and political struggle. This decision spared the main force units and lowered casualties considerably, but it did precipitate the furious allied pacification offensive during the summer of 1969, which lasted until the Cambodian incursion.

Because the pacification offensive shook the Front to an unprecedented degree and reduced its presence in many provinces, including Hau Nghia, to levels almost reminiscent of 1961, COSVN instituted a special program, entitled the Experimental Village Program, that was intended to find the best possible methods to help the insurgency get through this difficult period. The program itself and reaction to it from CORDS provided interesting evidence on the political situation in Hau Nghia province in the wake of the most intensive pacification campaign of the entire war—and the last to be undertaken with the support of American ground forces.

The Experimental Village Program, which began in October 1969 and lasted until the end of February 1970, was an intensive antipacification effort targeted against five villages near Saigon. Three of these were in Hau Nghia province—Tan My village in Duc Hue, Duc Lap village in Duc Hoa, and Duc Hoa district town itself. The other two villages were in Long An and

Gia Dinh. Three criteria were established for the choice of an appropriate village. First, the village had to have experienced a very high level of allied pacification activity. Second, the village had to have a particularly capable and stable Front apparatus in operation. Third, the village could not be in the total control of either the Front or the GVN.

The Front sent specially selected, district-level cadres to each village to guide and monitor the effort. In addition, each village received a platoon of troops to reinforce the local guerrillas. According to intelligence later gathered by CORDS, the program had five objectives:

1. An accelerated recruitment drive to get new party members and new members for the liberation association. Particular attention was placed on recruiting new members with legal GVN identification.
2. Increased efforts to penetrate the Regional and Popular Forces, Revolutionary Development teams, and People's Self Defense Forces.
3. Increased targeting of GVN village officials and RD Cadre for elimination. In conjunction with this, all persons in the village suspected of informing for the GVN were closely monitored. The targeted persons would be set up by the legal cadres and assassinated by the illegals.
4. Increased military activity, including raids and ambushes, tactical reconnaissance of GVN forces, and, particularly, harassment of People's Self Defense Forces and RD teams. This also included increased deployment of mines and booby traps.
5. Establishment of intensive indoctrination sessions for the villagers and mobilization of the people to resist the GVN and warn the VC when allied forces entered the area.[53]

Although the Experimental Village Program was clandestine, CORDS discovered its existence immediately upon its completion. A detailed examination of HES/70 figures did, indeed, show a regression in security for each village and an increase in abductions and assassinations. CORDS also learned that Front cadres reported to COSVN in March that 100 percent of the goals were achieved in Duc Lap, 80 percent in Tan My and Duc Hoa district town, and 50 percent and 35 percent in the other two villages.[54]

Upon receipt of this intelligence, Colby authorized a study to determine the validity of the Front's assessment and to determine whether the situation had altered since the end of the Experimental Village Program. The report was submitted in late August. Relying heavily on HES/70 figures, the report's author concluded that, although the Front made some headway while the Experimental Village Program took place, the GVN had recouped nearly all its losses and had made substantial gains in most areas during the summer of 1970. However, the author of the report for Colby was somewhat defensive about his reliance on HES/70 and admitted that his conclusions were tentative. In one area, the report was quite definite: During the period in question, March to August 1970 (immediately after the completion of the Experimental Village Program), Front military activity had reached an all-time low, and losses to the enemy continued to be painful. Considering the fact that this period coincided with the Cambodian incursion and the last American pacification offensive, there is no reason to question these rather matter-of-fact assertions. The "fog of war," however, envelops the rest of the study. For example, the author concluded that if the Front had been successful in recruiting new cadres in these villages, it was not reflected by HES/70. This judgment was not particularly helpful for either success or failure of a clandestine effort would, by definition, fail to register on the computer. The study did report that greater Front penetration of territorial forces and the PSDF was quite likely, thus confirming the opinion of the Hau Nghia advisory team. The HES/70 figures did not reveal a major increase in the assassination campaign in these villages, but the author of the study pointed out:

> What is not shown in the HES, however, is the extent of fear and paralysis which the GVN sometimes experiences at the local level when even one incident or assassination occurs.[55]

Lastly, the report concluded there was little evidence that the Front had succeeded in increasing its indoctrination efforts, although, here again, a clandestine effort was involved. The essential conclusion was that any progress initially achieved by the Experimental Village Program had been more than reversed by the GVN. However, expressing a candor rarely found in CORDS documents, the author acknowledged that the data gathered by the district advisors, upon which HES was based, was suspect:

> In many cases, advisors continue to overlook the fact that the peasants oftentimes look with skepticism on the activities of the government or simply exercise discretion in neither praising nor condemning either side in the political battle. Oftentimes unconsidered is the feeling of true nationalism which the people may continue to identify with what has now become the Communist cause. The difficulties in gauging the loyalties of a people who often look on their foreign allies as aggressors, or at least with a tinted eye, cannot be overemphasized.[56]

Ambassador Colby was unhappy with the CORDS report and complained that it "really just regurgitates the HES. . . . I would like to be a little better convinced that I am looking at more than our computers alone."[57] Wanting more substantial information, Colby sent a member of his staff to Hau Nghia province to visit the villages in question and obtain the views of the advisory team concerning both the Experimental Village Program and the overall situation in Hau Nghia. The findings of this visit to Hau Nghia must have been very sobering for CORDS. The village of Tan My in Duc Hue district received the most comprehensive review. Tan My was located in an area where the Popular Forces, in the opinion of the PSA, had given up the war. The description of the situation in Tan My sent to

Colby provides an interesting look at a Hau Nghia village during or just after the high tide of the allied pacification effort:

a. The VCI numbers about 13 or 14 which lives in a heavily mined area, but never leaves the village. VCI presence outnumber GVN government. The VCI are part of a network of relatives in the area with a VC having perhaps as many as 80–100 relatives.
b. The GVN has a village chief, 29 years old, who is from Hiep Hoa and stays at the outpost by the Hiep Hoa road. He rarely goes to the hamlets. Village police are ineffective and won't visit some hamlets unless escorted by a company of RF.
c. The RF Group (of three companies) does not stop VC movement in the Tan My area.
d. The VCI have a popular image of being poor, sincere, and honest. People sympathize with them. When taxes are paid to the Front the people do not believe there is a rake-off. Conversely, when people in Tan My apply for basic GVN documentation, they do expect to have to pay speed money. Hoi Chanh pay 2–3000$ for GVN identity papers.
e. Some VCI have rallied/captured but there is no real change of heart. The ralliers cannot live at home. Two weeks ago a cadre who rallied after capture was killed 60 meters from his house in Duc Lap in the evening.[58]

The opinions Colonel Weissinger, the PSA, gave to Colby's assistant on the other two villages were little more encouraging. Despite the large number of Duc Lap cadres killed, captured, or enticed to rally, Colonel Weissinger agreed with the Front estimate of 100 percent support in the village. Concerning Duc Hoa district town, the PSA suggested that, although not much reliable information existed, a strong Front presence would not surprise him. Colonel Weissinger furthermore added that the Front's apparatus was still very strong in Trang Bang district and that, though Front losses had been very high in Cu Chi district, there was no way to tell how the people viewed the GVN.[59]

As Colby knew, Colonel Weissinger's views on the situation had particular value. His background in the field of counterinsurgency was very extensive. In 1959, as a member of Special Forces, he began an association with the newly established Special Warfare School at Fort Bragg. In the spring of 1961, he helped found the Military Assistance Advisory Course, which was used to train thousands of officers destined for advisory duties. Five years later, he was assigned to a staff position in Vietnam. He was made PSA for Hau Nghia province in October 1969 and served in that position until the end of April 1971.

After the war, Colonel Weissinger stressed the psychological strength of the Front as a key to its victory. The Front, he recalled, maintained the psychological initiative in Hau Nghia even at the time of the most intensive allied pacification effort of the entire war. Despite terrible losses, enough Front cadres remained convinced of victory to prevent the pacification campaign from succeeding:

One of the underlying beliefs that I have, and it is unshakable by the way, is that there was a basic difference, possibly in the cultural background, possibly in the people, but certainly in the motivation of the North Vietnamese and Viet Cong, on one hand, and the followers of the GVN, on the other. I talked to dozens of cadre, and they were genuine cadre, not just people whom we suspected. I was struck, time and again, with the terribly strong belief they had in what they were doing. They absolutely believed, and I mean every one of them, that they were going to win eventually. They didn't believe in a military victory at that time, I don't think any of them did, but they all believed in the inevitable, final, political victory or combination military-political victory. That was a universal belief with them. It was right down inside the skin, they believed it so strongly.

These remarks reflected a serious situation facing the GVN, in that their enemy was not ready to capitulate. However, taken alone, this perception did not mean defeat for Saigon; there are many examples in history of one force believing totally in victory, only to be ultimately crushed. What made the situation desperate for the GVN, if Colonel Weissinger's assessment is correct, was that a goodly number of GVN officers and officials also believed that eventually the Front and the North would prevail:

Many Vietnamese officials would talk freely about the war with me or other advisors on the team. I think particularly of a couple of district chiefs and an intelligence officer, killed by the NVA after the war, that I knew very well. They typified, to me, the views of the more honest, knowledgeable, and perceptive Vietnamese officers. They also believed that the Viet Cong and the North were going to win the war. That belief was always in the back of their minds. There was a real fear of the eventual outcome of the war. This fear was very widespread.

Interestingly enough, Lt. Col. Carl Bernard, another man who understood Vietnam and counterinsurgency, had made exactly the same observation. In a letter to Robert Komer composed in October 1969, after Bernard's transfer out of Hau Nghia, he wrote:

There are at least four Vietnamese officers I know who are withdrawing their commitment to the GVN. They are trying to become candidates for something besides elimination in the event of a VC take-over! Their actions and words indicate that they do not want to "offend the VC" any more than is absolutely necessary to maintain their positions. I am not just newly piqued by typical Vietnamese inaction; I am convinced of a malaise that is coming over the middle ranks of some GVN officials, as they prepare for our withdrawal and its consequences. As a result of the VC concentration on the people and this malaise, the population, to whom we wish to "give" the benefits of freedom and democracy, is slipping through our fingers.

Obviously, such attitudes, if widely held, could only cripple the allied war effort. During the war, Colonel Weissinger reported to CORDS that a "whole web of understandings," often implicit, existed between the enemy and government officers and officials. As revealed in the province reports, there was a very good reason to search for such accommodations because the assassination campaign, though not quite as ruthless as during 1969, continued to rage on in 1970.

Nor, according to Colonel Weissinger, could U.S. forces do more to help by the time of their withdrawal. These forces had, he believed, virtually crushed the Front's military units, and there was little else they could do, especially in the face of a pronounced drop in morale, noticed by many observers, that had reached very serious proportions by 1970:

> When we left, after all of those damned years, we couldn't find a squad, we couldn't find four or five people to come up against in a military way. We had all kinds of units and all kinds of conventional power, but it just couldn't be applied in any meaningful way because we had already accomplished our military mission. We had rid the country of overt, organized military opposition. I know in Hau Nghia that to find five people together was a big night toward the end. So, we cleaned the country. We had even, mistakenly or not, gone into the sanctuaries. We cleaned them out to give the South Vietnamese some more breathing room. We couldn't have done anything more.
>
> Our army forces were in real trouble. They were untrained and undisciplined because they had nothing to bounce themselves against. And all of the bad things that went through our army about that period hurt us very badly. We couldn't have kept the army in there anyway. There was not a job for them to do. We had to get them out.
>
> So, from my point of view, and I can't be dislodged from this, we did all we could do with military power. We rid the country of large enemy forces and armed every South Vietnamese who would stand still long enough to accept a rifle. Winning was not in the cards. The South Vietnamese were afraid of that tough enemy. They were more afraid of the dedication, persistence, and uncompromising attitude of these people than they were of their numbers. It was just something we couldn't eradicate. In some villages, we got the Front cadres down to two or three, but there were just enough to hang in there. There were always just enough cadres to impose that damn fear that permeated through the officials, and through the army.[60]

Therefore, as so well described by Colonel Weissinger, the GVN was faced with a virtually unbreakable vicious circle in Hau Nghia. Fear of immediate danger and fear of the ultimate outcome crippled the vigorous efforts required to establish meaningful security. Timid action, along with accommodation (whether explicit or implicit), in turn created an environment within which the Front could continue to operate and continue to engender fear. The description of the security situation given by Colonel Weissinger is sad testimony to the ultimate failure of the allied pacification campaign and, consequently, of the failure of the entire war effort:

> You have to remember that even in the period of 1971, when the enemy was pretty well down, there was not a single official, nobody, who spent the night outside the barbed wire. I mean nobody, they never did. In Hau Nghia province, we never had nighttime security except behind barbed wire. We knew where

all of the village chiefs lived. They either lived in a PF outpost or a company outpost but always behind barbed wire. No one lived in his home. Because of the favorable military situation and because it was so quiet, most people in Saigon considered Hau Nghia secure. But it was totally insecure at night, and that is all the enemy needed. They just kept up the pressure, kept the contact. So we never attained genuine security.

The thoughts expressed by Colonel Weissinger were not just the retrospective views of a single individual. Although opinions, of course, varied considerably, some degree of doubt concerning the future was nearly universal at the time among advisors and field-workers with long experience in Vietnam. On one occasion, the members of the Hau Nghia advisory team had the opportunity to give their frank appraisal of the overall situation in Vietnam. Just after the withdrawal of the 25th Division, the highly respected secretary of the army, Stanley Resor, toured Vietnam, inspecting the progress of Vietnamization; one of his stops was Hau Nghia province. While there, Secretary Resor had a long conversation with Colonel Weissinger and key members of the advisory team. He asked their opinion on the prospects of Vietnamization:

> The question was what did we think was going to happen? Put in another way, could the Vietnamese keep up the momentum? We expressed my belief and the strong belief of my best people, particularly the men working with Phoenix and intelligence matters, that there was nothing in our collective experience with ARVN, the RF/PF, the PSDF, or GVN in general that allowed us to expect the momentum to continue. We told Resor that we saw just the opposite. We predicted that the forward momentum would cease, followed by a period of balance, followed finally by retrogression. We also told him our beliefs were very common among good Vietnamese officers. We labored on these points. Secretary Resor didn't comment much, but at least he accepted that we were expressing honest beliefs. He certainly listened.

The prognosis delivered by the Hau Nghia advisory team (and their views were widely held in U.S. military circles at the time) was totally vindicated by events. What was striking was the nature of their prognosis. They did not stress the armed strength of the other side. Rather, they pointed to the vicious psychological dynamic that always crippled the GVN and poisoned the relations between it and its people.

The dynamic had two related components. Perceived virtue gave to the Front a moral ascendancy in Vietnam that the GVN was never able to counter. Here, Americans were irrelevant to the equation. Nothing the United States could do could alter in any way the perception that followers of the Front were fighting for something beyond individual self-interest, whether the aim was social revolution or national fulfillment. Even Vietnamese that opposed the revolution for one reason or another admired the tenacity and courage of the Front. In one way, American intervention made the situation worse: After 1966, followers of the Front could claim very plausibly that they were defending national sovereignty. In addition, the fighters that had the luck and fortitude to continue the struggle in the face of U.S. power were rewarded with even greater prestige.

The perception of the Front's virtue was tied to the more important issue of the perception of victory. It was certainly true that the agony of the struggle broke the will of many partisans of the revolution, and the ambiguities of the situation led others to genuinely give up or even switch sides. Yet, what is striking in retrospect (and was very clear at the time) was the absolute, unshakable confidence that so many of the revolutionaries had concerning their final victory. Evidently, this belief was shared by many opponents of the revolution. Many people on the side of the GVN were stunned by their eventual defeat, yet, supporters of the GVN almost always talked about victory in a very different manner than did their enemies in the Front. Backers of the GVN often argued that the United States would never allow Saigon to be defeated. But it was one thing to believe that you could not lose and another to believe that you are going to win. Many in the GVN seem to have foreseen an indefinite conflict that would perhaps dissipate in the distant future. In contrast, both the leaders in Hanoi and most of their followers sincerely talked in very concrete terms of total victory at a precise moment in the fairly near future. The political will evidenced by Hanoi and the Front was, from beginning to end, far deeper and more substantial than that shown by Saigon. Naturally, the GVN always claimed that it would win, but, obviously, not enough people found the claims believable. This state of affairs crippled the war effort.

It was in this subjective realm of perceptions that the U.S. Army had failed. Given the political restraints on the use of American ground forces, attrition was pointless unless the killing had purpose. The sacrosanct status of the DRV made the physical elimination of enemy manpower impossible. Therefore, the only thing that American soldiers could gain by killing their foes was to change the nature of the psychological equation in rural Vietnam. As the cadres and the most intrepid of the Front's fighters died (something that everyone in a locality would soon know), Americans hoped that fear would deter others from taking their place. To a large extent, this happened but never to the necessary degree. At the same time, if the military campaign were to have meaning, supporters of the GVN should have gained skill, élan, and, most importantly, confidence in victory. Had both of these things taken place, the GVN could then have harnessed the formidable material strength provided them by the United States and made something solid out of the physical control of the countryside that the U.S. Army had allowed them to gain. As it was, lethargy and defeatism characterized the GVN's efforts at all times.

In Hau Nghia province, early signs of retrogression of the GVN's position, predicted by Colonel Weissinger and the advisors, began appearing immediately after the withdrawal of the 25th Division in late 1970. Although difficult to document, the U.S. withdrawal undoubtedly raised enemy morale. Any doubts as to the outcome of the war held by South Vietnamese officials, soldiers, or civilians must also have been increased. Rumors of an American "sell-out" began with the first announcement of troop reductions.

To be sure, the residual benefits of the American-supported pacification campaign in Hau Nghia province continued to be evident for several months after withdrawal. As already mentioned, Front forces continued to avoid contact at all costs until the end of 1970. The Chieu Hoi numbers, however, dropped steadily as U.S. force levels declined. In addition, there was a slight, but noticeable decrease in the numbers of Front cadres "neutralized." In July, the last month during which the bulk of an American brigade operated in Hau Nghia, 140 Hoi Chanh rallied. In August, there were 70 surrenders, and, in December, the number fell to 42. The advisory team believed that this drop was due to several factors. Intelligence indicated that many people accepted the Front propaganda claim that American withdrawal would lead to a coalition government, which would mean Front victory. The advisors also concluded that the Front was growing more effective in controlling its supporters, a higher portion being "hard-core" as the less committed defected. Lastly, the advisors contended that assassinations of Hoi Chanh were deterring further defections and reminding the local population that the war would continue.[61]

Although none of this augured well for the future, the GVN's position in Hau Nghia was stronger at the end of 1970 than ever before in the entire history of the province. Nevertheless, the regression feared by Colonel Weissinger and many others became evident in 1971. In 1972, the war returned to Hau Nghia with a terrible vengeance.

11

Last Battles: 1971–1973

A Year of Preparation

Throughout 1971, the war in Vietnam proceeded on an unusually low level. There were no large military campaigns inside the borders of South Vietnam by either side. The GVN attempted to capitalize on the waning asset of American military strength by launching a daring offensive into Laos. Hanoi, principally occupied with continuing preparations for the great 1972 general offensive, was forced to delegate any excess resources to counter this threat. In rural Vietnam, the GVN hoped that the military trends of the past two years would continue, allowing it to bring even more area under control and raise its numerical force levels higher yet. The Front, buoyed by American withdrawal but still bascially left to its own devices, hoped to halt or slow the unfavorable trends in the countryside in anticipation of the great blow to come the next year.

The pattern of operations employed by both sides in Hau Nghia during 1971 was nearly identical to that in the last half of 1970. There were no large engagements during the entire year, a fact for which there are several reasons. In the first place, both ARVN (with much of its remaining American support) and PAVN were preoccupied with the fierce fighting of February and March, coming from ARVN's attempt to cut the Ho Chi Minh Trail in Laos. Second, the enemy was quite content to await further American troop withdrawals before risking large formations in battle once again. Third, the severed supply lines running from Sihanoukville to the Parrot's Beak had to be replaced by an extension of logistics down the Ho Chi Minh Trail. This situation was complicated for the Front by new ARVN raids into the sanctuaries. Apparently, the Ba Thu sanctuary was not fully in operation until 1 October 1971.[1]

Throughout 1971, most of the fighting in Hau Nghia province was between the RF/PF and Front local forces and guerrillas. These Front units required regular infusions of manpower from PAVN to keep them in the field. Although the precise ratio was unclear, undoubtedly Front forces in total were heavily outnumbered by either the Hau Nghia Regional Forces or Popular Forces. Both branches of the Hau Nghia militia were substantially increased in size throughout the year. The number of Regional Forces companies remained at 33, but they were used with greater frequency in battalion-level or multicompany operations. The complement of PF platoons was raised from 77 to 117.[2]

More important than any numerical increase was a noticeable improvement in the leadership of the Regional Forces. In January 1971, the GVN appointed Lt. Col. Nguyen Van Thanh as province chief. Strongly supported by the Hau Nghia advisory team, Thanh instituted an uncharacteristic shake-up in the RF command structure and disposed of a large number of indolent or incompetent officers. According to Lt. Col. Gerald Bartlett, the PSA from May 1971 to November 1972, Thanh replaced them with "the eight fightingest officers" in Hau Nghia.[3] The Hau Nghia RF received American helicopter transport and gunship support for a few months, but these assets were gone by the end of the year. However, as part of Vietnamization, the United States provided the Regional Forces with their own artillery units, thus greatly increasing the firepower available and blurring the distinction between the RF and ARVN. Given his quota of increased (although often inaccurate) artillery support, Thanh redeployed 17 companies from hamlet security duties to mobile operations against various enemy safe zones. American engineers supported these operations with "Rome Plow" bulldozers, clearing some 15,000 acres throughout the year.[4]

Fighting was steady but low-level. Reflecting Thanh's leadership, Regional Forces became more active. They claimed to have inflicted serious losses on the enemy and no doubt did, but South Vietnamese figures were considered even more debatable than American ones. RF operations did, however, continue to account for most of the Front cadres killed or wounded. No doubt, these operations also accounted for a high percentage of Front ralliers, although these numbers, ranging between 18 and 40 per month, remained much lower than in previous years. In general, the advisors were pleased with the increase in effective RF activity. Gen. Nguyen Van Minh, later the commanding general of III CTZ, stated publicly that Hau Nghia had "the best RF in the world, better than ARVN."[5] Inevitably, there was a negative component to the equation: The RF took much heavier casualties, sometimes over 100 a month, with nearly half coming from mines and booby traps.

Yet, it is quite apparent that the pattern described by Colonel Weissinger concerning the Hau Nghia RF/PF continued until the cease-fire in 1973. There is no reason to doubt Lieutenant Colonel Bartlett's claim that several RF units improved greatly in performance, but he also reported that those units with continued poor leadership did not improve despite training dispensed by the remaining U.S. MAT teams. He further observed that RF performance was "directly related" to the presence of the energetic Lieutenant Colonel Thanh. In addition, the village-based Popular Forces continued to sit out the war. Although Bartlett attributed the lack of PF activity to the improved security situation, believing these units had grown lax because they had little to fear, he reported that no progress had been made in upgrading the various units. He considered the problem of PF leadership "unsolvable," adding that it was no longer possible to find or identify all the platoon leaders. The PSDF, of which so much had been expected by Ambassador Colby, remained, in the words of a member of the advisory team during this period, a "paper army."[6] Despite its large nominal enrollment, the PSDF operated in only 77 hamlets, just over half of those in Hau Nghia. Its performance was often criticized, although one advisor hoped that its very existence might satisfy the urge on the part of some Hau Nghia teenagers to play with guns and thus make them less likely to join the Front.[7] Some PSDF defections to the Front did take place, however, and betrayal by some members was believed responsible for a violent attack on a Duc Hoa outpost.[8]

Despite the continuing problems hampering militia activities, the operations of those good units continued to account for a painful level of attrition among Front forces. Interrogations indicated that the Front was still faced with serious recruitment problems and that taxes gathered were less than in the previous year.[9] The Front assassination campaign was down somewhat from earlier periods, although an official or a Hoi Chanh was killed or wounded every few days throughout the year. The various projects planned were, for the most part, completed on schedule. The RD Cadre teams, long since reduced to ten men and working in only the most secure areas, were praised for their educational and election activities, although it was noted that "a poor team causes more damage than several good ones can repair."[10]

Nevertheless, regardless of continuing pressure from the GVN, the Front remained intact and once again showed its ability to react with at least some success to the GVN pacification campaign. In the first place, local force and guerrilla units received reinforcement from PAVN personnel, in addition to the dwindling numbers of local recruits. Significant numbers of PAVN replacements came in February and in July.[11] Consequently, standoff attacks by fire and small sapper assaults were once again frequent, after almost having ceased in the fall of 1970. During July, Front units began operating on a company level for the first time since the Cambodian incursion.[12] Front cadres received reinforcement from higher echelons, a sign that cadre losses continued to hurt—but a sign also that the Front apparatus continued to exist.[13] Most importantly, intelligence indicated that the Front was attempting to compensate for its seriously shrinking "illegal" apparatus by increasing the numbers of "legal" cadres. The advisors were well aware that this shift toward recruiting "legal" cadres posed a serious threat. They also believed that this change in Front policy may have accounted for some of the decrease in observable Front activity:

If the VCI program (of recruiting "legal" cadres) is successful, a significant number of GVN local officials and Territorial Forces may be entirely neutralized or even turned against the GVN. . . . Interrogations of prisoners from SR-1 confirm that organization of legal cadre is the strategy the VCI will follow in order to destroy the pacification program. Elimination of troublesome GVN officials will only be used as a last resort. Prime effort will be given towards neutralizing them or turning them against the GVN through the use of friends and family members recruited as legal cadre.[14]

Further reports came in later in the year that indicated deep and widespread penetration on the part of "legal" cadres. This intelligence, according to the province report, made a "deep impression" on the province chief. Somewhat later, in a letter to the new province chief, Lieutenant Colonel Bartlett commented, "As you know, the legal VCI in Hau Nghia are very strong. If there should be a cease-fire, these legal VCI will be a dangerous problem."[15] Most importantly, the course of events during the 1972 Easter Offensive showed clearly that Front cadres continued to be very active throughout Hau Nghia.

With Front "illegal" cadres active, although seriously weakened, and the "legal" cadres increasing in number, the Hau Nghia advisory team put more emphasis than ever on attacking these elusive enemies. Some time in 1970, to emphasize Vietnamization, the term "Phoenix" was replaced in all documents by its Vietnamese translation *Phung Hoang*. In any case, Phung Hoang continued to fail to accomplish what it was designed to do. As always, the number of targeted cadres killed or captured was relatively small because most eliminations came through military sweeps or the Chieu Hoi program. The program itself, during this period, became highly suspect to the Phung Hoang advisors, who feared that many Front cadres had surrendered in order to obtain "legal" status. The advisors also came upon unusually clear evidence of corruption in the Chieu Hoi program. Before leaving in early 1971, Colonel Weissinger had done some investigations into it and discovered how the scam worked. The Chieu Hoi center in Bao Trai was, in theory, given a small amount of money per rallier per day to cover expenses. The number of people at the center, however, was never anything near the number of ralliers reported. The GVN officials took the expense money and took bribes from ralliers for new GVN identification cards.

There were some very good American officers working with Phoenix in this phase of the war. Some success was gained in Duc Hue and Trang Bang districts, but, in both cases, this was due to the fact that the U.S. advisors were running these programs completely, with very little assistance (often offset by outright obstruction) from Vietnamese officials.[16] Two of the Front defectors cultivated by the Americans were adopted by the Hau Nghia advisory team and gave invaluable aid to the Phoenix Program. Both men were killed within a few months by the Front. Fear and corruption in the GVN proved to be powerful allies of the Front.

The situation grew even worse when, during May, more responsibility for Phung Hoang was transferred from the South Vietnamese military to the National Police.[17] This was a great disappointment for the advisors for the National Police, as always, was considered both inefficient and corrupt. In November, Lieutenant Colonel Bartlett reported on the unfortunate consequences of having the National Police more active with Phung Hoang:

> The failure of the National Police to participate in a program which they, in theory, have a major part, bodes ill for the future if this agency assumes primary responsibility for action against the VCI. This aura of gloom assumes greater significance when one views the major emphasis the VCI are placing

on organizing legal cadre and targeting them against GVN village/hamlet officials and territorial forces. The detection and neutralization of this type of cadre results from a strictly police type of investigative activity.[18]

Later, Bartlett again castigated the National Police:

Security operations by the National Police are almost totally ineffective with the exception of an occasional village police force. I believe this is principally due to the gross and blatant corruption in the organization at every level. . . . The corruption covered the entire operation from resources control to releasing VCI for money.[19]

Interesting evidence concerning the failure of Phoenix during this period comes from Brig. Gen. Stuart Herrington, who was a captain with the Hau Nghia advisory team from January 1971 until August 1972. For several months, Herrington ran the Phung Hoang program in Duc Hue district with considerable success. Later, he was appointed the province Phung Hoang advisor. In his view, Phung Hoang failed because it was a U.S. program not appropriate to the Vietnamese environment. Interestingly, he did not believe, as did Colonel Weissinger and others, that fear of retribution was a major cause for the failure. Rather, he pointed to three related factors. First, the various Vietnamese intelligence agencies were jealous of each other and wished to gain complete credit for any success obtained, thus hampering coordination. Second, he claims that jealousy was compounded with suspicion, with the military fearing that the National Police Special Branch had been penetrated by the Front. Most importantly, according to Herrington, the district chiefs did not want an effective Phung Hoang program, because the HES scores would decline and a concrete picture of Front activity would be seen in Saigon as a bad reflection on the ability of the district chief. This type of attitude, he noted, had the following results:

The District Chiefs feared Phoenix, and did not, unless brutally pushed by the boss, give it real command emphasis. The District Chief would publish all of the required directives in reference to targeting, black lists, etc., and he would order each organization to detail a man to the DIOCC. Everything was done, but there was no supervision, everyone was "going through the motions" which is precisely what all Vietnamese organizations wanted, with the exception of one Vietnamese officer, who agonized over Phoenix in my District, then gave up on it as hopeless.[20]

Since the war, some evidence has appeared indicating that Phoenix had more success against the Front than Americans thought at the time. Several DRV officials told journalist Stanley Karnow after the war that Phoenix had done serious damage to the Front. Truong Nhu Tang, a founding member of the NLF, singled out Hau Nghia as an area that was particularly hard hit from the Front's point of view. Discussing the 1970–1971 period of the war, Tang wrote, "In some areas, though, Phoenix was dangerously effective.

In Hau Nghia Province, for example, not far from our old base area, the Front infrastructure was virtually eliminated."[21]

It is not entirely evident why the two sides would have had such differing appreciations of Phoenix. The Front, after all, would have known if its structure was getting weaker, and the Americans would have known if their efforts to identify, target, and eliminate Front followers had succeeded. Several factors may account for the discrepancies of opinion. First, it is possible that the smallest but most secret component of the plan, involving the PRUs and other select GVN agencies, was more successful than admitted at the time. Only the highest CORDS officials would have been privy to this type of information. Perhaps the Phoenix personnel underestimated the indirect effects of the successes they did achieve. The loss of a single "legal" cadre could force reorganization of cells; if that cadre was a high one, the damage could be quite extensive. For instance, in early 1971, the Party's top cadre in An Tinh village, Trang Bang district, defected. The information he supplied led to many arrests and the destruction of a secret tunnel complex.[22]

Yet, the officials interviewed by Karnow talked about thousands of cadres eliminated and about losing influence in whole areas of the country. They described a very large-scale and persistent phenomenon, not the result of a few "dirty tricks" on the part of the CIA and its GVN counterparts. Possibly, semantic differences were part of the problem. As anyone who has dealt with Front documents can testify, the Front frequently used allied terms haphazardly. The term *strategic hamlet,* for example, was frequently used to describe any populated area where the GVN was strong. It was very possible that Front and Party officials used *Phoenix Program* as shorthand for all the of negative results stemming from the coercive elements of the overall pacification campaign. If this were the case, the accounts of the two sides are once again synchronized. The Americans knew very well that the Front political apparatus, as measured by "VCI neutralized," was hit very hard. They were disappointed, however, that the Front losses were attributable to general attrition and not often from specifically Phoenix operations. Front losses would have been more or less the same even if there had been no Phoenix Program at all; they just would have been tabulated differently. However, from the Front's point of view, a lost cadre was a lost cadre. The precise program that caused the loss would not have been that important. Tang, a non-Party official of the Front whose duties did not deal directly with either underground activities or Hau Nghia province, could easily have heard accounts of the furious 1970 pacification campaign in Hau Nghia province, which was one of the strongest allied efforts directed anywhere against the Front during the entire war.

Whatever the case, the attrition process that weakened the Front was not accompanied by any important change in allegiance on the part of the rural population in favor of the GVN. This was confirmed later by Herrington. It should be remembered that he was referring to the period during which the GVN was at or near its strongest position in Hau Nghia province:

The improved situation was due to damage inflicted on the enemy, an essentially negative process, as distinct from the positive steps which would result in enthusiasm and support of more of the population. True, we were building schools and clinics and the like, but the government still was viewed with basic cynicism by those who chose to pay attention to it at all, even by its ardent supporters, ironically. Reason: Corruption at all levels generally had the effect of angering the people.[23]

There is no reason to believe that Herrington or any other American associated with Hau Nghia province would disagree on this point, yet factors beyond corruption without doubt stood in the way of any basic change of political sentiment in the countryside. As acknowledged by Herrington, the only way for an individual to be reasonably certain of safety in Hau Nghia was to move to a district capital or Bao Trai, even during 1971. Although Hau Nghia must have appeared almost tranquil if compared to previous years, violence was still central to existence. People were killed every day, refugees continued to be present in large numbers, forced relocation of civilians took place on occasion, and kidnapping and assassination were common. Even if most American observers were correct in believing that the vast majority of the population was neutral (and this opinion was arguable), the fear and exhaustion caused by the war itself would very likely have neutralized political initiatives coming from any government, regardless of how pure in motive. Sadly for the people of Hau Nghia, dark days, perhaps the darkest of all, were still to come.

The 1972 Offensive

Despite the relative lull in the war during 1971, everyone involved knew that PAVN and what remained of the Front military forces were preparing to launch a large offensive in 1972 somewhere in South Vietnam. Indeed, a primary reason for launching the 1971 ARVN offensive into Laos had been to inhibit logistic preparations for the NVA's 1972 campaign. Consequently, as was certainly appreciated by the NVA command, strategic surprise was out of the question. Nevertheless, those working with military intelligence are always faced with a multitude of variables that hamper precise determination of an opponent's plans, a fact that never ceases to perplex and surprise political leaders. Inevitably, some miscalculations occurred on the part of U.S. and GVN military intelligence in early 1972. For a variety of reasons, the allies estimated that PAVN would make the major effort in the Central Highlands in an attempt to sever the country in two. In addition, U.S. intelligence believed that the attack would begin during or just after Tet, thus giving enemy forces the opportunity to operate through the whole of the dry season.

Neither of these assumptions proved correct. Although feverish activity was noted on the part of PAVN, the Tet holidays passed without major incident. Attack was still expected, but several weeks of waiting inevitably lessened vigilance. When the great blow finally fell on 30 March 1972, the major effort came from across the DMZ and Laos toward Quang Tri and Hue. Six days later, a second major front was opened with a drive on An Loc in northwestern III CTZ, which, if successful, would have threatened Saigon. On 23 April, the long-expected drive toward Kontum also began. The NVA experienced initial success everywhere. By the beginning of May, the GVN was fighting for its life.[24]

A comprehensive account of the 1972 campaign, which the enemy called the Nguyen Hue Offensive and the American press called the Easter Offensive, has yet to be written. In scope and in violence, it can only be compared with the Tet Offensive. Both sides employed armor and heavy artillery, and the Americans found the most fruitful role of the entire war for their powerful air force. More importantly, it was a splendid example of the suppleness and depth of Hanoi's warmaking capabilities. Ever since 1968, the Party's leadership had allowed the Front to shoulder the brunt of the fighting. Its military forces had been smashed and its political apparatus shredded. Yet, in return, the U.S. Army was back in the United States, never to return, and the bulk of South Vietnamese manpower was deployed in the populated areas on pacification duties, far from the highlands and border regions that Hanoi had always considered the decisive theater of war. The political phase that was preeminent for so long had served its purpose. The shift in emphasis from political to military struggle created new challenges and burdens for the GVN that ultimately it could not face.

In January 1972, an apprehensive mood was present in Hau Nghia and throughout all of South Vietnam. Front cadres were warning villagers to expect a great offensive during Tet that would lead to the "liberation" of South Vietnam.[25] As in the first month of 1968, small-unit fighting increased greatly, relative to preceding months. The advisory team reported that "the population outwardly remains calm, but signs of heightened tension during the Tet season is evident." There was good reason for tension because elements of four Front main force battalions, along with a PAVN regiment, were identified in Hau Nghia.[26] The wait continued in February, with intelligence predicting attacks on Hiep Hoa, Duc Lap, and Bao Trai. Nevertheless, no attacks came, and the advisory team was puzzled by the disappearance of several of the main force units previously identified. During March, Front forces avoided all possible contact, making it the quietest month in Hau Nghia of the whole war. One decidedly bad omen did appear, however, when many young members of the PSDF were "abducted." The advisory team admitted that it was unclear how many of these members had actually been abducted or had really deserted to join the Front.

In April, war returned to Hau Nghia province. The Front proclaimed a PSDF "general uprising." The great majority of PSDF members stayed behind the barbed wire, but approximately 70 deserted, taking 140 weapons with them. On 20 April, Lieutenant Colonel Thanh, the province chief who had singlehandedly transformed a good portion of the Hau Nghia Regional Forces, paid the price of courage and competence when he was assassinated by the Front. Two hamlet chiefs and four deputy hamlet chiefs were also assassinated. All of these men, including Thanh, were killed by PSDF traitors.

On 26 April, the 101st NVA Regiment left the Ho Bo Woods and occupied Trung Lap village in northeastern Cu Chi district and Phuoc Hiep village astride Highway 1, also in Cu Chi. The villagers were told to leave these villages and return to hamlets in remote areas from which many of the residents had been relocated. They were also told to say they would rather die than leave "ancestral lands" and return to GVN "concentration hamlets." Many villagers did as they were told, and both villages were devastated by ARVN artillery and American air power during counterattacks that forced PAVN to withdraw.

In May, two more NVA regiments left Ba Thu in Cambodia to attack villages in Hau Nghia, and much of the province was soon engulfed by fighting. By the end of June, several more main force units were also in Hau Nghia. Naturally, ARVN reacted, and elements of the 5th, 25th, and 21st ARVN Divisions operated in Hau Nghia at one time or another during the fighting. Several of the RF units, rebuilt by the late Lieutenant Colonel Thanh, distinguished themselves, to the surprise and great satisfaction of the advisors.[27]

Although GVN forces fought stubbornly, the violence aided the Front. Everywhere, the pattern was the same as first seen at Trung Lap, with Front cadres ordering villagers to build bunkers or, if they had been relocated, to return to old hamlets near Front strongholds. In addition, as usual, many militia units fought badly and suffered from a very high desertion rate; some of the deserters followed the Front banner. By the time of a lull in mid-July, half of the villages in Hau Nghia were wholly or partially occupied by PAVN or Front main force units. The worst hit were Trung Lap, which was occupied for a second time in June, and several hamlets of Trang Bang district town, which were held for five days. Other villages suffering partial occupation and destruction included Hiep Hoa, An Tinh, Tan My, and Loc Giang. Outposts and installations in many other villages were mortared or received sapper attacks. By the end of June, there were 30,000 war victims in Hau Nghia.[28]

During mid-July, most of the NVA units retreated from Hau Nghia. Due to the dispersed nature of attacks, it is very unlikely that they had intended to permanently seize any portion of the province. It was quite enough to disrupt the GVN's control in important villages and cause an exodus, whenever possible, to Front-controlled areas. In addition, any ARVN units engaged would be prevented from joining the crucial fighting near An Loc.

In any case, the lull in action, so typical of the monsoon period, was a lull in relative terms only. Front activities of every type were much increased in comparison with the summer of either 1970 or 1971. Propaganda directed at the RF/PF was kept up and continued to cause desertions, 209 in July. Local force units, which had dwindled to near extinction, were greatly strengthened, at least partially due to defections from the PSDF and the RF/PF.[29] The assassination campaign was greatly increased.

The GVN reacted as best it could. The RF and ARVN established at least nominal control over all of Hau Nghia's villages. Some of the villagers who had fled to Front areas were once again relocated to more "secure" locations. Large numbers of people were arrested by the National Police, but, as evidence was usually flimsy, most were released. In fact, the much-publicized Phung Hoang (Phoenix) program died in this period. In July, the National Police was given complete responsibility for Phung Hoang and the inefficiency and corruption feared by American advisors showed itself very quickly.[30] During the period of 1 October 1972 to 28 January 1973, the date of the cease-fire, 293 Front cadres were killed, captured, or rallied: Not a single one had been targeted for "neutralization."

The various village programs were obviously hindered by the fighting, although, ironically, the rice harvest during 1972 was a record, due to the large amount of miracle rice (nearly 17,000 hectares) that had been planted before the offensive.[31] It is easy to imagine the anguish that must have afflicted the American agricultural advisors, seeing success for the first time only to watch, in turn, the most violent battles of the war and a marked revival of the Front in Hau Nghia.

The village election program, from which so much had been hoped for, also came to an end. In August, in an effort to tighten administrative security, Saigon gave the province chiefs the power to remove hamlet or village officials. In Hau Nghia, several hundred officials were replaced, many sent back to their RF/PF units. As might be expected, the advisory team could not detect any anger or disappointment on the part of the villagers due to the abolition of elections.[32]

By October, it was very clear that negotiations in Paris, as a result of the military stalemate on the ground throughout South Vietnam, were going to produce a cease-fire in the very near future. Both sides prepared measures intended to prove their "control" over the greatest possible area of Hau Nghia. The National Police, whose chief was arrested in October because of corruption, prepared a list of 4,000 people to be detained when a cease-fire was imminent.[33] Meanwhile, the Front was busy distributing flags and banners. The fight that so obviously was coming began on 12 October, when the 101st PAVN invaded Trang Bang district. In the next three weeks, they were joined by elements of the 271st NVA Regiment and the 7th NLF Division, which contained a large number of replacements from North Vietnam. The GVN was reinforced by elite ARVN Ranger units. By the time PAVN retreated in early November, there were another 15,000 war victims in Hau Nghia.[34]

Tragically, the October negotiations in Paris did not lead to the expected cease-fire, and both sides in Hau Nghia therefore reverted to preparations for the inevitable last minute "land grab." Once again, Regional Forces units were sent to relocate hamlets. And once again, arrests were made and flags distributed, although it is not clear whether the 4,000 people targeted were actually detained. In any case, Hau Nghia was again submerged in battle in January when two NVA regiments entered the province. Heavy pressure was put on the district capitals of Duc Hue and Trang Bang districts, as well as on Bao Trai, indicating that the NVA might have planned to seize them. If so, they failed, but large portions of Hau Nghia were again contested. As described by the PSA, both sides were heavily engaged when the long-awaited cease-fire took place:

> The day of the cease-fire [28 January] was marked by continuous friendly artillery and mortar fire on all sides of the capital. By the last day of the month both sides seem to have settled down to a form of siege warfare. . . . The territorials were moving cautiously into enemy-occupied areas after intensive artillery and mortar barrages, while the enemy seemed to be digging in for a long stay and returning fire with mortars and recoilless rifles.[35]

A sad view of the situation in Hau Nghia comes from an account of a meeting held in May 1973. This meeting was hurriedly called by the ARVN commander of forces around Saigon in reaction to enemy buildups in Tay Ninh and Hau Nghia provinces. It was attended by the commander of the 25th ARVN Division, as well as the province chiefs from Long An, Tay Ninh, and Hau Nghia. The Hau Nghia province chief reported that, although the roads were open and the government had maintained a presence in every village, the people were openly selling rice and gasoline to the enemy for great profit. Furthermore, he was worried that the NVA would attack again with the intention of causing destruction and flight of the population to Front-controlled "shadow hamlets." Lastly, concern was expressed over the "seduction" by the Front of the young people of Hau Nghia province.

In short, after ten years of war, including five years of campaigning by the 25th Infantry Division, a sort of violent stalemate had been reached in Hau Nghia. Despite all of the blood spilled and treasure spent, the GVN could still not claim victory. The GVN held the villages and controlled the roads, but the Front apparatus was intact, and enemy main force units threatened attack from the safe areas and Cambodia. The population was open to "seduction." This description would have been equally applicable to Hau Nghia province in 1963.

The Last Act

Although "peace with honor" may have been a reality in Paris or the United States, the war in Vietnam continued without pause until 1975. The Paris Accords did, however, lead to the final departure of all American personnel from Hau Nghia province. Most of the huge colony of journalists also left Saigon. Consequently, there were few American witnesses to the course of events in Hau Nghia province after 1973. In 1974, while on a diplomatic assignment, Stuart Herrington made a quick trip to Bao Trai and found out that he was the first American to have been there in over a year. Consequently, it is not possible to follow in any detail the history of the war in Hau Nghia province after May 1973. The outlines, however, are sufficiently clear.[36]

At the time of the cease-fire, both sides were near exhaustion. In the short run, this aided Thieu greatly. Logistics were traditionally the weakest part of the Party's war effort, and Front and PAVN units were at the end of a long supply line that had run dry and would take months to be restored. The United States, on the other hand, had frantically worked to build up ARVN's stockpiles. No wonder the Party wanted a genuine cease-fire to serve as a temporary expedient. As it was, Thieu pushed his short-term advantage and tried to extend GVN control back into as many areas as possible that had been lost during 1972 and, in some places, to extend it even further. The GVN's many successes in this campaign emboldened him to pursue his policy of the "Four Nos": no territory surrendered, no coalition government, no neutralist political activity, and no negotiation with the Party. In addition, Thieu, like Westmoreland earlier, always worried that the Front would strive to take Tay Ninh city and use it as a capital for the Provisional Revolutionary Government (PRG). Consequently, the GVN concentrated very strong forces in and around Hau Nghia province.

The temporary military superiority held by the GVN blinded many people to the actual situation: Saigon's position was completely hopeless. The 1972 offensive had been a great and decisive victory for the DRV, and the post-cease-fire period was a lopsided endgame. The GVN had lost most of the Central Highlands and never regained them. Dubbed the "Third Vietnam" by journalists, the huge expanses of mountains and jungles controlled by the Party's forces served as the ultimate liberated zone. Thieu continued to garrison the area's cities, putting a sizable portion of ARVN in an untenable position once PAVN was resupplied. Hue was likewise nearly under siege. All this had been gained by Hanoi despite a withering U.S. air and artillery offensive and brilliant tactical leadership by the American military advisors who, in fact, commanded ARVN. It was only a matter of time before PAVN struck again, this time starting from a much stronger position—better supplied, better trained in the use of heavy weapons, and with no possibility of American intervention on the scale that took place in 1972. Once they had regained their composure after the Christmas bombings and the violent land campaign of late 1972, the Party leadership realized all of this. Strategic disputes continued, but they were phrased in an increasingly confident manner and dealt with the best way to finish off an already defeated foe.[37]

Starting with the 1973–1974 dry season, Hanoi did not miss a step.[38] Most of PAVN continued to reequip, and much effort was spent creating a series of all-weather roads down the Ho Chi Minh Trail and deep into South Vietnam. One terminus was in northern Trang Bang district; therefore, by 1975, it would have been possible to drive from Hanoi to Hau Nghia. PAVN and what was left of Front forces struck hard in a series of "strategic raids" around Saigon, Hue, and Danang. Many GVN outposts were overrun, and old strategic safe zones near Saigon lost after Tet 1968 were reclaimed by the Party's forces. In the Mekong Delta, for once the real locus of Hanoi's attention, the Front launched a furious assault on the pacification program and, in many areas, destroyed four years of "progress" in a few weeks. General Tra claimed that the Mekong Delta offensive brought the Front back to the position it had in Vietnam's ricebowl before 1968.[39] Attacked from every quarter, ARVN was forced to disperse even more than before.

Fortunately for the people of Hau Nghia province, they were temporarily spared from the latest round of violence. There had been several large conventional engagements in northern Trang Bang and Cu Chi, with ARVN and the Hau Nghia Regional Forces often performing well, but no attacks on the province itself. In May 1974, ARVN used Hau Nghia as the base for a large foray into Cambodia, the last GVN military offensive of the war. With the fighting taking place in Cambodia, the respite in Hau Nghia continued.

However, nothing could shield the GVN from the growing economic and social debacle that was under way. Leaders of the religious minorities, Catholics included, turned on Thieu. Inflation, an aftershock of the calamitous policies of OPEC (Organization of Petroleum Exporting Countries), ravaged the agricultural sector. ARVN units were going without pay. Corruption became frenzied. And to make matters worse, the United States was embroiled with Watergate.

In the fall, the slide began. General Tra's men started a steady advance in Tay Ninh province. Just to the north, they conducted a brilliant operation and captured Phuoc Long province, the first province to fall permanently during the entire war. As PAVN shattered ARVN in the Central Highlands, Tra pulled several battalions out of Ba Thu and had them move up to the west bank of the Vam Co Dong and prepare for a crossing near Hiep Hoa. By March of 1975, Front and PAVN forces were ready to attack Hau Nghia. Tra held his forces back, however, until other units could be prepared for an all-out attack on Saigon from the south, west, and northeast to coordinate with the PAVN juggernaut rushing down the coast. On April 29, a massive assault began across the Vam Co Dong, which included tanks and hundreds of vehicles. Fortunately for all concerned, ARVN abandoned the province without a fight and Hau Nghia was occupied within hours. The next day, PAVN tanks captured the Presidential Palace in Saigon and ended the war. Ironically, Hau Nghia province, long a Front stronghold, was one of the last areas where the flag of the Republic of Vietnam flew.

12

Reflections on the War

Although war continues in Southeast Asia at the time of this writing, the American role in it ended in 1975. Not surprisingly, given the magnitude of our defeat, participants in the war and a large number of scholars have come forward—and will continue to do so—with various views of the catastrophe. Because the issues raised are both painful and recent, nothing like a consensus is possible. In addition, many issues pertaining to the American conduct of the war are difficult to approach for solid data is not yet available. The fine volumes currently being produced by the Center for Military History will undoubtedly help future research by creating a basic, detailed, and reliable narrative framework. From the Vietnamese side, there is even more to be learned. Unfortunately, unless the political situation changes fundamentally, any history coming from Vietnam will have to be treated with great caution. The Republic of Vietnam, so difficult to understand while it existed, remains an analytical enigma and badly needs a historian. Nevertheless, for Americans the war is over, the outcome clear, and some start has to be made to analyze the greatest debacle in our history since the American Civil War.

A large number of interesting books and articles have appeared since 1975 concerning the American conduct of the Vietnam War. Some of the authors are former participants in the struggle; others are historians, political scientists, and journalists. Many of the authors argue that a different strategy or method of operation in Vietnam might have led to success. People holding this view do not necessarily believe that success would have been worth the cost, but many do. In general, those believing that the United States lost a war that it could have won fall into three groups.

A first group consists of former policymakers or their apologists, including Richard Nixon, Henry Kissinger, and General Westmoreland.[1] They argue that, even though leaders (never themselves of course) made some strategic mistakes and accepted unwise political constraints, the American effort had been largely successful by 1973. The Front was crushed, and the NVA was contained. The real failure, these men maintain, took place when Congress, stampeded by a shallow and uninformed press and a woefully misguided antiwar movement, abandoned a sovereign ally well on the way to victory.

The betrayal resulted from an evil brew of domestic politics, war weariness, and the Watergate scandal. It is further argued that, had Nixon remained in power and had Congress not been so perfidious, a stronger South Vietnam, potentially aided by American air power, would have either deterred attack in 1975 or defeated one if it came. The fact that the NVA fought the final battle singlehandedly is offered as evidence that the United States had been victorious against the Front. These individuals prove their contention that the South could have prevailed by focusing on NVA defeats during the Easter Offensive of 1972.

A second group exemplifies a near-consensus in the American military today.[2] Most notably represented by Harry Summers, these people maintain that once the decision to use force is made (a political decision to be sure) it should be applied quickly and decisively. Pure firepower, sophisticated weaponry, and tactical refinement must never substitute for strategy. Force should never be employed unless the political will exists to support it. Vietnam is cited as a perfect example of how not to fight a war. According to this argument, the political constraints placed on the joint chiefs by President Johnson and other civilians forced General Westmoreland into a "no-win" strategy of attrition. Johnson's decision to raise the level of violence in small increments was a naive, academic, and politically cowardly response. It also allowed the enemy to dictate the tempo of the war. Many officers holding this view are quick to grant that it may have been a mistake to get involved in Vietnam in the first place. However, they contend that, once the decision to intervene was made, a rational conduct of the war would have included a mobilization of the reserves, a declaration of war, unrestricted bombing of the North, a naval blockade of North Vietnam, and a ground campaign aggressive enough to cut the Ho Chi Minh Trail and eject PAVN from South Vietnam. An ideal campaign would have involved ground operations in Cambodia, Laos and across the DMZ into North Vietnam. These measures, so this argument goes, should have been implemented as quickly as possible, and this relentless pressure should have stopped only when Hanoi agreed to a genuine, rather than a cosmetic, peace agreement.

A third argument is more popular with many academics and former participants in the village war. William Colby, Robert Komer, Guenter Lewy, and Andrew Krepinevich take this position.[3] This group contends that U.S. policymakers did not understand the "political" nature of the Vietnam War and thus allowed General Westmoreland to follow a futile strategy of attrition. Consequently, Americans neglected the key political and social issues, such as rural poverty, corruption, and administrative inefficiency, that fueled the insurgency. To compound the difficulty, these men maintain, MACV created a top-heavy, overly complicated, and unwieldy ARVN in the mirror image of the U.S. Army. Both American forces and their ARVN progeny misused military force by an unnecessary reliance on firepower, which brought politically counterproductive violence in civilian areas. Forces were also poorly deployed to fight the critical "other war." The insurgency was in the hamlets, not in the hinterlands, it is argued; therefore, the bulk of

American forces should have been deployed to reflect this reality. Instead of wasting resources on the "big battalion" war, MACV should have concentrated on rebuilding GVN forces and gaining security for the rural population. Furthermore, these men echo the stand of John Vann, arguing that the United States could have forced the GVN to "harness the revolution" through sweeping reform. According to this argument, a more sophisticated political strategy could have been created that would have appealed to non-Communist elements within the Front and led to the isolation of the Party.

Advocates of the third group share some common assumptions concerning the insurgency. First of all, they assume that control of the countryside by either player was thin: Most Vietnamese peasants, even in Front areas, were, in truth, neutral. Second, they argue that the problems facing the GVN stemmed from a governmental apparatus that was not responsive to the desires of the rural population—a major problem, no doubt, but one that Americans could have remedied by increasing aid and, more importantly, demanding reform. However, the Party's defects, the argument proceeds, were structural and beyond change. Party control was based on cynical propaganda, coercion, and terror. These analysts assume that communism per se was a bad thing for Vietnam, Asia, and the United States. The allies could have countered propaganda with reform, good deeds, and good example, and the Americans and the GVN could have broken the cycle of terror and coercion through proper force deployments and by giving the peasantry the military means to help protect themselves. In other words, if U.S. assistance had provided a credible promise of security and a better life, the people would have turned on their real enemy. The remaining "hard-core" remnant of dedicated Party members then could have been hunted down. Lastly, implicit in this argument is the contention that a more appropriate policy in the countryside, including a redeployment of ground forces to heavily populated areas and a general increase of resources allocated to the pacification campaign, would have led to a less violent war, allowing American participation to continue long enough to obtain victory over the Front. A revitalized GVN, supported by its own people, would then have been strong enough, with continued U.S. aid, to prevail over the long haul. Such arguments should sound familiar by now for they were the "party line" at CORDS.

Hau Nghia province was quite a small political entity, more likely to be of interest to an anthropologist than to a military historian. Yet, the sad history of Hau Nghia illustrates very well the enormous problems facing Americans as they attempted to do battle, physically and psychologically, with a powerful and determined enemy. Both sides, even if sometimes mistaken in strategy or tactics, used all their possible energy to prevail in this strategically important place. Furthermore, although the course of the war differed to some degree from province to province, Hau Nghia had certain characteristics that make possible some important generalizations concerning the wider war in Vietnam. It was quite typical of the entire upper Mekong Delta, the heartland of the insurgency, in terms of ethnic makeup, social structure, and economic base. Densely populated, ethnically Vietnamese, and primarily agricultural, it was exactly the type of province within which the Americans and the GVN had to prevail, within a reasonable amount of time, in order to be victorious. Ultimately, of course, despite an extraordinary military and political effort, victory eluded the allies. And regrettably, the factors that led to failure in Hau Nghia province cast serious doubt on each of the three arguments summarized above that suggest an alternative conduct of war would have led to the continued independence of a non-Communist South Vietnam.

One central conclusion, made clear by the war in Hau Nghia province, bears directly on each of the assertions that a change in policy would have led to success: The Party's analysis of the situation in rural Vietnam in 1965 was correct and ours was wrong. Recall for a moment that Party cadres believed that the GVN never had nor ever could obtain legitimacy because of structural factors that could not be changed. The Party viewed the inefficiency and wholesale corruption that characterized the GVN at every level as the inevitable result of social contradictions. An urban, Westernized, and largely Catholic elite, the Party maintained, could never create a just society—or one viewed as just by the peasantry—in a poor, rural Asian country. The Party argued, with considerable justification, that Diem and his successors had kept intact the French colonial apparatus, with the Americans assuming the role of protector.

It does not require a Marxist analysis to confirm these assumptions, and a goodly number of Americans, such as John Vann, agreed with most of them. Where Vann and others parted company with the Party was on their belief that the GVN, if pressured sufficiently by the Americans, could have reformed and revitalized itself and attracted non-Communist progressives away from the Front. Such prospects did not worry Party cadres, believing as they did that revolution—a fundamental redistribution of wealth and power—was sought by enough of the peasantry to neutralize any reform efforts by the GVN. In addition, if any reform was identified with the Americans, this could only justify the Party's contention that the GVN was a "puppet" of the foreigners and add fuel to the most widely heralded and supported goal of the Front—expulsion of the United States from Vietnam.

So, it did not really matter whether or not the Front had the support of a majority of the peasantry. It is very possible that Vann and others were right when they claimed that most peasants did not care who ruled in Saigon and just wanted to be left alone. The Party had what it needed, the support of the most politically aware and most determined segment of the peasantry. There can be no doubt that, in Hau Nghia and several other provinces, the Front had a virtual lock on the "best and brightest" of the rural youth. The revolutionary movement that had demolished the GVN in Hau Nghia by 1965, although controlled from the outside, was locally recruited and self-sustaining. To be sure, as charged by the Americans, the Front was ruthless in its tactics, unquestionably more so than the GVN. Yet, no revolutionary movement has ever succeeded on terrorism alone.

Enough people in Hau Nghia accepted the ideas of the Front to provide the social and political base for a legitimate government. The situation facing the GVN in Hau Nghia at the time of U.S. intervention was just the opposite—the only support it could find came from a few Catholic hamlets and ARVN artillery. This is not to argue that the Front was more virtuous than the GVN; it was, however, much stronger. These were facts of life in Hau Nghia and several other provinces, and they would have faced the Americans regardless of what course of action was adopted.

Three consequences followed from the fact that the Front and not the GVN possessed legitimacy in much of rural Vietnam. In the first place by 1965 (and probably much earlier), the Front had gained moral ascendancy over the GVN. Once again, this is not to argue that, in absolute terms, the Front was morally superior to the GVN. At present, Vietnam is a sad, oppressed, and destitute country. No doubt, many people in rural Vietnam deeply regret the outcome of the war. However, while the war was on, as confirmed by scores of reports and interrogations received by the Americans at Hau Nghia in every phase of the conflict, peasants perceived the followers of the Front as honest, efficient, and genuinely concerned about the people's welfare. They perceived GVN officials, on the other hand, as aloof and corrupt. The dedication and courage of enemy fighting men, compared with the listless performance that characterized most GVN forces, was widely acknowledged and admired by U.S. troops. No matter how hard and terrifying the war was for American or South Vietnamese soldiers, fighters for the Front led an absolutely hellish existence. They lived in holes, regularly faced hunger and disease, were subjected to air strikes, napalm and artillery bombardment, and lacked decent medical care. Whatever the actual validity of the "body count" figures, there can be no doubt that joining the Front was the most dangerous choice by far that could have been made by young people in Vietnam. Yet, enough Front cadres remained totally convinced that they would prevail to keep the general population's perceptions concerning the outcome of the war very much in doubt. Put another way, the GVN, even with massive American support, could never create the essential foundation for strong and resilient morale—the perception that it could win. The collapse in 1975 is very intelligible in this light.

From this situation follows the second consequence of the lack of legitimacy that faced the GVN: A genuine revival of government support or an actual change in allegiance on the part of the rural population could not have taken place while the war was in progress. As we have seen, any progress the GVN achieved in the countryside was due to measures that weakened the Front, chiefly through military attrition. All efforts to change the fundamental attitudes of the people of Hau Nghia toward the GVN failed, if American records are accurate. An undetermined but substantial number of peasants always either supported the Front or were sympathetic toward it. An even larger number of people were in doubt over the eventual outcome of the struggle, an attitude that encouraged neutrality. To be sure, the GVN did have its supporters in Hau Nghia and many more elsewhere. There were good commanders, good soldiers, good officials, and even a few good policemen—but never enough of them. Recall that the Hau Nghia Popular Forces, the units most responsible for hamlet security, were next to worthless, a very good indication that a great many people felt little reason to take major risks to protect the state. In this regard, Americans usually missed the point. When they constructed a political equation for Vietnam, it always resembled a hypothetical public opinion poll that asked whether most people in South Vietnam supported the GVN or the Front. The question they should have asked was which side were more people willing to die for. Had they asked the second question, they would not have liked the answer.

Last, if it is correct to assume that no real possibility existed to change the political allegiance of the rural population to one of genuine support of the GVN, it must follow that the only way for the GVN and the Americans to have prevailed was to have crushed the Front militarily. As has been seen, this very nearly occurred. Indeed, had South Vietnam been an island, the GVN undoubtedly would have survived. But South Vietnam, of course, was not an island. Consequently, considering the geography and terrain of Vietnam and the great strength of the Front in much of the country by 1965 (especially in provinces like Hau Nghia), crushing the Front inevitably would have been a very time-consuming process, regardless of the means chosen to do so.

More specific conclusions drawn from Hau Nghia also bear on the matter of alternative strategies. In the first place, Nixon and Westmoreland are wrong to maintain that Congress sabotaged a basically successful war effort after 1973. On the contrary, if the situation in Hau Nghia province at the time of the cease-fire is any guide, the GVN was in a nearly hopeless situation. Although the insurgency in Hau Nghia and throughout Vietnam had been seriously weakened by 1973, it was still intact, and, as we have seen, the Front had halted its downward spiral. At the time of the 1975 NVA offensive, Americans estimated that about 40,000 guerrillas were active in South Vietnam. Some, but not all, were northerners. During the Easter Offensive in 1972, it will be recalled, local force units in Hau Nghia were greatly strengthened due to desertions from territorial units and the PSDF. Furthermore, during that offensive, the NVA, with some Front aid, had seized a third of the country, mostly in the Central Highlands. Called Third Vietnam, this area was sparsely populated and contained less than 10 percent of the population. However, hamlets in this area, including some in Hau Nghia, were fully mobilized for revolutionary warfare. The continued existence of the insurgency had serious consequences for the GVN. As long as the Front existed, the spell of fear and possible doom continued to blanket the countryside. Weariness generated by years of unending war threatened to bring exhaustion and psychological collapse at any moment. Equally important, the bulk of the military manpower available to the GVN was tied down by the insurgency until the very end. In January 1975, there were nearly 500,000 men in the RF/PF, mostly involved with the pacification campaign. In addition, fifteen ARVN regiments were deployed in the Mekong

Delta, far from areas of strategic importance. The drain on the South Vietnamese finances from such a military establishment was severe, and, by 1975, the economy had started to collapse and the political system disintegrate.

Also, the strategic situation was positively dreadful from the point of view of the GVN even before 1975, particularly in the Central Highlands. Although the 1972 fighting is sometimes portrayed as an ARVN victory, the reality was more complex and far less favorable. Despite the recapture of Quang Tri in September 1972 (ARVN's last success), the GVN, even with the help of American air power, was unable to regain most of the territory lost. In 1974 the NVA was victorious in a series of middle-sized battles. It was just such a series of encounters that led to the loss of Phuoc Long province in northwestern III CTZ during January 1975. It is difficult to believe that, had he still been in power, President Nixon would have chosen to reopen hostilities to counter gradual aggression. Even if he had done so, massive air support of the type employed in 1972 would have taken some time to deliver because many of the air assets were no longer in Asia. In addition, the NVA had studied its defeats during 1972 and had instituted several tactical refinements. So, whereas the threat of U.S. air power might have deterred a massive attack in 1975, the North could have responded by finding the threshold at which the Americans would intervene and then exerting pressure just below it. Above all, most ARVN units could match PAVN only through greatly superior firepower. Fighting in Hau Nghia showed that, at every level and despite numerous tactical blunders, PAVN and Front military forces were superior to their GVN counterparts in morale and determination. They were, after all, ultimately able to defeat a sizable army without any friendly air support whatsoever, an impressive military achievement. Unfortunately for the GVN, by 1975, the NVA for the first time had reached at least parity in most fields of land weaponry. There is nothing the United States could have done to prevent the DRV from strengthening its armed forces. Furthermore, it is difficult to believe that a few extra billions of dollars in military aid for the GVN would have made a fundamental difference. Consequently, particularly considering the total and wretched nature of the rout during 1975, more U.S. aid and even the reintroduction of American air power could have, at most, delayed the collapse.

The U.S. military's claim that a rapid and decisive use of force would have led to victory is more plausible, but it, too, has difficulties. As the experience in Hau Nghia province made very clear, the Front was highly dependent upon aid from the DRV once it decided to emphasize main force operations after 1964. Supplies from the DRV, particularly in the field of heavier armament, were required if the Front were to finish off ARVN. They were even more necessary if the Front main force units had any hopes of engaging American units in pitched battle. The sanctuaries in Cambodia offered an excellent place to rest and prepare units. They also frustrated, to a large degree, American efforts in 1966–1967 to trap large enemy units.

As we have seen, the temporary loss of the sanctuaries, along with the permanent loss of the Sihanoukville supply line, injured the Front in Hau Nghia quite seriously. Furthermore, there is little doubt that the U.S. Army had the capabilities, especially if reinforced, to have cut the Ho Chi Minh Trail, neutralized the sanctuaries, and isolated Front forces from outside aid.

If the DRV would have been sufficiently frightened by more vigorous bombing, such actions might possibly have led the North to end direct aid to the insurgency and withdraw PAVN. It does not necessarily follow, however, that the North could have or would have tried to end hostilities in South Vietnam. The Front was nominally independent. Had necessity demanded, its political apparatus could have operated without guidance or assistance. It is inconceivable that the Front would have laid down its arms without a fight and yielded the huge portion of rural Vietnam, including Hau Nghia province, that it controlled and administered by 1965. Had the Front chosen to fight on alone, it would have faced serious problems. American units could have operated at squad and company levels at a much earlier date than they, in fact, felt safe to do so, and large offensives would not have been possible. This last point, however, might have been a blessing in disguise for the Front. Had the insurgency been forced to stand on the defensive, the manpower and cadres squandered during the two Tet Offensives would have been saved. It is possible, although not at all certain, that a massive show of force by the Americans might have shaken the conviction held by Front followers that victory was inevitable. However, no increase of military effort against the North in 1965–1966 would have altered the weakness of the GVN in the countryside. The U.S. military still would have had to assist GVN forces in an interminable pacification campaign. Above all, it would have been very difficult to counter a decision by the Front to lower the level of the war, conserve strength, and wait out the Americans no matter how long it took.

Had the United States chosen to go all-out militarily, more serious difficulties would have faced Washington if the DRV had chosen to fight. This would have been a very likely decision (unless vetoed by both Peking and Moscow), particularly if American forces had invaded the North above the DMZ, as urged by the joint chiefs. A land campaign in any part of North Vietnam would have presented daunting problems to the United States. North Vietnamese villages, to varying degrees, were all organized for a "people's war." Front-controlled villages and hamlets in Hau Nghia province were painful and frustrating to deal with for American forces, even with indigenous assistance from the South Vietnamese. In the North, Americans would have faced alone the tactical nightmares created by guerrilla warfare.

Americans would have faced a more serious problem in the strategic realm. The only way U.S. forces could have forced the NVA into a set-piece battle would have been to threaten geographic objectives absolutely vital to the DRV. Yet, not even the most ambitious contingency plans advocated an all-out invasion of the DRV. Consequently, PAVN divisions, unless they chose to fight to the end for the Ho Chi Minh Trail itself, would have been free to withdraw. As fighting in Hau Nghia province showed time and again, enemy units could be bombed, shelled, and bludgeoned but almost never trapped. Therefore, at some point, both sides would have formed a line, creating a situation similar to that in Korea during 1952–1953. Had such a situation developed, American forces would have faced a war of attrition with a much higher level of casualties than actually were endured. As soon as U.S. divisions stood in place, the tactical initiative would have passed to the NVA. The enemy would not have been compelled to either destroy American forces or seize territorial objectives. Rather, they would have concentrated on killing Americans with selective assaults, sapper attacks, and artillery bombardment. Recall that, except for 1969, the marines facing PAVN near the DMZ suffered the highest level of American casualties by a wide margin. (Interestingly, the dubious distinction of the "bloodiest" province in Vietnam during 1969 fell to Tay Ninh, which was the scene of vicious fighting between the army and the NVA. As we have seen, it was a very violent year for the 25th Division, which operated there along with other units.)

Of course, NVA losses would have been very painful and perhaps might have led to an acceptable settlement. On the other hand, grim tenacity marked every phase of the enemy's war effort. And North Vietnam would not have lacked moral support from the outside world. As it was, except for some very good clients like South Korea, America's closest friends refused to strongly support the war; the Canadian government even provided sanctuary to young men evading the draft. An all-out "aggressive" war against the DRV would have caused the United States to be treated like an international leper. In addition, it is reasonable to conjecture that a massive American military effort, which would have required higher draft calls, the cancellation of student draft deferments, and mobilization of reserves, could not have been made unless accompanied by political efforts within the United States to justify the action as absolutely vital to national security. In the resulting atmosphere, it would have been extremely difficult for American forces to sit behind a human Maginot Line in the Vietnamese and Laotian jungle, regardless of tactical wisdom. On the contrary, great pressure would have existed to push on ever deeper into North Vietnam in an attempt to break the enemy's will as quickly as possible. Had the United States yielded to this pressure, a very explosive situation would have developed, including the very real possibility of Chinese intervention that, in turn, could have led to general war. Consequently, although a much more vigorous military effort as early as possible would have offered some prospects for eventual success, we must conclude that these prospects were not bright and may well have entailed a debacle far greater than the one suffered.

The American experience in Hau Nghia province also illustrates why a different approach toward fighting the "village war" or the "people's war" would probably not have led to a successful conclusion. If anything, the case that the United States needlessly lost the war in the countryside is more difficult to support than the one that advocated increased military activity as the path to victory. Indeed, the "other war" argument is based upon a major historical distortion and fundamentally wrong assumptions on the nature of U.S. forces available and the nature of revolutionary war in Vietnam.

In the first place, it is often claimed that American leaders, particularly in the military, did not understand the need for a vigorous pacification campaign and were interested only in big battles leading to higher "body counts." This was never true in either practice or theory. As we have seen, the pacification campaign was theoretically crucial for the success of West-moreland's strategy. And the whole rationale for fighting Front main force and NVA units in their base areas was to provide a "shield" behind which the GVN could rebuild its forces, which had been nearly shattered in 1965, and to allow it to reestablish a basic presence in the countryside. Although it is true that Westmoreland and others underestimated the difficulties involved and ordered some operations, such as CEDAR FALLS, that probably were not worth the effort, the enemy was hurt, ARVN was saved, and the GVN was able to reenter large areas of rural Vietnam.

American arms temporarily rescued the GVN in 1965, but our intervention coincided with a massive intervention on the part of the NVA at a rate initially faster than the U.S. buildup. Immediate operations against the guerrillas in the countryside throughout Vietnam either would have required a far greater number of American troops than anyone envisioned (a number that would have taken a long time to build up anyway) or it would have required spreading American resources very thin—a strategy that MACV, given enemy main force strength, considered much too risky. With the number of serious moments faced by the 25th Division, such as the attack on Company A in April 1966, caution was most understandable. MACV also realized the disastrous propaganda implications of even a small-scale American Dien Bien Phu, further intensifying Westmoreland's desire to operate in strength. It is also necessary to consider that some of the safe zones that were the targets of the "big-unit war" were in direct proximity to heavily populated areas and crucial allied bases. We shall never know how the enemy would have reacted had the big battles not been fought, but it is reasonable to assume that they would have found targets of opportunity. The Party's great strength gave it a large number of options.

Furthermore, even Westmoreland, archvillain in the eyes of the "other warriors," authorized a large number of pacification operations by American units from the very beginning of the war. There was probably not a single month during their entire stay in Hau Nghia that some 25th Division units were not engaged directly in support of the pacification campaign. During the rainy seasons of both 1966 and 1967, such operations were the major effort of the entire division, and, after Tet of 1968, the 25th participated in a furious pacification campaign in Hau Nghia province. To a certain degree, this occurred with every American division. Therefore, it is not true that MACV did not realize the importance of pacification or failed to give it considerable support.

Nor was there ever a shortage of counterinsurgency theory within the U.S. military. Although most officers were trained to fight a large-scale conventional war, scores of others, in tandem with many civilian analysts, had long experience in the various Vietnamese pacification programs before American intervention. These men were well briefed on counterinsurgency theories developed by other countries over the years, which, despite a few differences, were essentially the same: It is no coincidence that a history of the pacification campaign in Hau Nghia province must read the way a broken record sounds. This fact was not at all due to conceptual difficulties for the techniques to defeat an insurgency have been demonstrated time and again in this century alone. The concept of operations in an insurgency was and always has been completely secondary to the balance of forces.

Some people have argued that the formation of CORDS was a major advance and should have been done much sooner. No doubt, CORDS did provide a more rational organizational framework and helped somewhat. Yet, at what point a more efficient arrangement would have made any real difference is not clear. Even the most perfect organizational chart would have been irrelevant in the period of 1965–1966: The GVN had precious little territory to pacify. Indeed, CORDS was formed in May 1967, but the pacification campaign in difficult areas, such as Hau Nghia province, did not begin to show signs of significant progress until 1969. Therefore, we must conclude that the pacification campaign's uneven but undeniable progress in weakening the Front did not result not from any major change in operations but reflected a change in the balance of forces. As countless interrogations showed, the combination of American military pressure and the psychological and physical losses suffered by the Front during their offensives of 1968 and 1969 crippled the insurgency and allowed the GVN to extend its physical control over areas where its presence had been very tenuous, as in Hau Nghia. The main force defeats of this period also allowed U.S. troops to disperse more freely and concentrate their attention on the village war to an unprecedented degree. The weakening of the Front and the extension of GVN control allowed the creation of a much larger militia that, through the presence of a few good units, kept up the attrition. Unfortunately for the alies, weakening the Front absolutely required a long and bloody campaign, and it is difficult to see how it could have been quickened substantially.

It is also very difficult to see how a greatly different mode of operation on the part of American ground forces could have been implemented in practice, considering the realities of the battlefield in Vietnam. Advocates of the "village war," during hostilities and since, were very critical of the use of U.S. and ARVN firepower, contending that it was both wasteful and counterproductive politically. No doubt, this argument has some merit. Certainly, harassing fire by American artillery was used excessively and quite wastefully. Nevertheless, the issue of what one Hau Nghia senior advisor called the "too little-too much violence dilemma" was much more complicated. Critics maintained that American forces should have employed more discriminating small-unit tactics during combat in populated areas. Theoretically, perhaps, they were right. However, the fact remains that a casualty-conscious, conscript force like the U.S. Army in Vietnam was bound to use the maximum amount of force within reason. In Vietnam, as in any other war, it was true that "fire kills," and it would have been disastrous for American morale to have asked "grunts in the grass" to use ground assaults when more effective means were available to deal with the enemy. As it was, the unique frustrations of combat in Vietnam helped lead to the greatest psychological crisis ever faced by the U.S. Army, a trauma that took years to recover from. Guenter Lewy quotes an American officer as having said, "I'll be damned if I permit the United States Army, its institutions, its doctrine, and its traditions to be destroyed just to win this war."[4] Professor Lewy used this quote as an example of the mental attitude that prevented a more rational conduct of the war. In reality, however, this officer's remark is one of the most perceptive to come from the war. The morale, cohesion, combat skill, and integrity of the U.S. armed forces were indeed more important than whatever we were fighting for in Vietnam. The sad fact remains that a theoretically perfect conduct of the village war would have required a U.S. Army in which every officer was like General Weyand, every advisor like John Vann, and every trooper like one of sensitive young volunteers helping with MEDCAPs. That the army was something else should surprise no one.

Many "other warriors" have criticized the United States for not insisting on American command of all forces, as was done in Korea. Although such an arrangement was never wanted by either the GVN or MACV, it probably could have been obtained. Nevertheless, it is difficult to see the decisive benefit of such an arrangement. In Korea, American command meant operational control. For whatever reason, a stronger will to resist was present on the part of the Koreans than the Vietnamese, and the enemy of that earlier war lacked the determination and skill of the Front and the DRV. The few operations where ARVN units were directly under American command, such as Operation FAIRFAX, were not very successful. In such cases, the Vietnamese often left everything to the Americans. In addition, U.S. command would have given even greater force to the "puppet GVN" propaganda line used by the Front. Various "encadrement" proposals were put forward that would have utilized combined American-Vietnamese units, even on the hamlet level, and some were tried on a limited basis. Some officers in the marines claimed such an arrangement met with a degree of success in the northern provinces. Even if true, large-scale use of such a plan would have put great strain on the limited number of interpreters and, more to the point, American volunteers at the enlisted level who did not dislike or hate the Vietnamese. Above all, American command or encadrement would have implied a permanent American presence. The French could employ such methods because they wanted to stay indefinitely. The Americans did not, and opponents of such arrangements argued quite convincingly that this approach would delay the day that Vietnamese forces could fend for themselves. As it was, U.S. units, including the 25th Division in Hau Nghia, spent abundant time training, supporting, and fighting with South Vietnamese units of all types.

Above all, those arguing that a more concentrated effort on the hamlet and village level would have brought success are in error because they implicitly assume that South Vietnamese society was as malleable as clay. As shown over and over again during the war in Hau Nghia province, the best that the GVN could do was attempt to crush the Front. With the aid of U.S. forces, it very nearly succeeded. Yet, all American efforts, as best exemplified by the RD Cadre Program, failed to bring about a fundamental change in political attitudes in the rural population. The most difficult idea to accept for many Americans in Vietnam was that the GVN was inefficient and corrupt because it was inefficient and corrupt. It is no doubt true that many governments around the world are and have been far more corrupt and repressive than the GVN. It is even probable that many people serving the GVN genuinely believed that they had something of value to offer the people they governed. However, because of the accident of geography, the GVN was faced with an insurgency that could lay claim to a great victory over colonialism, that was extremely strong politically, and that was guided by a determined and powerful ally controlling every inch of land bordering the country. In such circumstances, despite intense effort and great dedication (not to mention the blood and treasure expended), any American hope of "harnessing the revolution" and making a weak society strong was doomed. All that remained was force, coercion, and violence, and, however successfully used, it was not enough.

So we come, at last, full circle. The value of the history of the war in a small place like Hau Nghia province lies in pointing out that the military and political situation facing the United States and the government of South Vietnam in the larger arena was intractable, given the realities existing in those nations and in the world. The United States did not fail in Vietnam because of tactical errors that were open to remedy. The errors made were on a much higher level. The American military seriously underestimated the difficulties involved in dealing with enemy forces. And the civilian leadership, particularly under Johnson, underestimated the strength and tenacity of the enemy and overestimated the willingness of its own people and soldiers to continue the struggle indefinitely. In short, American leaders, both civilian and military, committed a strategic blunder that has brought many a general to grief: They chose the wrong battlefield. Tragically, this error brought violent consequences that Americans must contemplate for a very long time, indeed.

Notes

Chapter 1

1. Good accounts of the Diem period can be found in Ronald H. Spector, *Advice and Support: The Early Years of the U.S. Army in Vietnam 1941–1960* (New York, 1985); R. B. Smith, *An International History of the Vietnam War: Revolution Versus Containment 1955–61* (New York, 1983); Jeffrey Race, *War Comes to Long An: Revolutionary Conflict in a Vietnamese Province* (Berkeley, Calif., 1972), pp. 1–141; Gabriel Kolko, *Anatomy of a War: Vietnam, The United States, and the Modern Historical Experience* (New York, 1985), Parts 1 and 2.

2. David Chanoff and Doan Van Toai, *Portrait of the Enemy* (New York, 1986), pp. 26–27.

3. Chester L. Cooper, et al., *The American Experience with Pacification in Vietnam: An Overview* (Contract Study, Institute for Defense Analysis, Arlington, Va., 1972), Vol. 3 (hereafter cited as Cooper, *American Experience with Pacification*), pp. 119–20; *The Pentagon Papers: The Defense Department History of United States Decision-making on Vietnam*, Senator Mike Gravel edition (Boston, 1971), Vol. 1, p. 255.

4. Ibid., pp. 32–39.

5. Phillip B. Davidson, *Vietnam at War: The History: 1946–1975* (Novato, Calif., 1988), pp. 256–59; Spector, *Advice and Support The Early Years*, pp. 311–13; Race *War Comes to Long An*, pp. 73–74.

6. Ibid., p. 21.

7. Gerald Cannon Hickey, *Village in Vietnam* (New Haven, Conn., 1964), p. 205.

8. Race, *War Comes to Long An*, p. 26.

9. *Pentagon Papers*, Vol. 2, pp. 306–8; Race, *War Comes to Long An*, pp. 24–26; Hickey, *Village in Vietnam*, pp. 204–5.

10. Robert L. Sansom, *The Economics of Insurgency in the Mekong Delta of Vietnam* (New York, 1970), p. 25, cited in Charles Stuart Callison, *Land-to-the-Tiller in the Mekong Delta: Economic, Social and Political Effects of Land Reform in Four Villages of South Vietnam* (Lanham, Md., 1983), p. 39.

11. Callison, *Land-to-the-Tiller in the Mekong Delta*, pp. 37–42; Race, *War Comes to Long An*, pp. 56–60; Spector, *Advice and Support: The Early Years*, pp. 308–10.

12. Callison, *Land-to-the-Tiller in the Mekong Delta*, pp. 48–51, 57; *Pentagon Papers*, Vol. 1, pp. 254–55.

13. Race, *War Comes to Long An*, pp. 56–62.

14. Chanoff and Toai, *Portrait of the Enemy*, pp. 42–43.

15. Ibid., pp. 84, 94–97.

16. Spector, *Advice and Support: The Early Years*, p. 312.

17. Ibid., p. 313.

18. Ibid., pp. 333–35; Race, *War Comes to Long An*, pp. 62–63.

19. Cooper, *American Experience with Pacification*, Vol. 3, p. 132.
20. Ibid., pp. 135–46; *Pentagon Papers*, Vol. 1, p. 256;
21. Race, *War Comes to Long An*, p. 100.
22. Ibid.
23. Ibid., p. 112.
24. *Pentagon Papers*, Vol. 1, p. 259; Smith, *An International History of the Vietnam War: Revolution Versus Containment*, pp. 165–66.
25. *Pentagon Papers*, Vol. 1, pp. 259, 336–38; Race, *War Comes to Long An*, pp. 38–39, 104–17.
26. *Pentagon Papers*, Vol. 1, p. 338; Spector, *Advice and Support: The Early Years*, pp. 337–39.
27. *Pentagon Papers*, Vol. 1, pp. 266–67.
28. Bernard Fall, *The Two Vietnams* (New York, 1967), pp. 106, 123.
29. William R. Corson, *The Betrayal* (New York, 1968), p. 41.
30. *Pentagon Papers*, Vol. 1, pp. 257, 268; Fall, *Two Vietnams*, p. 324; Spector, *Advice and Support: The Early Years*, passim.
31. William Colby and Peter Forbath, *Honorable Men: My Life in the CIA* (New York, 1978), pp. 160–62; Fall, *Two Vietnams*, pp. 324–26; Corson, *The Betrayal*, p. 41; Robert B. Asprey, *War in the Shadows: The Guerrilla in History* (Garden City, N.Y., 1975), Vol. 2, p. 845.
32. Fall, *Two Vietnams*, p. 326.
33. *Pentagon Papers*, Vol. 1, p. 306.
34. Cooper, *American Experience with Pacification*, pp. 151–52.
35. Race, *War Comes to Long An*, p. 62.
36. Ibid., pp. 122–23; Fall, *Two Vietnams*, pp. 360–365.
37. *Pentagon Papers*, Vol. 2, p. 134.
38. Ibid.
39. Ibid., p. 32; R. B. Smith, *An International History of the Vietnam War: The Kennedy Strategy* (New York, 1985), pp. 21–35, 55–77.
40. *Pentagon Papers*, Vol. 2, pp. 2, 34.
41. Ibid., p. 101.
42. Ibid.
43. Ibid., p. 100.
44. Ibid., p. 135.
45. Ibid., pp. 20–21.
46. Ibid., p. 20.
47. Ibid., pp. 20–21, 52–53.
48. Ibid., p. 120.
49. Ibid., pp. 120–26.
50. Colby and Forbath, *Honorable Men*, pp. 223–24.
51. *Pentagon Papers*, Vol. 2, pp. 137–43; Smith, *An International History of the Vietnam War: The Kennedy Strategy*, pp. 55–60.
52. Truong Nhu Tang, *A Vietcong Memoir: An Inside Account of the Vietnam War and Its Aftermath* (New York, 1985), pp. 46–47.
53. Ibid., pp. 149–59.
54. Fall, *Two Vietnams*, p. 376; Smith, *An International History of the Vietnam War: The Kennedy Strategy*, pp. 166–71.
55. *Pentagon Papers*, Vol. 2, pp. 153, 175.
56. Ibid., pp. 186–87.
57. Gen. Bruce Palmer, Jr., *The 25-Year War: America's Military Role in Vietnam* (New York, 1984), p. 12.

58. Interview, Thomas Mellen, Major General USA (Ret.), September 5, 1989.

59. Asprey, *War in the Shadows*, pp. 1007–8; Fall, *Two Vietnams*, p. 382.

60. Ibid., pp. 374–75; *Pentagon Papers*, Vol. 2, pp. 153–58; Race, *War Comes to Long An*, pp. 190–91.

61. Fall, *Two Vietnams*, pp. 381–82; *Pentagon Papers*, Vol. 2, pp. 154–56.

62. Bui Diem, with David Chanhoff, *In The Jaws Of History* (Boston, 1987), p. 88.

63. *Pentagon Papers*, Vol. 2, pp. 158, 273–74; Race, *War Comes to Long An*, p. 173.

64. *Pentagon Papers*, Vol. 2, pp. 277–78, 462–72.

65. Ibid., pp. 283, 316–19.

66. Ibid., p. 523.

67. Ibid.

68. Ibid., pp. 523–25.

69. Ibid., pp. 482, 527.

70. Gen. William C. Westmoreland, *A Soldier Reports* (Garden City, N.Y., 1976), p. 84.

71. *Pentagon Papers*, Vol. 2, pp. 524–25.

72. Ibid., pp. 472–74; Race, *War Comes to Long An*, p. 136.

Chapter 2

1. Letter to author from Col. James Bremer, 14 September 1989; John C. Donnell and Gerald C. Hickey, *The Vietnamese "Strategic Hamlets": A Preliminary Report*, Rand Corporation, August 1962.

2. *Hau Nghia Handbook*, Advisory Team #43, 1968, CMH Hau Nghia File; *Hau Nghia Factor Analysis*, Appendix to U.S. Department of the Army, Office of the Deputy Chief of Staff for Military Operations, *A Program for the Pacification and Long Term Development of South Vietnam*, 1966 (hereafter cited as PROVN).

3. R. Michael Pearce, *Evolution of a Vietnamese Village: Part 1—The Present After Eight Months of Pacification* (Contract Study, Rand Corporation, Santa Monica, Calif., 1965), p. 6 (hereafter cited as Pearce, *Vietnamese Village*); *Hau Nghia Factor Analysis* in PROVN.

4. *Hao Nghia Factor Analysis* in PROVN.

5. Tang, *A Vietcong Memoir*, p. 125; Spector, *Advice and Support: The Early Years*, p. 330.

6. Tang, *A Vietcong Memoir*, pp. 76, 168.

7. *Hau Nghia Factor Analysis* in PROVN; *Hau Nghia Handbook*, Advisory Team #43, 1970, CMH Hau Nghia File.

8. *Interview with Vietnam War Participant*, Ch-24, 10-9-66, Indochina Archive.

9. *Studies of the National Liberation Front of South Vietnam*, Rand Corporation, AG-316, AG xi, Indochina Archive.

10. *Interviews Concerning the National Liberation Front of South Vietnam*, Rand Corporation, File AG-517 (AG xxxiv), Indochina Archive; Douglas Pike, *Viet Cong: The Organization and Techniques of the National Liberation Front of South Vietnam* (Cambridge, Mass., 1966), p. 388.

11. *Interrogation Report from Duc Hue District Intelligence and Operations Coordinating Center*, 11 April 1971, CMH Hau Nghia File, pp. 1–4 (hereafter cited as Duc Hue DIOCC).

12. Donnell and Hickey, *The Vietnamese "Strategic Hamlets"*.

13. Gloria Emerson, *Winners and Losers: Battles, Retreats, Gains, Losses, and Ruins from the Vietnam War* (New York, 1985), pp. 285–86.

14. Letter to author from Gerald Hickey, 6 July 1989.

15. Pearce, *Vietnamese Village,* p. 5; Fall, *Two Vietnams,* p. 376; Chanoff and Toai, *Portrait of the Enemy,* p. 16.

16. *Studies of the National Liberation Front of South Vietnam,* Rand Corporation, AG-346, AG xiii, Indochina Archive.

17. *Hau Nghia Handbook,* Advisory Team #43, 1970, CMH Hau Nghia File.

18. Douglas Pike, *Viet Cong;* Race, *War Comes to Long An.*

19. Headquarters, II Field Force Vietnam, *Operational Report—Lessons Learned,* 1 May–31 July 1966, p. 29. (hereafter cited as II Field Force ORLL, followed by appropriate date).

20. Race, *War Comes to Long An,* pp. 28–29

21. Ibid., pp. 160–61.

22. Tang, *A Vietcong Memoir,* p. 64.

23. Callison, *Land-to-the-Tiller in the Mekong Delta,* pp. 57, 65.

24. Race, *War Comes to Long An,* p. 60.

25. Pike, *Viet Cong,* p. 276.

26. Kolko, *Anatomy of a War,* p. 126.

27. Hickey, *Village in Vietnam,* pp. 243–47.

28. *Studies of the National Liberation Front of South Vietnam,* Rand Corporation, File AG-373, AG xiii, Indochina Archive.

29. Callison, *Land-to-the-Tiller in the Mekong Delta,* pp. 52–55.

30. *Interviews Concerning the National Liberation Front of South Vietnam,* Rand Corporation, AG-517, AG xxxiv, Indochina Archive.

31. *Interview with Vietnam War Participant,* Simulmatics Corporation, 7/27–8/2, 1966, Indochina Archive; Callison, *Land-to-the-Tiller in the Mekong Delta,* n. 61, p. 52.

32. *Interview with Vietnam War Participant,* JUSPAO, 1-13-67; *Interviews Concerning the National Liberation Front of South Vietnam,* Rand Corporation, AG-517, AG xxxiv, Indochina Archive.

33. *Studies of the National Liberation Front of South Vietnam,* Rand Corporation, AG-346, AG xiii, Indochina Archive.

34. *Interview with Vietnam War Participant,* JUSPAO, 1-13-67, Indochina Archive.

35. *Interviews Concerning the National Liberation Front of South Vietnam,* Rand Corporation, AG-517, AG xxxiv, Indochina Archive.

36. *Studies of the National Liberation Front of South Vietnam,* Rand Corporation, AG-346, AG xiii, Indochina Archive.

37. *Interviews Concerning the National Liberation Front of South Vietnam,* Rand Corporation, AG-474, AG xxx, Indochina Archive.

38. Tran Van Tra, *Vietnam: History of the Bulwark B2 Theatre: Vol. 5: Concluding the 30-Years War* (Hanoi, 1982), p. 35, Southeast Asia Report No. 1247, Indochina Archive.

39. *Interviews Concerning the National Liberation Front of South Vietnam,* Rand Corporation, AG-517, AG xxxiv, Indochina Archive.

40. Ibid, p. 5.

41. *Studies of the National Liberation Front of South Vietnam,* Rand Corporation, AG-64, AG i, Indochina Archive.

42. Ibid.

43. Ibid.

44. *Interview with Vietnam War Participant,* Simulmatics Corporation, CH-5, 7/27–8/2, 1966, Indochina Archive.

45. *Interview with Vietnam War Participant,* Simulmatics Corporation, CH-24, 10-9-66, Indochina Archive.

46. Ibid.

47. Ibid, p. 5.

48. *Studies of the National Liberation Front of South Vietnam,* Rand Corporation, AG-346, AG XIII, Indochina Archive.

49. *Interview with Vietnam War Participant,* Simulmatics Corporation, CH-24, 10-9-66, Indochina Archive.

50. *Interview with Vietnam War Participant,* Simulmatics Corporation, CH-5, 7/27–8/2, 1966, Indochina Archive.

51. Ibid.

52. *Interview with Vietnam War Participant,* Senior Captain, North Vietnamese Army, JUSPAO Field Development Division, 2/7/68, Indochina Archive.

53. Michael B. Cook and Captain David Pabst, Reports and Evaluation Division, CORDS, *A Study of Pacification and Security in Cu Chi District, Hau Nghia Province,* 29 May 1968, CMH Hau Nghia File, p. 9 (hereafter cited as Cook and Pabst *Pacification in Cu Chi District*).

54. Ibid., p. 8.

55.*Studies of the National Liberation Front of South Vietnam,* Rand Corporation, AG-64, AG I, Indochina Archive.

56. *Interview with Vietnam War Participant,* Simulmatics Corporation, CH-5, 7/27–8/2, 1966, Indochina Archive.

57. Bui Diem, *In the Jaws of History,* pp. 109–10.

58. Pearce, *Vietnamese Village,* p. 19.

59. Ibid., pp. 18–19.

60. Ibid., p. 4.

61. *Hau Nghia Handbook,* Advisory Team #43, 1968, CMH Hau Nghia File.

62. Pearce, *Vietnamese Village,* p. v.

63. *Interview with Vietnam War Participant,* H-18, February 1966, Indochina Archive.

64. *Interview with Vietnam War Participant: Research on Defoliation and Crop Destruction Operations: Five Interviews from Cu Chi,* H-1, Indochina Archive.

65. *Studies of the National Liberation Front of South Vietnam,* Rand Corporation, AG-346, AG XIII, Indochina Archive.

66. *Studies of the National Liberation Front of South Vietnam,* Rand Corporation, AG-316, AG XI, Indochina Archive.

67. "Trang Bang," in *Army,* January 1976, p. 34.

68. Westmoreland, *A Soldier Reports,* p. 84. Jeffrey J. Clarke, *Advice and Support: The Final Years, 1965–1973* (Washington, D.C., 1988) p. 42.

69. Pearce, *Vietnamese Village,* p. III.

70. Ibid., pp. 14–16.

71. Ibid., pp. 30–31.

72. Ibid., p. 61.

73. Ibid., p. 26.

74. Ibid., pp. 33–37.

75. Ibid., pp. 53–54.

76. Ibid., pp. 9–10, 68–71.

77. Ibid., pp. 47–51, 59.

78. Ibid., pp. 41–44.

79. Ibid., pp. 46–48.

80. Race, *War Comes to Long An,* pp. 168–75.

81. *Hau Nghia Factor Analysis* in PROVN.

82. Pearce, *Vietnamese Village*, p. 2.
83. *Hau Nghia Handbook*, Advisory Team #43, 1970, CMH Hau Nghia File.
84. Palmer, *25-Year War*, p. 22.
85. Ibid.
86. Daniel Ellsberg, *Papers on the War* (New York, 1972), pp. 143–44.
87. Ibid., p. 148.
88. Ibid., p. 149.
89. Tang, *A Vietcong Memoir*, p. 88.
90. Ellsberg, *Papers on the War*, p. 153.
91. Ibid., p. 144.
92. Ibid., p. 155.
93. *Pentagon Papers*, Vol. 2, p. 576.
94. Ibid., pp. 576–80.
95. *Hau Nghia Factor Analysis* in PROVN.
96. Ibid.
97. Ibid.

Chapter 3

1. Guenter Lewy, *America in Vietnam* (New York, 1978), pp. 95, 102.
2. Ibid., pp. 302–3.
3. A. J. Bacevich *The Pentomic Era: The US Army Between Korea and Vietnam* (Washington, D.C., 1986), n. 26, pp. 167–68.
4. Ibid., p. 86.
5. *Pentagon Papers*, Vol. 3, pp. 394–97.
6. Westmoreland, *A Soldier Reports*, p. 126.
7. *Studies of the National Liberation Front of South Vietnam*, Rand Corporation, AG-373, AG xiii, Indochina Archive.
8. Headquarters, 173d Airborne Brigade (Separate), *Operation MARAUDER*, undated, CMH.
9. Ibid.
10. Ibid.
11. Ibid.
12. Ibid.
13. Headquarters, 173d Airborne Brigade (Separate), *Summary of Civil Affairs, Civic Action and Psychological Operations from 5 May 1965 through 20 January 1966*, 28 January 1966, CMH.
14. Ibid.
15. II Field Force ORLL, 1 May–31 July 1966, pp. 29–31; Hung P. Nguyen, "Communist Offensive Strategy and the Defense of South Vietnam" in Lloyd J. Matthews and Dale E. Brown, eds., *Assessing the Vietnam War, A Collection from the Journal of the U.S. Army War College* (Washington, D.C., 1987), pp. 101–22.
16. *Pentagon Papers*, Vol. 4, p. 325.
17. Operation FRESNO After-action Report, 10 April 1966, Appendix 1 in 25th ORLL, 1 May–31 July 1966.
18. *Interview with Vietnam War Participant*, Rand Corporation, H-18 (h-1), February 1966, Indochina Archive.
19. Nguyen, "Communist Offensive Strategy," p. 105.
20. Tra, *History of the Bulwark B2 Theatre*, p. 38.
21. *Studies of the National Liberation Front of South Vietnam*, Rand Corporation, AG-373, AG xiii; AG-474, AG xxx, Indochina Archive.

22. *Studies of the National Liberation Front of South Vietnam*, Rand Corporation, AG-346, AG XIII, Indochina Archive.

23. Tom Mangold and John Penycate, *The Tunnels of Cu Chi* (New York, 1985), pp. 18–19.

24. *Interview with Vietnam War Participant*, Simulmatics Corporation, CH-5, 7/27-8/2, 1966, Indochina Archive.

25. Headquarters, Advisory Team #43, *Hau Nghia Province Report*, December 1966 (hereafter cited as Hau Nghia PR, followed by appropriate date.)

26. Lewy, *America in Vietnam*, pp. 172–73; Clarke, *Advice and Support: The Final Years*, p. 42.

27. Neil Sheehan, *Bright Shining Lie: John Paul Vann and America in Vietnam* (New York, 1988), p. 510.

28. Clarke, *Advise and Support: The Final Years*, p. 47.

29. Westmoreland, *A Soldier Reports*, pp. 169–76; Clarke, *Advice and Support: The Final Years*, Chapter 7.

30. *Pentagon Papers*, Vol. 2, pp. 440–42.

31. Ibid., p. 463.

32. Ibid., p. 479.

33. Ibid., p. 479.

34. Ibid., pp. 479–80.

35. John Paul Vann, *Harnessing the Revolution in South Vietnam*, 10 September 1965, CMH, p. 7.

36. Ibid., passim.

37. Ibid., p. 8.

38. PROVN., p. 100.

39. Ibid., pp. 1, 70, 100.

40. *Pentagon Papers*, Vol. 2, pp. 579–80.

41. Ibid., pp. 379–80, 500–2, 576–80.

42. Westmoreland, *A Soldier Reports*, pp. 144–51.

43. Ibid., p. 120.

44. Ibid., pp. 144–53.

Chapter 4

1. Westmoreland, *A Soldier Reports*, pp. 163–64; Interview with Maj. Gen. Thomas Mellen, USA (Ret); Interview with Col. Thomas Ferguson, USA (Ret); Interview with Col. Carl Quickmire, USA (Ret).

2. Davidson, *Vietnam at War*, pp. 325–27, 375–77.

3. 25th ORLL, 1 February–30 April 1966, pp. 9–10.

4. Ibid., p. 26.

5. After-action Report, Operation CIRCLE PINES, Appendix A, 25th ORLL, 1 February–30 April 1966, p. 1.

6. *Special Summary of Action-Company A, 2d Battalion, 27th Infantry, 5 April 1966*, Appendix B, 25th ORLL, 1 February–30 April 1966.

7. After-action Report, Operation CIRCLE PINES, Appendix A, 25th ORLL, 1 February–30 April 1966, p. 8.

8. Ibid., pp. 10–12.

9. 25th ORLL, 1 May–31 July 1966, pp. 1–5.

10. 25th ORLL, 1 August–31 October 1966, pp. 1–5.

11. 25th ORLL, 1 May–31 July 1966, pp. 3, 9, 10.

12. 25th ORLL, 1 August–31 October 1966, p. 31.

13. 25th ORLL, 1 May–31 July 1966, p. 9.

14. Shelby L. Stanton, *The Rise and Fall of an American Army: U.S. Ground Forces in Vietnam, 1965-1973* (Novato, Calif., 1985), pp. 97, 134.

15. Lt. Gen. Bernard Rogers, *CEDAR FALLS-JUNCTION CITY: A Turning Point* (Washington, D.C.: 1974), pp. 30, 77, 140, 158.

16. 25th ORLL, 1 May–31 July 1967, pp. 1–11.

17. 25th ORLL, 1 August–31 October 1967, pp. 1–7.

18. 25th ORLL, 1 November 1967–31 January 1968, p. 5.

19. Ibid., pp. 1–7.

20. Headquarters, II Field Force Vietnam, TET OFFENSIVE After-action Report, 31 January–18 February 1968, pp. 4–6. (hereafter cited as II Field Force TET AAR).

21. Rogers, *CEDAR FALLS-JUNCTION CITY*, p. 157.

22. 25th ORLL, 1 July–31 October 1966, pp. 6–11.

Chapter 5

1. *Pentagon Papers*, Vol. 2, pp. 515–48.

2. Ibid., pp. 548–54.

3. Ibid., pp. 529–30.

4. Ibid.

5. Ibid., p. 575.

6. Robert Shaplen, *The Road from War* (New York, 1970), pp. 163–65.

7. *Pentagon Papers*, Vol. 2, p. 562

8. Ibid., Vol. 2, p. 608

9. Cooper, *American Experience with Pacification*, pp. 250–67.

10. Ibid.

11. Colby and Forbath, *Honorable Men*, pp. 232–34; Shaplen, *The Road from War*, pp. 36–37.

12. *Pentagon Papers*, Vol. 2, p. 568.

13. Ibid., pp. 554, 568–72, 581.

14. Don Luce and John Sommer, *Vietnam—The Unheard Voices* (Ithaca, N.Y., 1969), pp. 152–53.

15. Asprey, *War in the Shadows*, Vol. 2, p. 1131.

16. Corson, *The Betrayal*, Appendix B.

17. Luce and Sommer, *Unheard Voices*, pp. 221–22.

18. "25th Division Pacification Operations in Hau Nghia Province," 7 August 1966, Appendix A of 25th ORLL, 1 May–31 July 1966, p. 2 (hereafter cited as "25th Pacification Operations").

19. Ibid., p. 14.

20. Letter to author from Oliver Davidson, 20 March 1976.

21. Palmer, *The 25-Year War*, pp. 58–59; Col. Thomas Ferguson tape, July 1989.

22. Col. Thomas Ferguson tape, July 1989.

23. *Pentagon Papers*, Vol. 2, pp. 381–82. Clarke, *Advice and Support: The Final Years, 1965–1973*, pp. 184–86.

24. "25th Pacification Operations," p. 6.

25. Ibid., pp. 4–7.

26. After-action Report, Operation MAILI, Appendix B, 25th ORLL, 1 May–31 July 1966, p. 6.

27. "25th Pacification Operations," p. 6.

28. After-action Report, Operation SANTA FE, Appendix D, 25th ORLL, 1 May–31 July 1966, p. 5.

29. "25th Pacification Operations," p. 10.

30. After-action Report, Operation SANTA FE, Appendix D, 25th ORLL, 1 May–31 July 1966, p. 5.

31. Luce and Sommer, *Unheard Voices*, pp. 213–14.

32. After-action Report, Operation SANTA FE, Appendix D, 25th ORLL, 1 May–31 July 1966, pp. 5, 14.

33. 25th ORLL, 1 February–30 April 1966, p. 25.

34. "25th Pacification Operations," p. 10.

35. Hau Nghia PR, July 1966.

36. "25th Pacification Operations," p. 8.

37. 25th ORLL, 1 August–31 October 1966, p. 13.

38. II Field Force ORLL, 1 May–31 July 1966, p. 65.

39. Letter to author from Oliver Davidson, 20 March 1976.

40. Ibid.

41. Interview with Oliver Davidson, 21 March 1976.

42. Hau Nghia PR, November 1966.

43. *Pentagon Papers*, Vol. 2, pp. 393–94; Clarke, *Advice and Support: the Final Years, 1965–1973*, pp. 189–91.

44. Interview with Oliver Davidson, 21 March 1976.

45. Ibid.

46. Hau Nghia PR, December 1966.

47. 25th ORLL,1 May–31 July 1966, pp. 36, 40–41.

48. Hau Nghia PR, August 1966.

49. Hau Nghia PR, November 1966.

50. *Studies of the National Liberation Front of South Vietnam*, Rand Corporation, AG-346, AG XIII, Indochina Archive.

51. Hau Nghia PR, December 1966.

52. Hau Nghia PR, October 1966.

53. Interview with Oliver Davidson, 21 March 1976.

54. Ibid.

55. Hau Nghia PR, September 1966.

56. Ibid.

57. Hau Nghia PR, August and September 1966.

58. Hau Nghia PR, October 1966.

59. Hau Nghia PR, July 1966.

60. Interview with Lt. Col. Andrew Rutherford, 8 September 1989.

61. Hau Nghia PR, July 1966.

62. Hau Nghia PR, November 1966.

63. Hau Nghia PR, December 1966.

64. Ibid.

65. Hau Nghia PR, October 1966.

66. *Pentagon Papers*, Vol. 2, p. 529.

67. Interview with Maj. Gen. Thomas Mellen, 5 September 1989; interview with Col. Thomas Ferguson, 28 November 1989.

68. *Pentagon Papers*, Vol. 4, p. 348.

69. *Pentagon Papers*, Vol. 4, p. 464.

70. Cooper, *American Experience with Pacification*, pp. 269–71.

71. 25th ORLL, 1 May–31 July 1967, pp. 2–10.

72. 25th ORLL, 1 May–31 July 1967, 1 August–31 October 1967, and 1 November 1967–31 January 1968.

73. 25th ORLL, 1 May–31 July, 1966.

74. Letter to author from Oliver Davidson, 20 March 1976.

75. Hau Nghia PR, April 1967.

76. Hau Nghia PR, November 1967.

77. Headquarters, MACCORDS III Corps Tactical Zone, *III Corps Tactical Zone Overview,* July 1967 (hereafter cited as III CTZ Overview, followed by the appropriate date); Hau Nghia PR, July 1967.

78. 25th ORLL, 1 August–31 October 1967, p. 19.

79. 25th ORLL, 1 May–31 July, p. 61.

80. 25th ORLL, 1 August–31 October 1967, p. 4.

81. Ibid., p. 41.

82. Oliver Davidson Papers: memo to Hau Nghia PSA, 2 August 1967; memo to John Paul Vann, DEPCORDS III CTZ, 16 October 1967; memo to W. Wilson DEPCORDS III CTZ, 12 December 1967.

83. Oliver Davidson Papers: memo to John Paul Vann, DEPCORDS III CTZ, 16 October 1967.

84. John Paul Vann, *Improvement of Security Within South Vietnam,* 12 November 1967, CMH.

85. Westmoreland, *A Soldier Reports,* pp. 206–7.

86. 25th ORLL, 1 August–31 October 1967.

87. Taped interview with Lt. Col. Frank Chance.

88. Hau Nghia PR, September and October 1967.

89. Hau Nghia PR, November 1967.

90. 25th ORLL, 1 November 1967–31 January, 1968, p. 29.

91. Ibid., pp. 7–9; 25th ORLL, 1 August–31 October 1967, pp. 1–4; 25th ORLL, 1 November 1967–1 January 1968, pp. 3–5.

92. Interview with Oliver Davidson, 21 March 1976.

93. *Interview with Vietnam War Participant,* JUSPAO Field Development Division, 2/7/68, Senior Captain, North Vietnamese Army, Indochina Archive.

94. Office, Assistant Secretary of Defense (Systems Analysis), *Southeast Asia Analysis Report,* CMH, October 1968; *Pentagon Papers,* Vol. 4, pp. 456–538.

95. Lewy, *America in Vietnam,* pp. 442–53.

96. Ibid.

97. Cook and Pabst, *Pacification in Cu Chi District,* p. 7.

98. Oliver Davidson Papers: memo to Dunlop, POL, 21 November 1967.

99. Letter to author from Oliver Davidson, 20 March 1976; Hau Nghia PR, October 1967.

100. Cook and Pabst, *Pacification in Cu Chi District,* p. 35.

101. Hau Nghia PR, May 1967.

102. Oliver Davidson Papers: memo to John Paul Vann, DEPCORDS III CTZ, 21 November 1967.

103. Oliver Davidson Papers: fact sheet *Election Hau Nghia, Trang Bang District,* 24 March 1967.

104. Oliver Davidson Papers: memo to Dunlop, POL, 30 August 1967.

105. Ibid.

106. Hau Nghia PR, August 1967.

107. Frances FitzGerald, *Fire in the Lake* (Boston, 1972), pp. 448–51; Shaplen, *Road from War,* p. 158; III CTZ Overview, August 1967.

108. III CTZ Overview, December 1967.

109. Hau Nghia PR, April 1967.

110. Hau Nghia PR, April 1967.

111. Hau Nghia PR, May 1967.

112. Hau Nghia PR, September and October 1967.
113. Hau Nghia PR, May 1967.
114. Hau Nghia PR, November 1967.
115. Hau Nghia PR, August 1967; Cook and Pabst, *Pacification in Cu Chi District*, p. 12.
116. 25th ORLL, 1 July–31 October 1967.
117. III CTZ Overview, December 1967.

Chapter 6

1. Peter Braestrup, *Big Story: How the American Press and Television Reported and Interpreted the Crisis of Tet 1968 in Vietnam and Washington*, (Garden City, N.Y., 1978), p. 54.
2. Ibid., p. 49.
3. Ibid., p. 50.
4. Ibid., p. 51.
5. Ibid., pp. 51–53.
6. Cable from Robert Komer, director of CORDS, to Lt. Gen. Le Nguyen Khang, commanding general, III CTZ, 1 January 1968, CMH Hau Nghia File.
7. Braestrup, *Big Story*, p. 54.
8. II Field Force ORLL, 1 August–31 October 1967, p. 4.
9. John Paul Vann, *Improvement of Security Within South Vietnam*, 12 November 1967, CMH.
10. Braestrup, *Big Story*, p. 57.
11. Cooper, *American Experience with Pacification*, pp. 288–99.
12. II Field Force ORLL, *TET AAR*, pp. 2–5.
13. 25th ORLL, 1 November 1967–31 January 1968, pp. 1–5.
14. II Field Force TET AAR, pp. 4–8.
15. *New York Times*, 8 January 1968, p. 5, and 10 January 1969, p. 4.
16. II Field Force TET AAR, pp. 7–8.
17. Ibid., p. 8; Westmoreland, *A Soldier Reports*, p. 318.
18. II Field Force TET AAR, p. 8.
19. Ibid., pp. 9–14.
20. Davidson, *Vietnam at War*, pp. 393–404; Interview with Lt. Gen. Phillip Davidson, 15 December 1989.
21. Davidson, *Vietnam at War*, pp. 1–28; Westmoreland, *A Soldier Reports*, pp. 310–30; 25th ORLL, 1 February–30 April 1968, pp. 1–8, and 1 May–31 July 1968, pp. 1–12; Department of Defense Intelligence Information Report #6029 1059 68, Captured Document, *Report on Activities During the First Six Months of 1968, Cu Chi District*, 25 November 1968, CMH Hau Nghia File (hereafter cited as Captured *Cu Chi District Report*); Asprey *War in the Shadows*, Vol. 2, pp. 1218–28; Advisory Detachment, Political Warfare College, Advisory Team #34, *Speech by VC POW*, 22 June 1968, CMH Hau Nghia File (hereafter cited as *POW Speech*).
22. II Field Force AAR, p. 1–38.
23. *POW Speech*.
24. II Field Force TET AAR, pp. 25–26; II Field Force ORLL, 1 May–31 July 1968, p. 19.
25. II Field Force TET AAR, p. 27.
26. Ibid., pp. 27–28.
27. Ibid., p. 15.
28. Ibid., p. 17; Hau Nghia PR, February 1968.

29. Cook and Pabst, *Pacification in Cu Chi District*, p. 11; Hau Nghia PR, February 1968; II Field Force TET AAR.

30. II Field Force TET AAR, p. 90; Hau Nghia PR, February 1968.

31. Hau Nghia PR, February 1968.

32. Hau Nghia PR, March and April 1968.

33. Ibid.; 25th ORLL, 1 February–30 April 1968, pp. 1–24.

34. Hau Nghia PR, March 1968; II Field Force ORLL, 1 February–30 April 1968, p. 46.

35. Hau Nghia PR, May 1968.

36. 25th ORLL, 1 May–31 July 1968, pp. 1–24.

37. Ibid., p. 12.

38. Hau Nghia PR, February 1968.

39. Lt. Gen. George Griffin, RF/PF Inspection Dept., Team #4, *Inspection Report of Hau Nghia Sector*, 10 July 1968, CMH Hau Nghia File.

40. Memo to Conlon from David Brown, "The Situation in Hau Nghia Province," 17 June 1968, CMH Hau Nghia File.

41. CORDS III CTZ Rural Technical Team Field Survey Report, *Duc Hue District: The TET Attacks and After*, 15 May 1968, CMH Hau Nghia File.

42. Hau Nghia PR, February 1968.

43. Hau Nghia PR, May 1968.

44. Hau Nghia PR, April 1968.

45. Hau Nghia PR, February and April 1968.

46. Oliver Davidson Papers: Notes on Trang Bang, 22–23 April 1968.

47. CORDS III CTZ Rural Technical Team Field Survey Report, *The Agony of Phuoc Hiep Village*, 11 April 1968, CMH Marshall File; *Relief of War Victims in Cu Chi District, Hau Nghia Province*, 18 April 1968, CMH Marshall File; Republic of Vietnam, Office of Prime Minister, *Relief of War Victims in Hau Nghia*, April 1968, CMH Hau Nghia File.

48. 25th ORLL, 1 February–30 April 1968, p. 48.

49. Ibid.

50. Hau Nghia PR, February 1968.

51. Memo to John Vann from PSA Lt. Col. Carl Bernard, "Assessment of Recent Attacks on Pacification," 19 May 1968, CMH Hau Nghia File.

52. Cook and Pabst, *Pacification in Cu Chi District*, p. 6.

53. Ibid.; Oliver Davidson Papers: memo to John Paul Vann, "Situation in Trang Bang District, Hau Nghia," 14 May 1968.

54. Ibid.

55. Duc Hue DIOCC, pp. 7–8.

56. Hau Nghia PR, June 1968.

57. Ibid.

58. Hau Nghia PR, February and April 1968.

59. Lt. Col. Carl Bernard, *The War in Vietnam, Observations and Reflections of a Province Senior Advisor*, report prepared for Robert Komer, October 1969, from the author's collection.

60. Captured *Cu Chi District Report*, p. 7.

61. Ibid., p. 6.

62. Ibid., p. 28.

63. Ibid.

64. Duc Hue DIOCC, pp. 8–9.

65. Letter to author from Maj. Stuart Herrington, undated (1978).

66. *Interview with Vietnam War Participant,* Senior Captain, North Vietnamese Army, JUSPAO Field Development Division, 2/7/68, Indochina Archive.

67. Race, *War Comes to Long An,* p. 270.

68. Dale Pfeiffer, III CTZ Field Evaluator, *Evaluation of the Pacification Techniques of the 2d Brigade, U.S. 25th Infantry Division,* 20 December 1968, CMH Hau Nghia File (hereafter cited as Pfeiffer, *Pacification Techniques of 2d Brigade*).

69. Ibid.; Hau Nghia PR, August 1968.

70. Hau Nghia PR, July 1968.

71. Ibid.

72. Hau Nghia PR, October 1968.

73. Ibid.

74. Memo from Maj. Gen. R. Wetherill to John Vann, 7 November 1968; letter from William Colby, DEPCORDS, to Tran Thien Khiem, Minister of Interior, 18 November 1968, CMH Hau Nghia File.

75. Hau Nghia PR, August 1968.

76. Hau Nghia PR, September 1968.

Chapter 7

1. Colby, *Honorable Men,* pp. 260–61; Lewy, *America in Vietnam,* pp. 134–35; Cooper, *American Experience with Pacification,* pp. 288–99.

2. Cooper, *American Experience with Pacification,* pp. 288–99.

3. MACCORDS Fact Sheet, *III CTZ Accelerated Pacification Campaign (APC),* 31 January 1969, CMH Hau Nghia File.

4. Circular from Lt. Col. Risher, *Upgrading of Hamlets to GVN Control,* 16 December 1968, CMH Marshall File; memo to William Colby from R. M. Montague, "Problem in Hau Nghia," 14 January 1969, CMH Hau Nghia File.

5. Hau Nghia PR, January 1969.

6. MACCORDS Fact Sheet, *III CTZ Accelerated Pacification Campaign (APC),* 31 January 1969, CMH Hau Nghia File.

7. Hau Nghia PR, January 1969.

8. III CTZ Overview, December 1968.

9. Hau Nghia PR, January 1969.

10. Pfeiffer, *Pacification Techniques of 2d Brigade.*

11. Letter to author from Lt. Col. David Harrington, 19 April 1976.

12. Oliver Davidson Papers: Trang Bang District Notes, February 1969; letter to Lt. Col. Carl Bernard, 9 December 1968; letter to John Paul Vann, 10 December 1968; letter to Dick Meyer, 24 December 1968; *Trang Bang Weekly Activities Report,* 14 December 1968 and 21 December 1968.

13. Hau Nghia PR, January 1969.

14. Lewy, *America in Vietnam,* p. 452.

15. Oliver Davidson Papers: Trang Bang District Notes, February 1969.

16. Oliver Davidson Papers: *Le Loi Report,* 30 December 1968.

17. Letter to author from Lt. Col. David Harrington, 19 April 1976.

18. Hau Nghia PR, December 1968.

19. Office of the Assistant Secretary of Defense (Systems Analysis), "Southeast Asia Analysis Report," October 1968, p. 23.

Chapter 8

1. Interview with Colonel Donald Marshall, August 1989, Davidson, *Vietnam at War*, pp. 552–53.

2. Cooper, *American Experience with Pacification*, pp. 299–304.

3. *Interview with Vietnam War Participant*, Medical Orderly, SR1, JUSPAO, 3-8-71, Indochina Archive.

4. *Interview with Vietnam War Participant*, Senior Captain-SRI, Deputy Commander Quyet Thang Regiment, C1973(III), Indochina Archive.

5. 25th ORLL, 1 February–30 April 1969, pp. 1–8, Appendix I; 1 May–31 July 1969, pp. 1–31; II Field Force ORLL, 1 February–30 April 1969, pp. 16–31; 1 May–31 July, pp. 2–16.

6. II Field Force ORLL, 11 February–30 April 1969, p. 20; 1 May–31 July 1969, p. 16.

7. 25th ORLL, 1 May–31 July 1969, pp. 1–3, 31.

8. 25th ORLL, 1 February–30 April 1969, p. 29; 1 May–31 July 1969, p. 43.

9. Henry Kissinger, *White House Years* (Boston, 1979), p. 226.

10. Ibid., p. 247.

11. Lewy, *America in Vietnam*, p. 146.

12. Hau Nghia PR, February 1969.

13. Hau Nghia PR, April 1969.

14. Hau Nghia PR, May 1969.

15. 25th ORLL, 1 May–31 July 1969, pp. 1–3.

16. MACCORDS Fact Sheet, Hau Nghia Province, June 1969, CMH Hau Nghia File; 25th ORLL, 1 August–31 October 1969, pp. 3–5.

17. 25th ORLL, 1 August–31 October 1969, pp. 1–5.

18. Ibid., p. 46.

19. MACCORDS Fact Sheet, Hau Nghia Province, April 1970, CMH Hau Nghia File.

20. Hau Nghia PR, October 1969 and December 1969.

21. 25th ORLL, 1 August–31 October 1969, p. 18.

22. Ibid., pp. 18–21.

23. Letter from Maj. Gen. Ellis Williamson, USA (Ret.) to author, 29 August 1989.

24. 25th ORLL, 1 November 1969–31 January 1970, p. 49.

25. Ibid., p. 14.

26. II Field Force ORLL, 1 November 1969–31 January 1970, p. 6.

27. 25th ORLL, 1 August–31 October 1969, p. 42.

28. 25th ORLL, 1 November 1969–31 January 1970, p. 9.

29. Ibid., p. 14; Hau Nghia PR, August 1969.

30. 25th ORLL, 1 November 1969–31 January 1970, p. 30.

31. *Interview with Vietnam War Participant*, Second Lieutenant, NVA 228th Regiment (Hau Nghia province), JUSPAO, C 1973, Indochina Archive.

32. Duc Hue DIOCC, pp. 8–11.

33. Ibid., p. 12.

34. 25th ORLL, 1 August–31 October 1969, p. 46.

35. III CTZ Overview, December 1969.

Chapter 9

1. Colby and Forbath, *Honorable Men*, p. 230.

2. Ibid., p. 234.

3. Race, *War Comes to Long An*, p. 231.

4. L. P. Holliday, A. W. Jones, and R. Rhyne, eds., *Final Report: Seminar on Area Security and Development (Pacification)* (Rand Corporation, June 1969), Report #4, *The Insurgency Environment*, pp. 1–14, CMH.

5. Lewy, *America in Vietnam*, pp. 279–85; Colby and Forbath, *Honorable Men*, pp. 266–89.

6. Hau Nghia Province Profile, April 1970, CMH Hau Nghia File.

7. Ibid.

8. Hau Nghia P.R., September 1969 and December 1969.

9. Ibid.

10. III CTZ Overview, May 1969.

11. Hau Nghia PR, June 1969.

12. Hau Nghia Province Profile, July 1970, CMH Hau Nghia File.

13. CORDS III CTZ Rural Technical Team Field Survey Report, *Terrorism in Cu Chi and Trang Bang Districts*, 1 September 1969, CMH Hau Nghia File.

14. Lewy, *America in Vietnam*, pp. 280, 289.

15. Hau Nghia PR, December 1969.

16. Cooper, *American Experience with Pacification*, p. 288.

17. Letter to author from Dr. E. R. Worthington, 19 April 1976.

18. Hau Nghia Province Profile, April 1969 and January 1970, CMH Hau Nghia File.

19. Hau Nghia Province Profile, January 1970, CMH Hau Nghia File.

20. Palmer, *The 25-Year War*, p. 44.

21. Colby and Forbath, *Honorable Men*, pp. 351–55.

22. Hau Nghia PR, December 1969.

23. Hau Nghia PR, June 1969.

24. Hau Nghia PR, February 1969.

25. III CTZ Overview, December 1969.

26. Hau Nghia PR, October 1969.

27. Cooper, *American Experience with Pacification*, p. 315.

28. Hau Nghia PR, August 1969.

29. Hau Nghia PR, October 1969.

30. Hau Nghia PR, April 1969.

31. Hau Nghia PR, September 1969.

32. Hau Nghia PR, August 1969.

33. See Chapter 1.

34. Cooper, *American Experience with Pacification*, p. 314.

35. Interview with Oliver Davidson, 21 March 1976.

36. Hau Nghia PR, February 1969, March 1969, July 1969, and October 1969.

37. III CTZ CORDS Local Survey Detachment Report, *Hamlet Elections in My Thanh Dong and Hiep Hoa Villages, Hau Nghia*, 25 April 1969, CMH Hau Nghia File.

38. III CTZ CORDS Local Survey Detachment Report, *General Situation in Hiep Hoa Village, Duc Hue District, Hau Nghia Province*, 17 July 1969, CMH Hau Nghia File.

39. Pacification Research Program Digest of Reports, #22, *Study on Village Committees in Binh Duong and Hau Nghia Province*, April 1970, CMH Hau Nghia File.

40. III CTZ CORDS Local Survey Detachment Report, *The Concept of Opposition in III CTZ*, July 1969, CMH Marshall File.

41. Hau Nghia PR, August 1969.

42. Memo for record, Charles Whitehouse, "General Tri's Views on Political Events in Hau Nghia," 18 July 1970, CMH Hau Nghia File.

43. III CTZ Overview, August 1969.

44. Memo to Lars Hydle, POLAD III CTZ, from Lt. Col. Carl Bernard, 7 March 1969; letter to Charles Cooper from Lt. Col. Carl Bernard, undated; memo from Major David Harrington to Lt. Col. Carl Bernard, 10 March 1969, CMH Hau Nghia File.

45. III CTZ Rural Technical Team Survey Report, *The Refugees in Loc Khe Hamlet, Hau Nghia Province, at the Crossroad,* 14 January 1970, CMH Hau Nghia File.

46. Memo to Lars Hydle, POLAD III CTZ, 7 March 1969; memo to Lt. Col. Carl Bernard from Funicello, "Chieu-Hoi Center at U.S. 25th Division," 3 February 1969, CMH Hau Nghia File.

47. III CTZ Overview, January 1968 and March 1968.

48. Cook and Pabst, *Pacification in Cu Chi District.*

49. Memo to Robert Komer from Brig. Gen. Earl F. Cole, Acting Assistant Chief of Staff, CORDS, 19 August 1968, CMH Hau Nghia File.

50. Memo to Brig. Gen. Earl Cole from Col. James Loomes, Chief OAD, 30 October 1968, CMH Hau Nghia File.

51. Lt. Col. John Brenna, Evaluation Report, GS III CTZ, Field Evaluator, *Province Administration, Hau Nghia,* 17 August 1968, CMH Hau Nghia File; Oliver Davidson Papers: letter to John Vann, 9 December 1968.

52. See Note 50.

53. Interview with Oliver Davidson, 21 March 1976.

54. Memo to William Colby from R. M. Montague, "Problem in Hau Nghia," 14 January 1969.

55. Letter to Robert Komer, U.S. ambassador to Turkey, from Lt. Col. Carl Bernard, May 1969, CMH Hau Nghia File; letter to author from Lt. Col. David Harrington, 19 April 1976; interview with Maj. Gen. Ellis Williamson, April 1976.

56. Hau Nghia PR, January 1970.

Chapter 10

1. Richard M. Nixon, *R. N.: The Memoirs of Richard Nixon* (New York, 1978), pp. 404–5; Kissinger, *White House Years,* pp. 34–36.

2. Tang, *A Vietcong Memoir,* p. 212.

3. Davidson, *Vietnam at War,* pp. 559–60.

4. 25th ORLL, 1 February–30 April 1970, pp. 1–3.

5. Cooper, *American Experience with Pacification in Vietnam,* pp. 318–19.

6. MACCORDS Fact Sheet, Hau Nghia Province, 15 January 1970, CMH Hau Nghia File.

7. 25th ORLL, 1 February–30 April 1970, p. 46.

8. Ibid., pp. 1–3; Hau Nghia PR, January 1970.

9. 25th ORLL, 1 February–30 April 1970, p. 46.

10. Ibid., p. 18.

11. Hau Nghia PR, February 1970.

12. 25th ORLL, 1 August–31 October 1970, pp. 1–3.

13. 25th ORLL, 1 May–31 July 1970, p. 13.

14. II Field Force ORLL, 1 May–31 July 1970, pp. 23–24.

15. Tang, *A Vietcong Memoir,* p. 183.

16. Hau Nghia PR, April 1970.

17. 25th ORLL, 1 May–31 July 1970, p. 7.

18. Ibid., p. 21.

19. Hau Nghia PR, April 1970.

20. *Interview with Vietnam War Participant*, Medical Orderly, SR1 Main Force, 38–71, Indochina Archive.

21. Duc Hue DIOCC, pp. 12–13.

22. Hau Nghia PR, May 1970.

23. 25th ORLL, 1 August–31 October 1970, pp. 1–23.

24. Hau Nghia PR, August 1970.

25. 25th ORLL, 1 August–31 October 1970, p. 27.

26. II Field Force ORLL, 1 August–31 October 1970, pp. 17–19.

27. Hau Nghia PR, October 1970.

28. Hau Nghia PR, December 1970.

29. Ibid.

30. Hau Nghia PR, February 1971.

31. Hau Nghia PR, December 1970.

32. Hau Nghia PR, August 1970.

33. Memorandum from Frank Walton, director, Public Safety Directorate, CORDS, to Brig. Gen. Tran Van Hai, director general, National Police, 19 September 1970, CMH Hau Nghia File.

34. Hau Nghia PR, May 1970.

35. Hau Nghia PR, January 1970.

36. Lewy, *America in Vietnam*, pp. 279–85.

37. Hau Nghia Province Profile, June 1970, CMH Hau Nghia File.

38. Memorandum from Colonel Jack Weissinger, Hau Nghia PSA, to DEPCORDS, II FFV/MR3, "RF/PF Results 1970 (Hau Nghia)," 16 February 1971, CMH Hau Nghia File.

39. Ibid.

40. Hau Nghia PR, May 1970; June 1970; July 1970; January 1971.

41. Hau Nghia PR, October 1970.

42. Memorandum from John R. Mossler to Brig. Gen. David Henderson, Acting Assistant Chief of Staff, CORDS, "Sugar Cane—MR 3," 3 November 1970, CMH Hau Nghia File.

43. Hau Nghia PR, April 1970.

44. Hau Nghia PR, September 1970.

45. Hau Nghia PR, December 1970.

46. Memorandum from Colonel S. W. Smithers to Maj. Gen. Cao Hao Hon, CPDC/CC, "Inspection Trip to Hau Nghia," 5 May 1970, CMH Hau Nghia File; Hau Nghia PR, April 1970; CORDS III CTZ Rural Technical Team Survey Report, *Village/Hamlet Elections in Trang Bang and Duc Hoa*, 18 May 1970, CMH Hau Nghia File.

47. Race, *War Comes to Long An*, pp. 270–73.

48. II Field Force ORLL, 1 February–30 April 1970, p. 68.

49. Lewy, *America in Vietnam*, pp. 186–89.

50. Hau Nghia PR, October 1970.

51. Ibid.

52. Race, *War Comes to Long An*, pp. 270–73.

53. CORDS Study, *Considerations Concerning the Experimental Anti-Pacification Program Conducted by People's Revolutionary Party in Selected Villages of SR2 from October 1969 through February, 1970*, undated, pp. 3–4, CMH Hau Nghia File.

54. Ibid.

55. Ibid., p. 6.

56. Ibid, p. 9

57. Memorandum from William Colby to Richard Funkhouser, deputy for CORDS, MR3, 16 October 1970, CMH Hau Nghia File.

58. Memorandum from Frank Scotton to William Colby, "Notes from 25 October Visit in Hau Nghia," 26 October 1970, CMH Hau Nghia File.

59. Ibid.

60. Ibid.

61. Hau Nghia PR, July 1970; August 1970; September 1970; July 1970; December 1970.

Chapter 11

1. Hau Nghia PR, October 1971.

2. Lt. Col. Gerald T. Bartlett, *Final Report: Tour, 19 May 1971–14 November 1972,* undated, CMH Hau Nghia File.

3. Ibid.

4. Hau Nghia PR, August 1971.

5. See Note 2.

6. Letter to author from Maj. Stuart Herrington, undated (1978).

7. Hau Nghia PR, April 1971 and October 1971.

8. Hau Nghia PR, August 1971.

9. Hau Nghia PR, April 1971.

10. Hau Nghia PR, July 1971.

11. Hau Nghia PR, February 1971 and July 1971.

12. Hau Nghia PR, July 1971.

13. Hau Nghia PR, June 1971.

14. Hau Nghia PR, November 1971.

15. Memo from Lt. Col. Gerald Bartlett to Lt. Col. Nguyen Van Thanh, Hau Nghia Province Chief, "Suggestions to Improve the Security Situation and Security Forces of Hau Nghia," 20 March 1972, CMH Hau Nghia File.

16. See Notes 2, 6.

17. Hau Nghia PR, May 1971.

18. Hau Nghia PR, November 1971.

19. See Note 2.

20. Letter to author from Maj. Stuart Herrington, undated (1978). Herrington recorded his experiences in Hau Nghia in *Silence Was a Weapon: The Vietnam War in the Villages* (Novato, Calif., 1982).

21. Stanley Karnow, *Vietnam: A History,* (New York, 1984), pp. 601–2; Tang, *A Vietcong Memoir.*

22. Mangold and Penycate, *The Tunnels of Cu Chi,* p. 266.

23. See Note 6.

24. Davidson, *Vietnam at War,* 605–11; Ray Bonds ed., *The Vietnam War: The Illustrated History of the Conflict in Southeast Asia* (New York, 1980), pp. 218–28.

25. Hau Nghia PR, January 1972.

26. Ibid.

27. See Note 6.

28. Hau Nghia PR, April 1972; May 1972; June 1972; July 1972; October 1972.

29. Hau Nghia PR, June 1972 and July 1972.

30. Hau Nghia PR, September 1972.

31. Hau Nghia PR, December 1972.

32. Hau Nghia PR, August 1972.

33. Hau Nghia PR, November 1972.
34. Hau Nghia PR, November 1972.
35. Hau Nghia PR, January 1973.
36. Arnold Isaacs, *Without Honor: Defeat in Vietnam and Cambodia* (New York, 1984) is a good journalistic account. The military campaign is outlined in Col. William E. Le Gro, *Vietnam from Cease-fire to Capitulation,* (Washington, D.C., 1981).
37. Tra, *History of the Bulwark B2 Theatre,* pp. 124–25.
38. The best account of military events in this period is found in Le Gro, *Vietnam from Cease-fire to Capitulation.*
39. Ibid., p. 87.

Chapter 12

1. Nixon, R. N.: *The Memoirs of Richard Nixon;* Kissinger, *White House Years;* Westmoreland, *A Soldier Reports.*
2. Harry Summers, *On Strategy: A Critical Analysis of the Vietnam War* (New York, 1984); Palmer, *The 25-Year War* is also a good example.
3. William Colby puts his case in both *Honorable Men: My Life in the CIA* (with Peter Forbath) and *Lost Victory: A Firsthand Account of America's Sixteen-Year Involvement in Vietnam* (Chicago, 1989) (with James McCarger). Robert Komer puts a similar argument in a milder form in *Bureaucracy at War: U.S. Performance in the Vietnam Conflict,* (Boulder, Colo., 1986). See also Lewy, *America in Vietnam;* Krepinevich, *The Army in Vietnam;* and Thomas Thayer, *War Without Fronts: The American Experience in Vietnam* (Boulder, Colo., 1985).
4. Lewy, *America in Vietnam,* p. 138.

Glossary of Terms, Abbreviations and Acronyms

AAR — After-action report
AID — Agency for International Development
AO — Area of operations
APC — Accelerated Pacification Campaign
APC — Armored personnel carrier
ARVN — Army of the Republic of Vietnam

Bde — Brigade

CA — Civic Action
CAP — Combined action platoon
Chieu Hoi — GVN program to encourage defectors or "ralliers" from the Front (also known as "Open Arms")
CIA — Central Intelligence Agency
CLIP — Combined Lightning Initial Project
CMH — Center of Military History
COMUSMACV — Commander, U.S. Military Assistance Command, Vietnam
CORDS — Civil Operations and Revolutionary (Rural) Development Support
COSVN — Central Office for South Vietnam (DRV's central body for the direction of the war in the South)
CRIP — Combined Reconnaissance and Intelligence Platoon
CTZ — Corps Tactical Zone, the basic military subdivision of South Vietnam (Hau Nghia was in III CTZ, which included the eleven provinces surrounding Saigon.)

DIA — Defense Intelligence Agency
DIOCC — District Intelligence and Operation Coordinating Center
DMZ — Demilitarized Zone
DOD — Department of Defense
DRV — Democratic Republic of Vietnam (North)

FFV — Field Force, Vietnam (U.S. corps-equivalent headquarters; II FFV controlled U.S. forces in III CTZ)
Front — National Liberation Front

GVN — Government of Vietnam (South)

H&I	Harassment and interdiction fire
HES	Hamlet Evaluation System
Hoi Chanh	Name given to a defector ("rallier") under the Chieu Hoi program
HQ	Headquarters
ICEX	Intelligence Coordination and Exploitation
JCS	Joint Chiefs of Staff
KIA	Killed in action
Lao Dong	Vietnamese Workers' Party (Communist Party of North Vietnam; see Party)
LTT	Land-to-the-Tiller Law
LRRP	Long Range Reconnaissance Platoon
MAAG	Military Assistance Advisory Group (preceded MACV)
MACCORDS	Civil Operations and Revolutionary Development Support division of MACV (same as CORDS)
MACV	Military Assistance Command, Vietnam
MAT	Mobile Advisory Team
MEDCAP	Medical Civic Action Program
MORD	Ministry of Revolutionary Development
MR	Military region
NLF	National Liberation Front
NLFA	National Liberation Front Army
NP	National Police
NSC	National Security Council
NVA	North Vietnamese Army
OB	A territorial force
OCO	Office of Civil Operations
OPEC	Organization of Petroleum Exporting Countries
Party	People's Revolutionary Party (southern branch of the Vietnamese Workers' Party [Lao Dong])
PAVN	People's Army of Vietnam (North Vietnamese Army, also called NVA)
PF	Popular Forces
Phoenix	English name for the Phuong Hoang program
Phuong Hoang	GVN program to "neutralize" VCI
PIOCC	Province Intelligence and Operation Coordinating Center
PLA	People's Liberation Agency
POW	Prisoner of war
PRG	Provisional Revolutionary Government
PROVN	*A Program for the Pacification and Long-term Development of South Vietnam* (a report commissioned in 1965 by the U.S. Army deputy chief of staff for military operations, completed in 1966)
PRP	People's Revolutionary Party (see Party)
PRU	Provincial Reconnaissance Unit

PSA	Provincial senior advisor
PSDF	People's Self Defense Force
RD	Revolutionary Development
RDC	Revolutionary Development Cadre
RF	Revolutionary Forces
RF/PF	Revolutionary Forces/Popular Forces
ROE	Rules of engagement
ROTC	Reserve Officers' Training Corps
R&R	Rest and recreation
RTT	Rural Technical Team
SRI	Subregion I (one of several military and political regions established by COSVN to coordinate operations against Saigon; included in SRI were Trang Bang and Cu Chi districts)
SRII	Subregion II (see SRI; included in SRII were Duc Hue and Duc Hoa districts)
TAOR	Tactical area of responsibility
Territorials	GVN militia, including Regional Forces (RF) and Popular Forces (PF)
Tet	Vietnamese lunar New Year holiday
USIA	U.S. Information Agency
USO	United Services Organization
USOM	U.S. Operations Mission
VC	Viet Cong
VCI	Viet Cong infrastructure
VIS	Vietnamese Information Service

Selected Bibliography

As befits an important locale in the Vietnam War, Hau Nghia province figures prominently in several books. Duc Hue and Duc Hoa districts were part of Long An province until 1963 and therefore are part of the story told by Jeffrey Race in *War Comes to Long An*. John Paul Vann's time on the Hau Nghia advisory team is recounted in Neil Sheehan's *A Bright Shining Lie*. Stuart Herrington described his 1971–1972 tour with the advisory team in *Silence Was a Weapon*. Two British journalists, Tom Mangold and John Penycate, depict tunnel warfare in *The Tunnels of Cu Chi*. The American 25th Division's war is chronicled by Larry Heineman in *Close Quarters*, one of the greatest Vietnam novels. The books listed below were helpful in my research.

Albright, John, and Cash, John A. *Seven Firefights in Vietnam*. Washington, D.C.: Government Printing Office, 1971.

Anderson, Charles R. *The Grunts*. San Rafael, Calif.: Presidio Press, 1976.

Asprey, Robert B. *War in the Shadows: The Guerrilla in History*. 2 vols. Garden City, N.Y.: Doubleday and Company, 1975.

Bacevich, A. J. *The Pentomic Era: The US Army Between Korea and Vietnam*. Washington, D.C.: National Defense University Press, 1986.

Berman, Larry. *Planning a Tragedy: The Americanization of the War in Vietnam*. New York: W. W. Norton & Company, 1984.

Blaufarb, Douglas S. *The Counter Insurgency Era: U.S. Doctrine and Performance; 1950 to the Present*. New York: Glencoe Free Press, 1977.

Bonds, Ray, ed. *The Vietnam War: The Illustrated History of the Conflict in Southeast Asia*. New York: Salamander Book, Crown Publishers, Inc., 1980.

Braestrup, Peter. *Big Story: How the American Press and Television Reported and Interpreted the Crises of Tet 1968 in Vietnam and Washington*. Garden City, N.Y.: Anchor Books, 1978.

Callison, Charles Stuart. *Land-to-the-Tiller in the Mekong Delta: Economic, Social and Political Effects of Land Reform in Four Villages of South Vietnam*. Lanham, Md.: University Press of America, 1983.

Chanoff, David, and Toai, Doan Van. *Portrait of the Enemy*. New York: Random House, 1986.

Cincinnatus [pseud.]. *Self-Destruction: The Disintegration and Decay of the United States Army During the Vietnam Era*. New York: W. W. Norton & Company, 1981.

Clarke, Jeffrey J. *Advice and Support: The Final Years, 1965–1973*. Washington D.C.: Center of Military History, U.S. Army, 1988.

Colby, William, and Forbath, Peter. *Honorable Men: My Life in the CIA*. New York: Simon and Schuster, 1978.

Colby, William, and McCargar, James. *Lost Victory: A Firsthand Account of America's Sixteen-Year Involvement in Vietnam.* Chicago: Contemporary Books, 1989.

Collins, Brig. Gen. James Lawton, Jr. *The Development and Training of the Vietnamese Army 1950–1972.* Vietnam Studies. Washington, D.C.: Government Printing Office, 1975.

Corson, William R. *The Betrayal.* New York: W. W. Norton & Company, 1968.

Davidson, Phillip B. *Vietnam at War: The History 1946–1975.* Novato, Calif.: Presidio Press, 1988.

Diem, Bui, with Chanhoff, David. *In the Jaws of History.* Boston: Houghton Mifflin Company, 1987.

Duan, Le. *The Vietnamese Revolution: Fundamental Problems and Essential Tasks.* New York: International Publishers, 1971.

Eckhardt, Brig. Gen. George S. *Command and Control 1950–1969.* Vietnam Studies. Washington, D.C.: Government Printing Office, 1974.

Ellsberg, Daniel. *Papers on the War.* New York: Simon and Schuster, 1972.

Emerson, Gloria. *Winners and Losers: Battles, Retreats, Gains, Losses, and Ruins from the Vietnam War.* New York: Random House, 1976.

Enthoven, Alain C., and Smith, K. Wayne. *How Much Is Enough? The Defense Programs 1961–1969.* New York: Harper and Row, 1971.

Ewell, Lt. Gen. Julian J., and Hunt, Brig. Gen. Ira A. *Sharpening the Combat Edge: The Use of Analysis to Reinforce Military Judgment.* Vietnam Studies. Washington, D.C.: Government Printing Office, 1974.

Fall, Bernard B. *Hell in a Very Small Place.* New York: Lippincott, 1967.

———. *Last Reflections on a War.* New York: Schocken Books, 1972.

———. *The Two Vietnams.* New York: Frederick Praeger, 1967.

———. *Vietnam Witness.* New York: Frederick Praeger, 1966.

FitzGerald, Frances. *Fire in the Lake.* Boston: Little, Brown and Company, 1972.

Fulton, Brig. Gen. William B. *Riverine Operations 1966–1969.* Vietnam Studies. Washington, D.C.: Government Printing Office, 1973.

Gelb, Leslie. *The Irony of Vietnam: The System Worked.* Washington, D.C.: Brookings Institute, 1979.

Giap, Vo Nguyen. *People' s War, People's Army.* New York: Bantam Books, 1968.

Gravel, Mike. *The Pentagon Papers.* 4 vols. Boston: Beacon Press, 1970.

Halberstam, David. *The Best and the Brightest.* Greenwich, Conn.: Fawcett Publications, Inc., 1973.

———. *Making of a Quagmire.* New York: Random House, 1964.

Harrison, James P. *The Endless War: Vietnam's Struggle for Independence.* New York: Columbia University Press, 1989.

Hasmer, Stephen T., and Kellen, Konrad. *The Fall of South Vietnam: Statements by Vietnamese Military and Civilian Leaders.* New York: Crane Russak and Company, Inc., 1980.

Hay, Lt. Gen. John H., Jr. *Tactical and Material Innovations.* Vietnam Studies. Washington, D.C.: Government Printing Office, 1974.

Heineman, Larry. *Close Quarters.* New York: Popular Library, 1977.

Helmer, John. *Bringing the War Home: The American Soldier in Vietnam and After.* New York: The Free Press, 1974.

Herr, Michael. *Dispatches.* New York: Alfred Knopf, 1978.

Herring, George C. *America's Longest War: The United States and Vietnam 1950–1975.* New York: John Wiley and Sons, 1979.

Herrington, Stuart A. *Peace with Honor? An American Reports on Vietnam 1973–1975.* Novato, Calif.: Presidio Press, 1983.

————. *Silence Was a Weapon: The Vietnam War in the Villages.* Novato Calif.: Presidio Press, 1982.

Hickey, Gerald Cannon. *Village in Vietnam.* New Haven, Conn.: Yale University Press, 1964.

Hung, Nguyen Tien, and Schecter, Jerrold L. *The Palace File: Vietnam Secret Documents.* New York: Perennial Library, 1989.

Isaacs, Arnold. *Without Honor: Defeat in Vietnam and Cambodia.* New York: Vintage Books, 1984.

Jones, James. *Viet Journal.* New York: Delacorte Press, 1974.

Kahin, George McT. *Intervention: How America Became Involved in Vietnam.* Garden City, N.Y.: Anchor Books, 1987.

Karnow, Stanley. *Vietnam: A History.* New York: Penguin Books, 1984.

Kinnard, Douglas. *The War Managers.* Hanover, N.H.: University Press of New England, 1977.

Kissinger, Henry. *White House Years.* Boston: Little, Brown and Company, 1979.

Kolko, Gabriel. *Anatomy of a War: Vietnam, the United States, and the Modern Historical Experience.* New York: Pantheon Books, 1985.

Komer, Robert. *Bureaucracy at War: U.S. Performance in the Vietnam Conflict.* Boulder, Colo.: Westview Press, 1986.

Krepinevich, Andrew F. *The Army and Vietnam.* Baltimore: The Johns Hopkins University Press, 1986.

Le Gro, Col. William E. *Vietnam from Cease-fire to Capitulation.* Washington, D.C.: Center of Military History, U.S. Army, 1981.

Levy, Charles J. *Spoils of War.* Boston: Houghton Mifflin Company, 1974.

Lewy, Guenter. *America in Vietnam.* New York: Oxford University Press, 1978.

Luce, Don, and Sommer, John. *Vietnam—The Unheard Voices.* Ithaca, N.Y.: Cornell University Press, 1969.

Mangold, Tom, and Penycate, John. *The Tunnels of Cu Chi.* New York: Berkeley Book, 1985.

Matthews, Lloyd J., and Brown, Dale E., eds. *Assessing the Vietnam War: A Collection from the Journal of the U.S. Army War College.* Washington, D.C.: Pergamon-Brassey's International Defense Publishers, 1987.

McChristian, Brig. Gen. Joseph A. *The Role of Military Intelligence 1965–1967.* Vietnam Studies. Washington, D.C.: Government Printing Office, 1974.

Nixon, Richard M. *R. N.: The Memoirs of Richard Nixon.* New York: Grosset and Dunlap, 1978.

Owen, Brig. Gen. J.I.H., ed. *Brassey's Infantry Weapons of the World 1950–1975.* New York: Bonanza Books, 1978.

Palmer, General Bruce, Jr. *The 25-Year War: America's Military Role in Vietnam.* New York: A Touchstone Book, 1984.

Parker, F. Charles. *Strategy for a Stalemate: Vietnam.* New York: Paragon House, 1989.

Pike, Douglas B. *PAVN: People's Army of Vietnam.* Novato, Calif.: Presidio Press, 1986.

————. *Viet Cong: The Organization and Techniques of the National Liberation Front of South Vietnam.* Cambridge, Mass.: MIT Press, 1966.

Race, Jeffrey. *War Comes to Long An: Revolutionary Conflict in a Vietnamese Province.* Berkeley: University of California Press, 1972.

Raskin, Marcus G., and Fall, Bernard B. *The Vietnam Reader.* New York: Vintage Books, 1965.

Rogers, Lt. Gen. Bernard. *CEDAR FALLS-JUNCTION CITY: A Turning Point.* Vietnam Studies. Washington, D.C.: Government Printing Office, 1974.

Schell, Jonathan. *The Real War.* New York: Pantheon Books, 1987.

Schlight, John, ed. *The Second Indochina War: Proceedings of a Symposium Held at Airlie, Virginia, 7–9 November 1984.* Washington, D.C.: Center of Military History, U.S. Army, 1986.

Scholl-Latour, Peter. *Death in the Rice Fields: An Eyewitness Account of Vietnam's Three Wars 1945–1979.* New York: Penguin Books, 1986.

Shaplen, Robert. *The Lost Revolution: The U.S. in Vietnam 1946–1966.* New York: Harper and Row, 1966.

———. *The Road from War.* New York: Harper and Row, 1970.

Shawcross, William. *Sideshow: Kissinger, Nixon and the Destruction of Cambodia.* New York: Pocket Books, 1979.

Sheehan, Neil. *A Bright Shining Lie: John Paul Vann and America in Vietnam.* New York: Random House, 1988.

Smith, R. B. *An International History of the Vietnam War: Revolution Versus Containment 1955–61.* New York: St. Martin's, 1983.

———. *An International History of the Vietnam War: The Kennedy Strategy.* New York: St. Martin's, 1985.

Spector, Ronald H. *Advice and Support: The Early Years of the U.S. Army in Vietnam 1941–1960.* New York: Free Press, 1985.

Stanton, Shelby L. *Green Berets at War: U.S. Army Special Forces in Southeast Asia 1956–1975.* Novato, Calif.: Presidio Press, 1985.

———. *The Rise and Fall of an American Army: U.S. Ground Forces in Vietnam, 1965–1973.* Novato, Calif.: Presidio Press, 1985.

———. *Vietnam Order of Battle.* New York: Exeter Books, 1987.

Summers, Harry G. *On Strategy: A Critical Analysis of the Vietnam War.* New York: Dell, 1984.

Tang, Truong Nhu. *A Vietcong Memoir: An Inside Account of the Vietnam War and Its Aftermath.* New York: Vintage Books, 1985.

Thayer, Thomas. *War Without Fronts: The American Experience in Vietnam.* Boulder, Colo.: Westview Press, 1985.

Thompson, Sir Robert K. G. *No Exit from Vietnam.* New York: David McKay Company, 1969.

Weigley, Russel F. *The American Way of War: A History of United States Military Strategy and Policy.* New York: Macmillan Publishing Company, 1973.

Westmoreland, General William C. *A Soldier Reports.* Garden City, N.Y.: Doubleday and Company, 1976.

Wiesner, Louis A. *Victims and Survivors: Displaced Persons and Other War Victims in Viet Nam, 1954–1975.* Westport, Conn.: Greenwood Press, 1989.

Zagoria, Donald S. *Vietnam Triangle.* New York: Pegasus, 1967.

About the Book and Author

Some of the most active debate about the Vietnam War today is prompted by those who believe that the United States could have won the war either through an improved military strategy or through more enlightened social policies. Eric Bergerud takes issue with both of these positions. Carefully analyzing the entire course of the war in a single key province, *The Dynamics of Defeat* shows that the Vietnam War was a tragedy in the true sense of the word: American policy could not have been much different than it was and could only have led to failure.

Examining the war at the operational level, where political policy is translated into military action, *The Dynamics of Defeat* provides a case study of the efficacy on the ground of policies emanating from Washington. Many of the policy alternatives now proposed in hindsight were actually attempted in Hau Nghia to one degree or another. Bergerud is able on that basis to critique these policies and to offer his own conclusions in a thought-provoking but utterly unpolemical fashion.

Based on extensive research in U.S. Army archives and many personal interviews with those who experienced the war in Hau Nghia, *The Dynamics of Defeat* is a story full of violence, frustration, and numbing despair, but also one rich with lessons for American foreign policy.

Eric M. Bergerud, after doing extensive research at the Center for Military History in Washington, D.C., received his Ph.D. in history from the University of California, Berkeley, in 1981. He teaches history at Lincoln University. He has taught courses on the Vietnam War at San Francisco State University and the University of California at Berkeley. He lives in Albany, California, with his wife and son. He is also the author of *Red Thunder, Tropic Lightning: The World of a Combat Division in Vietnam* (Westview, 1993).

Index

Abrams, Creighton, 223, 224, 238, 241, 242
Accelerated Pacification Campaign (APC), 223–239, 242, 247, 249, 289
Advisors. *See* United States, advisors
Agency for International Development (AID), 33, 106–107, 142, 155. *See also* Vann, John Paul
Agglomeration Centers plan, 19–20
Agroville Program, 20, 37
AID. *See* Agency for International Development
ALA MOANA (Operation), 164
Ambushes, 52, 70, 75, 79, 94, 96, 119, 123, 132, 134, 138, 147, 149, 150, 151, 153, 213, 265, 266, 273, 291, 296
Amnesty plans, 143–144
An Hoa village, 66, 296
Animals, 172, 251
Ann-Margret, 120
Anti-Communist Denunciation Campaign, 14
An Tinh village, 233, 234, 314, 317
APC. *See* Accelerated Pacification Campaign
Ap Chanh hamlet, 74, 75
APCs. *See* Armored personnel carriers
Ap Doi Mois. *See* New Life hamlets
Area security strategy, 35
Armored personnel carriers (APCs), 87, 118, 125, 136

Army of the Republic of Vietnam (ARVN), 29, 40, 151, 176, 179, 195, 236, 238, 265, 309, 328
  Cambodia operations, 286, 287, 293, 321
  casualties, 22, 27, 38, 42, 204, 222
  coups. *See* Coups/coup attempts
  desertions, 73, 82, 103
  firepower use, 297, 324, 329, 333
  49th Regiment, 275, 286
  and French colonial rule, 24
  intelligence, 229, 257
  Laos offensive, 315
  mortars, 74
  and 1972 offensive, 329
  officers, 104, 114, 202, 230, 261, 304
  pacification duties, 142, 175, 224, 225, 261, 262
  political intrigues in, 103
  and province chiefs, 15, 29–30
  Ranger battalions, 222, 318
  and rural areas, 24–25, 74. *See also* Hop Tac Program; Strategic Hamlet Program
  and Tet Offensive, 207, 216, 223
  25th Division, 73, 79, 103–104, 147, 149, 165, 225, 227, 228, 232, 236, 266, 289, 317
  and U.S. forces, 153–154, 164, 226–228, 231–232, 248, 249, 257, 274–276
  U.S. influence and control, 24
  and Viet Minh, 24
  weaknesses, 26, 42, 79–80, 82–83, 148

weaponry, 210
ARVN. *See* Army of the Republic of Vietnam
Assassinations, 4, 27, 235, 261–262, 308, 316. *See also* National Liberation Front, extermination campaign; People's Revolutionary Party, extermination policy
Atheism, 108
Atrocities, 155, 170, 223, 292
ATTLEBORO (Operation), 126
Attrition ratio, 167

Bacevich, A. J., 89
Balance of forces, 235–236, 333
Ball, George, 90
Bao An (Civil Guard), 19, 25, 26–27, 75
Bao Dai (emperor), 12, 15, 38, 269
Bao Trai hamlet, 53, 70, 76, 78, 151, 161, 164, 165, 166, 195–196, 216, 236, 243, 251, 266, 272, 273, 315, 318, 319
BARKING SANDS (Operation), 164–165, 166, 167, 175
Bartlett, Gerald, 310, 312–313
Bataan, 86
Ba Thu area, 214, 265, 288, 309. *See also* Cambodia
Battle of the Bulge, 86, 194
Ben Cat district, 35, 37–38
Ben Chua area, 252
Ben Sec village, 100
Ben Tuong hamlet, 35, 38
Bergson, Henry, 251, 274, 290–291
Bernard, Carl, 212, 235, 273, 275, 276, 277, 278, 279–280, 304
B-52 aircraft, 72, 134, 243, 286
Bien Hoa, 199, 244
Biggart, Homer, 52
Binh Dinh province, 83, 193
Binh Duong province, 35, 50, 93, 104, 121
Binh Tuy province, 107
Binh Xuyen, 13
Boardman, Phil, 227

Body counts, 135, 162, 167, 168, 174, 238, 280, 332. *See also* Casualties
Boi Loi Woods, 100, 125, 127, 134, 137, 154, 195
Bombardments, 70, 71–72, 73, 91, 95, 136. *See also* United States Army and Air Force, firepower use
Booby traps, 95, 121, 133, 134, 135, 150, 171, 258, 310. *See also* Mines
Bowman, C. W., 129–131, 135, 172
Bremer, James, 280
Brothels, 120
B2 Theater, 54, 93, 197
Buddhists, 38, 46, 53, 104, 113, 230
Bui Diem, 38, 68
Bulldozers, 310
Bunker, Ellsworth, 193, 242
Bunkers, 233–234, 258

CA. *See* Civic Action projects
Cadres, 15–16, 50, 98–99, 159, 199, 249, 252, 255, 301, 314
  captured, 264, 294, 318
  casualties, 259–260, 310, 318
  defectors, 159
  in Hau Nghia, 259–260, 262, 294
  illegal, 257–258, 301, 311, 312
  imprisonment of, 294
  legal, 258, 261, 301, 311–312, 314
  Party membership of, 257–258
  regroupee, 64–65
  reinforcements, 311
  Rural Development (GVN), 69
  and taxation, 214–215, 257
  and Tet Offensive, 199, 218
  training, 64
  See also Revolutionary Development Cadre program
Call, Michael, 133
Cambodia, 71, 72, 101–102, 120, 194, 247, 248, 253, 256, 264–265, 283, 286–289, 294, 321, 329
Canada, 331

Can Lao party, 14, 48
Cao Dai sect, 13, 39, 46, 66, 296
Cao Van Vien, 73
Capital Military District, 195, 198
Captured prisoners/weaponry, 246, 249, 264, 287
Casualties, 215, 218, 249, 254, 318
    cadres, 259–260, 310, 318
    civilian, 63, 72, 82, 89, 109, 167, 168, 169, 170, 171, 174, 212, 213, 274, 286, 297
    estimates, 167–168
    North and South Vietnam, 169
    RF/PF, 210, 310
    See also under individual combatant groups
Catholics, 20, 30, 38, 39, 46, 48, 66, 103, 177, 230, 296, 321, 326
Cease-fires, 199, 205, 223, 296, 319
CEDAR FALLS (Operation), 115, 124, 126, 137, 224, 332
Censuses, 69, 144
Central Highlands, 315, 320, 321, 328, 329
Central Intelligence Agency (CIA), 32, 82, 145, 159, 162, 169, 178, 255–256, 257
Central Nam Bo Propaganda Culture Indoctrination Section, 58
Chance, Frank, 208
Checkmate tactic, 154, 164
Chieu Hoi Program, 143, 158–159, 165, 215, 221, 225, 249, 260, 308, 312
Children, 173
China, 86–87, 95
Chinh-Hunnicutt affair, 157
Cholon, 200
CIA. *See* Central Intelligence Agency
CIRCLE PINES (Operation), 122–124, 126
Civic Action Cadre teams, 15–16, 50
Civic Action (CA) projects, 165, 176, 212
Civil Guard. *See* Bao An
Civilians, 169, 171, 173, 176. *See also* Casualties, civilian; Peasantry

Civil Operations and Revolutionary Development Support (CORDS), 28, 142, 156, 159, 177–178, 179, 211, 223, 224, 225, 236, 242, 254, 256, 257, 261, 268, 269, 279, 284, 294, 297, 301, 325, 333
Civilian Self Defense Force, 242
Class issues, 57, 58, 60, 81, 103, 230
CLIP. *See* Combined Lightning Initial Project
CMH. *See* United States, Center of Military History
Cochin, 16, 24
Colby, William, 32, 107, 145, 211, 221, 223, 256, 267, 277, 301, 302, 311, 324
Collectivization, 108
COLORS UP (Operation), 225
Combat villages/hamlets, 48–49, 94, 175
Combined Campaign Plans, 142, 166, 241
Combined Lightning Initial Project (CLIP), 166
Combined Reconnaissance and Intelligence Platoon (CRIP), 166, 225
Conferences of 1966 and 1967 (GVN-US), 141–142, 143–144
Cong An, 14, 18, 19, 24
Conner, Robert, 119, 136, 170, 175
Conscription, 4, 23, 61, 103, 221, 290
Cordon and Search operations, 166
CORDS. *See* Civil Operations and Revolutionary Development Support
Corps Tactical Zones (CTZ), 54
    III, 179, 194, 195, 196, 225, 251, 254, 271
Corruption, 3, 15, 16, 17, 18, 20, 23, 30, 37, 40, 48, 51, 81, 83, 86, 102, 109, 110, 113, 156, 221, 230, 231, 261, 262, 271, 294, 312, 315, 321, 324, 326, 335

Corvée labor, 51, 103. *See also*
    Forced labor
COSVN. *See* People's Revolutionary
    Party, Central Office in South
    Vietnam
Counterinsurgency, 28, 89, 105, 333
Counter-Terror Teams, 256
County Fair tactic, 152–153, 164
Coups/coup attempts, 30, 32, 35, 38,
    39, 41, 53
CRIP. *See* Combined Reconnaissance
    and Intelligence Platoon
Crop damage, 71, 77, 166, 233, 274.
    See also Defoliation
Crouch, Samuel, 135
CTZ. *See* Corps Tactical Zones
Cu Chi district/district town, 47, 48,
    50, 52, 67, 71, 83, 101, 178, 195,
    206, 211, 212, 246, 261, 303
    local force units, 217, 218
    25th Division (U.S.) base camp in,
    119–121, 131, 134, 244–245, 266,
    276, 289, 290, 291, 292
Culture shock, 170

Danang, 113, 320
Dan va dam (talking and fighting),
    283
Dan Ve (village militia), 19, 26, 27,
    75
Dau tranh, 56, 57, 100, 103, 197, 201
Davidson, Ollie, 147, 155, 158, 159–
    160, 165, 168, 175, 177, 179,
    211, 233, 234, 270
Defectors, 36, 159, 296, 311, 312. *See
    also* Desertions; Ralliers
Defoliation, 70–71, 73
Democracy, 269–270. *See also*
    Elections
Democratic Republic of Vietnam
    (DRV), 4, 13
    collectivization in, 57
    forces/supplies, 114, 138, 196. *See
    also* North Vietnamese Army;
    People's Army of Vietnam
    and negotiations, 197

    strategic debate in, 121
    villages, 330
Demonstrations, 49
Depopulation policy, 72, 109
DePuy, William, 148
Desertions, 73, 82, 103, 154, 159,
    210, 252, 288, 316, 317, 328. *See
    also* Defectors; Ralliers
Development projects. *See* Villages,
    development
Diem. *See* Ngo Dinh Diem
Diem regime, 11–38, 39, 40, 48, 105
    anti-Party activities, 14, 15–16, 19,
    20, 21
    and ARVN–province chiefs
    coordination, 29–30
    land policy, 17, 55–56
    police. *See* Cong An
    resettlement programs, 19–20
    and rural areas, 15–16, 17, 21, 22,
    23, 26, 269. *See also* Strategic
    Hamlet Program
    terrorist policy, 14, 21
    See also Ngo Dinh Diem
Dien Bien Phu, 24
DIOCC. *See* District Intelligence and
    Operation Cooordinating Center
District chiefs, 313
District Intelligence and Operation
    Coordinating Center (DIOCC),
    259, 294
Dong Hoa Bac hamlet, 80
Donnel, John C., 50, 52
Doves, 169, 202
Draft evasion, 61, 331. *See also*
    Conscription
Drugs, 290, 291
DRV. *See* Democratic Republic of
    Vietnam
Duc Hanh B hamlet, 149, 150, 151,
    178
Duc Hoa district/district town, 69–
    70, 73, 76, 164, 166, 171, 178,
    195, 206, 231, 253, 266, 295,
    298, 300, 301, 303

Duc Hue district, 46, 47, 49, 81, 164, 195, 207, 210, 220, 253, 266, 267, 279, 295, 312, 318
Duc Lap village, 73–76, 77–78, 149, 150–151, 273, 300, 301
Duong Van Minh, 29, 38
Durbrow, Eldridge, 30
Dust, 129–130

EAGLE FLIGHTS (helicopter raids), 250
Easter Offensive. *See* North Vietnamese Army, 1972 campaign
Education, 77
Elections, 177–178, 242, 261, 270, 271, 293, 298, 318
Elite, 62, 83, 103, 156
  and creation of a just society, 326
  and Diem, 20
  and peasantry, 3, 110, 299, 326
Ellsberg, Daniel, 78–79. *See also Pentagon Papers*
Encadrement proposals, 334
Enthoven, Alain, 163–164
Executions, 177
Experimental Village Program, 300–301

FAIRFAX (Operation), 166, 334
Fall, Bernard, 24, 25, 27–28, 81
Farmers' Liberation Association, 55, 60
Ferguson, Thomas, 128
Filhol Plantation, 100, 119, 134
Firebase Gold at Suoi Tre, 126
Flexible response doctrine, 117
Food shortages, 252–253, 288
Forced labor, 20, 49, 50–51
Foreign Affairs, 241
Fort Bragg, Special Warfare School, 89
Four Nos policy (Thieu), 320
Free fire zones, 70, 71–72, 88, 109, 134, 264
French colonial period, 3, 46, 47, 66, 108

land ownership, 16, 56
warfare during, 71, 89, 114–115, 166, 257, 334
See also Sûreté
French Groupement Mobile 100, 114

Geneva Accords, 12, 13, 17, 47
Geneva Conference (1954). *See* Geneva Accords
Geographically Phased National Level Operation Plan for Counterinsurgency, 33
Gia Dinh province, 42, 100
Gilpatric, Roswell, 28
Giltner, Thomas A., 170–171, 227, 229
Go Cao hamlet, 273
Go Teams, 149, 150
Government of Vietnam (GVN), 242
  and Accelerated Pacification Campaign, 234–239
  Civil Guard. *See* Bao An
  conferences with Lyndon Johnson, 141–142, 143–144
  Defense, Department of, 26
  disposition of forces, 97
  elite officials, 62, 83
  instability of, 39, 42, 104, 113
  intelligence, 313, 315
  Interior, Department of, 26
  as landlord, 17, 268
  legitimacy, 3, 4, 23, 39, 42, 326, 327
  militia. *See* Bao An; Dan Ve; Militia forces
  Ministry of Revolutionary Development (MORD), 143, 145
  Ministry of Rural Construction, 143
  mobilization of forces, 40
  National Executive Council, 29
  navy, 265
  secret police. *See* Cong An
  and U.S. military shield, 177
  and U.S. troop withdrawals, 304–305, 307

victory/defeat attitudes, 307, 327
See also Army of the Republic of
Vietnam; Diem regime; Republic
of Vietnam
Green Berets, 266–267. See also
United States Army and Air
Force, Special Forces
GVN. See Government of Vietnam
Guam Conference of March 1967,
141
Guerrillas, 94, 95, 96, 205, 207, 225,
228, 229–230, 238, 249, 262,
284, 309, 311, 328. See also
National Liberation Front, local
forces

Hackin, Dennis, 200
Haig, Alexander, 283
Hamburger Hill, 247
Hamlet Evaluation System (HES),
179, 242, 248, 278–279, 284–
285, 293, 301–302, 313
Hammer and anvil maneuver, 122
H&I. See Harassment and interdiction
Hanoi general uprising (1945), 13,
202
Harassment and interdiction (H&I),
135
Harkins, Paul, 36
Harrington, David, 231, 232–233,
235, 243, 296
Hau Nghia province, 1–2, 42, 321
advisory team, 306, 308, 310, 312,
316
agriculture, 46–47, 56
assassinations in, 261
balance of forces, 235–236. See also
Hau Nghia province, control by
GVN vs. NLF
casualties in, 318
climate, 46, 129–130. See also
Monsoons
commerce in, 161, 179, 268
control by GVN vs. NLF, 82, 116,
162, 205, 215, 222, 224, 225–
226, 234–239, 254, 293, 317,

327, 333. See also Hau Nghia,
security; Hamlet Evaluation
System
establishment of, 11, 53
and generalizations concerning
Vietnam War, 325–326
geography, 45–46
GVN assets in, 102–105, 226
HES scores in, 279, 285
homeless families in, 212
importance of, 102, 117
local forces' strengths, 94
military environment, 127–139
name of, 53
neutral zones, 66
NLF 1969 offensive in, 247–254
pacification in, 153, 212, 224, 248–
249, 286, 293, 308, 332, 333. See
also Pacification campaign/
programs
personnel quality, U.S., 233
personnel quality, Vietnamese, 232
population, 46, 56, 102, 175, 236
province reports, 156, 220, 267
rainy season campaign of 1964,
69–70
refugees in, 297. See also Refugees
relocations, 70
roads, 79, 149, 165–166, 179, 266,
268, 280–281, 319. See also
Highway 1; Road activities
security, 75, 79, 105, 147, 161–162,
163, 176, 179, 209, 210, 211,
215, 248, 305–306
stalemate in, 319
support for Viet Minh-NLF, 67–68,
116
Tet Offensive in, 205–215
and U.S. troop withdrawals, 307
Vietnamization in, 286
Hawaii, 149
Headley, Jerry, 229, 231
Hearts and Minds Program, 141, 153
Helicopters, 87, 118, 125, 135, 138,
232, 250, 266, 310
Helping Hands program, 149, 152,
165, 173

"Heroic American Killer" (title), 168
Heroism, 132
Herrington, Stuart, 218, 313, 314–315, 319
HES. *See* Hamlet Evaluation System
Hickey, Gerald, 15–16, 45, 50, 52
Hiep Hoa village, 49, 63, 69–70, 151–152, 161, 207, 214–215, 218, 253, 271, 317
 sugar mill, 80, 152, 207, 264, 265, 266, 267, 297
Highlands, 100
Highway 1, 46, 52, 100, 119, 136, 164, 165, 166, 200, 206, 211
Hoa Hao sect, 13, 39, 66
Hoa Khanh village, 70
Ho Bo Woods area, 72, 100, 122, 125, 127, 134, 137, 154, 195, 224
Ho Chi Minh, 13, 14, 18, 48
Ho Chi Minh Trail, 101, 309, 320, 330
Hoc Mon Bridge, 200–201
Hoi Chanh. *See* Ralliers
Hop Tac Program, 40–42, 68–69, 83. *See also* Duc Lap village
Hue, 113, 223, 320
Humphrey, Hubert, 193
Hunnicutt, Cecil F., 157

ICEX. *See* Intelligence Coordination and Exploitation
ID cards, 75
Indoctrination, 57, 64, 109, 159, 216, 246, 301, 302. *See also* Propaganda
Inflation, 18, 77, 161, 268, 321
Insects, 130
Intelligence, 23, 178–179, 194, 257. *See also* Central Intelligence Agency; *under individual combatant groups*
Intelligence Coordination and Exploitation (ICEX), 257
Intelligentsia, 39, 271
Interrogations, 172, 255, 260, 275–276

Iron Triangle, 100, 126, 127, 164

JCS. *See* United States, Joint Chiefs of Staff
Johnson, Harold K., 81, 193
Johnson, Lyndon, 112–113, 141–142, 177, 193, 197, 324, 335
Joint operations, 226, 249, 263, 265, 285. *See also* Army of the Republic of Vietnam, and U. S. forces
JUNCTION CITY (Operation), 126, 137

Kaye, Danny, 120
Kennedy, John, 28, 31, 117. *See also* Kennedy administration
Kennedy administration, 87, 89, 105–106. *See also* Kennedy, John
Kestell, Bill, 208, 209, 230
Khiem Cuong hamlet, 53
Kidnappings, 74, 152, 315, 316
Kissinger, Henry, 241, 246–247, 283, 323
Kolb, Gerald, 128, 136
KOLEKOLE (Operation), 164–165, 167, 175
Kolko, Gabriel, 57
Komer, Robert, 28, 107, 142, 145, 194, 211, 221, 223, 257, 275, 277, 324
Korean War, 104, 115, 277, 331, 334
Krepinevich, Andrew, 107, 324

Land issues, 55–60, 268–269
 ownership, 16, 17, 56–57, 58, 299
 reform, 4, 30, 57, 59, 268, 298–300
 rents, 16–17, 56, 59, 299
Land-to-the-Tiller Law (LTT), 298–300
Language issues, 156
Lansdale, Edward, 28, 32, 78, 105–106, 108
Laos, 309, 315
Law 10/59, 19
Lazarin, Jay, 132–133, 171–172, 175

Leaflet airdrops, 92, 154–155, 158
Le Duan, 14, 121, 196–197
Le Duc Tho, 101
Lewy, Guenter, 107, 112, 169, 324, 334
Liberated zones, 70, 101, 175
Liuci, Jeri, 200–201
Loc Giang village, 49, 59, 72, 175, 176–177, 317
Lodge, Henry Cabot, 41, 78, 107, 113, 142, 143, 145, 147, 162
Long An province, 17, 56, 83, 93, 104, 193, 219, 254
Long Binh, 198, 199, 244
Long Range Reconnaissance Platoon (LRRP), 265
Lon Nol, 286, 287
Lowlands, 100
LRRP. *See* Long Range Reconnaissance Platoon
LTT. *See* Land-to-the-Tiller Law

MAAG. *See* Military Assistance Advisory Group
McGarr, Lionel, 29
Machine guns, 95
McNamara, Robert, 36, 162–163, 194
MACV. *See* Military Assistance Command, Vietnam
Mai Chi Tho, 101
MAILI (Operation), 149–151, 153
Malaria, 98, 130
Manila Conference of 1966, 141, 144
MARAUDER (Operation), 90–92, 224
Ma Sanh Nhon, 216, 231–232, 273, 274–276, 279–280
MATs. *See* Mobile Advisory Teams
MEDCAPs. *See* Medical Civic Action Programs
Medical Civic Action Programs (MEDCAPs), 149, 152, 165, 173, 272
Medical evacuation, 98, 133
Mekong Delta, 16, 17, 46, 102, 148, 197, 320, 325, 328–329
Middle class, 39, 110

Military Assistance Advisory Group (MAAG), 24, 33, 34
Military Assistance Command, Vietnam (MACV), 36, 41, 71, 73, 100, 106, 111–112, 113, 115, 142, 153, 157, 168, 223, 238, 243, 324–325, 332, 333. *See also* Westmoreland, William
Militia forces, 26–27, 94, 159, 161, 166–167, 179, 208, 216, 223–224, 225, 264, 265, 333. *See also* Bao An; Dan Ve; Popular Forces; Regional Forces
Mines, 79, 80, 94, 96, 121, 130, 135, 147, 153, 171, 215, 235, 310
antipersonnel, 95, 229
fear of, 133
See also Booby traps
Mobile Advisory Teams (MATs), 166, 233, 295–296, 310
Monsoons, 126, 127, 130, 148, 164, 176, 220, 317
Montagnard hill tribes, 32, 104
Morale. *See* United States Army and Air Force, morale
Moral issues, 2, 6, 170. *See also* National Liberation Front, psychological/moral strength
MORD. *See* Government of Vietnam, Ministry of Revolutionary Development
Mortars, 74, 95, 96, 120, 131, 166, 167, 206, 235, 243, 272, 273, 284, 319
Murders, 172. *See also* Assassinations
Murphy, Jim, 244–245
My Lai, 292

Napalm, 136
National Liberation Front (NLF), 27, 40, 116, 125, 138, 161, 169, 300–308
advantages of, 96–97
agents, 207, 210, 256, 261
aid for, 237, 329
antipacification program. *See* Experimental Village Program

battlefields concept, 99–100
cadres. *See* Cadres
casualties, 5, 91, 125, 126, 127,
 138, 167, 169, 204, 208, 209,
 218, 219, 238, 246, 249, 300
combat strength, 238
demonstrations by, 49
and development programs, 272
disposition of forces, 97
establishment of, 27
extermination campaign, 238, 256,
 258–259, 261–262, 301, 302,
 305, 311, 315, 317. *See also*
 People's Revolutionary Party,
 extermination policy
headquarters, 101
integration of forces, 96–97
intelligence, 94–95
local forces, 93, 94, 137, 195, 205,
 209, 249, 250, 252, 309, 311, 317
main forces, 93, 94, 100, 101, 122,
 137, 138, 176, 196, 205, 209,
 212, 219, 225, 248–249, 286,
 300, 316, 329, 333
morale, 252, 254, 284, 286, 288,
 307
9th Division, 126, 127, 209, 219,
 245
non-Communists in, 27, 143, 325
offensive of 1969, 242–254
organizations, 55, 60
propaganda, 98–99, 210, 211, 225,
 238, 268, 270, 317, 334. *See also*
 Cadres; *under* People's
 Revolutionary Party
psychological/moral strength, 303–
 304, 306–307, 327
rainy season campaign of 1964,
 69–70
and ralliers, 159
recruitment, 61–62, 72, 77, 161,
 215–216, 239, 252, 268, 301, 311
replacements, 195, 219, 309, 311
in rural areas, 4, 16, 76, 82, 83,
 150, 161, 196, 272. *See also*
 People's Revolutionary Party, in
 rural areas

Security Affairs Section, 258–259,
 261
supplies, 96, 98
taxation, 49, 59, 82, 96, 195, 214–
 215, 218, 257, 268, 303, 311
and Tet Offensive, 197–199, 201,
 216, 219. *See also* Tet Offensive,
 in Hau Nghia Province
weaknesses, 97–99, 201
weaponry, 95, 138, 195, 196
See also Hau Nghia province,
 control by GVN vs. NLF;
 People's Revolutionary Party
National Police (NP), 102, 149, 178,
 248, 255, 257, 259, 312–313, 318
Nation building, 3, 5, 105, 111
Neil, Alan, 228, 291
Nepotism, 30
New Life hamlets, 144, 178, 211
New Rural Life hamlets, 69
New York Times, 195
Ngo Dinh Diem, 13–15, 36, 255, 269
 as bachelor, 48
 death, 11, 38, 53
 establishment of Hau Nghia, 11,
 53
 and United States, 12, 24
 See also Diem regime
Ngo Dinh Nhu, 11, 14, 29, 30, 35,
 36, 37, 38, 48, 50, 51, 52, 53
Nguyen, Hung P., 97
Nguyen Be, 145, 146–147
Nguyen Cao Ky, 103, 104, 143
Nguyen Chi Thanh, 121, 197
Nguyen Duc Thang, 143, 145
Nguyen Hue Offensive. *See* North
 Vietnamese Army, 1972
 campaign
Nguyen Khanh, 40, 42, 68
Nguyen Ngoc Loan, 178
Nguyen Van Minh, 310
Nguyen Van Thanh, 310, 316, 317
Nguyen Van Thieu, 4, 103, 104, 143,
 152, 199, 221, 223, 257, 263,
 276, 286, 293, 298, 319–320, 321
Nguyen Vo Giap, 14, 121, 196–197,
 283

Nhon. *See* Ma Sanh Nhon
Nhu. *See* Ngo Dinh Nhu
Nighthawk tactic, 266
Night operations, 136–137, 236
Nixon, Richard, 213, 237, 241, 247,
    323, 328, 329. *See also* Nixon
    administration
Nixon administration, 235, 246–247,
    283, 287. *See also* Nixon, Richard
NLF. *See* National Liberation Front
Nolting, Frederick, 29, 31, 32
North Vietnamese Army (NVA), 114,
    127, 169, 176, 195, 205, 208,
    222, 228–229, 262, 286, 315,
    329, 331
    1972 campaign, 315–319, 324, 328
    See also People's Army of Vietnam
NP. *See* National Police
NSC. *See* United States, National
    Security Council
NVA. *See* North Vietnamese Army

OCO. *See* United States, Office of
    Civil Operations
O'Daniel, John, 24
O'Hare, Richard, 230, 264, 265, 272,
    279
Oil spot strategy, 35, 75, 144
One-war concept, 241–242
Ong Ba, 46, 52, 57
OPEC. *See* Organization of
    Petroleum Exporting Countries
Open Arms Program, 143. *See also*
    Chieu Hoi Program
Operations, major vs. minor, 122. *See
    also individual operations;* Search
    and destroy operations
Opposition political parties, 271
Organizational issues, 26, 28, 29, 333
Organization of Petroleum Exporting
    Countries (OPEC), 321
Other war. *See* Village war

Pacification campaign/programs, 77–
    78, 81, 88, 111, 161, 163, 179,
    223–239, 241–242, 293, 328,
    332–333

    and coercion, 224
    confusion in, 155
    duration of, 220
    GVN vs. U.S. views of, 143–144
    1966 plan, 144–145
    1968 plan, 194
    in 1969, 248–249
    in 1970, 284
    operational priorities, 220
    and Tet Offensive, 210–211
    and U.S. Army, 147–155
    See also Duc Lap village; Hau
        Nghia, pacification in; *individual
        programs*
Palmer, Bruce, 36, 37, 78, 148, 267
Pancrazio, John, 154, 226–227, 228
Parallel wars concept, 115. *See also*
    United States Army and Air
    Force, division of labor with
    South Vietnamese forces
Paris Accords, 319. *See also* Peace
    talks
Parrot's Beak (Cambodia), 101, 264–
    265, 286, 309
PAVN. *See* People's Army of Vietnam
Peace talks, 205, 237, 243, 318, 319
Pearce, Donald, 206, 207, 211, 213–
    214, 272, 275, 276, 278
Pearce, R. Michael, 73, 74, 76, 77–78
Peasantry, 2, 26, 34–35, 108, 110
    and ARVN soldiers, 74
    and GVN legitimacy, 3, 326
    land ownership, 17, 56–57. *See also*
        Land issues
    middle-level, 59–60
    neutrality of, 325, 326
    poverty, 45, 58–59, 324
    social status, 57
    support for insurgency, 38, 76, 82,
        83
    and Viet Minh, 16–17
    youth, 23, 61, 326
    See also Casualties, civilian;
        Civilians; Pacification campaign/
        programs; Strategic Hamlet
        Program; Villages
Pentagon Papers, 25, 28, 29–30, 157

People's Army of Vietnam (PAVN),
   93, 101, 107, 121, 197, 208, 209,
   219, 229, 245, 285, 315, 329
troop strength, 94
See also North Vietnamese Army
People's Liberation Army (PLA), 27,
   42, 123–124, 125
People's Republic of China. *See*
   China
People's Revolutionary Party (PRP),
   6, 13, 237, 309, 311
anticlericalism, 52, 66
armed struggle, 21–22, 47
cadres, 62–65. *See also* Cadres
Central Committee, 21, 54
Central Office in South Vietnam
   (COSVN), 48, 54, 93, 101, 196–
   197, 217, 219, 242–243, 246, 285,
   286, 300
and class structure in countryside,
   58
committees, 54–55
defects, 325
and Diem's land policy, 17–18
extermination policy, 18–19, 22,
   67–68. *See also* National
   Liberation Front, extermination
   campaign
and Geneva Accords, 12, 13, 14–
   15, 47
intelligence, 55
and mobilization in South, 42
Nam Bo Regional Committee, 20
organization, 54–55, 257
and PLA, 27
politburo, 197, 242
political vs. armed strategy, 14, 18,
   19, 20–21
propaganda, 55, 57, 60, 71, 74,
   76–77, 269. *See also*
   Indoctrination; *under* National
   Liberation Front
in rural areas, 22, 23, 37, 39, 55–
   68. *See also* National Liberation
   Front, in rural areas
self-criticism sessions, 64, 68
and Strategic Hamlet Program, 37

and Tet offensive, 197, 198, 201–
   203, 216, 242–243
See also National Liberation Front;
   Republic of Vietnam, People's
   Revolutionary Party in
People's Self Defense Force (PSDF),
   211, 263, 267–268, 269, 293,
   296–297, 301, 311, 316, 328. *See*
   also Dan Ve
PF. *See* Popular Forces
Pham Ngoc Thao, Albert, 35
Phan Truong Chinh, 103, 157, 165,
   166
Phoenix program, 194, 211, 242, 257,
   259–262, 284, 312–314, 318
Phung Hoang, 312. *See also* Phoenix
   program
Phuoc Hiep village, 317
Phuoc Long province, 321, 329
Pike, Douglas, 56–57
PIOCC. *See* Province Intelligence and
   Operation Coordinating Center
PLA. *See* People's Liberation Army
Plain of Reeds, 46, 47, 71
Pleiku, 118
Plonka, Del, 133
Popular Forces (PF), 75, 80, 82, 159,
   167, 207, 209–210, 215, 222,
   236, 237, 242, 262–268, 269,
   288, 289, 293, 294, 295, 301,
   302, 309, 310, 328
Porter, William, 142
PRG. *See* Provisional Revolutionary
   Government
Program for the Pacification and Long-
   Term Development of South
   Vietnam, The (PROVN), 82–83,
   110–112, 241
Propaganda, 55, 57, 60, 71, 74, 76–
   77, 98–99, 145, 155, 199, 210,
   211, 225, 243, 269. *See also*
   Indoctrination; National
   Liberation Front, propaganda
Province chiefs, 15, 29–30, 83, 109,
   111, 154, 225, 231, 269, 270,
   271, 318

Province Intelligence and Operation
  Coordinating Center (PIOCC),
  259
Provincial Reconnaissance Units
  (PRU), 149, 256–257, 314
Provincial Route 8, 149
Provincial Route 10, 266
Provisional Revolutionary
  Government (PRG), 320
PROVN. *See Program for the
  Pacification and Long-Term
  Development of South Vietnam,
  The*
PRP. *See* People's Revolutionary
  Party; Republic of Vietnam,
  People's Revolutionary Party in
PRU. *See* Provincial Reconnaissance
  Units
PSA. *See* United States, Province
  Senior Advisors
PSDF. *See* People's Self Defense
  Force
Psychological warfare, 154
Public opinion, 31, 88, 112, 163–164,
  197, 202, 237, 284, 328

Quang Tri, 329
Quickmire, Carl, 131–132

Race, Jeffrey, 23, 55, 219
Ralliers, 143, 144, 158, 159, 165, 242,
  249–250, 252, 254, 260, 261,
  285–286, 288, 303, 308, 310, 318
Rand Corporation study, 73. *See also*
  Pearce, R. Michael
RDC. *See* Revolutionary Development
  Cadre program
RD Cadre Program. *See*
  Revolutionary Development
  Cadre program
Real New Life hamlets. *See* New Life
  hamlets
RECOVERY (Operation), 219
Reforms, 326. *See also* United States,
  and sovereignty issues
Refugees, 92, 176, 234, 249, 297, 315

Regional Forces (RF), 75, 159, 167,
  209–210, 215, 222, 225, 236,
  237, 242, 262–268, 288, 289,
  293, 294–295, 301, 309–310, 317,
  318
Religion, 52, 66. *See also individual
  religions and sects*
Relocations, 51, 52, 70, 297, 315, 318
Republic of Vietnam, 5
  Army. *See* Army of the Republic of
    Vietnam
  currency, 49
  People's Revolutionary Party (PRP)
    in, 27
  See also Diem regime; Government
    of Vietnam
Resor, Stanley, 306
Revolutionary Development Cadre
  (RDC) program, 16, 142, 145–
  147, 159–161, 162, 178, 211, 220,
  223–224, 237, 248, 256, 257,
  263, 274, 301, 311, 335
Revolutionary virtue, 62, 63
RF. *See* Regional Forces
Rice, 47, 96, 100, 127, 164, 165, 175,
  252, 262, 319
  miracle rice project, 220–221, 268,
  297, 318
Ridgway, Matthew, 277
Rifles, 95, 210, 225, 229, 267
Ringworms, 130
Ripe situation (concept), 21
Road activities, 154, 165–166, 173,
  208
Roadrunner tactic, 154, 164, 166
Rocket propelled grenades (RPG), 95,
  125
Rockets, 243
ROE. *See* Rules of engagement
Rogers, Bernard, 137
Ross, Jim, 291–292
Rostow, Walter, 28, 90, 113, 194
RPG. *See* Rocket propelled grenades
Rules of engagement (ROE), 88, 214,
  278
Rumors, 171
Rusk, Dean, 90

Rutherford, Andrew, 153–154, 156–157, 158, 161

Safe zones, 137, 243, 332
Saigon
    area surrounding, 28, 35, 39, 41, 42, 54, 68, 100, 127, 197, 204, 244, 245, 286, 289, 319, 320
    defense of, 195, 238
    Presidential Palace, 321
    slums, 196
    and Tet offensive, 198, 206, 209
    See also Capital Military District
Sanctuaries. *See* Cambodia
Sandbagging, 291
Sappers, 216, 243–244, 245, 276, 284
Schell, Jonathan, 100
Schools, 272
Seaman, Jonathan, 126
Search and destroy operations, 2, 5, 34, 35, 115, 121, 124–125, 132, 137, 154, 224. *See also individual operations*
Security issues, 52, 74, 76, 80, 82, 83, 121, 141, 148, 209, 212, 220, 234, 241, 263, 293–297, 325. *See also* Hau Nghia province, security
Self-help projects, 81, 165, 242
Sexual morality, 65
Shaplen, Robert, 143
Sihanouk, Norodom (Prince), 286
Sihanoukville, 287, 309, 330
"Situation and Missions for 1959" (Party document), 20
Slums, 196
Sniping, 79, 82, 88, 96, 119, 147
Sources, 6, 7–9
Soviet Union, 14, 95
SRI. *See* Subregion I
SRII. *See* Subregion II
Stillwell, Richard, 37
Stone, Sidney, 199, 200
Strategic Hamlet Program, 33–38, 50–53
Subregion I (SRI), 195, 217, 250

Subregion II (SRII), 195, 288
Sugarcane, 47, 71, 175, 297
Sully, François, 52
Summers, Harry, 324
SUNRISE (Operation), 35, 50
Suoi Tre, 126
Sûreté, 255
Systems Analysis, at the Pentagon, 238

Tactical area of responsibility (TAOR), 121, 122
Tan Hoa village, 207
Tanks, 118, 125, 136
Tan My village, 300, 301, 302–303, 317
Tan Phu Trung village, 206–207, 212–213
Tan Son Nhut, 198, 199
    Airbase, 100, 200
TAOR. *See* Tactical area of responsibility
Taxation, 36, 39, 49, 59, 72, 82, 100, 214–215, 218, 268
    rice, 96, 262
    See also National Liberation Front, taxation
Taylor, Maxwell, 29, 36, 37, 90
Tay Ninh City, 22, 101, 245, 320
Tay Ninh province, 59, 66, 93, 121, 224, 245, 247, 254, 319, 321, 331
Territorials. *See* Popular Forces; Regional Forces
Terrorism, 39, 107, 176, 326. *See also* Diem regime, terrorist policy; National Liberation Front, extermination campaign; People's Revolutionary Party, extermination policy
Tethered goat tactic, 245, 267
Tet offensive, 127, 242–243, 300, 330
    assumptions underlying, 198, 199
    beginning of, 199
    failure of, 202–204
    in Hau Nghia Province, 205–215

"military defeat, psychological
victory" interpretation, 197, 205
of 1969, 242–254, 300, 330
origins, 193–199
planning of, 198–199, 201–202, 219
results of, 215–222
in Saigon area, 198, 199–205
U.S. view of, 204–205
Thieu. *See* Nguyen Van Thieu
Thompson, R.G.K., 33, 34–35, 283
Three Merging Points for One Goal,
201–202, 203
Tra. *See* Tran Van Tra
Tra Cu, 265, 266, 267
Trang Bang district/district town, 49,
52, 195, 208, 211, 222, 236, 246,
266, 289, 296, 297, 298, 303,
312, 317, 318, 320
Tran Van Tra, 62, 97, 197, 219, 320,
321
Tropic Lightning Divsion. *See* United
States Army, 25th Infantry
Division
Tru gian. See People's Revolutionary
Party, extermination policy
Trung Lap village, 48, 52, 122–123,
317
Truong Chinh, 14, 196, 283
Truong Dinh Dzu, 177
Truong Nhu Tang, 80–81, 283–284,
287–288, 314
Tunnels, 47, 94, 98, 119, 175, 258
II FFV. *See* II Field Force Vietnam
II Field Force Vietnam (II FFV), 121,
127, 154, 194, 195, 289

Unification, 60, 99
United Service Organization (USO),
120
United States
advisors, 1, 105–106, 109, 111, 116,
149, 156–158, 159–160, 161, 165,
176, 178, 206, 212, 221, 222,
232, 235, 247–248, 259, 262,
263, 265, 266, 272, 276–280,
292–293, 298, 306, 308, 310,
311, 312

aid programs, 31, 68, 106–107
Air Force. *See* United States Army
and Air Force
antiwar movement, 246. *See also*
United States, public opinion in
Army. *See* United States Army and
Air Force
Center of Military History (CMH),
6, 7, 323
Congress, 323–324, 328
conscription, 87
control of war, 11–12, 31, 33, 40,
334
criticism of military policy, 24,
107–110
Defense Department, 30, 168, 169
dependence on military operations,
2–3, 5
efforts frustrated, 155–167
elections in, 202
Embassy (Saigon), 113–114, 216
ground forces deployment, 43, 47
hatred of, 99, 114, 150, 171, 196,
230, 273, 274
and Hop Tac Program, 41, 42
incorrect assessments, 37
intelligence, 23, 196, 207, 210, 246,
315. *See also under* United States
Army and Air Force
interagency battles, 155
Joint Chiefs of Staff (JCS), 90, 118,
163
lack of policy options, 3–5
and land reform, 298
Marines, 42, 87, 90, 331, 334
National Security Council (NSC),
29
Navy, 265–266
Office of Civil Operations (OCO),
142, 156
Officer Candidate Schools, 290
and organizational changes, 26, 28,
29
Province Senior Advisors (PSA), 1,
157, 158, 160, 165, 176, 178,
212, 221, 222, 235, 247–248,

262, 277. *See also individual advisors;* United States, advisors
public opinion in, 163–164, 197, 202, 237, 284
reasons for defeat of, 323–325
refugee policy, 92
and Revolutionary Development Cadre program, 146–147
and rural issues, 3–4, 5
and sovereignty issues, 28, 30, 31–32, 106–107, 111–112, 113, 115
State Department, 30, 106
and Tet offensive, 204–205
troop requests, 169
troop withdrawals, 197, 205, 237, 247, 262, 289–293, 297, 307, 308
United States Army and Air Force
air power, 70, 71, 72, 91, 134, 138, 243, 286, 316, 317, 329, 330. *See also* United States Army and Air Force, bombing in North Vietnam
ally relations, 272–276, 335. *See also* Army of the Republic of Vietnam, and U.S. forces
bands (music), 152
bombing in North Vietnam, 90, 107, 113, 114, 330
casualties, 88, 123, 124, 127, 128, 131, 133, 138–139, 167, 174, 201, 204, 209, 217, 237, 245, 246, 247, 273, 274. *See also under* United States Army, 25th Infantry Division
casualty consciousness, 87, 174, 334
Combat Command system, 86
combat contingents, 87–88
cruelty of, 172, 213
discipline, 87, 88, 237, 290
division of labor with South Vietnamese forces, 114, 115
draftee intelligence requirements, 290
82nd Airborne Division, 238
field strength, 131

firepower use, 89, 91, 98, 109, 121, 124, 132, 135–136, 138, 173–174, 175, 214, 245, 273–274, 278, 324, 333
1st Cavalry Division, 238
1st Infantry Division, 286
intelligence, 131, 132, 152, 199, 243, 259, 260. *See also under* United States; United States Army, 25th Infantry Division
kindness of, 173
and Korean War, 86–87
mail for, 128
medical support, 87, 133
morale, 87, 119, 128–129, 229, 230, 237, 291, 292, 305
night operations, 136–137, 236
9th Infantry Division, 248, 289
officers, 128, 136, 174, 275, 290
101st Airborne Division, 220, 222, 238
173d Airborne Brigade, 90–92, 278
organizational adaptability, 117–118
psychological crisis in, 334
racial strife in, 290, 291
redeployments (1970), 289
respect for enemy, 228–230, 327
as shield for GVN, 177, 209, 332
Special Forces, 32, 89, 251, 266–267
support personnel, 86
tours of duty, 120
training, 128, 170
25th Infantry Division. *See* United States Army, 25th Infantry Division
veterans, 170, 172
village relations, 92, 114, 152, 170–173, 213, 233–234, 273, 274
village war, 147–155. *See also* Pacification campaign/programs
withdrawals. *See* United States, troop withdrawals
and World War II, 85–86, 104
United States Army, 25th Infantry Division, 47, 92, 104–105, 117, 118–139, 152, 154–155, 162,

164–166, 170–171, 172, 174–177,
    195, 208, 209, 225, 226–234,
    235, 249–251, 331, 335
  and advisors, 157–158, 275–280
  casualties, 201, 217, 237, 245, 289,
    292, 295
  departure of, 289–293
  intelligence, 94, 250, 251
  morale, 128–129
  and pacification, 148, 153, 175,
    179, 220, 284, 332
  rules of engagement, 214, 278
  2d Brigade, 164, 195, 217, 225,
    286, 289
  and Tet Offensive, 199–201
  Wolfhounds, 123, 148, 152, 200,
    251, 274, 290–291. *See also*
    MAILI (Operation)
United States Information Agency
    (USIA), 142
Urban areas, 196, 202, 203
Urbanites, 110. *See also* Elite
USIA. *See* United States Information
    Agency
USO. *See* United Service
    Organization
USOM. *See* U.S. Operations Mission
U.S. Operations Mission (USOM),
    106, 107

Vam Co Dong. *See* Vam Co River
Vam Co River, 134–135, 157, 164,
    209, 220, 251, 264, 289, 321
Vandenberg, Dan, 173, 227–228, 245,
    291
Vann, John Paul, 36–37, 78, 79, 81,
    83, 107–110, 113, 143, 166, 194,
    206, 221, 260, 277, 278–279,
    280, 325, 326
Vann thesis, 107–110
VC. *See* Viet Cong
VCI. *See* Viet Cong, infrastructure
Viet Cong (VC), 6, 28, 52, 168
  infrastructure (VCI), 256, 260, 284,
    303, 314
  See also Cadres; Guerrillas;
    National Liberation Front; North

    Vietnamese Army; People's Army
    of Vietnam
Viet Minh, 16–17, 24, 47, 56, 66
Vietnamese Information Service
    (VIS), 211
Vietnamization, 283, 286, 287, 306,
    310, 312
Vietnam War Memorial, 168
Villages
  checkbooks, 269, 270
  combat villages/hamlets, 48–49,
    94, 175
  compensation for damage in, 234,
    271, 273, 297
  councils, 15, 269, 270
  development, 268–272, 275
  as NLF military bases, 93–94
  tactical situations fighting in, 175–
    177
  Village Self Development Program,
    269–272, 298
  See also Land issues; Peasantry;
    Relocations; Village war
Village war, 111, 113, 141, 331–332,
    333, 334. *See also* Pacification
    campaign/programs; Warfare,
    village vs. large-unit
VIS. *See* Vietnamese Information
    Service
Vo Huu Hanh, 280
Vung Tau, 146, 147

WAHIAWA (Operation), 125
Walt, Lew, 90
Warfare
  big-unit, 88, 107, 115, 125–126,
    148, 241, 247, 325, 332. *See also*
    Search and destroy operations
  guerrilla vs. conventional, 24, 25
  mobility in, 26, 96
  rich man's, 87
  small-unit actions, 138, 278, 334
  village vs. large-unit, 88, 107, 241,
    248, 334. *See also* Village war;
    Warfare, big-unit
  war of attrition, 5, 35, 115, 132,
    138, 324, 331

War Zone C, 101, 126, 127, 164, 195, 224

War Zone D, 33

Watergate, 287, 321, 323

Weaponry, 13, 27, 65, 82, 94, 95, 116, 125, 131, 203, 210, 229, 329

Weissinger, Jack, 294, 295–296, 303–304, 304–306, 312, 313

Westmoreland, William, 41, 42, 73, 90, 107, 111–112, 113, 114, 115, 118, 126, 143, 157, 166, 169, 193–194, 196, 241, 323, 324, 328, 332

Weyand, Frederick C., 105, 121, 124, 127, 128, 148, 152, 162, 196, 207–208

Wheeler, Earle, 194

Whitehouse, Charles, 271

Williams, Samuel, 22, 24

Williamson, Ellis, 224–225, 250, 275, 276, 278, 279, 280

Willis, Michael, 129, 134, 227, 228, 290

Wolfhounds. See under United States Army, 25th Infantry Division

Women, 65, 273

Women's Liberation Association, 55, 60

World War II, 19, 25, 85–86, 99, 104, 194, 226, 238

Xom Hue hamlet, 50–52

Year of Strategic Hamlets, 36

YELLOWSTONE (Operation), 195

Youth Liberation Association, 60